EQUALITY and the CHARTER

[redacted]

EQUALITY

and the

CHARTER

Ten Years of Feminist Advocacy Before the Supreme Court of Canada

Women's Legal Education and Action Fund

1996
Emond Montgomery Publications Limited

Printed in Canada.

Edited, designed, and typeset by WordsWorth Communications, Toronto.

Canadian Cataloguing in Publication Data

Main entry under title:

Equality and the Charter : ten years of feminist
advocacy before the Supreme Court of Canada

ISBN 0-920722-84-9

1. Women – Legal status, laws, etc. – Canada – Cases.
2. Sex discrimination against women – Law and legislation – Canada – Cases. I. Women's Legal Education and Action Fund.

KE4399.A7E68 1996 342.71′0878 C96-931077-3
KF4758.A7E68 1996

Contents

Appendices

Foreword

The participation of third parties as intervenors in court cases is an issue on which views may legitimately differ. Some view it as incompatible with the adversarial nature of our litigation process and particularly inappropriate in criminal litigation where the defence should face off only against the prosecution. Some rule it out on purely pragmatic grounds: it adds time to the length of the proceedings, produces more paperwork and clutters up the issues with tangential and sometimes irrelevant evidence and argument. Personally, I found it invaluable in most cases.

I was privileged to sit on the Supreme Court of Canada when the first cases under the Canadian Charter of Rights and Freedoms worked their way up to our Court. I used to wish we could save them up until we had several under each section so that we could see how they might apply in different contexts. I had a real apprehension that what we might say about freedom of expression or fundamental justice in the context of one case might have appalling implications in the context of another. It was impossible to envisage the full range of circumstances that might trigger the application of the section. Moreover, and perhaps more importantly, it might not be in the interests of counsel advancing a particular interpretation or application to draw the judges' attention to its impact and implications in other cases. And who knows? Counsel on the other side may not be gifted with a particularly vivid or wide-ranging imagination!

Enter the intervenor whose proper role, I believe, is to distance him or herself from the narrow facts of the case, to paint a broader picture and to assist the court by hypothesizing a wide range of contexts in which the section might be invoked, all with a view to discerning its purpose and delineating and defining its contours.

If an applicant for intervenor status was not going to do this but was merely going to create an imbalance in the court process by reinforcing the arguments of one or other of the existing adversaries, a grant of status would not only not be helpful, it would be harmful and unfair.

I have referred to sections of the Charter as if it were an ordinary piece of legislation but, of course, it is not. In deciding Charter cases the court is engaging in much more than dispute resolution between the parties. It is discharging the most onerous of all its responsibilities, that of balancing the fundamental human rights of legislative and executive power of the state, a responsibility that was laid upon it by the High Court of Parliament itself. Experience with the Charter has shown that while this calls for a two-step process, first to determine whether a protected right has been violated and, second, whether that violation constitutes a reasonable limit on the right when viewed in the context of society as a whole, it is that second step that poses the greatest challenge to the judiciary. As many commentators have pointed out, most judges have a thorough knowledge of the law and an extensive familiarity with the adjudicative process; it is in the achievement of the proper balance between citizen and state that we falter. Legislators may find the balance through their political ideologies; citizens may perceive it in their own self-interest; but how do judges find it in their mandated stance of impartiality and neutrality? Is it to be found through different levels of scrutiny or different degrees of deference? Or is this to elevate process over substance and acknowledge the limitations of the law in the search for human values?

I am pleased to write this foreword to LEAF's collection of intervenor facta because they made such an impressive contribution to the decisions in many of the leading Charter cases that came before the Supreme Court of Canada during my tenure. They were clear and concise and represented a real effort on the part of a very diligent and dedicated group of counsel to discharge the role of intervenor at its highest and most challenging level.

Bertha Wilson
November 1995

Acknowledgments

In 1985, the Women's Legal Education and Action Fund (LEAF) was founded to contribute to the goal of advancing women's equality in Canada. The founding mothers had a dream that Canadian law could grow and expand to encompass equality for all women. LEAF works toward this dream through litigation using the constitutional guarantees of the Canadian Charter of Rights and Freedoms.

LEAF is just one among the many organizations and individuals advancing the goal of women's equality in Canada. LEAF has succeeded, in part, because it chose a specific role for itself within the women's movement and the legal system.

The founding of LEAF was only the final step in a strategy focused on the Charter of Rights and Freedoms. Between 1982, when the Charter generally was enacted, and 1985, when the equality provisions came into effect, women and men committed to the dream published articles, edited books, held a National Symposium on Equality Rights, researched legal action funds, audited statutes, and spoke across the country on the significance of the Charter for women. Their labour prepared the ground, ensuring strong roots for LEAF that would enable it to grow and flourish.

The dream of equality is shared by thousands of women and men across Canada of all ages and all races, and from all walks of life. For many, the dream was born of the pain and rage of injustice and inequality. Women face discrimination not just as women, but as women of colour, as aboriginal women, as women with disabilities, as lesbians, as women in poverty, as older women. Women being sexually harassed, women refused registration as status Indians, women who could not pass on their names to their children, women cut off social assistance because they had male friends, pregnant women denied benefits, domestic workers who were refused overtime pay, women seeking the protection of rape shield laws—all had been denied equal benefit of the law.

LEAF has broken new ground in the way it presents cases, as well as in the cases it takes. By providing judges with the social and cultural history of legal issues, LEAF has made possible new approaches to equality arguments.

In addition to public funding, LEAF's work has been supported by a remarkable community of dedicated women and men. The facta in this book represent ten years, many thousands of volunteer and paid hours, and millions of dollars. Those dollars have been given in many ways. People have attended LEAF's Person's Day breakfasts and the LEAF Roadshow. They have taken part in the LEAF Foundation's Branching Out endowment campaign.. And year after year, they have sent annual donations—the sap that has enabled LEAF to grow.

We thank all LEAF donors for their confidence in LEAF, and for their support. It is impossible to name everyone who has contributed to LEAF's creation, evolution, and successes over the past ten years. LEAF's achievements have been built on the commitment and insights of lawyers, scholars, and community activists both in Canada and abroad whose efforts to secure equality for women and disempowered men pre-date the founding of LEAF and have continued in legal and non-legal arenas throughout LEAF's existence.

A number of individual women have made extraordinary contributions to LEAF and its role in advancing women's equality in and through law, either through the genius of their work on particular cases or the sheer volume of time and labour they have devoted to LEAF's enterprise over many years. However, singling out such women ultimately misrepresents the collective dynamics of LEAF's casework and law reform initiatives. No factum was inspired or authored by a single intelligence; no argument escaped multiple revisions and reshaping from consultative and committee processes; no factum emerged independent of its predecessors and the collective experience and thinking that animated them.

Many of the women who have participated in this collective enterprise have served LEAF in different capacities over time. We would like to express our gratitude to each of the different constituencies that have contributed to LEAF's history while acknowledging that the work of each is interdependent and that many paid and unpaid LEAF supporters have served in more than one branch of this organization, often simultaneously, during the past ten years, as well as in other organizations.

Every part of LEAF's work represents the collective, and often unpaid, labour of many people—a coming together of exceptional effort and ability that has produced exceptional results.

We wish to thank:

- The founding mothers.

- The members of the National Legal Committee, who have assumed the heavy responsibility of managing LEAF's legal work, including setting priorities and ensuring that the work is always first rate.

- The lawyers, scholars, and community activists who have served on subcommittees and provincial legal committees, and as case counsel. They have donated their energy and expertise to conceive and draft in written and oral argument the equality claims in LEAF facta and briefs.

- The staff of LEAF, who have sustained the work, weathered the growing pains, coordinated a nationwide network of volunteers, met impossible deadlines, and held us all together.

• The law firms that have donated a variety of legal services: lawyers to do research and act as counsel; support staff to transform pleadings, intervenor applications and facta from draft to final form; and facilities for meetings.

• The litigants, who permitted their private legal claims to become test cases in the interests of advancing or protecting the equality of others.

• Our coalition partners, whose varied expertise tested and enriched the substance and effectiveness of the legal arguments.

• All the LEAF volunteers in every province and territory, who served in branches, chapters and committees that supported the legal work through fund raising, public education, finance, personnel, or strategic planning.

This book is, in the tradition of LEAF, a collective effort. We thank Nancy Ruth (Jackman), the Women's Program of Status of Women of Canada, and Mary Eberts for their financial support.

We thank the following women, who worked on the manuscript: Karen Busby, Mary Eaton, Mary Eberts, Glenna Johnston, Cathy Laurier, Carissima Mathen, Bert MacBain, Sheila McIntyre, Elizabeth Nastasi, Jane Novak, Helena Orton, Bettina Quistgaard, Jane Rounthwaite, Sharon Seenath, Elizabeth Shilton, Shona Stone, Wendy Sutton, Sheila Ward.

We thank Bertha Wilson for her encouraging words in the foreword.

We also thank the publisher, Emond Montgomery, for supporting this project.

In the field of women's equality, there is still much to be done. The law has the power to include people in its protections and benefits, but it also has the power to exclude. LEAF has spent much of its time defending existing provisions for equality that have been threatened by legal challenges.

We believe, however, that the increasing demand for copies of these facta reflects the growing importance of equality law. By publishing the facta, we hope to increase the reach and influence of the stories they tell about women's lives and how law and legal theories have the capacity to diminish or improve our lives as women. We hope they will plant the seeds for a vigorous new flowering of women's equality under Canadian law.

Introduction

> 15. (1) Every individual is equal before and under the law and has the right to equal protection and equal benefit of the law without discrimination, and in particular, without discrimination based on race, national or ethnic origin, colour, religion, sex, age, or mental or physical disability.
>
> (2) Subsection (1) does not preclude any law, program or activity that has as its object the amelioration of conditions of disadvantaged individuals or groups, including those that are disadvantaged because of race, national or ethnic origin, colour, religion, sex, age, or mental or physical disability.
>
> 28. Notwithstanding anything in this Charter, the rights and freedoms referred to in it are guaranteed equally to male and female persons.[1]

The story of the Women's Legal Education and Action Fund (LEAF) is a story about women undertaking law reform and legal analysis in a very particular way. Using traditional legal tools, they continually assert women's right to be recognized as "human beings equally deserving of concern, respect and consideration."[2] This book presents a portion of these women's work, with a minimum of embellishment. It is 10 years since LEAF launched its first case. Certainly it is time for an overview but in the arena in which LEAF operates—litigation of Charter issues before Canada's highest courts—10 years is a brief interlude. It is not yet possible to judge LEAF's effect on equality jurisprudence in this country in a definitive way. However, it is possible to present what LEAF has done.

LEAF, occasionally in coalition with other organizations, has submitted 23 facta (the briefs used in legal appeals) to the Supreme Court of Canada. They are found on the following pages. There are cases in lower courts in which LEAF's work was significant,[3] but this book is limited to the Supreme Court of Canada because, arguably, that is where our greatest influence has been. This limitation also provides thematic consistency, for the facta possess a continuity of language and argument that is occasioned by the legal forum for which they were written.

---

[1] Canadian Charter of Rights and Freedoms, Part I of the Constitution Act, 1982, being Schedule B of the Canada Act 1982 (UK), 1982, c. 11.

[2] *Andrews v. Law Society of British Columbia*, per McIntyre J, at 171.

[3] See Appendix H.

This book will be of interest to feminist activists, legal practitioners and historians, students of equality theory and advocacy, and people who have followed and supported LEAF's work. The facta represent a sizeable portion of LEAF's legal history. They are impressive for both their technical and creative quality. They also provide a means to assess whether LEAF has been able to sustain its feminist roots while transforming its beliefs into legal action.

A History of LEAF

On April 17, 1985, section 15 of the Canadian Charter of Rights and Freedoms became law. On the same day, the creation of LEAF was formally announced. The link was intentional, for the women[4] who founded LEAF were among the many who affected Canadian constitutional history by ensuring that their views were considered during the constitutional negotiations on the equality sections of the Charter: sections 15 and 28. Their success convinced these women that they had a continuing role to play to ensure that the promise of section 15 was converted into tangible gains.

The LEAF founders' conviction sprang from their understanding that the development of true equality in Canadian society could not be achieved through constitutional amendment alone. To continue and expand upon the influence gained at the constitutional table, many of these women concluded that they needed to participate in the ensuing law reform and constitutional litigation. The task of conceiving and implementing a strategy for this participation was facilitated by the three-year delay between the Charter's proclamation in 1982 and section 15's enactment in 1985. However, as Sherene Razack notes in her book *Canadian Feminism and the Law*, the idea of a legal action fund was percolating among the core LEAF group as early as 1981.[5]

A number of conferences and consultations were organized. A group known as the Charter of Rights Educational Fund (CREF) organized the Study Days on January 15 and February 19, 1983. The study days attracted more than 170 participants from Canada and the United States who pondered issues ranging from the systemic nature of sex discrimination to the exact meaning of section 28 of the Charter. CREF also struck a committee to undertake an audit of federal and Ontario legislation in violation of section 15. The enormous document was released in January 1985.[6] Similar audits, mostly spearheaded by women, took place across the country.[7] These initiatives, impressive in themselves, were all the more so when arrayed against the relative inaction of the federal and

---

[4] Some men were also involved in founding LEAF, and today many men are among LEAF's supporters.

[5] Sherene Razack, *Canadian Feminism and the Law* (Toronto: Second Story Press, 1991), at 36.

[6] Charter of Rights Education Fund, *Report on the Statute Audit Project: A Preliminary Analysis of Selected Federal and Ontario Laws Based on the Sex Equality Provisions of the Canadian Charter of Rights and Freedoms* (Toronto: 1985).

[7] See, for example, Charter of Rights Coalition (BC), *Women's Equality and the Charter of Rights and Freedoms: Preliminary Review of Selected British Columbia Legislation.*

provincial governments in undertaking similar surveys, when this was the very purpose for which section 15 was delayed three years.

The Canadian Advisory Council on the Status of Women funded a research study to identify the type of agency that would enable women to both develop expertise on equality rights and influence the application and interpretation of those rights. Entitled *Women and Legal Action*, the study was released in October 1984. After examining landmark legal cases for Canadian women, existing advocacy organizations in Canada, and the American experience with litigation funds, the study concluded that "... a legal action fund to concentrate on issues of sex-based discrimination is an essential component of an effective strategy to promote the interests of women in the Canadian legal system."[8]

The result of these various initiatives was a rich resource for LEAF in coming years: a starting point for LEAF's equality analysis and a focus to its litigation.[9]

Litigation is an expensive business. Between August 1984 and April 1985, LEAF's founders principally applied themselves to the daunting task of generating sufficient capital to establish the operations of an organization devoted to legal activity. They were successful, in no small part, because among them were some of the most prominent feminist lawyers, activists, and fund-raisers in the country. In fact, the creation of LEAF in such a short period of time is a clear illustration of privilege transformed into progressive social activity.

Today, LEAF is a non-profit organization governed by a national board of directors. Branches and chapters exist across Canada. Board and committee members are volunteers. There is a national office in Toronto with paid staff as well as an office in Vancouver run by West Coast LEAF, a legally separate organization.

LEAF's mandate is two-fold: to participate in litigation that promotes equality for women and to educate the public about this litigation and its relationship to women's equality. Litigation is overseen by a committee of the board called the National Legal Committee. The Legal Committee is composed of women who possess extensive litigation experience and/or a sophisticated understanding of equality issues.

The mandate of the Legal Committee is to select and manage LEAF's litigation. This responsibility entails working toward the development of a comprehensive theory of substantive equality for all women, developing fundamental principles of legal analysis, establishing case and project selection criteria, and setting priority issue areas.

Cases come to LEAF's attention in a variety of ways: through regular examination of case law digests; through an informal network of lawyers, academics, and women's organizations; and through the approximately 1,000 inquiries LEAF receives from the public each year.

---

[8] M. Elizabeth Atcheson, Mary Eberts, and Beth Symes, *Women and Legal Action* (1984: Canadian Advisory Council on the Status of Women), at 163.

[9] Charter of Rights Education Fund, *Study Day Papers* (Toronto, 1985).

Once a case is identified, it is, assessed according to certain selection criteria. These criteria have changed during the past 10 years. In April 1985, the women who founded LEAF agreed upon the following criteria:

1. The case would be an equality rights case.

2. It would arise under the Charter, or equivalent provisions of other provincial legislation.

3. It would be a test case: it would involve breaking new ground, challenging a discriminatory law or advancing the interpretation of equality rights guarantees, and would have the potential to improve women's rights significantly.

4. It would present strong enough facts so that there would be little chance of its being decided on grounds that did not require an equality analysis.

5. Ideally, it would result in significant gains for women, or gains for a significant number of women.

6. It would be of special interest to LEAF if it raised issues of multiple discrimination, or discrimination on grounds other than and in addition to sex.

These criteria were developed at a time when LEAF's staff and board envisioned their work as proactive: identifying discriminatory law and practices and initiating court actions to eliminate them. As will be discussed in the next section, this vision was severely tested by the plethora of cases in which LEAF had to respond to challenges raised by others. The criteria were also closely tailored to sponsoring individual cases—a practice that proved to be prohibitively expensive. They did not necessarily address the issues that arise in interventions, the activity that has come to dominate LEAF's legal work.

Over the years, the guidelines have been further developed to reflect LEAF's current work and priorities. They currently read as follows:

1. The case must promote substantive equality for women; ideally, a case will result in significant gains for women, or gains for a significant number of women.

2. Preference will be given to cases arising under the Charter. A case arising under provincial human rights legislation may be taken if it otherwise meets the criteria.

3. The case must involve breaking new ground and/or establishing a legal precedent that affects the collective interests of women. (Note that the words "test case" have been removed because interventions are not generally recognized as test-case litigation.)

4. The case must enable the Court to decide the equality issue, or, in the alternative, it must otherwise advance the equality jurisprudence.

5. Regardless of the merits of the case, it must also lend itself to fashioning a remedy capable of concretely advancing women's equality rights.

6. Cases that allow for follow-up with respect to education, monitoring, and implementation of a successful decision will be given preference.

7. The Legal Committee will give priority to cases that will address issues of multiple discrimination and diversify LEAF's caseload.

Before being adopted, cases are summarized for the Legal Committee in a case proposal. Aside from detailing the precise nature of the equality issues, case proposals address other questions unique to LEAF's litigation philosophy including: avenues for addressing the inequality besides litigation; coalition and consultation possibilities; and the case's potential impact on women who experience diverse forms of discrimination.

Litigating Equality for Women: Underlying Principles

LEAF acknowledges that inequality is a continuing state for many different groups in society. However, LEAF's particular mandate is to address the inequalities experienced by women. With this in mind, three main principles animate LEAF's equality theory:

1. Women as a group, compared with men as a group, experience widespread and pervasive discrimination.
2. Women who are oppressed on the basis of, for example, their race, class, sexual orientation, religion or disability, experience inequality different in degree and/or kind, in various contexts.
3. Law can be an effective tool for egalitarian social change.

In accordance with the first principle, LEAF recognizes that women suffer sex-based discrimination in specific and concrete areas of their lives, such as: physical safety, access to fulfilling and fairly paid work, family and childcare responsibilities, reproductive choice, and economic security. In addition, LEAF recognizes that these concrete forms of discrimination represent persistent attacks on women's dignity, autonomy, credibility, power, and membership in community.[10]

Once the systemic inequality of women is understood as a pervasive social and legal condition, LEAF argues that litigating equality for women under section 15 of the Charter must proceed in a particular way. From the inception of its Supreme Court of Canada litigation, beginning with the *Andrews* case, LEAF advocated a purposive approach to section 15.

LEAF argues that the purpose of section 15 is to redress injustices and enhance the position of those groups who have been and remain subject to systemic discrimination. With respect to women, section 15 must be used to reject laws and practices that reinforce and shape their disempowerment. Conversely, section 15 supports laws and practices that promote women's equal enjoyment of legal, political, economic, and social benefits that historically have been reserved for men as a group.

The purposive approach to equality is articulated in LEAF's work in a variety of ways. LEAF firmly rejects any approach to equality which contains or promotes what is called the "similarly situated test." This approach, also known as the Aristotelian or formal equality approach, posits that equality is achieved by treating like persons alike,

[10] *Andrews v. Law Society of British Columbia*, LEAF Factum, paragraph 57.

and unalike persons unalike. As a test of rational consistency, it accords well with what are known as process claims. Process claims relate to the law's administration; they do not and cannot address how law is made, to whom it applies, its impact on oppressed groups, or its contribution to systemic inequality.

What the similarly situated test cannot answer are the following questions: how are persons or groups found to be alike? how are they found to be unalike? who determines the categories for comparison? what are the underlying criteria that form the basis for the comparison? As the Ontario Court of Appeal held in an early Charter case, these unanswered questions represent the fatal defect of the similarly situated test:

> It is not always clear whether persons are or are not similarly situated, and whether, even if they are not, this is relevant to a section 15 inquiry. ... It is usually possible to find differences between classes of persons, and, on the basis of these differences, conclude that persons are not similarly situated. However, what are perceived to be "differences" between classes of persons could be the result of stereotypes based on existing inequalities which the equality provisions of the Charter are designed to eliminate, not perpetuate.[11]

In other words, the similarly situated test carries with it the risk of importing into an equality analysis the values of an unequal society. For example, differences that arise through socially imposed disadvantage may become the criteria for unequal treatment that maintains and even promotes that disadvantage. When the subjects compared are men and women, the problem becomes particularly acute because biological and gender differences (both real and perceived) may be classed as differences that justify disadvantageous treatment of women; the historical refusal to recognize women's particular needs during and after pregnancy and childbirth is one example.

LEAF has also developed arguments to build upon the recognition in human rights law that discrimination often assumes indirect and unintentional forms. Very few laws deliver blatantly unequal treatment of women. Instead, much discrimination occurs indirectly and is attributable to systemic biases that are difficult to identify and more difficult still to eliminate. Many laws can be shown to have developed in accordance with standards for entitlement or recognition of social needs that appear neutral but are actually based upon male experience.[12]

Laws can be deficient both in what they do and what they fail to do. For example, until recently, sexual harrassment was not recognized as an actionable harm in the human rights or criminal law context. This is understandable only if one adopts the view that men's exploitation of women's sexuality is not only *not* harmful, it is natural. Even after sexual harrassment was deemed unacceptable conduct, there continued to be resistance to recognize it as an important obstacle to women's equality because the term

---

[11] *Century 21 Ramos Realty Inc. v. The Queen* (1987), 58 OR (2d) 737, at 756-57.

[12] Helena Orton, "Litigation for Equality—LEAF's Approach to Section 15 of the Charter," March 1989, at 5, in Karen Busby et al., eds., *Equality Issues in Family Law*.

appears gender-neutral and could, in theory, refer to harrassment of men by women. In reality, sexual harrassment is something that is almost exclusively done to women by men. Moreover, the sexual exploitation of any person is intrinsically linked with a socially ascribed status that is uniquely female. Looked at in this broader way, sexual harrassment can be seen for what it is, and indeed what the Supreme Court has recognized as such: sex-based discrimination.[13]

The second principle by which LEAF operates is that different women experience inequality differently. Although LEAF's mandate states that the organization seeks to promote equality for all women in Canada, LEAF recognizes that inequality is experienced in many ways and on many levels. Women experience disadvantage not only because of their sex but because of other characteristics such as race, national or ethnic origin, sexual orientation, or disability. Where multiple discrimination is experienced by the same person or groups of persons, the resulting inequality may call for a very different analysis.

LEAF has been criticized for failing to address women's inequality in all its complexity and diversity. This criticism is not without foundation. Because LEAF's founding board and staff were white, middle class professional women, there was legitimate skepticism of LEAF's ability to respond to and incorporate the interests and experiences of diverse women. Furthermore, the nature of the litigation process, and in particular the intervention process, is such that schedules and time constraints are often non-negotiable and extremely limiting. This makes it difficult to engage in the kind of extensive consultation with women and women's organizations which is essential if the final product is to reflect women's diverse realities in a respectful and meaningful way. In responding to court deadlines, LEAF has, on occasion, taken shortcuts that were insufficiently attentive to the impact of LEAF's positions on more marginalized women. Furthermore, it must be acknowledged that the goal of a comprehensive equality theory that accommodates women's differences is an elusive one. The issues raised are uniquely difficult, as is translating them into legal theory and argument.

It bears pointing out that LEAF's internal struggle to become more responsive to the needs of all women mirrors the struggle in the greater feminist community.[14] Feminist legal theorists have been confronted with the stark reality that, in choosing to examine women's experience without reference to their particular and unique realities, they render those women with the bleakest realities invisible.[15] To its credit, LEAF has not shied away from this daunting challenge, and has organized a three-fold response: organizational, theoretical, and experiential.

---

[13] *Janzen and Govereau v. Platy Enterprises Ltd. et al.*, [1989] 1 SCR 1252.

[14] See, for example, Marlee Kline, "Race, Racism and Feminist Legal Theory" (1989), 12 *Harvard Women's Law Journal* 115.

[15] Martha Minow, "Feminist Reason: Getting It and Losing It" (1988), 38 *Journal of Legal Education* 47, at 56.

Organizationally, LEAF adopted a Diversification Policy in 1990,[16] which it applies in many ways: actively pursuing a broad representation of women throughout the organization; recognizing the importance of inclusiveness and accountability in its administration and governance processes; and selecting and litigating cases that will involve and affect the greatest possible number and range of women. The development and adoption of the policy has been a long-term commitment. Perhaps the policy's most important accomplishment to date is that it has forced LEAF to confront the barriers to diversity posed by LEAF's commitment to litigation, an activity that relies upon skills and qualifications obtainable only through privileged processes.

On a theoretical level, LEAF's staff and National Legal Committee attempt to incorporate into their legal work the conflicting insights that often accompany the recognition of women's difference. All case proposals must address the potential impact of a case on different groups of women. More specifically, LEAF demands that serious and sustained thought be given to the question: how will a particular case, and the equality strategy LEAF adopts, impact on the most disadvantaged women in society?

Finally, to broaden its knowledge and understanding of different women's lives, LEAF has relied to an ever-increasing degree upon the insight and expertise of other women's organizations. In particular, LEAF has approached these organizations for assistance in forming the analysis around particular cases. That is why, more recently, LEAF has intervened not in its own name but as one member of a coalition.

The move to coalition work has had several implications. It has highlighted the difficulty of putting a theory of inclusiveness into practice. It is difficult to condense complex legal and social issues into a 20-page factum, even when only one organizational viewpoint—LEAF's—must be reflected. It is more difficult when many organizations are involved whose viewpoints are diverse and often conflicting.

Coalition work has further acknowledged the expertise of women who are not formally trained in the study of law but who have clear insight into how the law works to oppress women. Organizationally and through its membership, LEAF has the aura that comes from being a player in the legal arena. This imparts to LEAF, and the women behind it, a particular kind of privilege, which in part explains LEAF's continued access to the legal process. However, feminist litigation requires blending the power of the legal process with the rich detail and nuances of women's reality. It is crucial for the litigation process to take note of the varied ways in which the law actually operates in women's lives, which are not immediately apparent to those who make the arguments in court.

Finally, by including more and different women in the discussion and activity surrounding a case, LEAF has fundamentally changed its litigation processes. In this work to increase its experience base and expertise, LEAF perhaps comes closest to employing the consciousness-raising that many scholars have identified as critical to a feminist method.[17]

---

[16] Copy available from the National Office on request.

[17] See, for example, Richard F. Devlin, "Normos and Thanatos (Part B): Feminism as Jurisgenerative Transformation or Resistance Through Partial Incorporation?" (1990), *Dalhousie Law Journal* 123, at 171.

LEAF's third principle is a commitment to the law's utility as a tool for egalitarian social change. LEAF believes that women need to participate in Charter litigation based on principles of substantive equality—that is, principles designed to make changes in the material conditions of women's lives. This belief has been stringently tested over the past 10 years. LEAF has had to reassess its expectations as well as its strategies. Significantly, however, LEAF has never abandoned this founding belief.

LEAF's first annual report, *LEAF Litigation: Year One*, stated: "The primary focus of LEAF is to do proactive work. The ability to control the litigation agenda, to decide the timing and the substance of the challenges, is one very significant reason why women find LEAF empowering."[18] Adopting the strategy of advocacy groups such as the National Association for the Advancement of Coloured People, LEAF's founders hoped the organization could occupy the field of women's equality litigation, become recognized as an expert, and, by selecting appropriate cases, ensure that small but important progressive steps were made.[19]

This proactive vision was severely tested by early equality cases that often involved male litigants who sought to undermine benefits achieved by feminist law reform. For example, men challenged the criminalization of sexual assaults, previously viewed as consensual, between older men and underage girls. Men also lost no time challenging evidentiary rules designed to ensure fair, non-sexist treatment of complainants during sexual assault trials. On other fronts, men challenged laws such as those providing economic assistance to single mothers, which were enacted to address the severe hardship of the most impoverished women.

In these and other cases, LEAF participated simply to ensure that existing positive schemes for women were not dismantled. This participation was different from what LEAF originally envisioned. Instead of initiating a challenge on behalf of a woman or women adversely affected by existing laws, LEAF's role was as an intervenor—a third party permitted to make arguments in order to assist the court in its deliberations.

These developments had several implications for LEAF's litigation strategy. First, because an intervenor must always obtain leave of the court to participate, LEAF had to expend resources to ensure its right to intervene, both in particular cases and through policy work on the need for public interest interventions. Second, as intervenor, LEAF had to deal with the case as framed by the parties. Third, LEAF had to act within very short timelines and be in a state of continual readiness. Fourth, in its role as an intervenor, LEAF could not easily maintain contact with individual women litigants and the complexities of their lives.

Because of these and other difficulties that are not limited to LEAF, many feminists strongly oppose Charter litigation as a means to effect progressive social change. The

[18] Mary Eberts and Gwen Brodsky, *LEAF Litigation: Year One*, March 31, 1986, at 8.

[19] Razack, supra, at 52.

critique of Charter litigation includes the following perceived problems: it is undemocratic because it judicializes what are in fact political issues;[20] it drains women's resources, especially financial, that are better deployed in more overtly radical activities;[21] it is the domain of privileged men in which women are at a profound disadvantage;[22] and it is illusory because it fosters the belief that real change is possible, when in fact existing social and political structures remain intact and may even be strengthened.[23]

These are powerful charges of which women engaged in law reform and litigation must take note. LEAF does not have simple answers to these concerns. However, LEAF's experience over the past 10 years has allowed it to develop strategies to deal with these limitations.

Certainly the judiciary is an unrepresentative segment of society. However, elected institutions are no more representative and in recent years have been positively hostile to women's concerns and indeed equality issues in general. That members of the bench are not accountable in the same sense as elected representatives is not entirely negative since their independence is accompanied by the freedom to accept politically unpopular arguments. Similarly, their lengthy and uninterrupted tenures provide groups such as LEAF the opportunity to create and implement strategies that recognize that equality-seeking is a long-term endeavour.

With respect to allocating women's resources, there is no doubt that litigation is tremendously expensive. But it is wrong to assume that the women who support LEAF's work have abandoned other methods of effecting social change. Litigation is simply one strategy among many. At some point, however, it is a strategy that must be considered because inevitably legal schemes will be vulnerable to Charter attack. In the words of one commentator, "[the] women's movement cannot abjure the Charter. The Charter will not abjure us."[24] Challenges to progressive legislation cannot go unanswered. The early section 15 cases present a striking display of the clash between two possible methods of Charter interpretation: a civil libertarian model focused on individual rights and freedoms, and a systemic model that continually presses for the recognition and amelioration of existing group-based inequalities. LEAF, indeed women in general, cannot afford to shun this battle.

---

[20] Michael Mandel, *The Charter of Rights and the Legalization of Politics in Canada* (Toronto: Wall and Thompson, 1989), chapter 2.

[21] Judy Fudge, "The Effects of Entrenching a Bill of Rights upon Political Discourse: Feminist Demands and Sexual Violence in Canada" (1989), 17 *International Journal of Sociology and the Law* 445, at 457.

[22] Elizabeth Shilton, "Charter Litigation and the Policy Processes of Government: A Public Interest Perspective" (1992), 30:3 *Osgoode Hall LJ* 653, at 654.

[23] Allan Hutchinson, "Waiting for Coraf (or the Beatification of the Charter)" (1991), 41 *University of Toronto LJ* 332.

[24] Shilton, supra, at 655.

As well, the law *itself* often operates as a clear and direct impediment to women's equality. For example, women's legal status has been impaired or even denied through discriminatory provisions such as those found in the immigration and Indian acts. Their exercise of reproductive autonomy has been criminalized. The systemic legal barriers that adversely affect women's daily lives require, at some point, the pursuit of legal remedies to remove them.

Certainly, women are at a preliminary disadvantage when they litigate under the current conditions of male power and privilege, which are paramount in the legal arena. However, within LEAF itself, litigation has come to encompass processes quite alien to its conventional meaning. LEAF's continued success, and the success of other organizations, in obtaining leave to intervene in a variety of cases is evidence that the parameters within which such cases are defined can be influenced and even changed. LEAF's interventions in private civil actions[25] have illustrated that equality issues arise in cases traditionally considered too narrow and individualistic to warrant the application of public law principles. LEAF's interventions in criminal cases, perhaps the archetype of the individual rights model of Charter interpretation, sends a clear message that the criminal law involves more than the rights of an accused person measured against the state's interest in law and order; it involves women's rights to equal protection of the criminal law and equal security of the person. In both civil and criminal law cases, LEAF's intervention arguments set precedents merely by the fact that the Court allowed them to be made.[26]

Finally, there is the argument that the Charter is illusory and dangerous because it precludes real systemic change. What constitutes real systemic change is a matter of debate and an issue on which women can legitimately differ. Some scholars point to feminist equality challenges as a bright light in an otherwise gloomy 10 years of Charter litigation.[27] Certainly, there are cases presented in this book that represent significant symbolic and material gains for women.

Criticisms of the Charter's efficacy as a tool for egalitarian social change must be balanced against the realization that the Charter is a fact of our legal and social universe. Although most women did not specifically ask for a constitutionally entrenched bill of rights, the women who founded and continue to support LEAF responded to the Charter's advent by demanding that it harm women as little as possible and live up to its rhetorical claims. These women welcomed the challenges posed by the Charter, and their work over the past 10 years highlights the Charter's potential not only to vouchsafe women's equality, but to advance it.

---

[25] *Norberg v. Wynrib*, [1992] 2 SCR 226; *K.M. v. H.M.*, [1992] 3 SCR 6; and *Moge v. Moge*, [1992] 3 SCR 813.

[26] Sharon Lavine, "Advocating Values: Public Interest Intervention in Charter Litigation" (1992-93), 2 *National Journal of Constitutional Law* 26.

[27] Richard Sigurdson, "The Left-Legal Critique of the Charter: A Critical Assessment" (1993), 13 *Windsor Yearbook of Access to Justice* 117, at 130-34.

The Book's Organization

The facta are presented in chronological order—that is, in the order that the cases were heard by the Supreme Court. Readers may perceive themes among the facta—for example, a great many of the facta were presented in criminal cases concerning male sexual violence. However, the facta have not been grouped by subject matter, chiefly because these cases occurred over a 10-year period and it would be misleading to present LEAF as having a uniform and unchanged position on issues such as violence against women, equality in employment, or women's place in the family. LEAF's work is constantly changing and developing, and what is appropriate in one case is not necessarily appropriate in another one five years later. However, LEAF's *approach* to equality remains constant, and it is this aspect of our work that we hope will be most evident, regardless of the particular factual context in which the case arose.

Each factum is preceded by the briefest of information—that is, the who, what, where, and when of the case. The case briefings have scrupulously avoided why LEAF advanced the argument and whether the argument was effective both in structure and articulation. The facta are simply reproduced so that more disinterested scholars, practitioners, and activists may evaluate the approach and execution of LEAF's arguments in each case.

Each factum is followed by the outcome of the decision, which has principally been adopted from the head notes found in the Supreme Court Reporter. However, head notes are written for a general readership, and some portions of the decision that address equality issues may be left out. In such cases, we have taken the liberty of amending the head note to include these passages and they are set off in italics. The reader is cautioned that the head notes are meant to give only a flavour of the actual decisions and cannot substitute for the entire judgment.

Every case presented here has a history that could easily be the subject of a much longer work. However, this book is not meant to address the very broad social, political, and historical questions legitimately raised in these cases, but to showcase LEAF's particular contribution to these critical issues for Canadian women. We hope that through reading these facta, you derive some measure of the satisfaction we felt in writing them.

Carissima Mathen
December 1995

Facta

IN THE SUPREME COURT OF CANADA
(ON APPEAL FROM THE COURT OF APPEAL FOR THE PROVINCE OF BRITISH COLUMBIA)

BETWEEN:

THE LAW SOCIETY OF BRITISH COLUMBIA

Appellant
(Respondent)

AND:

THE ATTORNEY GENERAL OF BRITISH COLUMBIA

Appellant
(Respondent)

AND:

MARK DAVID ANDREWS

Respondent
(Petitioner)

AND:

GOREL ELIZABETH KINERSLY

(Co-Respondent)

AND:

THE ATTORNEY GENERAL OF ALBERTA
THE ATTORNEY GENERAL OF SASKATCHEWAN
THE ATTORNEY GENERAL OF ONTARIO
PROCUREUR GENERAL DE LA PROVINCE DE QUEBEC
THE ATTORNEY GENERAL OF NOVA SCOTIA
FEDERATION OF LAW SOCIETIES OF CANADA
CANADIAN ASSOCIATION OF UNIVERSITY TEACHERS AND
ONTARIO CONFEDERATION OF UNIVERSITY FACULTY ASSOCIATIONS
WOMEN'S LEGAL EDUCATION AND ACTION FUND
COALITION OF PROVINCIAL ORGANIZATIONS OF THE HANDICAPPED

Intervenors

Factum of the Women's Legal Education and Action Fund (LEAF)

Andrews v. The Law Society of British Columbia and the Attorney General of British Columbia

INTRODUCTION

Mark David Andrews, a British citizen residing in British Columbia, applied to the provincial law society for a lawyer's practising certificate. Although he possessed the academic and professional requirements, the law society rejected his application because he was not a Canadian citizen as required by section 42 of the Barristers and Solicitors Act. Andrews challenged section 42 of the Act on the basis that it discriminated against non-citizens contrary to section 15 of the Charter. Note that section 15 does not expressly mention citizenship as a prohibited ground of discrimination.

The Supreme Court of British Columbia held that although citizenship was an analogous ground of prohibited discrimination, section 42 of the Barristers and Solicitors Act was not discriminatory because its distinction between citizens and non-citizens was a rational basis for determining eligibility to practise law.

The British Columbia Court of Appeal overturned this ruling and held that the Barristers and Solicitors Act did indeed violate section 15 of the Charter and was not saved under section 1 of the Charter. In its decision, the Court affirmed that equality is defined according to the similarly situated test—that is, persons who are similarly situated be similarly treated and persons who are differently situated be differently treated. The Court also articulated its analysis of the relationship between sections 15 and 1: there must be an initial determination that the impugned legislation is unreasonable or unfair; only after this determination is made will the analysis shift to section 1 of the Charter, at which point the question becomes whether "a fair-minded person, weighing the purposes of legislation against its effects on individuals adversely affected, and giving due weight to the right of the legislature to pass laws for the good of all, would conclude that the legislative means adopted are unreasonable or unfair."

The Court of Appeal's ruling caused concern to equality advocates and others. The Court's reliance upon the similarly situated test mandated a narrow, formalistic reading of the equality guarantees that would undermine the possibility that section 15 would promote the substantive equality of disadvantaged groups. The Court's approach placed the onus on individuals to prove the unreasonableness of laws, rather than placing the onus on lawmakers to justify laws that deny fair treatment. Also of concern was the Court's reference to legislative expedience (the right to pass laws for the good of all) in the Court's analysis of discrimination. This seemed to leave no room for consideration of section 1 of the Charter and, indeed, suggested that laws advancing majoritarian interests at the expense of minorities would be constitutional unless the majority of people agreed that such laws were unfair.

Therefore, when the Law Society obtained leave to appeal to the Supreme Court of Canada, LEAF sought and obtained intervenor status to address "what approach should be taken by this Court in analyzing section 15 of the [Charter] and in determining its relationship to section 1." Intervenors that supported either an expansive approach to section 15 or the recognition of citizenship as an analogous ground of discrimination were the Coalition of Provincial Organizations of the Handicapped, the Canadian Association of University Teachers, and the Ontario Confederation of University Faculty Associations. Intervenors who generally supported either the law society and/or the Attorney General of British Columbia were the attorneys general for Ontario, Quebec, Nova Scotia, Saskatchewan, and Alberta, and the Federation of Law Societies of Canada.

FACTUM

PART I: FACTS

1. The Women's Legal Education and Action Fund (LEAF) offers no comment on the facts as outlined by the Appellants and Respondents.

PART II: ISSUES

2. LEAF takes no position on the constitutional validity of the citizenship requirements in section 42 of the Barristers and Solicitors Act, RSBC 1979, c. 26. In any event, there does not seem to be enough in the record to support an analysis of this question in the fashion LEAF recommends for the analysis of equality questions under section 15.

3. LEAF restricts its arguments to the question of what approach should be taken by this Court in analyzing section 15 of the Canadian Charter of Rights and Freedoms and in determining its relationship to section 1 of the Charter.

> Canadian Charter of Rights and Freedoms, Constitution Act, 1982, as enacted by Canada Act 1981 (UK), 1982, c. 11.

4. Although it does not restrict itself to this perspective, LEAF acknowledges that its approach to section 15 and equality is that of an advocate for women's equality.

5. LEAF will argue that the approach developed by the Court of Appeal of British Columbia in the decision appealed from was erroneous in several respects, and will propose for the consideration of this Court a purposive analysis of sections 15 and 1.

PART III: ARGUMENT

The Context for Interpreting Section 15

Human Rights and Equality Values

6. It is submitted that the interpretation of section 15 and the determination of its relationship to section 1 should be consistent with the decisions of this Court on the interpretation of the Charter, the meaning and significance of equality, and the importance to be accorded human rights and respect for human dignity.

7. In particular, it is to be remembered that this Court has adopted a purposive approach to the interpretation of the Charter, looking to the value that the right or freedom seeks to protect and rejecting a narrow and technical interpretation.

Law Society of Upper Canada v. Skapinker, [1984] 1 SCR 357, at 366.

Hunter v. Southam Inc., [1984] 2 SCR 145, at 156-57.

Singh et al. v. Minister of Employment and Immigration, [1985] 1 SCR 177, at 209, 218-19.

R v. Oakes, [1986] 1 SCR 103, at 119.

8. This Court has identified equality as one of the fundamental values of society, against which the objects of all legislation must be measured.

Oakes, supra, at 136.

9. This Court has acknowledged the importance of promoting the equality of particular groups.

R v. Big M Drug Mart Ltd., [1985] 1 SCR 295, at 337-38.

Société des Acadiens v. Association of Parents for Fairness in Education et al., [1986] 1 SCR 549, at 579.

Caldwell v. Stuart, [1984] 2 SCR 603, at 626.

10. This Court has also decided that the interests of true equality may require differentiation in treatment.

Big M Drug Mart Ltd., supra, at 347.

11. It has, moreover, recognized that dominant groups in society should not be permitted to use the Charter to cut back legislative measures designed for the advancement of the less advantaged.

Edwards Books and Art Ltd. v. The Queen, [1986] 2 SCR 713, at 779.

12. This Court has acknowledged the importance of human rights legislation in a series of decisions which ruled that persons may not contract out of their rights under human rights legislation, and established the primacy of human rights legislation over other statutes. Human rights legislation has been characterized by this Court as quasi-constitutional.

Ontario Human Rights Commission v. The Borough of Etobicoke, [1982] 1 SCR 202.

Insurance Corporation of British Columbia v. Heerspink et al., [1982] 2 SCR 145, at 157-58, per Lamer J.

The Winnipeg School Division No. 1 v. Craton et al., [1985] 2 SCR 150.

Ontario Human Rights Commission and Theresa O'Malley v. Simpsons-Sears Ltd., [1985] 2 SCR 536, at 546-47.

13. This Court's respect for human rights legislation and equality principles reflects the trend in Canadian public policy and legislation over the past century toward increasing the substantive equality of those groups previously excluded from power and full participation in society. Anti-slavery legislation, extension of the franchise, and the right to hold public office, reform of family law, and enactment of human rights legislation all reflect this growing commitment to egalitarian goals.

Walter S. Tarnopolsky and William Pentney, *Discrimination and The Law: Including Equality Rights Under the Charter* (Toronto: DeBoo, 1985), at part I, "Background and Setting."

Mary Eberts, "The Rights of Women" in *The Practice of Freedom*, Ronald St. J. MacDonald and John P. Humphrey, eds. (Toronto: Butterworths, 1979), 225, at 225-36.

Lynn Smith, "A New Paradigm for Equality Rights" in *Righting the Balance: Canada's New Equality Rights*, Lynn Smith, ed. (Saskatoon: The Canadian Human Rights Reporter Inc., 1986), 353, at 357.

N. Colleen Sheppard, "Equality, Ideology and Oppression: Women and the Canadian Charter of Rights and Freedoms" in *Charterwatch: Reflections on Equality*, Christine Boyle et al., eds. (Toronto: Carswell, 1986), 195, at 198-200.

14. In recent years, the range of prohibited grounds of discrimination in human rights legislation has been extended, from the original grounds of race, religion, and ethnic origin to include sex, marital status, family status, age, disability, and, in some jurisdictions, political belief, sexual orientation, and record of offences.

Walter S. Tarnopolsky and William Pentney, *Discrimination and the Law*, supra, at part II, "The Prohibited Grounds of Discrimination."

15. Similarly, both the decisions of this Court and human rights legislation itself have expanded the concept of discrimination to include indirect and unintentional discrimination.

Simpsons-Sears Ltd., supra, at 546-50.

Canadian Odeon Theatres Ltd. v. Saskatchewan Human Rights Commission and Huck, [1985] 3 WWR 717 (Sask. CA), leave to appeal denied June 3, 1985: 60 NR 240 (SCC).

Human Rights Code, 1981, SO 1981, c. 53, as amended 1984, c. 58, s. 39; 1986, c. 64, s. 10.

The Yukon Territory Human Rights Act, SY 1987, c. 3, s. 11.

The British Columbia Human Rights Act, SBC 1984, c. 22, s. 13(1.1).

The Quebec Charter of Human Rights and Freedoms, RSQ 1977, c. 12, s. 10.

16. This Court has recognized the need for effective remedies to redress conditions which prevent women from achieving equality in the workplace in two recent decisions under the Canadian Human Rights Act.

Action Travail des Femmes v. Canadian National Railway Company, [1987] 1 SCR 1114.

Robichaud v. Canada (Treasury Board), [1987] 2 SCR 84.

17. This Court has also recognized the importance of protecting the rights of disadvantaged persons in contexts outside both the Charter and human rights legislation.

E. (Mrs.) v. Eve, [1986] 2 SCR 388.

18. It is thus submitted that the interpretation of section 15 should be informed by egalitarian principles and the necessity to protect the rights of historically disadvantaged persons, and by the strong recognition of the place of equality values and human rights legislation in the Canadian legal system. The concept of equality in section 15 should be no less broad.

Legislative History and Purpose

19. It is also submitted that the interpretation of section 15 should take account of its legislative history.

20. The legislative history and language of section 15 suggests that it continues the guarantee of evenhandedness in the legal process which had been provided by paragraph 1(b) of the Canadian Bill of Rights, although it is clear both from the history and the language of section 15 that the section is not confined to safeguarding process rights.

21. In particular, the legislative history of section 15 shows an intention that the equality guarantees of section 15 would reach not only the process but also the substance of the law, affect all levels of government, and be entrenched in the Constitution. The language of section 15 was shaped so as to eliminate certain specific problems disclosed by judicial interpretation of paragraph 1(b), problems which had deprived it of any strength as a guarantee of equality, for women or any other disadvantaged group.

Peter Hogg, "A Comparison of the Canadian Charter of Rights and Freedoms with the Canadian Bill of Rights" in *Canadian Charter of Rights and Freedoms: Commentary*, Walter S. Tarnopolsky and Gerald Beaudoin, eds. (Toronto: Carswell, 1982), 1, at 19-20.

Laskin's Canadian Constitutional Law, Neil Finkelstein, ed. (Toronto: Carswell, 1986, fifth ed.), vol. 2, at 1267-73.

Walter S. Tarnopolsky, "The Equality Rights" in *Canadian Charter of Rights and Freedoms: Commentary*, Tarnopolsky and Beaudoin, supra, 395, at 396, 421-22.

Special Joint Committee of the Senate and House of Commons on the Constitution of Canada, *Minutes of Proceedings and Evidence—Feb. 2-13, 1981*, at 5A:2, 9:81, 19:30, 22:10-11, 22:55-60.

Motion tabled by Minister of Justice in House of Commons, February 13, 1981, at 5.

Robin Elliot, "Interpreting the Charter—Use of the Earlier Versions as an Aid" (1982), *UBC Law Review Charter Edition* 11-57.

Mary Eberts, "Women and Constitutional Renewal" in *Women and the Constitution*, Audrey Doerr and Micheline Carrier, eds. (Ottawa: Minister of Supply and Services Canada, 1981), at 3-27.

Beverley Baines, "Women, Human Rights and the Constitution" in *Women and the Constitution*, supra, at 31-63.

Leslie A. Pal and F. L. Morton, "Bliss v. Attorney-General of Canada: From Legal Defeat to Political Victory" (1986), 24 *Osgoode Hall LJ* 141.

22. Moreover, section 28 was added to the Charter to confirm and strengthen that instrument's commitment to the equality of women.

"Summary of Conference Resolutions" in *Equality Rights and the Canadian Charter of Rights and Freedoms*, Anne Bayefsky and Mary Eberts, eds. (Toronto: Carswell, 1985), at 634-44.

Katherine de Jong, "Sexual Equality: Interpreting Section 28" in *Equality Rights and the Canadian Charter of Rights and Freedoms*, supra, at 493.

23. The history of the Charter's guarantees of substantive equality clearly shows that they were intended to benefit individuals and groups which historically have had unequal access to social and economic resources, either because of overt discrimination or because of the adverse effects of apparently neutral forms of social organization premised on the subordination of certain groups and the dominance of others. In this factum, we refer to these intended beneficiaries as the powerless, the excluded, the disadvantaged.

24. It is submitted that this purpose of promoting the equality of the powerless, excluded, and disadvantaged should animate interpretation of the guarantees of substantive equality in section 15.

25. It is further submitted that this Court is entitled to recognize, in formulating its approach to the equality guarantees, that the groups intended to benefit from these guarantees, whether enumerated in the section or akin to those so enumerated, have not yet achieved equality.

26. For example, a recent Parliamentary survey heard evidence which confirms that women have not yet achieved equality, that serious barriers remain and that new areas of need are emerging. It affirmed commitments made in government *Speeches from the Throne* in 1984 and 1986 giving women's equality national priority.

House of Commons, Standing Committee on Secretary of State, *Fairness in Funding: Report on the Women's Program*, May 26, 1987.

27. The compendious nature of section 15 has received judicial recognition in the Ontario Court of Appeal, and its commitment to equality for the disadvantaged, powerless and excluded has been confirmed in Parliament.

Reference Re an Act to Amend the Education Act (1986), 53 OR (2d) 513 (CA), at 554, per Howland CJO and Robins JA, affirmed in *Re Blainey and Ontario Hockey Association* (1986), 54 OR (2d) 513 (CA), at 524-25, per Dubin JA:

> In our view, s. 15(1) read as a whole constitutes a compendious expression of a positive right to equality both in the substance and the administration of the law. It is an all-encompassing right governing all legislative action. Like the ideals of equal justice and equal access to the law, the right to equal protection and equal benefit of the law now enshrined in the Charter rests on the moral and ethical principle fundamental to a truly free and democratic society that all persons should be treated by the law on a footing of equality with equal concern and equal respect.

Equality for All, Report of the Parliamentary Committee on Equality Rights, October 1985 (Boyer Report), at 5-6.

Toward Equality, The Response to the Report of the Parliamentary Committee on Equality Rights by the Department of Justice Canada, at 2-4.

28. The commitment of section 15 to the achievement of substantive equality for powerless, excluded, and disadvantaged groups is also reflected in other guarantees in the Charter which promote and preserve the diversity and distinctive interests of identifiable groups.

Canadian Charter of Rights and Freedoms:

Religious minorities: ss. 2, 15, and 29.

Language rights: ss. 14, 15, and 16 to 23.

Multiculturalism: ss. 14, 15, and 27.

Native peoples: ss. 15 and 25 and s. 35 of the Constitution Act, 1982.

Women: ss. 15 and 28.

Equality for All, supra, at 1-5, 9-16, 33-36, 69-74, 129-31.

Jennifer Bankier, "Equality, Affirmative Action, and the Charter: Reconciling 'Inconsistent' Sections" in *Research Studies of the Commission on Equality in Employment*, Judge Rosalie Silberman Abella, Commissioner, April 1985, at 307, 314 (footnote 10).

Mary Jane Mossman, "Gender, Equality, and the Charter" in *Research Studies of the Commission on Equality in Employment*, supra, at 299-304.

Implications of Adopting the Purposive Approach

29. It is submitted that this Court can take into account both the legislative history of section 15 and the place of section 15 in the evolving societal commitment to equality

by acknowledging that both process claims and claims to substantive equality can be dealt with under the section.

30. It is further submitted that the Court can follow a purposive approach to the section with respect both to process and to substantive equality claims. In the case of the process claims, the Charter purpose against which a provision will be measured is that of furthering the social interest in access to justice. Such a purpose is allied to the Diceyan purpose earlier suggested for paragraph 1(b) of the Canadian Bill of Rights. It ensures that section 15 is complementary to the provisions of the Charter dealing with legal rights. For reasons developed more fully below, the intervenor submits that the concepts of disadvantage, powerlessness, or exclusion need not play as large a role in the analysis of process claims as they would do in claims for substantive equality.

31. It is submitted that the purpose which informs the analysis of claims to substantive equality is that described in paragraphs 23 and 24 above—namely, the purpose of promoting the substantive equality of the powerless, excluded, and disadvantaged.

32. Accepting such an equality promoting purpose has implications for the analysis of claims to equality under section 15.

Implications with Respect to the Enumerated Grounds

33. Some of the terms in section 15 indicate clearly the type of disadvantage which is meant to be addressed by the equality guarantees—e.g., mental and physical disability. Others are all encompassing on their face—e.g., race, sex. These latter grounds appear to place on the same footing the equality claims of those who have been historically disadvantaged (like women and people of colour) and those who, traditionally, have been members of the dominant group (men and whites). In assessing claims to substantive equality brought under section 15, it is submitted that a court should bear in mind that the purpose of the section is to promote the equality of those who have been disadvantaged. While not categorically ruling out the equality claims of members of a dominant group, a purposive approach would lead a court to interpret section 15 in such a way that these claims would be viewed with caution.

34. In applying the purposive approach, a Court will have to determine which of the groups described by an apparently all encompassing term (sex, national origin) is dominant and which disadvantaged. The historical and contemporary record will make such determinations relatively straightforward in some cases; indeed, the record is so clear in these instances that a categorical determination may be made. It is submitted, for example, that there is widespread agreement in society that women and people of colour have been disadvantaged in Canadian society. In other situations, the determination will depend more closely on the context of the inquiry—e.g., members of traditionally dominant religious groups may, in some contexts, be in a minority and in need of certain guarantees (see, for example, the legislative protection for non-Catholic teachers in the Catholic system incorporated into Ontario Bill 30).

An Act to Amend the Education Act, SO 1986, c. 21, sections 136-1 and 136-1a.

35. The foregoing approach meshes well with the Court's statement that the Charter's guarantees should not be used by dominant groups in society to cut back legislative measures designed for the advancement of the disadvantaged. It is submitted that the equality claim of a member of a dominant group could often be a disguised attempt to invalidate legislation aimed at attacking a persistent disadvantage affecting the counterpart subordinate group. For example, attacks by men on legislation creating certain sexual assault offences, affording protections to victims of sexual assault, or providing financial assistance to low-income single mothers, may be seen in this light.

Edwards Books and Art Ltd., supra.

36. Because of the need to address the asymmetry inherent in inequality, it is submitted that a proper test for applying the substantive equality guarantees of section 15 need not aim at creating perfect symmetry in each case. As the disadvantaged must be the beneficiaries of legislative change if they are to achieve equality, section 15 is meant to accommodate legislation which favours the disadvantaged over the advantaged. This preference is apparent in the express language of subsection 15(2). Moreover, the language of subsection 15(2) colours the interpretation to be placed on the language of subsection 15(1), indicating, in our submission, that any test developed for assessing whether a denial of substantive equality has occurred should be one that does not prejudice the interests of the disadvantaged.

37. It is further submitted that the Court should not adopt a narrow approach to the interpretation of the grounds listed in section 15. A ground which seems to be non-enumerated—e.g., pregnancy—is actually an aspect of a "sex" distinction. Since only women become pregnant, any disadvantage visited upon a pregnant person is inevitably a disadvantage visited upon a woman. The intervenor criticizes in this regard the decision in *Bliss v. AG Canada*. Because of the sexual element in the subordination of women, it will also be seen that sexual harassment can be a "sex" distinction amenable to examination under section 15.

Bliss v. AG Canada, [1979] 1 SCR 183, at 190-91.

38. Similarly, the Court should not require that an inequality in substance be visited upon all women in order to constitute a denial of equality on the basis of sex. Distinctions focusing particularly on prostitutes as a class or on pregnant women are nonetheless distinctions on the basis of sex. The intervenor criticizes in this regard the reasoning in certain cases under the Canadian Bill of Rights.

R v. Lavoie (1970), 16 DLR (3d) 647 (BC Co. Ct.), at 652, per Schultz J.

R v. Beaulne, Ex p. Latreille (1971), 16 DLR (3d) 657 (Ont. HCJ), at 659, per Houlden J.

39. In its first two and a half years of women's equality litigation, the intervenor has found that cases of explicit "facial" distinctions against women are comparatively few, yet sex inequality in society is pervasive and damaging. The greatest harm is done by distinctions which are facially neutral. It is thus important, in its submission, that courts develop a sensitivity to "impact" or "adverse effect" analysis. Approaching an

issue with such sensitivity will often reveal that an issue which seems to be one involving a non-enumerated ground may actually raise, in substance, an issue of sex equality. In the employment context, for example, certain height and weight requirements, neutral on the surface, are actually proxies for a more explicit requirement to hire male workers.

40. In the past two decades, scholarship about women has begun to document the different reality of women's lives. Such scholarship, where it is available, can illuminate issues of sexual inequality by revealing the persistent and systemic patterns of dominance and subordination in society (i.e., revealing the structural inequality in the labour market, as was done in the *Action Travail des Femmes* case). Accordingly, in preference to supposition and stereotype, this scholarship should be relied upon when assessing the condition of women.

With Respect to the Non-Enumerated Grounds

General Principles

41. It is submitted that a non-enumerated ground may appear as proxy for an enumerated ground. For example, citizenship restrictions may in some cases be used to restrict opportunities for members of visible minority groups (although on the record in this case, it is not possible to say that citizenship is used in this fashion). Where it can be shown that this is occurring, the analysis should proceed as if the enumerated ground were overtly employed.

42. Although in many cases a sensitive analysis of the problem will show that it is not at all a problem involving a non-enumerated ground (but rather a problem involving an enumerated ground), in some cases the basis of distinction complained of will be a non-enumerated ground unrelated to any enumerated ground.

43. It is submitted that the language of section 15 clearly shows that the enumerated grounds are not intended to be exhaustive; legislative history and judicial interpretation reflect that this point is commonly understood.

Minister of Justice and Attorney General of Canada, *Government Response to Representations for Changes to Proposed Resolution*, January 12, 1981, at 4.

Motion Tabled by Minister of Justice in House of Commons, supra, at 6.

Equality for All, supra, at 5.

Andrews v. Law Society of British Columbia, [1986] 4 WWR 242 (BC CA), at 253.

44. The intervenor's survey of equality cases brought under section 15 to August 14, 1987 shows that far more claims involving non-enumerated grounds have come forward than have claims involving enumerated grounds.

Appendix A.

45. In our submission, unlimited reception of claims truly based on non-enumerated grounds will dilute the effectiveness of the guarantees of substantive equality. In an effort not to extend protection to interests which seem intuitively not to merit protection

under section 15, courts may develop such a stringent test for establishing denial of equality that a genuine claim, on a ground enumerated in section 15 or akin to an enumerated ground, would be unsuccessful.

46. It is accordingly submitted that limits should be imposed in providing access to the equality guarantees on the basis of the non-enumerated grounds. Aside from process claims discussed below, only claims based on non-enumerated grounds which are proxies for enumerated grounds or akin to enumerated grounds should be permitted.

Process Claims

47. It is submitted that a significant class of claims advanced on non-enumerated grounds are actually claims relating to the process of the law. As such, these claims would fall under the protection of the opening words of section 15, "equality before the law." It is appropriate to separate this class of case from those involving claims of denial of substantive equality, and to permit access to the process guarantees whether the basis of the distinction is enumerated or non-enumerated. Such a generous approach accords with the traditional respect for the rule of law and the social interest in evenhanded administration of justice. Although in some cases these process claims will involve substantive enactments (e.g., Criminal Code provisions), it is submitted that they should be regarded as "process" issues and dealt with as such.

R v. Hamilton; R v. Asselin; R v. McCullagh (1986), 17 OAC 241 (CA).

48. Dealing with a claim as a process issue means, essentially, that the applicant need not show a disadvantage of the sort described immediately below in the context of the guarantees of substantive equality. Similarly, it may be appropriate for the Court to require of the applicant a showing only that he or she has been treated differentially in a way that is not "reasonable" or "fair" in order to establish the breach of the process guarantee.

Substantive Claims

49. It is submitted that in each case where a claim of denial of substantive inequality is advanced on a non-enumerated ground, the Court should determine on the facts whether it involves a denial of substantive equality of the sort meant to be within section 15. We refer to these categorizations as "akin" to the enumerated grounds.

50. To guide such a factual inquiry into whether a category raises concerns of substantive inequality, the Court may wish to inquire:

(a) whether and to what extent it is related to an enumerated ground (e.g., marital status and sex, citizenship and national origin);

(b) whether it is institutionalized throughout society so as to affect, in a systematic and cumulative way, dignity, respect, access to resources, physical security, credibility, membership in community, or power; and

(c) whether it has a social history of disempowerment, exploitation, and subordination to and by dominant interests.

51. How this analysis might work is shown by its application in the case of women. Widely acknowledged indices of second class citizenship which have led to the recognition that women are a disadvantaged group include women's unequal pay, allocation to disrespected work, demeaned physical characteristics; targeting for rape, domestic battery, sexual abuse as children, and systematic sexual harassment; depersonalization, use in denigrating entertainment, and forced prostitution. For women, these abuses occur in an historical context characterized by disenfranchisement, preclusion from property ownership, exclusion from public life, and a sex-based poverty and devaluation of women's contributions in all spheres of social life which continue down to the present day.

Catharine MacKinnon, *Feminism Unmodified: Discourses on Life and Law* (Harvard University Press, 1987), 23-25, 40-41, 169-70, and 277-79.

52. An approach like that described in paragraphs 49 and 50 would eliminate from consideration under section 15 those cases where the only complaint of disadvantage amounts to the fact that a distinction is being made in the law under consideration. For example, two groups of business owners treated differently under a business licensing statute would not be entitled to claim the protection of section 15 where the different treatment is not based on an enumerated or akin ground, or not a genuine process claim.

53. Human rights legislation and international instruments will assist the Court in establishing what grounds are "akin" to those enumerated in section 15.

International Covenant on Civil and Political Rights, in force for Canada 19 August 1976, GA Res. 220 (XXI), 21 UNGAOR, Supp. (No.16) 52, UN Doc. A/6316 (1966).

European Convention for the Protection of Human Rights and Fundamental Freedoms, signed 4 November 1950, entered into force 3 September 1953, 213 UNTS 222.

Universal Declaration of Human Rights, adopted and proclaimed by the General Assembly, 10 December 1948, GA Res. 217A (III), UN Doc. A/810, at 71 (1948).

International Covenant on Economic, Social and Cultural Rights, adopted 16 December 1966, in force for Canada 19 August 1976, GA Res. 220 (XXI), 21 UNGAOR, Supp. (No.16) 49, UN Doc. A/6316 (1966).

Application of the Purposive Interpretation and Relationship to Section 1

54. It is submitted that an initial question in any section 15 application or analysis is whether the claim relates to a process or a substantive interest.

55. Where the claim involves an alleged denial of substantive equality, the applicant would have to demonstrate his or her entitlement to the protection of the section by outlining the nature of his or her disadvantage. This may involve showing that he or she is characterized by an enumerated ground (e.g., mental or physical disability) or by the "disadvantaged" aspect of a neutral enumerated ground (e.g., is a woman, a person of colour). In other cases, such a demonstration would involve showing how he or she is disadvantaged even though a member of a traditionally dominant group. For example, a

single father who wished to assert under section 15 a claim to "mother's" allowance, would have to show that he is disadvantaged (i.e., impecunious) even though a member of a traditionally dominant group, before he could advance a claim to substantive equality under section 15. In yet other cases, this initial stage will involve a demonstration of disadvantage in the context of a non-enumerated ground. The intervenor contemplates that the showing of disadvantage could either be categorical (i.e., membership in a group that is accepted as disadvantaged) or contextual (though a member of a traditionally dominant group, the applicant is disadvantaged in the particular context of this case).

56. The applicant would also have to show how the disadvantage outlined is related to the purpose and provisions of the legislation being impugned.

57. The applicant would also have to demonstrate an impairment of his or her equality. Given the approach to section 15 outlined in the previous section of this factum, the intervenor suggests that the inquiry here might focus on establishing to a civil standard of proof the impact of the impugned provision either in purpose or effect on values like dignity, respect, access to resources, physical security, credibility, membership in community, and power.

58. It is submitted that there is no basis in the language of section 15 for importing a "reasonableness" or "fairness" standard into the analysis of substantive equality claims under section 15. To import such a reasonableness or fairness standard in effect means that a court would be reading section 15 as if it provided that every individual is equal before and under the law and entitled to the equal protection and equal benefit of the law "to the extent that such entitlement is reasonable or fair." It is submitted that any assessment of reasonableness which is needed for purposes of a claim to substantive equality could be done in the context of section 1.

59. It is submitted that all substantive grounds, enumerated or akin, which are entitled to protection under section 15, should be accorded the same level of protection. In other words, there should be only one level of scrutiny under section 15, and that a rigorous one. One level of scrutiny for all claims of substantive equality will work because the section 1 analysis permits the Court to examine the justification for departures from equality. Accordingly, a ground like age need not be afforded a lower level of scrutiny simply because one can envision several instances where differential treatment on the basis of age may seem intuitively acceptable. Rather, the acceptability of those examples can be assessed under section 1.

60. If a violation of section 15 is established using the foregoing analysis, the party seeking to uphold the legislation under section 1 would have to establish a purpose for it that meets the tests set out by this Court in Oakes; similarly, the relationship between the purpose and the means chosen to fulfill it would have to withstand scrutiny.

Oakes, supra, at 138-40.

Submissions on the Decision Under Appeal

61. Madam Justice McLachlin, speaking for the Court, said that the essential meaning of the section 15 guarantee of equality is to require that persons who are

similarly situated be similarly treated and conversely that persons who are differently situated be differently treated. She then said that the nature of the analysis under section 15 is to determine whether a fair-minded person, weighing the purposes of the impugned legislation against the effects on the individuals adversely affected and giving due weight to the right of the legislature to pass laws for the good of all would conclude that the legislative means are unreasonable or unfair in the sense of being unduly prejudicial.

Andrews, supra, at 248 and 252-53. Case Under Appeal at 97 and 103.

62. The intervenor agrees with the movement in the *Andrews* case away from mere formal differentiation and toward a substantive test for determining whether an infringement of the equality guarantees has occurred. The substantive test outlined above by the intervenor requires an applicant to explain his or her disadvantage, how it relates to the legislation at issue, and how the provision impairs his or her equality. On the other hand, requiring only the formal establishment of some distinction before the analysis shifts to section 1 is really an approach which is designed to deal with formal, or facial, denials of equality. As stated above, most denials of equality which affect the disadvantaged are not evident on the surface of the legislation. However, often provisions intended to promote the equality of the disadvantaged will present a superficial differentiation between the disadvantaged (who are meant to benefit from the legislation) are the advantaged (who are not). Thus, a test which emphasizes mere distinctions might well impair the realization of the purpose of section 15 because it might facilitate attacks on legislation aimed at removing disadvantage.

63. It is submitted, however, that the definition of equality and the analytical approach propounded in *Andrews* suffer from the following shortcomings.

64. In our submission, it is desirable to reject quite clearly the purely formal or Aristotelian concept of equality when dealing with claims to substantive equality under section 15. This "similarly situated" definition of equality is essentially a rule of rational consistency, and thus comports well with claims to procedural equality. However, it says nothing about human rights to dignity and respect, and thus is not a test which will prove helpful in determining whether a substantive denial of equality has occurred.

65. The "similarly situated" rule is already embodied in the rule of law. The rule of law is satisfied if officials enforce rules impartially against all those to whom they apply, blind to differences that are irrelevant from the standpoint of the policy or principle of the rules. To say that likes should be treated alike in the formal sense of equality is to say only that laws should be laws. Such a standard may not be out of place in analyzing process claims, which deal with the administration of these laws and, on a larger scale, access to the legal process. However, this formal approach does not assist in deriving the underlying meaning of equality in the context of a claim to substantive equality.

66. This flaw inherent in the similarly situated approach is demonstrated in the reasoning of Tysoe JA in *R v. Gonzales*, who interpreted the guarantee of "equality

before the law" in the Canadian Bill of Rights to mean, "They shall be entitled to have the law as it exists applied equally and without fear or favour to all persons to whom it relates or extends." His interpretation was specifically rejected by Hall J in his concurring judgment in *R v. Drybones* and impliedly rejected in the result of that case.

R v. Gonzales (1962), 37 CR 56 (BC CA), at 62, per Tysoe JA.

R v. Drybones, [1970] SCR 282, at 299-300, per Hall J.

67. Moreover, as was recognized by Madam Justice McLachlin, the similarly situated rule requires reference to underlying criteria which the rule itself does not articulate and it thus often imports *sub silentio* the values of an unequal society into its equality standard. This weakness has also been noted by the Ontario Court of Appeal:

> [I]t is not always clear whether persons are or are not similarly situated, and whether, even if they are not, this is relevant to a section 15 inquiry.

It is usually possible to find differences between classes of persons and, on the basis of these differences, conclude that the persons are not similarly situated. However, what are perceived to be "differences" between persons or classes of persons could be the result of stereotypes based on existing inequalities which the equality provisions of the Charter are designed to eliminate, not perpetuate.

Century 21 Ramos Realty Inc. v. The Queen (1987), 58 OR (2d) 737, at 756-57.

68. The similarly situated rule presumes that all persons are similarly situated in most respects. The error in this assumption is illustrated by its application in cases of sex equality. Because men and women are not similarly situated with respect to their reproductive capacities, the rule is said to permit different treatment where there is a biological difference. There are, however, a number of problems with this approach.

The most important problem is the inherent contradiction it contains. The law is trying both to admit and to deny that differences exist between women and men. The result is confusion. For example, judges confound biological differences with socially determined differences, or in confirming biological differences they justify detrimental differential treatment. Professor Catharine MacKinnon captures the essence of the problem when she writes:

> The relationship between woman's anatomy and her social fate is the pivot on which turns [*sic*] all attempts, and opposition to attempts, to define or change her situation. At every turn, nature appears hand in glove with culture, so that the special definition of woman's place within man's world appears to conform exactly to her differences from him. But the same reality can be seen as the fist of social dominance hidden in the soft glove of reasonableness—the ideology of biological fiat.

N. Colleen Sheppard, *Charterwatch: Reflections on Equality*, supra, at 277.

69. It is submitted that this Court should not adopt the "reasonable and fair" analysis propounded by the Court of Appeal in *Andrews* for the following reasons.

70. It is submitted that the Court in *Andrews* adopted a two-step approach to section 15, first deciding on the basis of the "similarly situated" analysis whether there is a

denial of equality and then proceeding under the "without discrimination" rubric to ask whether such a denial is "reasonable" or "fair."

71. It is submitted that the without discrimination rubric does not give rise to a "reasonable" or "fair" test: rather, it reflects the preoccupation in the guarantees of substantive equality with those who have traditionally been the victims of discrimination. Thus, this echo of the language of human rights codes should not be taken as an invitation to assess the fairness of denials of equality, but instead should provide a reminder of the egalitarian purpose of section 15.

72. In deciding that the words "without discrimination" in section 15 necessitate a test of reasonableness and fairness, the *Andrews* Court both ignores the egalitarian content of section 15 expressed in the words "equal before and under the law" and "equal protection and equal benefit of the law," and invents an unprecedented meaning for "discrimination."

Simpsons-Sears Ltd., supra, at 551-52.

73. The balancing of means and ends is, according to the *Oakes* test, the role of section 1. As the Federal Court of Appeal said in *Smith Kline*, "If a category must be shown to be unreasonable or unfair before it can be said to give rise to a breach of equality rights, it is difficult to see how there can ever be room for application of s. 1." The reasonable and fair test propounded in *Andrews* in fact leaves no, or almost no, room for the application of section 1. Although the Court in Andrews suggests a possible application for section 1, that application is markedly more restricted than that developed in cases like *Oakes* and applied to other sections of the Charter.

Smith Kline & French Laboratories Ltd. et al. v. Attorney-General of Canada (1986), 12 CPR (3d) 386 (FCA), at 393.

Oakes, supra, at 138-39.

74. At the same time that it effectively moves the "means and ends" analysis from section 1, governed by *Oakes*, to section 15, *Andrews* omits or changes aspects of the *Oakes* approach in ways that significantly weaken the Charter's commitment to equality. In particular,

(a) *Oakes* requires that the purpose of legislation be evaluated against fundamental values, including equality, and *Andrews* does not;

(b) the test of reasonableness in *Andrews* is more onerous than in *Oakes* in that it requires the applicant to show undue prejudice, a requirement that is nowhere mandated by the words of section 15; and

(c) *Oakes* requires that there be a rational connection and proportionality between the object and the means chosen, and *Andrews* does not, so that an equality rights limitation that is out of proportion with its ends could still survive section 15 analysis.

75. The Court in *Andrews* places the burden of proving unreasonableness, unfairness, or irrationality on the equality-seeker, a requirement that is neither supported by

the text of section 15 nor in keeping with the approach outlined in *Oakes*. Under the *Andrews* test, the equality-seeker must show that the limit is not a reasonable one and demonstrably justified, whereas section 1 and *Oakes* require the party relying on the provision to assume the burden of showing that it is reasonable and demonstrably justified. The result of so collapsing the section 1 analysis into section 15, with a reversal of the burden of proof, is that a limit which could not survive section 1 scrutiny might never be subjected to it.

76. Nowhere in the language of the Charter is there a requirement that courts defer to a "right of the legislature to pass laws for the good of all." An early version of section 1 of the Charter was amended to remove from it this type of justification for a limit on a Charter right. Moreover, such a requirement is tantamount to saying that there is a presumption of constitutional validity, whereas this Court has said that such a presumption is not compatible with the innovative and evolutive nature of the Charter.

Robin Elliot, *UBC Law Review Charter Edition*, supra, at 24-25.

AG Manitoba v. Metropolitan Stores (MTS) Ltd. et al., [1981] 1 SCR 110, at 125.

77. The similarly situated definition of equality in Andrews has been widely accepted by Canadian courts, including provincial courts of appeal. In addition, the *Andrews* "reasonable and fair" analysis of section 15 has been adopted by several courts of appeal. However, for all of the reasons stated above, it is submitted that this Court should decline to approve the approach taken in *Andrews* to the section 15 guarantees of substantive equality, although it may wish to explore what aspects of it are useful in the context of a process claim.

Re McDonald and the Queen (1985), 51 OR (2d) 745 (CA).

R v. R.L. (1986), 14 OAC 318 (CA).

Bregman v. Attorney General of Canada (1986), 18 OAC 82 (CA).

R v. LeGallant (1986), 6 BCLR (2d) 105 (CA).

Ramos, supra.

78. The *Andrews* "reasonable and fair" limitation on equality has been rejected by the Nova Scotia Court of Appeal and the Federal Court of Appeal.

Smith Kline, supra.

Reference Respecting the Family Benefits Act, unreported, November 27, 1986 (NS CA).

79. Variations on the approaches discussed thus far appear in the decisions of the BC Court of Appeal in *Rebic* and *Shewchuk*; the Federal Court of Appeal in *Smith Kline*, and the Nova Scotia Court of Appeal in the *Reference Respecting the Family Benefits Act*. The approaches adopted in these cases differ from one another but none scrutinizes the impugned legislation in light of the purpose of section 15.

Rebic v. Collver Prov. J and Attorney General for British Columbia (1986), 2 BCLR (2d) 364 (CA).

Shewchuk v. Ricard (1986), 28 DLR (4th) 429 (BC CA).

Smith Kline, supra.

Reference Respecting the Family Benefits Act, supra.

PART IV: NATURE OF ORDER SOUGHT

80. It is, accordingly, respectfully requested that this Court adopt a purposive approach to the interpretation of section 15, which would recognize both the legal process and substantive aspects to equality, and acknowledge that the purpose of the substantive equality guarantees is to promote the equality of hitherto powerless, excluded and disadvantaged groups.

81. LEAF takes no position on the nature of the Order to be granted in this Appeal.

THE OUTCOME

Head Notes—Andrews v. The Law Society of British Columbia and the Attorney General of British Columbia

Held:

Section 15(1) of the Charter

Per Dickson CJ and McIntyre, Lamer, Wilson, and L'Heureux-Dubé JJ: Section 15(1) of the Charter provides for every individual a guarantee of equality before and under the law, as well as the equal protection and equal benefit of the law without discrimination. This is not a general guarantee of equality; its focus is on the application of the law. No problem regarding the scope of the word "law" arose in this case because legislation was under attack.

The concept of equality ... as embodied in s. 15(1) of the Charter ... is a comparative concept, the condition of which may only be attained or discerned by comparison with the condition of others in the social and political setting in which the question arises. It must be recognized ... however, that every difference in treatment between individuals under the law will not necessarily result in inequality and, as well, that identical treatment may frequently produce serious inequality. (p. 164) [T]he main consideration must be the impact of the law on the individual or group concerned. Recognizing that there will always be an infinite variety of personal characteristics, capacities, entitlements and merits among those subject to a law, there must be accorded, as nearly as may be possible, an equality of benefit and protection and no more of the restrictions, penalties or burdens imposed upon one than another. (p. 165)

The [similarly situated] test ... is seriously deficient in that it excludes any consideration of the nature of the law. (p. 166) [M]ere equality of application to similarly situated groups or individuals does not afford a realistic test for a violation of equality rights. For, as has been said, a bad law will not be saved merely because it operates equally upon those to whom it has application. Nor will a law necessarily be bad because it makes distinctions. (p. 167) [T]he test cannot be accepted as a fixed rule or formula for the resolution of equality questions arising under the Charter. Consideration must be given to the content of the law, to its purpose, and its impact upon those to whom it applies, and also upon those whom it excludes from its application. The issues which will arise from case to case are such that it would be wrong to attempt to confine these considerations within such a fixed and limited formula. (p. 168)

It is not every distinction or differentiation in treatment at law which will transgress the equality guarantees of s. 15 of the Charter. It is, of course, obvious that legislatures may—and to govern effectively—must treat different individuals and groups in different ways. Indeed, such distinctions are one of the main preoccupation of legislatures. The classifying of individuals and groups, the making of different provisions respecting such groups, the application of different rules, regulations, requirements and qualifications to different persons is necessary for the governance of modern society. ... [F]or the accommodations of differences, which is the essence of true equality, it will frequently be necessary to make distinctions. (pp. 168-69)

The right to equality before and under the law and the rights to the equal protection and benefit of the law contained in s. 15 are granted with the direction contained in s. 15 itself that they be without discrimination. Discrimination is unacceptable in a democratic society because it epitomizes the worst effects of the denial of equality, and discrimination reinforced by law is particularly repugnant. ... It is against this evil that s. 15 provides a guarantee. (p. 172)

Discrimination is a distinction which, whether intentional or not but based on grounds relating to personal characteristics of the individual or group, has an effect which imposes disadvantages not imposed upon others or which withholds or limits access to advantages available to other members of society. Distinctions based on personal characteristics attributed to an individual solely on the basis of association with a group will rarely escape the charge of discrimination, while those based on an individual's merits and capacities will rarely be so classed.

Generally, the principles applied under the Human Rights Acts are equally applicable to questions of discrimination under s. 15(1). However, the Charter requires a two-step approach to s. 15(1). The first step is to determine whether or not an infringement of a guaranteed right has occurred. The second step is to determine whether, if there has been an infringement, it can be justified under s. 1. The two steps must be kept analytically distinct because of the different attribution of the burden of proof; the citizen must establish the infringement of his or her Charter right and the state must justify the infringement.

The grounds of discrimination enumerated in s. 15(1) are not exhaustive. Grounds analogous to those enumerated are also covered and the section may be even broader than that although it is not necessary to answer that question in this case since the ground advanced in this case falls into the analogous category.

[The] "enumerated or analogous grounds" approach ... adopts the concept that discrimination is generally expressed by the enumerated grounds. The analysis of

discrimination in this approach must take place within the context of the enumerated grounds and those analogous to them. (pp. 179-80)

The words "without discrimination" require more than a mere finding of distinction between the treatment of groups or individuals. These words are a form of qualifier built into s. 15 itself and limit those distinctions which are forbidden by the section to those which involve prejudice or disadvantage. The effect of the impugned distinction or classification on the complainant must be considered. Given that not all distinctions and differentiations created by law are discriminatory, a complainant under s. 15(1) must show not only that he or she is not receiving equal treatment before and under the law or that the law has a differential impact on him or her in the protection or benefit of the law but must show in addition that the law is discriminatory.

A rule which bars an entire class of persons from certain forms of employment, solely on the grounds of a lack of citizenship status and without consideration of educational and professional qualifications or the other attributes or merits of individuals in the group, infringes s. 15 equality rights. Section 42 of the Barristers and Solicitors Act is such a rule.

Per La Forest J: The views of McIntyre J as to the meaning of s. 15(1) were substantially agreed with in so far as relevant to the question of whether or not the impugned provision amounted to discrimination based on "irrelevant personal differences" such as those listed in s. 15 and, traditionally, in human rights legislation. The opening words of s. 15 referring more generally to equality, however, may have a significance that extends beyond protection from discrimination through the application of law. Nevertheless, all legislative classifications need not be rationally supportable before the courts; s. 15 was not intended to be a tool for the wholesale subjection of legislation to judicial scrutiny.

The impugned legislation distinguished the respondents from other persons on the basis of a personal characteristic which shares many similarities with those enumerated in s. 15. Citizenship is typically not within the control of the individual and is, at least temporarily, a characteristic of personhood which is not alterable by conscious action and which in some cases is not alterable except on the basis of unacceptable costs. Non-citizens are a group of persons who are relatively powerless politically and whose interests are likely to be compromised by legislative decisions.

Citizenship, while properly required for certain types of legitimate governmental objectives, is generally irrelevant to the legitimate work of government in all but a limited number of areas. Legislating citizenship as a basis for distinguishing between persons, here for conditioning access to the practice of a profession, harbours the potential for undermining the essential or underlying values of a free and democratic society embodied in s. 15. Legislative conditioning on the basis of citizenship may, in certain circumstances, be acceptable in the free and democratic society that is Canada, but that legislation must be justified by the government under s. 1 of the Charter.

Section 1 of the Charter

Per Dickson CJ and Wilson and L'Heureux-Dubé JJ: The legislation at issue was not justified under s. 1.

The objective of the legislation was not sufficiently pressing and substantial to warrant overcoming the rights protected by s. 15. Given that s. 15 is designed to protect those groups who suffer social, political, and legal disadvantage in our society, the burden resting on government to justify the type of discrimination against such groups is appropriately an onerous one.

The proportionality test was not met. The requirement of citizenship is not carefully tailored to achieve the objective that lawyers be familiar with Canadian institutions and customs and may not even be rationally connected to it. Most citizens, natural-born or otherwise, are committed to Canadian society but that commitment is not ensured by citizenship. Conversely, non-citizens may be deeply committed to our country. Even if lawyers do perform a governmental function, citizenship does not guarantee that they will honourably and conscientiously carry out their public duties: that is a function of their being good lawyers, not of citizenship.

Per La Forest J: While in general agreement with McIntyre J about how the legislation must be approached under s. 1 in balancing the right infringed by the legislation against its objectives, the legislation fails to meet the test of proportionality.

Citizenship neither ensures the objectives of familiarity with Canadian institutions and customs nor of commitment to Canadian society. Restriction of access to the profession to citizens is over-inclusive. Less drastic methods for achieving the desired objectives are available.

While certain state activities may, for both symbolic and practical reasons, be confined to those who are full members of our political society, such restriction should not apply to the legal profession as a whole. The practice of law is primarily a private profession. A lawyer working for a private client does not play a role in the administration of justice requiring citizenship. Ordinary lawyers are not privy to government information and there are rules to restrict lawyers from obtaining confidential governmental information. Their situation differs from those involved in government policy-making or administration.

Per McIntyre and Lamer JJ (dissenting): The citizenship requirement is reasonable and sustainable under s. 1 given the importance of the legal profession in the government of the country. The measure was not disproportionate to the object to be attained. Non-citizens are encouraged to become citizens and the maximum delay imposed upon the non-citizen from the date of acquisition of permanent resident status is three years. It is reasonable to expect that the newcomer who seeks to gain the privileges and status within the land and the right to exercise the great powers that admission to the practice of law will give should accept citizenship and its obligations as well as its advantages and benefits.

IN THE SUPREME COURT OF CANADA
(ON APPEAL FROM THE COURT OF APPEAL FOR ONTARIO)

BETWEEN:

HER MAJESTY THE QUEEN

Appellant

(Respondent)

AND:

CANADIAN NEWSPAPERS COMPANY LIMITED

Respondent

(Appellant)

AND:

WOMEN'S LEGAL EDUCATION AND ACTION FUND, ONTARIO COALITION OF RAPE CRISIS CENTRES, BARBRA SCHLIFER COMMEMORATIVE CLINIC, WOMEN'S COLLEGE HOSPITAL SEXUAL ASSAULT CARE CENTRE TEAM, METROPOLITAN TORONTO SPECIAL COMMITTEE ON CHILD ABUSE, METRO ACTION COMMITTEE ON PUBLIC VIOLENCE AGAINST WOMEN AND CHILDREN, BROADSIDE COMMUNICATIONS, LTD., AND WOMENHEALTHSHARING, INC.

Intervenors

AND:

ATTORNEY GENERAL OF ONTARIO

Intervenor

AND:

PROCUREUR GENERAL DE LA PROVINCE DE QUEBEC

Intervenor

Factum of the Women's Legal Education and Action Fund (LEAF)

Canadian Newspapers v. Canada

INTRODUCTION

This case arose in the context of section 442(3) of the Criminal Code, which allows for a publication ban on the identity of sexual assault complainants in several circumstances. Where the complainant requests it, as happened in this case, the ban must be imposed by the trial judge. At trial, Canadian Newspapers Company Ltd. made a civil application to have section 442(3) declared unconstitutional on the basis that, by making the ban mandatory in certain circumstances, the section violated the right of freedom of the press guaranteed by section 2(b) of the Charter. The trial judge upheld section 442(3) and ordered the publication ban. He found that section 442(3)'s objective was to remove some of the historic barriers that have made complainants reluctant to come forward when they have been sexually assaulted. In his view, given the purpose of the provision, the mandatory ban on publication was a reasonable limit under section 1 of the Charter.

Canadian Newspapers appealed to the Ontario Court of Appeal, which reversed the ruling and held that section 442(3)'s infringement of freedom of expression was not justified under section 1. Although Chief Justice Howland agreed that the limitation placed by the provision upon freedom of the press was reasonable, he went on to consider the possible impact of the provision on the accused. Howland CJO found that in some cases a complainant may have made false allegations, or may have previously falsely accused other persons. In such cases, the mandatory nature of the ban could prevent these facts from emerging and, therefore, infringe an accused's right to a fair trial. Note, however, that the accused was not a party to these proceedings; the plaintiff throughout was Canadian Newspapers.

The Crown appealed to the Supreme Court. LEAF intervened, in coalition with the Ontario Coalition of Rape Crisis Centres, the Barbra Schlifer Commemorative Clinic, the Women's College Hospital Sexual Assault Care Centre Team, the Metropolitan Toronto Special Committee on Child Abuse, the Metro Action Committee on Public Violence Against Women and Children, Broadside Communications, Ltd., and Women HealthSharing, Inc., to argue that the ban protected and promoted the complainants' right to equality. The Attorneys General for Ontario and Quebec also intervened in support of the section.

FACTUM

PART I: FACTS

1. Intervenors are rape crisis and treatment centres, policy, research, litigation, organizing and action groups on behalf of victims of sexual violence, and women's publishing concerns. They are equality advocates for women and children with particular experience in the areas of sexual violence against women and children, the preconditions for access to justice by sexually offended individuals, equal access to freedom of expression by women, and equality rights of disadvantaged groups.

2. Intervenors bring extensive expertise on the equality, liberty, security, and extensive needs of women and children survivors of sexual offences on the basis of direct contact with victims, relevant legal and social research and scholarship, policy development in the public and private sectors, work with agencies of government, and the practice of medicine, counselling, journalism, and law.

3. Challenged here is section 442(3) of the Criminal Code ("section 442(3)"), which provides for mandatory non-publication of the names and identities of victims of sexual assault at the discretion of the victim or prosecutor.

Criminal Code, 1953-54, c. 51, s. 442(3).

4. Victims of sexual assault often do not report the crimes against them because of fear of revenge, dread of the attitudes of police and courts, experience of not being believed, and feelings of humiliation and shame.

Reported and Unreported Crimes, Exhibit "A" to Affidavit of Carolyn Kobernick, Case on Appeal ("CA"), 97-99.

Rape: Guidelines for a Community Response, Exhibit "B" to Affidavit of Carolyn Kobernick, CA, 131 and 137.

5. Uncontroverted expert testimony at trial establishes that sexual assault victims are often unwilling to report crimes and to proceed with prosecutions if their names and identities may be publicized, and that reporting of sexual assault would drop if section 442(3) protections were eliminated.

Testimony of Doreen Carol Boucher, CA, 72-75.

6. The factual support for section 442(3) provided by the record in this case is universally confirmed by the extensive experience of intervenors.

PART II: ISSUES

7. Intervenors adopt the statement of points in issue as defined by this Court in its Order of June 6, 1985.

PART III: ARGUMENT

Introduction

8. Intervenors submit that section 442(3) should be upheld in its entirety under sections 1, 2(b), 7, 15, and 28 of the Canadian Charter of Rights and Freedoms ("the Charter").

Canadian Charter of Rights and Freedoms, Constitution Act, 1982, as enacted by Canada Act 1981 (UK), 1982, c. 11.

9. Intervenors submit that section 442(3) raises no issues under section 2(b) of the Charter because Canadian Newspapers have no legitimate interest in the "expression" of names and identifying information of victims of sexual assault.

10. If section 442(3) is found to raise expressive concerns, the provision is, alternatively, submitted to be constitutional as an equality, expression, liberty, and security measure under sections 2(b), 7, 15, and 28 of the Charter. Publication of identities of victims of sexual assault against their will significantly threatens equal access to justice, equal security, and expressive equality of Canadian women and children, materially undermines their liberty, and threatens their physical security and sense of security. Section 442(3) promotes these interests.

11. Intervenors agree with the Appellant and the Ontario Court of Appeal that the Respondents have no standing to raise section 11(d) fair trial issues in this action. All arguments concerning the gains to sexual assault defendants if section 442(3) were discretionary or eliminated are fair trial arguments that Canadian Newspapers have no standing to make.

Reasons for Judgment (Howland CJO), CA, at 197.

Re Southam Inc. and The Queen (No. 1) (1983), 41 OR (2d) 113 (CA), at 117.

12. Intervenors approach the Charter as a whole, considering each provision in light of the others, prior to balancing conflicts of rights under section 1. This preserves the integrity of the Charter's design, the purpose of each Charter-protected right, and the distinctive role of section 1 as more than a second venue for substantive judgments better approached first as matters of substantive rights.

13. Should the case be resolved under section 1, Intervenors submit that Charter-based equality, liberty, security, and expressive interests of women and children justify section 442(3) as a reasonable limit on any expressive interests of newspapers and (if found properly raised), any section 11(d) fair trial rights of sexual assault defendants.

14. Intervenors submit that the Ontario Court of Appeal was correct in recognizing that section 442(3) serves an urgent social interest in encouraging reporting of sex offences. It was correct in holding that section 442(3) does not infringe section 11(d) in that trials remain public. That Court was further correct when, on the basis of these recognitions, it did not void section 442(3) entirely as a violation of speech and fair trial rights, as it was urged to do.

Reasons for Judgment (Osborne J), CA, 151-52.

15. However, the Ontario Court of Appeal erred in giving courts discretion to deny victims' requests for protection under section 442(3) by not recognizing the significance for Charter-based equality of the mandatory feature of the provision.

16. Charter-based equality, expression, liberty, and security rights provide the increment of constitutional support needed to uphold the mandatory victim-driven aspect of section 442(3).

17. At stake in this case are the practical conditions under which victims of sexual assault, overwhelmingly women and children, must rely on government equally to protect and vindicate their legal rights—hence the social conditions under which all women and children, the primary target groups for sexual assault, can live on a daily basis.

Respondents Have No Valid Expressive Interest in Publicizing the Identities of Victims of Sexual Assault

18. The name and identity of sexual assault victims is not "conscience, religion, thought, belief, or opinion" or part of their "expression," in the sense the Charter protects. The Charter does not expressly protect freedom of information or freedom to publicize, nor has it been interpreted to do so.

19. The expressive status of the names and identities of victims of sexual assault is nil. Under section 442(3), everything can be broadcast or published about the issue of sexual assault, the trial, and the victim—except who she personally is. Indeed, the victim's identity can be publicized by word of mouth, just not by the mass media; it can be fully publicized if she consents. A witness for the Respondents stated below that a section 442(3) order "would effectively preclude the reporting of the proceedings at trial." As the trial judge recognized in the instant case, the press can inform the public concerning a marital rape trial without disclosing the victim's identity.

Affidavit of Michael Grieve, CA, 63.

Reasons for Judgment (Osborne J), CA, 152-53.

20. Since the accused is on trial, not the victim, the victim deserves at least as much protection as an accused, and "[t]he public need not be aware of the identity of the accused in order to be informed about the legal issues being litigated." Where necessary, as here, to protect the victim's identity, and only for this reason, the defendant's identity could be covered by section 442(3), with no loss to public information.

R v. P. (1978), 41 CCC (2d) 377 (Ont. HC), at 379.

21. Broadcasting or publishing a sexual assault victim's name and identity against her will does not further the values on which section 2(b) is based, such as the dignity and worth of the person or the rule of law. Section 442(3) promotes these values.

R v. Keegstra (1984), 19 CCC (3d) 254 (Alta. QB), at 266-67.

22. Courts are less likely to protect one person's freedom of expression if it denies the freedom of expression of others. Some courts have upheld prohibitions on some

forms of expression which, in effect, cancel their expressive value by silencing the speech of others.

R v. Keegstra, supra, at 268.

R v. Zundel (1987), 58 OR (2d) 129 (CA), at 155.

Section 442(3) Promotes Equality Rights

23. Section 15 of the Charter provides both a constitutional right to equality and equal access to other Charter-protected rights ("equal benefit of the law"), including those of liberty, security, and expression. Section 28 further provides equal access by women and men to the Charter's guarantees. Section 442(3) effectuates the Charter's guarantee of freedom from discrimination on the basis of two enumerated grounds—age and sex—by supporting equal access to the criminal justice system, equal liberty and security, and equal freedom of expression.

Section 442(3) Advances Sexual Equality by Promoting Equal Access to Justice by Women

Equality Rights Must Be Approached Purposively

24. This Court has interpreted Charter guarantees in light of the interests they are meant to protect, adopting an expansive and broad rather than a narrow and technical approach. The interpretation of sections 15 and 28, and their relationship to other Charter provisions and to section 1, has taken this approach.

Law Society of Upper Canada v. Skapinker, [1984] 1 SCR 357, at 366.

Hunter v. Southam Inc., [1984] 2 SCR 145, at 156-57.

Singh et al. v. Minister of Employment and Immigration, [1985] 1 SCR 177, at 209, 218-19.

R v. Big M Drug Mart Ltd., [1985] 1 SCR 295, at 337-38.

R v. Oakes, [1986] 1 SCR 103, at 119.

25. This Court has identified equality as one of the fundamental values of society, against which the objects of all legislation must be measured.

Oakes, supra, at 136.

26. This Court has acknowledged the importance of promoting the equality of particular groups.

Big M Drug Mart, supra, at 337-38.

Société des Acadiens v. Association of Parents for Fairness in Education et al., [1986] 1 SCR 549, at 579.

Caldwell v. Stuart, [1984] 2 SCR 603, at 626.

27. It is submitted that sections 15 and 28, taken together, disclose an intent to promote the equality of women.

28. The legislative history of section 15, including changes in its drafting, reveals a clear intent that its equality guarantees be strong and reach the substance as well as process of law.

Peter Hogg, "A Comparison of the Canadian Charter of Rights and Freedoms with the Canadian Bill of Rights" in *Canadian Charter of Rights and Freedoms: Commentary*, W. Tarnopolsky and G. Beaudoin, eds. (Toronto: Carswell, 1982), 1, at 19-20.

Mary Eberts, "Women and Constitutional Renewal" in *Women and the Constitution*, A. Doerr and M. Carrier, eds. (Ottawa: Minister of Supply and Services Canada, 1981), at 3-27.

29. Section 28 was added to the Charter to confirm and strengthen its commitment to the equality of women.

"Summary of Conference Resolutions" in *Equality Rights and the Canadian Charter of Rights and Freedoms*, A. Bayefsky and M. Eberts, eds. (Toronto: Carswell, 1985), at 634-44.

30. Legislatures may confine legislative reforms to urgent concerns of needy constituencies.

Edwards Books and Art Ltd. v. The Queen, [1985] 2 SCR 713, at 772.

31. Women's status calls for legislative attention and Charter recognition as an equality problem. Acknowledged indices of all-pervasive second class citizenship, from unequal pay to physical victimization, have led to the recognition that women are socially unequal to men. Despite some "formal equality" under law, women are properly termed a disadvantaged or disempowered group.

House of Commons, Committee on Secretary of State, *Fairness in Funding: Report on the Women's Program* (May 26, 1987).

Sexual Assault Is a Sex Equality Issue

32. Victims of sexual assault are, overwhelmingly, women; perpetrators of sexual assault are, overwhelmingly, men. Sexual violation of women by men is both an indication and a practice of inequality between the sexes, specifically of the low status of women relative to men.

33. Only a fraction of rapes are reported. Only a fraction of reported rapes are prosecuted. Only a fraction of prosecuted rapes result in convictions. Rape sentences are often short. Most rapists, therefore, continue to live in society either undetected or unpunished and unrehabilitated.

House of Commons Debates, Official Report (1st Sess. 32nd Parl., vol. XIII, July 8, 1981), at 11349.

House of Commons Debates, Official Report, supra (Dec. 17, 1981), at 14187.

34. In sum, victims of sex crimes, largely women, are comparatively disadvantaged relative to the perpetrators of sex crimes, largely men. A systemic situation of inequality

between the sexes thus exists in the social practice of sexual violence, the victims of which are women, and in the operation of the criminal justice system, which *de jure* outlaws sexual violence but *de facto* permits men to engage in it on a wide scale.

Forced Publicity of the Identities of Sexual Assault Victims Is a Sex Equality Issue

35. Because of the place of sexual assault in the denigrated status of women under existing conditions of sex inequality, for a woman to be known as a victim of sexual violence is always stigmatic, frequently humiliating, and sometimes dangerous. A direct relationship thus exists between the ability of a sexual assault victim to control the conditions under which her victimization will become public knowledge and her willingness to report the crime against her.

Testimony of Doreen Carol Boucher, CA, supra.

36. Because sexual assault is still widely regarded as a statement of the victim's character, morals, and desires, media publicity harms reputations and deters reporting.

37. As the courts below recognized, when identifying information about a female who has been a victim of sexual violence is involuntarily disclosed, the impact on her employment opportunities, family and personal life, emotional well-being, dignity, reputation, physical security, and future can be devastating. The long-term effects of involuntary disclosure can include rejection by family members, ostracism from the community, deteriorated work relationships, termination of employment, further terrorization, harassment and assault, and silencing.

38. When assailants are unlikely to be reported, due to complainants' fear of publicity or whatever reason, the victim population is subjected to heightened risk of crime.

39. While intervenors see no value in the publication of victim identities, intervenors see positive value in news coverage of rape cases otherwise. Such accounts can diminish the aura of shame and secrecy surrounding sexual assault, reduce the isolation of victims from one another and from information about sexual assault, reduce public ignorance about the nature and extent of the problem, and counter public apathy. Intervenors also, in general, oppose publication bans on defendant names and identities, since other victims of the same abuser (of whom there are often many) are less likely to be found.

40. Uncertainty as to whether one's identity will be published or broadcast upon reporting a sexual offence is a significant barrier to reporting. Only a mandatory non-publication rule—leaving the choice of publicity primarily with the victim—provides the certainty that permits all victims to know, at the time they are making the decision to report, that reporting their offence will not further injure them through its publication. All women and children, as target classes for sexual assault, thus have a material interest in section 442(3) as helping to provide them equal access to the judicial process.

Section 442(3) Is Protected by Sections 15 and 28 of the Charter

41. Section 15 must be given prospective effect to give it a purposive interpretation. Regardless of the timing of the commencement of an application, each section of

the Charter must be interpreted in light of all its provisions, including the equality rights provisions. In any event, legislation that invokes equality defences should not be judicially modified prior to an opportunity for full constitutional defence.

42. In cases arising under human rights legislation, this Court has recognized the need to secure the rights of historically disadvantaged persons such as women through protecting positive relief measures that improve their condition. Such measures have been characterized as "quasi-constitutional." It is submitted that women's rights should be at least as expansive under the Charter as under human rights codes. Acts specifically mandated by statutes that promote sex equality should receive at least as much protection under the Charter as acts authorized, but not specifically mandated by statutes that promote sex equality, have received under human rights codes.

Insurance Corporation of British Columbia v. Heerspink et al., [1982] 2 SCR 145, at 157-58.

Action Travail des Femmes v. Canadian National Railway Company, [1987] 1 SCR 1114.

Robichaud v. Canada (Treasury Board), [1987] 2 SCR 84.

43. Just as statutes that are neutral on their face as to sex or age can be based on discriminatory attitudes and can have unintended or non-consciously discriminatory effects, such statutes can be based on egalitarian purposes or have the result of advancing equality in their applications.

Yick Wo v. Hopkins, 118 US 356 (1886).

Ontario Human Rights Commission and Theresa O'Malley v. Simpsons-Sears Ltd., [1985] 2 SCR 536, at 546-47.

44. The clear result of section 442(3) is to advance the equality of women by providing equal access to criminal redress for sexual violation through reducing the consequences of reporting such crimes, of which women are disproportionately the victims, and that are signals and integral to the maintenance of women's second class social status.

45. This Court has recognized that dominant groups in society should not be permitted to use the Charter to cut back legislative measures designed for the advancement of the less advantaged.

Edwards Books and Art Ltd., supra, at 779.

46. While a proper legislative purpose cannot save a law that violates the Charter any more than a proper private motive can save a practice that discriminates under human rights legislation, both the legislature's purpose and the impact of its legislation are relevant in assessing the constitutionality of a statute.

Action Travail des Femmes, supra.

AG Quebec v. Quebec Association of Protestant School Boards, [1984] 2 SCR 66.

Big M Drug Mart Ltd., supra.

47. The legislature tailored section 442(3) to sex offences, victims of which are mostly women and children. It noted scholarship documenting underreporting of rape, cited women's fear of public stigma and humiliation as special factors in their non-reporting, and connected these factors to women's social status.

House of Commons Debates, Official Report (1st Sess. 30th Parl., vol. IX), no. 18, 1975, 9204 and 9225.

48. Parliament has twice reconsidered a version of section 442(3) giving courts discretion over non-publication orders. Both times it expressly readopted the mandatory provision, consciously choosing to leave the publicity decision with the victim(s) and their representatives.

Bill C-15, An Act To Amend the Criminal Code and the Canada Evidence Act (2nd Sess., 33rd Parl., assented to June 30, 1987), House of Commons, s. 13(3) (First Reading).

Minutes of the Proceedings and Evidence of the Legislative Committee on Bill C-15, House of Commons, March 17, 1987.

Bill C-15, supra, s. 14(3) (as passed).

Bill C-89, An Act To Amend the Criminal Code [Victims of Crimes] (2nd Sess., 33rd Parl., First Reading November 5, 1987).

49. Counsel for the Defendant argued at trial that in some rape cases, "the real victim is the person accused by the alleged victim," apparently on the assumption that women fabricate rape charges. On this theory, publication of victim identities would presumably produce a wide-ranging inquiry into their sexual associations. Rejection of such assumptions underlies current public policy, exemplified by provisions that exclude sexual history and character evidence in sexual assault cases. The right to publicize a victim's name would thus punish and deter grounded as well as ungrounded charges, a distinction usually left to the trial process.

Cross-examination by Mr. Petrone, CA, 75.

Criminal Code, supra, section 246.6.

50. Allowing judicial and media discretion over publicity is based on the view that the likely veracity of some sexual assault victims can be distinguished from that of others prior to trial. This reveals a false assumption that certain women are knowably likely to be fabricating rape charges under certain factual conditions. Only a trial can make this determination.

51. The protections of the Charter are not designed only for individuals, but also for groups, so that group members can be aware of the equality of treatment or respect afforded their group and share the sense that they can expect equality of treatment and respect as well.

Kask v. Shimizu, [1986] 28 DLR (4th) 64, at 69.

52. Because of the risks of forced publicity, the right of victims of sexual assault to non-publication of their name and identity promotes reporting and prosecution of sex

crimes. Removal of that right practically precludes equal access to the criminal process for many women and children on the basis of their sex (women), age (boys), and age and sex (girls).

Section 442(3) Advances Equality for Boys and Girls by Promoting Equal Access to Justice by Children

53. Children are often victims of sexual abuse, overwhelmingly by adult men. The powerlessness of children enhances their vulnerability to sexual abuse and places them at a disadvantage in the legal system.

Ministry of Justice and Attorney General of Canada, *Sexual Offences Against Children* (Badgley Report) (1984), 30-32, 196-98, 927-28.

54. The legislature expanded section 442(3) with children specifically in mind, now covering more sex crimes of which children are the victims, and witnesses under 18 years of age.

Bill C-15, supra.

55. The publicity associated with trials is often so traumatic for child victims or witnesses of sex crimes that it is decided that justice is not worth the cost. When, for whatever reason, child victims do not benefit from the existing publication ban on victim identification, the added burden of exposure makes testifying in court more traumatic and sometimes impossible.

56. Courts have previously recognized that children are damaged by publicizing their involvement in crimes, whether as perpetrators or victims. Press is excluded and identifying information protected in young offender proceedings because protecting youth from the damaging effects of publicity is more important than any speech interests involved. Such provisions are constitutional.

Re N. v. The Queen (1979), 48 CCC (2d) 97, at 103.

Re Southam Inc. and The Queen (No. 1) (1984), 16 CCC (3d) 263, at 271 and 282.

Re Canadian Newspapers and The Queen (1984), 16 CCC (3d) 495, at 508-9.

57. A Charter defeat of section 442(3), which applies to children as well as adults, could be used to undermine existing non-publication protections for child victims and witnesses in other statutes.

Child and Family Services Act, SO 1984, c. 55, s. 41(8).

Young Offenders Act, SC 1980-81-82-83, c. 110, s. 38(1).

58. Juxtaposing the Ontario Court of Appeal's decision in this case with the Young Offenders Act yields the perverse possibility that publication of a victim's name depends upon the perpetrator's age—protection being more certain if one is violated by a child than by an adult.

59. Boys are protected from disadvantage under section 15 on the basis of their age. Section 15 protects girls doubly: on the basis of both age and sex. Section 443(3) vindicates both Charter concerns.

Section 442(3) Ameliorates the Disadvantaged Status of Women and Children

60. Section 15(2) is an integral part of section 15 as a whole and a guide to its interpretation. Section 15(2), by sheltering equality initiatives from specious equality-based attacks, reveals that one purpose of section 15 is to ensure that the law benefits those disadvantaged by inequality.

61. Women and children are each socially disadvantaged and disempowered in specific ways. Children are disadvantaged relative to adults in physical strength and size, psychic vulnerability to adult authority, economic dependence, social power, relative lack of credibility, and deprivation of social voice. Women are disadvantaged relative to men economically, socially, politically, as targets for physical and sexual violence, and in access to credibility and expression.

62. Section 15(2) directs particular constitutional sensitivity toward those who are disadvantaged on the basis of sex (women), age (boys), and sex and age (girls), in this case women and children victims of sexual assault.

63. One apparent purpose of the legislature in passing section 442(3) was to protect women and children victims of sexual assault, as its recent expansions make clear.

Bill C-15, supra, s. 14.

64. Section 442(3), a provision designed to ameliorate the condition of two enumerated disadvantaged groups, therefore furthers the purpose section 15(2) underlines for section 15 as a whole.

Section 442(3) Enhances the Liberty and Personal Security of Women and Children, Their Sense of Security, and Their Equal Access to These Rights

65. Section 7 of the Charter provides everyone with the legal right to liberty and security of the person without deprivation except for reasons of fundamental justice. Section 442(3) effectuates section 7 by opening the criminal process to victims of sex offences and making it more predictable that sex offenders will be brought to justice, increasing the freedom of movement, security, and sense of security of women and children by reducing the threat of sexual assault upon them.

Section 442(3) Enhances Women's and Children's Liberty, Security, and Sense of Security

66. Protected security centres on physical security. In addition, "serious state-imposed psychological stress, at least in the criminal law context," has been recognized to breach security of the person. While not granting an absolute right of protection from emotional distress or upset, section 7 security includes psychic freedom, such as from the threat of physical punishment or suffering, along with freedom from such punishment itself. It also includes personal dignity.

Morgentaler v. The Queen, unreported decision of the SCC, File #19550 (opinion of Dickson CJ, at 15) (opinion of Wilson J, at 16).

Singh et al., supra.

R.L. Crain Inc. v. Couture (1984), 6 DLR (4th) 478 (Sask. QB), at 502.

67. Protected liberty centres on liberty of the person in the physical sense, especially freedom of movement, but includes "more than freedom from captivity." It encompasses more than actual physical restraint but less than the full range of freedom of conduct.

Parkdale Hotel Ltd. v. AG Canada (1986), 27 DLR (4th) 19 (FCTD), at 34.

R v. Robson (1985), 19 DLR (4th) 112 (BC CA), at 115 and 119.

R v. Neale (1986), 28 CCC (3d) 345, leave to appeal to SCC refused Jan. 15, 1987.

68. Fundamental justice is broader than, and includes, natural justice.

Reference Re Section 94(2) of the Motor Vehicle Act, [1985] 2 SCR 486.

69. "Rights" under section 7 have wide generic meaning.

Re Cadieux and Dir. of Mountain Institution (1984), 13 CCC (3d) 330 (FCTD), at 338.

70. Principles of fundamental justice permit review of the substance of a deprivation, including the history of the right, its legislative tradition, and community standards.

R.L. Crain, supra, at 507 and 510.

71. Canadian women's interest in personal security from assault is threatened by the involuntary publicizing of their identities as sexual assault victims. Victims who avoid publicity by non-reporting are, in effect, violated with official impunity. Their offenders, in turn, remain at large to terrorize and assault others, whose security is reduced and whose liberty—in the sense of freedom of movement—is often curtailed in an effort to avoid them. Victims who do not report because of fear of publicity are vulnerable to further assault by their offenders who remain at large. Victims who do report may be further harassed, threatened, and individually targeted for assault as a result of publication.

72. The history of section 442(3) reveals concern for women's personal security from sexual assault. Community intolerance for legal disincentives to reporting sexual assault was expressed and influenced the passage of the provision.

House of Commons Debates, supra, at 9204 and 9225.

73. Section 442(3), therefore, delivers principles of fundamental justice by enhancing the liberty, security, and sense of security of actual and prospective victims of sexual assault.

Equal Personal Security and Liberty Are at once Principles of Fundamental Justice and Guaranteed by Sections 15 And 28 of the Charter

74. Breach of section 7 principles of fundamental justice may give rise to a Charter claim. Access to justice for violations of the person and equitable treatment by law are both principles of fundamental justice.

The Queen v. Operation Dismantle (1983), 3 DLR (4th) 193 (FCA), per LeDain, Marceau, and Hugessen JJ.

75. Sections 15 and 28 guarantee equal access to all Charter-protected rights, including section 7 liberty and security.

76. Women often isolate themselves, avoiding events or places, as a precaution against sexual assault. Threat of sexual assault is threat of punishment for being female. Men, who are not subjected to the constant threat of rape and other forms of sexual assault as women are, have correspondingly greater security of the person, sense of security, and liberty of movement in society.

77. Both the criminal law against sex offences and section 442(3) attempt to equalize these social inequalities by prohibiting violations of the physical person and encouraging their reporting.

78. Barriers to reporting and prosecuting sexual assault differentially impact women and children, in effect denying victims the equal benefit and protection of the laws against sexual assault on the basis of sex and age.

79. Section 442(3) promotes equal liberty and security of women and children by increasing the likelihood that their violators will be brought to justice without further injury to their person through publication and by moving toward a society in which sexual offences could be reported and more effectively prosecuted. In such a society, women and children would have freedom of movement and personal security that they cannot have so long as sexual offences are, as a practical matter, permitted. They would also have the sense of security that such changes would make practical, rather than living in well-founded and constant fear of being sexually violated with impunity.

80. The constitutionality of section 442(3) is, therefore, supported by section 7 and by sections 15 and 28 grants of equal access to section 7 rights.

Women's Right to Equality of Expression Is Promoted by Section 442(3) and Undermined by Making It Discretionary

81. One purpose of section 2(b) is to guarantee freedom of expression in furtherance of other Charter-protected rights. Section 442(3), by assuring that publicity of a sexual assault victim's identity is voluntary, supports victim speech hence equal entry into the legal process. Substituting judicial and media discretion for victim and prosecutorial discretion silences victim speech, restricting protected access to expression and to justice.

82. Sexual assault silences women. It restricts the probability and potency of their public and private speech, including survivors' ability to express themselves, their legitimacy to many hearers, and their credibility to officials.

83. Forced publicity makes women feel blamed, targeted, endangered and judged for the sexual assault against them. Added to the pain of the assault itself, this has a devastating silencing effect. Faced with choosing between the danger and indignity of publicity

they cannot control or suffering in silence, many have chosen the latter. If women cannot choose how they will be publicized as sexual assault victims, they will speak less.

84. Section 442(3) gives the victim choice over the conditions under which her name and identity can be publicized. The choice to report is a choice to go on the public record. The choice to prosecute is a choice to enter the public arena. Section 442(3) makes the choice to have one's name broadcast and published a further choice. The issue is thus not whether or not publication occurs, or state interference with publication, but whether the decision to publicize the victim's identity will be made by the victim and her representatives or by a judge and the media.

85. The prohibition authorized by section 442(3) is clear, concrete, narrow, limited and tailored to its objectives. The public is not excluded from trials. Any information about the trial other than the name and identity of the victim can be published. The victim can choose to disclose her identity. Broader rights to ban publication of information have been granted to criminal defendants on no stronger Charter justification.

Re Global Communications and AG Canada (1984), 44 OR (2d) 609 (CA), at 625.

86. A victim-driven disclosure system enhances freedom of expression by giving women opportunities for freedom of speech. Much information on sexual assault has been first revealed in the feminist press because it provides a situation for publicity that victims control. Victim control in this area thus promotes values upon which freedom of expression is based: the search for truth, self-fulfilment, and participation in government and public dialogue.

87. Voyeurism can be masked as freedom of expression. Courts have noted, in giving effect to section 28, that "if true equality between male and female persons is to be achieved it would be quite wrong … to ignore the threat to equality" posed by some expressive materials, in that case pornography.

R v. Red Hot Video Ltd. (1985), 18 CCC (3d) 3, at 23.

Sask. HRC v. Waldo (1984), 5 CHRC D/2074, at 2080-81.

88. Courts have found that Charter rights, including the right to freedom of expression, are not absolute.

Zundel, supra, at 147.

Retail, Wholesale & Department Store Union, Local 580 v. Dolphin Delivery Ltd., [1986] 2 SCR 573, at 588.

89. Sex equality interests have, at times, taken precedence over speech interests prior to reaching section 1. Similar results have been reached by US courts in the absence of an equivalent to section 1.

Red Hot Video Ltd., supra.

Waldo, supra.

Pittsburgh Press Co. v. Pittsburgh Commission on Human Relations, 413 US 376 (1973).

Keegstra, supra.

90. Statutory and judicial non-publication bans on particular information in judicial proceedings have been upheld as constitutionally permissible limits upon freedom of the press, often based on fair trial safeguards, usually to protect accused perpetrators of crimes, typically men.

Global Communications, supra.

R v. Banville (1983), 145 DLR 595 (NB QB).

Re Southam Inc. and The Queen (No. 2) (1982), 70 CCC (2d) 264 (Ont. HC).

91. Measuring the interest on each side of this case, section 442(3) is seen substantially to further women's and children's sections 15, 28, 2(b), and 7 interests, while restricting the newspapers' interest in section 2(b) very little to not at all. Making section 442(3) protections discretionary by judges and the media would further the values of section 2(b) little if at all, while substantially undermining the values sections 15, 28, 2(b), and 7 exist to promote.

In the Alternative, Section 442(3) Restricts Expressive (and Trial) Rights Within Reasonable Limits that a Free and Democratic Society Dedicated to Equality Can Demonstrably Justify

92. Under section 1, the usual procedure is to place the burden of justification on those seeking to limit the Charter-protected right.

Oakes, supra.

93. In the instant case, both sides claim a basis in the Charter for their interests: Respondents for newspapers and those accused of sexual assault, and Applicants and Intervenors for sexually victimized women and children. It is submitted that a proper methodology for resolving such conflicts of rights under section 1 would place equal onus on each side and resolve the conflict on the merits of persuasion, giving priority to Canadian values over the value choices of other free and democratic societies, where necessary.

94. The rights and freedoms guaranteed by the Charter are not absolute. "It may become necessary to limit rights and freedoms in circumstances where their exercise would be inimical to the realization of collective goals of fundamental importance."

Oakes, supra, at 136.

95. When considered with other rights under section 1, Canadian courts have found the right to freedom of expression is not absolute.

Red Hot Video Ltd., supra.

Re Luscher and Deputy Minister Revenue Canada (1985), 17 DLR (4th) 503 (FCA), at 510.

Re Ontario Film & Video Appreciation Society and Ontario Board of Censors (1983), 147 DLR (3d) 58 (Ont. HC), at 64.

96. As Dickson CJC has noted concerning free speech prior to the Charter, while free speech is a fundamental value,

> it is equally obvious that free speech or expression is not an absolute, unqualified value. Other values must be weighed with it. Sometimes these other values supplement, and build on, the value of speech. But in other situations there is a collision. When that happens the value of speech may be cut back if the competing value is a powerful one. Thus, for example, we have laws dealing with libel and slander, sedition and blasphemy. We also have laws imposing restrictions on the press in the interests of, for example, ensuring a fair trial or protecting the privacy of minors or victims of sexual assault.

Fraser v. Public Service Staff Relations Board, [1985] 2 SCR 455, at 467.

97. The expressive and fairness losses to newspapers and defendants in not being able to publicize the names and identities of victims of sex offences are negligible. The equality, security, liberty, and expressive losses to women and children of such involuntary publicity is proportionally substantial. In "attempt[ing] to balance the limitation of the right with the evil or harm done to others," section 442(3) limits protected rights to a *de minimus* degree, while its invalidation would visit substantial trauma and risk on those whom Intervenors represent, effectively excluding many from justice for their sexual violations.

Black v. Law Society of Alberta (1986), 27 DLR (4th) 527 (Alta. CA), at 567.

Keegstra, supra, at 274-75.

98. The Ontario Supreme Court has ruled that the mandatory non-publication of identities of young offenders is a reasonable limitation upon freedom of the press. As amended, the Young Offenders Act extends this protection to victims and witnesses.

Re Southam Inc. and The Queen (1985), 16 CCC (3d) 262 (Ont. SC).

Young Offenders Act, supra.

99. Sex and age equality are collective goals of fundamental—indeed superordinate—importance.

100. The US Constitution contains no equivalent to section 1.

101. The US Constitution, while on its face perhaps more readily lending itself to an interpretation that would elevate speech above other rights, especially when pursued by legislation, does not hold freedom of speech to be absolute. No "right to publicity" exists of the sort the Respondents attempt to enshrine here. Freedom of speech is balanced by interests in child protection, personal reputation, harmony and peace among groups, the moral fabric and quality of community life for all groups, and other public goods.

New York v. Ferber, 458 US 747 (1982) (harm to children).

Gertz v. Robert Welch, 418 US 323 (1974) (libel).

Miller v. California, 413 US 15 (1973) (obscenity).

Beauharnais v. Illinois, 343 US 250 (1952) (group libel).

102. While few non-publication orders and no mandatory closure or non-publication provisions have been upheld by the US Supreme Court under First Amendment

attack, no non-publication provision, even one involving sex offences, has ever been defended against a First Amendment attack on sex or age equality grounds.

Cox v. Cohn, 420 US 469 (1975).

Richmond Newspapers v. Virginia, 448 US 555 (1980).

Globe Newspaper Co. v. Sup. Ct., 457 US 596 (1982).

Nebraska Press Assn. v. Stuart, 427 US 539 (1976).

KNPX Broadcasting v. Arizona Sup. Ct., 459 US 1302 (1982).

103. The public's right to know, to the limited extent recognized under the First Amendment, has never encompassed the right to know the name of a victim of sexual assault. Even the question whether state law may punish publication or broadcast of a rape victim's name remains unsettled under US law.

Pell v. Procunier, 417 US 817 (1974).

Houchins v. KQED, 438 US 1 (1978).

Florida Star v. BJF, 499 So. 2d 883 (Fla. App. 1986), 56 USLW 3414 (Dec. 16, 1987).

104. The American interpretation of expressive rights urged by the Respondents to prohibit publication protections has not, on any evidence available or offered, solved the problem of rape non-reporting in the United States.

105. The US Constitution contains no express guarantee of equality on the basis of sex or age. Sex equality has constitutional dimension in the United States only by interpretation.

106. In the United States, the legal system justifies closed trials for juvenile offenders, usually boys, based on the rationale that minors deserve special protection, but prohibits states from extending the same solicitude to minor rape victims, usually girls, under the First Amendment. This is gender inequality by law.

Globe Newspaper v. Superior Court, 102 S. Ct. 2613, at 2623 (Burger CJ, dissenting).

Gordon Gidlund, "Case Comment, Globe Newspaper Co. v. Superior Court" (1983), 1 *J Law & Inequality* 389, at 401.

107. The US Constitution permits legislatures to go further in pursuing equality rights than would be required by the equality guarantee itself.

Katzenbach v. Morgan, 384 US 641 (1966).

City of Rome v. United States, 446 US 156 (1980).

108. The fact that US courts do not limit a right guaranteed under both constitutions does not make a Canadian limit on that right unreasonable.

Global Communications, supra.

109. Canadian values deserve priority in section 1 cases. "[T]he court must come back, ultimately … to the facts of our own free and democratic society to answer the

question whether the limit imposed on the particular guaranteed freedom has been demonstrably justified as a reasonable one."

Southam Inc. (No. 1), supra, at 130.

110. As stated by the judge at trial in this case, upholding section 442(3) under section 1, "This is a Canadian solution to a problem that I am sure exists in all jurisdictions."

Reasons for Judgment (Osborne J) CA, 154.

111. Section 1 allows limits on rights demonstrably justified in "a free and democratic society." Intervenors submit that equality is essential to democracy and requisite to freedom. Tolerating inequality is, therefore, inconsistent with freedom and democracy.

112. Sex and age equality, entrenched as constitutional rights, are distinctively Canadian value priorities.

113. Section 442(3) promotes sex and age equality.

114. Section 442(3) is therefore justified as a reasonable limit on speech and trial rights (if any) in a free and democratic society such as Canada.

PART IV: NATURE OF ORDER SOUGHT

115. Intervenors therefore submit that section 442(3) does not infringe freedom of expression under section 2(b).

116. Intervenors further submit that, taking the Charter as a whole, section 442(3) is protected as a provision to ensure the equality, liberty, security, and speech of women and children under sections 2(b), 7, 15, and 28.

117. Intervenors alternatively submit that if section 442(3) is found to limit the Charter-protected rights of some, and is not constitutional as furthering more important Charter-protected rights of others, it is nonetheless a justified limit on those rights in a free and democratic society under section 1.

118. Intervenors respectfully request that the appeal be allowed setting aside the judgment of the Ontario Court of Appeal and that section 442(3) be upheld in its entirety.

All of which is respectfully submitted.

THE OUTCOME

Head Notes—Canadian Newspapers v. Canada

Held: The appeal should be allowed.

Section 442(3) of the Code infringes the freedom of the press guaranteed by s. 2(b) of the Charter. Freedom of the press is an important and essential attribute of a free and democratic society, and measures which prohibit the media from publishing information deemed of interest obviously restrict that freedom.

The limit imposed by s. 442(3) on the freedom of the press is justifiable under s. 1 of the Charter. Section 442(3) purports to foster complaints by victims of sexual assault by protecting them from the trauma of widespread publication resulting in embarrassment and humiliation. Encouraging victims to come forward and complain facilitates the prosecution and conviction of those guilty of sexual offences. The overall objective of the publication ban imposed by s. 442(3) is to favour the suppression of crime and to improve the administration of justice. This objective undoubtedly bears on a "pressing and substantial concern" and is of sufficient importance to warrant overriding a constitutional right. The provision has a rational connection to the objective it is designed to serve and imposes only minimal limits on the media's rights. Section 442(3) applies only to sexual offence cases, it restricts publication of facts disclosing the victim's identity and it does not provide for a general ban but is limited to instances where the complainant or prosecutor requests the order or the court considers it necessary. Nothing prevents the media from being present at the hearing and reporting the facts of the case and the conduct of the trial. Only information likely to reveal the complainant's identity is concealed from the public. Therefore, it cannot be said that the effects of s. 442(3) are such an infringement on the media's rights that the legislative objective is outweighed by the abridgement of freedom of the press.

[S]exual assault is one of the most unreported [of the most serious crimes]. The main reasons stated by those who do not report this offence are fear of treatment by police or prosecutors, fear of trial procedures and fear of publicity or embarrassment. ... Since fear of publication is one of the factors that influences the reporting of sexual assault, certainty with respect to non-publication at the time of deciding whether to report plays a vital role in that decision. (pp. 131-32)

A discretionary provision under which a judge would retain the power to decide whether to grant or refuse the ban on publication would not be effective in attaining Parliament's pressing goal, since it would deprive the complainants of the assurance that, upon request, their identity would not be disclosed, an important factor in their decision to report the crime.

[A]n absolute ban on publication is the only means to reach the desired objective.

Section 442(3) of the Code does not infringe the accused's right to a public hearing guaranteed by s. 11(d) of the Charter. The mandatory ban on publication does not prevent the public or the press from attending trial proceedings; it only restricts publication of facts disclosing the complainant's identity.

The question as regards the accused's right to a fair hearing should not be answered since it was not an issue properly raised before this Court.

IN THE SUPREME COURT OF CANADA

(ON APPEAL FROM THE SASKATCHEWAN COURT OF APPEAL)

BETWEEN:

JOSEPH BOROWSKI

Appellant

(Plaintiff)

AND:

THE ATTORNEY GENERAL FOR CANADA

Respondent

(Defendant)

AND:

WOMEN'S LEGAL EDUCATION AND ACTION FUND

REAL WOMEN OF CANADA

INTERFAITH COALITION ON THE RIGHTS AND WELL-BEING OF WOMEN AND CHILDREN

Intervenors

Factum of the Women's Legal Education and Action Fund (LEAF)

Borowski v. Attorney-General of Canada

INTRODUCTION

In 1978, Joseph Borowski sought a declaration from a Saskatchewan court that subsections (4), (5), and (6) of section 251 of the Criminal Code—which legalized access to abortions under limited circumstances—violated the Federal Bill of Rights (the claim was eventually amended to include reference to the Charter), because in his view the subsections violated the foetus's right to life. In addition, Borowski sought a declaration that any Acts of Parliament which authorized the expenditure of public moneys for abortions would be similarly unconstitutional. Borowski's application failed at both the Saskatchewan Court of Queen's Bench and Court of Appeal. In 1987, Borowski was granted leave to appeal to the Supreme Court of Canada. By the time the appeal date was set, the Supreme Court had already struck down section 251 in *Morgentaler v. The Queen* on unrelated grounds.

In *Morgentaler*, a majority of the Court held that the delayed access to abortions caused by section 251 violated women's right to security of the person as guaranteed by section 7 of the Charter. Quite deliberately, the Court did not address the question of foetal rights. However, as a result of *Morgentaler*, a serious issue existed whether the Borowski appeal was moot. The Court reserved judgment on the mootness question and proceeded to hear the substantive arguments of the parties and intervenors. LEAF intervened to address the particular equality issues that arise upon the restriction of women's reproductive choice. The Interfaith Coalition on the Rights and Wellbeing of Women and Children and REAL Women of Canada intervened to generally support Borowski's arguments.

FACTUM

PART I: FACTS

1. LEAF agrees with the description of the procedural history of this appeal contained in paragraphs 1 to 7 inclusive of the factum of the Respondent.

2. LEAF submits that the Appellant's claim that the woman and the foetus are separate entities fundamentally distorts reality. It treats the pregnant woman as nothing more than a container for the foetus, an unconnected, unconcerned, and invisible life support system. The reality is that the foetus's "small domain" is a woman's womb (Appellant's Factum, paragraph 22); the placenta, dubbed an "external organ of the child," is an internal part of the woman's uterus (paragraph 27); the implantation of the fertilized egg in the "wall of the uterus" (paragraph 17) and the growth and development of the foetus in the "amniotic sac" (paragraph 20) all occur within the body of a woman. The events and processes described by the Appellant are happening to a pregnant woman, they occur within her body, and form part of her experience of pregnancy.

3. The Appellant's snapshot of "intrauterine life" requires a wider lens to reveal that the "uterus" belongs to a woman with constitutionally protected rights. We invite the Court to take judicial notice that the foetus exists within the body of a woman. Medical technologies that can visualize the foetus in utero should not be used to deny the foetus's complete physical dependence on the pregnant woman. They in fact emphasize rather than undermine unity between the treatment and status of the foetus and the treatment and status of the pregnant woman.

PART II: ISSUES

4. The constitutional questions on this appeal are set out in the Respondent's factum at page 6. This Intervenor uses the term "foetus" throughout this factum to refer to the zygote, embryo, or foetus, rather than "child en ventre sa mère." In addition, this Honourable Court is asked to consider whether these constitutional questions should be answered.

PART III: ARGUMENT

Should the Constitutional Questions Be Answered?

6. This Honourable Court granted standing to Mr. Borowski to challenge the validity of legislation, namely section 251 of the Criminal Code. The proceedings in the courts below make clear that the validity of section 251 of the Code has been at stake throughout. This Honourable Court has held that section 251 is unconstitutional and void. Accordingly, the basis—and the only rationale—for Mr. Borowski's status to sue no longer exists.

R v. Borowski, [1981] 2 SCR 575, at 598.

Borowski v. AG Canada et al., [1984] 1 WWR 15 (Sask. QB), at 31.

Borowski v. Attorney General of Canada, [1987] 4 WWR 385 (Sask. CA), at 387 and 409.

R v. Morgentaler (No. 2), [1988] 1 SCR 30.

7. These circumstances evoke the observations of then Chief Justice Laskin (with whom Mr. Justice Lamer concurred) in his dissenting reasons in this Court's original standing decision:

> Courts do not normally deal with purely hypothetical matters where no concrete legal issues are involved, where there is no lis that engages their processes or where they are asked to answer questions in the abstract merely to satisfy a person's curiosity or perhaps his or her obsessiveness with a perceived injustice in the existing law. Special legislative provisions for references to the courts to answer particular questions (which may be of a hypothetical nature) give that authority to governments alone and not to citizens or taxpayers.
>
> *R v. Morgentaler (No. 1)*, [1981] 2 SCR 575, at 579.

8. The circumstances of the present appeal also evoke the cautionary words of Chief Justice Dickson in *R v. Morgentaler*:

> In my opinion, it is neither necessary nor wise in this appeal to explore the broadest implications of s. 7 as counsel would wish us to do. I prefer to rest my conclusions on a narrower analysis than that put forward on behalf of the appellants. I do not think it would be appropriate to attempt an all-encompassing explication of so important a provision as s. 7 so early in the history of Charter interpretation. The Court should be presented with a wide variety of claims and factual situations before articulating the full range of s. 7 rights.
>
> *Morgentaler (No. 2)*, supra, at 51e-h.

9. The absence of a legislative context for the present case has several consequences. It means that there is no government action to attract the operation of the Charter through section 32. There is no specific allegation of any particular violation of Charter rights and, accordingly, no opportunity to assess the validity of legislation under section 1 of the Charter.

10. Thus, this case as pursued by the Appellant presents none of the usual opportunities for the careful weighing of interests which characterizes constitutional adjudication. Rather, it boldly seeks to establish new rights: "Borowski seeks to establish the personhood of unborn children."

> M. Shumiatcher, "I Set Before You Life and Death" (1986), 24 *UWO L Rev.* 1, at 25.

11. LEAF submits that this invitation to develop rights for the foetus where none before existed should be refused. To make new constitutional rights where there is an ample and balanced evidentiary record and a concrete legislative context would itself be a departure from the past practice of this Honourable Court. To do so with regard to an abstract question and with a record generated in the context of only one of the many issues raised by that question would be an even greater novelty. As has been pointed out, "It is not for the courts to manufacture a constitutional right out of whole cloth."

> *Morgentaler (No. 2)*, supra, at 141a-b, per McIntyre J.

12. A decision that the foetus has constitutional protection will have ramifications for matters as diverse—and as factually and morally complex—as in vitro fertilization and embryo transplants, foetal surgery, coerced medical treatment for the mother over her religious objections, and whether a brain dead woman should be kept alive to nourish the foetus until its birth, or allowed to die. It could affect settled law in both the

civil and criminal areas. The evidentiary record in this appeal simply does not provide the factual basis necessary to inform such a momentous legal decision as a determination that the foetus has constitutional status.

13. Because of the reality of complete foetal dependence on the woman, no direct societal involvement with, or relationship to, a foetus is possible. In all pregnancy-related cases, society's relationship to the foetus must be—and in fact necessarily is—mediated by the woman within whose body it is.

Janet Gallagher, "Prenatal Invasions & Interventions: What's Wrong with Fetal Rights" (1987), 10 *Harvard Women's LJ* 9, at 13.

14. Thus, any creation by this Court of new constitutional rights for the foetus has the potential to place at risk the rights and autonomy of women in a variety of circumstances. A woman's practices with respect to nutrition, contraception, and sexual activity, for example, both before and during pregnancy, her right to refuse (or accept) medical treatment during pregnancy, and allocation of decision-making rights between the pregnant woman and the state when prenatal caretaking conflict all could be affected.

Edward W. Keyserlingk, "The Unborn Child's Right to Prenatal Care (Part I) and (Part II)," 3 *Health Law in Canada* 10, at 31.

W.W. Watters et al., "Response to Edward W. Keyserlingk's Article: The Unborn Child's Right to Prenatal Care," 4 *Health Law in Canada* 32.

Edward W. Keyserlingk, "Clarifying the Right to Prenatal Care," 4 *Health Law in Canada* 36.

In re A.C., 533 A.2d 611 (DC App., 1987).

California v. Stewart, San Diego Judicial District, State of California, February 26, 1987.

In the Matter of Jaclyn Jeffery, State of Michigan Court of Appeals, 1987.

Poole et al. v. Santa Clara County Kaiser Hospital et al., in the Superior Court of the State of California, 1986.

15. This case originally dealt only with abortion. No intervenors were permitted to participate in the trial to adduce evidence or present argument. The Appellant's claims are now unlimited by abortion legislation, extending to any issues affecting the potential interests of a foetus. The scientific literature shows disagreement on the circumstances in which medical and other interventions on behalf of a foetus are indicated, and also about their efficacy. Theories contend over the time at which the state should interest itself in the fate of a foetus, and the physiological and philosophical basis upon which such an interest should be based. It would be a regrettable step, in these circumstances, for this Honourable Court to decide a question that has such potential for profound impairment of the rights of women.

Borowski v. Minister of Justice of Canada et al., [1983] 3 WWR 505 (Sask. QB).

L.J. Nelson et al., "Compelled Medical Treatment of Pregnant Women" (1988), 259 *JAMA* 1060, at 1061, 1064-65.

16. By contrast, a decision of this Honourable Court that the foetus has no rights under section 7 or 15 of the Charter of Rights and Freedoms would not result in a fundamental change of the status quo. In particular, such a decision would still leave scope for governmental legislation in the interest of the foetus, the possibility recognized in the *Morgentaler* decision. It would also be consistent with the prior development of the common law and criminal jurisprudence, which take live birth as the starting point for the recognition of rights, even if those rights can in some instances have retrospective application.

Factum of the Respondent, paragraphs 41 to 50.

R v. Sullivan and Lemay, British Columbia Court of Appeal, July 28, 1988, Reasons for Judgment.

Re F., [1988] 2 All ER 1193 (CA).

17. A decision refusing to recognize new constitutional rights for the foetus would not be tantamount to acknowledging a constitutional right to abortion. The circumstances in which any such right exists, and the constitutional and legal basis for it, would remain to be determined in a future case, building upon the decision of this Honourable Court in *R v. Morgentaler*. A decision in this appeal that the foetus has rights under section 7 or 15 would, however, inhibit the principled exploration of the impact of the Charter's sex equality guarantees upon the abortion issue.

Paragraphs 52-56, infra; *Morgentaler (No. 2)*, supra, at 171h-72e.

18. It is submitted that the rationale underlying the present legal position of the foetus is a sound one. Human rights should be reserved for persons already born. The time of birth provides a clear and recognizable time at which rights can vest. Unlike the "moment" of conception, which is unknowable, and the point of foetal viability, which varies in every case and depends on the state and availability of medical knowledge and technology, the time of birth can be readily ascertained, remains constant, and marks the beginning of social interaction between human beings.

19. Accordingly, it is submitted that this Court should decline to answer the abstract questions posed in this appeal.

20. In the alternative, it is submitted that the Court should hold that the foetus does not have rights under section 7 or 15 of the Charter.

The Canadian Charter of Rights and Freedoms

A Preferred Point of Departure

21. The Appellant's factum barely mentions the existence, let alone the rights, of the pregnant woman. In this, it exhibits a not atypical characteristic of foetal rights advocates: that of portraying the foetus as an autonomous "space-hero" and the pregnant woman as the "empty space" in which he floats.

R.P. Petchesky, "Fetal Images: The Power of Visual Culture in the Politics of Reproduction" (1987), 13 *Feminist Studies* 263, at 270-71.

22. In this view the woman registers as a void insofar as her own rights or even existence are concerned. When foetal rights activists contemplate her impact upon foetal rights, her existence is acknowledged, but viewed as a clear threat. She is seen as separate from her own foetus, and menacing to it, either by presenting a hostile environment to its development or by actively refusing some proposed medical intervention. She is a force to be either erased or controlled, managed or circumscribed in the interests of the foetus.

Keyserlingk, supra.

23. LEAF, by contrast, submits that the focus of rights concerns during pregnancy must be on the woman. A pregnant woman is a live, independent, and autonomous person who is unquestionably intended and entitled to benefit from the Charter's guarantees of constitutionally entrenched rights and freedoms. Personhood is a social and legal judgment, not in itself a biological fact. The legal rights of a woman, who is a person, cannot be sacrificed to a foetus, which may or may not become a person.

24. Since 1982, this Honourable Court has recognized the rights of women both inside and outside the Charter context. These decisions affirm a woman's right to be free from sexual harassment, the integrity of a woman's reproductive capacity, and the legitimacy of state action to enhance women's employment opportunities.

E. (Mrs.) v. Eve, [1986] 2 SCR 388.

Action Travail des Femmes v. Canadian National Railway Company, [1987] 1 SCR 1114.

Robichaud v. Canada (Treasury Board), [1987] 2 SCR 84.

R v. Chase, [1987] 2 SCR 293.

Morgentaler (No. 2), supra.

25. Madam Justice Wilson recognized in the *Morgentaler* case that a decision by a woman concerning whether to continue her pregnancy

> ... is a decision that deeply reflects the way the woman thinks about herself and her relationship to others and to society at large. It is not just a medical decision: it is a profound social and ethical one as well. Her response to it will be the response of the whole person.

Morgantaler (No. 2), supra, at 171g-h.

26. Implicit in this statement is an entirely appropriate respect for women's capacity to exercise the moral and ethical responsibility for such grave decisions. LEAF submits that decisions about prenatal caretaking and termination of pregnancy, which inescapably implicate a woman's physical integrity, more properly lie with the woman than with a state- or self-appointed guardian of the foetus.

27. Thus, LEAF submits that the Charter rights of all women can and must be the starting point and standard against which the argument urging creation of constitutional rights for the foetus must be scrutinized.

Women's Rights Under the Charter: Generally

28. Section 7 of the Charter provides that everyone has the right to life, liberty, and security of the person and the right not to be deprived thereof except in accordance with the principles of fundamental justice. Section 15 guarantees that every individual is equal before and under the law and has the right to the equal protection and equal benefit of the law without discrimination on the basis, inter alia, of sex. Section 28 states that the rights referred to in the Charter are guaranteed equally to male and female persons.

29. As this Intervenor has argued before, to require that the sexes be "similarly situated" before their treatment can be subjected to a legal equality mandate is to preclude the most deep, urgent, and pervasive sex inequality from being addressed by the Charter. This argument takes on a special dimension in the context of this case, because there is no comparison in the lives of men with women's role in reproduction. Only women, and never men, become pregnant, and experience directly and immediately the physiological, social and economic ramifications of pregnancy. Only women directly experience "the childbearing year" each time a human child is produced.

30. Historically, women's role in childbearing has provided an occasion and pretext for women's social and legal disadvantagement. Examples include patronizing and cruel obstetrical and gynaecological practices; restrictions on pregnant (or married) women's employment on grounds of alleged danger to the foetus, purported incapacity of pregnant women, exclusion from the public domain on alleged grounds of propriety or simply questions of taste; criminalization of birth control technology and information; and refusal to recognize that discrimination based on pregnancy is discrimination based on sex.

"A History of Midwifery in Canada" in *Report of the Task Force on the Implementation of Midwifery in Ontario* (1987), 218-23.

Canadian Air Line Flight Attendants' Association v. Pacific Western Airlines Ltd. (1979), 105 DLR (3d) 477 (BC SC), affirmed at (1981), 124 DLR (3d) 688 (BC CA).

R v. Palmer, [1937] 2 DLR 609 (Ont. Mag. Ct.), affirmed at [1937] 3 DLR 493 (Ont. CA).

Royal Commission on the Status of Women in Canada, Report, para. 206-10, at 277-88.

Bliss v. AG Canada, [1979] 1 SCR 183.

31. The uniqueness of women's reproductive situation does not justify disadvantaging, hence unequal, treatment by law. Laws cannot alter the reproductive capacities of men and women, but they can and do prescribe the social and legal consequences which attach to them. Biology may dictate that only women can become pregnant, but the legislature and the courts have a full range of options on how to treat pregnant women. One should not attribute to nature or biology the hardships imposed by man-made law.

32. The Charter of Rights is an instrument intended by its framers to relieve against disadvantage. Accordingly, when viewing the rights of women under sections 7, 15, and 28, LEAF submits that this Honourable Court should recognize that women are entitled

to the full amplitude of life, liberty, security of the person, and of equality. Bearing children creates no exceptions from these rights and no burdens upon them; rather, it creates social and legal requirements for their full realization. Section 28 alone, which does not explicitly impose any "similarly situate" requirement and should not be interpreted as doing so, ensures no less.

33. The Appellant argues that sections 7 and 15 should be used to protect the foetus. LEAF submits that sections 7, 15, and 28 of the Charter are important instruments, which should be used to overcome the historical and systemic discrimination against women, address women's material inequality and accommodate their biological capacities. Judicial application and interpretation of these sections should not be used in the way the Appellant suggests because the result would be to force women, the traditional caretakers and nurturers of children, to pay for their reproductive capabilities with their rights to life, liberty, and security of the person, equality before and under the law, and the equal benefit and protection of the law.

Section 7

34. The potential invasions of women's life, liberty, and security, which might be authorized in the name of newly minted rights for the foetus, are extensive.

35. Edward Keyserlingk, for example, proposes a right to prenatal care that would include "from conception onwards, claims to affirmative or positive care, duties, obligations and protections and not only claims to the avoidance of harmful acts … ." Some elements of the right could be exercised in utero "by means of court-ordered protective mechanisms," which could include granting of injunctions against certain acts being done or decisions taken, appointment of guardians to make certain decisions on behalf of the foetus, allowing a state welfare authority to supervise the mother, and separation of the parents where the interaction between them produces intolerable levels of stress for the foetus.

Keyserlingk, supra (Pt. I), 12; (Pt. II), 32-34.

36. He also envisions the creation of a duty "of a sexually active and fertile woman who is not practising birth control, and who intends to carry to term a child who may be conceived, to take reasonable precautions and preventive measures to protect a foetus which might be conceived."

Keyserlingk, supra (4 *Health Law in Canada*), at 36.

37. In practical terms, such rights in the foetus and duties in the mother could give rise not only to forced caesarians but also to

> … court orders prohibiting pregnant women from using alcohol, cigarettes, or other possibly harmful substances, forbidding them from continuing to work because of the presence of fetal toxins in the workplace, forcing them to take drugs or accept intrauterine blood transfusions, requiring pregnant anorexic teenagers to be force-fed, forcing women to undergo prenatal screening and diagnostic procedures such as amniocentesis, sonography, or fetoscopy, or mandating that women submit to in utero or extrauterine surgery for the fetus.

L.J. Nelson et al., "Forced Medical Treatment of Pregnant Women: 'Compelling Each to Live as Seems Good to the Rest' " (1986), 37 *The Hastings Law Journal* 703, at 756.

38. Isolated cases of forced intervention in prenatal care, which have already occurred in the United States and Canada, are a warning of the dangers inherent in curtailing women's liberty and security, sometimes in the name of a medical prognosis later proved unfounded. It is striking that the women subjected to this coercion are often poor, disadvantaged, and members of racial, religious, or linguistic minorities, in other words, those least able to assert their rights.

Factum of the Respondent, paragraphs 51 to 55.

V.E.B. Kolder et al., "Court-Ordered Obstetrical Interventions," (1987), 316 *New England Journal of Medicine* 1192, at 1193.

39. In *R v. Morgentaler*, the majority of this Court recognized that a restrictive criminal law prohibition against abortion improperly infringed a pregnant woman's section 7 rights. In LEAF's submission, that decision illuminates the approach to section 7 that should inform this appeal.

40. In *Morgentaler*, Chief Justice Dickson concluded:

> Forcing a woman, by threat of criminal sanction, to carry a foetus to term unless she meets certain criteria unrelated to her own priorities and aspirations, is a profound interference with a woman's body and thus a violation of security of the person.

Morgantaler (No. 2), supra, at 56j-57a.

41. Madam Justice Wilson held that a woman's decision to terminate her pregnancy is a part of her liberty and security of the person. She explained how the right to decide to make fundamental personal decisions is a necessary aspect of human dignity, a prerequisite to pursuing one's own conception of a full and rewarding life, and a principle embodied in numerous Charter sections.

Morgantaler (No. 2), supra, at 171b-d, and 173f-174a.

42. Madam Justice Wilson further held that a woman's "security of the person" protected in section 7, is infringed when the woman is treated as the "passive recipient of a decision made by others as to whether her body is to be used to nurture a new life."

Morgantaler (No. 2), supra, at 173h-j.

43. She classified the abortion decision as a matter of personal morality and individual conscience within the protection of section 2(a) of the Charter. The criminal prohibition against abortion constituted a substantive breach of the principles of fundamental justice because it endorsed and enforced "one conscientiously-held view at the expense of another."

Morgantaler (No. 2), supra, at 175i-176b, and 179e-i.

44. There is no common law principle that supports the appropriation of one person's body, life, and person to the affirmative service of another. For example, a judge in

the United States has refused to order a woman to undergo a caesarian section after acknowledging that he lacked the right to force her to donate an organ to a child of hers, even if that child were dying.

L.J. Nelson et al., supra, para. 15, at 1065, n. 66.

McFall v. Shimp, 10 D & C 3d 90 (1978).

In Re George, 630 SW 2d 614 (1982).

45. A foetus, as a potential human being, could have no greater claim on the liberty and freedom of a potential rescuer than a fully capacitated and existing human being.

Section 15

46. Taken together, the legislative history and text of sections 15 and 28 of the Charter disclose an intent to promote the equality of women.

"Summary of Conference Resolutions," Appendix VII, in A. Bayefsky and M. Eberts, eds., *Equality Rights and the Canadian Charter of Rights and Freedoms* (1985), 634-44.

N.C. Sheppard, "Equality, Ideology, and Oppression" in C.L.M. Boyle et al., *Charterwatch: Reflections on Equality* (1986), 195, at 221-22.

W.S. Tarnopolsky, "The Equality Rights" in W.S. Tarnopolsky and G.A. Beaudoin, eds., *Canadian Charter of Rights and Freedoms* (1982), 395, at 423.

47. Section 15 explicitly recognizes, especially in subsection 2, that amelioration of disadvantage is an integral part of the equality guarantee. Many of the present-day disadvantages of women arose in association with their capacity for and role in child-bearing, and the restrictions placed on women because of a narrow view of their "biological destiny."

48. While pregnancy may be a voluntary condition in the case of individual women, for women as a group, pregnancy is not voluntary. For women to bear children is an obvious social imperative.

49. The social context of sex inequality has denied women control over the reproductive uses of their bodies. Women have been socially disadvantaged in controlling sexual access to their bodies because of social learning, lack of information, inadequate or unsafe contraceptive technology, social pressure, custom, poverty and enforced economic dependence, sexual force, and ineffective enforcement of laws against sexual assault. As a result, they often do not control the conditions under which they become pregnant.

50. Similarly, under conditions of social inequality on the basis of sex, women have been allocated primary responsibility for the intimate care of children. Social custom, pressure, economic circumstances and lack of adequate day care (public or private) have meant that women often do not control the circumstances under which they rear children, hence the impact of those conditions on their own life chances.

51. Men as a group are not comparably disempowered by their reproductive capacities and are not generally required by society to spend their lives caring for children to the comparative preclusion of other life pursuits.

52. Women's reproductive capacity is thus an integral part of women's "equality problem," along a spectrum of situations. Whether or not they actually have children, all women are disadvantaged by societal norms that limit their options in the public domain because of childbearing and childrearing. Women who become pregnant and have children face additional circumscriptions of their role outside the family, because of custom and because society's resources are not usually allocated in a way that would assist women's childbearing and childrearing activities. These circumscriptions affect even those women whose pregnancies and childrearing are voluntary.

53. This inequality has important implications for the interpretation of the Charter's equality guarantees. For women of reproductive age, the guarantee of sex equality should be interpreted so as to reduce or minimize state-sanctioned interference with women's full development as human beings, socially, economically, and politically. For women who are pregnant, and carrying the foetus to term, regard for sex equality should prohibit state-sanctioned interference with their physical being and authority to make prenatal caretaking decisions. Women's equality rights should also preclude state coercion into motherhood: the kind of coercion that results when the state bars women's access to abortion.

54. Forced maternity in this broader sense must be clearly understood as a problem of sex inequality. Access to abortion is necessary as a means for women to survive in their unequal circumstances. However difficult an abortion decision may be for an individual woman, it may provide some relief in a life otherwise led in conditions that preclude choice in ways she cannot control. Women's access to legal abortion to ensure that women and men have more equal control of their reproductive capacities, more equal opportunity to plan their lives, and more equal ability to participate fully in society than if legal abortion did not exist. Because motherhood without choice is a sex equality issue, legal abortion should be seen as a sex equality issue.

55. The reasons why women choose abortion are numerous, personal, and profound. As long as contraceptive devices fail, are risky, or are unavailable there will be many women, who in the course of their lives, while planning and preparing for other things, will be confronted with the intrusive and immediate reality of an unwanted pregnancy. There will be teenage girls who will only want to finish growing up. There will be single women who cannot carry the emotional, financial, and social burdens of being single mothers. There will be married women pregnant either too soon, too late, or too often. There will be families with sufficient numbers or overwhelming problems. The guarantees in sections 15 and 28 require that in all these circumstances the Charter must provide women faced with unwanted pregnancies a secure right to control the number, timing, and spacing of their children.

56. Among its other consequences, legal recognition of foetal personhood would undermine the possibility of recognizing an abortion right, depriving women of sex

equality in a unique, unprecedented, and discriminatory manner. First, such a deprivation of reproductive control would further women's historical relegation to social subordination and second class citizenship, a legal position that the Charter's equality provisions propose to eliminate. Second, all direct victims of deprivation of reproductive control through such a recognition would be of one sex: female. Third, women's self-determination and autonomy would be burdened by law in a way that men's are not. Thus, elevation of the constitutional status of the foetus as sought by the Appellant would both indicate and institutionalize sex inequality.

57. Women have traditionally been those primarily concerned with the life, health, welfare, and life possibilities of the foetus and of children. This is in part because what happens to the foetus, happens to the woman. Legal recognition of foetal personhood would effectively grant the foetus (or its guardians) legal rights over the woman's body, when the philosophically and jurisprudentially desirable position is for the state to recognize that the woman must have legal and decision-making rights over her own body and over the foetus.

58. The Court must be careful not to create a time in a woman's life when, because of her unchosen biological capacities, she is outside the constitutional protection of the expansive equality rights entrenched in section 15.

S. Martin, "Persisting Equality Implications of the Bliss Case" in K. Mahoney and S. Martin, eds., *Equality and Judicial Neutrality* (1987), 195.

59. This Honourable Court, in the *Morgentaler* decision, did not consider the question of abortion in the context of section 15. However, the Court did accept, in varying degrees, that control over her own body, and her reproductive capacity, bear an important relationship to the security, liberty, and integrity of a woman.

60. LEAF submits that for the Court now to create rights for the foetus would curtail the woman's physical integrity, and her right, vis-à-vis the state, to make prenatal caretaking decisions. It would inhibit the further exploration or elaboration of the circumstances in which the woman would be entitled to abortion as of right.

61. Giving Charter rights to foetuses will result in the law imposing burdens on women that are not imposed on men. Historic and systemic patterns of discrimination against women will be allowed to continue and the traditional stereotype of women's role as a function of biological destiny, rather than personal choice, will be perpetuated.

Conclusion

62. If constitutional status is granted to the foetus, the Court would assume the task of reconciling two sets of potentially conflicting section 7 or 15 rights physically located in one body—that of the pregnant woman.

63. The Appellant's argument that some doctors are of the view that there are two "patients" in a medical procedure involving a pregnant woman provides no guidance to a court seeking to accommodate these competing interests. The medical community itself is divided as to whether the "two patients" view is an acceptable one. In practice,

implementation of the "two patients" view has produced coerced medical treatment for women. Moreover, the question of whether an entity is a person is a legal and political decision, not a medical one.

L.J. Nelson et al., supra, para. 15, 1060-61, and 1064-65.

64. Acknowledgment that the focus during pregnancy must remain on the woman's constitutional rights does not threaten the state's proper interest in the welfare of the foetus. It does signal how that interest in the foetus may be furthered. Regard for women's life, liberty, security of the person, and equality are consistent with pregnancy care that promotes the welfare of both woman and foetus by respecting the value of the woman in her own right. It is also consistent with the idea that the state should fulfil its interest in foetal welfare through legislation and policies that promote maternal welfare, and guarantee women's access to adequate and supportive health, financial, and social resources, while respecting their moral and physical integrity.

65. In a particular legislative context, the issue may arise as to whether a limit on a woman's section 7 or section 15 rights, imposed pursuant to a claim of state interest in the foetus, is reasonable and demonstrably justifiable under section 1. Such an inquiry is properly done in the context of a concrete legislative enactment, and as part of the incremental process of interpreting the Charter of Rights.

PART IV: NATURE OF ORDER SOUGHT

66. It is submitted that this Court should decline to answer the abstract questions posed in this appeal.

67. In the alternative, the Court should hold that the foetus does not have rights under section 7 or 15 of the Charter.

All of which is respectfully submitted.

THE OUTCOME

Head Notes—Borowski v. Attorney-General of Canada

Held: The appeal should be dismissed.

The appeal is moot and the Court should not exercise its discretion to hear it. Moreover, the appellant no longer has standing to pursue the appeal as the circumstances upon which his standing was originally premised have disappeared .

The doctrine of mootness is part of a general policy that a court may decline to decide a case which raises merely a hypothetical or abstract question. An appeal is moot when a decision will not have the effect of resolving some controversy affecting or potentially affecting the rights of the parties. Such a live controversy must be present not only when the action or proceeding is commenced but also when the court is called upon to reach a decision. The general policy is enforced in moot cases unless the court exercises its discretion to depart from it.

The approach with respect to mootness involves a two-step analysis. It is first necessary to determine whether the requisite tangible and concrete dispute has disappeared rendering the issues academic. If so, it is then necessary to decide if the court should exercise its discretion to hear the case. (In the interest of clarity, a case is moot if it does not present a concrete controversy even though a court may elect to address the moot issue.)

This appeal is moot as there is no longer a concrete legal dispute. The live controversy underlying this appeal—the challenge to the constitutionality of ss. 251(4), (5) and (6) of the Code—disappeared when s. 251 was struck down in *R v. Morgentaler (No. 2)*. None of the relief sought in the statement of claim was relevant. Three of the five constitutional questions that were set explicitly concerned s. 251 and were no longer applicable. The remaining two questions addressed the scope of ss. 7 and 15 of the Charter and were not severable from the context of the original challenge to s. 251.

A constitutional question cannot bind this Court and may not be used to transform an appeal into a reference. Constitutional questions are stated to define with precision the constitutional points at issue, not to introduce new issues, and accordingly, cannot be used as an independent basis for supporting an otherwise moot appeal.

The second stage in the analysis requires that a court consider whether it should exercise its discretion to decide the merits of the case, despite the absence of a live controversy. Courts may be guided in the exercise of their discretion by considering the underlying rationale of the mootness doctrine.

The first rationale for the policy with respect to mootness is that a court's competence to resolve legal disputes is rooted in the adversary system. A full adversarial context, in which both parties have a full stake in the outcome, is fundamental to our legal system. The second is based on the concern for judicial economy, which requires that a court examine the circumstances of a case to determine if it is worthwhile to allocate scarce judicial resources to resolve the moot issue. The third underlying rationale of the mootness doctrine is the need for courts to be sensitive to the effectiveness or efficacy of judicial intervention and demonstrate a measure of awareness of the judiciary's role in our political framework. The Court, in exercising its discretion in an appeal which is moot, should consider the extent to which each of these three basic factors is present. The process is not mechanical. The principles may not all support the same conclusion and the presence of one or two of the factors may be overborne by the absence of the third, and vice versa

The Court should decline to exercise its discretion to decide this appeal on its merits because of concerns for judicial economy and for the Court's role in the law-making process. The absence of an adversarial relationship was of little concern: the appeal was argued as fully as if it were not moot.

With respect to judicial economy, none of the factors justifying the application of judicial resources applied. The decision would not have practical side effects on the rights of the parties. The case was not one that was capable of repetition, yet evasive of review: it will almost certainly be brought before the Court within a specific legislative context or possibly in review of specific governmental action. An abstract pronouncement on foetal rights here would not necessarily obviate future repetitious litigation. It was not in the public interest, notwithstanding the great public importance of the question involved, to address the merits in order to settle the state of the law. A decision as to whether ss. 7 and 15 of the Charter protect the rights of the foetus is not in the public interest due to the potential uncertainty that would result from such a decision absent a legislative context.

In a legislative context any rights of the foetus could be considered or at least balanced against the rights of women guaranteed by s. 7 (p. 364).

A proper awareness of the Court's law-making function dictated against the Court's exercising its discretion to decide this appeal. The question posed here was not the question raised in the original action. Indeed, what was sought—a Charter interpretation in the absence of legislation or other governmental action bringing it into play—would turn this appeal into a private reference. The Court, if it were to exercise its discretion, would intrude on the right of the executive to order a reference and pre-empt a possible decision of Parliament by dictating the form of legislation it should enact. To do so would be a marked departure from the Court's traditional role.

The appellant also lacked standing to pursue this appeal given the fact that the original basis for his standing no longer existed. Two significant changes in the nature of this action occurred since standing was granted by this Court in 1981. Firstly, the claim is now premised primarily upon an alleged right of a foetus to life and equality pursuant to ss. 7 and 15 of the Charter. Secondly, the legislative context of original claim disappeared when s. 251 of the Code was struck down. Standing could not be based on section 24(1) of the Charter for an infringement or denial of a person's own Charter-based right was required. Here, the rights allegedly violated were those of a foetus. Standing could not be based on s. 52(1) of the Constitution Act, 1982 as this is restricted to litigants challenging a law or governmental action pursuant to power granted by law.

IN THE SUPREME COURT OF CANADA
(ON APPEAL FROM THE COURT OF APPEAL FOR MANITOBA)

BETWEEN:

SUSAN BROOKS

(Complainant-Appellant)

Appellant

AND:

CANADA SAFEWAY LIMITED

(Respondent)

Respondent

AND BETWEEN:

PATRICIA ALLEN AND PATRICIA DIXON, AND
THE MANITOBA HUMAN RIGHTS COMMISSION

(Complainants-Appellants)

Appellant

AND:

CANADA SAFEWAY LIMITED

(Respondent)

Respondent

AND:

WOMEN'S LEGAL EDUCATION AND ACTION FUND (LEAF)

Intervenor

Factum of the Women's Legal Education and Action Fund (LEAF)

Brooks v. Canada Safeway Ltd.

INTRODUCTION

Susan Brooks, Patricia Allen, and Patricia Dixon were employed as part-time cashiers at Canada Safeway in Manitoba. All three became pregnant in 1982 and applied for benefits under Safeway's health benefits plan. The Safeway plan provided general sickness and accident coverage for all employees who had completed three months service with the company. The plan covered pregnant women but suspended coverage for 10 weeks prior to and 7 weeks after birth. During that period, pregnant employees were enjoined from coverage for any illness whether related to their pregnancy or not. Instead, pregnant employees had to apply for benefits under the Unemployment Insurance Act, which were deficient in three respects: the Act provided a longer qualifying period; the Act provided a less comprehensive coverage scheme; and the Act's benefits were worth less in dollar terms. Brooks, Allen, and Dixon filed complaints with the Manitoba Human Rights Commission, alleging that the different treatment accorded to pregnancy in Canada Safeway's plan constituted discrimination on the basis of sex contrary to section 6 of the Manitoba Human Rights Act. A Human Rigths Commission adjudicator dismissed the claims, in part relying upon a 1979 decision of the Supreme Court of Canada, *Bliss v. Attorney-General of Canada*, which held that discrimination on the basis of pregnancy was not sex discrimination because not all women became pregnant. The Manitoba Court of Queen's Bench and Court of Appeal upheld the adjudicator's decision.

The women appealed to the Supreme Court of Canada. LEAF was the sole intervenor. One of the main purposes of LEAF's intervention was to challenge the prior decision in *Bliss*, and show how a purposive approach to section 15 led to the inescapable conclusion that discrimination against pregnant women was indeed discrimination on the basis of sex.

FACTUM

PART I: FACTS

The Intervenor concurs with the Statement of Facts of the Appellant.

PART II: ISSUES

1. Did the Court of Appeal for Manitoba err in interpreting the Manitoba Human Rights Act in that it concluded that the prohibition against sex discrimination in employment did not encompass a prohibition against discrimination based on pregnancy?

2. Did the Court of Appeal for Manitoba err in interpreting the Manitoba Human Rights Act in that it concluded that the prohibition against family status discrimination in employment did not encompass a prohibition against discrimination based on pregnancy?

3. Did the Court of Appeal for Manitoba err in concluding that a disability plan, such as the one offered by the Respondent Canada Safeway Limited, which offers less generous benefits to women employees who are pregnant, is not discriminatory within the meaning of the Manitoba Human Rights Act?

PART III: ARGUMENT

Did the Court of Appeal for Manitoba Err in Interpreting the Manitoba Human Rights Act in that It Concluded that the Prohibition Against Sex Discrimination in Employment Did Not Encompass a Prohibition Against Discrimination Based on Pregnancy?

That Pregnancy Discrimination Is Sex Discrimination Is the Only Conclusion Consistent with the Present-Day Understanding of Equality and the Right To Be Free from Discrimination

In the Context of Human Rights Jurisprudence

1. Recent decisions of this Honourable Court under human rights legislation show an approach to equality that goes beyond the formal principle of treating similarly situated persons similarly and recognizes the purpose of human rights legislation as connected with both equal opportunity and equal concern and respect. The Intervener agrees with the Appellant's submissions in paragraphs 17 and 18 of its Factum that human rights legislation has the status of public "fundamental law," which should be interpreted in a manner that gives effect to its purpose.

> *Ontario Human Rights Commission and Theresa O'Malley v. Simpsons-Sears Ltd.*, [1985] 2 SCR 536, 23 DLR (4th) 321, at 329.
>
> *Insurance Corporation of British Columbia v. Heerspink et al.*, [1982] 2 SCR 145, at 158.
>
> *The Winnipeg School Division No. 1 v. Craton*, [1985] 2 SCR 150, at 156.

Action Travail des Femmes v. Canadian National Railway Company, [1987] 1 SCR 1114, 8 CHRR D/4210, at D/4223.

Robichaud v. Canada (Treasury Board), [1987] 2 SCR 84, 8 CHRR D/4329.

2. A similar view of the meaning of equality is widely found in academic writing and in governmental studies.

Judge Rosalie Abella, *Equality in Employment: Royal Commission Report* (1984), at 1-18 and 254.

Walter Tarnopolsky and William Pentney, *Discrimination and the Law* (1985), at chapter XVI.

Beatrice Vizkelety, *Proving Discrimination in Canada* (1987), at 238-40.

3. In two recent decisions, this Honourable Court has found that human rights legislation provides remedies to assist women in overcoming particular sex-specific barriers against their entry into the paid work force.

Robichaud, supra, para. 1, at CHRR D/4330-33.

Action Travail des Femmes, supra, para. 1, at CHRR D/4232.

4. To generalize from the human rights jurisprudence, there are four possible ways to discriminate against members of particular groups:

(a) through a rule or practice that applies to all members of the group, such as the former prohibitions against women voting or entering the professions (total, direct discrimination);

(b) through a rule or practice that applies to all members of a group who also possess a particular characteristic, such as the rule at issue in the *Drybones* case, which affected all Indians who were intoxicated off a reservation (partial, direct discrimination);

(c) through a rule or practice that, although neutral on its face, disadvantages only or primarily members of one group compared with another, such as the Sunday closing rule at issue in *Edwards Books & Art Ltd. v. The Queen* or the requirement to work on a Saturday at issue in *Ontario Human Rights Commission and Theresa O'Malley v. Simpsons-Sears Ltd.* (indirect or systemic discrimination, which may be total or partial, depending upon the circumstances); and

(d) through a pattern of treatment that singles persons out for abuse on the basis of a condition of birth—i.e., gender (sex harassment is an example).

R v. Drybones, [1970] SCR 282, at 297.

Edwards Books & Art Ltd. v. The Queen, [1986] 2 SCR 713, at 766 and 808.

Ontario Human Rights Commission and Theresa O'Malley, supra, para. 1, at 332.

Catharine A. MacKinnon, *Sexual Harassment of Working Women: A Case Study of Sex Discrimination* (1979), at 208ff.

5. The Intervenor submits that discrimination based on pregnancy falls into the second category in paragraph 4 above when there is a straightforward pregnancy-based rule or practice, as in the instant case.

6. Discrimination against a subset of a group identified by a prohibited classification is nonetheless discrimination. For example, refusal to hire Roman Catholics who go to Mass while hiring those who do not go to Mass would still be discrimination because of religion. Failing to provide access to a building for persons in wheelchairs while providing access to those with other disabilities would still be discrimination because of disability. To say that pregnancy discrimination is not sex discrimination because there are, at any given time, non-pregnant women, is as illogical as it is to say that discrimination against observant Roman Catholics is not religious discrimination because there are non-observant Roman Catholics, or that inaccessibility for those in wheelchairs is not discrimination based on disability because there are those on crutches who can enter.

> *Canadian Odeon Theatres Ltd. v. Saskatchewan Human Rights Commission and Huck* (1985), 18 DLR (4th) 93 (Sask. CA), leave to appeal refused (1985), 18 DLR (4th) 93n (SCC).
>
> *Rand v. Sealy Eastern Ltd.* (1982), 3 CHRR D/938.
>
> *Wiens v. Inco Metals Company*, unreported, April 6, 1988, Ont. BI (Cumming J), at 33.

7. On the other hand, if a subset is defined by a factor that applies widely, so that the subset is not identified by a prohibited classification, it is not necessarily discriminatory. Thus, refusal to serve disorderly women in a public facility is not discriminatory if the management equally refuses to serve disorderly men.

8. Cases where the discrimination is "colourable" or where the effect of discriminating against the subset has an adverse impact on a group defined by a prohibited classification are exceptions to the principle stated in paragraph 7. An example of a "colourable" provision would be a rule disentitling from a benefit all those who live on an Indian reserve (in all likelihood this would be designed to disentitle Indians, although it may also catch others). An example of adverse impact discrimination would be height and weight requirements for employees where they are not bona fide occupational qualifications and have the effect of disproportionately excluding women or members of some racial groups from employment.

> *R v. Hayden*, [1983] 6 WWR 655, 3 DLR (4th) 361 (Man. CA), at DLR 364, leave to appeal refused 3 DLR (4th) 361.
>
> Compare *R v. Lefthand* (1985), 37 Alta. LR (2d) 223 (CA), at 231.
>
> *Chapdelaine and Gravel v. Air Canada et al.* (1988), 9 CHRR D/4449 (Can. H. Rts. Trib.), at D/4454.
>
> *Action Travail des Femmes*, supra, para. 1, at CHRR D/4216.

9. The instant case is comparable with *R v. Drybones*, although not exactly analogous because it is possible to be intoxicated off a reserve and not Indian; it is not

possible to be pregnant and not female. However, singling out a subset of a prohibited classification does not render the provision non-discriminatory. There can be no doubt that pregnant women are a subset of the group defined by a prohibited classification (sex), just as Indians intoxicated off a reserve were a subset of the group defined by a prohibited classification (Indians). Just as the only persons affected by the legislation struck down in *Drybones* were Indian, the only persons affected by the exclusion in the insurance plan in the instant case are women. The fact that all women are not caught by the distinction does not mean that the class of women is not affected.

Drybones, supra, para. 4, at 297.

In the Context of Modern Equality Theory

10. Historically, most sex discrimination litigation arose in cases where the only issue was whether the law should treat women the same as men when they met the very requirements that were set out for men in the law.

Mabel Penery French (1905), 37 NBR 359 (SC), at 363.

AG Canada v. Lavell, [1974] SCR 1349, at 1353.

Edwards v. AG Canada, [1930] AC 124, at 126-27.

11. This understanding of equality between the sexes is incomplete; it allows women to be equal to men only so long as and to the extent that they are the same as men.

Angela Miles, "Feminism, Equality and Liberation" (1985), 1 *Can. J Women and the Law* 42, at 64-68.

Catharine A. MacKinnon, "Difference and Dominance: On Sex Discrimination" in *Feminism Unmodified: Discourses on Life and Law* (1987), 32 and "Making Sex Equality Real" in L. Smith, G. Cote-Harper, R. Elliot, and M. Seydegart, eds., *Righting the Balance: Canada's New Equality Rights* (1986), 37.

Martha Minow, "Foreword: Justice Engendered" (1987), 101 *Harv. L Rev.* 10, at 32-33 and 38-45.

Laurence H. Tribe, "Reorienting the Mirror of Justice: Gender, Economics, and the Illusion of the 'Natural' " in *Constitutional Choices* (1985), 238.

12. This understanding of equality fails to deal with biological and social realities such as the different roles played by women and men in reproduction. Thus, rules governing behaviour in the workplace that assume that the "worker's" role in reproduction and childcare consists, after conception, in the provision of some assistance with childrearing (typically, not requiring any time off work) are inadequate to deal with female workers.

13. This understanding of equality fails to deal with socio-economic realities such as the common pattern of income-earning within marriage. Thus, separation of property in which the spouses are treated as theoretically equal economic units each acquiring and holding property has proved inadequate.

Rathwell v. Rathwell, [1978] 2 SCR 436.

Freda Steel, "The Ideal Marital Property Regime—What Would it Be?" in Elizabeth Sloss, ed., *Family Law in Canada: New Directions* (1985), 127 at 128-31.

14. Finally, this understanding of equality fails when confronted with the cultural reality that women have been expressly and effectively excluded from playing an equal role in public life and in the private business sector of the economy for most of our history, and that many of our institutions still reflect that history. Thus, an expectation that the political process or private institutions will readily respond to women's needs and concerns is unrealistic.

Action Travail des Femmes, supra, para. 1, at CHRR D/4229-32.

Royal Commission Report: Status of Women in Canada (1970), chap. 7, 333-56.

15. Legal reasoning often depends upon reasoning by analogy. However, there can be no reasoning by analogy where none exists. Pregnancy provides the paradigm case for women's situation having no analogy in men's lives.

16. The Intervenor submits that a theory or model of equality that fails to deal with the social, economic, biological, and cultural realities of women's lives is simply an inadequate theory, that a method of legal reasoning that requires analogies in order to identify inequalities is an inadequate method, and that an understanding of women's inequality entails recognition of the social subordination of women to men.

N. Colleen Sheppard, "Equality, Ideology and Suppression: Women and the Canadian Charter of Rights and Freedoms" in Christine Boyle, A. Wayne MacKay, Edward J. McBride, and John A. Yogis, eds., *Charterwatch: Reflections on Equality* (1986), 195 at 216-18.

Also see generally Catharine A. MacKinnon and other references, supra, para. 11.

17. Terms and conditions of employment set as standard in Canada have been (and still tend to be) those that contemplate a male worker—that is, a worker who may become a parent without childbearing, lactation (or, typically, subsequent nurturing) responsibilities, and who may in general count on the support of a wife in the domestic sphere.

See, for example, Unemployment Insurance Act, 1971, SC 1970-71-72, c. 48, s. 30.

Workers' Compensation Act, RSBC 1979, c. 437, s. 17, as am. SBC 1985, c. 68, s. 12.

18. Thus, only to the extent that women's career patterns fit within institutions and structures created by and for men, can they compete on an equal basis in the paid work force. The presumption of a male "norm" may mean that women in the paid work force must forego childbearing (and perhaps marriage) or operate under a distinct disadvantage if they undertake it.

Katherine Swinton, "Regulating Reproductive Hazards in the Workplace: Balancing Equality and Health" (1983), 33 *U of T LJ* 44, at 71-73.

19. The problem of combining paid work with motherhood affects a great many women. This is not because there is a high incidence of maternity among women workers

at any given time (the existing evidence suggests that it would be around 2%) but because many if not most women do become pregnant at some point in their lives. In 1983, the percentage of women who participated in the paid labour force was 52.6%. It is estimated that in 1984 this participation rate rose to 56%. Among women of childbearing age, the participation rate is highest. For example, it is estimated in 1987 that 74.4% of women between the ages of 25 and 44 participated in the paid labour force. Overall, women comprised 41.7% of the paid labour force in 1983 and 42.6% in 1985.

Statistics Canada, *Women in Canada—A Statistical Report*, 1985, 89-503E.

Statistics Canada, *The Labour Force*, November 1987, 71-001 (monthly).

Statistics Canada, *Women in the Workplace*, 1987, 71-534.

Monica Townson, "Economic Consequences of Maternity Leave" in Sheilah L. Martin and Kathleen E. Mahoney, eds., *Equality and Judicial Neutrality* (1987), 218, at 223.

20. The Intervenor submits that if human rights legislation does not protect women in the paid work force against discrimination based on pregnancy, pregnant women will be vulnerable to many forms of invidious differential treatment, including lower wages, loss of benefits and even dismissal, in the absence of specific legislation.

In the Context of the Advent of the Charter

21. The Canadian Charter of Rights and Freedoms is the "supreme law of Canada" by virtue of section 52 of the Constitution Act, 1982 and its provisions should be considered when interpreting human rights legislation. The Charter applies to the terms of provincial human rights legislation. Section 15 of the Charter gives individuals the right to equal protection and equal benefit of the law, including human rights laws. Since April 17, 1985, it has required that a term such as "sex discrimination" in a human rights statute be interpreted in a manner consistent with sections 15 and 28 of the Canadian Charter of Rights and Freedoms.

Re Blainey and Ontario Hockey Association (1986), 26 DLR (4th) 728 (Ont. CA), at 736, leave to appeal refused June 26, 1986 (SCC).

Approved in *Retail, Wholesale & Department Store Union, Local 580 v. Dolphin Delivery Ltd.*, [1986] 2 SCR 573, at 595-96.

Connell v. University of British Columbia; Harrison v. University of British Columbia (1988), 21 BCLR (2d) 145 (CA), at 149.

22. Although section 15 of the Charter was not in effect at the time at which the human rights complaint in this case arose, it is submitted that section 15 reflects our deep and ongoing values with respect to the meaning of equality and the importance of our legal system as a factor in the attainment of equality.

23. It is submitted that terms that are common to human rights legislation and the Charter, such as "sex," "religion," and "race" should, wherever possible, be interpreted in a manner that is consistent.

24. The legislative history of section 15 of the Charter, culminating in the inclusion of the wording "equal benefit of the law" and "equality under the law" suggests an intention to depart from the reasoning and the outcome of the *Bliss* case.

Walter S. Tarnopolsky, "The Equality Rights" in Walter Tarnopolsky and Gerald A. Beaudoin, eds., *Canadian Charter of Rights and Freedoms: Commentary* (1982), 395 at 421-22.

Anne F. Bayefsky, "Defining Equality Rights" in Anne F. Bayefsky and Mary Eberts, eds., *Equality Rights and the Canadian Charter of Rights and Freedoms* (1985), 1, at 3-25.

25. Under other sections of the Charter, this Honourable Court has approached equality-related issues in a manner consistent with the Intervenor's argument. In *Edwards Books & Art Ltd. v. The Queen*, the Court recognized that a system that is designed to meet the needs of the majority may have the effect of infringing the rights of particular groups whose needs are different. The three sets of Reasons of the majority in the *Morgentaler* case reflect an appreciation of the necessity for life alternatives to be reasonably available to women, consistent with the view of equality argued by this Intervenor.

Edwards Books & Art Ltd. v. The Queen, supra, para. 4, at 765 and 781.

R v. Morgentaler, [1988] 1 SCR 30, per Dickson CJ, at 56-60 and 70-73; per Beetz J, at 89-91, 101-6, and 121-22; per Wilson J, at 164-80.

26. This Court has said that Charter rights are to be given a purposive interpretation. The Women's Legal Education and Action Fund submits (as it did in its intervention in *Andrews v. Law Society of British Columbia*, argued in this Honourable Court in October 1987, decision reserved) that the primary purpose of the equality rights guaranteed in sections 15 and 28 of the Charter is to alleviate the disadvantage of historically disadvantaged, powerless, or excluded groups, such as women, through permitting review of governmental action or laws that, in their purpose or effect, perpetuate disadvantage. It submits that human rights legislation should also be interpreted purposively and that the primary purpose of anti-discrimination legislation such as the Manitoba Human Rights Act is similarly to alleviate the disadvantage of historically disadvantaged, powerless, or excluded groups, such as women, through providing remedies in particular instances of discrimination to individuals (or groups, where the legislation permits).

R v. Big M Drug Mart Ltd., [1985] 1 SCR 295, at 331; see also references in para. 1, supra.

27. The Intervenor submits that the disadvantage of women in the paid work force stems in considerable measure from the perpetuation of norms that are implicitly male, in that they do not take cognizance of workers as mothers or mothers as workers. If the definition of "sex discrimination" does not extend to discrimination against pregnant women or mothers, the purpose of human rights legislation in this respect cannot be fulfilled.

The Arguments for Finding Pregnancy Discrimination Not To Be Included Within the Meaning of Sex Discrimination Are Insupportable

28. There are two concerns that may underlie reluctance to find that pregnancy discrimination is sex discrimination. First, there may be a belief that pregnancy is a voluntary condition and that women who choose to become pregnant should be responsible for the consequences. Second, there may be a related belief that employers or society as a whole should not be expected to subsidize women who choose to become pregnant.

Reasons of Adjudicator, Case on Appeal, vol. I, 234; Respondent's Factum, para. 6.

29. There are serious problems with the argument that pregnancy is a voluntary condition and therefore one that should not properly be seen in the same light as sickness or disability. (At the same time, normal pregnancy is not the same as sickness or disability: it is a unique condition.)

30. While pregnancy may sometimes be a voluntary condition in the case of individual women, for women as a group pregnancy is not voluntary. The social imperatives for women to bear children are clear and obvious. It should not be socially disadvantageous for women to perform a function (reproduction) that benefits society as a whole. As recognized by this Court in cases under human rights legislation and under the Charter, it is sometimes necessary to view people as members of groups in order to understand the nature of the discrimination against them and create the appropriate remedies for it.

Action Travail des Femmes, supra, para. 1, at D/4226.

Edwards Books & Art Ltd., supra, para. 4, at 781.

31. Further, many pregnancies are not voluntary in the ordinary sense of the word. Some pregnancies are not the result of voluntary sexual activity but rather of coerced sex. Some other pregnancies are the result of voluntary sexual activity but are not desired or intended; rather, they are the consequence of unavailable, inadequate, or failed birth control.

32. Notably, other medical conditions arising unintentionally from voluntary activity (such as automobile accidents or sports injuries) are not excluded from the Respondent's insurance plan. Nor are any male-specific conditions excluded from the Respondent's insurance plan.

Case on Appeal, vol. II, p. 276. *General Electric Co. v. Gilbert*, 429 US 124 (1976), at 151-53, per Brennan J, dissenting.

33. Disadvantaging women who have children is inconsistent with viewing women as fully human. Wilson J stated in the *Morgentaler* decision (and the Intervenor submits that this statement is consistent with the Reasons of other members of the majority):

> The fact that the decision whether a woman will be allowed to terminate her pregnancy is in the hands of a committee is just as great a violation of the woman's right to personal autonomy in decisions of an intimate and private nature as it would be if a committee were established to decide whether a woman should be allowed to continue her pregnancy.

Morgentaler, supra, para. 25, per Wilson J, at 172.

34. With respect to the second concern, that it is inappropriate to subsidize women who become pregnant, in part this may rest upon the premise that pregnancy is a voluntary condition. For the reasons given above, the Intervenor submits that that is a mistaken premise: the voluntariness of individual pregnancies, even where it exists, is irrelevant to the issue whether it is discriminatory to disadvantage pregnant women.

35. As well, this concern may arise from the fundamental distinction that has been made between the nature of productive activity in the private and the public spheres. Recently, some political and economic theorists have argued that the line between work done in the "private" sphere (unpaid and in general unrecognized) and in the "public" sphere (paid and recognized as work, for example by inclusion in the Gross National Product) is arbitrary and works gravely to women's detriment.

Lorenne Clark and Lynda Lange, "Introduction," Lorenne Clark and Lynda Lange, eds., *The Sexism of Social and Political Theory* (1979), vii.

Margrit Eichler, "The Connection Between Paid and Unpaid Labour and Its Implication for Creating Equality for Women in Employment" in Judge Rosalie Abella (Commissioner), *Research Studies of the Commission on Equality in Employment* (1985), 537.

36. Although the bearing and rearing of children has traditionally been done by women in the private sphere (meaning that it is unpaid labour), undeniably bearing and rearing of children is work that is vital to our society. Notably, in many industrialized countries fully-paid (or close to fully-paid) maternity leave has been the norm.

Monica Townson, "Economic Consequences of Maternity Leave" in Sheilah L. Martin and Kathleen E. Mahoney, eds., *Equality and Judicial Neutrality* (1987), 218, at 221.

Monica Townson, "Introduction," *Paid Parental Leave Policies: An International Comparison with Options for Canada*, Task Force on Child Care, Background Papers Series 4, Status of Women Canada (1985), at 4-10.

37. If women are to enjoy an equal opportunity to participate in the life of our society, the social value of child bearing ought to be given full currency in the law.

Marc Gold, "Equality Before the Law in the Supreme Court of Canada: A Case Study" (1980), 18 *Osgoode Hall LJ* 336, at 426.

38. The Intervenor submits, therefore, that there is no principled basis for concerns based on perceptions of pregnancy as voluntary, or on perceptions of some unfairness in making benefits, including insurance benefits, available to pregnant women and new mothers. On the contrary, to act on those perceptions would be to perpetuate inequality, as reflected in the *Preamble to the United Nations Convention on the Elimination of All Forms of Discrimination Against Women*, 1980:

> Bearing in mind the great contribution of women to the welfare of the family and to the development of society, so far not fully recognized, the social significance of maternity and the role of both parents in the family and in the upbringing of children, and aware that the role of women in procreation should not be a basis for discrimination but that the

upbringing of children requires a sharing of responsibility between men and women and society as a whole ... .

39. The decision of this Honourable Court in *Bliss v. AG Canada* was followed by the courts below and is relied upon by the Respondent. The Intervenor submits that the *Bliss* case is distinguishable and, in the alternative, with respect, that it was wrongly decided.

Reasons of the Adjudicator, Case on Appeal, vol. I, 223-26.

Reasons of Simonsen J, Case on Appeal, vol. I, 253-55.

Bliss v. AG Canada, [1979] 1 SCR 183, 92 DLR (3d) 417.

40. It is submitted that the *Bliss* case is distinguishable because:

(a) The Court was dealing with an application to strike down federal legislation pursuant to the Canadian Bill of Rights, a federal statute that the courts were reluctant to see as permitting any departure from the principles of Parliamentary sovereignty.

(b) In *Bliss*, human rights legislation duly enacted by an elected legislature, aimed at promoting equality and preventing harmful discrimination, was not at issue.

(c) This Court's comments in *Bliss* on the meaning of sex discrimination were *obiter dicta* in that the basis for the decision was that section 1(b) of the Canadian Bill of Rights failed to extend to benefits rather than penalties, or to equality in the substance rather than the administration of the law, and that in any event there had been established a valid federal objective for the Unemployment Insurance Act.

Bliss, supra, para. 39, at DLR 421-25.

41. It is submitted in the alternative, and with respect, that the *Bliss* case was wrongly decided because:

(a) The Court and the parties were operating on the understanding of equality that was then prevalent—that (at least in the workplace) what was required was to treat women the same where they were "the same" as men. Thus, the Court had been led into error when it stated that any inequality was not created by the legislation, but by nature and that, therefore, there was no discrimination. Parliament, not "nature," enacted the Unemployment Insurance Act.

(b) The Court erred when it found that the legislation in *Bliss* was not discriminatory, even under the test for inequality that was then applied. The appellant, Stella Bliss, was disentitled to unemployment insurance benefits because of her condition even though she would have qualified for them otherwise. In other words, she was similarly situated to men who had paid premiums for the same period of time and who were unemployed, but ready and available for work. Despite being similarly situated in those respects, she was disentitled by the statute.

(c) The Court erred in logic in holding that pregnancy discrimination is not sex discrimination, for reasons given in paragraphs 6-9 above.

Bliss, supra, para. 39, DLR, at 421-22.

42. After the ruling in *Bliss*, Parliament moved to amend the Unemployment Insurance Act (to remove the disentitlement that Bliss had challenged) and the Canadian Human Rights Act (to add "pregnancy" to the definition of sex discrimination). In other jurisdictions, including Manitoba, subsequent legislation has also consistently taken the form of adding pregnancy to the definition of "sex." This is an expression of public policy in the area. It does not follow from the fact that a legislature has amended a human rights statute specifically to cover an area that it was not previously covered; amendments may be made in order to clarify, out of an abundance of caution.

Canadian Human Rights Act, SC 1976-77, c. 33, as am. SC 1980-81-82-83, c. 143, s. 3.

Human Rights Code, SM 1987, c. 44, s. 9(2)(f).

Saskatchewan Human Rights Code, SS 1979, c. 524.1, s. 2(o).

Individual's Rights Protection Act, RSA 1980, c. I-2, s. 7(1.1).

Human Rights Act, SY 1987, c. 3, s. 6(f).

Pregnancy Discrimination Act, 42 USCS, s. 2000 e(k).

Ontario Human Rights Commission and Theresa O'Malley, supra, para. 1, overruling (1982), 138 DLR (3d) 133 (Ont. CA), at 136.

Wiens, supra, para. 6, at 59 and 73-74.

Interpretation Act, RSM 1954, 128, s. 27(2).

43. The Respondent also relies upon decisions of this Court relating to whether it is sex discrimination to have a "no beards" rule for male employees.

Canada Safeway Ltd. v. Retail Store Employees Union Local 832 (1981), 37 NR 394.

Manitoba Human Rights Commission v. Canada Safeway Limited (1985), 58 NR 311.

44. It is fallacious to analogize between pregnancy and growing a beard. Facial hair serves no particular social function. On the other hand, reproduction is a central human concern. It is imperative to the survival of our species that women give birth. To compare the ability to grow facial hair with the ability to give birth is to trivialize the social role women play in giving birth. Further, men grow facial hair as fashion dictates. Whether women have babies is not a matter of fashion.

45. Whether or not discrimination based on possession of a beard is sex discrimination (that is not at issue here), discrimination based on pregnancy is. In any event, this Honourable Court did not discuss whether the "no beards" policy was sex discrimination in either of the cases cited by the Respondent. The decision of the Manitoba Court of Appeal in the 1985 human rights case has been persuasively criticized by academic commentators.

Tarnopolsky and Pentney, *Discrimination and the Law* (1985), at 8-51 to 8-54.

Recent Authority Supports the Inclusion of Pregnancy Discrimination Is Sex Discrimination

46. In a recent British Columbia Supreme Court decision, the issue was whether the British Columbia Human Rights Act prohibition against sex discrimination in employment prevented an employer from firing a woman whom it had just hired, upon learning that she was pregnant. Oppal J said:

> It may be unduly restrictive and somewhat artificial to argue that a distinction based on a characteristic such as pregnancy, which is shared only by some members of a group, is not discrimination against the whole group ... For discrimination which is aimed at, or has its effect upon some people in a particular group as opposed to the whole of that group, is not any the less discriminatory.

Century Oils (Canada) Inc. and Production Supply v. Christine Marie Davies and British Columbia Council of Human Rights, as yet unreported, British Columbia Supreme Court, January 28, 1988, at 10. See also the decisions cited by the Appellants at para. 7 of their Factum, and *Riggio v. Sheppard Coiffures Ltd.* (1988), 9 CHRR D/4520 (Ont. Hum. Rts. BI), at D/4525 and *Wiens*, supra, para. 6, at 59.

47. In the United Kingdom, since the *Turley* case cited by the Respondent, there have been decisions limiting its effect. For example, in one case the tribunal said:

> Finally Mr. Symons submitted that the equality clause did not operate in this case because there was a material difference between the applicant and male employees, other than the difference of sex. Putting his argument succinctly, he said that the different treatment afforded to the applicant when she was sick was not merely because she was a woman (which would be a difference of sex alone) but because she was a woman who had just become a mother (which, he said, is an additional difference). In our view this argument propounds a distinction without a difference, and we reject it for a number of reasons. First we consider that the difference between being a man, who only has to produce a sick certificate to qualify for benefit, and being a mother, who has to go further, is in our view clearly no more than a difference of sex within the meaning of s. 1(3). The section is not designed for such narrow distinctions as the difference between being a woman and being a mother.

Turley v. Allders Department Stores Ltd., [1980] ICR 66 (EAT).

Coyne v. Exports Credits Guarantee Department, [1981] IRLR 51, at 54; see also *Hayes v. Malleable Working Men's Club and Institute*, [1985] ICR 703 (EAT), at 708-9.

48. An American appellate court considered a case under Title VII of the Civil Rights Act against an airline that, as a rule, fired any of its female flight attendants who married and refused to hire women as flight attendants unless they were single. No male employees were subject to such a rule, although there were no male flight attendants. The Court said:

> The effect of the statute is not to be diluted because discrimination adversely affects only a portion of the protected class. Discrimination is not to be tolerated under the guise of physical properties possessed by one sex ... or through the unequal application of a seemingly neutral company policy.

Sprogis v. United Airlines Inc., 444 F.2d 1194 (7th Cir. 1971), at 1198 (cert. denied).

49. In a 1987 decision, the United States Supreme Court considered whether a California statute requiring employers to provide unpaid pregnancy leave of up to four months, and to reinstate returning employees to their same or similar jobs, violated federal legislation (the Pregnancy Discrimination Act amendment to Title VII of the Civil Rights Act) mandating the same treatment for pregnant women as other employees. The Court rejected the argument that the California statute violated the federal legislation, holding that both statutes were passed to promote equal opportunity in employment, and were not in conflict. The Court clearly believed that equality for women is promoted by accommodating the childbearing needs of working women, and noted that the California statute's approach was consistent with the dissenting opinion of Brennan J in *General Electric Co. v. Gilbert*, supra, para. 32, adopted by Congress in enacting the Pregnancy Discrimination Act. The majority Reasons in California Federal Savings state:

> By "taking pregnancy into account" California's pregnancy disability leave statute allows women, as well as men, to have families without losing their jobs.

California Federal Savings & Loan Association et al. v. Guerra, Director, Department of Fair Employment & Housing et al., 93 L Ed. 2d 613 (1987), at 629.

Pregnancy Discrimination Act, supra, para. 42.

50. In summary, the Intervenor submits that the Manitoba Court of Appeal erred in concluding that the prohibition against sex discrimination in employment in section 6(1) of the Manitoba Human Rights Act did not encompass discrimination based on pregnancy because such a conclusion is inconsistent with a purposive approach to the interpretation of human rights legislation, is inconsistent with a present-day understanding of the meaning of equality as reflected in judicial decisions, academic writing, and the Charter, is inconsistent with a logical approach to sex-specific distinctions, and is inconsistent with recent authority and public policy in the area.

Did the Court of Appeal for Manitoba Err in Interpreting the Manitoba Human Rights Act in that It Concluded that the Prohibition Against Family Status Discrimination in Employment Did Not Encompass a Prohibition Against Discrimination Based on Pregnancy?

51. The Intervenor agrees with the submissions of the Appellants and submits that family status discrimination must encompass a prohibition against discrimination based on pregnancy. A woman who is pregnant is about to become a mother, and discrimination against her because she is pregnant is based upon that future family status.

Did the Court of Appeal for Manitoba Err in Concluding that a Disability Plan, Such as the One Offered by the Respondent Canada Safeway Limited, Which Offers Less Generous Benefits to Women Employees Who Are Pregnant, Is Not Discriminatory Within the Meaning of the Manitoba Human Rights Act?

52. The Intervenor submits that a plan such as the one at issue in this case, which cuts off benefits to women because they are pregnant, is discriminatory within the meaning of section 6(1) of the Manitoba Human Rights Act, either on the basis of sex or, alternatively, family status. The point of an insurance program is to spread risks; if the goal were to ensure an even allocation of benefits to all participants regardless of need, the program would not be an insurance program but something else (such as a forced savings program).

53. Further, the Intervenor takes issue with the Respondent's suggestion that, because women may stand to gain more from the insurance program than men, it is proper to disentitle them from benefits. It is submitted that it is just as improper to disentitle women from benefits for that reason as it would be to disentitle from insurance benefits members of a particular racial or religious group who appear, statistically, to require a higher level of benefits in particular contexts. The fact that statistical differences may be established between groups does not immunize policies or practices distinguishing between those groups from the effect of human rights legislation.

City of Los Angeles, Department of Water and Power et al. v. Manhart et al., 55 L Ed. 2d 657 (1978), at 664-66.

PART IV: NATURE OF ORDER SOUGHT

54. The Intervenor respectfully requests that this appeal be allowed, that an order be made that the Respondent has discriminated against the Appellants, contrary to the provisions of section 6(1) of the Manitoba Human Rights Act, and that the Adjudicator be asked to determine an appropriate remedy pursuant to section 28 of the said Act. The Intervenor further requests that there be no costs against the Intervenor.

All of which is respectfully submitted.

THE OUTCOME

Head Notes—Brooks v. Canada Safeway Ltd.

Held: The appeals should be allowed.

Discrimination on the Basis of Pregnancy

The complete disentitlement of pregnant women during a seventeen-week period from receiving accident or sickness benefits under the respondent's plan constitutes discrimination by reason of pregnancy. Pregnant employees receive significantly less favourable treatment under the plan than other employees. The plan singles out pregnancy for disadvantageous treatment, in comparison with any other health reason which may prevent an employee from reporting to work.

Pregnancy, while it is not properly characterized as a sickness or an accident, is a valid health-related reason, in our society, for absence from work and as such should not have been excluded from the respondent's plan. The respondent's plan is designed to compensate employees who are absent from work for valid health-related reasons.

Pregnancy is clearly such a reason. ... It is to state the obvious to say that pregnancy is of fundamental importance in society. Indeed, its importance makes description difficult. To equate pregnancy with ... a decision to undergo medical treatment for cosmetic surgery ... is fallacious. (p. 1237)

Further, in distinguishing pregnancy from all other health-related reasons for not working, the plan imposed unfair disadvantages on pregnant women. Everyone in society benefits from procreation but one of its major costs is placed, under this plan, on one group in society—pregnant women. Removal of unfair disadvantages imposed on groups in society is a key purpose of anti-discrimination legislation. Finding that the respondent's plan is discriminatory furthers this purpose. In sum, where an employer enters the field of compensation for health conditions and then excludes pregnancy as a valid reason for compensation, the employer has acted in a discriminatory fashion. A plan would be considered discriminatory even if it did not exclude coverage for non-pregnancy-related illness and accidents. It is enough that the plan excludes compensation for pregnancy.

The respondent alleged that the decision to exclude pregnancy from the scope of its plan was not a question of discrimination, but a question of deciding to compensate some risks and to exclude others. Underinclusion may be simply a backhanded way of permitting discrimination. Once an employer decides to provide an employee benefit package, exclusions from such schemes may not be made, like in this case, in a discriminatory fashion.

Section 19(h)(vii) of the Unemployment Insurance Act, 1971 regulations, while it addresses employer plans which do not compensate pregnant women during the seventeen-week period, does not constitute a permissible distinction pursuant to s. 7(2) of the Manitoba Human Rights Act. Distinction along sex lines might have been permissible in employee benefit plans only if such regulations had been passed pursuant to s. 7(2). In the absence of regulations under that provision, discrimination in employee benefit packages is not permissible.

Discrimination on the Basis of Sex

Discrimination on the basis of pregnancy is discrimination on the basis of sex. The decision of this Court in *Bliss*, which reached the opposite conclusion, is inconsistent with the Court's approach to interpreting human rights legislation taken in subsequent cases and should no longer be followed. Pregnancy discrimination is a form of sex discrimination simply because of the basic biological fact that only women have the capacity to become pregnant. Appellants' disfavoured treatment under the plan flowed entirely from their state of pregnancy, a condition unique to women. Those who bear children and benefit society as a whole should not be economically or socially disadvantaged. It is thus unfair to impose all of the costs of pregnancy upon one-half of the population.

It is also wrong to believe that pregnancy-related discrimination could not be sex discrimination because not all women become pregnant. While pregnancy-based discrimination only affects part of an identifiable group, it does not affect anyone who is not a member of the group. Indeed, pregnancy cannot be separated from gender. The fact, therefore, that the plan did not discriminate against all women, but only against pregnant women, did not make the impugned distinction any less discriminating.

[There is no] useful analogy between a company rule denying men the right to wear beards and an accident sickness insurance plan which discriminates against female employees who become pregnant. The attempt to draw an analogy at best trivializes the procreative and socially vital function of women and seeks to elevate the growing of facial hair to a constitutional right. (pp. 1249-50)

[T]he respondent's argument that legislative amendments to preclude pregnancy-based discrimination in the aftermath of Bliss indicate that the term sex discrimination does not include pregnancy [is unpersuasive]. (p. 1250)

IN THE SUPREME COURT OF CANADA

(ON APPEAL FROM THE COURT OF APPEAL FOR MANITOBA)

BETWEEN:

DIANNA JANZEN AND TRACY GOVEREAU

(Complainants)

Appellants

AND:

PLATY ENTERPRISES LTD., AND PLATY ENTERPRISES LTD., CARRYING ON BUSINESS UNDER THE FIRM NAME AND STYLE OF PHAROS RESTAURANT, AND TOMMY GRAMMAS

(Respondents)

Respondents

AND:

WOMEN'S LEGAL EDUCATION AND ACTION FUND (LEAF)

Intervenor

Factum of the Women's Legal Education and Action Fund (LEAF)

Janzen and Govereau v. Platy Enterprises Ltd.

INTRODUCTION

Dianna Janzen and Tracy Govereau were employed at the Pharos Restaurant in Winnipeg in 1982. Both were sexually harassed by a cook who worked there. Complaints to the harasser and owner were ineffective. Both women filed complaints with the Manitoba Human Rights Commission, alleging discrimination on the basis of sex contrary to section 6 of the Manitoba Human Rights Act. The human rights adjudicator agreed that Janzen and Govereau had been subjected to persistent sexual harassment and were thus discriminated against on the basis of their sex. He awarded exemplary damages and damages for loss of income. The Manitoba Court of Queen's Bench upheld the adjudicator's finding of sex discrimination but significantly lowered the damages awarded to both women. The Court of Appeal, however, reversed the judgment on the grounds that sexual harassment was not sex discrimination:

> When a schoolboy steals kisses from a female classmate, one might well say that he is harassing her. He is troubling her; vexing her; harrying her—but surely he is not discriminating against her.

The Court also ruled that an employer could not be held liable for any sexual harassment perpetrated by its employee because harassment could not said to have occurred in the course of employment:

> [What] has patting the buttocks of a waitress to do with fulfilling the responsibilities as a cook?

Janzen and Govereau appealed to the Supreme Court. LEAF was the sole intervenor.

FACTUM

PART I: FACTS

1. The Intervenor concurs with the Statement of Facts of the Appellant save that it adds the following:

(a) Diana Janzen testified that the physical and emotional consequences of the harassment she endured included insomnia, vomiting, and inability to concentrate. The Adjudicator accepted this evidence "Totally."

See Reasons for Decision of the Adjudicator, Case on Appeal, vol. II, 496; Evidence of Janzen, vol. I, 133.

(b) The Adjudicator found that the harassment of Tracy Govereau by Tommy and Phillip was "devastating" to her. In this regard, Govereau testified that she "felt dirty, wasn't relaxed, couldn't sleep or concentrate in class." The adjudicator specifically found that the criticism of Govereau's work by Tommy and Phillip was "persistent and unjustified."

See Reasons for Decision of the Adjudicator, Case on Appeal, vol. II, 497; Evidence of Govereau, vol. I, 204-5.

(c) The Adjudicator found that the acts of Tommy and Phillip created a "poisoned work environment" for both complainants.

See Reasons for Decision of the Adjudicator, Case on Appeal, vol. II, 496-98.

(d) The witness Enns, whose evidence was accepted completely by the Adjudicator, testified that the physical (although not overtly sexual) contact that Tommy imposed upon her bothered her and made her feel apprehensive.

See Evidence of Enns, Case on Appeal, vol. I, 281; Reasons for Decision of the Adjudicator, vol. II, 497.

PART II: ISSUES

1. Is sexual harassment within the ambit of the prohibition against sex discrimination in section 6(1) of the Manitoba Human Rights Act?

2. Is an employer liable for sexual harassment perpetrated against its employees by its supervisory employees?

PART III: ARGUMENT

Sexual Harassment Is Sex Discrimination and Is Thus Within the Ambit of Section 6(1) of the Manitoba Human Rights Act

Purposive Approach

1. This Court has consistently articulated a purposive approach to human rights legislation, wherein it has sought to identify the social evil to be removed, and has given such legislation a "fair, large and liberal interpretation as will best ensure the attainment of [its] objects."

Robichaud v. Canada (Treasury Board), [1987] 2 SCR 84, at 88-90.

Action Travail des Femmes v. Canadian National Railway Company, [1987] 1 SCR 1114, at 1132-38.

Ontario Human Rights Commission and Theresa O'Malley v. Simpsons-Sears Ltd., [1985] 2 SCR 536.

2. In cases involving the Canadian Human Rights Act, this Court has enunciated one purpose of human rights legislation as follows:

> to give effect to the principle that every individual should have an equal opportunity with other individuals to live his or her life without being hindered by discriminatory practices.

It is submitted that this description properly characterizes a central purpose of the Manitoba Human Rights Act, as well.

Robichaud, supra, at 89.

Action Travail des Femmes, supra, at 1134.

3. This Court has recognized that the special nature and purpose of human rights legislation gives such legislation "not-quite constitutional" status.

Insurance Corporation of British Columbia v. Heerspink et al., [1982] 2 SCR 145, at 157-58.

Robichaud, supra, at 89.

4. Save for section 15, the Canadian Charter of Rights and Freedoms was in effect at the time the complaints in the case at bar arose. The Charter applies to provincial human rights legislation.

Appellants' Factum, Statement of Facts, 1, 4.

Re Blainey and Ontario Hockey Association (1986), 26 DLR (4th) 728, 736 (Ont. CA), leave to appeal refused June 26, 1986, SCC, approved in *Retail, Wholesale & Department Store Union, Local 580 v. Dolphin Delivery Ltd.*, [1986] 2 SCR 573, at 595-96.

5. In the course of addressing Charter rights, this Court has enunciated certain basic aspects of equality that, the Intervenor submits, should also inform the construction of human rights legislation, in view of the quasi-constitutional nature of the latter. In particular:

(a) This Court has acknowledged that a commitment to social justice and equality is one of the fundamental values of society.

R v. Oakes, [1986] 1 SCR 103, at 119.

(b) This Court has acknowledged the importance of promoting the equality of particular groups.

R v. Big M Drug Mart Ltd., [1985] 1 SCR 295, at 337-38.

Société des Acadiens v. Association of Parents for Fairness in Education et al., [1986] 1 SCR 549, at 579.

Caldwell v. Stewart, [1984] 2 SCR 603, at 626.

6. The principles set forth in paragraphs 1-5 above compel recognition that sexual harassment is a form of sex discrimination because it denies women equality of opportunity in employment because of their sex.

7. Notwithstanding that the present complaints arose before April 17, 1985, it is submitted that section 15 of the Charter should be considered in construing section 6(1) of the Manitoba Human Rights Act. In fact, that Act continued in force until December 10, 1987, when Manitoba's Human Rights Code was proclaimed. Further, terms that are common to human rights legislation and the Charter, such as "sex" and "race," among others, should be interpreted in a consistent manner. To do otherwise would undermine respect for the law, and undermine the consistent development of equality jurisprudence and section 15 jurisprudence in particular.

8. In *Andrews v. Law Society of British Columbia* (argued in this Honourable Court in October 1987, decision reserved), this Intervenor argued that the primary purpose of section 15 is to alleviate the disadvantages of the disempowered, including women. Sexual harassment in the workplace is a significant barrier to women's equality. Hence, section 15 confirms that sexual harassment is a form of sex discrimination.

The Sexual Harassment of Working Women Contributes to Women's Inequality

9. Sexual harassment in employment consists of the unwanted imposition of sexual requirements at work.

> *Brennan v. The Queen (Treasury Board) and Robichaud*, [1984] 2 FC 799, at 821 (FCA), reversed on other grounds (sub nom. *Robichaud v. Canada (Treasury Board)*), supra.
>
> *Zarankin v. Johnstone* (1984), 5 CHRR D/2274, at D/2274-5.
>
> Catharine MacKinnon, *Sexual Harassment of Working Women* (New Haven and London: Yale University Press, 1979), 1.

10. Sexual harassment both mirrors and reinforces a fundamental imbalance of power between men and women in the workplace and in society.

11. Victims and perpetrators of sexual harassment can be male or female. However, the victims are largely female, and the perpetrators largely male. This is so because of sex inequality in society. Because women have not yet attained equal economic status with men, the hiring, firing and advancement of women in the workplace is most frequently in the hands of men. Men are thus in a social position of economic dominance over women. Because the sexes have not yet attained sexual equality, men are socialized to aggressively initiate sexual interchanges with women, often heedless of women's desires. Men are thus in a social position of sexual dominance over women. Sexual harassment utilizes economic dominance to effect sexual coercion and sexual dominance to effect economic coercion. When sexual harassment is permitted to occur, the sexual proclivities of some men become employment standards for their female employees.

> MacKinnon, *Sexual Harassment of Working Women*, supra, at 1-27 and 143-92.
>
> Constance Backhouse and Leah Cohen, *The Secret Oppression: Sexual Harassment of Working Women* (Toronto: Macmillan of Canada, 1978), 39-41.
>
> Arjun P. Aggarwal, *Sexual Harassment in the Workplace* (Toronto: Butterworths, 1987), 1-4.

12. Attitudes, beliefs and traditional practices have as great an impact on the behaviour of the sexes as does biology. Non-biological constructs of sex, including gender identification and sex role behaviour, create some of the greatest barriers to women's equality. Such barriers are appropriate targets for human rights laws.

13. Our society has traditionally assigned to males the prerogative to initiate intimacy and conditioned them to find female powerlessness and submission erotic. This is a socially constructed aspect of gender identification and sex role behaviour. As reflected in sexual harassment, this social construct of sex creates a significant barrier to women's equality. This understanding of sexual harassment was grasped in one of the earliest adjudications on a sexual harassment complaint under the Manitoba Human Rights Act. In *Hufnagel v. Osama Enterprises Ltd.*, adjudicator Paul Teskey found that the plain and ordinary meaning of the word "sex" included "sexual instincts, desires or other manifestation pertaining to sex ... arising from differences of consciousness of sex." He concluded that sexual harassment is sex discrimination.

Hufnagel v. Osama Enterprises Ltd. (1982), 3 CHRR D/922, at D/924-25.

14. As a result of the generally disadvantaged status of women in Canadian society, men frequently hold positions in the employment hierarchy in which they control the working conditions, promotional opportunities, and employment tenure of female subordinates. Sexual harassment is a way of exploiting this economic control to secure sexual access to women. This Court has dealt with a case in which a victim who proved sexual harassment by her male supervisor recovered in a claim for sex discrimination made against her employer.

Robichaud, supra.

15. Even when men do not hold superior positions, in a formal sense, in the employment hierarchy, they may use sexual harassment as a tool for maintaining dominance and reminding women of their dependent, vulnerable, and precarious status in the workplace. This Court has recognized that the sexual harassment of women by male co-workers constitutes one means of systemic discrimination on the basis of sex.

Action Travail des Femmes, supra.

16. Whether women are harassed by co-workers or superiors, they are subjected to sexual harassment because of their sex. They are vulnerable because of their sex and the form of harassment used against them is selected because of their sex.

17. In situations of sexual harassment, women must satisfy sexual standards for their employment. Men typically labour under no such disability. A double standard is thus created at work: one for women that includes sexual requirements, one for men that does not.

18. Sexual harassment is pandemic in women's employment. It occurs in female job ghettos such as waitressing as well as in so-called "non-traditional" employment.

M.A. Hickling, "Employer's Liability for Sexual Harassment" (1988), 17 *Man. LJ* 124, manuscript, at 3-4.

Backhouse and Cohen, *The Secret Oppression*, supra, at 1-37 and 39-41.

19. Sexual harassment leads to job loss, as it did in the case on appeal. While many victims are fired, at least 50% of victims leave their jobs because of a "poisoned work environment," in which sexually harassing acts do not lead to direct employment consequences such as firing or denial of benefits, but so sully the work environment that they cause an employee anxiety and debilitation.

Aggarwal, *Sexual Harassment in the Workplace*, supra, at 3, 20-23, and 81-84.

20. Sexual harassment not only deprives women of a livelihood but deprives them of their physical and mental health. The unwelcome verbal and physical attentions endured by the Appellants Janzen and Govereau and the subsequent persistent and unjustified criticisms of their work resulted in both women suffering from physical and psychological symptoms of stress disorder.

Intervenor's Statement of Facts, paragraph 1.

21. A recent Royal Commission on Equality in Employment concluded that processes for dealing quickly and effectively with sexual harassment in the workplace are necessary to eliminate women's inequality.

Judge Rosalie Silberman Abella, *Equality in Employment: Royal Commission Report* (Ottawa: Supply and Services, 1984), 268, Recommendation 107.

The Analysis of Sex Discrimination Adopted by the Manitoba Court of Appeal Is Inconsistent with the Purposive Approach and Modern Equality Jurisprudence

22. The Intervenor adopts the Appellants' argument that the sex discrimination provisions of the Human Rights Act are not confined to addressing discrimination based "solely" on sex. Discriminatory activities that select the victim on the basis of the prohibited ground plus an additional factor, have been recognized by numerous courts and adjudicators as discrimination on the prohibited ground.

R v. Drybones, [1970] SCR 282.

Brennan, supra.

Re: Mehta and MacKinnon (1985), 19 DLR (4th) 148 (NS CA).

Rand v. Sealy Eastern Ltd. (1982), 3 CHRR D/938.

Phillips v. Martin Marietta Corporation, 91 S. Ct. 496 (1971).

Sprogis v. United Airlines Inc., 444 F.2d 1194 (7th Cir. 1971).

Bundy v. Jackson, 641 F.2d 934 (DC Cir. 1981).

23. The Intervenor submits that it is conceptually more accurate to state the problem of "sex-plus" discrimination as a problem of the appropriate definition of "sex" for human rights purposes.

24. It is submitted that in the case at bar, and the companion case, *Brooks v. Canada Safeway Ltd.*, the Manitoba Court of Appeal has confined the definition of "sex" to "biological gender." This narrow definition fails to recognize that in Canadian

society, and many other societies, to be female is also to be economically unequal and sexually subordinated.

Brooks v. Canada Safeway Ltd. (1986), 42 Man. R (2d) 27 (CA).

25. One reason why the Manitoba Court of Appeal chose such a narrow definition of "sex" was that it assumed that no other definition would permit a Court to determine whether conduct was discriminatory based on a clear and unequivocal categorization. Because, in the case at bar, the cook harassed some women but not all women the Court concluded that the cook's behaviour distinguished between persons to whom the cook was attracted and those to whom he was not, rather than between men and women.

Reasons for Decision of Mr. Justice Huband Case on Appeal, vol. II, 519-20 and 524-25.

Reasons for Decision of Mr. Justice Twaddle, Case on Appeal, vol. II, 569-71 and 575-76.

26. An understanding of "sex" that imports social and well as biological constructs into the definition allows us to recognize that the behaviour of the cook and the owner of Pharos effectively subsumed all female employees into a pool of potential victims to whom the cook could assert a right of sexual access if and when he chose. It was small comfort to those who were not the immediate object of such harassment to know that they had no control over whether or when sexual intimacy might be imposed upon them. Thus, the witness Carol Enns felt bothered and apprehensive although the cook's physical attentions to her were not overtly sexual. The end result is that not only were the individual complainants prevented from earning a living on a basis of equality, but all female employees were subordinated.

Intervenor's Statement of Facts, paragraph 1(d).

27. Another reason why the Manitoba Court of Appeal could not accept that the actions of the cook and owner of Pharos were sex discrimination was that the victim was a particular woman rather than women as a class or category. The Court allowed that sexual harassment could be sex discrimination only where the activity was a pretext for attacking women generally. Thus, it required that there be an intention to strike at women as a class or group, and not as individuals, before either sexual harassment or discrimination on the basis of pregnancy could be prohibited under the Human Rights Act.

Reasons for Decision of Mr. Justice Huband, Case on Appeal, vol. II, 520.

Reasons for Decision of Mr. Justice Twaddle, Case on Appeal, vol. II, 569 and 571.

28. The Intervenor submits that this Court has made clear that an intent to discriminate is not required to find a violation of human rights legislation.

Action Travail des Femmes, supra, at 1134-38.

Robichaud, supra, at 89-90.

O'Malley, supra, at 547-49.

29. Each woman is a member of the gender group "women." Each man is a member of the gender group "men." Most discrimination is directed against individuals one at a time on the basis of their membership in a group (for example, exclusion from accommodation or hiring only for menial, low-paid work), rather than against groups all at once (for example, facially discriminatory statutes or, at the most extreme, genocidal policies.) Similarly, most discrimination is not visited equally upon all members of a targeted group (for example, some women may not be hired on the basis of their sex, while other women who better satisfy standards applied only to women, are hired). Such practices are still recognized as discriminatory.

30. The analysis of sex discrimination adopted by the Manitoba Court of Appeal founders on assumptions about what is "natural" that are, in fact, based on gender stereotypes.

31. Just as this Court, in *Bliss*, concluded that any discrimination on the basis of pregnancy was discrimination by nature and not by Parliament, so the Manitoba Court of Appeal sees a male prerogative to initiate intimacy, whether in private life or in the employment sphere, as "natural." The conduct of the cook is described as "amorous." A "school boy stealing kisses" is offered as an analogy. It is the Manitoba Court of Appeal's failure to see that sex role behaviour is a product of social and cultural factors and appears natural only from a particular perspective, that leads the Court to see sexual harassment in inappropriately romantic and innocent terms.

Bliss v. AG Canada, [1979] 1 SCR 183, at 190.

Reasons for Decision of Mr. Justice Huband, Case on Appeal, vol. II, 510 and 520.

32. In *Brooks*, where benefits were denied not to all women, but only to some—those who were pregnant, the Manitoba Court of Appeal was unable to find sex discrimination. In the case at bar, the Court was unable to find sex discrimination because only some and not all women were victims. What the Court failed to see is that all women are potentially in the class for which protection is claimed. In the case of pregnancy, only women can ever be in the class; in the case of sexual harassment the class is composed overwhelmingly of women.

33. The Manitoba Court of Appeal's analysis of sex discrimination also founders on the assumption that, unless a male could be similarly situated, there can be no sex discrimination.

34. In *Brooks*, the Manitoba Court of Appeal could find no discrimination, let alone sex discrimination. It is submitted that the Court so concluded because a man could not become pregnant, and therefore could never be similarly situated. Thus, no general or "neutral" standard of treatment could be identified.

35. If sex discrimination cannot be found unless a male can be similarly situated, then women can be further excluded and disempowered with impunity on the basis of characteristics unique to women (whether biological or social).

36. *Brooks* and *Janzen* together illustrate the fallacy of an approach to sex discrimination proscriptions that defines sex as mere biology. By that approach, women will only be assisted by human rights legislation where differential treatment occurs to all members of the group "women" as defined by biological gender, but not for reasons unique to that biology.

37. By the above test, the instances in which human rights legislation can be of real aid in securing equality for women are almost nil.

38. In support of its narrow view of sex discrimination proscriptions, the Manitoba Court of Appeal relied on *Bliss v. AG Canada*. As this Intervenor argues in *Brooks*, *Bliss* is distinguishable and, in the alternative, with respect, was wrongly decided.

Reasons for Decision of Mr. Justice Twaddle, Case on Appeal, vol. II, 570.

Hickling, supra, at 12-14.

39. To define sex as mere biology is to defeat the purpose of human rights legislation. Gender-related characteristics need not be immutable. This understanding is apparent in the legion of cases that have concluded that the fact both sexes are capable of being harassed or of harassing is irrelevant to the recognition of sexual harassment as sex discrimination. However, that fact should not obscure that it is overwhelmingly women who are disadvantaged by sexual harassment. Nevertheless, if man or woman should harass another on the basis of gender, that behaviour is a form of sex discrimination.

Hickling, supra, at 5.

40. Sexual harassment is neither unique to individual personalities nor biologically mandated. Sexual harassment of women by men would rarely occur if women and men were social equals.

41. The analysis of sex discrimination enunciated in *Brooks* and in the case at bar has rendered the Manitoba Human Rights Act an instrument that denies protection for the rights of women as individuals and frustrates the quest for the empowerment of women as a group. Thus does the equality analysis of the Manitoba Court of Appeal collapse in upon itself and the purpose of human rights legislation becomes not an end—to secure a measure of social justice and equality for the disempowered; but, as defined by Twaddle JA, a means—a means "to confine discrimination to discrimination by category." It is respectfully submitted that this is the antithesis of the purposive approach to the interpretation of human rights legislation.

Reasons for Decision of Mr. Justice Twaddle, Case on Appeal, vol. II, 563.

42. To fail to recognize the sex inequality in sexual harassment is to neglect its negative impact on women's employment opportunities and is to reproduce the inequitable social situation of male superiority and female subordination. That inequitable situation is the very thing that human rights laws seek to eliminate when they proscribe sex discrimination as a factor in employment.

The Employer Is Liable for Sexual Harassment Perpetrated Against Its Employees by Its Supervisory Employees

43. In *Robichaud*, this Court has disposed of the second question to be addressed by the Intervenor. In this regard, the Intervenor adopts the arguments of the Appellants at paragraphs 27 and 28 of their Factum.

PART IV: NATURE OF ORDER SOUGHT

44. The Intervenor respectfully requests that this appeal be allowed and that an Order be made that the Respondents have discriminated against the Appellants contrary to section 6(1) of the Manitoba Human Rights Act.

All of which is respectfully submitted.

THE OUTCOME

Head Notes—Janzen and Govereau v. Platy Enterprises Ltd.

Held: The appeal should be allowed.

Sexual harassment is a form of sex discrimination. Sexual harassment in the workplace is unwelcome conduct of a sexual nature that detrimentally affects the work environment or leads to adverse job-related consequences for the victims of the harassment.

It is ... an abuse of power [and when it] occurs in the workplace, it is an abuse of both economic and sexual power. Sexual harassment is a demeaning practice, one that constitutes a profound affront to the dignity of the employees forced to endure it. (p. 1284)

By requiring an employee, male or female, to contend with unwelcome sexual actions or explicit sexual demands, sexual harassment in the workplace attacks the dignity and self-respect of the victim both as an employee and as a human being.

Perpetrators of sexual harassment and victims of the conduct may be either male or female. However, in the present sex stratified labour market, those with the power to harass sexually will predominantly be male and those facing the greatest risk of harassment will tend to be female. (p. 1284)

Here, the sexual harassment suffered by the appellants constituted sex discrimination for it was a practice or attitude which had the effect of limiting the conditions of employment of, or the employment opportunities available to, employees on the basis of a characteristic related to gender.

The fact that only some, and not all, female employees at the restaurant were subject to sexual harassment is not a valid reason to conclude that sexual harassment could not amount to discrimination on the basis of sex. Sex discrimination does not exist only where gender is the sole ingredient in the discriminatory action and where, therefore, all members of the affected gender are mistreated identically. While the concept of discrimination is rooted in the notion of treating an individual as part of a group rather than on the basis of the individual's personal characteristics, discrimination does not require uniform treatment of all members of a particular group. It is sufficient that the ascribing of a group characteristic to an individual is a factor in the treatment of that individual. If a finding of discrimination required that every individual in the affected group be treated identically, legislative protection against discrimination would be of little or no value. In nearly every instance of discrimination the discriminatory action is composed of various ingredients with the result that some members of the pertinent group are not adversely affected, at least in a direct sense, by the discriminatory action. To deny a finding of discrimination in the present circumstances would be to deny the existence of discrimination in any situation where discriminatory practices are less than perfectly inclusive. The crucial fact in this case is that it was only female employees who ran the risk of sexual harassment. Indeed, only a woman could be subject to sexual harassment by a heterosexual male, such as the offending employee. A man would not have been subjected to this treatment.

It strains credulity to argue that the sole factor underlying the discriminatory action was appellants' sexual attractiveness—a personal characteristic—and that gender was accordingly irrelevant. Sexual attractiveness cannot be separated from gender. These women were subject to a disadvantage because of their being women; no male employee in these circumstances would have been subject to the same disadvantage. Any female considering employment at the restaurant was a potential victim and as such was disadvantaged because of her sex.

The respondent Platy Enterprises Ltd. must be held liable for the actions of its employee given this Court's decision in *Robichaud*. The offending employee was acting in respect of his employment when he sexually harassed the appellants. His actions were clearly work related. His authority, which had been accorded to him by the respondent, and which derived from his control in running the restaurant and his purported ability to fire waitresses, gave him power over the waitresses. Respondent did not meet its responsibility to ensure that this power was not abused, even after the appellants made specific complaints

The Court of Queen's Bench should not have reduced the award of damages given to the appellants. The amounts were not inordinate in light of the seriousness of the complaints.

IN THE SUPREME COURT OF CANADA

(ON APPEAL FROM A JUDGMENT OF THE COURT OF APPEAL OF THE PROVINCE OF QUEBEC)

BETWEEN:

CHANTAL DAIGLE

RESPONDENT

(Applicant)

AND:

JEAN-GUY TREMBLAY

APPELLANT

(Respondent)

AND:

WOMEN'S LEGAL EDUCATION AND ACTION FUND (LEAF)

Intervenor

Factum of the Women's Legal Education and Action Fund (LEAF)

Daigle v. Tremblay

INTRODUCTION

Chantal Daigle and Jean-Guy Tremblay began dating in December 1988 and decided to live together early in 1989. In March of 1989, as their relationship began to deteriorate in part because of Tremblay's abuse, Daigle became pregnant. By May, Daigle was giving serious consideration to ending the relationship and her pregnancy. She left Tremblay shortly thereafter. On July 1, in her 18th week of pregnancy, Daigle arranged for an abortion.

Jean-Guy Tremblay applied to the Quebec Superior Court for a temporary injunction to prevent the abortion. He did so without Daigle's knowledge and the Court granted the injunction in her absence. After the injunction expired, Tremblay obtained an interlocutory injunction. The injunction was obtained on the following grounds: (1) as the biological father, Tremblay had a sufficient interest to request the injunction; (2) the foetus was a "human being" according to the Quebec Civil Code and under the Quebec Charter of Human Rights and Freedoms and therefore enjoyed a "right to life" under section 1 of the Quebec Charter; (3) the foetus's right to life was greater than Chantal Daigle's interest or right to security of the person as guaranteed under section 7 of the Canadian Charter of Rights and Freedoms. Daigle appealed this injunction to the Quebec Court of Appeal. The Court of Appeal, in a 3-2 decision, upheld the injunction.

Daigle obtained leave to appeal to the Supreme Court of Canada. The Court reconvened for an emergency hearing on August 8. By this time, Daigle was in her 22nd week of pregnancy. The ongoing delay caused by court proceedings created a potentially serious medical situation. Before the appeal, Daigle went through with the abortion. Nonetheless, the Court agreed to proceed in light of the significance of the issues raised.

In addition to LEAF, other intervenors who opposed the use of injunctions to restrict women's reproductive choice were the Canadian Abortion Rights Action League and the Canadian Civil Liberties Association. Tremblay's arguments were echoed and supported by the following intervenors: the Campaign Life Coalition, the Canadian

Physicians for Life, the Association des medecins du Quebec pour le respect de la vie, and REAL Women of Canada. The Attorneys General of Canada and Quebec also intervened.

FACTUM

PART I: FACTS

1. The facts in this appeal are fully covered in the exhibits filed by the Appellant in support of her motion for leave to appeal and are not contested, except that the Women's Legal Education and Action Fund will claim below that the lower courts neglected to take into account certain proven facts when weighing the rights of the appellants.

(a) The decisions of the lower courts erred in creating new fundamental rights—that is, the right to life of the foetus and the right to procreation of the putative father.

(b) The fundamental rights of the pregnant woman by virtue of the Canadian and Quebec Charters.

(c) The injunction is not an appropriate recourse in this case and constitutes an infringement of women's fundamental rights.

PART III: ARGUMENT

The Decisions of the Lower Courts Erred in Creating New Fundamental Rights—That Is the Right to Life of the Foetus and the Right to Procreation of the Putative Father

3. The Honourable Mr. Justice Viens concluded that the foetus is a human being within the meaning of the Quebec Charter of Human Rights and Freedoms, and on that basis enjoys the rights laid down in sections 1 and 2 of the Charter.

Reasons of the Honourable Mr. Justice Viens, at 20.

4. The Honourable Mr. Justice Bernier of the Court of Appeal ruled that the conceived but unborn child must not be deprived of the natural right to life, has the right to life and to the protection of those responsible for the conception of the foetus, has civil status and, from conception, has the right to be carried to term.

Reasons of the Honourable Mr. Justice Bernier, at 4-5.

5. The Honourable Mr. Justice Bernier did not refer to any text to back up his affirmations and expressly stated that he did not believe he should pronounce on the provisions of the Quebec Charter.

Reasons of the Honourable Mr. Justice Bernier, at 6.

6. The Honourable Mr. Justice Nichols decided that the patrimonial rights provided for in the Civil Code presuppose the fundamental right to life. He affirmed that the right has been recognized by custom and is implicitly sanctioned by law.

Reasons of the Honourable Mr. Justice Nichols, at 8-11.

7. The Honourable Mr. Justice Nichols reached this conclusion even though he recognized the absence of a constitutional guarantee in favour of the foetus, under both the Canadian and the Quebec Charters.

Reasons of the Honourable Mr. Justice Nichols, at 4.

8. He even said that it would have been preferable for the rights of the foetus to be specifically covered but this omission did not constitute a negation of such rights.

Reasons of the Honourable Mr. Justice Nichols, at 9.

9. The Honourable Mr. Justice Nichols nevertheless granted the foetus constitutional protection since the rights just recognized were in opposition to those expressly guaranteed to women.

Reasons of the Honourable Mr. Justice Nichols, at 10-11.

10. The Honourable Mr. Justice Lebel ruled that the foetus, at the stage of development it has reached in this case, appears to be both human and a being within the meaning of the Quebec Charter.

Reasons of the Honourable Mr. Justice Lebel, at 23.

11. After analyzing the provisions of the Civil Code, the Honourable Mr. Justice Lebel concluded that the foetus has a juridical personality separate from that of the pregnant woman and that this personality gives it the right to development and life.

Reasons of the Honourable Mr. Justice Lebel, at 25.

12. Although he admitted that the juridical personality of the foetus expressly recognized by the legislators is incomplete, the Honourable Mr. Justice Lebel ranked the rights stemming from the partial personality among the rights expressly recognized by the Charter. He actually proceeded to weigh the rights of the pregnant woman and those of the foetus as if the two enjoyed the same constitutional protection.

Reasons of the Honourable Mr. Justice Lebel, at 34.

13. We submit that, when adopting the Charter of Human Rights and Freedoms in 1975, the Quebec legislators expressly included all the fundamental rights then recognized by law, as indicated in section 51 of the Charter, which reads as follows:

> 51. The Charter shall not be so interpreted as to extend, limit or amend the scope of a provision of law ...

14. When the Charter was enacted, the Quebec legislators could not be ignorant of the jurisprudence, in both Civil Law and Common Law, to the effect that the foetus is not a person or a human being with a juridical personality, and that birth alone actualizes the potential rights of a foetus.

In civil law:

Articles 17.11, 18, and 608 of the Civil Code.

Section 61.16 of the Interpretation Act (RSQ, c. I-16).

Allard v. Monette (1928), 66 CS 291, at 302-3.

Lavoie v. Cité de Rivière du Loup, [1955] CS 452, at 457.

Julien v. J.E. Roy Inc. [1975] CS 401.

Montreal Tramways Co. v. Leveille, [1933] SCR 456.

In common law:

K. v K., [1933] 3 WWR 351 (Man. KB).

Solowan v. Solowan (1953), 8 WWR 288 (Alta. SC).

Roe v. Wade, 410 US 113 (1973).

15. In view of these authorities, we submit that the legislators would have expressed themselves more explicitly if they had wished to include the foetus under the protection of the Quebec Charter.

16. We submit that the Honourable Mr. Justice Viens and the Honourable Mr. Justice Lebel erred in including the foetus in their interpretation of the expression "human being." The legislators' intention was not unobtrusively to extend the term "person" to the foetus but simply to distinguish between natural persons and artificial persons or legal entities. This was the thrust of the clarification made by the then Minister of Justice, Jérôme Choquette, when he said at the Parliamentary committee hearings:

> You will note that, in some sections, you must understand that, when the Charter refers to a human being, it means a flesh and blood human being. When it refers to a person, it may refer to either a human being or a legal entity. (Translation of an excerpt from the *Journal des débats*, Commissions parlementaires, 3rd session, 30th Legislature, 1975, at 212-13.)

17. We respectfully submit that the Honourable Mr. Justice Lebel erred when he concluded that there had been an evolution of the law to include *a posteriori* the foetus in the expression "human being." In our opinion, the authorities do not support this affirmation.

In civil law:

Beaudoin and Renaud, Code civil annoté, vol. 1, 1989:

> A newborn, to be considered a human being, must be born living and viable, that is, have a life entirely independent from that of the mother. (translation)

Madeleine Caron, "Le Code civil quebécois, instrument du protection des droits et libertes de la personne?" Revue du Barreau canadien, vol. 56, no. 2, June 1978, at 197.

Edith Deleury, "Naissance et mort de la personne humaine ou les confrontations de la médecine et le droit" (1976), 17 Cahiers de droit 265.

Assurance-Automobile 9, [1984] CAS 489 and 491.

Monique Ouellette, *Droit des personnes et de la famille*, 3rd ed. (Montreal: Themis), at 27-31.

In common law:

Dehler v. Ottawa Civic Hospital (1979), 101 BLR (3d) 686 (Ont. HC), at 695, continued to (1980), 290 CR (2d) 677 (Ont. CA).

Baby R. (1988), 15 RFL (3d) 225 (BC SC).

Re F., [1988] 2 All ER 1193 (CA).

R v. Sullivan (1989), 65 CR (3d) 256 (BC CA).

18. We submit that it is erroneous in law to deduce the existence of fundamental rights not expressly guaranteed by the Charter from the statement of specific patrimonial rights as provided for in the Civil Code.

19. We submit that the Honourable Mr. Justice Bernier and the Honourable Mr. Justice Lebel transformed the suspensive condition attached to the patrimonial rights of the foetus into a source of fundamental rights in its favour.

20. We submit that the interpretation given the relevant provisions of the Civil Code by the Honourable Mr. Justice Viens and the Honourable Mr. Justice Lebel is contrary to section 51 of the Quebec Charter by extending the scope of the rights mentioned therein.

21. We submit that the exercise of rights guaranteed by the Charter must be limited only by the exercise of other rights guaranteed by the Charter. Since the rights of the pregnant woman are guaranteed, the lower court justices erred in limiting them.

22. The Honourable Mr. Justice Viens, the Honourable Mr. Justice Lebel, and the Honourable Mr. Justice Bernier recognized the interest of the respondent in seeking an injunction as the putative father of the foetus. They based their decisions respectively on the interest of the respondent in protecting his progeniture, his relationship of filiation, and the fruits of conception.

Reasons of the Honourable Justices Viens (at 24), Lebel (at 37), and Bernier (at 6).

23. We respectfully submit that the recognition, in this case, of the interest of the father as progenitor is equivalent to recognizing that he has a fundamental right to procreation, which does not exist in Quebec law.

24. We submit that the above reasoning applies to such a right.

The Fundamental Rights of the Pregnant Woman by Virtue of the Canadian and Quebec Charters

25. The new rights created by the appeal judgment are incompatible with the rights granted to women by sections 1, 3, 4, 5, and 10 of the Charter of Human Rights and Freedoms of Quebec and sections 7 and 15 of the Canadian Charter of Rights and Freedoms.

26. The Quebec Charter of Human Rights and Freedoms provides that women are the possessors of the right to life, personal security, inviolability, and freedom (section 1); of the fundamental freedoms, including freedom of conscience, freedom of religion, and

freedom of opinion (section 2); of the right to the safeguard of their dignity, honour, and reputation (section 4); of the right to respect for their private life (section 5); and of the right to full and equal exercise of their human rights and freedoms without distinction based on sex or pregnancy (section 10).

27. Analysis of the scope of the rights and freedoms guaranteed by the Quebec Charter must be made in the light of precedents established by virtue of the Canadian Charter, in view of the goals of the two Charters.

Andrews v. Law Society of British Columbia, [1989] 1 SCR 143, at 175, per McIntyre J.

28. In *Andrews*, this Court, in terms wholly consistent with the Quebec Charter, recognized that the promotion of the rights of specific disadvantaged groups and subgroups is consistent with, indeed helps define, Charter-based equality. This Court explicitly rejected the need for such groups first to be "similarly situated" with comparable groups.

29. The text of section 15 of the Charter, together with its legislative history, reveals an intent to promote the equality of women and eliminate disadvantages based on sex.

30. In *Andrews*, this Court also explicitly recognized that the purpose of the Charter's equality guarantees is to promote and advance the equality of disadvantaged groups.

31. As previously submitted by LEAF to this Court, women are a socially disadvantaged group, having been subjected to a distinctive second-class social and legal status including enforced poverty, educational deprivation, physical and sexual assault, sex-based denigration and exclusion, objectification and stigmatization, and deprivation of reproductive control.

32. In the abortion context, Madam Justice Wilson has expressed herself eloquently on this subject. Her analysis properly places reproductive issues in the context of sexual equality and requires that they be examined in the light of the equality of the sexes guaranteed under section 15, to eliminate the discrimination that exploits women's role as mothers.

R v. Morgentaler, [1988] 1 SCR 30, at 172.

33. Women often do not control the conditions under which they become pregnant. Up to the present day, the context of social inequality has denied women control over the reproductive uses of their bodies. Women have been socially disadvantaged in regard to control of sexual access to their bodies because of the particular socialization they receive, lack of information, inadequate or unsafe contraceptive technology, social pressure, custom, poverty and enforced economic dependence, sexual coercion, and the ineffective enforcement of laws against sexual assault. Nor do women control the social consequences of their pregnancies. Women's role in childbearing has provided a particular occasion and pretext for women's disadvantagement, including the exclusion of pregnant women from and stigmatization of women in society and work. Such consequences are not occasioned by the biology of pregnancy but by law and

society. In this case, the appellant's situation typifies these disadvantages in a number of ways, including the pressure to abandon birth control and the violent nature of the relationship.

34. Further, under conditions of social inequality on the basis of sex, women have been allocated primary responsibility for the intimate care of children. Social custom, pressure, economic circumstances, and lack of adequate day care have meant that women often do not control the circumstances under which they rear children, hence the impact of these conditions on their own life chances.

35. Men as a group are not comparably disempowered by their reproductive capacities—no one forces them to impregnate women or to bear children—and they are not generally required by society to spend their lives caring for children to the comparative preclusion of other life pursuits. In this case, the Honourable Mr. Justice Bernier specifically remarks upon the absence of an undertaking from Mr. Tremblay to take custody of the infant if the mother decides not to, or is physically or financially unable to do so. This is not to suggest that Miss Daigle's rights would be satisfied if he were.

Reasons of the Honourable Mr. Justice Bernier, at 3.

36. In sex equality terms, this case presents an attempt by a man to control the life of a woman by forcing her, through government intervention, to become a mother. The uncontradicted evidence concerning the respondent shows this: "She made the point that the applicant had no interest in the case other than to maintain control over her."

37. A woman's relation to the foetus is unique and inseparable: what happens to it, happens to her. He who controls it, controls her, as this case makes abundantly clear. Indeed, this case is an example of an attempt to control the woman through controlling the foetus. Several justices misconstrue this case as a conflict between the mother and the foetus. It is a conflict between a woman and a man over that woman's body, life, and relation to her foetus.

Reasons of the Honourable Justices Bernier (at 5-6), Nichols (at 12), and Lebel (at 11).

38. The Court of Appeal seeks to equate the man's relationship to the foetus with the woman's relationship to the foetus. The two cannot be equated—biologically, socially, or spiritually. The Court of Appeal creates a fictional equality in law where none exists in fact, equating in essence the presence of ejaculated sperm (which could as well come from incest or rape) resulting in impregnation with the nine-month experience of gestation and birth. It leaves the child hers by default while ignoring entirely the effect upon her or the foetus, specifically her concerns that her child should not be raised (nor should she continue her life) in a context of violence.

Reasons of the Honourable Justices Lebel (at 35), Nichols (at 12), and Viens (at 6-7).

39. The Court below recognizes the distinction between the sexes in their relation to the foetus, but attributes that distinction wholly to nature.

Reasons of the Honourable Mr. Justice Viens, at 24.

This logic is identical to the approach to pregnancy taken in *Bliss*, which was expressly repudiated by this Court in *Brooks*.

Bliss v. AG of Canada, [1979] 1 SCR 183.

Brooks v. Canada Safeway Ltd., [1989] 1 SCR 1219.

40. Sex equality is not promoted when the state supports the coerced reproductive use of a woman by a man. This is an ultimate state-enforced example, to adopt the words of Madam Justice Wilson, of "being treated as a means—a means to an end which she does not desire but over which she has no control."

Morgentaler, supra, at 173-74.

41. The Court of Appeal has stated that this is a matter of private law: "The question before this Court is about the right of the father to prevent the mother from terminating her pregnancy, a question at quite another level, namely that of private law." On the contrary, this is not, and cannot be, a "private" matter. If this man can go to court to force this woman to bear a child, the door is open for other men to do the same to other women they can get pregnant, by rule of law. This is a public matter of the status of the sexes.

Reasons of the Honourable Mr. Justice Bernier, at 4.

42. It is the woman who has the primary concern and interest in the life, health, welfare, and life possibilities of her foetus. The primacy of the woman's interest, and its defining place in the relation, has been recognized in contexts apart from the sex equality one, in which it is mandatory.

Paton v. British Pregnancy Advisory Service Trustees, [1979] 1 QB 276.

Mack v. Brandenburg (1988), 61 Alta. LR 236 (QB).

Danforth (father cannot be delegated authority over abortion that the constitution forbids to the state).

43. It is sex discrimination, prohibited by the Charters, for a court to do what a legislature is constitutionally prohibited from doing: disadvantage women by law. As this Court stated in *Andrews*, discrimination is that which, "based on grounds relating to personal characteristics of the individual or group … has the effect of imposing burdens, obligations, or disadvantages on such individual or group not imposed upon others." Because pregnancy can be experienced only by women, any forced pregnancy will always deprive and impact on one sex only. This is surely as great a sex inequality as is imposing the costs of pregnancy on one sex only, recognized by this Court in *Brooks*. Just as no man will ever become pregnant, no man will ever need an abortion, hence be in a position to be denied one by law. Leaving aside the parameters of possible legislation in this area, issues not raised in this case, the conclusion is inescapable that because only women can be disadvantaged, for a reason unique to their sex, through state-mandated restrictions on abortion in the present posture, deprivation of abortion as accomplished in this case violates women's constitutional right to sex equality.

Andrews, supra, at 174, per McIntyre J.

Brooks, supra.

44. Maternity imposed by a court is a deprivation of Charter-based sex equality. Access to abortion is a necessary means for women to survive in their unequal circumstances. However difficult an abortion decision may be for an individual woman, it may provide some relief in a life otherwise led in conditions that preclude choice in ways she cannot control—for example, rearing a child in an abusive relationship. Women's access to legal abortion is a remedial attempt to ensure that women and men have more equal control of their reproductive capacities, more equal opportunity to plan their lives, and more equal ability to participate fully in society than if legal abortion did not exist—a spectre clearly raised by this case.

45. This Court has defined discrimination to include that which "withholds or limits access to opportunities, benefits, and advantages available to other members of society."

Andrews, supra, at 174.

The Injunction Is Not an Appropriate Recourse in This Case and Constitutes an Infringement of Women's Fundamental Rights

46. LEAF accepts and adopts the arguments of CARAL in paragraphs 4 to 18 of its brief as intervenor.

47. In addition, LEAF maintains that the injunction procedure constitutes an infringement of the fundamental rights of women.

Time Frame

48. The recourse to an injunction necessarily causes additional delay in access to abortion. This delay can have the effect of endangering the woman's physical and psychological health. In this case, the appellant was about to have an abortion on July 8, at which time she was approximately 17 weeks pregnant, when she was informed that an injunction had been obtained *ex parte* to prevent her from having it. In the meantime, she had to appear before a justice of the Quebec Superior Court on July 17, before the Quebec Court of Appeal on July 20, and before this Court on August 8. The procedure has already caused a delay of at least 31 days, and it is not over yet.

49. The Canadian judicial system is not in a position to hear a series of new cases on abortion, most of which require rapid processing and are likely to raise difficult questions of fact.

Access

50. The injunction procedure creates problems of access to abortion even more insurmountable than those imposed by this Court in *Morgentaler*. The woman will have to be represented before the Court. For many women, this requirement presents a considerable financial obstacle to access to abortion. The urgent nature of the procedure obliges the woman to quickly find an attorney who will agree to represent her. The availability of attorneys varies considerably depending on the time of year and the locality.

51. Another serious obstacle to access to abortion is the public nature of the judicial process. A woman who does not want the publicity surrounding the judicial process may well exercise self-censorship and fail to follow up on her wish to have an abortion, for reasons entirely extraneous to the exercise of her fundamental rights. The injunction procedure exposes intimate, personal questions to public view, thereby constituting an infringement of the reasonable expectation of the right to privacy provided for in section 5 of the Quebec Charter.

Criteria

52. Under former section 251 of the Criminal Code, the criterion according to which an abortion might be obtained and which was supposed to guide the review of the therapeutic abortion committee was as follows: the pregnancy of the person of the female sex endangers or could endanger her life or health.

53. Two justices of this Court decided, in *Morgentaler*, that the criterion of health laid down by former section 251 of the Criminal Code was unconstitutional because it was vague and lent itself to a variety of interpretations by therapeutic abortion committees. The evidence offered in this case revealed that definitions of health varied considerably from one committee to another.

Morgentaler, supra, at 67-69, per Dickson J.

54. The judgment of the Quebec Court of Appeal, far from remedying the problem of vague criteria, presented a list of new, equally vague criteria that open the way to violation of women's sex equality rights.

55. The criteria set forth in the appeal judgment are as follows:

(a) whether the pregnancy was desired;

(b) the requirement of seeking serious or reasonable motives for the exercise of fundamental rights;

(c) whether the foetus was normal;

(d) the mother's state of health;

(e) the Court's right to consider the reasonableness of the motives of concern about damage to physical and psychological health alleged by the mother; and

(f) the viability of the foetus or the stage of pregnancy.

56. The administering of a test of reasonableness by the lower courts demonstrates that criteria that are shaky from the point of view of jurisprudence are capable of being interpreted in a manner detrimental to women by reflecting stereotypes or attributing little importance to their concerns.

57. In addition, the Superior Court and two justices of the Court of Appeal concluded that the pregnancy was "voluntary" or "desired" despite evidence brought by the appellant that she had stopped using contraceptives at the request of the respondent.

Reasons of the Honourable Justices Viens (at 5, 8), Lebel (at 3), Bernier (at 6), and Nichols (at 11).

58. Finally, the lower courts completely ignored the uncontested evidence that the appellant had left the respondent because of violence on his part and because she wanted an abortion to avoid being forced to continue her association with the respondent, an association that would have become unavoidable under the conditions of parenthood created by the birth of a child: she did not want to bring up a child in a violent atmosphere. In fact, the justices penalized the appellant for breaking off the relationship.

Reasons of the Honourable Justices Viens (at 3, 5, and 6), Bernier (at 6), and Lebel (at 35).

59. In an analogous manner, the Court of Appeal adopted a restrictive interpretation of the concept of health, considering only the physical health of the appellant, and concluded that her health, like that of the foetus, was in no way deficient.

Reasons of the Honourable Justices Bernier (at 6), Nichols (at 11), and Lebel (at 35).

This definition of health is more restrictive than the definition recommended by the Honourable Mr. Justice Beetz and concurred in by the Honourable Mr. Justice Estey in *Morgentaler*, namely, that the term "health," far from being vague, clearly means the mental or physical health of the pregnant woman.

Morgentaler, supra, at 108.

60. Section 251 of the Criminal Code, a legislative standard meant to define the circumstances of legal access to abortion, was repealed following the decision of this Court in *Morgentaler*. The Court of Appeal, calling the current situation a legal void, proceeded to fill the void by decreeing standards of jurisprudence whose purpose was to limit the right to abortion. We respectfully submit that this is a misuse of judiciary power and that the Court's approach ignores the standards established by this Court for justifying restrictions on constitutional rights.

61. In *Morgentaler*, this Court clearly recognized that restrictions on the right to abortion are protected by section 7 of the Canadian Charter. Any limitations of rights guaranteed by section 7 of the Canadian Charter or its equivalent in the Quebec Charter must accord with (1) the principles of fundamental justice and (2) section 1 of the Canadian Charter.

62. Access to abortion is also protected by sections 1, 3, 4, 5, and 10 of the Quebec Charter. Any limitation of the rights and freedoms guaranteed therein must be (1) provided for by law according to section 9.1 of the Charter, and (2) justified by the public interest and not only the private interests of another party, according to this same section 9.1.

63. Section 9.1 of the Quebec Charter is a standard equivalent to section 1 of the Canadian Charter.

Ford v. AG Quebec, [1988] 2 SCR 712.

64. The limitations on the right to abortion created by the Court of Appeal fail to accord with both section 1 of the Canadian Charter and section 9.1 of the Quebec Charter.

65. Fundamental to the establishment of the reasonableness of limits under section 1 of the Canadian Charter is the establishment of a pressing and substantial state interest in limiting the right.

Morgentaler, supra, at 180, per Wilson J.

66. The Court of Appeal articulates no state interest in issuing this injunction. On the contrary, it claims that the dispute is a private matter.

67. Moreover, any reliance on the father's interest to support a limitation would run counter to the holding of this Court in *Oakes* with respect to the interpretation of section 1.

68. To meet constitutional scrutiny, limits under section 1 of the Canadian Charter must be prescribed by a law that is precise and clearly articulated.

69. The limitations imposed by the Court of Appeal do not meet any of these standards, for reasons outlined above in this factum.

70. In addition, this Court should be particularly slow to uphold limits which would further disadvantage an already disadvantaged group.

71. Limitations generated ad hoc, and with a significant possibility of error, are particularly unacceptable in abortion situations where an interlocutory injunction is the functional equivalent of a permanent injunction.

Reasons of the Honourable Justices Viens (at 4), Bernier (at 2), and Lebel (at 11).

72. Calculating the stage of pregnancy to limit access to abortion by including the weeks elapsed following a Court order forbidding the interruption of the pregnancy is tantamount to using the delay caused by the judicial process as an intrinsic limitation on the rights guaranteed by the Charters. Such proceedings are likely to bring the administration of justice into disrepute (section 24 of the Canadian Charter).

PART IV: NATURE OF ORDER SOUGHT

We respectfully submit that the appeal of the appellant be allowed and the injunction quashed.

THE OUTCOME

Head Notes—Daigle v. Tremblay

Held: The appeal should be allowed.

The injunction must be set aside because the substantive rights which are alleged to support it—the rights accorded to a foetus or a potential father—do not exist.

A foetus is not included within the term "human being" in the Quebec Charter and, therefore, does not enjoy the right to life conferred by s. 1. The Quebec Charter, considered as a whole, does not display any clear intention on the part of its framers to consider the status of a foetus. It is framed in very general terms and makes no reference to the foetus or foetal rights, nor does it include any definition of the term "human being" or "person." This lack of an intention to deal with a foetus' status is, in itself, a strong reason for not finding foetal rights under the Quebec Charter. If the legislature had wished to accord a foetus the right to life, it is unlikely that it would have left the protection of this right in such an uncertain state. As this case demonstrates, a foetus' alleged right to life will be protected only at the discretionary request of third parties.

The difficult issue of whether a foetus is a legal person cannot be settled by a purely linguistic argument that the plain meaning of the term "human being" includes foetuses. Like a purely scientific argument, a purely linguistic argument attempts to settle a legal debate by non-legal means. What is required are substantive legal reasons which support a conclusion that the term "human being" has a particular meaning. As for the differing usage of the terms "human being" and "person" in the Quebec Charter, it does not lead to the conclusion that a foetus is included within the term "human being." The more plausible explanation is that different terms were used in order to distinguish between physical and moral persons.

A consideration of the status of the foetus under the Civil Code supports the conclusion that a foetus is not a "human being" under the Quebec Charter. The provisions of the Code providing for the appointment of a curator for an unborn child and the provisions granting patrimonial interests to such child do not implicitly recognize that a foetus is a juridical person. Articles 338 and 345, like art. 945, simply provide a mechanism whereby the interests of the foetus described elsewhere in the Code can be protected. They do not accord the foetus any additional rights or interests. In addition, the realization of the patrimonial interests of the foetus under arts. 608, 771, 838 and 2543 of the Code is subject to a suspensive condition that the foetus be born alive and viable. The recognition of the foetus' juridical personality is only a "fiction of the civil law" which is utilized in order to protect the future interests of the foetus. In view of the treatment of the foetus in the remainder of the Code, the term "human being" in art. 18 of the Code, which provides that "Every human being possesses juridical personality," cannot be construed as including foetuses. The Civil Code, therefore, does not generally accord a foetus legal personality. A foetus is treated as a person only where it is necessary to do so in order to protect its interests after it is born.

While Anglo-Canadian law is not determinative in establishing the meaning to be given to general terms in the Quebec Charter, it is instructive to consider the legal status of a foetus in that body of jurisprudence. In Anglo-Canadian law, a foetus must be born alive to enjoy rights. In light of the treatment of foetal rights in civil law and, in addition, the consistency to be found in the common law jurisdictions, it would be wrong to interpret the vague provisions of the Quebec Charter as conferring legal personhood upon the foetus.

The Canadian Charter cannot be invoked in this case to support the injunction. This is a civil action between two private parties and there is no state action which is being impugned. The respondent pointed to no "law" of any sort which he can claim is infringing his rights or anyone else's rights. The issue as to whether s. 7 of the Canadian

Charter could be used to ground an affirmative claim to protection by the state was not raised. This Court should generally avoid making any unnecessary constitutional pronouncement.

Finally, there is nothing in the Quebec legislation or case law to support the argument that the father's interest in a foetus he helped create gives him the right to veto a woman's decision in respect of the foetus she is carrying. The lack of legal basis is fatal to this argument.

IN THE SUPREME COURT OF CANADA

(ON APPEAL FROM THE FEDERAL COURT OF APPEAL)

BETWEEN:

JOHN ROSS TAYLOR AND
THE WESTERN GUARD PARTY

Appellants

AND:

CANADIAN HUMAN RIGHTS COMMISSION AND
THE ATTORNEY GENERAL OF CANADA

Respondents

AND:

THE ATTORNEYS GENERAL OF ONTARIO, QUEBEC, MANITOBA AND BRITISH COLUMBIA, CANADIAN CIVIL LIBERTIES ASSOCIATION, LEAGUE FOR HUMAN RIGHTS OF B'NAI BRITH CANADA, CANADIAN HOLOCAUST REMEMBRANCE ASSOCIATION, CANADIAN JEWISH CONGRESS AND WOMEN'S LEGAL EDUCATION AND ACTION FUND

Intervenors

Factum of the Women's Legal Education and Action Fund (LEAF)

Taylor and the Western Guard Party v. The Canadian Human Rights Commission et al.

INTRODUCTION

In 1972, the Western Guard Party was formed in Ontario to promote white supremacy; in 1976, John Ross Taylor became its leader. In 1977, Taylor supplied financing and prepared messages for a telephone hate-message line in Toronto. Callers could phone in and listen to the messages that were anti-Semitic and racist.

In 1979, the Canadian Human Rights Commission charged Taylor and the Western Guard with violating section 13(1) of the Canadian Human Rights Code. Section 13(1) makes it a discriminatory practice to transmit by telephone any matter that is likely to expose persons to hatred by reason of their membership in any group, against which group discrimination is prohibited by the Code. After finding that Taylor and the Western Guard had engaged in a discriminatory practice, a Commission tribunal issued a cease and desist order that was subsequently filed with the Federal Court for enforcement. Taylor and the Western Guard defied the order and continued to communicate their messages. The Federal Court Trial Division found Taylor and the Western Guard in contempt of court and Taylor served a prison term between October 1981 and March 1982.

In 1983, the Human Rights Commission filed another application with the Federal Court on the basis that Taylor and the Party had taped and broadcast four new hate messages. At the same time, Taylor and the Western Guard Party initiated a court challenge alleging that section 13(1) of the Human Rights Act violated freedom of expression as defined in section 2(b) of the newly enacted Canadian Charter of Rights and Freedoms. The Federal Court Trial Division dismissed Taylor and the Western Guard's constitutional challenge. Their subsequent appeal to the Federal Court of Appeal was also dismissed.

Taylor and the Western Guard then appealed to the Supreme Court of Canada. LEAF intervened to support the necessity and constitutionality of section 13(1), as did the Canadian Holocaust Remembrance Association, B'Nai Brith, the Canadian Jewish Congress, and the Attorneys General of Ontario, Quebec, and Manitoba. The Canadian Civil Liberties Association intervened in support of Taylor and the Western Guard.

FACTUM

PART I: FACTS

1. The Women's Legal Education and Action Fund (LEAF) offers no comment on the facts as outlined by the Appellants and Respondents herein, except to say that the facts as found below fall within section 13(1) of the Canadian Human Rights Act, RSC 1985, c. H-6, as amended (the "Act").

PART II: ISSUES

2. The constitutional questions are as framed by this Court pursuant to the order of Dickson CJC dated February 10, 1988.

PART III: ARGUMENT

3. LEAF submits that the repeated telephonic communication of hate messages is not protected expression under section 2(b) of the Canadian Charter of Rights and Freedoms (the "Charter"). As a recognized practice of discrimination, such communications promote inequality and are inconsistent with the reasons expression is protected. Reading the Charter purposively and as a whole, sections 15 and 28 support the constitutionality of section 13(1) prior to reaching section 1.

4. Should this Court decide to the contrary and reach section 1, LEAF respectfully submits that section 13(1) of the Act restricts expressive rights minimally, if at all, and it effectively furthers equality. The limits it imposes are demonstrably justified in a free and democratic society that has equality as a constitutional guarantee.

5. The case at bar, together with the closely related cases of *R v. Keegstra* and *Andrews and Smith v. The Queen*, raise constitutional issues of whether the Charter permits group hate communications to be regulated by law and the constitutional standards, if any, governing proof of truth or falsity of group defamation. While *Keegstra* and *Andrews and Smith* challenge a criminal provision limited to the wilful public promotion of group hatred, the case at bar challenges a civil law provision limited to the repeated telephonic communication of hate messages that expressly acknowledges group hatred or contempt as a discriminatory practice.

Hate Messages Promote Inequality—Since Section 13(1) of the Canadian Human Rights Act Protects and Promotes Equality, It Is Supported by Sections 15 and 28 of the Charter

6. This Court has identified equality as one of the underlying values and principles of a free and democratic society, the genesis of the rights and freedoms guaranteed by

the Charter, and the ultimate standard against which the objects of all legislation must be measured.

R v. Oakes, [1986] 1 SCR 103, at 136.

7. This Court has said that the section 15 guarantee "is the broadest of all guarantees in the Charter. It applies to and supports all other rights guaranteed by the Charter."

Andrews v. Law Society of British Columbia, [1989] 1 SCR 143, at 185.

8. In *Andrews v. Law Society of British Columbia*, supra, Wilson J stated at 154 that "s. 15 is designed to protect those groups who suffer social, political and legal disadvantage in our society." In assessing whether a group is discriminated against within the meaning of section 15, this Court in *R v. Turpin et al.*, [1989] 1 SCR 1296, at 1331 directed inquiry into "the larger social, political and legal context" and at 1333 enumerated "indicia of discrimination such as stereotyping, historical disadvantage or vulnerability to political and social prejudice."

9. Human rights legislation generally, and the Act in particular, constitute fundamental law. This Court has accepted this premise by elevating human rights legislation to quasi-constitutional status, by holding that persons may not contract out of their rights and by establishing the primacy of human rights legislation over other statutes.

Ontario Human Rights Commission v. The Borough of Etobicoke, [1982] 1 SCR 202, at 213.

The Winnipeg School Division No. 1 v. Craton et al., [1985] 2 SCR 150, at 153-54.

Ontario Human Rights Commission and Theresa O'Malley v. Simpsons-Sears Limited, [1985] 2 SCR 536, at 546-47.

Robichaud v. Canada (Treasury Board), [1987] 2 SCR 84, at 89-91.

Insurance Corporation of British Columbia v. Heerspink, [1982] 2 SCR 145, at 157-58.

10. The importance of human rights legislation was stressed by Dickson CJC in *Action Travail des Femmes v. Canadian National Railway Company*, [1987] 1 SCR 1114, as follows at 1134:

> Human rights legislation is intended to give rise, among other things, to individual rights of vital importance, rights capable of enforcement, in the final analysis, in a court of law. I recognize that in the construction of such legislation the words of the Act must be given their plain meaning, but it is equally important that the rights enunciated be given their full recognition and effect. We should not search for ways to enfeeble their proper impact.

11. Numerous studies have linked hate propaganda with discrimination.

The Report Arising out of the Activities of the Ku Klux Klan in British Columbia (McAlpine Report) (1981), at 40 and 60.

"Equality Now!" *The Report of the Special Parliamentary Committee on Participation of Visible Minorities in Canadian Society* (1984), at 35-40.

"Hatred and the Law," *Report of the Special Committee on Racial and Religious Hatred*, Canadian Bar Association (1984), at 8-12.

Group Defamation Submissions to the Attorney-General of Ontario (Lawlor Report) (1984), at 95-97.

"Hate Propaganda," *Working Paper 50*, Law Reform Commission of Canada (1986), at 32 and 39.

Life Together: A Report on Human Rights in Ontario (Symons Report) (1971).

Report of the Special Committee on Hate Propaganda in Canada (Cohen Report) (Ottawa: Queen's Printer, 1966).

12. The concrete adverse effects of the repeated telephonic communication of hate messages similar to those at bar were considered by the Human Rights Tribunal in *Nealy et al. v. Johnston et al.; Goldberg v. Church of Jesus Christ Christian-Aryan Nations*, (unreported, July 25, 1989), at 20-29. The Tribunal accepted the characterization of this practice as a "quite sophisticated propaganda technique" and found that it reinforced negative stereotypes, incited listeners to aggressive feelings or even violence, and encouraged violence as a pro-active means of defence against any who were seen as the enemies of racial purity. The Tribunal summarized as follows at 28:

> Simply put, its [the hate messages'] thrust is to deny the humanity of any group in Canadian society which does not conform to the promoters' perverted notions of "Aryan purity," and in doing so creates fear and anxiety within the membership of those groups which are targeted.

13. Negative stereotyping and the denial of a group's humanity can adversely affect individual members of the group. Their employment and education opportunities and the dignity afforded to them may depend as much on the reputation of the group as on their individual abilities. LEAF submits that no individual can receive equality of opportunity if surrounded by an atmosphere of group hatred or contempt.

Beauharnais v. Illinois, 343 US 250 (1951), at 263.

14. Section 13(1) expressly recognizes that the repeated telephonic communication of hate messages is a discriminatory practice and violates human rights. Section 13(1) prohibits the repeated telephonic communication of hate messages against groups identified by "race, national or ethnic origin, colour, religion, age, sex, marital status, family status, disability and conviction for which a pardon has been granted." Section 15 of the Charter guarantees freedom from discrimination on many of the same enumerated grounds. Both generate out of the same historic systemic discrimination affecting the same groups as were victimized by hate in the case at bar.

15. LEAF submits that some Charter rights require only that existing law be properly applied. Other Charter rights require affirmative legislation for their achievement. Equality is an example of the second. As noted by Dickson CJC in *Reference Re Public Service Employee Relations Act (Alta.)*, [1987] 1 SCR 313, at 361, the notion of "rights" is "said to impose a corresponding duty or obligation on another party to ensure the protection of the right." It is submitted that the upholding of section 13(1) as equality-

promoting legislation is an appropriate example of the latter. Just as Charter rights can be used to challenge legislation, they can be used to uphold legislation that furthers constitutional rights.

16. Parliament promotes equality and moves against inequality when it prohibits the repeated telephonic communication of hate messages in the Act. Similarly, regulations under the Broadcasting Act, RSC 1985, c. B-9, as amended, which prohibit "any abusive comment that, when taken in context, tends or is likely to expose an individual or a group or class of individuals to hatred or contempt on the basis of race, national or ethnic origin, colour, religion, sex, age or mental or physical disability" are a further recognition by Parliament of its duty to prevent discrimination and promote equality through the regulation of communication undertakings under its control.

Radio Regulations, 1986, SOR/86-982, s. 3(b).

Television Broadcasting Regulations, 1987, SOR/87-49, s. 5(b).

17. Government-sponsored group hatred would violate section 15 of the Charter. It follows that government action against group hate, because it promotes social equality, deserves special constitutional consideration under section 15. Indeed, the government would arguably be sponsoring group hatred if it permitted a public undertaking to be used to undermine the guarantee of equality rights in the Charter.

18. In addition to being protected by section 15, section 13(1) is protected by section 28 of the Charter. The fact that "sex" is a protected ground under the Act invokes a further constitutional basis for upholding section 13(1).

19. In the result, LEAF submits that since section 13(1) protects and promotes equality as comprehended by the Charter, it deserves special constitutional consideration prior to any consideration under section 1.

The Repeated Telephonic Communication of Hate Messages as Prohibited Under Section 13(1) Is Not Protected Under Section 2(b) of the Charter

Collision of Values and Rights Under Section 2(b)

20. This Court has recognized that the rights and freedoms guaranteed by the Charter are not absolute and are subject to limitations even before a section 1 inquiry is undertaken.

Operation Dismantle Inc. et al. v. The Queen et al., [1985] 1 SCR 441, at 489.

Jones v. The Queen, [1986] 2 SCR 284, at 300.

21. LEAF submits that each provision of the Charter must be read in light of or in the context of the others, prior to any recourse to section 1. This preserves the Charter's integrity, the purpose of all its provisions and the distinctive role of section 1.

22. This Court has held that freedom of expression is not absolute. In *Fraser v. Public Service Staff Relations Board*, [1985] 2 SCR 455, Dickson CJC stated at 463 and 467:

> All important values must be qualified, and balanced against, other important, and often competing, values. This process of definition, qualification and balancing is as much required with respect to the value of "freedom of speech" as it is for other values.
>
> ... Sometimes these other values supplement, and build on, the value of speech. But in other situations there is a collision. *When that happens the value of speech may be cut back if the competing value is a powerful one.* (emphasis added)

23. This Court has inextricably linked the value of equality with the concept of a free society. In *R v. Big M Drug Mart Ltd.*, [1985] 1 SCR 295, Dickson CJC stated at 336 that: "A free society is one which aims at equality with respect to the enjoyment of fundamental freedoms and I say this without any reliance upon s. 15 of the Charter." This suggests that the value of equality is an inherent limit on section 2(b) without reliance upon section 15. When read with section 15, the conclusion is inescapable that freedom of expression must be interpreted in a manner consistent with the equality rights of others.

24. LEAF submits that in the case at bar this Court is faced with the "collision" of competing values referred to in *Fraser*, supra. In these circumstances, freedom of expression ought to accommodate the guarantee of equality.

25. Moreover, LEAF submits that there is a further collision between freedom of expression and multiculturalism. All freedoms and rights in the Charter must be interpreted and applied in accordance with section 27 thereof, in a manner consistent with the preservation and enhancement of the multicultural heritage of Canadians.

> *Edwards Books and Art Ltd. v. The Queen*, [1986] 2 SCR 713, at 752.
>
> *Big M Drug Mart*, supra, at 360-61.

26. The repeated telephonic communication of hate messages contradicts and erodes the multicultural heritage of all Canadians, which section 27 affirms as a fundamental characteristic of Canadian society.

27. Parliament has recognized its duty to preserve, foster, and promote multiculturalism through enactment of the Canadian Multiculturalism Act, RSC 1985 (4th Supp.), c. 24, which makes reference to section 15 of the Charter and to the Act.

Content Regulation Under Section 2(b)

28. In *Irwin Toy Ltd. v. AG Quebec*, [1989] 1 SCR 927, this Court enunciated a test to be used to determine whether any particular activity is protected by section 2(b). Dickson CJC said at 978:

> [T]he first step in the analysis is to determine whether the plaintiff's activity falls within the sphere of conduct protected by the guarantee. Activity which (1) does not convey or attempt to convey a meaning, and thus has no *content* of expression or (2) which conveys a meaning but through a violent *form* of expression, is not within the protected sphere of conduct. (emphasis in original)

29. Hatred and contempt are vehicles for content, and as such are closer to form. Arguably, section 13(1) contains no express content element. Under section 13(1),

certain *people* are protected when they are subjected to a pattern of behaviour likely to expose them to hatred or contempt by telephonic means. In other words, to regulate matter because it is likely to expose protected groups to hatred or contempt because *they* are identifiable on the basis of a prohibited ground is not the same as regulating matter because *it* promotes hatred on a prohibited ground. The latter, as in *Keegstra*, contains a content element, the former, as here, merely identifies the *groups* who are subjected to this form of discrimination.

30. LEAF argued in *Keegstra* and *Andrews and Smith* that violations of section 281.2(2) of the Criminal Code, a provision that does contain a content element, nonetheless constitute a "violent form of expression." Violations of section 13(1) of the Act, a provision which contains no content restriction on expression as such, constitute even more clearly a "violent form of expression."

"Aryan Nation" videotape produced by Lawrence Ryckman (1985).

31. In any event, LEAF respectfully submits that the content/form distinction is more properly viewed as a continuum, with regulation of pure content at one end and more violent forms of expression at the other.

32. Virtually all human activity conveys some meaning. In *Irwin Toy*, supra, this Court at 970 expressly declined to exhaust the types of expression that may or may not be protected. Presumably, a practice of inequality like racial segregation would not become protected expression because it conveys a meaning, even if not always violently. The same sensitivity that recognized that a "violent form of expression" is unprotected would, in LEAF's submission, extend to the use of words when likely to expose people to hatred or contempt on prohibited grounds. The denial of equality rights through discriminatory practices deserves the same constitutional consideration under section 2(b) as does violence or threats of violence.

33. This Court has accepted that group-based harassment may be prohibited as discrimination even when it consists entirely of words, words with content. This Court noted with approval the view that a hostile or offensive working environment created by sexual harassment "is every bit the arbitrary barrier to sexual equality at the workplace that racial harassment is to racial equality." The Court treats inequality garbed as expression as inequality.

Janzen and Govereau v. Platy Enterprises Ltd. et al., [1989] 1 SCR 1252, at 1284.

Robichaud, supra.

34. The Appellants argue that to be likely to be exposed to hatred or contempt is anticipatory and not real. To so hold would be to require that hate messages be permitted to do even more damage to equality rights before intervention is possible. If hate mongering in this form is recognized as a discriminatory practice in itself, and the Appellants have not argued that it is not, it should be permissible to legislate against it.

35. Should this Court decide that section 13(1) requires further scrutiny, LEAF submits that the clear purpose of the section is to promote equality, not to restrict expression. The provision protects members of identifiable groups from the likelihood

of exposure to hatred or contempt. In this way, it is clearly aimed at controlling the unequal consequences of particular conduct, some of which are physical, rather than expression as such.

> Canada, Parliament, House of Commons Debates, February 11, 1977, at 2975-92.
>
> Canada, Parliament, House of Commons, Standing Committee on Justice and Legal Affairs, May 18, 1977, 12:24-30.

36. Moreover, hate mongering does not further any of the values underlying freedom of expression, as summarized in *Irwin Toy*, supra, at 976. The Appellants have not met their burden of proof to show that the effects of the telephone communications fit within the reasons expression is protected. In fact, the repeated telephonic communication of hate messages inhibits truth-seeking, because it intimidates the target groups from asserting the truth. Rather than encouraging community participation, group defamation restricts the participation of disadvantaged groups by undermining respect for them and spreading fear. If the individuals who engage in communicating such messages are thereby fulfilled, it is at the expense of others. Human flourishing is constrained by the atmosphere of fear and contempt engendered by telephone hate messages.

37. In *Irwin Toy*, supra, this Court did not have to consider a conflict between one constitutional right embodied in a statutory provision, equality, and another constitutional freedom, expression. LEAF submits that the purpose of promoting equality, a constitutionally entrenched guarantee, deserves greater judicial consideration than non-constitutional interests such as consumer protection, as recognized in *Irwin Toy*.

38. Furthermore, it is submitted that section 15(2) of the Charter strengthens this interpretation of the relation between section 15 and section 2(b). Section 15(2) clearly contemplates that the disadvantaged will be the beneficiaries of governmental acts, and defines such initiatives as consistent with constitutional equality. LEAF submits that to be consistent with section 15, any test developed to evaluate the constitutionality of equality-promoting legislation under section 2(b) should be one that does not prejudice the disadvantaged.

39. In the result, it is submitted that the repeated telephonic communication of hate messages falls outside the sphere of conduct protected by section 2(b) of the Charter.

In the Alternative, Section 13(1) Should Be Upheld Under Section 1 of the Charter

40. It is submitted that the task of section 1 in the case at bar is to balance the tension between harms that flow from regulating expression under section 13(1) and the harms that, unregulated by law, are actualized through the repeated telephonic communication of hate messages. LEAF submits that the importance of promoting equality, including equal access to expression by disadvantaged groups, and the absence of any significant infringement of freedom of expression, significantly weighs the balance in favour of upholding section 13(1) under section 1 of the Charter.

41. In *Irwin Toy*, supra, this Court at 990 and 993-94 distinguished between situations where the government mediates between different groups with competing interests

and those situations where government is the singular antagonist of the individual whose right has been infringed. In the case at bar, the Appellants cast themselves as victims of government, when in reality they are the aggressors in a social conflict between unequal groups. Section 13(1) advances the interests of the disadvantaged while the Appellants advance the interests of the advantaged.

42. This Court also acknowledged at 990 that where groups conflict, legislation inevitably draws a line between their claims. In such situations, LEAF submits that where Parliament has favoured disadvantaged groups in the sense of *Andrews v. Law Society of British Columbia*, supra, this Court should support that assessment.

43. The relative burdens of the parties under section 1 should be assessed in this context. LEAF submits that the Appellants must justify limiting the equality rights of disadvantaged groups just as the Crown must justify limiting freedom of expression.

44. In applying section 1, this Court is guided by the values and principles essential to a free and democratic society. These include, inter alia, respect for the inherent dignity of the human person, commitment to social justice and equality, and respect for cultural and group identity. This Court has recognized that it may become necessary to limit rights and freedoms in circumstances where their exercise would be inimical to the realization of collective goals of fundamental importance.

Oakes, supra, at 136.

Slaight Communications Inc. v. Davidson, [1989] 1 SCR 1038, at 1056.

45. It is submitted that the repeated telephonic communication of hate messages is antithetical to these essential values and principles, and that the requirements of "pressing and substantial concern" and proportionality are met.

Edwards Books and Art Ltd., supra, at 768.

46. In *Edwards Books and Art Ltd.* this Court was concerned at 779 to avoid use of the Charter as "an instrument of better situated individuals to roll back legislation which has as its object the improvement of the condition of less advantaged persons." The legislation under attack at bar has such an object; invalidating it would be such a misuse.

47. LEAF submits that legislative action taken to deter the repeated telephonic communication of hate messages goes some way to redress the imbalance of power between advantaged and disadvantaged groups. Protection from hate is necessary to protect freedom of expression and the inherent dignity and worth of all human beings in society.

48. LEAF submits that both the promotion of section 15 and section 28 equality rights and the preservation and enhancement of Canada's multicultural heritage under section 27 are pressing and substantial concerns.

49. A proscription against the repeated telephonic communication of hate messages is rationally connected to the objectives of equality and the preservation and enhancement of the multicultural heritage of Canada.

50. LEAF submits that section 13(1) does little, if any, damage to freedom of expression because the repeated telephonic communication of hate messages is contrary

to the principles and values that this Court has stated underlie the protection of freedom of expression. Any limit on freedom of expression is slight when compared with the deleterious effect group hatred has on target groups, their members, and society as a whole.

51. The application of section 13(1) is limited to disadvantaged groups enumerated in section 3 of the Act and in accordance with *Andrews v. Law Society of British Columbia*, supra, thus minimizing any impairment of freedom of expression.

52. LEAF submits that reliance on the "marketplace of ideas" as the appropriate protection for disadvantaged groups unless direct physical harm results from expression is in error. For a marketplace of ideas to function, there must be equality, including equal ability to speak and be heard. Because equality does not exist in Canadian society as a whole, the use of "the marketplace of ideas" concept to assess permissible limits on freedom of expression is fundamentally flawed when considering that the repeated telephonic communication of hate messages is targeted against disadvantaged groups. Advantaged groups "own" a disproportionate share of freedom of expression by virtue of their greater share of power and wealth. In a marketplace where some have a greater ability to speak and be heard than others, it is more likely that the ideas of the advantaged will emerge out of the competition of ideas, rather than the truth.

53. The case at bar is a challenge to section 13(1) on its face, but its facts do not expressly address all the protected groups whose interests are at stake. For example, if section 13(1) is invalidated, practices such as telephone pornography, which arguably discriminate on the basis of sex, could not be regulated by this means, without ever having a hearing on the merits. If the Act is unconstitutional, discriminatory forms of expression by telephone become protected expression. Would this mean that repeated telephonic sexual harassment would not be actionable discrimination, but the same sexual harassment in person would be? Should section 13(1) be declared unconstitutional, such questions would be resolved against the interests of the protected groups.

54. Dickson CJC, dissenting in *Reference Re Public Service Employee Relations Act (Alta.)*, supra, at 194 recognized that government intervention, rather than impeding the enjoyment of fundamental freedoms such as freedom of expression, may in some instances protect and enhance their enjoyment. LEAF submits that this analysis applies directly to the freedom of expression of disadvantaged groups, which is promoted by section 13(1).

55. In answer to the Appellants' submission that section 13(1) is unconstitutional because it does not allow for a defence of truth, LEAF submits that a defence of truth is not constitutionally required and may, at times, even be perverse where discrimination is the activity regulated. Advantaged and dominant groups often impose stereotypes on subordinate groups that socially shape them in the image of these stereotypes. It would be ironic if, having enforced such stereotypes, repeated hate communications became protected expression for the reason that they became, to some degree, accurate. Communications that spread hatred or contempt against disadvantaged groups can be invidious when there is some factual support for them as well as when they are provably false.

56. Section 13(1), therefore, constitutionally advances the equality of disadvantaged groups in the sense section 15 of the Charter exists to promote equality, and is a narrowly tailored and finely limited instrument that infringes protected expression little, if at all, while advancing equality substantially by section 1 standards.

PART IV: NATURE OF ORDER SOUGHT

57. In the result, LEAF respectfully submits that the first two constitutional questions posed be answered as follows:

Question #1: Yes.

Question #2: Yes.

58. LEAF takes no position with respect to the third and fourth constitutional questions.

All of which is respectfully submitted.

THE OUTCOME

Head Notes—Taylor and the Western Guard Party v. The Canadian Human Rights Commision et al.

Held (La Forest, Sopinka, and McLachlin JJ dissenting in part): The appeal should be dismissed. Section 13(1) of the Canadian Human Rights Act is constitutional.

Per Dickson CJ and Wilson, L'Heureux-Dubé, and Gonthier JJ: The activity described by s. 13(1) of the Act is protected by s. 2(b) of the Charter. Where an activity conveys or attempts to convey a meaning, through a non-violent form of expression, it has expressive content and thus falls within the scope of the word "expression" as found in the guarantee. The type of meaning conveyed is irrelevant. Section 2(b) protects all content of expression. In enacting s. 13(1), Parliament sought to restrict expression by singling out for censure particular conveyances of meaning. Section 13(1), therefore, represents an infringement of s. 2(b).

Hate propaganda messages against identifiable groups, such as the ones dealt with by s. 13(1), do not fall within the ambit of a possible s. 2(b) exception concerning expression manifested in a violent form. This exception speaks only of physical forms of violence, and extends neither to analogous types of expression nor to mere threats of violence.

Section 13(1) of the Act, which is sufficiently precise to constitute a limit prescribed by law under s. 1 of the Charter, constitutes a reasonable limit upon freedom of expression. First, Parliament's objective of promoting equal opportunity unhindered by discriminatory practices, and thus of preventing the harm caused by hate propaganda, is of sufficient importance to warrant overriding a constitutional freedom. Hate propaganda presents a serious threat to society. It undermines the dignity and self-worth of target group members and, more generally, contributes to disharmonious relations among various racial, cultural and religious groups, as a result eroding the tolerance and open-mindedness that must flourish in a multicultural society which is committed to the idea of equality. The international commitment to eradicate hate propaganda and Canada's commitment to the values of equality and multiculturalism enshrined in ss. 15 and 27 of the Charter magnify the weightiness of Parliament's objective in enacting s. 13(1).

Second, s. 13(1) of the Act is proportionate to the government's objective. The section is rationally connected to the aim of restricting activities antithetical to the promotion of equality and tolerance in society. When conjoined with the remedial provisions of the Act. s 13(1) operates to suppress hate propaganda and its harmful consequences. It also reminds Canadians of our fundamental commitment to equality of opportunity and the eradication of racial and religious intolerance. The fact that the international community considers such laws to be an important weapon against racial and religious intolerance strongly suggests that s. 13(1) cannot be viewed as ineffectual.

The guarantee of freedom of expression is not unduly impaired by s. 13(1). The section is not overbroad or excessively vague. Its terms, in particular the phrase "hatred or contempt," are sufficiently precise and narrow to limit its impact to those expressive activities which are repugnant to Parliament's objective. The phrase "hatred or contempt" in the context of s. 13(1) refers only to unusually strong and deep-felt emotions of detestation, calumny and vilification and, as long as human rights tribunals continue to be well aware of the purpose of s. 13(1) and pay heed to the ardent and extreme nature of feeling described in that phrase, there is little danger that subjective opinion as to offensiveness will supplant the proper meaning of the section. The absence in the Act of an interpretative provision to protect freedom of expression does not create in s. 13(1) an overly wide scope, for both its purpose and the common law's traditional desire to protect expressive activity permit an interpretation solicitous of this important freedom. Further, the absence of an intent component in s. 13(1) raises no problem of minimal impairment when one considers that the objective of the section requires an emphasis upon discriminatory effects. As in other human rights legislation, an intent to discriminate is not a precondition of a finding of discrimination. To import a subjective intent requirement into human rights provisions, rather than allowing tribunals to focus solely upon effects, would defeat one of the primary goals of anti-discrimination statutes. As for the possibility that imprisonment will be imposed upon an individual by way of a contempt order, intent is far from irrelevant in this regard, subjective awareness of the likely effect of one's message being a necessary precondition for the issuance of such an order by the Federal Court. Furthermore, the fact that s. 13(1) does not contain an exemption for truthful statements does not give it a fatally broad scope. Such an exemption is not mandated by the Charter in the context of s. 13(1).

Finally, by focusing upon "repeated" telephonic messages, s. 13(1) directs its attention to public, larger-scale schemes for the dissemination of hate propaganda, the very type of phone use which most threatens the aim underlying the Act.

The effects of s. 13(1) upon freedom of expression are not so deleterious as to make intolerable its existence in a free and democratic society. The section furthers a government objective of great significance and impinges upon expression exhibiting only tenuous links with the values underlying the freedom of expression guarantee. Hate propaganda contributes little to the aspirations of Canadians or Canada in the quest for truth, the promotion of individual self-development or the protection and fostering of a vibrant democracy where the participation of all individuals is accepted and encouraged. Moreover, operating in the context of the procedural and remedial provisions of the Act, s. 13(1) plays a minimal role in the imposition of moral, financial or incarceratory sanctions, the primary goal being to act directly for the benefit of those likely to be exposed to the harms caused by hate propaganda.

Assuming that the Charter applies to the Tribunal's cease and desist order, the latter does not unjustifiably infringe s. 2(b) of the Charter. Read in the context of the Tribunal's expansive reasons, the order was not too vague and obscure to enable the appellants to be held in contempt for failure to abide by its terms. The Tribunal's reasons are emphatically clear in describing the subject-matter found to constitute a discriminatory practice.

The failure of the appellants to raise the issue of bias in a timely fashion constituted a waiver of the right to challenge the jurisdiction of the Tribunal on that ground. Bias must be alleged at the earliest practical opportunity. Here, the issue had not been raised until the hearing before the Federal Court of Appeal, almost eight years after the Tribunal's order was rendered. In any event, since the appellants did not challenge the legitimacy of the Tribunal order directly, they could not attack it collaterally in the contempt proceeding. The appellants are bound by the cease and desist order and must obey it while it remains in force, regardless of how flawed it may be.

Per La Forest, Sopinka, and McLachlin JJ (dissenting in part): Section 13(1) of the Act infringes the guarantee of freedom of expression in s. 2(b) of the Charter. Where, as in this case, an activity conveys or attempts to convey a meaning or message through a non-violent form of expression, this activity falls within the sphere of the conduct protected by s. 2(b). This section protects all content of expression irrespective of the meaning or message sought to be conveyed. In enacting s. 13(1), Parliament intended to control attempts to convey a meaning by restricting the content of expression. The section does not prohibit communication by telephone. Rather, it regulates the content of such communications. Section 13(1), therefore, imposes a limit on s. 2(b).

Section 13(1) of the Act is sufficiently precise to constitute a limit prescribed by law under s. 1 of the Charter. By using the same wording as is found in the common law in defamation cases, Parliament has provided an intelligible standard for the Tribunal to apply.

Section 13(1) of the Act does not constitute a reasonable limit upon freedom of expression. While the legislative objectives of preventing discrimination and of promoting social harmony and individual dignity are of sufficient importance in our multicultural society to warrant overriding a constitutional freedom, s. 13(1) fails to meet the proportionality test.

First, s. 13(1) of the Act is not carefully tailored to its aims and lacks a rational connection with its objectives. While it is well designed to minimize many of the undesirable aspects of curbing free expression and its approach to curbing hate propaganda is far more appropriate than the all or nothing approach inherent in criminalization of such expression, s. 13(1) is too broad and too invasive and catches more expressive conduct than can be justified by its objectives. The use of the words "hatred" and "contempt," which are vague, subjective and susceptible of a wide range of meanings, extends the scope of s. 13(1) to cover expression presenting little threat of fostering hatred or discrimination. The absence of any requirement of intent or foreseeability of the actual promotion of hatred or contempt further broadens the scope of s. 13(1). Without a proof of harm or actual discrimination, s. 13(1) could well reach speech which is in fact anti-discriminatory. Finally, while the chilling effect of human rights legislation is likely to be less significant than that of a criminal prohibition, the vagueness of the law may deter more conduct than can legitimately be targeted.

Second, s. 13(1) does not interfere as little as possible with freedom of expression. No serious attempt was made to strike an appropriate balance between furthering equality and safeguarding free expression. There is no provision in the Act which protects freedom of expression. Section 13(1) simply applies to all expression "likely to expose a person or persons to hatred or contempt." Moreover, the overbreadth of the section, the absence of defences, in particular an exemption for truthful statements, and the inclusion of private communications between consenting individuals within the scope of s. 13(1) illustrate the significance of the infringement of the rights of the individual effected by s. 13(1). The section goes well beyond what can be defended as a reasonable limit on free speech justified by the need to combat discrimination against members of particular groups.

Third, the benefits to be secured by s. 13(1) of the Act fall short of outweighing the seriousness of the infringement which the section effects on freedom of expression. The limitation touches expression which may be relevant to social and political issues. Free expression on such matters has long been regarded as fundamental to the working of a free democracy and to the maintenance and preservation of our most fundamental freedoms. Such a limitation must be proportionate to the evil and sensitive to the need to preserve as much freedom of expression as may be compatible with suppressing that evil. Under s. 13(1), it is far from clear that the measure, broad as it is, is calculated to significantly diminish the evils of group discrimination.

The unconstitutionality of a law upon which a court order is based does not excuse a refusal to obey the order. Even an invalid court order must be followed until it is set aside by legal process. Since s. 13(1) of the Act is unconstitutional, it follows that the Tribunal's cease and desist order rendered pursuant to that section should be quashed. The effective date of the quashing of the order, however, must be the date that this judgment is issued. For the purposes of the contempt proceedings, the order must be considered to be valid until that date. Thus, the ultimate invalidity of the order was not a defence to the contempt citation and the appellants' convictions following the 1983 complaint must be affirmed. Since the wisdom or validity of the initial decree is a relevant consideration in determining the appropriate sanction, T's sentence should be reduced to three months imprisonment.

Appellants' contention that the findings of the Human Rights Tribunal were flawed because of an apprehension of bias must be rejected. The appellants raised this issue several years after the initial hearing. By failing to raise the issue at the outset of the proceedings, the appellants must be deemed to have impliedly waived any right to allege bias.

IN THE SUPREME COURT OF CANADA

(ON APPEAL FROM THE COURT OF APPEAL FOR ALBERTA)

BETWEEN:

HER MAJESTY THE QUEEN

Appellant

AND:

JIM KEEGSTRA

Respondent

AND:

CANADIAN JEWISH CONGRESS, WOMEN'S LEGAL EDUCATION AND ACTION FUND, INTER-AMICUS, B'NAI BRITH, CANADIAN CIVIL LIBERTIES ASSOCIATION, ATTORNEY GENERAL OF CANADA, ATTORNEY GENERAL OF NEW BRUNSWICK, ATTORNEY GENERAL OF QUEBEC, ATTORNEY GENERAL OF ONTARIO, AND ATTORNEY GENERAL OF MANITOBA

Intervenors

AND:

IN THE SUPREME COURT OF CANADA

(ON APPEAL FROM THE COURT OF APPEAL FOR ONTARIO)

BETWEEN:

DONALD CLARKE ANDREWS AND ROBERT WAYNE SMITH

Appellants

AND:

HER MAJESTY THE QUEEN

Respondent

CANADIAN JEWISH CONGRESS, WOMEN'S LEGAL EDUCATION AND ACTION FUND, INTER-AMICUS, B'NAI BRITH, CANADIAN CIVIL LIBERTIES ASSOCIATION, ATTORNEY GENERAL OF CANADA, ATTORNEY GENERAL OF NEW BRUNSWICK, ATTORNEY GENERAL OF QUEBEC, ATTORNEY GENERAL OF ONTARIO, AND ATTORNEY GENERAL OF MANITOBA

Intervenors

Factum of the Women's Legal Education and Action Fund (LEAF)

R v. Keegstra; R v. Andrews and Smith

INTRODUCTION

James Keegstra taught social studies to grade 9 and 12 students in Eckville, Alberta from the early 1970s until 1982. During this period, he taught his students social theories based on hatred of Jews and Judaism. The Lacombe Board of Education dismissed Keegstra from his position after he refused to alter his teaching. He was subsequently charged with the promotion of hatred under section 281(2) of the Criminal Code and committed for trial in June of 1984.

Section 281.2(2) (now section 319(2)) states:

> Every one who, by communicating statements, other than in private conversation, wilfully promotes hatred against any identifiable group is guilty of … (a) an indictable offence and is liable to imprisonment for a term not exceeding two years; or (b) an offence punishable on summary conviction.

Section 281.2(3) (now section 319(3)) provides for defences against conviction:

> No person shall be convicted of an offence under subsection (2) (a) if he establishes that the statements communicated were true; (b) if, in good faith, he expressed or attempted to establish by argument and opinion upon a religious subject; (c) if the statements were relevant to any subject of public interest, the discussion of which was for the public benefit, and if on reasonable grounds he believed them to be true; or (d) if, in good faith, he intended to point out, for the purpose of removal, matters producing or tending to produce feelings of hatred towards an identifiable group in Canada.

The Criminal Code defines "identifiable group" as "any section of the public distinguished by colour, race, religion or ethnic origin."

Keegstra made a pre-trial application to have the section struck down as an unconstitutional abridgement of freedom of expression as guaranteed under section 2(b) of the Charter. The Alberta Court of Queen's Bench ruled that the law did not violate freedom of expression and Keegstra was subsequently convicted. He appealed to the Alberta Court of Appeal, which reversed the conviction and struck down the section.

Donald Andrews and Robert Smith of the Nationalist Party of Canada published and distributed the *Nationalist Reporter*, which promoted white supremacist views. Andrews and Smith were each convicted under section 281.2(2) in 1985 and were given prison sentences of 12 and 7 months, respectively. The Ontario Court of Appeal dismissed the constitutional challenge of Andrews and Smith, and held that section 281 did not unjustifiably infringe freedom of expression. However, the Court reduced their sentences to three months and one month, respectively.

The cases were appealed to the Supreme Court of Canada. The appeals were heard together in December 1989.

LEAF intervened before the Supreme Court to defend the constitutionality of the promotion of hatred law, as did the League for Human Rights of B'Nai Brith; the Canadian Jewish Congress; Inter-amicus; and Attorneys General of Canada, New Brunswick, Quebec, Ontario, and Manitoba. The Canadian Civil Liberties Association intervened in support of Keegstra, Andrews, and Smith.

FACTUM

PART I: FACTS

1. The Women's Legal Education and Action Fund (LEAF) offers no comment on the facts as outlined by the Appellants and Respondents herein, except to say that the facts as found below fall within section 281.2(2).

PART II: ISSUES

2. The constitutional questions are as framed by this Court pursuant to the Order of Dickson CJC dated August 1, 1989.

PART III: ARGUMENT

3. LEAF respectfully submits that for the purpose of constitutional analysis the wilful public promotion of group hatred is as much an issue of equality as of expression because the promotion of group hatred erodes the equality rights of the members of the target group.

4. LEAF respectfully submits that the wilful public promotion of group hatred falls outside the protective ambit of section 2(b) of the Canadian Charter of Rights and Freedoms ("Charter") because it is a discriminatory practice and a violent form of expression.

5. Should this Court decide to the contrary and reach section 1, LEAF respectfully submits that section 281.2(2) of the Criminal Code restricts expressive rights minimally, if at all, as it effectively furthers equality. The limits it imposes are demonstrably justified in a free and democratic society that has equality as a constitutional guarantee.

Hate Propaganda Promotes Inequality—Because Section 281.2(2) [Now Section 319(2)] of the Criminal Code Protects and Promotes Equality, It Is Supported by Section 15 of the Charter

6. This Court has identified equality as one of the underlying values and principles of a free and democratic society, the genesis of the rights and freedoms guaranteed by the Charter, and the ultimate standard against which the objects of all legislation must be measured.

R v. Oakes, [1986] 1 SCR 103, at 136.

7. This Court has said that the section 15 guarantee "is the broadest of all guarantees in the Charter. It applies to and supports all other rights guaranteed by the Charter."

Andrews v. Law Society of British Columbia, [1989] 1 SCR 143, at 185.

8. In *Andrews*, supra, Wilson J stated at 154 that "s. 15 is designed to protect those groups who suffer social, political and legal disadvantage in our society." In assessing whether a group is discriminated against within the meaning of section 15, this Court in *R v. Turpin et al.*, [1989] 1 SCR 1296, at 1331 directed inquiry into "the larger social, political and legal context" and at 1333 enumerated "indicia of discrimination such as stereotyping, historical disadvantage or vulnerability to political and social prejudice."

9. In the larger context, group-based hatred promotes group disadvantage and, as such, is a practice of discrimination. Group-based enmity, ill will, intolerance, and prejudice produce exclusion, denigration, and subordination. Stereotyping and stigmatization of historically disadvantaged groups through hate propaganda shapes their social image and reputation, often controlling the opportunities of individual members more powerfully than their individual abilities do.

The Report Arising out of the Activities of the Ku Klux Klan in British Columbia (McAlpine Report) (1981), at 61-66.

"Equality Now!" *The Report of the Special Parliamentary Committee on Participation of Visible Minorities in Canadian Society* (1984), at 35-40.

"Hatred and the Law," *Report of the Special Committee on Racial and Religious Hatred*, Canadian Bar Association (1984), at 8-12.

Group Defamation Submission to the Attorney-General of Ontario (Lawlor Report) (1984), at 95-97.

"Hate Propaganda," *Working Paper 50*, Law Reform Commission of Canada (1986), at 32 and 39.

Life Together: A Report on Human Rights in Ontario (Symons Report) (1971).

10. LEAF submits that for the purpose of constitutional analysis, the wilful public promotion of group hatred is properly understood as a practice of inequality. For example, anti-Semitism promotes the inequality of Jews on the basis of religion and ethnicity. White supremacy promotes inequality on the basis of race, colour, and sometimes ethnic origin. As argued more fully below, hate propaganda is not mere expression of anti-Semitic or white supremacist opinion. It is a practice of discrimination similar to

sexual harassment and other discriminatory acts that take a verbal form, such as signs reading "Whites Only" or advertisements stating that a position is open only to men.

11. Section 281.2(2) criminalizes the wilful public promotion of hatred against groups identified by "colour, race, religion or ethnic origin." Section 15 of the Charter guarantees freedom from discrimination on the same enumerated grounds. Both generate out of the same historic systemic discrimination affecting the same groups as were victimized by hate in the cases at bar.

12. Government sponsored hatred on group grounds would violate section 15 of the Charter. Parliament promotes equality and moves against inequality when it prohibits the wilful public promotion of group hatred on these grounds. It follows that government action against group hate, because it promotes social equality as guaranteed by the Charter, deserves special constitutional consideration under section 15.

13. Quigley J recognized in *R v. Keegstra* (1984), 19 CCC (3d) 254 (Alta. QB), at 268 that the wilful public promotion of group hatred "negates or limits the rights and freedoms of such target groups, and in particular denies them the right to the equal protection and benefit of the law without discrimination."

14. LEAF therefore submits that section 15 provides the constitutional basis for section 281.2(2). Since section 281.2(2) protects and promotes equality as comprehended by the Charter, it deserves special constitutional consideration under section 15, prior to any consideration under section 1.

The Wilful Public Promotion of Group Hatred as Criminalized Under Section 281.2(2) Is Not Protected Under Section 2(b)

Collision of Values and Rights Under Section 2(b)

15. This Court has recognized that the rights and freedoms guaranteed by the Charter are not absolute, and are subject to limitations even before a section 1 inquiry is undertaken.

> *Operation Dismantle Inc. et al. v. The Queen et al.*, [1985] 1 SCR 441, at 489.
>
> *Jones v. The Queen*, [1986] 2 SCR 284, at 300.

16. LEAF submits that each provision of the Charter must be read in light of or in the context of the others, prior to any recourse to section 1. This preserves the Charter's integrity, the purpose of all its provisions, and the distinctive role of section 1.

17. This Court has held that freedom of expression is not absolute. In *Fraser v. Public Service Staff Relations Board*, [1985] 2 SCR 455 Dickson CJ stated at 463 and 467:

> All important values must be qualified, and balanced against, other important, and often competing, values. This process of definition, qualification and balancing is as much required with respect to the value of "freedom of speech" as it is for other values.
>
> ... Sometimes these other values supplement, and build on, the value of speech. *But in other situations there is a collision. When that happens the value of speech may be cut back if the competing value is a powerful one.* (Emphasis added.)

18. This Court has inextricably linked the value of equality with the concept of a free society. In *R v. Big M Drug Mart Ltd.*, [1985] 1 SCR 295 Dickson CJ stated at 336 that: "A free society is one which aims at equality with respect to the enjoyment of fundamental freedoms and I say this without any reliance upon s. 15 of the Charter." This suggests that the value of equality is embedded within section 2(b) without reliance upon section 15. When read with section 15, the conclusion is inescapable that freedom of expression must be interpreted in a manner consistent with the equality rights of others.

19. LEAF submits that in the cases at bar this Court is faced with the "collision" of competing values referred to in *Fraser*, supra. In these circumstances, freedom of expression ought to accommodate the guarantee of equality.

20. LEAF further submits that all freedoms and rights in the Charter must be interpreted and applied in accordance with section 27 thereof, in a manner consistent with the preservation and enhancement of the multicultural heritage of Canadians.

Edwards Books and Art Ltd. v. The Queen, [1986] 2 SCR 713, at 752.

Big M Drug Mart, supra, at 360-61.

21. The wilful public promotion of group hatred contradicts and erodes the multicultural heritage of all Canadians, which section 27 affirms as a fundamental characteristic of Canadian society.

Content Regulation Under Section 2(b)

22. In *Irwin Toy Ltd. v. AG Quebec*, [1989] 1 SCR 927, this Court enunciated a test to be used to determine whether any particular activity is protected by section 2(b). Dickson CJ said at 978:

> [T]he first step in the analysis is to determine whether the plaintiff's activity falls within the sphere of conduct protected by the guarantee . Activity which (1) does not convey or attempt to convey a meaning, and thus has no *content* of expression or (2) which conveys a meaning but through a violent *form* of expression, is not within the protected sphere of conduct. (Emphasis in original.)

23. LEAF submits that hate propaganda combines content and form. "Colour, race, religion or national origin" is content. The wilful public promotion of hatred is closer to form. Similar content to that conveyed by the Respondent Keegstra and Appellants Andrews and Smith is widely conveyed throughout society, but only becomes criminal when it takes the form of the wilful public promotion of group hatred on the enumerated grounds.

24. LEAF submits that the wilful public promotion of group hatred, while conveying meaning, is a violent form of expression and therefore is not protected by section 2(b).

25. LEAF submits that neither physical contact nor force are necessary to constitute a violent form of expression. For example, in the labour context false statements, threats and veiled threats by words and acts have been held to constitute violence.

Esco Operating Corporation v. Kaplan, 25 NYS 303, 144 Misc. 646 (NY Sup., 1932), at 309.

26. The violent and threatening nature of the wilful public promotion of hatred was recognized by the Cohen Committee in its "Report of the Special Committee on Hate Propaganda in Canada" as follows at 24:

> What matters is that incipient malevolence and violence, all of which are inherent in "hate" activity, deserves national attention.

27. This Court in *Irwin Toy*, supra, at 970 declined to exhaust the forms of expression that may or may not be protected. Presumably, a practice of inequality like racial segregation would not become protected expression because it conveys a meaning, even if not always violently. Enforcement of inequality need not be violent to be coercive. An official denial of equality rights to disadvantaged groups violates the Charter as clearly as does violence.

28. More particularly, the wilful public promotion of group hatred is a violent form of expression because it is an integral link in systemic discrimination that keeps target groups in subordinated positions through the promotion of fear, intolerance, segregation, exclusion, disparagement, vilification, degradation, violence, and genocide. In this sense, it goes beyond "imprudent speech." Its violent nature ranges from immediate psychic wounding and attack to well-documented consequent physical aggression.

M. Matsuda, "Public Response to Racist Speech: Considering the Victim's Story" (1989), *Michigan L Rev.* 2332.

R. Delgado, "Words that Wound: A Tort Action for Racial Insults, Epithets, and Name-Calling" (1982), 17 *Harvard Civil Rights Lib. LR* 133.

"They Don't All Wear Sheets: A Chronology of Racist and Far Right Violence, 1980-1986" (C. Lutz, comp.) (1987).

29. Cory JA (as he then was) observed the connection in *R v. Andrews* (1988), 65 OR (2d) 161 (CA) when he said at 179: "When expression does instill detestation it ... lays the foundation for the mistreatment of members of the victimized groups."

30. Through section 281.2(2), Parliament recognized that the wilful public promotion of group hatred is an act, an injury, and a consequence in itself. It is not merely an intention to act. To promote group hatred is, at a minimum, to act to further the social definition of the group as inferior, unequal, and rightly disadvantaged.

31. At the very least, it amounts to harassment on the basis of group membership. This Court has accepted that harassment, including the environmental form, is a practice of inequality resulting in legally recognized harm and loss, even when it consists of words. It is a form of discrimination, even if the action is words. Regulating harassment is not regulating the content of expression, although the expression has content. This Court treats inequality garbed as expression as inequality.

Janzen and Govereau v. Platy Enterprises Ltd. et al., [1989] 1 SCR 1252.

Robichaud v. Canada (Treasury Board), [1987] 2 SCR 84.

32. LEAF respectfully submits that the content/form of distinction in *Irwin Toy*, supra, is more properly viewed as a continuum, with pure regulation of content at one end and violent forms of expression at the other. Therefore, courts should take a sensitive approach, which would be more nuanced and practical than the doctrinal morass resulting from the American speech/action distinction urged by the Appellants Andrews and Smith.

33. In the alternative, should this Court find it necessary to proceed to the next step in the *Irwin Toy* analysis, LEAF submits that the purpose of the legislation is not to restrict freedom of expression but to promote equality. Further, while LEAF acknowledges that not all the consequences of group hate are "physical," neither are they confined to the mind. Social inequality is a group status, and as such is a major physical consequence of group hate.

34. LEAF submits that the effect of section 281.2(2) is not to restrict protected expression, because the wilful public promotion of group hate is inconsistent with the purposes for which expression is protected. It is submitted that the Respondent Keegstra and Appellants Andrews and Smith have not met the burden of proof put upon them to show that their expression has been restricted contrary to the reasons for which freedom of expression is protected.

35. The principles and values underlying the protection of freedom of expression were summarized by this Court in *Irwin Toy*, supra, as follows at 976:

> (1) seeking and attaining the truth is an inherently good activity; (2) participation in social and political decision-making is to be fostered and encouraged; and (3) the diversity in forms of individual self-fulfillment and human flourishing ought to be cultivated in an essentially tolerant, indeed welcoming, environment not only for the sake of those who convey a meaning, but also for the sake of those to whom it is conveyed.

36. The wilful public promotion of group hatred inhibits truth-seeking, because it intimidates disadvantaged groups from asserting the truth. Rather than encouraging community participation, group defamation restricts the participation of disadvantaged groups by undermining respect for them and spreading fear. If the individuals who engage in hatemongering are thereby fulfilled, it is at the expense of others. Human flourishing is constrained by the atmosphere of fear and contempt engendered by hate propaganda.

37. LEAF further submits that another effect of the wilful public promotion of group hatred is to chill the speech of the target groups. As recognized by Quigley J in *R v. Keegstra*, supra, at 268:

> [Section] 281.2(2) of the Code cannot rationally be considered to be an infringement which limits "freedom of expression," but on the contrary it is a safeguard which promotes it. The protection afforded by the proscription tends to banish the apprehension which might otherwise inhibit certain segments of our society from freely expressing themselves upon the whole spectrum of topics, whether social, economic, scientific, political, religious, or spiritual in nature. The unfettered right to express divergent opinions on these topics is the kind of freedom of expression the Charter protects.

38. In the further alternative, in *Irwin Toy*, supra, this Court did not have to consider colliding constitutional rights. LEAF submits that in cases of colliding Charter rights, this Court should ask, in its consideration of purpose and effect, whether the purpose of the legislation is to promote valid state interests and, if so, whether its effect is contrary to the reason expression is protected. The purpose of promoting equality, a constitutionally entrenched guarantee, deserves greater judicial consideration than non-constitutional interests, such as the protection of consumers in *Irwin Toy*.

House of Commons Debates, April 7, 1970, at 5577-78; April 9, 1970, at 5699; April 13, 1970, at 5790; November 17, 1969, at 889; and November 17, 1969, at 883-84.

39. In the result, it is submitted that the wilful public promotion of group hatred falls outside the sphere of conduct protected by section 2(b) of the Charter.

In the Alternative, Section 281.2(2) Should Be Upheld Under Section 1 of the Charter

40. It is submitted that the task of section 1 in the cases at bar is to balance the tension between any harms that flow from regulating expression under section 281.2(2) and the harms that, unregulated by law, are actualized through the wilful public promotion of group hatred. LEAF submits that the importance of promoting equality, including equal access to expression by disadvantaged groups, and the absence of any significant infringement of freedom of expression, significantly weighs the balance in favour of upholding section 281.2(2) under section 1 of the Charter.

41. In *Irwin Toy*, supra, this Court at 990 and 993-94 distinguishes between situations where the government mediates between different groups with competing interests and those situations where government is the singular antagonist of the individual whose rights have been infringed. In the cases at bar, the Respondent Keegstra and Appellants Andrews and Smith cast themselves as victims of government, when in reality they are the aggressors in a social conflict between unequal groups. Section 281.2(2) advances the interests of the disadvantaged while hatemongers advance the interests of the advantaged.

42. This Court also acknowledged at 990 that "Where the legislature mediates between the competing claims of different groups in the community, it will inevitably be called upon to draw a line marking where one set of claims legitimately begins and the other fades away." LEAF respectfully submits that Parliament has made a reasonable assessment as to where the line, in the case of disadvantaged groups, is most properly drawn and this Court ought not to "second guess" that assessment.

43. The relative burdens of the parties under section 1 should be assessed in this context. LEAF submits that the Respondent Keegstra and Appellants Andrews and Smith must justify limiting the equality rights of disadvantaged groups just as the Crown must justify limiting freedom of expression.

44. In applying section 1, this Court is guided by the values and principles essential to a free and democratic society. These include, inter alia, respect for the inherent dignity of the human person, commitment to social justice and equality, and respect for

cultural and group identity. This Court has recognized that it may become necessary to limit rights and freedoms in circumstances where their exercise would be inimical to the realization of collective goals of fundamental importance.

Oakes, supra, at 136.

Slaight Communications Inc. v. Davidson, [1989] 1 SCR 1038, at 1056.

45. It is submitted that the wilful public promotion of group hatred is antithetical to these essential values and principles, and that the requirements of "pressing and substantial concern" and proportionality are met.

Edwards Books and Art Ltd., supra, at 768.

46. It is generally accepted that section 281.2(2) springs from the recommendations of the Cohen Committee. Quigley J, in terms that expressly recognized equality-seeking goals, characterized the objective of the provision in *R v. Keegstra*, supra, as follows at 271:

> The object of the legislation is obviously to control hatemongers from spreading their hatred to others and to give some protection to the target groups that the law heretofore did not protect .... [It is also] to create a public conscience or a minimum standard for expected behaviour in Canadian society. This legislation manifests such a purpose and has as its objective the protection of certain segments of society from the wilful promotion of hatred and the injurious consequences thereof.

47. In *Edwards Books and Art Ltd.*, supra, this Court was concerned at 779 to avoid use of the Charter as "an instrument of better situated individuals to roll back legislation which has as its object the improvement of the condition of less advantaged persons." The legislation at bar has such an object; invalidating it would be such a misuse.

48. In *Slaight Communications Inc. v. Davidson*, supra, this Court recognized that under section 1 an inequality interest (not one of recognized constitutional dimension) can outweigh a section 2(b) right. This Court was "concerned to avoid constitutionalizing inequalities of power in the workplace *and between societal actors in general*." (Emphasis added.) Similarly, in *Canadian Newspapers Co. v. AG Canada*, [1988] 2 SCR 122, this Court used section 1 in finding that the interest of sexual assault victims in withholding their names and identities from the media outweighed an infringement of section 2(b). Section 1 owes no less to rights of constitutional dimension. This Court's observation in *Slaight* at 194 applies directly: "constitutionally protecting freedom of expression would be tantamount to condonation of an abuse of an already unequal relationship."

49. LEAF submits that legislative action taken to deter the wilful public promotion of group hatred goes some way to redress the imbalance of power between advantaged and disadvantaged groups. Protection from hate propaganda is necessary to protect freedom of expression and the inherent dignity and worth of all human beings in society.

50. LEAF submits that both the protection of section 15 equality rights and the preservation and enhancement of Canada's multicultural heritage under section 27 are pressing and substantial concerns.

51. A proscription against the wilful public promotion of group hatred is rationally connected to the objectives of equality and the preservation and enhancement of the multicultural heritage of Canada.

52. LEAF submits that section 281.2(2) does little, if any, damage to freedom of expression because the wilful public promotion of group hatred is contrary to the principles and values which this Court has stated underlie the protection of freedom of expression. Any limit on freedom of expression is slight when compared with the deleterious effect the wilful public promotion of group hatred has on target groups, their members, and society as a whole.

53. LEAF urges this Court to reject the argument of the Respondent Keegstra and Appellants Andrews and Smith that protection of the most offensive expression is the test of protected expression under the Charter. Instead, the expression of the most unequal must be protected. The application of section 281.2(2) to the wilful public promotion of group hatred is limited to disadvantaged groups in accordance with *Andrews v. Law Society of British Columbia*, supra, thus minimizing any impairment of freedom of expression.

54. LEAF submits that reliance on the "marketplace of ideas" as the appropriate protection for disadvantaged groups, unless direct physical harm results from expression, is in error. For a marketplace of ideas to function, there must be equality, including equal ability to speak and be heard. In the case of children in a classroom, as in *Keegstra*, the free marketplace of ideas does not exist because equality between students and teachers does not exist. The power imbalance, with its opportunity for abuse, renders the concept inappropriate.

Statement of Facts, Factum of the Appellant, Her Majesty The Queen, at 2.

55. Further, because equality does not exist in Canadian society as a whole, the use of "the marketplace of ideas" concept to assess permissible limits on freedom of expression is fundamentally flawed when considering that the wilful public promotion of hatred is targeted against disadvantaged groups. Advantaged groups "own" a disproportionate share of freedom of expression by virtue of their greater share of power and wealth. In a marketplace where some have a greater ability to speak and be heard than others, it is more likely that the ideas of the advantaged will emerge out of the competition of ideas, rather than the truth.

A.B. Volume 10 at 2058-70 (Exhibit 82, a student essay).

56. Finally, it is submitted that Kerans JA in *R v. Keegstra* (1988), 43 CCC (3d) 150 (Alta. CA) erred in determining that section 281.2(2) is overly broad in that it does not require the successful promotion of hatred. The reasoning of the Ontario Court of Appeal in *R v. Andrews*, supra, is to be preferred.

57. As outlined above, the wilful public promotion of group hatred in and of itself constitutes a harm. To wait for further consequences of that harm to manifest themselves in society is to ignore the lessons of history.

Ambrose Doskow and Sidney Jacoby, "Anti Semitism and the Law in Pre-Nazi Germany," *Contemporary Jewish Record* 498.

58. LEAF respectfully submits that the historical connection between racism and violence is a record against which to consider a legal response to racist speech. The fact that six million Jews were murdered in a public campaign of group hate promoting racial superiority should guide this Court in developing the law of freedom of expression and the treatment of the wilful public promotion of hatred under the Charter.

Section 11(d) of the Charter Is Not Infringed by Section 281.2(3)(a) [Now Section 319(3)(a)] of the Criminal Code

59. LEAF adopts the arguments of the Appellant Her Majesty the Queen with respect to this question.

60. LEAF further submits that section 281.2(3)(a) is mischaracterized as a reverse onus provision. Pursuant thereto defendants are not required to disprove an element of the offence, but rather are offered a defence to it. Generally, hate propaganda is false; however, no constitutional command prescribes that falsity be an element of the offence to be proved by the Crown. It is constitutionally sufficient that Parliament provide that defendants may, as a defence, prove the truth of their utterances.

In the Alternative, Section 281.2(3)(a) Can Be Upheld Under Section 1 of the Charter

61. LEAF adopts the arguments of the Appellant Her Majesty the Queen with respect to this question.

PART IV: NATURE OF ORDER SOUGHT

62. It is respectfully submitted that the constitutional questions posed be answered as follows:

Question #1: No.

Question #2: Yes.

Question #3: No.

Question #4: Yes.

All of which is respectfully submitted.

THE OUTCOME

Head Notes—R v. Keegstra; R v. Andrews and Smith

Held (La Forest, Sopinka, and McLachlin JJ dissenting): The appeal should be allowed. Sections 319(2) and 319(3)(a) of the Code are constitutional.

Freedom of Expression

Per Dickson CJ and Wilson, L'Heureux-Dubé, and Gonthier JJ: Communications which wilfully promote hatred against an identifiable group are protected by s. 2(b) of the

Charter. When an activity conveys or attempts to convey a meaning, through a non-violent form of expression, it has expressive content and thus falls within the scope of the word "expression" as found in the guarantee. The type of meaning conveyed is irrelevant. Section 2(b) protects all content of expression. In enacting s. 319(2) of the Code, Parliament sought to prohibit communications which convey meaning. Section 319(2), therefore, represents an infringement of s. 2(b).

Communications which are intended to promote hatred against identifiable groups do not fall within the ambit of a possible s. 2(b) exception concerning expression manifested in a violent form. This exception refers only to expression communicated directly through physical harm. Hate propaganda is not analogous to violence. It conveys a meaning that is repugnant, but the repugnance stems from the content of the message and not from its form. As for threats of violence, they are not excluded from the definition of expression envisioned by s. 2(b).

Sections 15 and 27 of the Charter, which deal with equality and multiculturalism, and the international agreements signed by Canada on the prohibition of racist statements, should not be used to interpret the scope of s. 2(b). It is inappropriate to attenuate the s. 2(b) freedom on the grounds that a particular context so requires. The large and liberal interpretation given to freedom of expression indicates that the preferable course is to weigh the various contextual values and factors in s. 1 of the Charter. This section both guarantees and limits Charter rights and freedoms by reference to principles fundamental in a free and democratic society.

Section 319(2) of the Code constitutes a reasonable limit upon freedom of expression. Parliament's objective of preventing the harm caused by hate propaganda is of sufficient importance to warrant overriding a constitutional freedom. Parliament has recognized the substantial harm that can flow from hate propaganda and, in trying to prevent the pain suffered by target group members and to reduce racial, ethnic and religious tension and perhaps even violence in Canada, has decided to suppress the wilful promotion of hatred against identifiable groups. Parliament's objective is supported not only by the work of numerous study groups, but also by our collective historical knowledge of the potentially catastrophic effects of the promotion of hatred. Additionally, the international commitment to eradicate hate propaganda and Canada's commitment to the values of equality and multiculturalism in ss. 15 and 27 of the Charter strongly buttress the importance of this objective.

Section 319(2) of the Code is an acceptably proportional response to Parliament's valid objective. There is obviously a rational connection between the criminal prohibition of hate propaganda and the objective of protecting target group members and of fostering harmonious social relations in a community dedicated to equality and multiculturalism. Section 319(2) serves to illustrate to the public the severe reprobation with which society holds messages of hate directed towards racial and religious groups. It makes that kind of expression less attractive and hence decreases acceptance of its content. Section 319(2) is also a means by which the values beneficial to a free and democratic society—in particular, the value of equality and the worth and dignity of each human person—can be publicized.

Section 319(2) of the Code does not unduly impair freedom of expression. This section does not suffer from overbreadth or vagueness; rather, the terms of the offence indicate that s. 319(2) possesses definitional limits which act as safeguards to ensure that it will capture only expressive activity which is openly hostile to Parliament's objective, and will thus attack only the harm at which the prohibition is targeted. The word "wilfully" imports into the offence a stringent standard of mens rea which significantly restricts the reach of s. 319(2) by necessitating the proof of either an intent to promote hatred or knowledge of the substantial certainty of such a consequence. The word "hatred" further reduces the scope of the prohibition. This word, in the context of s. 319(2), must be construed as encompassing only the most severe and deeply felt form of opprobrium. Further, the exclusion of private communications from the scope of s. 319(2), the need for the promotion of hatred to focus upon an identifiable group and the presence of the s. 319(3) defences, which clarify the scope of s. 319(2), all support the view that the impugned section creates a narrowly confined offence. Section 319(2) is not an excessive impairment of freedom of expression merely because the defence of truth in s. 319(3)(a) does not cover negligent or innocent error as to the truthfulness of a statement. Whether or not a statement is susceptible to classification as true or false, such error should not excuse an accused who has wilfully used a statement in order to promote hatred against an identifiable group. Finally, while other non-criminal modes of combatting hate propaganda exist, it is eminently reasonable to utilize more than one type of legislative tool in working to prevent the spread of racist expression and its resultant harm. To send out a strong message of condemnation, both reinforcing the values underlying s. 319(2) and deterring the few individuals who would harm target group members and the larger community by communicating hate propaganda, will occasionally require use of the criminal law.

The effects of s. 319(2) are not of such a deleterious nature as to outweigh any advantage gleaned from the limitation of s. 2(b). The expressive activity at which s. 319(2) is aimed constitutes a special category, a category only tenuously connected with the values underlying the guarantee of freedom of expression. Hate propaganda contributes little to the aspirations of Canadians or Canada in either the quest for truth, the promotion of individual self-development or the protection and fostering of a vibrant democracy where the participation of all individuals is accepted and encouraged. Moreover, the narrowly drawn terms of s. 319(2) and its defences prevent the prohibition of expression lying outside of this narrow category. Consequently, the suppression of hate propaganda represents an impairment of the individual's freedom of expression which is not of a most serious nature.

Per La Forest, Sopinka, and McLachlin JJ (dissenting): Section 319(2) of the Code infringes the guarantee of freedom of expression. Where, as in this case, an activity conveys or attempts to convey a meaning or message through a non-violent form of expression, this activity falls within the sphere of the conduct protected by s. 2(b). This section protects all content of expression irrespective of the meaning or message sought to be conveyed, no matter how offensive it may be. The government's purpose in enacting s. 319(2) was to restrict freedom of expression by curtailing what people may say. Section 319(2), therefore, imposes a limit on s. 2(b).

The promotion of hatred in this case does not assume a form which falls outside the protected sphere of s. 2(b). The accused's communications were offensive and propagandistic, but they do not constitute threats in the usual sense of that word. The accused's statements did not urge violence against the Jewish people. They were not made with the intention and do not have the effect of compelling Jewish people or anyone else to do one thing or another. Nor do the accused's statements constitute violence. Violence, as discussed in *Dolphin Delivery* and *Irwin Toy*, connotes actual or threatened physical interference with the activities of others. Moreover statements promoting hatred are not akin to threats or violence. There is nothing in the form of such statements which subverts democracy or our basic freedoms in the way in which violence or threats of violence may. Finally, to suggest that speech, like hate propaganda, which undermines the credibility of speakers belonging to particular groups does not fall within s. 2(b) of the Charter, is to remove from the protection of the Charter an enormous amount of speech which has long been accepted as important and valuable.

Sections 15 and 27 of the Charter and the international convenants signed by Canada on the prohibition of racism do not reduce the scope of expression protected by s. 2(b) so as to exclude the accused's statements. First, to do so would be to exclude statements from the protection of s. 2(b) on the basis of their content, an approach which this Court has rejected. Second, given that the protection under s. 2(b) is aimed at protecting individuals from having their expression infringed by the government, it would be a misapplication of Charter values to thereby limit the scope of that individual guarantee with an argument based on s. 15, which is also aimed at circumscribing the power of the state. Third, it would be extremely difficult to balance in the abstract conflicting values such as equality and multiculturalism against freedom of expression. Assuming such balancing were to be done, it would be more appropriately made under s. 1 of the Charter than under s. 2(b). Fourth, Canada's international obligations, and the accords negotiated between international governments, may well be helpful in placing Charter interpretation in a larger context but these obligations are not determinative or limitative [sic] of the scope of the Charter guarantees. The provisions of the Charter, though drawing on a political and social philosophy shared with other democratic societies, are uniquely Canadian. As a result, considerations may point, as they do in this case, to a conclusion regarding a rights violation which is not necessarily in accord with those international covenants. Unlike the international covenants, which exclude hate propaganda from the guarantee of speech, the Charter posits a broad and unlimited right of expression under s. 2(b), a right which can only be cut back under s. 1.

Section 2(b) does not protect only justified or meritorious expression. Historical legal limitations on expression which conflict with the larger Canadian conception of free speech must be rejected. While in this case it may be easy to achieve near-unanimous consensus that the statements contribute nothing positive to our society, experience shows that in other cases it may be difficult to draw the line between speech which has value to democracy or social issues and speech which does not. Attempts to confine the guarantee of free expression only to content which is judged to possess redeeming value or to accord with the accepted values strike at the very essence of the value of the freedom, reducing the realm of protected discussion to that which is comfortable and compatible with current conceptions. If the guarantee of free expression is to be meaningful, it must protect expression which challenges even the very basic conceptions about our society. A true commitment to freedom of expression demands nothing less.

Section 319(2) of the Code does not constitute a reasonable limit upon freedom of expression. While the legislative objectives of preventing the promotion of hatred, of avoiding racial violence and of promoting equality and multiculturalism are of sufficient importance to warrant overriding the guarantee of freedom of expression, s. 319(2) fails to meet the proportionality test.

Section 319(2) does, to some degree, further Parliament's objective. However, the rational connection between s. 319(2) and its goals is tenuous as there is not a strong and evident connection between the criminalization of hate propaganda and its suppression. Section 319(2) may in fact detract from the objectives it is designed to promote by deterring legitimate expression. Law-abiding citizens, who do not wish to run afoul of the law, could decide not to take the chance in a doubtful case. Creativity and the beneficial exchange of ideas could be adversely affected. At the same time, it is unclear that s. 319(2) provides an effective way of curbing hate mongers. Not only does the criminal process attract extensive media coverage and confer on the accused publicity for his dubious causes, it may even bring him sympathy.

Section 319(2) of the Code does not interfere as little as possible with freedom of expression. Section 319(2) is drafted too broadly, catching more expressive conduct than can be justified by the objectives of promoting social harmony and individual dignity. The term "hatred" in s. 319(2) is capable of denoting a wide range of diverse emotions and is highly subjective, making it difficult to ensure that only cases meriting prosecution are pursued and that only those whose conduct is calculated to dissolve the social bonds of society are convicted. Despite the requirement of "wilful promotion," people who make statements primarily for non-nefarious reasons may also be convicted under s. 319(2). A belief that what one says about a group is true and important to political and social debate is quite compatible with, and indeed may inspire, an intention to promote active dislike of that group. Such a belief is equally compatible with foreseeing that promotion of such dislike may stem from one's statements. The absence of any requirement that actual harm or incitement to hatred be shown further broadens the scope of s. 319(2), and it is unclear, in practice, if the s. 319(3) defences, including the defence of truth, significantly narrow the ambit of s. 319(2). Moreover, not only is the category of speech caught by s. 319(2) defined broadly, the application of the definition of offending speech—i.e., the circumstances in which the offending statements are prohibited is virtually unlimited. Only private conversations are exempt from state scrutiny. Given the vagueness of the prohibition of expression in s. 319(2), there is again a danger that the legislation may have a chilling effect on legitimate activities important to our society by subjecting innocent persons to constraints born out of a fear of the criminal process. Finally, the process by which the prohibition is effected—the criminal law—is the severest our society can impose and is arguably unnecessary given the availability of alternate and more appropriate and effective remedies.

Any questionable benefit conferred by s. 319(2) of the Code is outweighed by the significant infringement on the guarantee of freedom of expression. Section 319(2) does not merely regulate the form or tone of expression, it strikes directly at its content. It is capable of catching not only statements like those at issue in this case, but works of art and the intemperate statement made in the heat of social controversy. While few may actually be prosecuted to conviction under s. 319(2) and imprisoned, many fall within the shadow of its broad prohibition. Section 319(2) touches on the vital values upon which s. 2(b) of the Charter rests: the value of fostering a vibrant and creative society through the marketplace of ideas; the value of the vigourous and open debate essential to democratic government and preservation of our rights and freedoms; and the value of a society which fosters the self-actualization and freedom of its members. An infringement of this seriousness can only be justified by a countervailing state interest of the most compelling nature. However, the claims of gains to be achieved at the cost of the infringement of free speech represented by s. 319(2) are tenuous. Indeed, it is difficult to see how s. 319(2) fosters the goals of social harmony and individual dignity.

Presumption of Innocence

Per Dickson CJ and Wilson, L'Heureux-Dubé, and Gonthier JJ: Section 319(3)(a) of the Code, which provides that no person shall be convicted of wilfully promoting hatred "if he establishes that the statements communicated were true," infringes the presumption of innocence guaranteed in s. 11(d) of the Charter. The real concern under s. 11(d) is not whether the accused must disprove an element of the offence or prove a defence. What is decisive is the final effect of the impugned provision on the verdict. If, as in this case, an accused is required to prove some fact on a balance of probabilities to avoid conviction, the impugned provision violates the presumption of innocence because it permits a conviction in spite of a reasonable doubt in the mind of the trier of fact as to the guilt of the accused.

Section 319(3)(a) of the Code constitutes a reasonable limit on the presumption of innocence. Parliament's objective in employing a reverse onus is pressing and substantial. The objective behind s. 319(3)(a) is closely connected with the purpose of s. 319(2). Harm is created whenever statements are made with the intention of promoting hatred, whether or not they contain an element of truth. If the defence of truth is too easily used, Parliament's objective under s. 319(2) will suffer unduly. It is therefore in the furtherance of that same objective that truthfulness must be proved by the accused on a balance of probabilities.

Section 319(3)(a) meets the proportionality test. First, the section has a rational connection to the purpose of preventing the harm caused by hate propaganda. The reverse onus in the truth defence operates so as to make it more difficult to avoid conviction where the wilful promotion of hatred has been proven beyond a reasonable doubt. Second, the section also represents a minimal impairment of the presumption of innocence. By requiring the accused to prove that his statements are true on a balance of probabilities, Parliament made a concession to the importance of truth in freedom of expression values without excessively compromising the effectiveness of s. 319(2). Any less onerous burden would severely skew the equilibrium. Third, the importance of preventing the harm caused by hate propaganda is not outweighed by Parliament's infringement of s. 11(d). The reverse onus found in the truth defence represents the only way in which the defence can be offered while still enabling Parliament to prohibit hate propaganda effectively through criminal legislation; to require that the state prove beyond a reasonable doubt the falsity of a statement would excuse much of the harmful expressive activity caught by s. 319(2) despite minimal proof as to its worth.

Per Sopinka and McLachlin JJ (dissenting): Section 319(3)(a) of the Code infringes s. 11(d) of the Charter. Under s. 319(2), where the Crown proves beyond a reasonable doubt that the accused wilfully promoted hatred against an identifiable group, the accused will escape liability if, under s. 319(3)(a), he "establishes that the statements communicated were true." By placing the burden of establishing the truth of the statements on the accused, Parliament has contravened the basic principle that the accused need not prove a defence. When an accused is required to prove some fact on a balance of probabilities to avoid conviction, the provision violates the presumption of innocence because it permits a conviction in spite of a reasonable doubt in the mind of the trier of fact as to the guilt of the accused.

Section 319(3)(a) of the Code does not constitute a reasonable limit upon the right to be presumed innocent. The section lacks the required degree of proportionality. It is difficult to discern a rational connection between the aims of s. 319(3)(a) and its requirement that the accused prove the truth of his statements. Further, s. 319(3)(a) does not impair s. 11(d) as little as possible. Because of its superior resources, the state is in a better position than the accused to determine whether or not a statement is true or false. If such a determination is impossible, it should not be ruled out that the statements could be more valuable than harmful. These considerations suggest that s. 319(3)(a)'s infringement of the presumption of innocence is neither minimal nor, given the importance of the infringement in the context of prosecutions under s. 319(2), sufficient to outweigh the dubious benefit of such a provision. Parliament intended the truth to be a defence and falsehood to be an important element of the offence created by s. 319(2). That fact, coupled with the centrality of the presumption of innocence in our criminal law, indicates that only a countervailing state interest of the most compelling kind could justify the infringement. It is difficult to see, however, what benefits s. 319(2) in fact produces in terms of stemming hate propaganda and promoting social harmony and individual dignity.

Per La Forest J (dissenting): It is unnecessary to consider the issues respecting the right to be presumed innocent in s. 11(d) of the Charter.

IN THE SUPREME COURT OF CANADA

(ON APPEAL FROM THE COURT OF APPEAL FOR BRITISH COLUMBIA)

BETWEEN:

MARY CHARLOTTE SULLIVAN
AND GLORIA JEAN LEMAY

Appellants

AND:

REGINA

Respondent

AND BETWEEN:

REGINA

Appellant
(Crown)

AND:

MARY CHARLOTTE SULLIVAN
AND GLORIA JEAN LEMAY

Respondents
(Accused)

AND:

WOMEN'S LEGAL EDUCATION AND ACTION FUND (LEAF)

Intervenor

Factum of the Women's Legal Education and Action Fund (LEAF)

R v. Sullivan and Lemay

INTRODUCTION

In the spring of 1984, after a foetus they were attempting to deliver died in its mother's birth canal, midwives Mary Sullivan and Gloria Lemay were charged with two counts of criminal negligence. The first count was laid under section 203 of the Criminal Code for causing death (to the foetus). The second count was laid under section 204 of the Criminal Code for causing bodily harm (to the mother). A different section of the Criminal Code—section 206—defines, for the purposes of death occurring in the context of pregnancy and childbirth, a "human being" as a child who has been born alive.

Sullivan and Lemay were acquitted of criminal negligence causing bodily harm to the mother because in the trial judge's view the mother had suffered only superficial bruising. However, they were convicted of criminal negligence causing death because the court held that a child in the process of being born is a "person" within the meaning of section 203, despite the fact that it is expressly not defined as a "human being" under section 206.

On appeal, the British Columbia Court of Appeal reversed the decision and substituted a conviction of criminal negligence causing bodily harm on the basis that the baby was not a "person" but part of the mother as defined by section 206 of the Code. Therefore, the court held, by causing the unborn child's death, Sullivan and Lemay caused bodily harm to the mother.

Sullivan and Lemay appealed this conviction to the Supreme Court of Canada on the grounds that the unborn child was not a part of its mother but was indeed a "person." The Crown cross-appealed Sullivan and Lemay's acquittal of criminal negligence causing death.

LEAF intervened to argue that the foetus is not a "person" within the meaning of section 203 of the Criminal Code, or indeed any other kind of entity separate from the woman in whose body it is. REAL Women of Canada also intervened to argue that the foetus should be considered a legal person.

FACTUM

PART I: FACTS

Procedural History

1. The Appellants were charged with criminal negligence causing death to a person, namely, "the baby of Jewel Voth" (first count), and criminal negligence causing bodily harm to a person, namely Jewel Voth (second count), contrary to sections 203 and 204 respectively, of the Criminal Code (now sections 220 and 221).

2. The criminal proceedings arose from the attendance of the Appellants in the home of Jewel Voth to assist in the birth of her first child. The precise event giving rise to the charge was described by the trial judge as "the death of a child in the course of a home birth where contractions ceased after the head was delivered and the two accused were unable to deliver the rest of the child," She found that "the head was born alive and that the child died when the accused were unable to complete this delivery."

Reasons for Judgment of Her Honour Judge Godfrey ("Reasons"), Appeal Case, at 18 and 29.

3. Her Honour Judge Godfrey found the accused guilty on the first count, holding that the definition of "person" in section 203 is broad enough to cover the situation where "the child was alive when the head was born and died because the accused were unable to complete the birth." She declined to convict the accused of causing bodily harm to Jewel Voth, who, she says "miraculously suffered only what in effect would be bruising." However, she states that had she reached the opposite conclusion with respect to the "person" argument, she would have found the accused guilty of criminal negligence causing bodily harm to Jewel Voth "because I would have concluded that the child was a part of Jewel Voth at the time of its death."

Reasons, Appeal Case, at 31-32.

4. The Court of Appeal concluded that the trial judge erred in interpreting the term "person" so as to produce a conviction on the first count. It entered a conviction on the second count, reasoning that "from the conclusion that the line of demarcation as a matter of law is live birth, in our opinion, for the purpose of count 2, the child when it is in the birth canal remains part of the mother, as a matter of law."

Reasons, Appeal Case, at 58.

5. The Appellants appeal their conviction on the second count and seek to convince this Honourable Court that neither the trial judge nor the Court of Appeal was correct. They refer to the foetus in this case as "baby Voth" and argue that it was neither a person (as found by the trial judge) nor part of the mother (a concluded by the Court of Appeal). Rather, they argue that "baby Voth" was "an entity separate and apart from its mother," and had a "separate existence, in law, in the womb." Accordingly, they argue, they cannot be convicted of either of the offences with which they are charged.

Appellants' Factum, paras. 2, 13, 24, 29, and 35.

6. Responding to the appeal, the Crown argues that the interpretation of the word "person" by the Court of Appeal is entirely consistent with all the leading authorities on the point, and states that the Appellants' position that the common law recognizes the foetus as an entity separate and apart from the mother is incorrect. However, the Crown also brings its own appeal against the decision of the Court of Appeal, raising the issue of whether the Court erred in holding that a foetus is not a "person" within the meaning of section 203 of the Criminal Code.

Respondent's (Crown's) Factum, paras. 25-26, at 13-14.

Appellant's (Crown's) Factum, para. 16, at 5.

7. LEAF has been granted status to intervene in the appeals of both the Appellants and the Crown. This factum responds to the issue raised by both appeals.

The Facts

8. In addition to the facts set out by the Appellants and the clarifications and additions of the Crown, LEAF highlights the following facts:

(a) The trial judge found Ms. Voth to be "an astonishingly precise and careful witness" and "very reliable in terms of describing what was going on in her own body. ..." Ms. Voth made considerable efforts to provide herself with adequate and sensitive care during her pregnancy. Mr. Voth's evidence was that if the baby had been delivered safely, Jewel Voth "would have been happy."

Reasons, Appeal Case, at 18-20 and 28.

(b) Dr. Morrell, the family physician seen by Jewel Voth, noted in the initial physical examination that she had a narrow sub-pubic arch, but the trial judge accepted Ms. Voth's evidence that this was never communicated to her.

Reasons, Appeal Case, at 19.

(c) The trial judge found that during the pregnancy the Voths became "disenchanted" with both Dr. Morrell and the hospital where he had his privileges. They first decided to stay with the hospital, in spite of this, so that they could have Dr. Morrell attend the birth. Later, Jewel Voth tried to discuss the option of a home birth with Dr. Morrell. He attempted to dissuade her with "a graphic description" of a woman who had haemorrhaged very badly after delivery and had been saved only because she was in hospital. The reasons of the trial judge contain no reference to any other advice on the advantages and disadvantages of home birth being received from Dr. Morrell. Eventually, Ms. Voth decided not to have Dr. Morrell attend the birth. The trial judge attributed this decision to Ms. Voth's reaction to his policy on episiotomies.

Reasons, Appeal Case, at 18-19.

(d) The trial judge agreed that the skill offered by a competent midwife would certainly seem to enhance the birth process for women.

Reasons, Appeal Case, at 24.

(e) The Voths initially hired Mary Sullivan for private pre-natal classes and as a labour coach for their hospital delivery. While continuing to see Dr. Morrell for pre-natal visits, Jewel Voth eventually made plans with Ms. Sullivan to have a home birth.

Reasons, Appeal Case, at 18-19.

(f) Gloria Lemay was Ms. Sullivan's "teacher" and the two of them generally operated as a team. The Appellant had no formal training, and sought therefore to be assessed by the trial judge on a more lenient standard than that which would be applied to persons with such training.

Reasons, Appeal Case, at 30 and 23.

(g) The Crown at trial advanced three types of "bodily harm" that had been done to Jewel Voth: pain in the leg from a lengthy period of squatting, the pain and irritation to her stomach and back from fundal pressure exerted in an ambulance attendant's attempt to expel the baby, and a cut made when an episiotomy was started.

Reasons, Appeal Case, at 31.

(h) The trial judge noted that the ambulance attendant was a "power lifter," who was pushing as hard as he could on the fundus, and observed, "It is astonishing that nothing ruptured." Ms. Voth's labour began at 11:00 p.m. in the evening and the baby's head emerged at 2:00 p.m. the next day. When she was admitted to hospital at least half an hour after that she was showing "symptoms of exhaustion ... fever ... sunken eyes ... volume depletion."

Reasons, Appeal Case, at 32 and at 12, 21, and 30.

PART II: ISSUES

9. In this factum, LEAF deals with the following issues that are argued by the parties to these appeals:

(a) Does criminal negligence during the process of childbirth causing the full-term foetus not to be born alive constitute the death of a person within the meaning of section 203 (now 220) of the Criminal Code?

(b) Does criminal negligence during the process of childbirth causing the full-term foetus not to be born alive constitute bodily harm to the woman giving birth, within the meaning of section 204 (now 221) of the Criminal Code?

10. LEAF will argue, using sections 7, 15, 28, and 1 of the Charter, that:

(a) the foetus is not a "person" within the meaning of section 203 of the Criminal Code, or any other kind of entity separate from the woman in whose body it is;

(b) the foetus is in and of the woman for the purposes of section 204 of the Criminal Code; LEAF thus states that it is a mischaracterization of the Court of

Appeal's reasons to say that it held that the foetus is "simply a disposable part of the woman's body," as do the Appellants in paragraph 29 of their factum, and urges this Honourable Court to reject such mischaracterization; and

(c) Jewel Voth suffered "bodily harm" within the meaning of section 204 of the Criminal Code:

(i) through the death of her full term foetus; and

(ii) through the physical consequences of unduly prolonged labour and the Appellants' failed attempts to complete the birth.

PART III: ARGUMENT

Interpretation of Sections 203 and 204 of the Criminal Code Must Be Guided by the Charter's Guarantee of Sex Equality

The Interpretation of the Legal Status of the Foetus and Legal Treatment of Pregnant Women Raise Constitutional Sex Equality Issues

11. LEAF invokes the Charter's sex equality guarantees in order that they might shape the interpretation by this Honourable Court of the language of sections 203 and 204 of the Criminal Code. Entailed in this focus on the sex equality guarantees is a restoration of the pregnant woman to a central place in the legal analysis. Resulting from such a focus, in LEAF's submission, will be an interpretation of the Code, consistent with the Charter, that furthers women's equality rather than entrenching inequality. Why such an approach is necessary can be appreciated by considering what has happened in this case to Jewel Voth herself.

12. Jewel Voth desired a baby. She experienced pregnancy, a lengthy, painful, and wasted delivery, and anguish due to the loss of that expected baby. Yet Jewel Voth has receded into the background of this case as legal issues relating to the characterization of the foetus are defined and then debated. The issues have been structured in a way that fails to place the pregnant woman, in whose body a foetus is, at the centre of the legal analysis.

13. The legal status of the foetus—even of a full-term foetus—cannot be addressed without addressing the legal status of the woman in whose body it is. Similarly, analysis of bodily harm to a woman in the circumstances of this case should not focus on what happened to the foetus disconnected from the woman seeking to give birth.

14. The Canadian Charter of Rights and Freedoms addresses the legal status of women in the following sections, among others:

> 7. Everyone has the right to life, liberty and security of the person and the right not to be deprived thereof except in accordance with the principles of fundamental justice.
>
> 15.(1) Every individual is equal before and under the law and has the right to the equal protection and equal benefit of the law without discrimination and, in particular, without discrimination based on race, national or ethnic origin, colour, religion, sex, age or mental or physical disability.

(2) Subsection (1) does not preclude any law, program or activity that has as it object the amelioration of conditions of disadvantaged individuals or groups including those that are disadvantaged because of race, national or ethnic origin, colour, religion, sex, age or mental or physical disability.

28. Notwithstanding anything in this Charter, the rights and freedoms referred to in it are guaranteed equally to male and female persons.

15. This Honourable Court has given a purposive interpretation to section 15, describing its purpose as the promotion of the equality of socially disadvantaged groups. Through its use of examples, and its post-Charter interpretation of human rights legislation, it has also recognized that women are a group disadvantaged on the basis of sex.

Robichaud v. Canada (Treasury Board), [1987] 2 SCR 84, at 89-92, per La Forest J.

Action Travail des Femmes v. Canadian National Railway Company, [1987] 1 SCR 1114, at 1142-45, per Dickson CJC.

Andrews v. Law Society of British Columbia, [1989] 1 SCR 143, at 170-75, per McIntyre J.

Brooks v. Canada Safeway Ltd., [1989]1 SCR 1219, at 1223 and 1241-50, per Dickson CJC.

Janzen and Govereau v. Platy Enterprises Ltd. et al., [1989] 1 SCR 1252, at 1276-82 and 1284-85, per Dickson CJC.

R v. Turpin et al., [1989] 1 SCR 1296, at 1330-33, per Wilson J.

16. In particular, this Court has recognized that women have been socially disadvantaged because they bear children. In the context of human rights legislation, it has held that disadvantaging women on the basis of pregnancy constitutes discrimination on the basis of sex.

Brooks, supra, paragraph 15.

17. The Court's section 7 jurisprudence has supported a woman's security of the person and liberty in the context of decisions about procreation.

R v. Morgentaler, [1988] 1 SCR 30, at 56-63 and 73, per Dickson CJC, and at 171-73, per Wilson J.

Development of Doctrine Concerning the Legal Relation of Woman and Foetus Must Not Further Entrench Sex Inequality

18. LEAF's approach to interpretation of sections 203 and 204 proceeds from the recognition that pregnancies occur within a context of sex inequality, an inequality that encompasses women's experiences of fertility and infertility, conception and contraception, pregnancy and the end of pregnancy whether through miscarriage, abortion, or birth and child-rearing. The point is not just the obvious one that only women directly experience pregnancy and birth, but that it is women who because of their sex are subjected to social inequality as a result of the whole range of experiences around procreation.

19. Although reproduction has major consequences for both women and men, its impact on women and men is not the same, because of the conditions of social inequality within which women live and experience pregnancy and childbirth. Women often do not control the social conditions under which they become pregnant. The social context of inequality between men and women often denies women control over the reproductive use of their bodies because it denies women control over sexual access to their bodies. Sexual access is often forced or pressured. Frequently, contraception is inadequate or unsafe and sex education misleading or unavailable. Poverty and enforced economic dependence often undermine women's physical integrity and sexual self-determination. It is not realistic to rely on the individual woman's sense of self-respect as a bulwark against these life circumstances; social supports for that self-respect are simply too frail.

Margrit Eichler, "Unmarried Parenthood," at 231-41 in *Families in Canada Today*, 2d ed. (Toronto: Gage, 1988).

Catharine MacKinnon, "Rape: On Coercion and Consent," at 171-83 and 295-99 in *Toward a Feminist Theory of the State* (Cambridge: Harvard University Press, 1989).

Linda MacLeod, *Battered But Not Beaten* (Canadian Advisory Council on the Status of Women, 1987), at 3- 7 and 19-30.

Committee on Sexual Offences Against Children and Youth, *Report: Sexual Offences Against Children* (Ottawa: Supply and Services, 1984), at 195-233.

20. Further, the social consequences both of being pregnant and of not being pregnant are not controlled by women, whatever their age or social station. Historically, women's role in childbearing has provided an occasion for women's social disadvantage. Women's autonomy in making fertility decisions has been affected by a number of outside influences, ranging from government enforced sterilization to availability and management of programs ostensibly intended to benefit the infertile. Decision-makers in health care and government have left women little choice about the type of care they will receive during pregnancy, who will attend them in childbirth, and whether the birth will be in hospital or not; social and economic support for pregnant women are often seriously inadequate.

Mabel Penery French (1905), 37 NBR 359 (SC), at 366, per Barker J.

E. (Mrs.) v. Eve, [1986] 2 SCR 388, at 400-401, 418-24, 427-30, and 434, per La Forest J.

Walker et al. v. Pierce, 560 F.2d 609 (4th Cir., 1977).

Christine Overall, "Infertility," chapter 7 in *Ethics and Human Reproduction* (Boston: Allen & Unwin, 1987), at 137-65.

Task Force on the Implementation of Midwifery in Ontario, Report (Toronto: Queen's Printer, 1987), at 69-70 and 79-82.

Murray Enkin et al., "Social, financial and psychological support during pregnancy and childbirth," at 11-15 in *A Guide to Effective Care in Pregnancy and Childbirth* (Toronto: Oxford University Press, 1989).

21. After birth, women are traditionally allocated primary responsibility for the intimate care of children. However, women often do not control the circumstances under which they rear children, because of poverty, inadequate housing, lack of day care, and the structuring of the world of paid work on the assumption that everyone in it—women included—has a life cycle like the male's and the same freedom from childcare responsibilities that has long characterized male workers. In those circumstances, women certainly do not, and cannot, control the impact that childrearing will have in their own lives.

Canadian Advisory Council on the Status of Women, *Women and Labour Market Poverty* (1990), at 7-35.

National Council of Welfare, *Report: Women and Poverty Revisited* (Ottawa: Supply and Services, 1990), at 38-83 and 128-129.

Margrit Eichler, "Types of Childcare Used," at 318-24 in *Families in Canada Today*, supra, paragraph 19.

Pat Armstrong, *Labour Pains: Women's Work in Crisis* (Toronto: Women's Press, 1984), at 19-21 and 47.

Linda MacLeod, *Wife Battering in Canada* (Ottawa: Supply and Services, 1980), at 28-31.

22. By contrast, men are not comparably disempowered by society through their reproductive capacities. No one forces them to impregnate women or to bear children. They are not generally required by society to spend their lives caring for children to the comparative preclusion of other life pursuits.

23. Thus, it is women who are caught, in varying degrees, between the reproductive consequences of sexual use and aggression on the one side and the economic and other consequences of the sex role allocations of labour in the market and family on the other. Women are prevented from having children they do want and forced to have children they do not want and cannot want because they cannot responsibly care for them. LEAF submits that this reality is best described as one of sex inequality.

24. To say that women face sex inequality as a result of—and in—their procreative functions is to acknowledge that in our society procreation is socially gendered. That is, differences between men and women exist, in spite of the camouflaging effects of gender neutral language, and those differences are socially constructed, not biologically determined. When a teenager gets pregnant because of the negative social connotations associated with contraception, it is a young woman who is pregnant. When miscarriage results from physical assault it is a woman who was beaten. When there is not enough money for another child, and no access to abortion, it is a woman who is forced to have a child she cannot responsibly care for. When there is no choice between a home and a hospital delivery, it is the labouring woman who is forced to take risks she has not chosen either in hospital or at home. When someone must care for the children, it is almost always women who do it, without their work being valued either in terms of money or cultural status.

25. Establishing equality between the sexes in the reproductive sphere would require reciprocity of respect, parity of regard for physical dignity and personal integrity,

shared work, and a mutuality of sexual initiative and control over intimacy. To be able to realize these values, women need at least full citizenship, non-impoverishment, racial and cultural equality, and sexual self-determination.

26. A legal system committed to equality for women in the reproductive sphere might well contain laws ensuring that pregnant women are entitled to full information in order to enable them to make an informed choice about a home or hospital birth. It might ensure that fully-trained midwives with adequate support service are available, and that appropriate measures, short of the criminal law, exist to ensure the professional competence of such midwives. It is the result of the continued inequality of women in our society that Jewel Voth had to make her decisions in this case without the benefit of any such measures.

27. Although paid considerable lip service, these values and goals are not lived as social norms and only unevenly inform law. LEAF submits that to be consistent with the Charter's mandate of sex equality in the reproductive area, legal interpretation must be guided by these values and goals, and may not further entrench social realities to the contrary. Accordingly, LEAF urges that this Honourable Court adopt an interpretation of the Criminal Code sections at issue here that will enhance women's equality (rather than further entrench their inequality) by ensuring that the status of the foetus is not considered apart from the woman who carries it.

Development of Doctrine Concerning the Legal Relations of Woman and Foetus, To Be Consistent with Charter Sex Equality Guarantees, Must Take into Account the Experiences of Pregnant Women

28. Because our legal system has been developed historically almost entirely by men, without the presence of women as equal participants, and in a society characterized by the subjection of women, it has tended to view pregnancy from the standpoint of the outsider or observer rather than the participant. While some of the approaches of that legal system, like the conclusion that the foetus does not become a person until fully emerged in a living state from the body of the woman, may coincide with the approaches that might characterize a legal system and a society where women are equal partners, the "outsider" perspective of our legal system has produced two phenomena that are particularly troublesome in the context of this case. One of these phenomena relates to our method of legal reasoning—particularly reasoning by analogy—and its ability fully to encompass the experience of pregnancy. The second of these phenomena concerns the substantive treatment of pregnancy and the foetus in our law. In this case, these two phenomena intersect, providing a difficult challenge to our legal system and a serious potential threat to women's equality rights.

29. To describe the first of these phenomena, LEAF points out that traditionally, legal method proceeds by analogy and distinction, making it tempting to compare the relationship between a pregnant woman and her foetus to relations already mapped by law. However, there are no adequate legal analogies to pregnancy and childbirth and attempts to find them distort reality. Had women not been excluded from participation in the legal system, the unique relationship between the woman and her foetus and the

experience of pregnancy in the life of a woman—hardly new facts—might have engendered their own fundamental legal concepts and doctrines, as elaborate as, for example, the doctrines dealing with the legal relationship between partners in a commercial venture or between employer and employee.

30. Recognizing these shortcomings in our method of conceptualizing the legal relations of woman and foetus produces a method of analysis that seeks to incorporate the perspective of women in the development of legal doctrine relating to reproductive issues. Such a method is an analytical approach consistent with equality as a goal of the legal system because it expands the point of view informing development of legal doctrine beyond the outsider's perspective to include the perspective from the experience of women (distinguished from the subjective perceptions of all women or any individual woman).

31. This Court recognized the validity of approaching the elaboration of legal doctrine in a manner that recognizes the realities of women's lives in *R v. Lavallee*. That decision was based upon a recognition that it is predominantly women who experience spousal abuse and that, in the interests of equality, legal doctrine had to be made to respond to women's experience of threats to life or health within the context of an abusive relationship. It was not necessary to assume that all women shared these experiences to conclude that the adaptation of legal doctrine was appropriate.

R v. Lavallee, [1990] 1 SCR 852, 108 NR 31, at 342-47, per Wilson J.

Tremblay v. Daigle, [1989] 2 SCR 530, at 536-37.

32. Turning now to explore the impact of the outsider's perspective on substantive law in this area, LEAF notes that the outsider standpoint has led, especially in recent times, to a tendency to focus on observing and controlling the pregnant woman in the interest—and the name—of her foetus. Those sharing this focus have tried to give it legal shape, by urging that courts intervene, on behalf of the foetus, in pregnancy and childbirth—and even in the lives of non-pregnant, but fertile, women. Recent technological innovation have fuelled the development of this phenomenon. For example, ultrasound viewing of the foetus has provided the basis for seeing the foetus as a free-floating independent entity, rather than situated within and interconnected with the pregnant woman. Seeing a foetus from an outside perspective, often opposed to the woman, rather than in terms of its relationship with the pregnant woman, clearly poses grave risks to women's equality and ultimately to the welfare of the foetus as well. It ignores the fact that throughout history women have been the primary guardians of the welfare of the foetus.

Anne Oakley, "Getting to Know the Foetus," at 155-86 in *The Captured Womb: History of the Medical Care of Pregnant Women* (New York and Oxfordshire: Basil Blackwell, 1984, 1986).

Rosalind Pollack Petchesky, "Foetal Images: The Power of Visual Culture in the Politics of Reproduction," at 57-80 in Michelle Stanworth, ed., *Reproductive Technologies: Gender, Motherhood and Medicine* (Minneapolis: U of Minnesota Press, 1987).

Isabel Grant, "Forced Obstetrical Intervention: A Charter Analysis" (1989), 39 *U of T LJ* 217.

Edward Keyserlingk, "Clarifying the Right to Prenatal Care," 4 *Health Law in Canada* 36, paragraph 40, infra.

33. Positions adopted by others in this case reveal the influence of both these results of the "outsider" perspective. The arguments of the Appellants and the Intervenor, REAL Women, that the foetus is a separate entity or a person, see the foetus as an entity independent of the pregnant woman. At the other end of the continuum, to characterize the essence of Court of Appeal's conclusion as a holding that the foetus is "simply a disposable part of the woman's body," reveals the shortcoming of argument by analogy in this area of the law, ignores the complexity and uniqueness of the relations between a woman and her foetus, and submerges the woman's experience of pregnancy.

Appellants' Factum, paras. 15 and 29.

34. By contrast, LEAF's argument focuses on the relationship between a pregnant woman and her foetus, aims to grasp its uniqueness, and situates pregnancy in the legal and social context of sex inequality in a way that makes clear the relationship of this case to women's equality rights in the reproductive area. To do so is essential because while the issues in this case focus on the Criminal Code, the submissions of the parties to the two appeals make it clear that any decision on whether the term "person" includes the child in the process of birth, or whether a full-term foetus being born is part of the woman giving birth, will have potentially far reaching implications for women, both in jurisprudence under the Canadian Charter of Rights and Freedoms and in the law generally.

Interpretation of Sections 203 and 204 of the Criminal Code

The Foetus Is Not a Person

35. The foetus is not a person or any other kind of separate entity, as has been recognized in our legal system. This conclusion is the only one consistent with the equality of women as guaranteed by the Charter.

36. The position in the case law that a foetus becomes a "person" when it has fully emerged in a living state from the body of its mother is consistent with adopting the perspective of the pregnant woman and with the facts that the pregnancy is the woman's and the foetus stays in her body until the point of completed live birth.

Reasons of the Court of Appeal, Appeal Case, at 54-56.

Tremblay, supra, at 552-65.

37. The election of complete live birth at the time and place to establish rights as a "person" is consistent with women's experience of pregnancy and birth. While pregnant women may have different attitudes toward the personhood of the embryo or foetus, depending on the particular woman's religious belief, stage of the pregnancy, desire for the child, and many other factors, and these views may change over the course of pregnancy, the empirical reality of the fully emerged live child is something around

which all of these experiences can converge. As well, both the pregnant woman, who has experienced the pregnancy as a process interior to her, and her partner, for whom it has been an exterior process, begin at birth to share an exterior perspective on the newborn child.

38. Moreover, establishing the full emergence of the live child at the beginning of personhood takes account of the fact that live birth, even of the full-term foetus, is not inevitable. As Jewel Voth found to her sorrow, the perils of the birth process, while now diminished through improved maternal health, and availability of professional help, have not been removed altogether.

39. LEAF adopts the submissions of the Crown as respondent in its factum at paragraph 25 to 27, and urges that this Honourable Court decline to accept the positions advanced by REAL Women and the Appellants, which separate foetus and woman and could endow the foetus with an identity and rights of its own.

Respondent's (Crown's) Factum, at 13-15.

40. A foetus so independently endowed is potentially capable, if only through the interventions of others, of having legal relations with persons other than the pregnant woman (e.g., the father or a curator). The definition of its interests by those others almost invariably brings them into conflict with the rights and interests of the woman.

In re AC, 573 A.2d 1236 (DC App., 1990)

Raleigh Fitkin-Paul Morgan Memorial Hospital v. Anderson, 201 A.2d 537 (NJ SC, 1964).

Jefferson v. Griffin Spalding County Hospital Authority et al., 274 SE 2d 457 (Ga. SC, 1981).

Taft v. Taft, 446 NE 2d 395 (Mass., 1983).

In re Ruiz, 500 NE 2d 935 (Ohio CA, 1986).

Cox v. Franklin City, Court of Common Pleas, 537 NE 2d 721 (Ohio CA, 1988).

In re Troy D., Minor, 216 Cal. App. 3d 889 (Calif. CA, 1990).

Paton v. British Pregnancy Advisory Service Trustees, [1979] 1 QB 276, affirmed at [1987] 1 All ER 1230 (sub nom. *C. v. S.*) and *Paton v. United Kingdom* (1980), 3 EHRR 408.

Re F. , [1988] 2 All ER 1193 (CA).

Tremblay, supra.

Mack v. Brandenburg (1988), 61 Alta. LR 236 (QB).

Baby R. (1988), 15 RFL (3d) 225 (BC SC).

Re Children's Aid Society of Belleville and T. (1987), 59 OR (2d) 204 (Prov. Ct. Fam. Div.).

Re Children's Aid Society for the District of Kenora and J.L. (1981), 134 DLR (3d) 249 (Ont. Prov. Ct. Fam. Div.).

41. Clothing the foetus with independent legal and constitutional rights may lead to the foetus having a right to the use of a woman's body, or a right to medical treatment that overrides the welfare of the pregnant woman—rights to be asserted over the woman by the putative father, a doctor, a self-appointed foetal curator, or an arm of the state. The approaches of both the Appellants and the Intervenor REAL Women could lead to a legal analysis in which the pregnant woman is treated as either not present at all (the "born in the imagination" approach promoted-by technological imaging of the foetus) or simply present as a breeding container. Neither is consistent with equality for women.

David R. Field, "Maternal Brain Death During Pregnancy: Medical and Ethical Issues" (1988), 260 *JAMA* 816.

The Foetus Is In and Of the Pregnant Woman

42. For the purposes of section 204 of the Code, what is important is that the foetus is in the woman's body. This is the case right up to the point where the child has fully emerged in a living state from her body, as recognized by section 206 (now 223) of the Code. Even a full-term foetus whose head has been (in the words of the trial judge) "born," is still largely in the woman's body.

43. Not only is a foetus in the woman but it is also "of" her in that it is interconnected with her in many intricate and intimate ways.

44. While in and of the pregnant woman, the foetus is not just another body part, as the Appellants characterize the Court of Appeal decision. It is not analogous to an appendix, which is the Appellants' suggested comparison. The foetus and the pregnancy are not even analogous to those parts of the woman's body, like her breast and vagina, which have specific gender connotations. A sex equality perspective lets us see that what is a foetus to others is lived by the pregnant woman through her pregnancy. Pregnancy is not, in fact or in social meaning, like a "body part," even a female body part. Pregnancy has many cultural meanings which have significant consequences for women. It can be an emblem of female inferiority or adulation, of elevation or denigration, of heightened or lowered social status. It can bring pain or joy, fear or hope, dream or dread of the future, and closeness or estrangement between women and between women and men. It can give a new sense of the meaning of life and new depth to the experience of family. It can attract violence against the woman, sentimentality towards her, and attempts to control her, and it can give rise to financial cost and disadvantage and the need for difficult decisions. Women have lost jobs and have been stigmatized and excluded from public life because they are pregnant—jobs and access they had in spite of being biological females. No body part, not even one evidently emblematic of gender (like a breast), has the profound and distinct effect on women's social destiny that pregnancy and the possibility of pregnancy can have.

45. The intimate and complex connections between the pregnant woman and her foetus are unique, and feature many ways in which the foetus is quite unlike a body part. The foetus is ordinarily created through intercourse, a social relation which has impregnation as a consequence. During pregnancy, a woman experiences wide-ranging physiological

change that only the pregnancy initiates; without the foetus, they will not occur. From its outset, the connection between the pregnant woman and her foetus is expected to end and it inevitably does end, whether through spontaneous or planned abortion or through birth. Further, the foetus carried to term involves the commitment of almost one year of a woman's life to the creation of a child.

46. Yet the foetus is deep within the body of a pregnant woman, connected to many of her body's systems. The two are jointly nourished. There is no access to the foetus except through the pregnant woman; whatever happens to the foetus happens to the pregnant woman but not always in the same way, and whatever happens to the pregnant woman happens to the foetus but not always in the same way. Through her body, the pregnant woman perceives and experiences the foetus in ways that no one else can duplicate; she alone can witness the foetus and its development through her own senses without the intermediation of technology.

47. Viewing the foetus, either as a person or as a person-like separate entity, or alternatively as just another body part of the pregnant woman, does not capture the unique reality of pregnancy. These views illustrate the limitations of attempting to conceptualize the foetus from an outside perspective, which abstracts the foetus from it context, namely the woman.

48. The reasons of the British Columbia Court of Appeal on this point do not turn on a conclusion that the foetus is "simply a disposable part of the woman's body." The Court of Appeal first concluded that the learned trial judge had erred in holding that the foetus in the process of birth was a "person" for the purposes of section 203 of the Criminal Code, given the clear line of demarcation at live birth that had been established for centuries at common law.

Reasons of the Court of Appeal, Appeal Case, at 4-55.

49. The Court of Appeal said:

> From the conclusion that the line of demarcation as a matter of law is live birth, in our opinion, for the purpose of count 2, the child when it is in the birth canal remains part of the mother, as a matter of law.

Reasons, Appeal Case, at 58.

50. The conclusion of the Court of Appeal on this point is consistent with the position argued by LEAF, although conceptually reached through a different route. The Court held that as a matter of law, when there is harm to a foetus that has not yet fully proceeded in a living state from a woman's body, there is bodily harm to the pregnant woman. On the facts of this case, the Court of Appeal concluded that there was bodily harm to Jewel Voth. LEAF submits that that conclusion was correct. Recognizing that the foetus is in the woman's body and central to her pregnancy reveals that harm to a full-term foetus in the process of birth is harm to the woman giving birth. The interpretation of section 24 given by the Court of Appeal furthers the purposes of sections 15, 7, and 28 of the Charter. The opposite interpretation (namely, that, when third-party negligence harms a full-term foetus in the process of birth, there is not bodily harm to the pregnant woman) would work against the purposes of those sections.

Jewel Voth Suffered Bodily Harm

51. LEAF submits that the issue of bodily harm to Jewel Voth should be considered in light of this Honourable Court's observation that "[t]he importance of maintaining the physical integrity of a human being ranks high in our scale of values, particularly as it affects the privilege of giving life." Although stated in the context of a proposed involuntary sterilization, this expression of values is quite appropriate in the context of the treatment during labour of a pregnant woman.

E. (Mrs.), supra, at 434.

52. "Bodily harm" is not defined in the Criminal Code within the context of causing bodily harm by criminal negligence (section 204), but rather in the context of the assault offences. In that context it is defined as any hurt or injury to the complainant that interferes with the health or comfort of the complainant and that is more than merely transient or trifling in nature.

Criminal Code, 1990, s. 267(2), as enacted by 1980-81-82-83, c. 125, s. 19.

53. This definition appears to have been adopted from the common law definition of bodily harm:

> Bodily harm has its ordinary meaning, and includes any hurt or injury that interferes with the health or comfort of the person. It is also referred to as such, [sic] hurt or injury need not be permanent but must be more than merely transient and trifling ...

R v. Maloney (1976), 28 CCC (2d) 323, at 326, per Lesage Co. Ct. J.

54. Because the definition set out in section 267(2) evolved from the common law, LEAF submits that it should not be confined to the assault offences, but should also be used for purposes of determining criminal negligence causing bodily harm within the meaning of section 204.

R v. Martineau (SCC, September 1, 1990), Reasons of Madam Justice L'Heureux-Dubé, at 18.

55. The dictionary definition of "hurt" includes "damage," "harm," "wrong," or "detriment." The definition of "injury" includes "hurt or loss caused to or sustained by a person," as well as "harm," "detriment," and "damage." "Bodily" is defined as including "of the nature of body," "corporeal," "physical," "in the manner of, or with regard to, the body."

Shorter Oxford English Dictionary, 1973, at 211, 999, and 1075.

56. LEAF submits that Jewel Voth sustained a hurt, harm, or loss that interfered with her health and comfort and was not merely transient and trifling, within the meaning of section 204 of the Code.

(i) Through the Death of Her Foetus Because It Was In Her and Of Her

57. Seeing harm to the full-term foetus in the process of birth as bodily harm to the birthing woman emphasizes the interconnected experience of the woman and her foetus, and the high degree to which she remains physically implicated especially at this late stage of pregnancy.

58. The process of birth itself, like pregnancy, is something that happens in and to the body of the woman. Each woman experiences it profoundly and uniquely, her body systems functioning in complex ways to deliver a baby into the world. Harm to the child being born is harm to the woman in her experience of birth, and of birthing the foetus; it is harm to something in her and of her in complex physiological and psychological senses. As such it is harm to the woman, well within the definition of "bodily harm" set out above at paragraphs 51 to 56.

59. Death of a foetus during birth is something that is uniquely experienced by a pregnant woman. Failure of the state to recognize it as harm is failure to recognize harm in a situation specific to women, and as such, is a violation of women's equality rights.

Gillian Forrest, "Care of the Bereaved After Perinatal Death," chapter 85 in Murray Enkin et al., ed., *Effective Care in Pregnancy and Childbirth* (Toronto: Oxford University Press, 1989), at 1422.

60. Recognizing the woman as the harmed party for the purposes of section 204 of the Code is consistent both with this Court's respect for bodily integrity as it relates to procreation and with the Charter's sex equality guarantees. It is also consistent with the right in section 7 of the Charter to security of the person, a right extended equally to females and males by section 28. Such recognition is, moreover, in keeping with section 1 of the Charter. Section 1 in and of itself does not create rights in the foetus. Moreover, the section requires that the purpose and effect of legislation be tested against fundamental democratic values, including equality. The interpretation of the Code put forward by LEAF in this case advances the equality of women and is therefore consistent with section 1 of the Charter.

(ii) Physical Consequences of Prolonged Labour

61. A focus on the pregnant woman reveals another kind of bodily harm within the meaning of section 204 of the Criminal Code. Jewel Voth suffered bodily harm through the physical consequences of unduly prolonged labour and the Appellants' failed attempt to complete the birth.

62. One of the bases for the trial judge's holding that the midwives were guilty of criminal negligence causing death (of the foetus) was her finding that in undertaking this birth, the midwives both failed to have and to use reasonable knowledge, skill, and care. She further found that the midwives showed reckless disregard for the life and safety of the child in failing to recognize the symptom of exhaustion in the mother, the fever, the sunken eyes, the volume depletion; and in "wasting precious time applying fundal pressure to the mother's uterus, with the knowledge of potential harm to the mother. ..."

Reasons, Appeal Case, at 29-30.

63. To acknowledge the suffering of Jewel Voth only in the context of the harm to the full-term foetus, and not in the context of allegations that bodily harm was caused to her, fails to recognize the significance to a woman of that woman's suffering. Such an analysis is inconsistent with women's right to equality before the law.

64. Registering the fact that the injury and suffering of the woman during a negligently conducted childbirth (both because of what happens to her body during the process and because of its unhappy results) are the woman's injury and suffering is to place the woman at the centre of the legal analysis, where she belongs. It is also fitting recognition of the fact that labour and childbirth are, even now, perilous for the woman. Injury, and even death, have not been banished from late twentieth-century obstetrics.

PART IV: NATURE OF ORDER SOUGHT

65. For the foregoing reasons, LEAF asks that this Honourable Court uphold the judgment of the Court of Appeal.

All of which is respectfully submitted.

THE OUTCOME

Head Notes—R v. Sullivan and Lemay

Held in *Sullivan and Lemay v. The Queen* (L'Heureux-Dubé J dissenting): The appeal from the Court of Appeal's judgment substituting a conviction of criminal negligence causing bodily harm should be allowed.

Held in *R v. Sullivan and Lemay*: The appeal from the Court of Appeal's judgment acquitting Sullivan and Lemay of criminal negligence causing death should be dismissed.

Per Lamer CJ and Wilson, La Forest, Sopinka, Gonthier, Cory, McLachlin, and Stevenson JJ: From the wording of s. 206, a foetus is not a "human being" for the purposes of the Code. The introduction of the criminal negligence provisions in 1954 was not intended to change the meaning of "person" and that term, as used in s. 203 of the Code, is synonymous with the term "human being."

A court of appeal has no jurisdiction to disturb a verdict of acquittal unless there has been an appeal by the Crown from that acquittal. An exception occurs, however, where the Kienapple rule is applicable.

That rule provides that where an accused has been charged with and found guilty of two offences arising under the same delict, he or she is convicted of only one of the charges and a conditional stay is entered with respect to the other.

The Kienapple rule has no application here. First, there is an insufficient legal nexus between the two offences; count 1 requires proof of the death of the foetus while count 2 requires proof of bodily harm to the mother. The two charges, while they may involve the same general conduct, involve two separate consequences. Second, the acquittal entered by the trial judge on the charge of criminal negligence causing bodily harm was an acquittal on the merits and was not entered pursuant to a finding of guilt on the first count. Sullivan and Lemay could have been convicted on both counts. Even if no independent bodily harm was found to have occurred, it would still not be impossible for Sullivan and Lemay to have been convicted on both counts.

It would not have been illogical to find that bodily harm was done to [the mother] through the death of the foetus which was inside of and connected to her body and, at the same time, to find that the foetus was a person who would be the victim of criminal negligence causing death. (p. 506)

The Court of Appeal had no jurisdiction under s. 613 to substitute a conviction of criminal negligence causing bodily harm.

No compelling policy reasons were put forward for granting a further exception which would extend the Court of Appeal's jurisdiction to substitute a conviction for an acquittal in the absence of a Crown appeal.

Per L'Heureux-Dubé J (dissenting in *Sullivan and Lemay v. The Queen*): The Crown's appeal from the acquittal entered by the Court of Appeal should be dismissed as proposed by Lamer CJ. The appeal by Sullivan and Lemay should also be dismissed since the Court of Appeal had jurisdiction to enter a conviction pursuant to s. 613(8) of the Criminal Code. The trial judge specifically considered the question of guilt on the second count of causing bodily harm by criminal negligence. She would have convicted if she had not concluded that the child was not part of the mother.

IN THE SUPREME COURT OF CANADA

(ON APPEAL FROM THE COURT OF APPEAL FOR ONTARIO)

BETWEEN:

STEVEN SEABOYER

Appellant

AND:

HER MAJESTY THE QUEEN

Respondent

AND:

THE ATTORNEY GENERAL OF CANADA, THE ATTORNEY GENERAL OF QUEBEC, THE ATTORNEY GENERAL OF SASKATCHEWAN, CANADIAN CIVIL LIBERTIES ASSOCIATION, AND WOMEN'S LEGAL EDUCATION AND ACTION FUND ET AL.

Intervenors

IN THE SUPREME COURT OF CANADA

(ON APPEAL FROM THE COURT OF APPEAL FOR ONTARIO)

BETWEEN:

NIGEL GAYME

Appellant

AND:

HER MAJESTY THE QUEEN

Respondent

AND:

THE ATTORNEY GENERAL OF CANADA, THE ATTORNEY GENERAL OF QUEBEC, THE ATTORNEY GENERAL OF SASKATCHEWAN, THE ATTORNEY GENERAL OF MANITOBA, THE CANADIAN CIVIL LIBERTIES ASSOCIATION, AND WOMEN'S LEGAL EDUCATION AND ACTION FUND ET AL.

Intervenors

Factum of the Women's Legal Education and Action Fund (LEAF)

Seaboyer and Gayme v. The Queen

INTRODUCTION

Steven Seaboyer and Nigel Gayme, two men charged with sexual assault in separate cases, sought to admit evidence concerning their victims' past sexual histories as part of their defence. In particular, both men wished to draw attention to the women's relationships with other men. They were not permitted to adduce this evidence because of two sections of the Criminal Code then in force: sections 246.6 and 246.7. Section 246.6 rendered inadmissible most evidence concerning the past sexual history of a complainant with parties other than the accused. Section 246.7 prohibited the accused from introducing evidence of a complainant's general sexual reputation to challenge the complainant's credibility. After their respective trial judges disallowed particular questions that would have violated those sections of the Criminal Code, Seaboyer and Gayme together applied to the Supreme Court of Ontario for rulings quashing the orders committing their cases to trial, on the grounds that sections 246.6 and 246.7 violated principles of fundamental justice under section 7 and infringed their right to a fair trial under section 11(d) of the Charter. The Court agreed and struck down both sections. The Crown appealed to the Court of Appeal, a majority of which upheld section 246.7. However, with respect to section 246.6, the Court agreed that it might exclude relevant evidence in exceptional circumstances. The Court therefore decided that section 246.6 would be inoperative in cases where it could be shown that the provision violated the Charter rights of the accused. The Court restored the order committing the cases for trial, with the proviso that the accused would have the right to apply for a constitutional exemption under which the trial judge could allow some of their questions to be put to the complainants. Seaboyer and Gayme appealed to the Supreme Court of Canada. LEAF intervened—in coalition with the Barbra Schlifer Commemorative Clinic, Metro Action Committee on Public Violence Against Women and Children, Metropolitan Toronto Special Committee on Child Abuse, Women's College Hospital Sexual Assault Care Centre, and Canadian Association of Sexual Assault Centres—to support the purpose and operation of the Criminal Code sections. Other intervenors who supported the legislation were the Attorneys General of Canada, Quebec, and Saskatchewan. The

Canadian Civil Liberties Association intervened to argue that the sections infringed the accused's right to a fair trial.

FACTUM

PART I: FACTS

1. The Intervenors are rape crisis and treatment centres, and policy, research, litigation, organizing, and action groups working on behalf of survivors of sexual abuse and assault. As a group, they are equality advocates for women and children with particular experience in the areas of sexual violence. This coalition is dedicated to protecting and advancing the equality and security rights of women and children under Canadian law.

2. The Intervenors bring to these cases extensive expertise on the equality and security needs of women and children who are victims of sexual offences, on the basis of direct contact with victims, relevant legal and social research and scholarship, policy development in the public and private sectors, counselling and law.

PART II: ISSUES

3. The points in issue are set out in the Factums of the Appellants.

4. The Intervenors take no position on the issues raised in paragraphs 4 and 5 of the Appellant Seaboyer's factum, and paragraphs 49-52 of the Appellant Gayme's factum.

5. The Intervenors submit that section 246.6 (now section 276) and section 246.7 (now section 277) of the Criminal Code should be upheld. The Intervenors argue that:

(a) evidence of the type excluded by these sections has no impact on section 7 or section 11(d) Charter rights; such evidence is either irrelevant or of very limited probative value and highly prejudicial to victims and to the administration of justice;

(b) in the alternative, if this Court finds that these sections have some impact on Charter-protected rights, the sections are nevertheless justifiable because of the role they play in protecting and enhancing the rights of women and children to equal protection and benefit of the law, and in particular to equal security of the person, as mandated by sections 7, 15, and 28 of the Charter.

PART III: ARGUMENT

Legislative Purpose and Intent

6. The law of sexual assault has played a unique role in the history of women's inequality. Historically as a matter of common law, women, the victims of rape, were not legal persons. Rape was treated by the law more like a property offence than like an offence against the person: a property offence committed by one man against another man's property. Women were also disenfranchised. Therefore laws relating to sexual

assault were developed, promulgated, and administered by men, the perpetrator group, without regard to the experience and perspective of women, the victim group, and without regard to sex equality values or law.

Constance B. Backhouse, "Nineteenth Century Canadian Rape Law, 1800-92" in *Essays in the History of Canadian Law*, vol. II, D.H. Flaherty, ed. (Toronto: Osgoode Society, 1983), at 200-47.

L. Clark and D. Lewis, *Rape: The Price of Coercive Sexuality* (Toronto: Women's Press, 1977), at 110-24.

7. If rape law had taken sex equality into account, it would have taken into account the following:

(a) The victims of sexual assault in Canada, as elsewhere, are overwhelmingly female; the perpetrators of sexual assault are overwhelmingly adult males.

(b) Sexual assaults that are not committed against adult women are overwhelmingly committed against children, mostly by older males.

(c) Only a fraction of sexual assaults are reported. Only a fraction of reported sexual assaults are prosecuted. Only a fraction of prosecuted sexual assaults result in convictions.

(d) On a conservative estimate, at least one in four Canadian women will be sexually assaulted at least once in her life. One half of these women will be sexually assaulted before the age of seventeen.

J. Brickman and J. Briere, "Incidence of Rape and Sexual Assault in an Urban Canadian Population" (1985), *Int. J of Women's Studies* 195.

"Sexual Offences Against Children," Report of the Committee on Sexual Offences Against Children and Youths (Badgley Report) (Ottawa: Ministry of Supply and Services, 1984), at 175-233 and 351-65.

Solicitor General of Canada, Canadian Urban Victimization Survey, "Female Victims of Crime" (1985) and "Reported and Unreported Crimes" (1984).

Felony Arrests: Their Prosecution and Disposition in New York City's Courts, Vera Institute of Justice Monograph, at 6-9.

K.E. Renner and C. Wackett, "Sexual Assault: Social and Stranger Rape" (1987), 6 *Can. J of Com. Mental Health* 49, at 53-55.

K.M. Williams, *The Prosecution of Sexual Assaults* (Washington: Institute for Law and Social Research, 1978), at 19-40.

Diana E.H. Russell, *Sexual Exploitation: Rape, Child Sexual Abuse and Workplace Harrassment* (Beverley Hills: Sage, 1984), at 41-53.

8. The law of sexual assault has historically evidenced a suspicion that women's accusations of sexual abuse were uniquely likely to be fabricated. Thus the law required that rape complaints be recent, and that sexual crimes alone among violent crimes against the person be corroborated. It was not possible to prosecute rape in marriage.

Juries were cautioned that victim testimony in rape cases be viewed with special scepticism.

Backhouse, supra, at 220-26 and 233-35.

N. Brooks, "Rape and the Laws of Evidence" (1975), 23 *Chitty's LJ* 1.

V. Berger, "Man's Trial, Women's Tribulation: Rape Cases in the Courtroom" (1977), 77 *Col. LR* 1, at 21-22.

9. In the context of the above substantive criminal law rules, evidentiary rules were developed permitting wide-ranging cross-examination of the complainant on her previous sexual history and sexual reputation. These matters were regarded as relevant to the complainant's credibility, and to whether or not she had consented to the act.

10. Women have never been proven more likely than men to lie about sexual activity or anything else. False accusations of sexual assault have never been shown more difficult to disprove than false accusations of any other crime. There is no basis to suggest that sexual assault is more frequently falsely reported.

11. The law of evidence reflected deeply entrenched fallacies about women and their sexuality. For example, a widely used treatise on evidence, as late as 1970, stated that:

> (1) Modern psychiatrists have amply studied the behaviour of errant young girls and women coming before the courts in all sorts of cases. Their physical complexes are multifarious, distorted partly by inherent defects, partly by diseased derangements or abnormal instincts, partly by bad social environment, partly by temporary physiological or emotional conditions. One form taken by these complexes is that of contriving false charges of sexual offenses by men.
>
> (2) No judge should ever let a sex offence charge go to the jury unless the female complainant's social history and mental makeup have been examined and testified to by a qualified physician.

J.H. Wigmore, *Evidence in Trials at Common Law*, vol. 3A, rev. J.H. Chadbourne (Boston: Little, Brown & Co., 1970), at 924a (736-37).

12. Legal doctrines developed against this historical background continued to shape the criminal law in Canada until the mid-1970s, when Parliamentary law reform began to acknowledge some of the realities of sexual assault and its place in the status of women.

13. Sections 276 and 277 were part of a process of change designed to make the criminal justice system more accessible to women and child survivors of sexual assault, to protect their dignity and self-respect within the trial process, and to protect their bodily integrity and personal autonomy by improving the odds that their abusers would be brought to justice.

SC 1980-81-82, c. 125.

House of Commons, Debates:

18 November 1975: 9204 and 9224-25.

19 November 1975: 9247-48, 9251-52, 9259 and 9261.

8 July 1981: 11300-01 and 11342-44.

17 December 1981: 14165-66.

20 July 1982: 19499-500.

4 August 1982: 20041-42.

Standing Committee on Justice and Legal Affairs, Minutes of Proceedings and Evidence:

22 April 1982, 77:27-46.

14. These legislative reforms involved a recognition that traditional practices and procedures of the criminal courts "stacked the deck" against the victims of sexual assault in ways that were unique to these offences and ungrounded in reality. As women were gaining a public voice, the received myths became less acceptable as a foundation for legal doctrine and criminal procedure.

15. The process described above commenced in 1976 with Parliament's first package of reforms of sexual assault law. Part of this package was section 142 of the Criminal Code.

SC 1974-75-76, c. 93.

16. Although section 142 was designed to protect victims from intrusive and irrelevant cross-examination, it was interpreted by the courts as broadening the scope for cross-examination of complainants about prior sexual history and reputation, in that it made a complainant compellable on these issues, and allowed the defence to impeach her credibility by calling witnesses to testify with respect to her reputation, previously regarded as a collateral issue.

R v. Forsythe, [1980] 2 SCR 268.

R v. Konkin, [1983] 1 SCR 388, at 398, per Wilson J, dissenting.

17. In 1982, partly in response to this jurisprudence, Parliament passed a second package of legislative reforms, including what are currently sections 276 and 277 of the Code.

SC 1980-81-82, c. 125.

18. These reforms were enacted after careful study and review by Parliament, involving extensive committee hearings in which representatives of groups of women who had been sexually assaulted were heard. A variety of detailed, comprehensive, and authoritative studies and Royal Commission reports, including a report from the Law Reform Commission of Canada, were reviewed.

Standing Committee on Justice and Legal Affairs, Minutes of Proceedings and Evidence:

27 April 1982, 78:4-7 and 25-28.

6 May 1982, 82:30-49.

1 June 1982, 91:3-56 and 91A:1-10.

9 June 1982, 95:3-25.

See also citations, para. 13, supra.

19. Parliament enacted these provisions knowing that only 1 in 10 rape cases is ever reported, and that the conviction rate is lower for rape than for other indictable offences. The reforms were explicitly designed to ensure that laws against sexual assault would be more equitably and effectively enforced. They clearly promote sex equality.

See citations, para. 13, supra.

20. These provisions were enacted with the purpose of protecting and enhancing the equality of victims of sexual assault, and providing them with equal benefit of the criminal law and equal protection within the criminal justice system.

See citations, para. 13, supra.

Equality Rights Under the Charter

21. This Court has identified equality as one of the fundamental values of our society, against which the objects of all legislation must be measured. This Court has also said that the section 15 guarantee "is the broadest of all guarantees [in the Charter]. It applies to and supports all other rights guaranteed by the Charter."

R v. Oakes, [1986] 1 SCR 103, at 136.

Andrews v. Law Society of British Columbia, [1989] 1 SCR 143, at 185.

22. In this Court's developing jurisprudence, while section 15 does not itself guarantee social equality, equal law is seen as a means to an equal society, as well as an end in itself. Thus, the purpose of section 15 "is to ensure equality in the formulation and application of the law. The promotion of equality entails the promotion of a society in which all are secure in the knowledge that they are recognized at law as human beings equally deserving of concern, respect and consideration."

Andrews, supra, at 171.

23. This Court has acknowledged the importance of promoting the equality of disadvantaged groups. In the words of Wilson J, "section 15 is designed to protect those groups who suffer social, political and legal disadvantage in our society."

Andrews, supra, at 154.

R v. Turpin et al., [1989] 1 SCR 1296, at 1332-33.

Sexual Assault as an Equality Issue

24. It is submitted that the social practice of sexual assault constitutes discrimination on the basis of sex and age. Its treatment by the legal system therefore implicates the equality rights of women and children.

25. Just as women are sexually harassed based on their sex, women are sexually assaulted based on their sex. The Supreme Court has quoted with approval a scholar's argument that sexual harassment is used in a sexist society to "underscore women's difference from, and by implication, inferiority with respect to the dominant male group" and to "remind women of their inferior ascribed status." The same is true of sexual assault.

Janzen and Govereau v. Platy Enterprises Ltd. et al., [1989] 1 SCR 1252, at 1285.

26. Children are sexually assaulted because of their age and sex.

27. For purposes of the laws against sexual assault, women and children are groups disadvantaged by social inequality within the meaning of section 15.

28. Sexual assault is categorical and group-based. Just as "no man would have been subjected to [sexual harassment]," men are not under most circumstances subjected to sexual assault by women, nor are adult men treated in the way children of both sexes are treated by those who sexually assault them. Just as "[a]ny female considering employment at the ... [r]estaurant was a potential victim ... and as such was disadvantaged because of her sex," any woman and child in an unequal society is a potential victim of sexual assault and as such is disadvantaged because of age and sex.

Janzen and Govereau, supra, at 1288-91.

29. In sex-unequal societies, both sexes are taught to accept sexual aggression by men against women as normal to some degree. Male sexual exploitation of women is fostered by traditional gender roles in which male sexuality embodies the role of the aggressor, female sexuality embodies the role of the victim, and some force is romanticized as acceptable. Sexual assaults frequently occur in the context of normal social events, often by an assailant who is known to the victim. A third of all college men say they would rape women if they could be assured they would not get caught.

Renner and Wackett, supra, at 49-56.

N.M. Malamuth, "Rape Proclivity Among Males" (1981), 37 *J of Soc. Issues* 139.

J.V.P. Check and N.M. Malamuth, "Sex Role Stereotyping and Reactions to Depictions of Stranger Versus Acquaintance Rape" (1983), 45 *J of Pers. and Soc. Psych.* 344.

R. Gunn and C. Minch, *Sexual Assault: The Dilemma of Disclosure. The Question of Conviction* (Winnipeg: U of Man., 1988), at 3-12 and 44-46.

30. Women occupy a disadvantaged status as victims of aggression. Rape and the fear of rape, function cross-culturally as a mechanism of social control over women, enabling men to assert dominance over women and maintaining the existing system of gender stratification. Rape operates as both a symbol and reality of women's subordinate social status to men.

M.T. Gordon and S. Riger, *The Female Fear* (New York: The Free Press, 1989), at 8-22.

S. Brownmiller, *Against Our Will: Men, Women and Rape* (New York: Bantam, 1975), at 1-188.

31. Thus, sexual assault cannot be legally treated by the law as just another "gender neutral" crime, in other words a crime in which gender does not matter. Rather, the criminal law of sexual assault must be measured by constitutional equality standards.

Role of Sections 276 and 277 in Promoting and Enhancing Section 15 and Section 7 Rights of Women and Children

32. It is submitted that permitting a sexual assault victim to be questioned at large about her past sexual conduct and sexual reputation elicits evidence that is irrelevant and prejudicial. Such evidence:

(a) reduces the likelihood that sexual assaults will be reported;

(b) subjects her to demeaning and dehumanizing experiences in the trial process that undermine her credibility, expose her to public contempt, and trivialize her violation;

(c) reduces the likelihood that her violation will be recognized as such and that anyone will be brought to account for it; and

(d) reduces the likelihood that further violations, both of herself and other women, will be deterred.

See articles cited in paras. 33-34, infra.

33. Contemporary empirical research supports the conclusion that the admission of sexual history in sexual assault trials independently reduces the possibility of conviction and lowers sentences. Once a woman is "sexualized" by the introduction of this evidence, it becomes the "pivot of the case." When their female victims are shown not to conform to traditional sex roles, men who rape are less likely to be convicted, and if convicted are less likely to receive a severe sanction. Evidence of past sexual activities in effect transforms the courtroom into a sexual spectacle.

La Free, "Variables Affecting Guilty Pleas and Convictions in Rape Cases: Toward a Social Theory of Rape Processing" (1980), 58 *Social Forces* 833.

La Free, G.D.B. Reskin, and C.A. Visher, "Juror's Responses to Victim's Behaviour and Legal Issues in Sexual Assault Trials" (1985), 32 *Soc. Prob.* 389-407.

E. Borgida and P. White, "Social Perception of Rape Victims" (1978), 2 *Law and Human Behaviour* 339.

L.L. Holmstrom and A.W. Burgess, *The Victim of Rape: Institutional Reactions* (New Jersey: Transaction Books, 1983), at 157-220.

T.W. McCahill, L.C. Meyer, and A.M. Fischman, *The Aftermath of Rape* (Toronto: Lexington Books, 1979), at 190-91.

34. Any evidence of sexual activity outside marriage leads jurors to doubt the defendant's guilt in cases in which consent or a lack of sexual activity is pleaded. It has been shown that juries use victims' past sexual conduct to mitigate defendants' culpability. Even unfounded and unrebutted questions concerning past sexual behaviour plant suspicions and do serious damage to the victim's credibility. This is often adopted as a deliberate defence strategy. Simulated jury studies indicate that, once a victim is asked about her sexual past, if she refuses to answer, she is perceived as sexually active, and as more responsible for having precipitated the rape, than victims who were not asked.

K. Catton, "Evidence Regarding the Prior Sexual History of an Alleged Rape Victim—Its Effect on the Perceived Guilt of the Accused" (1975), 33 *U of T Fac. LR* 165.

A. Cann, L.J. Calhoun, and J.W. Selby, "Attributing Responsibility to the Victim of Rape: Influence of Information Regarding Past Sexual Experience" (1979), 32 *Human Relations* 57.

35. Research such as this has led many states in the United States to restrict the admissibility of evidence about rape complainants' sexual history in court.

Harriet R. Galvin, "Shielding Rape Victims in the State and Federal Courts: A Proposal for the Second Decade" (1986), 70 *Minnesota LR* 763, at 768-77.

36. In sex-unequal societies, sexual activity is thought to be degrading to women, although not to men. Public knowledge of details of a woman's sexual past, voluntary or involuntary, destroys her standing as a credible member of the community. As a result, public disclosure of sexual activity is experienced as humiliating, and is avoided by victims even at the cost of protected rights.

37. The prospect of participating in such a process with the results outlined above, acts as a powerful disincentive for women to make legitimate rape complaints, and to pursue vindication of their violations through the legal system.

Canadian Urban Victimization Survey, "Reported and Unreported Crimes," supra, at 3.

Gunn and Minch, supra, at 35-82.

Holmstrom and Burgess, supra, at 58.

38. When a victim's sexual history or reputation with others may be introduced at a sexual assault trial, she does not receive equal access to justice. It is not merely the victims' sensibilities that are at stake, but their equal human status in court and in society. The issue is not privacy, but equality.

39. Just as Charter rights can be used to challenge legislation, they can be used to uphold existing legislation that furthers and promotes Charter rights. Section 15 "has a large remedial component." Victims of sex crimes need remedial legislation like sections 276 and 277 to promote their right to equal access to justice in a sex unequal society.

R v. Keegstra, [1990] 3 SCR 697.

Andrews, supra, at 171.

McKinney v. University of Guelph, unreported decision of SCC, per Wilson J, dissenting, at 115-16.

40. While changes in statistical reporting procedures since the new reform package was introduced make direct comparisons difficult, and relevant provisions of the law have been under constitutional attack virtually since they were passed, the data available suggests that the new law has had some positive impact on reporting rates for sexual assault.

K.E. Renner and S. Sahjpaul, "The New Sexual Assault Law: What Has Been Its Effect" (1986), 28 *Can. J of Crim.* 407.

Impact of Excluded Evidence on Appellants' Constitutional Rights

41. It is submitted that evidence of victim sexual history and reputation excluded by sections 276 and 277 is virtually always totally irrelevant to a determination of the facts. Where it may have some marginal relevance to an issue in the case, its probative value is easily outweighed by its prejudicial effect—i.e., its unreliability, its unwarranted and disproportionate impact on trial outcomes, and its negative impact on other process goals, such as reporting and deterrence, which promote equality.

Priest v. Rotary, 98 FRD 755 (US DC, 1983).

42. Constitutional guarantees of fair trial rights do not include the right to present irrelevant evidence.

R v. Corbett, [1988] 1 SCR 670, at 687-88, 744, per La Forest J dissenting on other grounds.

People v. Thompson, 257 NW 2d 268 (Mich. CA, 1977).

43. Relevance is a basic principle governing the admissibility of evidence. No evidence is admissible that is not relevant. As a matter of public policy, more important interests have at time outweighed relevance, and produced exclusionary rules such as solicitor-client privilege, hearsay rules, spousal immunity, and the general principle that no evidence should be admitted if its probative value is outweighed by its prejudicial effect.

R. Cross, *Evidence*, 5th ed. (London: Butterworths, 1979), at 17-31.

R.J. Delisle, *Evidence: Principles and Problems*, 2d ed. (Toronto: Carswell, 1989), at 9-18.

44. It is submitted that the impugned provisions of the Criminal Code function simply to bring the rules of evidence in sexual assault cases into line with the rules of evidence in other criminal cases by providing an appropriate and necessary counterbalance to the systemic bias against women and child victims in the criminal justice system.

C. Boyle and S.W. Rowley, "Sexual Assault and Family Violence: Reflections on Bias" in *Equality and Judicial Neutrality*, K. Mahoney and S. Martin, eds. (Toronto: Carswell, 1987), 312, at 323-25.

L. Vandervort, "Mistake of Law and Sexual Assault: Consent and Mens Rea" (1987), 2 *CJWL* 233.

T.B. Dawson, "Sexual Assault Law and Past Sexual Conduct of the Primary Witness: The Construction of Relevance" (1988), 2 *CJWL* 310.

E.A. Sheehy, "Canadian Judges and the Law of Rape: Should the Charter Insulate Bias?" (1989), 21 *Ottawa LR* 741.

R v. Bird and Peebles (1984), 40 CR (3d) 41 (Man. QB).

Priest v. Rotary, supra.

45. While relevance is a legal concept, it is essentially a matter grounded in empirical experience. Facts that are regarded, as a matter of experience, as likely to be associated with other facts are seen as "tending to prove or disprove" those other facts, and therefore as relevant evidence to establish those other facts.

46. Beliefs about relevance are derived from the experience of the person who is making the determination about relevance. The consequence is that those with power can define their experience as objective fact. Because social power in our society has historically been distributed along gender lines, and men have been able to impose their experience on the social definition of reality, male experience of sexual relationships and relations, and male perceptions of women's experience of sex and sexual relationships in the sexual assault area have dominated and informed concepts of legal relevance.

47. Due to sex inequality in society, women's perceptions and experience of sex and sexual relationships are not the same as men's.

C. MacKinnon, *Toward a Feminist Theory of the State* (Cambridge: Harvard, 1989), at 126-54.

48. Historically, women who have ever had sex outside marriage were regarded as untruthful; sexual activity outside traditional marriage was therefore regarded as relevant to the credibility of female witnesses. This rule was not applied to men, because "unchaste" men were not regarded as untruthful. There is no basis in fact for predicating a judgment of truthfulness on a person's sexual experience.

49. Historically, women who consented to sex with one man or some men outside marriage were regarded as more likely to consent to sex with any man. "Unchastity" was therefore regarded as relevant to consent. In fact, women clearly understand that men are distinct and different from each other, and that the fact that a woman consented to enter into sexual relations with one man tells us nothing useful about whether she would consent to enter into similar relations with a different man. It certainly tells us nothing useful about the factual issue of whether or not she did consent on a particular occasion.

50. Section 276 recognizes that in some situations the accused may put evidence of the complainant's sexual history before the court. These exceptions, while arguably overbroad, amply provide for fair trials in all situations in which potentially relevant evidence of any significant probative value might be adduced.

Dawson, supra, at 317-21.

51. It is submitted that in all of the hypothetical situations outlined in the Appellants' factums, evidence of sexual history and/or sexual reputation is either totally irrelevant, admissible pursuant to the exceptions provided for in section 276, or, in the alternative, of very low probative value and highly prejudicial to the interests of the administration of justice, and the complainant. These examples present scenarios arguing the relevance of similar fact patterns and propensity, character, motive for false accusation, unchastity going to lack of credibility, and fantasy. They seek to shape the law according to misogynist stereotypes holding that women who are or have been

sexually active are available for, and interested in, further sexual activity, and that they fabricate allegations of sexual assault. The examples involving prostituted women obscure the irrelevance of past sexual exchanges for money to a present allegation of rape, and fail to acknowledge that whether or not the sexual exchange on the occasion in issue was to be for a fee is clearly admissible. All these examples seek to show "what kind of woman" the complainant "is" to divert attention from the issue at trial: what the defendant did or did not do to her. The "demeanour" examples are particularly obnoxious.

Dawson, supra, at 317-25.

52. It is further submitted that the hypotheticals presented by the Appellants in their factums illustrate the very problem the law was designed to correct. They are substantially reflective of what scholars term "rape myths." Studies indicate that men who believe in the assumptions behind such scenarios would be more likely to rape, and less likely to recognize that what they were doing was rape.

M.R. Burt and R.S. Albin, "Rape Myths, Rape Definitions and Probability of Conviction" (1981), 11 *J of App. Soc. Psych.* 212.

M.R. Burt, "Justifying Personal Violence: A Comparison of Rapists and the General Public" (1983), 8 *Victimology* 131.

53. Arguments that evidence not provided for in the exceptions is relevant reflect gender-biased assumptions about female sexuality. The construction of rules of evidence on gender-biased assumptions that disadvantage women violate sections 7, 15, and 28 of the Charter.

See citations, supra, para. 44.

54. The Appellant Seaboyer argues that the problems that precipitated the laws under examination will not recur if they are declared inoperative because we will now have a "modern common law approach" based on "present day views of sexual relationships" (para. 93). Presumably this means that judges and juries will no longer accept the myths about women's sexuality that were at the root of previous unacceptable treatment of complainants. It is submitted that no support for this has been provided by the Appellants.

55. Generally consistent patterns in sentencing in sexual assault cases in the lower courts, together with the comments provided by trial judges in imposing sentence, make it clear that in many cases the judges who would be exercising the discretion do not understand the enormity of the crime of sexual assault, the impact on the victim, the violence inherent in coerced sex, the power exercised by men over women in our society as a result of sex-unequal institutions and other power structures, and the systemic role of sexual assault and threats of sexual assault in maintaining sex-unequal power relations in our society. No decision should be made in these cases on the assumption that trial judges and triers of fact understand and accept sex equality principles, and that their decisions on relevance will be informed by them.

R v. Lavallee, [1990] 1 SCR 852, at 872-75.

P. Marshall, "Sexual Assault, the Charter and Sentencing Reform" (1988), 63 CR (3d) 216.

Informa Inc., *Sexual Assault: Measuring the Impact of the Launch Campaign*, Report Prepared for the Ontario Women's Directorate, August 1988.

56. The legislative history demonstrates that the impugned legislation was passed because Parliament found that exercises of judicial discretion failed to reflect concerns for sex equality, and concerns for the dignity, bodily integrity, and equal security of the person of women victims. No evidence has been produced to suggest that these Parliamentary findings do not continue to be valid.

See paras. 12-20, supra.

57. Where law reform has left the admissibility of sexual conduct evidence to the discretion of the trial judge, "such evidence is often admitted on highly questionable grounds and decision making in this area is more a reflection of prejudice against the complainant than of relevance to the accused's case in any real and acceptable sense."

Z. Adler, "The Relevance of Sexual History Evidence in Rape: Problems of Subjective Interpretation," [1985] *Crim. LR* 768, at 770.

58. Sections 7 and 11(d) values invoked by the accused include justice and fairness with respect to the interests of the state as representative of the public, and the protection of the integrity of the administration of justice as well as the accused's interests. It is submitted that "fairness" must recognize the legitimate interests of the complainant.

R v. Corbett, supra, at 745, per La Forest J, dissenting on other grounds.

59. American state courts have, almost without exception, upheld rape shield laws, rejecting contentions that the particular statute constituted a denial of due process or of a fair trial.

C. Backhouse and L. Schoenroth, "A Comparative Survey of Canadian and American Rape Law" (1983), 6 *Can.-US LJ* 48, at 70-71.

Equality Issues Raised by the Defence of Mistaken Belief in Consent

60. In *R v. Pappajohn*, this Court found that mistaken belief in consent was a defence available in sexual assault cases even where there was no reasonable basis for the mistake.

R v. Pappajohn, [1980] 2 SCR 120.

61. As reflected in *Pappajohn*, the legal concept of mistaken belief in consent defines the boundaries of criminal behaviour without regard to the bodily integrity and sense of self-worth of the victim, or to the liberty and security interests of the victim. It transforms consent from something the women does into something the man thinks.

62. It provides no incentive for men to inform themselves about women's sexuality in general, or on the particular occasion. It promotes a state of law in which stereotypical, even pornographic, myths about women's sexuality are sanctioned by law, and thus become validated in the eyes of jurors. It makes it possible for a man to be acquitted of rape regardless of the amount of force used.

63. Parliament, in response to such equality concerns and in the interests of maintaining criminal sanctions against forcing women to engage in sexual relations to which they do not consent, has now codified in section 265(4) the defence in order to limit its scope. Concurrently, it also codified the nature of the sexual history evidence relevant to this defence in section 276(1)(c). It is submitted that these provisions are constitutional exercises of Parliament's authority to define the scope of criminal conduct, maintaining *mens rea* requirements while focusing trials on case-specific facts rather than stereotypes.

Standing Committee on Justice and Legal Affairs, Minutes of Proceedings and Evidence:

22 April 1982, 77:32.

28 July 1982, 107:125-130.

64. It is submitted that even as codified by Parliament there is serious reason to doubt whether the defence of mistaken belief in consent can withstand section 15 scrutiny in view of its impact on women's equality rights.

Sheehy, supra, at 761-68.

65. It is further submitted that in light of its implications for sex equality it should be narrowly interpreted. So interpreted, no relevant evidence whatsoever would be excluded by sections 276 and 277.

Section 1 Issues

66. Section 1 has recently been described by this Court as the locus in which "the fundamental values and aspirations of Canadian society" are brought together.

Keegstra, supra.

67. The Chief Justice, as he then was, comments that "promoting equality is an undertaking essential to any free and democratic society ... The principles underlying s. 15 of the Charter are thus integral to the section 1 analysis." Where the objective of the legislation is to promote equality, that objective is enhanced "in light of the Charter commitment to equality, and the reflection of this commitment in the framework of section 1."

Keegstra, supra.

68. This Court has recognized that where Charter challenges involve legislation mediating the claims of different groups, the analysis under s.1 involves different considerations than where the conflict is strictly between an individual and the state as "singular antagonist."

Irwin Toy Ltd. v. AG Quebec, [1989] 1 SCR 927, at 994.

Edwards Books and Art Ltd. v. The Queen, [1986] 2 SCR 713.

United States of America v. Cotroni, [1989] 1 SCR 1469, at 1489-90.

69. It is submitted that in a free and democratic society in which equality is a paramount value, the impugned sections accord more than due weight to the rights of the accused in balancing those rights against the equality rights of women and children.

70. It is submitted that where it is clear that the issue involved is a complex and sensitive social issue, and where Parliament engaged in a thoughtful process of deliberation, involving due consideration of the competing rights and interests involved, of the social conditions, and of evolving sensitivity to issues of sex equality, this Court should defer to the Parliamentary compromise between the interests of the respective groups involved in the absence of clear and convincing evidence that some other balance would be more appropriate under the Charter. "[A]s courts review the results of the legislature's deliberations, particularly with respect to the protection of vulnerable groups, they must be mindful of the legislature's representative functions."

Irwin Toy, supra, at 993.

71. Where the rights in conflict are those of women and men, this Court must have regard to section 28 of the Charter, and avoid any interpretation of the Charter that allows the rights of men to override the rights of women.

Constitutional Exemption Approach Does Not Give Adequate Protection to the Equality and Security Rights of Women and Child Victims

72. The Ontario Court of Appeal attempted to resolve the issues before it by upholding the legislative provisions, but recognizing the right of any defendant who could demonstrate a constraint on his particular rights to claim a "constitutional exemption" from the statutory restrictions on cross-examination of complainants.

73. The constitutional exemption approach is simply a species of judicial discretion, and suffers from all the constitutional flaws inherent in that concept in this type of case, as outlined in paragraphs 53-57 above.

74. Judicial discretion also fails to provide certainty to victims that their rights and interests will be respected and vindicated by the criminal justice system.

75. Victims need to be sure they will receive this protection at the time they make a decision to report. This Court has recognized that there is a compelling social interest in the reporting of the crime of sexual assault, and that assured protections of the privacy and dignity of the victims are essential to persuade victims to report.

Canadian Newspapers Co. v. AG Canada, [1988] 2 SCR 122, at 130.

76. The "compromise" reached by the Ontario Court of Appeal fails to confront the group nature of the equality right to be protected here. The legislation, by contrast, promotes the equality rights of women and children as groups because it promotes reporting, increases the likelihood that guilty persons will be convicted, and therefore deters the crime of sexual assault. The constitutional exemption solution goes only so far as to protect those individual victims whose cases get as far as the trial of their victimizers, and whose dignity, privacy, and equality are deemed worthy of protection on a case-by-case basis.

PART IV: NATURE OF ORDER SOUGHT

77. The Intervenor Women's Legal Education and Action Fund et al. submits that the constitutional questions should be answered as follows:

(a) No.

(b) If yes, yes.

All of which is respectfully submitted.

THE OUTCOME

Head Notes—Seaboyer and Gayme v. The Queen

Held (L'Heureux-Dubé and Gonthier JJ dissenting in part): The appeals should be dismissed; however, s. 276 of the Criminal Code is inconsistent with ss. 7 and 11(d) of the Charter and that inconsistency is not justified under s. 1 of the Charter. Section 277 is not inconsistent with the Charter.

Per Lamer CJ and La Forest, Sopinka, Cory, McLachlin, Stevenson, and Iacobucci JJ: It is fundamental to our system of justice that the rules of evidence should permit the judge and jury to get at the truth and properly determine the issues. Nothing is to be received which is not logically probative of some matter requiring to be proved and everything which is thus probative should be received absent some other ground for its exclusion. A law which prevents the trier of fact from getting at the truth by excluding relevant evidence in the absence of a clear ground of policy or law justifying the exclusion runs afoul of our fundamental conceptions of justice and what constitutes a fair trial. The trial judge must balance the value of the evidence against its potential prejudice. Virtually all common law jurisdictions recognize a power in the trial judge to exclude evidence on the basis that its probative value is outweighed by the prejudice which may flow from it. The prejudice must substantially outweigh the value of the evidence before a judge can exclude evidence relevant to a defence allowed by law.

Sections 276 and 277 of the Code are to be measured against this yardstick. They have the capacity to deprive a person of his or her liberty and they violate the fundamental principles underlying our justice system if they exclude evidence whose probative value is not substantially outweighed by its potential prejudice.

Section 277 excludes evidence of sexual reputation for the purpose of challenging or supporting the credibility of the plaintiff. The idea that a complainant's credibility might be affected by whether she has had other sexual experience is today universally discredited. There is no logical or practical link between a woman's sexual reputation and whether she is a truthful witness. Section 277 excludes evidence which can serve no legitimate purpose in the trial but does not touch evidence which may be tendered for valid purposes. It accordingly does not infringe the right to a fair trial

Section 276 has the potential to exclude evidence which is relevant to the defence and whose probative value is not substantially outweighed by the potential prejudices to the trial process. It constitutes a blanket exclusion, subject to three exceptions—rebuttal evidence, evidence going to identity, and evidence relating to consent to sexual activity on the same occasion as the trial incident. The value of the excluded evidence will not always be trifling when compared with its potential to mislead the jury.

Two fundamental flaws mark s. 276. First, the different purposes for which evidence may be tendered are not distinguished. The legislation misdefines the evil to be addressed as evidence of sexual activity, when in fact the evil to be addressed is the narrower evil of the mis-use of evidence of sexual activity for irrelevant and misleading purposes—the inference that the complainant consented to the act or that she is an unreliable witness. The result of this misdefinition of the problem is a blanket prohibition of evidence of sexual activity, regardless of whether the evidence is tendered for an illegitimate purpose or for a valid one. Secondly, a "pigeon-hole approach" is adopted which is incapable of dealing adequately with the fundamental evidentiary problem, that of determining whether or not the evidence is truly relevant, and not merely irrelevant and misleading. This amounts, in effect, to predicting relevancy on the basis of a series of categories.

Section 276 has the potential to exclude otherwise admissible evidence which may be highly relevant to the defence. Such evidence is excluded absolutely, without any means of evaluating whether in the circumstances of the case the integrity of the trial process would be better served by receiving it than by excluding it. Given the primacy in our system of justice of the principle that the innocent should not be convicted, the right to present one's case should not be curtailed absent an assurance that the curtailment is clearly justified by even stronger contrary considerations.

The existence of other exclusionary rules of evidence does not support the contention that such rules are not contrary to the principles of fundamental justice or to our notion of what constitutes a fair trial. These rules are based on the justification that the evidence excluded is likely to do more harm than good to the trial process. They, moreover, admit of a great deal of flexibility, allowing considerable discretion to the trial judge to admit evidence in cases where the value of the evidence outweighs its potential prejudice.

Courts in other jurisdictions have found it necessary to curtail the effect of legislation similar to s. 276 of the Criminal Code so as to permit accused persons to present evidence relevant to their defence. This fact reinforces the conclusion that the legislation offends the principles of fundamental justice underlying a fair criminal trial.

The operation of s. 276 permits the infringement of the rights enshrined in ss. 7 and 11(d) of the Charter. In achieving its purpose—the abolition of the outmoded, sexist-based use of sexual conduct evidence—it overshoots the mark and renders inadmissible evidence which may be essential to the presentation of legitimate defences and hence to a fair trial. In exchange for the elimination of the possibility that the judge and jury may draw illegitimate inferences from the evidence, it exacts as a price the real risk that an innocent person may be convicted. The price is too great in relation to the benefit secured and cannot be tolerated in a society that does not countenance in any form the conviction of the innocent.

Section 276 is not saved under s. 1 of the Charter. It addresses a pressing and substantial objective but the rights infringed are not proportionate to the pressing objective. Section 276 is rationally connected to the objective because it helps to exclude unhelpful and potentially misleading evidence of the complainant's prior sexual conduct. It does not however impair the right as little as possible. Even assuming that this case, which is criminal and therefore a contest between the State and the accused, might fall into the class where the State is given more latitude in fixing a balance between competing interests, the degree of impairment effected by s. 276 is still not appropriately restrained. The section excludes relevant defence evidence whose value is not clearly outweighed by the danger it presents and is therefore overbroad. Finally, there is no balance between the objective and the injurious effect of the legislation. A provision which rules out probative defence evidence which is not clearly outweighed by the prejudice it may cause to the trial strikes the wrong balance between the rights of complainants and the rights of the accused. The line must be drawn short of the point where it results in an unfair trial and the possible conviction of an innocent person.

The doctrine of constitutional exemption should not be applied here. The exemption, while perhaps saving the law in one sense, dramatically alters it in another. Applying this doctrine would not achieve the end of substantially upholding the law which Parliament enacted. It would import the discretion of the trial judge, which was an element that the legislature specifically chose to exclude from the provision. The will of the legislature would become even more obscured with the addition of a host of judge-made procedures which have been proposed to effect this judicial amendment to the legislation. The result, too, will set up a regime based on discretion and common law notions of relevancy, which is precisely what striking down would do. Finally, this solution would delegate to the trial judge the task of determining when the legislation should not be applied. This result has the effect of placing on the accused the burden of showing that the decision to exclude evidence is unconstitutional.

Striking down s. 276 does not revive the old common law rules of evidence which permitted evidence of sexual conduct and condoned invalid inferences from it. These rules, like other common law rules of evidence, must be adapted to conform to current reality. Evidence of sexual conduct and reputation in itself cannot be regarded as logically probative of either the complainant's credibility or consent. The twin myths which s. 276 sought to eradicate have no place in a rational and just system of law.

The inquiry as to what the law is, in the absence of s. 276 of the Code, must be considered in light of the fundamental principles governing the trial process and the reception of evidence. Legitimate uses should be preserved and illegitimate uses abolished. This approach of a general exclusion because of the impossibility of predicting in advance what evidence may be relevant in a particular case. Trial judges are not free to act on whim.

The following principles apply:

1. On a trial for sexual offence, evidence that the complainant has engaged in consensual sexual conduct on other occasions (including past sexual conduct with the

accused) is not admissible solely to support the inference that the complainant is by reason of such conduct (a) more likely to have consented to the sexual conduct at issue in the trial; or (b) less worthy of belief as a witness.

2. Evidence of consensual sexual conduct on the part of the complainant may be admissible for purposes other than an inference relating to the consent or credibility of the complainant where it possesses probative value on an issue in the trial and where that probative value is not substantially outweighed by the danger of unfair prejudice flowing from the evidence.

[T]he following are examples of admissible evidence:

(A) Evidence of specific instances of sexual conduct tending to prove that a person other than the accused caused the physical consequences of the rape alleged by the prosecution;

(B) Evidence of sexual conduct tending to prove bias or motive to fabricate on the part of the complainant;

(C) Evidence of prior sexual conduct, known to the accused at the time of the act charged, tending to prove that the accused believed that the complainant was consenting to the act charged ... ;

(D) Evidence of prior sexual conduct which meets the requirements for the reception of similar act evidence, bearing in mind that such evidence cannot be used illegitimately merely to show that the complainant consented or is an unreliable witness;

(E) Evidence tending to rebut proof introduced by the prosecution regarding the complainant's sexual conduct. (pp. 635-36)

3. Before evidence of consensual sexual conduct on the part of a victim is received, it must be established on a *voir dire* (which may be held *in camera*) by affidavit or the testimony of the accused or third parties that the proposed use of the evidence of other sexual conduct is legitimate.

4. Where evidence that the complainant has engaged in sexual conduct on other occasions is admitted on a jury trial, the judge should warn the jury against inferring from the evidence of the conduct itself, either that the complainant might have consented to the act alleged, or that the complainant is less worthy of credit.

Section 52 of the Constitution Act, 1982, does not confer jurisdiction on a tribunal to determine whether a law is constitutional. That jurisdiction must be found in the legislation which defines the powers of the body. The jurisdiction of a judge on a preliminary hearing is conferred exclusively by Part XVIII of the Criminal Code. A justice presiding over a preliminary inquiry does not have the jurisdiction to grant a remedy under s. 24 of the Charter because a preliminary inquiry is not a "court of competent jurisdiction" under that section. The Criminal Code gives the magistrate no jurisdiction which would permit him to hear and determine the question of whether or not a Charter right has been infringed or denied. The preliminary inquiry judges therefore did not have the power to determine the constitutionality of ss. 276 and 277 of the Criminal Code.

It was unnecessary to consider whether the refusal of the preliminary inquiry judges to determine the constitutional question was an error of jurisdiction so as to be reviewable.

The right to appeal from the rulings of preliminary inquiry judges is restricted to questions of loss or excess of jurisdiction. Charter violations do not give rise to jurisdictional errors. In criminal cases, Charter review will generally take place at the trial stage. The only exception to this rule would appear to be cases where no other remedy, existing or prospective, lies for a wrong under the Charter.

Appeals from rulings on preliminary inquiries are to be discouraged. While the law must afford a remedy where one is needed, the remedy should, in general, be accorded within the normal procedural context in which an issue arises, namely the trial. Such restraint will prevent a plethora of interlocutory appeals and the delays which inevitably flow from them. It will also permit a fuller view of the issue by the reviewing courts, which will have the benefit of a more complete picture of the evidence and the case.

Per L'Heureux-Dubé and Gonthier JJ (dissenting in part):

Sexual assault is not like any other crime. In the vast majority of cases the target is a woman and the perpetrator is a man. ... Unlike other crimes of a violent nature, it is for the most part unreported. Yet by all accounts, women are victimized at an alarming rate and there is some evidence that an already frighteningly high rate of sexual assault is on the increase. The prosecution and conviction rates for sexual assault are among the lowest for all violent crimes. Perhaps more than any other crime, the fear and constant reality of sexual assault affects how women conduct their lives and how they define their relationships with the larger society. (p. 648)

These statistics indicate that prejudicial beliefs may distort our perception of what actually happens. Rape myths still present formidable obstacles for complainants in their dealings with the very system charged with discovering the truth. From the making of the initial complaint down to the determination of the issue at trial, stereotype and mythology are at work, lowering the number of reported cases, influencing police decisions to pursue the case, thereby decreasing the rates of arrest, and finally distorting the issues at trial and, necessarily, the results.

Parliament intervened on two notable occasions. First, it repealed s. 142 of the Code and enacted a provision designed to alleviate some of the problems caused by the virtually unrestricted inquiry into a complainant's previous sexual history allowed at common law. Judicial interpretation of the section thwarted any benefit that might have accrued to the complainant. In fact, the provision, as judicially interpreted, provided less protection to the complainant than that offered at common law. Second, a sweeping reform was introduced in 1982 for the protection of the integrity of the person, the protection of children and special groups, the safeguarding of public decency, and the elimination of sexual discrimination. Sections 246.6 and 246.7 (now ss. 276 and 277) under scrutiny here were enacted as part of that reform.

The concept of relevance has been imbued with stereotypical notions of female complainants and sexual assault. This is plain from the common law which held that evidence of "unchasteness" was relevant to both consent and credibility. Any connection between the evidence sought to be adduced and the fact or matter of which it was supposedly probative must be bridged by stereotype (that "unchaste" women lie and "unchaste" women consent indiscriminately) in order to make sense.

Any relevancy decision is particularly vulnerable to the application of private beliefs whether the test be one of experience, common sense or logic. Generally the determination of what is relevant will not be problematic. However, there are certain areas of inquiry where experience, common sense and logic are informed by stereotype and myth. This area of the law has been particularly prone to the use of stereotype in determinations of relevance and again this appears to be the unfortunate concomitant of a society which to a large extent, holds these beliefs. Recognition of the large role that stereotype may play in such determinations has had surprisingly little impact in this area of the law.

It is contradictory to conclude that "truth" has been found if only stereotype renders a determination of relevancy understandable. And it is perverse to suggest that an objective application of the law of evidence mandates the admission of evidence which exhibits "rank prejudice." The examination of, and responsibility for, individual decision making is excluded. The application of "logic" and "common sense" may, in any given case, show "rank prejudice."

The irrelevance of most evidence of prior sexual history is clear once the mythical basis of relevancy determinations in this area of the law is revealed. Nevertheless, Parliament has provided broad avenues for its admissibility in setting out exceptions to the general rule in s. 276. Moreover, all evidence of the complainant's previous sexual history with the accused is prima facie admissible under those provisions. Evidence that is excluded by these provisions is simply irrelevant in a decision-making context free of myth and stereotype.

The exclusion of "pattern" evidence and "habit" evidence is not unconstitutional; the mythical basis of these arguments denies their relevance. "Pattern of conduct evidence" usually occurs where the complainant has had consensual sexual relations in circumstances that look much like those supporting the assault allegation. Such evidence is almost invariably irrelevant. It is highly prejudicial to the integrity and fairness of the trial process and, in any event, is nothing more than a prohibited propensity argument. Arguments in its favour depend for their vitality on the notion that women consent to sex based upon such extraneous considerations as the location of the act, the race, age or profession of the alleged assaulter and/or considerations of the nature of the sexual act engaged in. Consent is to a person and not to a circumstance; the use of the words "pattern" and "similar fact" deny this reality. Such arguments are implicitly based upon the notion that women will, in the right circumstances, consent to anyone and, more fundamentally, that "unchaste" women have a propensity to consent.

Evidence characterized as habitual, as being more specific than character and as denoting one's regular response to a repeated situation, too, is inadmissible. Adopting such an argument here would lend support to the stereotypical proposition that "unchaste" women have a propensity to consent. No analogy can be drawn between this behaviour and volitional sexual conduct.

The relevance of evidence of mistaken belief in consent in some cases does not conclusively demonstrate the infirmity of the provision. No relevant evidence regarding the defence of honest but mistaken belief in consent is excluded by the legislation under attack here. Assuming that both the trier of fact and the trier of law are operating in an intellectual environment that is free of rape myth and stereotype about women, any evidence excluded by this subsection would not satisfy the "air of reality" that must accompany this defence nor would it provide reasonable grounds for the jury to consider in assessing whether the belief was honestly held. The structure of the exception set out in s. 276(1)(c) is thus not offensive to the defence of honest belief.

Evidence of prior acts of prostitution or allegations of prostitution are properly excluded by the provision. This evidence is never relevant and, moreover, is highly prejudicial. A prostitute is not generally more willing to consent to sexual intercourse and is no less credible as a witness because of that mode of life. There is no understandable reason for asking complainants in sexual assault cases if they are prostitutes.

Refutation of stereotype strikes at the heart of the argument that s. 276 does not allow evidence going to show motive to fabricate or bias. Clearly, most such alleged motives or bias will not be grounded in the complainant's past sexual history. Moreover, much of this evidence depends for its relevance on certain stereotypical visions of women—that women lie about sexual assault and that women who allege sexual assault often do so in order to get back in the good graces of those who may have their sexual conduct under scrutiny. Evidence that a complainant has made prior false allegations of sexual assault is admissible under the existing provision, however, because this evidence does not involve the admission of her previous sexual history.

The evidence excluded by s. 276 is simply irrelevant because it is based upon discriminatory beliefs about women and sexual assault. This provision provides wide avenues for the introduction of sexual history evidence that is relevant. Paradoxically, some of the exceptions may be cast overly broadly with the unfortunate result that a large body of evidence may still be improperly admitted on the basis of specious relevancy claims. Even if relevant sexual history evidence is excluded, such exclusion is proper because of its extremely prejudicial effect on the trial of the legal issues. The trial judge has a long-recognized discretion to exclude otherwise relevant evidence. Hence a determination that something is relevant does not answer the further question whether, regardless of its relevance, there exists some rule or policy consideration that nevertheless mandates exclusion of the proffered evidence.

Relevant evidence may be excluded for many reasons and such exclusions play a significant and important role in the traditional law of evidence. Some evidence is excluded in order to protect values that our society holds dear. Other evidence may be excluded because of its inherent unreliability. As well, evidence will be excluded if it distorts rather than enhances the search for truth. The exclusion of evidence of sexual history, rather than negatively affecting decisions of guilt and innocence, rationalizes such determinations. Evidence of sexual history transforms the guilt or innocence determination into an assessment of whether or not the complainant should be protected by the law of sexual assault.

Neither "fairness" nor "the principles of fundamental justice" mandate the constitutional invalidity of s. 276. Rather, in order to achieve fairness and to conduct trials in accordance with fundamental tenets of criminal law, this provision must be upheld in all of its vigour.

An accused does not have a constitutional right to adduce irrelevant evidence. Accordingly, to the extent that much, if not all, of the evidence excluded by s. 276 is irrelevant, there is no constitutional issue. An accused, furthermore, does not have the right under the Charter, whether under the rubric of a right to a fair trial or the right to make full answer and defence, to adduce evidence that prejudices and distorts the fact-finding process at trial. Notions of a "fair trial" and "full answer and defence" do not recognize a right in the accused to adduce any evidence that may lead to an acquittal. Such propositions cast ss. 7 and 11(d) in an extremely narrow fashion and deny meaningful content to notions of "fairness" and "principles of fundamental justice."

Because it excludes only irrelevant or prejudicial evidence, s. 276 passes constitutional muster. The accused, on any meaningful and purposive interpretation of the rights involved, has no right to adduce such evidence. Rather than making the ordinary rules of evidence inapplicable and putting an accused charged with sexual assault in a separate and worse position than persons charged with other serious crimes, the provision ensures that the ordinary rules of evidence are applied. Parliament has excluded no evidence that is not properly excluded both at common law and under the Charter.

Sections 7 and 11(d) of the Charter protect not only the accused but other interests as well. The exact nature of the other interests involved depends upon the nature and aspect of the right considered. The complainant, and indeed the community at large, have an interest in the reporting and prosecution of sexual offences. They also have a legitimate interest in ensuring that trials of such matters are conducted in a fashion that does not subordinate the fact-finding process to myth and stereotype. However, a discussion of the community or group interests involved is not strictly necessary as the competing interest in this case, that of ensuring that trials and thus verdicts are based on fact and not on stereotype and myth, is not one belonging solely to any group or community but rather is an interest which adheres to the system itself; it maintains the integrity and legitimacy of the trial process. This interest is so closely intertwined with the interests of complainants and of the community that the distinction may be unimportant in reality.

The recognition of the accused's unfettered right to adduce all relevant evidence seriously misconstrues the phrase "principles of fundamental justice." Clearly, these principles have developed with an eye to values and interests beyond those of the accused, and thus such values and interests are pertinent in constitutional inquiries. The argument that an accused is prevented from adducing all relevant evidence going to innocence has little weight in this inquiry and must give way to other considerations. Sexual history evidence excluded by the provision is either irrelevant or so prejudicial that its minimal probative value is overwhelmed by its distorting effect on the trial process. It operates as a catalyst for the invocation of stereotype about women and about rape.

Unless one accepts the paradoxical assertion that an accused has the right to a biased verdict, or that the principles of fundamental justice constitutionalize the discriminatory application of the law, the provisions cannot be constitutionally impugned. (pp. 701-2)

The Code provision, even if found to be unconstitutional in its effect, is justified under s. 1 of the Charter.

By enacting this provision, Parliament sought to minimize sexual discrimination in the trials of sexual offences through the elimination of irrelevant and/or prejudicial sexual history evidence. A further legislative goal, intimately linked to the first, was to encourage women to report their victimization.

Sections 15 and 28 of the Canadian Charter of Rights and Freedoms mirror the values which motivate the intervention of Parliament. (p. 703)

The importance of Parliament's objectives in the reform of the law of sexual assault is amplified by the nature of the harm done and by the fact that its legislative effort gives voice to values that are paramount in a free and democratic society.

The measures were proportional. The effort on the part of Parliament to exclude sexual history evidence at trial, evidence which is largely irrelevant and biased, is rationally connected to the stated objectives of ridding the law in this area of discriminatory beliefs and of encouraging increased reporting of such offences.

The measures impair the rights of the accused as little as possible.

In the face of a previous legislative provision that was emasculated by the courts and on the heels of this, the continued application of stereotype, Parliament's measured and considered response was to codify those situations wherein sexual history evidence may be both relevant and sufficiently probative such that its admission was warranted. Parliament exhibited a marked, and justifiedly so, distrust of the ability of the courts to promote and achieve a non-discriminatory application of the law in this area. In view of the history of government attempts, the harm done when discretion is posited in trial judges and the demonstrated inability of the judiciary to change its discriminatory ways, Parliament was justified in so choosing. ... Discretion in judges is antithetical to the goals of Parliament. (pp. 706-7)

Parliament weighed the claims of different groups and attempted to balance their concerns. The courts are not better situated than or even as well situated as Parliament to determine whether the "least drastic means" have been chosen. The appropriate standard of review at this stage of the proportionality inquiry is one of reasonableness—whether the government had a reasonable basis for concluding that the legislative solution they chose impaired rights as little as possible given the government's pressing and substantial objective. The legislative choice was, at a minimum, reasonable.

The nature of the problem facing Parliament did not admit of a solution through the exercise of discretion of trial judges. That discretion saturated the law in this area with stereotype and society is still not rid of such beliefs. Discretionary decision making in this area is absolutely antithetical to the achievement of government's pressing and substantial objectives.

Lastly, the effects of the measures were not so deleterious as to outweigh the importance of the objective. The exclusion of largely irrelevant and highly prejudicial sexual history evidence does not significantly entrench upon an accused's right to a fair trial or an accused's right to make full answer and defence. The provision still permits the accused wide avenues of admissibility to adduce evidence of sexual history which is relevant and sufficiently probative that its admission is not outweighed by its discriminatory effect.

Although it is not necessary to consider the doctrine of constitutional exception, the same rationales which make the doctrine inapplicable highlight the infirmity of the guidelines suggested by the majority.

IN THE SUPREME COURT OF CANADA
(ON APPEAL FROM THE COURT OF APPEAL FOR MANITOBA)

BETWEEN:

DONALD VICTOR BUTLER

Appellant

AND:

HER MAJESTY THE QUEEN

Respondent

AND:

WOMEN'S LEGAL EDUCATION AND ACTION FUND,
GROUP AGAINST PORNOGRAPHY, ATTORNEY GENERAL OF
CANADA, ATTORNEYS GENERAL OF BRITISH COLUMBIA,
ALBERTA, ONTARIO, AND QUEBEC

Intervenors

AND:

CANADIAN CIVIL LIBERTIES ASSOCIATION,
BRITISH COLUMBIA CIVIL LIBERTIES ASSOCIATION,
MANITOBA ASSOCIATION FOR RIGHTS AND LIBERTIES

Intervenors

Factum of the Women's Legal Education and Action Fund (LEAF)

Butler v. The Queen

INTRODUCTION

In August of 1987, Winnipeg police raided the Avenue Video Boutique and seized the store's entire inventory of videos, magazines, and sexual paraphernalia. Owner Donald Butler was charged with 173 violations of the anti-obscenity provision of the Criminal Code: section 163 (at the time of this case, section 159). Among other things, section 163 forbids selling "obscene materials," which are defined as any publication a dominant characteristic of which is the undue exploitation of sex, alone or in combination with crime, horror, cruelty, and violence. Butler re-opened his store in October and was again arrested and charged with 77 additional violations.

At trial, Butler argued that section 163, by limiting the distribution of obscene materials, infringed freedom of expression contrary to section 2(b) of the Charter. In addressing the Charter challenge, the trial judge, Wright J, acknowledged that obscene expression, including graphic sexual imagery, was a form of expression entitled to be protected by section 2(b) of the Charter. In his analysis of section 1 of the Charter, Wright J stated that expression could never be suppressed to control social morality or encourage decency. The only legitimate grounds for restricting pornography, he concluded, were: to protect people from involuntary exposure; to protect the vulnerable, for example children, from exposure or participation; or to prevent the circulation of material that effectively reduces the human, equality, or other Charter rights of individuals. Applying this standard, Wright J found that only eight of the films seized from the Avenue Video Boutique were obscene. He acquitted Butler on the charges related to the other 242 items.

The Crown appealed the acquittals and Butler cross-appealed the conviction. A majority of the Manitoba Court of Appeal entered convictions on the ground that the materials in question fell outside the protection of the Charter because they constituted purely physical activity and involved the undue exploitation of sex and the degredation of human sexuality. Therefore, the materials were not "expression" and were not protected by section 2(b).

Butler appealed to the Supreme Court. LEAF was granted status to intervene as were the Group Against Pornography (GAP), the Attorney General of Canada and the Attorneys General of British Columbia, Alberta, Ontario, and Quebec. The following intervenors argued that the Criminal Code provisions unjustifiably infringed freedom of expression: the Canadian and British Columbia Civil Liberties Associations, and the Manitoba Association for Rights and Liberties.

FACTUM

PART I: FACTS

1. LEAF directs this Court's attention to the following facts in the record in order to set the context for the argument that follows.

2. The materials seized and prosecuted in the within action constitute the entire inventory of a pornography store in Winnipeg, Manitoba, and therefore constitute a naturalistic rather than selective sample.

3. The vast majority of the subject materials are visual materials in which actual women are presented as used, hurt, or abused for sex for men.

4. In these materials, inter alia, women are presented as being raped. Sometimes they act as if they are enjoying it; sometimes they scream, resist, and try to run. Sex acts are presented being performed on subordinates by superiors or caretakers, including employer on employee, priest on penitent, doctor on nurse, and nurse on patient. Adult women are presented as children, with child-like (shaved) pubic areas, teddy bears, hair ribbons, and saddle shoes. Some participants appear to be children. Women are shown having sex with women, as sex for men. An Asian woman is subjected to racist insults as part of forced fellatio and rape. Women are presented as being sexually insatiable. Women are simultaneously or serially penetrated in every orifice by penises or objects. Women are presented as gagging on penises down their throats. Women lick men's anuses. Women are bound with rings through their nipples, and hung handcuffed from the ceiling. Men ejaculate all over women, including on their faces and into their mouths. In these contexts, women are referred to and described as "pussy," "cunt," "split beavers," "hole," "bitch," "hot titties and twats," "dyke meat," and "chocolate box."

Exhibits 2, 3, 4, 5, 6, 9, 14, 20, 29, 33, 46, 50, 55, 56, 60, 62, 64, 66, 70, 71, 78, 79, 80, 85, 86, 87, 162, 168, 169, 171, 173, 174, 175, 176, 186, 189, and 190.

5. A small number of the subject materials present men engaging in sexual aggression against other men, analogous to the ways women are treated in the materials described above. Men are slapped with belts. A man is anally penetrated with a rifle. Men are presented as being raped. Men's genitals are bound. They are in dog collars and in chains. Men lick other men's anuses and are forced to lick urinals during anal intercourse. Men are presented as gagging on penises down their throats. Men urinate on men and ejaculate into their mouths. Boys are presented with genitals exposed, surrounded by toys.

Exhibits 11, 22, 4, 7, 23, 12, 15, 17, 30, 34, 42, 44, 59 and 76.

PART II: ISSUES

6. The constitutional questions are as framed by this Court pursuant to the Order of Lamer CJC dated January 23, 1991.

PART III: ARGUMENT

Introduction

7. LEAF submits that pornography amounts to a practice of sex discrimination against individual women and women as a group. Historically obscenity law was justified on the basis of morality, a rationale that has been the subject of much criticism and obscures pornography's discriminating effects on women. LEAF submits that the regulation of pornography can be constitutionally justified using a harms-based equality approach that focuses on the actual harms done by and through pornography.

8. LEAF submits that some pornography is not protected by section 2(b) of the Canadian Charter of Rights and Freedoms (the "Charter"), either because it constitutes a violent form of expression or because it is a discriminating form of expression proscribed by section 28 of the Charter, which applies to and controls section 2(b). LEAF submits further and in the alternative that under section 1 of the Charter, any infringement of free expression is outweighed by the social interest in equality in society.

The Historical Development of Obscenity Law

9. Originally, obscenity law was meant to prevent moral corruption through exposure to sexually explicit materials. An overlapping but broader purpose was to prevent offence to public sensibilities. Underlying assumptions informing these views were and are that women's naked bodies are indecent, sexual displays are immodest, unchaste, and impure, homosexuality is repulsive and sex outside of traditional marriage or in other than traditional configurations is a sin.

R v. Sidle (1663), 82 ER 1036 (KB).

R v. Curl (1727), 93 ER 849 (KB).

R v. Hicklin (1868), LR 3 QB 360 (QB).

R v. Beaver (1905), 9 OLR 418 (CA).

R v. McCormick (unreported, Ont. Co. Ct, January 10, 1980).

Luscher v. MNR (1983), 149 DLR (3d) 243 (Customs app.), reversed on other grounds (1985), 57 NR 386 (FCA).

10. The traditional approach went far to obscure the actual harms that pornography does to women. No recognition of the impact of pornography on the status and treatment of women was possible when the only harms of pornography are thought to be harms to the morals of consumers and infractions of moral rules. In the result, obscenity law, by ignoring the exploitation of women, often implicitly functioned as an instrument to legitimize and enforce women's disadvantaged status.

C. MacKinnon, "Not a Moral Issue" (1984), 2 *Yale L & Policy Rev.* 321.

11. In Canada, obscenity law has evolved over time to go beyond morality toward a recognition of actual harms. A significant step was taken in 1959 when the law as amended to define obscenity as crime, horror, cruelty, and violence combined with sex, as well as the undue exploitation of sex itself.

12. Notwithstanding this amendment, the way in which obscenity law was judicially interpreted was that "undue exploitation of sex" depended upon sexual explicitness. LEAF submits that the community standards test applied was gender biased insofar as its reference point was male consumers and audiences.

R v. Campbell (1974), 17 CCC (2d) 130 (Ont. Co. Ct), at 135-36.

R v. Odeon Morton Theatres Ltd. et al. (1974), 16 CCC (2d) 185 (Man. CA), at 197.

R v. Kleppe (1977), 35 CCC (2d) 168 (Ont. Prov. Ct.), at 173-74.

R v. Gray (1982), 65 CCC (2d) 353 (Ont. HC), at 355.

13. Some courts assiduously and deliberately avoided identifying harm of any kind. Notwithstanding the accumulating evidence of harm, other courts still took the approach of criminalizing "dirt for dirt's sake."

R v. Coles Co. Ltd., [1965] 2 CCC 304 (Ont. CA), at 322-23.

R v. Prairie Schooner News Ltd. (1970), 1 CCC (2d) 251 (Man. CA), at 254-55.

R v. Video World Ltd. (1986), 22 CCC (3d) 331 (Man. CA), at 342-43; leave denied [1987] 1 SCR 1255 (SCC).

R v. Periera-Vasquez (1988), 64 CR (3d) 253 (BC CA), at 269.

14. The traditional failure of obscenity law to focus on real harms has also, in LEAF's submission, contributed to a host of problems, weaknesses, and potential legal disabilities for which obscenity law has long been criticized. These include vagueness, subjectivity, gender bias, potential for abuse as a mechanism of censorship, difficulties of proof and effective enforcement, and lack of compelling governmental interest to guide interpretation.

15. As long as obscenity law remained preoccupied with explicitness, it was particularly unable to address the explosion of visual pornography in the 1970s and 1980s. This material features incest, forced intercourse, sexual mutilation, humiliation, beatings, bondage, and sexual torture, in which dominance and exploitation are directed primarily against women. Some of this material does not necessarily contain the degree of explicitness the courts required for obscenity, but causes real harm. For example, in the December 1984 issue of *Penthouse* (excerpted in Appendix 1) partially or fully naked Asian women are tightly bound and hanging from trees. Some courts convicted while others did not. In LEAF's submission this was because the community standards test was not properly anchored by a harms-based principle that found harms to women to be determinative.

R v. Odeon Morton Theatres, supra, at 198.

R v. Metro News Ltd. (1986), 29 CCC (3d) 35 (Ont. CA), leave denied November 6, 1986 (SCC).

R v. Arena Recreations (Toronto) Ltd. (1987), 46 Man. R (2d) 47 (QB).

R v. Regina News Ltd. (1988), 39 CCC (3d) 170 (Sask. CA).

G. Cowan, C. Lee, D. Levy, and Snyder, "Dominance and Inequality in X-Rated Videocassettes" (1988), 12 *Psych. of Women Q* 299.

N. Malamuth and B. Spinner, "A Longitudinal Content Analysis of Sexual Violence in the Best Selling Erotic Magazines" (1980), 16 *J of Sex Research* 226.

P. Dietz and A. Sears, "Pornography and Obscenity Sold in Adult Bookstores: A Survey of 5132 Books, Magazines, and Films in Four American Cities" (1987-88), 21 *U Mich. JL Ref.*

Pornography and Prostitution in Canada: Report of the Special Committee on Pornography and Prostitution, 1985 (Fraser Report), chapter 6.

The Emerging Canadian Approach: Identifying Real Harms

16. One of the earliest official recognitions in Canada of the gender-related harms of pornography is found in the *Report of the Standing Committee on Justice and Legal Affairs*, 1978 (MacGuigan Report), as follows at 3-4:

> The clear and unquestionable danger of this type of material is that it reinstates some unhealthy tendencies in Canadian Society. The effect of this type of material is to reinforce male-female stereotypes to the detriment of both sexes. It attempts to make degradation, humiliation, victimization and violence in human relationships appear normal and acceptable. A society which holds that egalitarianism, non-violence, consensualism and mutuality are basic to any human interaction, whether sexual or other, is clearly justified in controlling and prohibiting any medium of depiction, description or advocacy which violates these principles.

17. In sharp contrast to the older cases, but consistent with the legislative purpose, particularly with the language of the 1959 amendment, is a recent line of Canadian authority which has begun to acknowledge the harms pornography causes to women and to recognize the sex equality interest in its regulation. This line of cases uses the harms of pornography to women to interpret the content, reach, and rationale of the obscenity law. Whereas the traditional approach is concerned with materials deemed scurrilous, disgusting, indecent, and immoral, this line of cases identifies as obscene material that is dehumanizing, degrading, subordinating, and dangerous for women.

R v. Doug Ranking Company Ltd. et al. (1983), 36 CR (3d) 154 (Ont. Co. Ct.).

R v. Nicols (1984), 43 CR (3d) 54 (Ont. Co. Ct.).

R v. Ramsingh et al. (1984), 14 CCC (3d) 230 (Man. QB).

R v. Wagner (1985), 43 CR (3d) 318 (Alta. QB), affirmed (1986), 50 CR (3d) 175 (Alta. CA), leave denied 50 CR (3d) 175 (SCC).

R v. Red Hot Video Ltd. (1985), 45 CR (3d) 36 (BC CA), leave denied 46 CR (3d) xxv (SCC).

R v. Fringe Product Inc. et al. (1990), 53 CCC (3d) 422 (Ont. Dist. Ct.).

18. Illustrative of this line of authority is *R v. Wagner,* supra. There the trial court recognized as obscene sexually explicit materials in which pain was overtly inflicted or force used or threats of either were made. The court also recognized as obscene sexually explicit materials that were dehumanizing or degrading, and described this latter class of materials at 331 as follows:

> [M]en and women are often verbally abused and portrayed as having animal characteristics. Women, particularly, are deprived of unique human character or identity and are depicted as sexual playthings, hysterically and instantly responsive to male sexual demands. They worship male genitals and their own value depends upon the quality of their genitals and breasts. Thus in such films professional women, such as nurses and secretaries, are hired solely for the purpose of sexual gratification, without regard for their professional qualifications and abilities.

19. The trial court in *Wagner* found that repeated exposure to these types of pornography results in social harm, which Shannon J described at 336 as "increased callousness toward women on a personal level and less receptiveness to their legitimate claims for equality and respect."

20. Recognizing the context that section 28 of the Charter provides for interpreting obscenity law, Anderson JA, in *Red Hot Video*, supra, identified the harms of pornography as follows at 59:

> They constitute a threat to society because they have a tendency to create indifference to violence insofar as women are concerned. They tend to dehumanize and degrade both men and women in an excessive and revolting way. They exalt the concept that in some perverted way domination of women by men is accepted in our society. ...
>
> If true equality between male and female persons is to be achieved it would be quite wrong in my opinion to ignore the threat to equality resulting from the exposure to male audiences of the violent and degrading material described above. As I have said, such material has a tendency to make men more tolerant of violence to women and creates a social climate encouraging men to act in a callous and discriminatory way toward women.

21. In *R v. Butler* below, [1991] 1 WWR 97 (Man. CA), Helper JA in dissent at 141 noted that: "Evidence shows the circulation of such material may lead to an increase in the incidence of aggressive, harmful behaviour and further can lead to attitudinal changes that are antithetical to the Charter, specifically to section 28 of the Charter."

22. These findings and developments in judicial reasoning are consistent with a growing body of legal and social scholarship, evidence, expert and victim testimony, and official acknowledgment that pornography is a systematic practice of exploitation and subordination based on sex that differentially harms women.

23. The harms of pornography to women documented in this literature include dehumanization, humiliation, sexual exploitation, forced sex, forced prostitution, physical injury, child sexual abuse, and sexual harassment. Pornography also diminishes the reputation of women as a group, deprives women of their credibility and social and self worth, and undermines women's equal access to protected rights.

Fraser Report, supra, at 95-103.

Final Report of the Attorney General's Commission on Pornography (US, 1986), at 747-756 and 767-1035.

Metro Toronto Task Force on Public Violence Against Women and Children, Final Report (1984), at 66.

Report of the Joint Select Committee on Video Material (Australia, 1988), at 185-230.

Report of the Ministerial Committee of Inquiry into Pornography (New Zealand, 1988), at 38-45, 59-60, and 79-81.

Sexual Offences Against Children: Report of the Committee on Sexual Offences Against Children and Youths, (Badgley Report) 1984, chapter 55.

24. This Court in *Towne Cinema Theatres Ltd. v. The Queen*, [1985] 1 SCR 494, recognized some of the harms of pornography as potentially constituting undue exploitation of sex regardless of the community standards test and, LEAF submits, implicitly recognized the avoidance of harm as a purpose of section 163. In the words of Dickson CJC at 505:

> No one should be subject to the degradation and humiliation inherent in publications which link sex with violence, cruelty, and other forms of dehumanizing treatment ...
>
> Even if certain sex related materials were found to be within the standard of tolerance of the community, it would still be necessary to ensure that they were not undue in some other sense, for example in the sense that they portray persons in a degrading manner as objects of violence, cruelty, or other forms of dehumanizing treatment.

25. Discussing the *Towne Cinema* decision, one court recently linked the harms of pornography to the real-life context within which women live. In *Fringe Product*, supra, Charron J observed at 444 that: "The notion that dehumanization and degradation constitutes 'harm' from which our society has a right to guard itself against is implicit in *Towne Cinema Theatres Ltd. v. The Queen* ... ," and continued: "[this concern] remains pressing and substantial today in a society where, unfortunately, gender inequality and sexual violence exist as social problems.

26. An equality approach to pornography underlies the foregoing line of authority. In LEAF's submission this judicial approach should be made the explicit constitutional basis for the regulation of pornography in Canada.

Some Pornography Is Not Protected by Section 2(b) of the Charter Because It Is a Violent Form of Expression

27. Charter rights, including freedom of expression, are not absolute, but are subject to limitation prior to section 1.

Fraser v. Public Service Staff Relations Board, [1985] 2 SCR 455, at 463 and 467.

28. Pursuant to its decision in *Irwin Toy Ltd. v. AG Quebec*, [1989] 1 SCR 927, this Court protects from governmental restriction under section 2(b) all activity (including conduct) that has meaning except "violence as a form of expression." This Court stated

at 970 that it has not delineated precisely "when and on what basis a form of expression chosen to convey a meaning falls outside the sphere of the guarantee. But it is clear, for example, that a murderer or rapist cannot invoke freedom of expression in justification of the form of expression he has chosen." This is so because even though the conduct may express profound meaning, its harm outweighs its expressive value.

29. Expanding on what it is about murder and rape that deprives them of expressive protection, this Court has stated that direct acts of violence involving direct attacks on the physical liberty and integrity of others are not protected by section 2(b), and that violent expression is antithetical to the values underlying the guarantee of free expression.

Reference Re ss. 193 and 195.1(1)(c) of the Criminal Code, [1990] 1 SCR 1123, at 1185-86.

R v. Keegstra, [1991] 2 WWR 1, at 106, per McLachlin J in dissent.

30. Direct physical violence to real people is inflicted in order to make some pornography, particularly visual pornography. Some women are coerced into pornography and sexually assaulted so that pornography can be made of them. This is not the case with most hate propaganda, which, in order to be made, does not require violence against real people. LEAF submits that where physical harm becomes pornography, not only is the actual force or coercion outside the protection of section 2(b), but so is the resulting pornography.

Final Report of the Attorney General's Commission, supra, chapters 16 and 17.

31. LEAF submits that if anything can violate a person's physical liberty and integrity more than a sexual assault, it is the mass marketing of that assault as sexual entertainment. The pornography market provides a profit motive for physically harming people. It is also a mechanism for proliferating and making permanent the societally imposed stigma of sexual attacks. Pornography, which is made from assaults and which exacerbates the injury of those assaults, is no more worthy of protection as expression than are the assaults themselves.

Linda Lovelace, *Ordeal* (New Jersey: Citadel Press, 1980).

32. This approach to coerced or violent pornography is consistent with the way the US Supreme Court treats child pornography. Because using children to make sex pictures is regarded as child abuse, and the harm of their making is exacerbated by their circulation, sex pictures of children are regarded as child abuse. The Court has thus permitted, consistent with freedom of expression, criminalizing the entire chain of sale and distribution, as well as possession, as a means of eliminating these harms. The Court also recognized that in addition to harms to the child victims, harms can occur to third parties; for example, pedophiles may use child pornography to abuse other children.

New York v. Ferber, 458 US 747 (1982).

Osborne v. Ohio, 110 S. Ct. 1691, 1697 (1990).

33. Threats of violence may also fall outside the protective ambit of section 2(b). LEAF submits that because threats of violence are coercive, taking away free choice and undermining freedom of action, they should be excluded from the scope of section 2(b).

Retail, Wholesale & Department Store Union, Local 580 v. Dolphin Delivery Ltd., [1986] 2 SCR 573, at 588.

Irwin Toy, supra, at 970.

Rocket v. Royal College of Dental Surgeons, [1990] 2 SCR 232, at 245.

Keegstra, supra, at 106 (per McLachlin J in dissent).

34. LEAF submits that when explicit sex and express violence against women are combined, particularly when rape is portrayed as pleasurable or positive for the victim, the risk of violence against women is known to increase as a result of exposure. In particular, it is uncontroversial that exposure to such materials increases aggression against women in laboratory settings, increases attitudes that are related to violence against women in the real world, and increases self-reported likelihood to rape. As a result of exposure, a significant percentage of men, many not otherwise predisposed as well as the 25-35% who report some proclivity to rape a woman, come to believe that violence against women is acceptable. Such materials hence constitute direct threats of violence.

E. Donnerstein, "Pornography: Its Effect on Violence Against Women" in *Pornography and Sexual Aggression*, N. Malamuth and E. Donnerstein, eds. (1984), at 53.

N. Malamuth and J.V.P. Check, "The Effects of Mass Media Exposure on Acceptance of Violence Against Women: A Field Experiment" (1981), 15 *J of Research in Personality* 436.

E. Donnerstein and L. Berkowitz, "Victim Reaction in Aggressive Erotic Films as a Factor in Violence Against Women" (1981), 41 *J of Personality and Social Psychology* 710.

N. Malamuth, "Factors Associated with Rape as Predictors of Laboratory Aggression Against Women" (1983), 45 *J of Personality and Social Psychology* 432.

N. Malamuth, "Prediction of Naturalistic Sexual Aggression" (1986), 50 *J of Personality and Social Psychology* 953.

N. Malamuth and J.V.P. Check, "Aggressive-Pornography and Beliefs in Rape Myths: Individual Differences" (1985), 19 *J of Research in Personality* 299.

J.V.P. Check and T.H. Guloien, "Reported Proclivity for Coercive Sex Following Repeated Exposure to Sexually Violent Pornography, Nonviolent Dehumanizing Pornography, and Erotica" in *Pornography: Research Advances and Policy Considerations*, D. Zillman and J. Bryant, eds. (New Jersey: Erlbaum, 1989).

M. McManus, Introduction to Report of Attorney General's Commission on Pornography (Nashville: Rutledge Hill Press, 1986), at xviii (consensus of all researchers as released by Surgeon General Koop).

Exhibits 6, 20, 162 and 178 (examples of "positive outcome rape" scenarios).

Some Pornography Is Not Protected Under Section 2(b) by Virtue of Section 28

35. Section 28 of the Charter overrides every other provision therein. It mandates that all rights and freedoms, including freedom of expression, and equality rights, are guaranteed equally to women and men. Therefore, in LEAF's submission, section 28 engages section 2(b) prior to any recourse to section 1 and requires a balancing of speech interests and equality interests. Failure to strike such balance constitutes a breach of section 28.

36. The idea that each provision of the Constitution must be read in the light of the others is a familiar aid to the interpretation of sections 91 and 92 of the Constitution Act, 1867. In defining the various heads of power in sections 91 and 92, the courts have engaged in a process of "mutual modification" in order to accommodate apparently overlapping or conflicting provisions. Thus, the exclusive provincial power over property and civil rights in the province has been narrowed to exclude interprovincial and international trade-matters that come within Parliament's exclusive power over trade and commerce.

P. Hogg, *Constitutional Law of Canada*, 2d ed. (Toronto: Caswell, 1985), at 333.

37. Section 28 requires a purposive approach. The whole relationship between freedom of expression and the social role of pornography must be evaluated. The majority approach in *Keegstra*, supra, noted at 32 that so long as context is maintained, balancing within section 2(b) is not logically precluded. Indeed, McLachlin J performed such an assessment at 106 in her dissent.

38. Section 15 read with section 28 guarantees women equal access to equality rights. This Court has held that the section 15 equality guarantee "is the broadest of all guarantees. It applies to and supports all other rights guaranteed by the Charter."

Andrews v. Law Society of British Columbia, [1989] 1 SCR 143, at 185.

39. This Court has inextricably linked the value of equality with the concept of a free society. In *R v. Big M Drug Mart Ltd.*, [1985] 1 SCR 295, Dickson CJC stated at 336 that: "A free society is one which aims at equality with respect to the enjoyment of fundamental freedoms and I say this without any reliance upon section 15 of the Charter." Particularly in light of section 28, this suggests that the value of gender equality is imbedded within section 2(b) itself.

40. Constitutional equality, as construed in *Andrews*, supra, centres on eliminating the disadvantage of historically subordinated groups. This means that the Charter is not neutral on practices that promote inequality, but rather is a constitutional commitment to ending them.

41. Restriction of pornography on a harms-based equality rationale is not regulation because of content, although clearly it is tied to content. The purpose of regulation is not to restrict freedom of expression but rather to prevent harm.

42. It should be observed that just as conduct can express meaning, words can act. LEAF submits that it is unlikely that under section 2(b) this Court would protect sexual

harassment, obscene phone calls, child pornography, sex segregated employment advertisements, and similar forms of expression that amount to acts or practices of sex discrimination. Sex discrimination is typically accomplished through such forms of expression, which use words to both express and actualize group inferiority. In the context of pornography which, LEAF submits, is discriminatory, section 28 requires a balancing under section 2(b).

43. LEAF submits that applied to section 2(b), section 28 should also require the Appellant to demonstrate that the subject materials do not limit women's rights before the protection of section 2(b) can be claimed. When in addition, pornography requires coercion or violence to be made, it is further deprived of section 2(b) protection. Coercion or violence were not present in the materials considered in *Keegstra*, supra, nor was section 28 a factor there.

44. Materials that combine sex with aggression have perceptual effects that disadvantage women in society. They desensitize consumers to rape trauma and sexual violence. In one study, simulated juries after exposure were less able than the real juries to perceive an account of a rape as an account of a rape.

N. Malamuth and J.V.P. Check, "Penile Tumescence and Perceptual Responses to Rape as a Function of the Victim's Perceived Reactions" (1980), 10 *J of Applied Social Psychology* 528.

D. Linz, E. Donnerstein, and S. Penrod, "The Effects of Multiple Exposures to Filmed Violence Against Women" (1984), 34 *J of Communication* 130.

45. Other discriminatory effects are documented in the most advanced and recent research (most of which postdates the 1985 Fraser Report), which addresses materials not necessarily taking a violent form but which degrade and dehumanize women. Such material has been shown to lower inhibitions on aggression by men against women, increase acceptance of women's sexual servitude, increase sexual callousness toward women, decrease the desire of both sexes to have female children, increase reported willingness to rape, and increase the belief in male dominance in intimate relationships, among other known effects. For high-frequency consumers, these materials also increase self-reported sexually aggressive behaviour. While these effects are not invariant or always immediate, and do not affect all men to the same degree, there is no reason to think that these beliefs are not acted upon, given the pervasiveness of sex inequality and abuse in society.

D. Zillman and J. Bryant, "Effects of Massive Exposure to Pornography" in *Pornography and Sexual Aggression*, N. Malamuth and E. Donnerstein, eds. (New York: Academic Press, 1984), at 115.

J.V.P. Check and N. Malamuth, "Pornography and Sexual Aggression: A Social Learning Theory Analysis" (1986), 9 *Communication Yearbook* 181.

D. Zillman and J.B. Weaver, "Pornography and Men's Sexual Callousness Toward Women" in D. Zillman and J. Bryant, eds., supra.

D. Zillman and J. Bryant, eds., supra, at 45.

D.E.H. Russell, "Pornography and Rape: A Causal Model" (1988), 9 *Political Psychology* 41.

D. Zillman and J. Bryant, "Effects of Prolonged Consumption of Pornography on Family Values" (1988), *J of Family Issues* 518.

Check and Guloien, supra.

J.G. Buchman, "Effects of Nonviolent Adult Erotica on Sexual Child Abuse Attitudes," paper presented at meeting of American Psychological Association, August 1990, Boston, Massachusetts.

Exhibits 6, 9, 14, 20, 162, and 189.

46. These laboratory studies merely document what women know from their lives. Many women report that men abuse them through pornography. For example, in a study of 105 women staying in battered women's shelters in Ontario, 25% of the women reported being forced to perform acts which their partners had seen in pornography. In another study, specific pornography as spontaneously mentioned by rapists during the course of the rape in 25 of 193 rapes reported by 200 street prostitutes. Further studies find a substantial percentage of all Canadian women report they have been upset by someone trying to do something to them that came from pornography.

Public Hearings on Ordinances to Add Pornography as Discrimination Against Women, Minneapolis City Council, Government Operations Committee, December 12 and 13, 1983.

Susan Cole, *Pornography and the Sex Crisis* (Toronto: Amanita Press, 1989), at 44.

C.Y. Senn, "Women's Reactions to Violent Pornography, Nonviolent Pornography and Erotica" (1985), unpublished Master's Thesis, University of Calgary, Alberta.

E. Sommers and J.V.P. Check, "An Empirical Investigation of the Role of Pornography in the Verbal and Physical Abuse of Women" (1987), 2 *Violence and Victims* 189.

M.H. Silbert and A.M. Pines, "Pornography and Sexual Abuse of Women" (1984), 10 *Sex Roles* 857.

47. LEAF submits that pornography is not only a practice of discrimination that disadvantages women and treats them as second class citizens on the basis of sex, it also uses race and age to discriminate through gender. Pornography sexsualizes racism and racial stereotypes and eroticizes the vulnerability of children.

Exhibits 60, 64, and 80 (see excerpts in Appendix 2).

48. Individual men are also harmed by pornography, although this is exceptional in that this harm does not define the social status and treatment of men as a group. Indeed, there is no systematic data to support the view that men as such are harmed by pornography. However, LEAF submits that much of the subject pornography of men for men, in addition to abusing some men in the ways that it is more common to abuse women

through sex, arguably contributes to abuse and homophobia as it normalizes male sexual aggression generally.

Exhibits 11, 22, 23, and 42.

49. Given the role of section 28 and the violent materials in the case at bar, LEAF submits that, unlike in *Keegstra*, supra, expressive values are appropriately balanced under section 2(b).

50. Pornography furthers none of the values for which expression is protected, as summarized in *Irwin Toy,* supra, at 976. All the reasons that led this Court in *Keegstra* not to value hate literature highly in the section 1 balance, apply to pornography in the section 2(b) balance. LEAF submits that pornography is a form of hate propaganda against women. Hate propaganda was found by Dickson CJC in *Keegstra*, supra, at 41-44 to produce real harms. Additional reasons not to value pornography highly include the use of actual women to make the materials, the strong documentation of the connection between pornography and violence and discrimination, and its pervasiveness and acceptability in society as a medium for entertainment.

51. Pornography is made to produce male sexual excitement, erection, and masturbation through the harms outlined above. It is not made to further any search for truth. (This argument should not be confused with the position that pornography has no meaning. LEAF submits that all social practices, however invidious, have meaning.)

52. Contrary to the submission of the Appellant, pornography is not a form of political speech as traditionally protected. It does not present a critique of the status quo or a dissenting but repressed voice. Rather, it entrenches and embodies society's most repressive and anti-egalitarian norms, which is indefensible in a society that has equality as a constitutional guarantee.

53. LEAF submits that pornography lies about women and their sexuality; for example, that women live to be raped, love to be hurt, and are fulfilled by abuse. Pornography silences women's expression and inhibits truth-seeking and works to deprive women of public regard. Sex toys do not generally run for prime minister. The pervasive presence of pornography thus deters women's equal access to participation in community life.

54. If the humanity of men "flourishes" through pornography, it is at women's expense.

55. One risk of protecting pornography under section 2(b) prior to upholding its regulation under section 1 is not only dignifying a vicious traffic, but progressively eroding expression rights in favour of the more policy-oriented constitutional calculus performed under section 1.

To the Extent Section 163 Is Interpreted To Promote Sex Equality, Any Restraints It Imposes on Expression Are Demonstrably Justifiable in a Free and Democratic Society

56. LEAF submits, in the alternative, that if this Court does not accept the aforesaid arguments under section 2(b), they apply equally under section 1.

57. This Court has held in *Keegstra*, supra, at 49-50 that the principles underlying section 15 are integral to the section 1 analysis and that the objective of impugned legislation is enhanced insofar as it seeks to ensure the equality of all individuals in Canadian society.

58. Under section 1 this Court must balance the harms that flow from regulating expression under section 163 against the harms that are actualized through the promotion of women's inequality through pornography. Sex inequality in society provides the context in which pornography must be assessed for section 1 purposes. In this context, prohibiting pornography promotes equality.

59. LEAF submits that, in addition to the harms described above, pornography promotes systemic discrimination against women through systematic bias and subordination. The status and treatment of women is affected even for those who do not experience abuse related to pornography directly. When reduced to their sexual parts and seen in terms of how they can be sexually used, women are forced to live in a social climate of disrespect, denigration and comparative deprivation of human regard. Women's opportunities for autonomy and self-determination are undermined throughout society.

60. The values embodied in the Charter must be given preference over an interpretation of the statute that would run contrary to them. Where a statute can reasonably bear an interpretation that conforms with the Charter it should be interpreted in such a manner. Section 163 of the Criminal Code should thus be interpreted as in the *Wagner* line of authority.

Leroux v. Co-operators General Insurance Co. et al. (1990), 65 DLR (4th) 702 (Ont. HC), at 716-17.

AG Manitoba v. Metropolitan Stores (MTS) Ltd. et al., [1981] 1 SCR 110, at 125.

Dolphin Delivery Ltd., supra, at 602-3.

Hills et al. v. AG Canada, [1988] 1 SCR 513, at 558.

61. In *Keegstra*, supra, this Court observed that the very real harms of hate propaganda, and not its offensiveness, supported upholding legislation against it under section 1. Similarly, the real harms of pornography supports upholding section 163 on an equality rationale rather than in the historical manner that focused on morality and offensiveness.

62. Dickson CJC, dissenting in *Reference Re Public Service Employee Relations Act (Alta.)*, [1987] 1 SCR 313, recognized at 367 that government intervention, rather than impeding the enjoyment of fundamental freedoms such as freedom of expression, may in some instances protect and enhance their enjoyment. LEAF submits that this analysis applies directly to the freedom of expression of women, which is promoted by section 163, properly interpreted.

63. LEAF submits that if section 28 does not operate under section 2(b), it must be interpreted to control the balancing of interests under section 1 in favour of promoting equality, otherwise section 28 is meaningless.

64. In deciding on the proper balance, this Court is guided by the values and principles essential to a free and democratic society. These include, inter alia, respect for the inherent dignity of the human person, commitment to social justice and equality, and respect for cultural and group identity. This Court has recognized that it may become necessary to limit rights and freedoms in circumstances where their exercise would be inimical to the realization of collective goals of fundamental importance.

R v. Oakes, [1986] 1 SCR 103, at 136.

Slaight Communications Inc. v. Davidson, [1989] 1 SCR 1038, at 1056.

65. When interpreted to promote equality, section 163 is neither vague nor overbroad. The compelling and concrete interest in eliminating systemic social subordination provides a clear guide to interpretation and a limit that constrains any potential overreach in the statutory language.

66. Building on the *Wagner* line of authority to make more explicit the sex equality rationale for the regulation of pornography could sharpen and make more predictable the factual determination of the lower courts, and at the same time make more visible those harms of pornography that have been obscured in the past.

67. In *R v. Edwards Books and Art Ltd.*, [1986] 2 SCR 713, this Court was concerned at 779 to avoid use of the Charter as "an instrument of better situated individuals to roll back legislation which has as its object the improvement of the condition of less advantaged persons." The legislation at bar has such an object; invalidating it would be such a misuse. Without this obscenity law, neither adult nor child pornography will be regulated in Canada.

68. LEAF submits that pornography undermines the pursuit of equality and has little, if any, expressive value. The importance of promoting equality and the absence of any significant infringement of freedom of expression decisively weigh in favour of upholding section 163 under section 1 of the Charter.

PART IV: NATURE OF ORDER SOUGHT

69. LEAF respectfully submits that the constitutional questions posed be answered as follows:

Question #1: No.

Question #2: Yes.

70. LEAF further requests that this Court reconsider the Order of Stevenson J made on April 10, 1991 and direct that the Appellant bear his own costs of LEAF's intervention herein as a friend of the Court. In the alternative, LEAF requests an opportunity to make submissions in that regard at a later date.

All of which is respectfully submitted.

THE OUTCOME

Head Notes—Butler v. The Queen

Held: The appeal should be allowed and a new trial directed on all charges. Section 163 of the Criminal Code infringes s. 2(b) of the Charter but can be justified under s. 1 of the Charter.

Per Lamer CJ and La Forest, Sopinka, Cory, McLachlin, Stevenson, and Iacobucci JJ: While the constitutional questions as stated concern s. 163 in its entirety, this appeal should be confined to an examination of the constitutional validity of the definition of obscenity in s. 163(8). Section 163(8) provides an exhaustive test of obscenity with respect to publications and objects which exploit sex as a dominant characteristic. In order for a work or material to qualify as "obscene," the exploitation of sex must not only be its dominant characteristic, but such exploitation must be "undue." The courts have attempted to formulate workable tests to determine when the exploitation of sex is "undue." The most important of these is the "community standard of tolerance" test. This test is concerned not with what Canadians would not tolerate being exposed to themselves, but with what they would not tolerate other Canadians being exposed to. There has been a growing recognition in recent cases that material which may be said to exploit sex in a "degrading or dehumanizing" manner will necessarily fail the community standards test, not because it offends against morals but because it is perceived by public opinion to be harmful to society, particularly women.

Among other things, degrading or dehumanizing materials place women (and sometimes men) in positions of subordination, servile submission or humiliation. They run against the principles of equality and dignity of all human beings. (p. 479)

In the appreciation of whether material is degrading or dehumanizing, the appearance of consent is not necessarily determinative. The last step in the analysis of whether the exploitation of sex is undue is the "internal necessities" test or artistic defence. Even material which by itself offends community standards will not be considered "undue" if it is required for the serious treatment of a theme. Thus far the jurisprudence has failed to specify the relationship of these tests to each other.

The courts must determine as best they can what the community would tolerate others being exposed to on the basis of the degree of harm that may flow from such exposure. Harm in this context means that it predisposes persons to act in an anti-social manner, *as, for example, the physical or mental mistreatment of women by men, or, what is perhaps debatable, the reverse. Anti-social conduct for this purpose is conduct ... (p. 485)* which society formally recognizes as incompatible with its proper functioning. The stronger the inference of a risk of harm, the lesser the likelihood of tolerance. The portrayal of sex coupled with violence will almost always constitute the undue exploitation of sex. Explicit sex which is degrading or dehumanizing may be undue if the risk of harm is substantial. Explicit sex that is not violent and neither degrading nor dehumanizing is generally tolerated in our society and will not qualify as the undue exploitation of sex unless it employs children in its production. If material is not obscene under this framework, it does not become so by reason of the person to whom it is or may be shown or by reason of the place or manner in which it is shown.

The need to apply the "internal necessities" test arises only if a work contains sexually explicit material that by itself would constitute the undue exploitation of sex. The portrayal of sex must then be viewed in context to determine whether undue exploitation of sex is the main object of the work or whether the portrayal of sex is essential to a wider artistic, literary or other similar purpose. The court must determine whether the sexually explicit material when viewed in the context of the whole work would be tolerated by the community as a whole. Any doubt in this regard must be resolved in favour of freedom of expression.

Section 163 of the Code seeks to prohibit certain types of expressive activity and thereby infringes s. 2(b) of the Charter.

Meaning sought to be expressed need not be "redeeming" in the eyes of the court to merit the protection of s. 2(b), whose purpose is to ensure that thoughts and feelings may be conveyed freely in non-violent ways without fear of censure. (p. 489)

Activities cannot be excluded from the scope of the guaranteed freedom on the basis of the content or meaning being conveyed.

The infringement is justifiable under s. 1 of the Charter. Section 163(8), as interpreted in prior judgments and supplemented by these reasons, prescribes an intelligible standard.

[L]egislation proscribing obscenity is a valid objective which justifies some encroachment on the right to freedom of expression. (p. 497) To impose a certain standard of public and sexual morality, solely because it reflects the conventions of a given community, is inimical to the exercise and enjoyment of individual freedoms, which form the basis of our social contract. ... The prevention of "dirt for dirt's sake" is not a legitimate objective which would justify the violation of one of the most fundamental freedoms enshrined in the Charter. [However, Parliament may] have the right to legislate on the basis of some fundamental conception of morality for the purposes of safeguarding the values which are integral to a free and democratic society. ... [C]riminalizing the proliferation of materials which undermine another basic Charter right may indeed be a legitimate objective. (pp. 492-93)

The overriding objective of s. 163 is not moral disapprobation but the avoidance of harm to society, and this is a sufficiently pressing and substantial concern to warrant a restriction on freedom of expression. One does not have to resort to the "shifting purpose" doctrine in order to identify the objective as the avoidance of harm to society.

In assessing whether the proportionality test is met, it is important to keep in mind the nature of the expression which has been infringed. (p. 499)

The kind of expression which is sought to be advanced does not stand on an equal footing with other kinds of expression which directly engage the "core" of the freedom of expression values. ... [T]he targeted material is expression which is motivated, in the overwhelming majority of cases, by economic profit. (pp. 500-1)

There is a sufficiently rational link between the criminal sanction, which demonstrates our community's disapproval of the dissemination of materials which potentially victimize women and restricts the negative influence which such materials have on changes in attitudes and behaviour, and the objective. While a direct link between obscenity and harm to society may be difficult to establish, it is reasonable to presume that exposure to images bears a causal relationship to changes in attitudes and beliefs.

The message of obscenity which degrades and dehumanizes is analogous to that of hate propaganda. (p. 501)

Section 163 of the Code minimally impairs freedom of expression. It does not proscribe sexually explicit erotica without violence that is not degrading or dehumanizing, but is designed to catch material that creates a risk of harm to society. Materials which have scientific artistic or literary merit are not caught by the provision. Since the attempt to provide exhaustive instances of obscenity has been shown to be destined to fail, the only practical alternative is to strive towards a more abstract definition of obscenity which is contextually sensitive. The standard of "undue exploitation" is thus appropriate. Further, it is only the public distribution and exhibition of obscene materials which is in issue here.

Once it has been established that the objective is the avoidance of harm caused by the degradation which many women feel as "victims" of the message of obscenity, and of the negative impact exposure to such material has on perceptions and attitudes towards women, it is untenable to argue that these harms could be avoided by placing restrictions on access to such material. Making the materials more difficult to obtain by increasing their cost and reducing their availability does not achieve the same objective. (p. 507)

Given the gravity of the harm, and the threat to the values at stake, there is no alternative equal to the measure chosen by Parliament. Serious social problems such as violence against women require multi-pronged approaches by government; education and legislation are not alternatives but complements in addressing such problems. Finally, the effects of the law do not so severely trench on the protected right that the legislative objective is outweighed by the infringement.

Per L'Heureux-Dubé and Gonthier JJ: Sopinka J's reasons were generally agreed with, subject to the following comments. The subject matter of s. 163 of the Code, obscene materials, comprises the dual elements of representation and content, and it is the combination of the two that attracts criminal liability. Obscenity is not limited to the acts prohibited in the Code: Parliament ascribed a broader content to it because it involves a representation. Obscenity leads to many ills. Obscene materials convey a distorted image of human sexuality, by making public and open elements of human nature that are usually hidden behind a veil of modesty and privacy. These materials are often evidence of the commission of reprehensible actions in their making, and can induce attitudinal changes which may lead to abuse and harm.

Parliament through s. 163 prohibits, and does not regulate, the circulation of obscene materials. In determining whether they are obscene, the impugned materials must therefore be presumed available to the Canadian public at large, since restrictions on availability are the result of regulatory measures which fall outside the purview of these provisions.

Explicit sex with violence will generally constitute undue exploitation of sex, and explicit sex that is degrading or dehumanizing will be undue if it creates a substantial risk of harm, as outlined by Sopinka J. Explicit sex that is neither violent nor degrading or dehumanizing may also come within the definition of obscene in s. 163(8). While the content of this category of materials is generally perceived as unlikely to cause harm, there are exceptions, such as child pornography. As well, it is quite conceivable that the representation may cause harm, even if its content as such is not seen as harmful. While the actual audience to which the materials are presented is not relevant, the manner of representation can greatly contribute to the deformation of sexuality, through the loss of its humanity, and make it socially harmful. The likelihood of harm, and the tolerance of the community, may vary according to the medium of representation, even if the content stays the same. The overall type or use of the representation may also be relevant. The assessment of the risk of harm here depends on the tolerance of the community. If the community cannot tolerate the risk of harm, then the materials, even though they may offer a non-violent, non-degrading, non-dehumanizing content, will constitute undue exploitation of sex and fall within the definition of obscenity.

Section 163 of the Code is aimed at preventing harm to society, a moral objective that is valid under s. 1 of the Charter. The avoidance of harm to society is but one instance of a fundamental conception of morality. In order to warrant an override of Charter rights the moral claims must be grounded; they must involve concrete problems such as life, harm and well-being, and not merely differences of opinion or taste. A consensus must also exist among the population on these claims. The avoidance of harm caused to society through attitudinal changes certainly qualifies as a fundamental conception of morality. It is well grounded, since the harm takes the form of violations of the principles of human equality and dignity.

Obscene materials debase sexuality. They lead to the humiliation of women, and sometimes to violence against them. This is more than just a matter of taste. (p. 524)

IN THE SUPREME COURT OF CANADA

(ON APPEAL FROM THE COURT OF APPEAL FOR BRITISH COLUMBIA)

BETWEEN:

LAURA NORBERG

Appellant

(Plaintiff)

AND:

MORRIS WYNRIB

Respondent

(Defendant)

AND:

WOMEN'S LEGAL EDUCATION AND ACTION FUND (LEAF)

Intervenor

Factum of the Women's Legal Education and Action Fund (LEAF)

Norberg v. Wynrib

INTRODUCTION

In February of 1986, a woman commenced a civil action against her physician for insisting that she have sex with him in exchange for the painkillers to which she was addicted. Although she approached the physician after she had formed an addiction, she claimed that once he became aware of her condition, he did not take steps to treat her properly, but instead offered her the drugs in return for sexual relations.

The woman claimed general and punitive damages for sexual assault, professional negligence, and breach of a doctor's fiduciary duty to a patient. The trial judge and later the British Columbia Court of Appeal dismissed her claims for the following reasons. Both courts held that she could not claim damages for sexual assault because she had consented to the acts. The trial judge dismissed the negligence claim on the ground that she had not suffered any real injury. While the Court of Appeal did not agree with that conclusion, it found she was not entitled to any damages for the physician's negligent behaviour because she had contributed to her injuries by seeking out drugs that she knew would only further her addiction. With respect to the claim for breach of fiduciary duty, the Court of Appeal held that, in a doctor-patient relationship, this breach only arose through a breach of confidentiality, which was not the case here.

Norberg appealed to the Supreme Court of Canada. LEAF was the sole intervenor.

FACTUM

PART I: FACTS

1. The Intervenor ("LEAF") is an advocacy organization engaging in test case litigation, research, and public education to secure equal rights for women as guaranteed by the Canadian Charter of Rights and Freedoms. LEAF has developed expertise regarding issues affecting equal access to justice for sexual assault survivors. This factum has been prepared without the benefit of receiving the Respondent's factum.

Sexual Assault Is a Sex Equality Issue

2. Sexual assault is a social practice that harms women as women, because they are women. Just as women are sexually harassed based on their sex, women are sexually assaulted in other ways based on their sex. This Court has recognized that sexual harassment is used to "underscore women's difference from, and by implication, inferiority with respect to the dominant male group" and to "remind women of their inferior ascribed status." The same is true of sexual assault.

Janzen and Govereau v. Platy Enterprises Ltd., [1989] 1 SCR 1252, at 1285.

3. Women occupy a disadvantaged status in society as targets for coerced sex. Sexual assault, and the fear of sexual assault, function cross-culturally as a mechanism of social control over women, enabling men to assert dominance over women and maintaining the existing system of gender stratification. Sexual assault operates as both a symbol and reality of women's subordinate social status to men.

The Common Law Should Be Developed in a Manner Consistent with the Values in the Canadian Charter of Rights and Freedoms

4. In *Retail, Wholesale & Department Store Union, Local 580 v. Dolphin Delivery Ltd.*, McIntyre J, for this Court, stated that:

> the judiciary ought to apply and develop principles of the common law in a manner consistent with the fundamental values enshrined in the Constitution. ... In this sense, then, the Charter is far from irrelevant to private litigants whose disputes fall to be decided at common law.

[1986] 2 SCR 573, at 603.

5. LEAF submits that the Court should develop common law principles in a manner most consistent with promoting the constitutional rights of such disadvantaged groups as women and persons with disabilities. These include the right to equal benefit and protection of the law (section 15 of the Charter) and the equal right to security of the person (sections 7 and 28).

Andrews v. Law Society of British Columbia, [1989] 1 SCR 143.

R v. Swain, [1991] 1 SCR 933.

6. Dr. Wynrib was Ms Norberg's general physician. She told him in the context of the doctor-patient relationship that she was addicted to fiorinal. He did not treat her addiction. Instead, he used this information for his own sexual benefit. On about a dozen occasions, he asked her to his bedroom, put a bottle of fiorinal on the dresser, kissed and touched her sexually and got on top of her and made motions of sexual activity, and later gave her fiorinal pills or a prescription. The British Columbia Supreme Court and Court of Appeal dismissed her civil claims for sexual assault and negligent prolongation of her chemical dependence.

Case at 102, I.16-22, at 97, I.7-24, at 87, I.6-29, at 94, I. 17, at 95, I.4, and 361-405.

7. The development of tort doctrine in this case will have a direct bearing on the degree to which women receive the equal protection and benefit of the law, and in particular, the degree to which harms experienced by women are recognized by the legal system. It raises questions, which are of particular significance to women, about the appropriate legal response to the use of positions of power to harm or exploit vulnerable people. The Court's decision will do the following:

(a) help determine the degree to which the harms suffered by victims of batteries commonly termed "sexual assault" will be recognized and redressed;

(b) affect the ability of people who need medical assistance to consult doctors safely and without experiencing sexual exploitation; and

(c) affect the legal protection offered to people suffering from a chemical dependence.

The Reality of Sexual Assault

8. At least 90 percent of sexual assaults involve female victims. Most perpetrators of sexual assault are male. Clinical studies of rapists have found that two factors operate in their selection of a rape victim: availability and vulnerability.

Canadian Urban Victimization Survey No. 4, "Female Victims of Crime" (1985), Ministry of the Solicitor General, Supply and Services Canada, at 2.

Report of the Committee on Sexual Offences Against Children and Youth: Sexual Offences Against Children and Youth, vol. 1 (Ottawa: Canadian Government Publishing Centre, 1984) (Chair: R.F. Badgley), at 196-98 and 213-15.

S. Katz and M.A. Mazur, *Understanding the Rape Victim. A Synthesis of Research Findings* (New York: John Wiley & Sons, 1979), at 153.

9. Some women are more vulnerable than others:

(a) People with disabilities are at least 150 percent as vulnerable to sexual abuse as individuals of the same age and sex who are not disabled. Recent research showed that 27 percent of the offenders were special service providers and that the more severely disabled the victims were, the more likely they were to be abused by a service provider.

Dick Sobsey, "Sexual Offences and Disabled Victims: Research and Practical Implications" (1988), 6:4 *Vis-à-vis: A National Newsletter on Family Violence*, Canadian Council on Social Development, at 1.

(b) American studies have shown that black women are substantially overrepresented in rape statistics of victims.

Katz and Mazur, supra, at 39-44.

(c) It is increasingly acknowledged that women who consult professionals are at risk of sexual exploitation. This makes it dangerous for women to seek help. Just as sexual harassment is a barrier to sex equality in the workplace, the threat and reality of sexual assault are barriers to sex equality in access to medical and other professional services.

The Preliminary Report of the Task Force on Sexual Abuse of Patients, An Independent Task Force Commissioned by the College of Physicians and Surgeons of Ontario (May 27, 1991) (Chair: Marilou McPhedran).

Glen O. Gabbard, ed., *Sexual Exploitation in Professional Relationships* (Washington: American Psychiatric Press, Inc., 1989).

Peter Rutter, MD, *Sex in the Forbidden Zone: When Men in Power—Therapists, Doctors, Clergy, Teachers and Others—Betray Women's Trust* (Los Angeles: Jeremy P. Tarcher, Inc., 1989).

Janzen and Govereau, supra.

(d) Young women are particularly vulnerable to sexual assault, especially by those known to them.

Canadian Urban Victimization Survey No. 4, supra, at 2-3.

Laws Reinforcing Inequality

10. The law's response to sexual assault has played a unique role in the history of women's inequality. The law has contributed to the disadvantage women suffer by offering distinctive and unusual protections to persons accused of sexual assault.

C. Boyle, *Sexual Assault* (Toronto: Carswell, 1984), ch. 1.

11. In the past decade, the criminal law has progressed toward recognizing the seriousness of the problem of sexual assault for women. Significant changes in the criminal law of sexual assault have removed husbands' immunity and corroboration warnings, and have ensured that the names of complainants will not be published against their wishes. LEAF submits that it would be consistent with this trend to ensure that tort law provides effective redress for all forms of sexual assault.

Boyle, supra, ch. 3, at 47-49.

Canadian Newspapers Co. v. AG Canada, [1988] 2 SCR 122.

12. LEAF submits that the decisions of both courts below effectively condone sexual assault of women in general, and in particular, the sexual exploitation of chemically dependent women, in the following ways:

(a) by applying a standard of "consent" that enables aggressors to coerce sexual submission without civil liability;

(b) by denying recovery to litigants regarded as "immoral," thus making them targets for incompensable abuse; and

(c) by failing to recognize and treat as significant the harms of sexual assault and prolonged chemical dependence.

PART II: ISSUES

13. From a sex equality perspective, the issues of consent, *ex turpi causa* and damages in this case raise the following issues:

(a) Consent: How should the law of consent to battery in cases of sexual assault protect against abuse of the power arising from the social inequality of the parties?

(b) *Ex Turpi Causa*: Should the law treat chemical dependency and perceived sexual immorality as reasons for denying recovery in tort?

(c) Damages: How should damages be assessed in order to recognize the true harm caused by sexual assault and prolonged chemical dependence?

PART III: ARGUMENT

Consent: How Should the Law of Consent to Battery in Cases of Sexual Assault Protect Against Abuse of the Power Arising from the Social Inequality of the Parties?

14. LEAF submits that the legal standard set for consent to batteries termed "sexual assault" should restrain abuses of power. Failure to do so denies women the equal protection and benefit of tort law.

Analysis in Courts Below

15. The trial judge made the following findings of fact and law relevant to consent:

(a) "[Ms Norberg was] addicted to the heavy use of tranquillizers and painkillers."

(b) "[Ms Norberg] returned to Dr. Wynrib. She stated that she was desperate."

(c) "At no time did [Ms Norberg] refuse his advances either directly or indirectly. … She simply did not want to believe what was happening."

(d) "By apparently voluntarily submitting to the doctor's advances … [Ms Norberg] gave her implied consent to the sexual contact. … She obviously had deep misgivings about engaging in this conduct. … Clearly she did not wish to do so. However, at no time did she express her feelings to [Dr. Wynrib] that she did not wish to engage in sexual activities with him."

(e) "It cannot be said that Dr. Wynrib either exercised force or threats of it."

(f) "While her willingness to engage in sexual activity was obviously inspired by the prescriptions which the doctor would provide, nevertheless her implied consent was voluntary."

Case, at 365, II. 18-20, at 366, II. 5-10, at 367, I. 1, 1-12, 25-27, and 32-38.

16. Neither the trial judge nor the Court of Appeal articulated a standard of consent, but the adoption by the Court of Appeal of the trial judge's findings suggest that:

(a) Unless coercion is effected by overt threats or physical force, or unless the woman actively refuses or lacks cognitive capacity, a woman will be held to have consented to sexual contact;

(b) The vulnerability of Ms Norberg arising from the doctor-patient relationship, her chemical dependence, and her sex, does not require a doctor to refrain from sexual contact with her.

17. LEAF submits that both courts below adopted an unduly broad definition of consent which did not address the distinction between consent and coerced submission in the context of unequal power. They reached conclusions as to the existence of consent without consideration of the inequalities of sex, disability (chemical dependence), and the confidential relationship, here between doctor and patient. They describe Ms Norberg's submission as if it were consent freely exercised under conditions of equality.

Catharine A. MacKinnon, *Toward a Feminist Theory of the State* (Cambridge: Harvard University Press, 1989), at 175.

John G. Fleming, *The Law of Torts*, 7th ed. (Sydney: The Law Book Co. Ltd., 1987), at 73.

18. LEAF submits that such an approach is inconsistent with the legal principle of sex equality. The practical result is to permit more powerful members of society to prey with impunity upon more vulnerable members. The message to the public is that if you have power you are permitted to use it; if you do not have power, you must resist the exercise of power with the power that you do not have. This approach misdescribes the exploitation of social disadvantage as a free exchange between equals.

19. The findings of the courts below suggest that consent is present where a person in a position of power forces a person in a position of less power to make a choice between two unwanted alternatives: in this case, between unsupervised chemical withdrawal (with its pain and dangers) and unwanted sexual activity (with its pain, indignities, and dangers). Such a forced choice should not be seen as the exercise of autonomy.

20. The standard used in the courts below can be criticized as reflecting the interests of those (mostly males) in a position to exploit their power to gain sexual access to vulnerable others. The standard classifies certain pressures (e.g., threats and force) as illegitimate and other pressures (e.g., offers of drugs to a chemically dependent person) as legitimate. Such a standard places the obligation on people subjected to "legitimate" pressure to withstand that pressure, rather than on those having greater power to avoid exerting such pressure.

21. This standard might be appropriate with respect to social, economic, physical, and psychological equals but is not appropriate when there is inequality of such aspects of power. The gender implications are clear with respect to sexual assault, where the vulnerable people are likely to be women and children, while the more powerful people are likely to be men.

Inequalities of Power

22. Other areas of law commonly recognize and control relationships of power and vulnerability:

(a) Such doctrines as duress, undue influence, and unconscionability provide relief against unfair contracts. Unconscionability applies where there has been an "unfair advantage gained by an unconscientious use of power by a stronger party against a weaker." An element of unconscionability is "inequality in the position of the parties arising out of ignorance, need or distress of the weaker, which left him in the power of the stronger."

Morrison v. Coast Fin. Ltd. (1965), 55 DLR (2d) 710 (BC CA), at 713.

(b) Doctrines and statutory protections have developed to protect the structurally weaker party in certain legally recognized relationships, such as fiduciary, consumer, employment, and tenancy relationships.

(c) This Court has recognized the connection between power, exploitation, and gender in the field of sexual harassment.

Janzen and Govereau, supra, at 1281 and 1284.

(d) With respect to all assaults, section 265 of the Criminal Code distinguishes between consent and submission, and recognizes both that consent may be absent even where there are no overt signs of resistance and that the relative positions of the complainant and the accused can determine whether there was consent or submission. "[N]o consent is obtained where the complainant submits or does not resist by reason of … (d) the exercise of authority."

(e) Consent is no defence to several offences regarding sexual contact with children. While women should not be legally seen as the same as children, these offences reflect an understanding that an inequality of power arising from youth may mean sexual contact is exploitive and/or a breach of trust rather than an exchange between equals.

Criminal Code, RSC 1985, c. C-46, ss. 151, 152, and 153(1).

23. Similar insight should inform the distinction between consent and coerced submission in the tort law of sexual assault. Achieving equality requires the recognition of social hierarchies. In this case, the factors to be recognized are sex, disability, and the confidential relationship (here between doctor and patient), factors that combined and interacted synergistically.

Andrews, supra.

R v. Turpin et al., [1989] 1 SCR 1296.

Sex

24. Ms Norberg is a woman, and as such is socially vulnerable to sexual abuse. Women as a group have suffered systematic political, social, and economic disadvantage.

A persistent signal and instance of such disadvantage is coerced sexual activity, usually by men. Forms of sexual coercion can range from threats of death or injury to the withholding of jobs, shelter, money, medical treatment, approval, and spiritual comfort. On the basis of sex, Ms Norberg suffered "the unwanted imposition of sexual requirements in the context of a relationship of unequal power."

Janzen and Govereau, supra, at 1256.

Catharine A. MacKinnon, *Sexual Harassment of Working Women: A Case of Sex Discrimination* (London: Yale University Press, 1979), at 1.

Disability

25. Ms Norberg was suffering from chemical dependence on prescription drugs for which she needed treatment. The Canadian Human Rights Act recognizes that such dependence is a disability. A woman with a disability is particularly vulnerable to sexual assault. Her need to accommodate her disability presents an opportunity for the exertion of pressure and for exploitation. Doctors can prescribe drugs and are therefore in a position to exploit chemical dependence on prescribed drugs.

Canadian Human Rights Act, RSC 1985, c. H-6, s. 25.

Doctor-Patient Relationship

26. Ms Norberg was a patient seeking assistance from a doctor. A person needing and seeking help is inherently less powerful than the person in a position to provide it. People with special expertise, especially professionals, are accorded power and authority by others. It may be difficult to resist someone licensed and expected to act in one's best interests.

Shirley Feldman-Summers, "Sexual Contact in Fiduciary Relationships" in Gabbard, ed., supra, at 193.

Confidential Relationship

27. Ms Norberg disclosed the confidential fact of her vulnerability (dependence on prescription drugs) to Dr. Wynrib because he was her doctor. This knowledge (combined with his authority to prescribe drugs) gave him power over her, which he chose to exploit to his sexual advantage.

Gabbard, ed., supra.

Nanette Gartrell et al., "Psychiatrist-Patient Sexual Contact: Results of a National Survey 1: Prevalence" (1986), 143 *American Journal of Psychiatry* 1126.

Thomas Lyon, "Sexual Exploitation of Divorce Clients: The Lawyer's Prerogative?" (1987) 10 *Harvard Women's LJ* 159.

Sheldon H. Kardener et al., "A Survey of Physicians' Attitudes and Practices Regarding Erotic and Nonerotic Contact with Patients" (1973), 130 *American Journal of Psychiatry* 1077.

28. Some aspects of Ms Norberg's vulnerability could be legally recognized by labelling the relationship with Dr. Wynrib a "fiduciary" one. LEAF submits that, whether or not the Court chooses to use the label "fiduciary" here, the standard for consent in the tort of sexual assault should recognize inequalities of power.

Implications for Tort Law

29. The list of factors in tort law demonstrating coerced submission, rather than consent, should be open to new legal and social knowledge and development. The commentary to the American Restatement of the Law of Torts suggests that the types of duress that will vitiate consent are not settled or limited to past cases. "Age, sex, mental capacity, the relation of the parties and antecedent circumstances all may be significant."

Restatement, Second, Torts, para. 892B, at 376.

30. While developments in criminal sexual assault law may be instructive, tort issues should receive independent analysis. The special protections for criminal defendants have no place in a civil context because there is no risk of unjust incarceration.

31. It is consistent with both sex equality principles and the purposes of tort law to adopt a perspective on consent consistent with the interests of members of a disadvantaged group targeted for sexual assault, rather than a perspective consistent with the interests of those in a position to exploit a disadvantaged group's relative powerlessness.

32. Thus, LEAF submits that, as a general principle, the courts should find that consent to sex does not exist where the defendant occupies a position of such power, trust or authority that the plaintiff is left no free choice to decline to have sex. Such an approach to consent is informed by a commitment to sex equality.

33. In unequal relationships such as with therapists, doctors, and teachers, sexual behaviour of which a victim complains should generally be regarded as tortious because in such relations "a man holds in trust the intimate, wounded, vulnerable, or undeveloped parts of a woman. ... [T]he factors of power, trust and dependency remove the possibility of a woman freely giving consent to sexual contact."

Peter Rutter, MD, supra, at 25.

34. LEAF submits that the position a doctor occupies in the doctor-patient relationship should be seen as a paradigm of a position of power, trust, and authority. The impropriety of sexual contact between doctor and patient is so fundamental that it is in the Hippocratic Oath: "In every house where I come I will enter only for the good of my patients, keeping myself far from all intentional ill-doing and all seduction, and especially from the pleasures of love with women or with men. ..."

Stedman's Medical Dictionary, 25th ed. (1990), at 717.

35. There is growing recognition of the harm of sexual contact in the doctor-patient and like relationships, which a number of American states have introduced legislation to address. For example, California has created a cause of action for injuries caused by sexual contact with a therapist during the period of treatment and two years afterward. "Consent" is not a defence.

The Preliminary Report of the Task Force on Sexual Abuse of Patients, supra.

Denise LeBoeuf, "Psychiatric Malpractice: Exploitation of Women Patients" (1988), 11 *Harvard Women's LJ* 83.

Cal. Civil Code, para. 43.93(b)(1), (2) (Deerings, 1990).

36. All doctor-patient relationships inherently contain such vulnerability, difference of power and potential for abuse that the law should place the responsibility for avoiding sexual contact with patients on the doctor. This should certainly be the case where groups enumerated in section 15 of the Charter are also involved, as between male doctors and women patients.

37. Because of the exploitation of the confidential information that Ms Norberg was chemically dependent, this case is an extreme example of one in which the Court should not find consent. A sex equality approach to consent would aim to decrease the sexual exploitation of members of disadvantaged groups in contexts of power imbalances like lawyer-client, teacher-student, spiritual adviser-advisee. This would have the effect of enhancing women's access to safe and objective legal, medical, and spiritual services and avoid compounding social inequalities, which it is the purpose of section 15 of the Charter to oppose through law.

Ex Turpi Causa: Should the Law Treat Chemical Dependency and Perceived Sexual Immorality as Reasons for Denying Recovery in Tort?

38. Application of an *ex turpi causa* defence in tort further enables the advantaged to prey on the disadvantaged. Victims should not be placed outside the protection of tort law, thus enabling others to harm or exploit them without liability, simply on the basis that they have engaged in illicit acts or acts perceived by the Court to be immoral.

39. A tortfeasor may benefit from the victim's participation in the tortious activity. For example, Dr. Wynrib wanted sex. It was available to him only because he prolonged Ms Norberg's chemical dependence on prescribed drugs. Enabling such a tortfeasor to escape liability for damages effectively allows him to profit from his own tort. This is contrary to public policy.

40. The majority of the BC Court of Appeal relied "far more heavily upon illegal than upon immoral conduct" in denying Ms Norberg damages. It apparently relied upon the illegality in Ms Norberg's acquisition of fiorinol and the perceived immorality of its use, and on the perceived immorality of Ms. Norberg's participation in sexual activity outside marriage.

Case, at 387, II. 30-35.

Chemical Dependency

41. Canadian studies have shown that women receive more prescriptions for all drugs than do men, and in particular, that women receive more prescriptions for mood-modifying drugs than men. Many more women than men receive prescriptions for tranquillizers. Barbiturates in particular are known to cause dependence. Therefore, it

appears that women are particularly likely to be chemically dependent on prescription drugs.

P.S. Stephenson and G.A. Walker, "Psychotropic Drugs and Women" (1980), 2 *Bioethics Quarterly*, at 20.

R. Cooperstock and M. Sims, "Mood-Modifying Drugs Prescribed in a Canadian City: Hidden Problems" (1971), 61 *American Journal of Public Health*, at 1007.

D.R. Wesson, MD, and D.E. Smith, MD, *Barbiturates: Their Use, Misuse, and Abuse* (New York: Human Sciences Press, 1977), at 33.

42. Suffering sexual abuse is believed to lead to chemical dependence.

D. Finkelhor, PhD, and A. Browne, PhD, "The Traumatic Impact of Child Sexual Abuse: A Conceptualization" (1985), 55:2 *Amer. J Orthopsychiatry*, at 530.

Dembo et al., "Physical Abuse, Sexual Victimization, and Illicit Drug Use: Replication of a Structural Analysis Among a New Sample of High-Risk Youth" (1989), 4:2 *Violence and Victims*.

L. Lapierre, *Canadian Women: Profile of Their Health*, Statistics Canada Health Division, Ministry of Supply and Services, 1984.

43. It is common to blame individuals dependent on prescribed drugs for the dependency, rather than the medical and pharmaceutical practices that develop and continue the dependency, or the violence, sexual abuse and other factors that may cause the dependency. For example, "double-doctoring" is considered by psychiatrists to be part of the pattern of chemical dependency. The offence may in effect blame chemically dependent people for the status of being dependent on prescribed drugs.

H.I. Kaplan, MD, and B.J. Sadock, MD, *Synopsis of Psychiatry Behavioral Sciences Clinical Psychiatry* (Baltimore: Williams & Wilkins, 1988), at 228.

Kathleen McDonnell, ed., *Adverse Effects: Women and the Pharmaceutical Industry* (Toronto: Women's Educational Press, 1986).

Saskatchewan Health Joint Committee on Drug Utilization, Report No. 4, *Utilization of Mood-Modifying Drugs in Saskatchewan: 1977*, Part II (Regina, Sask., 1979).

44. LEAF submits that barring tort recovery to a victim of chemical dependence, whether on the basis that the dependence is "immoral" or on the basis of the illegality of the victimless crime which is a symptom of the dependence, is improperly "blaming" the victim. It invites sexual and other exploitation of chemically dependent women.

Sexual Immorality

45. The decisions of the courts below (and the obiter in *Hegarty v. Shine*, [1878] LR 2 Ir. 273) punished women for sexual activity outside marriage. In both cases, the women were denied compensation because of the perceived immorality that more powerful men created and exploited or at least enjoyed.

46. Application of the sexual immorality bar to compensatory recovery can mean that a person who rejects even unlegislated "morality" (for example, by being the subject of pornography) becomes an "outlaw" deprived of legal protection, and thus an easy target for incompensable abuse (such as negligent medical treatment or physical and mental abuse).

Summary

47. LEAF submits that either a chemical dependency bar or a sexual immorality bar to recovery in tort will make women targets for incompensable abuse on the basis of sex and therefore the defence of *ex turpi causa* should not be applied.

Damages: How Should Damages Be Assessed in Order To Recognize the True Harm Caused by Prolonged Chemical Dependence and Sexual Assault?

48. LEAF submits that the principles for assessment of damages for the harms suffered in sexual assault and prolonged chemical dependence should recognize the very real physical, psychological, and emotional harm suffered. Failure to compensate adequately such harms trivializes the offensive conduct, reminds women of their inferior ascribed status, and enforces that status. It fails to recognize harms suffered by women and therefore fails to give women equal protection and benefit of the law. It also refrains from using tort law's potential to deter sexual assault.

Analysis of Courts Below

49. The courts below did not award damages for either sexual assault or prolonged chemical dependence. Locke JA, dissenting, would have awarded $1,000 nominal damages for prolonged chemical dependence. In assessing this, he said the following:

> I do not regard it as reasonably foreseeable on the facts of this case that the defendant could ever reasonably have thought that the other party to this transaction would be so overtaken by these human feelings as to sustain mental damage. On this ground I would dismiss any action in tort for this type of damage as not being sustainable.
>
> Case, at 397, II. 24-32.
>
> As to damages [for being] left drug dependent for a year or more ... there is no specific evidence ... that her life during this drug-dependent period was unpleasant, beyond the presumed unhappy life of one a slave to drugs ... she has recovered, or is at least free from physical effects except for the craving, which perhaps will never leave her ... nothing but nominal damages should be awarded. I award $1,000 ... I would not award punitive damages.
>
> Case, at 404-5, II. 28-12.

General Damages

50. LEAF submits that the harms suffered by victims of both sexual assault and drug dependence include fear and anxiety, depression, nightmares, loss of self-esteem, self-hatred, and self-recrimination. Victims of sexual assault may additionally suffer

sexual dysfunction and a profound inability to trust and form or maintain relationships with people like those who harmed them (often men and/or caregivers).

Deanna Nass, *The Rape Victim* (Iowa: Kendall/Hunt Publishing Company, 1977), at 123 and 133.

Koss and Harvey, *The Rape Victim, Clinical and Community Approaches to Treatment* (Massachusetts: Stephen Greene Press, 1987), at 31-41.

Goodman and Gilman, *The Pharmacological Basis of Therapeutics*, 8th ed. (New York: Pergamon Press, 1990), at 536-37.

51. The courts award large sums as general and exemplary damages in cases involving trespass to land and nuisance. LEAF submits that the violation of a woman's physical, emotional, and psychological security should merit at least as much legal redress as the loss of or interference with a person's property. On a relative scale, the equality values requiring protection of women against unwanted sexual contact should rank equal to, if not higher than, those associated with the protection of property.

Horseshoe Bay Retirement Society et al. v. SIF Development Corp. et al. (1990), 66 DLR (4th) 42 (BC SC) ($33,172 general damages and $100,000 punitive damages for trespassing and cutting down trees).

Kates v. Hall, unreported, BC CA No. CA011265, February 8, 1991 ($34,000 general damages and $26,000 punitive damages for trespassing and cutting down 13 trees).

Shewish et al. v. MacMillan Bloedel Limited (1990), 48 BCLR (2d) 290 (CA) ($58,000 damages for trespass for value of timber taken).

Epstein v. Cressey Development Corporation (1990), 48 BCLR (2d) 311 (SC) ($25,000 general damages and $45,000 punitive damages for trespass in installing 25-foot rods in soil).

52. The following cases not cited by Ms Norberg involve damages for sexual assault:

Brander v. Brander, unreported, Manitoba Queen's Bench, March 25, 1991, Winnipeg, CI 97-01-24465. (General damages of $100,000 for psychological trauma and aggravated damages of $50,000 awarded for sexual abuse by father of daughter over nine-year period. Psychological evidence indicated the plaintiff was one of the worst cases of sexually damaged persons encountered by the professionals and that she had a number of sexual and social difficulties and would need continuing psychotherapy.)

N. (J.L.) v. L. (A.M.) (1988), 47 CCLT 65, [1989] 1 WWR 438, 56 Man. R (2d) 161 (QB) ($65,000 general damages for sexual assaults by stepfather of stepdaughter over six-year period beginning when she was age six).

A.K.M. v. M.B., unreported, Ontario, June 22, 1990 ($50,000 award to girl sexually assaulted by her priest and who experienced stress, suicidal thoughts, depression, anxiety, fears of intimacy, inability to trust others, avoidance, and withdrawal).

Wiebe v. Haroldson (1989), Saskatchewan QB No. 3571/85 ($10,000 general damages and $40,000 punitive damages for one incident of sexual assault).

Q. v. Minto Management Ltd. (1985), 15 DLR (4th) 581 (Ont. HCJ). (General damages of $40,000 for an isolated sexual assault at night in the plaintiff's apartment. The plaintiff's suffering included loss of weight, becoming more security-conscious, and experiencing a period of "feeling dirty" and fear, as well as indignity and humiliation.)

C. v. M. (1988), Ontario Dist. Ct. No. 3233349/88. (General damages of $40,000 for an isolated sexual assault by the plaintiff's companion. The plaintiff's complaints included humiliation, degradation, shock, anxiety, depression, thoughts of suicide, sleepless nights, mistrust of others (particularly men), and lost self-respect.)

53. Aggravated damages should be available to compensate for intangible injuries, such as distress and humiliation suffered by a plaintiff.

Vorvis v. ICBC (1989), 58 DLR (4th) 193 (SCC), at 202.

Punitive Damages

54. Commission of sexual assaults is so socially reprehensible that it merits condemnation by the court and an award of punitive damages.

Robitaille v. Vancouver Hockey Club Ltd. (1981), 30 BCLR 286 (CA).

Wiebe, supra.

Weisenger v. Mellor (1989), unreported, BC SC No. 871938.

55. Punitive damages should be awarded for sexual assault involving exploitation of a position of trust and power. Here, the sexual assaults occurred in the doctor-patient relationship and made use of confidential information obtained in the course of that relationship. In addition, Dr. Wynrib negligently and for his own gain prolonged and exploited the very disability for which Ms Norberg sought and deserved proper medical treatment.

56. Punitive damages should be awarded for deliberate conduct resulting in a personal benefit for the tortfeasor. Here, Dr. Wynrib's deliberate conduct prolonged Ms. Norberg's chemical dependence, and Dr. Wynrib derived a personal benefit from it in the form of sexual gratification.

PART IV: NATURE OF ORDER SOUGHT

57. Based on the principles outlined above, LEAF submits that this appeal should be allowed and judgment entered for the Plaintiff against the Defendant for significant damages together with solicitor-client costs throughout.

All of which is respectfully submitted.

THE OUTCOME

Head Notes—Norberg v. Wynrib

Held: The appeal should be allowed.

Per La Forest, Gonthier, and Cory JJ: The sexual assault alleged here fell under the tort of battery—the intentional infliction of unlawful force on another person. One defence to this tort is consent, express, or implied. It has long been held that consent will be vitiated where it is obtained by force or threat of force, by fraud or deceit as to the nature of the defendant's conduct, or where it is given under the influence of drugs. The vitiating factors, however, are not limited to these. The concept of consent as it operates in tort law is based on a presumption of individual autonomy and free will. In some circumstances, a position of relative weakness can interfere with the freedom of a person's will. Accordingly, our notion of consent must involve an appreciation of the power relationship between the parties.

In certain circumstances, consent will be considered to be legally ineffective if it can be shown that there was such a disparity in the relative positions of the parties that the weaker party was not in a position to choose freely. Ordinarily, a special "power dependency" relationship will be required. The existence of one of these special relationships, however, is not necessarily determinative of an overwhelming power imbalance. The factual context of each case must be evaluated to determine if there has been legally effective consent. The doctrine of unconscionability used to address the issue of voluntariness in contract law provides insight into the issue of consent in tort law which, to be genuine, must be voluntary.

In "power dependency" relationships, a two-step process is involved in determining whether or not there has been legally effective consent to a sexual assault. An inequality between the parties must first be proved, and then exploitation. A consideration of the type of relationship at issue may provide a strong indication of exploitation. Community standards of conduct may also be of some assistance.

There was a marked inequality in the respective powers of the parties here. The appellant was addicted to the heavy use of tranquilizers and pain killers. Her drug dependence placed her in a vulnerable position and diminished her ability to make a real choice.

An unequal distribution of power is frequently a part of the doctor-patient relationship. The respondent's medical knowledge and knowledge of the appellant's addiction, combined with his authority to prescribe drugs, gave him power over her. The second step of exploitation was also satisfied. The respondent abused his power over the appellant and exploited the information he obtained concerning her weakness to pursue his own personal interests. The sex-for-drugs relationship was markedly divergent from what the community would consider acceptable.

Respondent's assertions of compassion and interest in appellant's well-being did not square with his flagrant disregard for her need for treatment. If he were truly interested in her well-being, he would have helped her overcome her addiction. The argument that appellant took advantage of an old and lonely doctor would have had more credence had appellant initiated the sex-for-drugs arrangement.

The principle of *ex turpi causa non oritur actio* did not apply so as to bar the appellant's recovery for damages. To apply this doctrine would be to deny the appellant's claim on the same basis that she succeeded in the tort action: because she acted out of her desperation for the addictive drug. Public policy would not countenance giving to the appellant with one hand and then taking away with the other. The offence of "double-doctoring" was irrelevant here because no causative link existed between the injury and the crime. The appellant, if she had been relying on the respondent alone for her drug supply rather than "double-doctoring," would have suffered the same harm.

The tort of battery is actionable without proof of damage and liability is not confined to foreseeable consequences. Aggravated damages, where general damages are assessed taking into account any aggravating features of the case, may be awarded if the battery has occurred in humiliating or undignified circumstances. These must be distinguished from punitive or exemplary damages which are awarded to punish the defendant and make an example of him or her to deter others from committing the same tort. Here the appellant was entitled to aggravated damages for the indignity of the sexual assault. Respondent's conduct merited condemnation by the court. Although not harsh, vindictive or malicious, it was nevertheless reprehensible and it offended the ordinary standards of decent conduct in the community. Further, the exchange of drugs for sex by a doctor in a position of power is conduct that cries out for deterrence and an award of punitive damages was accordingly appropriate.

Per L'Heureux-Dubé and McLachlin JJ: *Only the principles applicable to fiduciary relationships and their breach encompass the true relationship between the parties and the gravity of the wrong done by the defendant. (paraphrased from passage at p. 269)*

The fiduciary duty which existed here was breached. The plaintiff was entitled to recover the appropriate damages at equity.

The doctor-patient relationship can be conceptualized as a creature of contract or of tort but its most fundamental characteristic, rooted in the trust inherent in the relationship, is its fiduciary nature. The foundation and ambit of the fiduciary obligation are conceptually distinct from the foundation and ambit of contract and tort. In negligence and contract the parties are taken to be independent and equal actors, concerned primarily with their own self-interest. Consequently, the law seeks a balance between enforcing obligations by awarding compensation when those obligations are breached, and preserving optimum freedom for those involved in the relationship in question. The essence of a fiduciary relationship, by contrast, is that one party exercises power on behalf of another and pledges himself or herself to act in the best interests of the other. When breach occurs, the balance favours the person wronged.

A fiduciary relationship is marked by the following characteristics: (1) the fiduciary has scope for the exercise of some discretion or power; (2) the fiduciary can unilaterally exercise that power or discretion so as to affect the beneficiary's legal or practical interests; and (3) the beneficiary is peculiarly vulnerable or at the mercy of the fiduciary holding the discretion or power. A physician owes his or her patient the classic duties associated with a fiduciary relationship—"loyalty, good faith, and avoidance of conflict of duty and self-interest."

That one party in a fiduciary relationship holds power over the other is not in and of itself wrong. Wrong occurs, however, if the risk inherent in entrusting the fiduciary with such power is realized and the fiduciary abuses the power entrusted to him or her.

A fiduciary duty arises because that power or discretion may be used to affect the beneficiary in a damaging way. Fiduciary duties are not confined to the exercise of power which can affect the legal interests of the beneficiary, but extend to the beneficiary's "vital non-legal or 'practical' interests." Fiduciary obligation is not confined to legal rights such as confidentiality and conflict of interest and undue influence in the business sphere. Here, societal and personal interests which are vital and substantial are being protected, and not what have been traditionally regarded as legal interests.

The third requirement is that of vulnerability. The beneficiary of a fiduciary relationship need not be per se vulnerable. It is only where there is a material discrepancy, in the circumstances of the relationship in question, between the power of one person and the vulnerability of the other that the fiduciary relationship is recognized by the law. Where the parties are on a relatively equal footing, contract and tort provide the appropriate analysis.

Women, who can so easily be exploited by physicians for sexual purposes may find themselves particularly vulnerable. Female patients are disproportionately the targets of sexual exploitation by physicians. (paraphrased from p. 297)

The doctrine applied notwithstanding a number of alleged conditions of defeasibility.

The short answer to the arguments based on wrongful conduct of the plaintiff is that she did nothing wrong in the context of this relationship. She was not a sinner, but a sick person, suffering from an addiction which proved to be uncontrollable in the absence of a professional drug rehabilitation program. The law might accuse the plaintiff of "double-doctoring" and moralists might accuse her of licentiousness; but she did no wrong because not she but the doctor was responsible for this conduct. He had the power to cure her of her addiction, as her successful treatment after leaving his "care" demonstrated, but instead chose to use his power to keep her in her addicted state and to use her for his own sexual purposes. An application of the clean hands maxim here amounts to nothing more than "blaming the victim."

Even taking a somewhat ... cautious approach ... as to when a doctor-patient relationship is characterized by sufficient power imbalance to render sexual contact between the parties a breach of the physician's fiduciary obligations, I can only agree that where such a power imbalance exists it matters not what the patient may have done, how seductively she may have appeared, or how self-interested her conduct may have been—the doctor will be at fault if sexual exploitation occurs. (p. 287)

Treating this case on the basis of breach of fiduciary duty adds a great deal, besides perhaps a duty of confidence and non-disclosure, to an action in tort or contract. The scope of the fiduciary obligation is not narrowly confined to matters akin to the duty not to disclose confidential information. Fiduciary obligations "must be reserved for situations that are truly in need of the special protection that equity affords," and the situation here is precisely one that is "truly in need of the special protection that equity affords." Given that the principles apply here to protect the plaintiff's interest in receiving medical care free of exploitation at the hands of her physician, the consequences are most significant. The defences based on the alleged fault of the plaintiff, so pressing in tort, may carry little weight when raised against the beneficiary of a fiduciary relationship.

Equity has always held trustees strictly accountable in a way the tort of negligence and contract have not. Foreseeability of loss is not a factor in equitable damages. Certain defences, such as mitigation, may not apply.

[T]he most significant consequence of applying the doctrine of fiduciary obligation to a person in the position of [the defendant is that] without doing so the wrong of a physician's abusing his or her position to obtain sexual favours from his or her patient ... can neither be fully comprehended in law nor adequately compensated in damages. (bits and pieces from the long paragraph beginning at p. 290)

Viewing the relationship at issue here as fiduciary will not open the floodgates to unfounded claims based on the abuse of real or perceived inequality of power. The ambit of the fiduciary obligation must be defined in a way that encompasses meritorious claims while excluding those without merit. The prospect of the law's recognizing meritorious claims by the powerless and exploited against the powerful and exploitive should not alone serve as a reason for denying just claims.

Damages should be assessed according to the principles which generally govern damages for breach of fiduciary duty, keeping in mind that the remedy awarded need not be confined to that given in previous situations if the requirements of fairness and justice demand more, and that reference to the principles of assessment in contract and tort may be of assistance in so far as they are relevant. The goal of equity is to restore the plaintiff as fully as possible to the position he or she would have been in had the equitable breach not occurred. Where the traditional equitable remedies of restitution and account are not available, equity awards compensation in their stead. In awarding damages the same generous, restorative remedial approach, which stems from the nature of the obligation in equity, applies. The fiduciary, being the person with the advantage of power, assumes full responsibility and cannot be heard to complain that the victim of his or her abuse cooperated in his or her defalcation or failed to take reasonable care for his or her own interests.

[The defendant's] breach of his duty to [the plaintiff] caused the following losses or injuries to her: (1) prolongation of her addiction; and (2) sexual violation (p. 295)

Punitive damages were appropriate here.

Per Sopinka J: Consent, either express or implied by conduct, is a defence to a claim of battery. Consent must be genuine and cannot be obtained by force, duress, or fraud or deceit as to the nature of the defendant's conduct, or under the influence of drugs. The factors relating to consent must be applied on a case-by-case basis rather than by the establishment of categories of individuals or relationships where apparent consent will never or rarely be considered valid. Certain relationships, particularly those in which there is a significant imbalance in power or those involving a high degree of trust and confidence, may require the trier of fact to be particularly careful in assessing the reality of consent.

The sexual contact, although clearly against appellant's wishes, was not without her consent. Her addiction, while it clearly inspired her willingness to engage in sexual activity, did not interfere with her ability to reason or her capacity to consent to the sexual activity which took place. The doctor did not exercise such control or authority that her submission could not be considered genuine consent. Indeed, appellant admitted to playing on respondent's loneliness. There is no basis on which to set aside the conclusion of the courts below on the issue of consent.

There is a fundamental difference between the issue of consent in tort law and the doctrine of unconscionability. The weight of academic and judicial opinion is that the doctrine of unconscionability operates to set aside transactions even though there may have been consent or agreement to the terms of the bargain. It is not that this doctrine vitiates consent; rather fairness requires that the transaction be set aside notwithstanding consent. The doctrine of unconscionability and the related principle of inequality of bargaining power are still evolving and are not yet completely settled areas of contract law. Importing the principles of unconscionability into the context of a battery claim has the potential to obscure the real question of whether, in all the circumstances, the plaintiff actually consented to the touching which constituted the alleged battery. The facts of this case are more accurately reflected by acknowledging that the appellant consented to the sexual contact and by considering the respondent's conduct in light of his professional duty towards the appellant.

Respondent's professional duty arose out of the doctor-patient relationship which is essentially based in contract. Breach, however, can be subject to action in either contract or tort. While certain obligations that arise from a doctor-patient relationship are fiduciary in nature, other obligations are contractual or based on the neighbourhood principle which underlies the law of negligence. Fiduciary duties should not be superimposed on common law duties. Whether the appellant relies on contract or negligence, the duty to treat was not vacated by consent. The abandonment of the contractual relationship between the parties required their mutual consent supported by consideration. The doctor-patient relationship here, notwithstanding any relationship independent of it, continued and was not abandoned. Neither the parties nor the medical community had any reason to believe that the parties had mutually abandoned their contract. Even if the contract were ended, the duty subsisted independently and formed the basis of the action in tort.

The plaintiff's consent to the defendant's conduct did not excuse the defendant from the obligations of his duty. He owed a professional responsibility both to the plaintiff and to the state not to mistreat her in a medical way by extending her period of addiction without proper treatment regardless of her wishes. Absent a clear statement by the respondent to the appellant that he was no longer treating her as her physician and an unequivocal consent to the cessation of treatment, the duty to treat the appellant continued until she attended at the rehabilitation centre on her own initiative and was treated.

The appellant's claim was not barred by *ex turpi*. Its application to defeat a tort action has been rare. Emphasis is now placed on preserving the administration of justice from the taint that would result from the approval of a transaction that a court ought not to countenance.

The sexual acts were causally connected to the failure to treat and must form part of the damage suffered by the appellant. Punitive damages, however, should not be awarded because the basis of liability is the breach of professional duty. While the sexual episodes are an element of damage, they are not the basis of liability.

IN THE SUPREME COURT OF CANADA

(ON APPEAL FROM THE FEDERAL COURT OF APPEAL)

BETWEEN:

THE CANADIAN COUNCIL OF CHURCHES

Appellant

(Plaintiff)

AND:

HER MAJESTY THE QUEEN

THE MINISTER OF EMPLOYMENT & IMMIGRATION

Respondents

(Defendants)

AND:

WOMEN'S LEGAL EDUCATION AND ACTION FUND (LEAF), CANADIAN DISABLITY RIGHTS COUNCIL, THE COALITION OF PROVINCIAL ORGANIZATIONS FOR THE HANDICAPPED, QUEBEC MULTI ETHNIC ASSOCIATION FOR THE INTEGRATION OF HANDICAPPED PEOPLE, B'NAI BRITH CANADA

Intervenors

Factum of the Women's Legal Education and Action Fund (LEAF) and Canadian Disability Rights Council (CDRC)

Canadian Council of Churches v. The Queen

INTRODUCTION

In 1987, the Canadian government proposed certain amendments to the Immigration Act: Bills C-55 and C-84. The amendments changed the procedures for determining whether applicants came within the United Nation's definition of a "Convention refugee." Among the controversial features of this legislation were (1) the designation of "safe countries" to which refugees could be deported; and (2) measures to prevent immigrants and refugees from physically reaching Canada before making their claims. (The emphasis of the legislation in preventing refugees from landing in Canada was a response to the 1985 Supreme Court of Canada ruling, *Singh v. The Minister of Employment and Immigration*, which held that anyone who was physically present in Canada, regardless of status, was entitled to the full protection of the Charter. The Court found that the treatment of refugee claimants by the Department of Immigration ran afoul of the Charter and ruled that refugee claims could not be denied without an oral hearing.)

This overhaul of the Canadian refugee determination process was heavily criticized by human rights advocates, church groups, and organizations working with refugees. Prominent among these advocates was the Canadian Council of Churches (the "Council"), a federal corporation representing a broad group of member churches. Immediately after Bills C-55 and C-84 became law on January 1, 1989, the Council sought a declaration that most of the new provisions violated the Charter and the Canadian Bill of Rights because they threatened the personal security of refugees. In an extensive Statement of Claim filed in Federal Court, the Council sought to invalidate 91 provisions of the new Immigration Act.

The federal government responded with a motion to dismiss the Council's application on the basis that the Council had no standing to contest the legislation. Originally, litigation by individuals was limited to situations in which a person could claim that a direct personal or proprietary interest had been harmed by the actions of another. Only the Attorney General was permitted to litigate matters that were deemed to be in the public interest, such as the constitutional validity of legislation. The Supreme Court of Canada eventually developed a three-part test to allow for public-interest litigation by groups other than the Attorney General. The test required an applicant to show: a serious issue as to the invalidity of the legislation being raised; a genuine interest as a citizen in the validity of the legislation; and no reasonable, effective or practical means by which the issue might otherwise be brought before the court.

The Federal Court Trial Division dismissed the government's motion. However, on the government's appeal, the Federal Court of Appeal took a narrower view of public-interest standing. It held that since many of the Council's claims were speculative and others could be pursued by a individual refugee claimant, the Council could pursue only four of the provisions it claimed were unconstitutional.

The Council appealed to the Supreme Court. The government cross-appealed, arguing that the Council should have been totally barred from contesting the legislation on any grounds. LEAF and the Canadian Disability Rights Council were granted leave to intervene together and urged the Court to expand access to public-interest litigation in a manner consistent with section 15's formal and substantive equality guarantees. The Coalition of Provincial Organizations for the Handicapped, the Quebec Multi Ethnic Association for the Integration of Handicapped People, and B'Nai Brith Canada also intervened separately to advance equality arguments.

FACTUM

PART I: FACTS

1. LEAF and CDRC adopt the statements of the appellant concerning the nature of its appeal, its constitutional challenge, the decision of Mr. Justice Rouleau and the decision of the Federal Court of Appeal.

> Appellant's Factum, paragraphs 1-2 (at 1), 9-10 (at 34),11-14 (at 5-6) and 15-19 (at 6-8), and Appendix A.

2. LEAF is a national, federally incorporated, not-for-profit organization founded in 1985 to secure equality rights for Canadian women under the Canadian Charter of Rights and Freedoms and comparable instruments at the provincial/territorial level. To this end, it engages in test case litigation, research, and public education.

3. CDRC is a national federally incorporated, not-for-profit, public-interest advocacy organization founded on May 4, 1987 to secure equality rights for people with disabilities by means of strategic test case litigation under the Charter and human rights legislation, and to undertake related research and public consultation. CDRC is made up of member organizations from the national, provincial/territorial and local levels, all of which represent persons with various mental and physical disabilities.

4. The litigation experience of LEAF and CDRC includes:

(a) acting as public-interest litigants, including interventions in the Supreme Court of Canada, provincial Courts of Appeal, and the Federal Court of Canada;

(b) sponsoring a public-interest group that initiates litigation or acts as an intervenor;

(c) sponsoring an individual who in a representative capacity makes group-based claims; and

(d) sponsoring the initiation of litigation by an individual who is a member of a disadvantaged group.

PART II: ISSUES

5. The appellant raises the question of whether the Federal Court of Appeal erred in holding that:

(a) the appellant should be denied standing to challenge certain provisions of the Immigration Act;

(b) certain claims contained in the amended Statement of Claim failed to disclose a reasonable cause of action; and

(c) certain claims described in the Statement of Claim were hypothetical or premature.

6. LEAF and CDRC address the issue of standing. Certain of their arguments in this regard necessarily and incidentally address the issue of prematurity. The issue of reasonableness of the cause of action is not addressed.

7. LEAF and CDRC propose a consideration of standing that is based on the Charter, and in particular, on the guarantees in section 15 thereof of equality before and under the law and of the right to the equal protection and equal benefit of the law. We explore in Part III how those guarantees affect the law of standing, both with respect to direct, "party" interests and also with respect to what has come to be known as "public-interest" standing. These arguments relate primarily to standing to challenge legislation on the ground that it violates the Charter.

PART III: ARGUMENT

The Traditional Basis of Private and "Public-Interest" Standing

8. The nature of the interest required by a private party who seeks standing to claim declaratory or injunctive relief where a question of public right or interest is raised was laid down in cases involving the private action for public nuisance. The interest required has thus been defined with respect to the role of the Attorney General as the guardian of public rights. Only the Attorney General has the standing to assert "a purely public right or interest" either on her or his own motion or at the instigation of another person. Consent of the Attorney General must be given for these so-called "relator" proceedings, and the decision about consent is not subject to review. Absent such consent, a private

party may proceed only upon showing either that interference with some public right interferes at the same time with some private right or that the plaintiff has suffered some special damage peculiar to herself or himself as a result of interference with a public right.

Finlay v. Canada (Minister of Finance), [1986] 2 SCR 607, at 617-620.

9. In this formulation, the "private right" has been said to be a right the invasion of which gives rise to an actionable wrong within the categories of private law—for example, a breach of contract or trust or the commission of a tort, or a right created by statute for the benefit of a plaintiff.

Finlay, supra, at 619.

10. When these ideas have been applied to cases where the validity of legislation or government action is at issue, the requirement of a special interest has been construed to mean that the plaintiff must establish "some special interest in the operation of the legislation beyond the general interest that is common to all members of the relevant society" or the general interest of the public in constitutional behaviour by government.

R v. Borowski, [1981] 2 SCR 575, at 576 (per Laskin CJ dissenting).

11. Private interest standing is available as of right if the applicant can satisfy the requirements of the test. If there is insufficient private interest to support an action, then the plaintiff must seek "public-interest" standing, the granting of which is within the discretion of the court.

Finlay, supra.

12. For public-interest standing, three criteria must be met: (1) there must be a serious issue; (2) the plaintiff must have a genuine interest as a citizen in the validity of the legislation; and (3) there must be no other reasonable and effective manner in which the issue may be brought before the court.

Canadian Council of Churches v. Canada, [1990] 2 FC 534, at 541.

Borowski, supra, at 598 (per Martland J).

13. LEAF and CDRC argue below that these two tests for standing constitute serious limitations on the right of access to the courts, which is essential for disadvantaged persons fully to realize their rights under the Charter. The disadvantaged, because of their life circumstances, often do not have the kinds of proprietary or pecuniary interests that would entitle them to, as of right, private standing. Judicial interpretation of the public-interest test has favoured those whose interests are most closely analogous to the rights underlying private interest standing. As a result of these restrictive interpretations, the very persons intended to benefit from the Charter lack the means to enforce its guarantees, a lack which compounds and exacerbates the effects of their exclusion from the legislative process. To deny access to justice to persons who are the most fragile, most marginalized, most isolated and most frightened is a profound denial of the equality before the law which underlies all of the Charter's guarantees, and is an essential foundation of the rule of law in a democratic society.

Equality Guarantees and Access to Justice

14. LEAF and CDRC propose that this Honourable Court review the basis upon which standing in public law matters has been granted, in light of the basic constitutional guarantees of equality which mandate equal access to justice. These guarantees are twofold: the specific provisions of the Charter, and the fundamental principles underlying the rule of law in a democratic society.

Charter Equality Guarantee

15. Decisions of this Court dealing with section 15 of the Charter, and with the human rights principles informing the Charter's equality guarantees, recognize that inequality has more than an individual dimension, adversely affecting members of historically disadvantaged groups through systemic practices, policies, and institutionalized barriers. Accordingly, remedies for inequality must also have a group dimension, and promote systemic equality, not just rectification of isolated individual harms. In establishing these principles, the Court is upholding the intention of the framers of the Charter and human rights codes.

Andrews v. Law Society of British Columbia, [1989] 1 SCR 143, at 154, 168, and 174.

Janzen and Govereau v. Platy Enterprises Ltd. et al., [1989] 1 SCR 1252.

Brooks v. Canada Safeway Ltd., [1989] 1 SCR 1219.

Action Travail des Femmes v. Canadian National Railway Company, [1987] 1 SCR 1114, at 1145.

R v. Turpin et al., [1989] 1 SCR 1296, at 1332-33.

16. An important aspect of this Court's approach to equality is its recognition that more important than simply the immediate or linear consequences of conduct may be taken into account in determining whether a denial of equality, or discrimination, has occurred. This acknowledgment of indirect effects reflects an understanding that actions can have long-term group consequences that may, upon examination, prove discriminatory, whereas an examination of more short-term, or individual, consequences of those actions may show either no discrimination or may fail to reveal its actual extent. This approach also recognizes that rules of general application that are constitutional on their face can have disparate and disadvantaging effects on particular disadvantaged groups.

Ontario Human Rights Commission and Theresa O'Malley v. Simpsons-Sears Ltd., [1985] 2 SCR 536.

William Black and Lynn Smith, "The Equality Rights" in Beaudouin and Ratushny, eds., *The Canadian Charter of Rights and Freedoms,* 2d ed. (Toronto: Carswell, 1989), at 564-67.

17. The Court signalled in *Andrews* that it would adopt a purposive approach to the Charter's equality guarantees and in subsequent decisions has recognized the central importance of promoting the equality of those groups who suffer social, political, and

legal disadvantage. In so doing, the Court has exhibited a welcome sensitivity to the nature of those disadvantages.

R v. Swain, [1991] 1 SCR 933.

8. LEAF and CDRC submit that these principles of constitutional equality shaped in the context of substantive rights apply as well to the determination of standing to initiate litigation for the enforcement of those rights. This Court's purposive approach to section 15 of the Charter requires that the rules governing standing to seek relief under section 52 of the Constitution Act, 1982 promote the equal benefit and protection of constitutional equality guarantees for disadvantaged groups and their members. This is so whether those rules relate to which persons or groups may have standing as of right, or to the exercise of judicial discretion to determine that an individual or group may have "public-interest" standing.

The Rule of Law in a Democratic Society

19. There is, moreover, an even deeper constitutional foundation for the re-evaluation of standing in Charter cases that reaches the normative level on which equality is fundamental to the rule of law.

20. This Court has identified equality as one of the underlying principles of a free and democratic society:

> A free society is one which aims at equality with respect to the enjoyment of fundamental freedoms and I say this without any reliance upon s. 15 of the Charter. Freedom must surely be founded in respect for the inherent dignity and the inviolable rights of the human person.

R v. Big M Drug Mart Ltd., [1985] 1 SCR 295, at 313-14.

21. Equality, as one of the fundamentals of a democratic society, is an important standard against which to assess the reasonableness and justifiability of limits on Charter rights.

R v. Oakes, [1986] 1 SCR 103, at 136.

22. This recognition of equality as a fundamental democratic value, underlying all Charter guarantees (including the specific guarantee of equality) has significant implications for the issue of standing. Equal access to justice must be regarded as an integral aspect of equality. Without access to court to defend—or, just as importantly, to assert—rights, citizens cannot be said to be truly equal. A right cannot be considered "inviolable" if it cannot be vindicated in court; a freedom is not "fundamental" if it may not be protected at the instigation of its holder.

23. Equal access to justice is also an essential foundation of the rule of law, to which the preamble of the Charter refers. If the rule of law is to be more than an utopian dream or an unrealized judicial ideal, there must be standing rules that permit access to the process for determining what the legal rules are and how they are to be interpreted and applied. Such access cannot be restricted to the privileged, for judicial decision

making in a framework determined only by the privileged will reflect the perspectives and interests of only the privileged. Rather, the judge-made rules of access to the courts should strive to encompass the deprived, the excluded, the silenced, and the dispossessed, whether as individuals or in groups.

BCGEU v. AG British Columbia, [1982] 2 SCR 214, at 229.

24. Equal access to justice also has critical implications for the development of the substance of the law. Courts decide the cases that are brought to them; the courts' caseload, as determined by litigants, determines what areas of the law will be developed. Precedent from areas actively litigated could well control decision making in areas that are not. A caseload that arises from the interests of the advantaged is very likely to create a body of law that privileges the interests of the advantaged, at the expense by omission or partiality of the disadvantaged.

Raoul Colinvaux, *The Law of Insurance*, 5th ed. (London: Sweet & Maxwell, 1984), at 11-12.

25. Applying both the substantive norm of constitutional equality and the deeper systemic concerns about equality in a democratic society to the analysis of the standing issue resonates very well with this Court's view of the important relationship between equality and participatory democracy. Equal laws, produced by equal access to law, enhance democratic accountability rather than diminish it.

26. Although this Court has held that equality is an essential attribute of a democratic society, there are many disadvantaged groups whose access to the democratic system exists in name only. Although they have the right to vote and to hold office (for some, comparatively recent acquisitions), they have, in practice, almost no access to institutions of decision making. Representation of disadvantaged persons in legislative assemblies, for example, is very low, because of barriers that are just beginning to be identified.

Canadian Charter of Rights and Freedoms, ss. 3 and 4.

Peter Hogg, *Constitutional Law of Canada*, 2d ed. (Toronto: Carswell, 1985), at 723.

Provincial Elections Act, SBC 1939, c. 16, ss. 2-5, as amended by SBC 1945, c. 26, s. 2 and SBC 1947, c. 28, ss. 5-14A.

Canadian Disability Rights Council (CDRC) v. Canada (1988), 21 FTR 268 (FCTD).

Sylvia B. Bashevkin, *Toeing the Lines: Women and Party Politics in English Canada* (Toronto: University of Toronto Press, 1986), at 70-79.

27. Exclusion from the legislative process is paralleled by exclusion from the judicial process. Barriers impairing access to justice in Canada include discrimination on the basis of disability, race, and gender. Taken singly, each of these factors can be very disadvantaging. Multiple disadvantages, experienced simultaneously, produce even graver limitations on participation.

Ontario, *Study of Access to Legal Services by the Disabled* (Commissioner: R.S. Abella) (Toronto: Queen's Printer, 1983), at 31-60.

Dodds v. Murphy (July 11, 1989), Toronto 1566/89 (Ont. SC) [unreported] (Gray J), at 13-24.

CDRC, supra.

Nova Scotia, Royal Commission on the Donald Marshall Jr. Prosecution, *Commissioner's Report: Finding and Recommendations*, 1989, vol. 1 (Halifax: Queen's Printer, 1989) ("Marshall Report"), at 275-97.

Alberta, *Justice on Trial: Report of the Task Force on the Criminal Justice System and Its Impact on the Indian and Métis People of Alberta* (Alberta: Queen's Printer, 1991) (*Justice on Trial*), vol. 1 at, 1-1 to 1-8.

Alberta, *Policing in Relation to the Blood Tribe: Report of the Public Inquiry*, vol. 2: Executive Summary (Alberta: Queen's Printer, 1991), at 7-13.

Sheila L. Martin and Kathleen E. Mahoney, eds., *Equality and Judicial Neutrality* (Toronto: Carswell, 1987), at iii-v, 402-9.

Sherene Razack, *Canadian Feminism and the Law* (Toronto: Second Story Press, 1991), at 133.

Isabel Grant and Lynn Smith, "Gender Representation in the Canadian Judiciary" in Law Reform Commission of Ontario, *Appointing Judges: Philosophy, Politics and Practice* (Toronto: Queen's Printer, 1991), at 60-63.

Canada, Department of Justice Bureau of Review, *Evaluation of the Divorce Act, Phase II: Monitoring and Evaluation* (Ottawa: Queen's Printer, May 1990) (Task Report), at 43 and 136-37.

28. There is evidence that this form of lack of access to justice is also occurring in the context of enforcement of Charter rights.

Gwen Brodsky and Shelagh Day, *Canadian Charter Equality Rights for Women* (Ottawa: Canadian Advisory Council on the Status of Women, 1989), at 130-44.

29. Effective exclusion of disadvantaged persons from a means of enforcing their Charter rights denies them what could be a remedy for action or inaction by a majoritarian legislature that deprives them of equality. This not only perpetuates their existing disadvantage; it compounds the harm of their exclusion from the democratic process and the alienating and disempowering effects of that exclusion.

30. The implicit obligation of legislatures to adhere to the Charter in framing legislation cannot by itself mean that the interests of the disadvantaged will be so effectively included in the legislative process that they need not be attended to in the judicial process. Much Canadian legislation pre-dates the coming into force of the Charter and the three-year delay in bringing into force section 15 was not used, as had been intended by its framers for an overhaul of legislation that offended the equality guarantees—at least in part because governments took a narrow view of what those guarantees required.

Saskatchewan, *Compliance of Saskatchewan Laws with the Canadian Charter of Rights and Freedoms: Discussion Paper* (Regina: Minister of Justice and Attorney General of Saskatchewan, 1984).

Equality Rights Statute Law Amendment Act, 1986, RSO 1986, c. 64.

Statute Law (Canadian Charter of Rights and Freedoms) Amendment Act, RSC 1985, c. 26.

Charter of Rights Educational Fund, *Report on the Statute Audit Project* (Toronto: CREF, 1985).

Charter of Rights Coalition (BC), *Women's Equality and the Charter of Rights and Freedoms* (The Legal Services Society of British Columbia, 1984, 1985).

31. Moreover, the disadvantaged and the advantaged will often have quite different views and interests concerning what is necessary to achieve compliance with the Charter and there has been judicial recognition that it is necessary to adopt the perspective of the disadvantaged in order to understand the discriminatory impact of a law. Given the underrepresentation of the disadvantaged in legislative assemblies, they have no direct way of ensuring that their concerns are addressed when legislation is framed. The need for the courts to act as a countervail, to repair legislative omissions, thus remains; in performing this task, access to the perspective of the disadvantaged is essential.

Zylberberg v. Sudbury Board of Education (Director) (1988), 65 OR (2d) 641 (CA), at 654-55.

Andrews, supra, at 152-53.

32. A right of access to the courts for the disadvantaged assumes particular importance in light of the fact that equality-promoting legislation directly affecting the rights of the majority or the powerful may confer private standing on already advantaged groups to challenge such legislation as a direct violation of their rights.

R v. Hess, [1990] 2 SCR 906.

R v. Keegstra, [1991] 2 WWR 1.

Phillips v. Nova Scotia (Social Assistance Appeal Board) (1986), 34 DLR (4th) 633 (NS CA).

Athabasca Tribal Council v. Amoco Canada Petroleum Company Ltd., [1981] 1 SCR 699.

Metropolitan Toronto Condominium Corporation Number 624 v. Ramdial and Salmon, unreported, January 29, 1988, Toronto M159582/88 (Ont. Dist. Ct.).

33. Thus, unless the disadvantaged have comparable access to the courts to press their claims for equality, the Charter may effectively operate as an instrument for the powerful to roll back the few gains of the disadvantaged. Such an outcome would be inconsistent with both section 15 of the Charter and the holdings of this Court.

Edwards Books and Art Ltd. v. The Queen, [1986] 2 SCR 713, at 779.

34. Access to court in order to bring a civil proceeding is markedly different from the kind of "access" to court inherent in defending a civil or criminal proceeding

brought by another. A party originating an action has greater opportunity to control the timing of the case, the framing of the issues involved, and the resources that will be deployed than that party would have if defending a proceeding brought at a time and on grounds chosen by another.

35. While the opportunity for the disadvantaged to seek to intervene in challenges to equality-promoting legislation is of some assistance in addressing questions of access, it is no substitute for the opportunity to initiate cases that address limitations or denials of equality. Intervenor status also has some serious procedural limitations. Decisions denying or allowing standing may not be reported or reported with reasons. The principles upon which standing is awarded, or denied, may thus be inaccessible, either for purposes of information, or importantly, for purposes of enhancing courts' accountability for the exercise of their discretion.

36. Intervenor status at the appellate level offers no opportunity to adduce evidence that would illuminate the extent and nature of the reasons for the legislation, or the disadvantage it addresses. It may come too late to put an individual claim of denial of equality in the proper systemic context. The intervenor at the appellate level has no control over the process, and cannot effectively address the issue of remedy.

37. Thus, LEAF and CDRC submit that a full right of access to justice will include the right of access to court to define and pursue rights and interests at a party's own initiative. Access that consists only of the "right" to defend oneself from the initiatives of others, or to seek a limited role in matters raised by others that may profoundly affect one's rights, is only a partial vindication of that access to justice, which is an essential part of the rule of law in a democratic society.

The Traditional Means in Determining Standing: Substantive and Systemic Equality Concerns

38. According privileged access to the courts based on private, proprietary interests, as does the traditional standing test, reinforces the disparity in power between those who are advantaged and those who are not. The advantaged are more likely to have established, recognized interests. The documented poverty of many disadvantaged persons means that they are much less likely to be able to base their claims on proprietary interests. Moreover, the disadvantaged may be advancing newer interests and as yet untried claims, since their perspective has only lately, and still partially, been brought into the formulation of legal principles. To allow the advantaged access to court as of right, while the disadvantaged petition for discretionary standing, exhibits a systemic preference for established interests that may themselves play a part in the creation of the disadvantage complained of.

Study of Access to Legal Services by the Disabled, supra, at 31-32.

Marshall Report, supra, vol. 1, at 163-64.

Justice on Trial, supra, vol. 1, at 8-1 to 8-3.

Doe v. Metropolitan Toronto (Municipality) Commissioners of Police (1990), 1 OR (3d) 416 (Div. Ct.), leave to appeal to CA denied Feb. 4, 1991.

Irwin Toy Ltd. v. AG Quebec, [1989] 1 SCR 927, at 1003-4.

Jones v. Van Zandt, 45 US (5 How.) 215 (1847).

Ableman v. Booth, 62 US (21 How.) 506 (1859).

Queen v. Hepburn, 11 US (7 Cranch) 290 (1813).

Scott v. Negro Ben, 10 US (6 Cranch) 3 (1810).

Re Drummond Wren, [1945] OR 788 (Chambers).

39. In order to address this problem, LEAF and CDRC submit that this Court should re-evaluate the traditional basis of affording private (or as-of-right) standing. Because of the close conceptual relationship that now exists between as-of-right standing and public-interest standing, such a re-evaluation of the former will inevitably influence the approach to the latter.

40. LEAF and CDRC propose that this re-evaluation proceed from a re-thinking of what interests merit or support access to the courts, particularly in Charter cases. The present narrow approach to this question fails to serve either the interests of those who depend on judicial remedies to actualize their Charter rights, or the institutional interest of the courts themselves in having the perspective of the disadvantaged to inform decision making and effective use of judicial resources. The approach suggested by LEAF and CDRC is intended to broaden the category of those who receive standing as of right, so that the disadvantaged are no longer reliant largely on judicial discretion for access to the courts in Charter cases.

41. Whether or not this Honourable Court determines that equality concerns mandate a change to the basis for as-of-right standing, LEAF and CDRC argue that the principles governing the exercise of judicial discretion with respect to "public-interest" standing are in need of re-evaluation. The present formulation fails to take into account the barriers to access that affect the disadvantaged, and the important "public interest" in ensuring real access to justice.

Private, As-of-Right, Standing

42. LEAF and CDRC submit that this Honourable Court should adopt an approach to "private" standing in constitutional cases that is more in keeping with the Charter's remedial purposes. What is necessary to arrive at such an interpretation may be seen by reviewing some of the elements of the present approach to "as-of-right" standing.

43. For example, it was held in *Finlay* that a strong, indirect, financial interest in the interrelationship between the Canada Assistance Plan and a provincial welfare program did not entitle a recipient under that provincial program to allege, as of right, that continued payments by Canada to the province were illegal because of the province's alleged breach of conditions under the Plan. He was required to seek "public-interest" standing.

44. *Finlay* was not a constitutional case. However, the approach in *Finlay* may make it necessary to observe that, in the constitutional context, a test of private entitlement to sue that does not acknowledge the more extended or systemic effects of

action or legislation is inconsistent with jurisprudence holding that such effects of legislation or actions, including less direct effects, can give rise to a claim for a violation of equality rights.

45. Similarly, strict insistence on the violation of a private right of the sort that can be vindicated in a tort action is inappropriate in the equality and anti-discrimination context because of the decision of this Court that the remedy for discrimination lies not in tort but rather in complaints under human rights legislation.

Seneca College of Applied Arts & Technology v. Bhadauria, [1981] 2 SCR 181.

46. The criteria for determining whether a right is private, and not public, take as the paradigm of a private right one that accrues to an individual. They thus fail to accommodate the concept of a group right or a right with a systemic dimension, or an individual claim on a group-based ground. Such a right is broader than an individual right but is more specific than a general public interest. To use such criteria for standing to bring court actions contrasts with the approach of human rights legislation, which conceptually and procedurally accommodates the possibility of group wrongs, group complaints, and group remedies.

Action Travail des Femmes, supra.

Saskatchewan Human Rights Code, part IV, s. 27.

47. It may thus be seen that the traditional test for as-of-right standing in a public law matter emphasizes the individual over the group or group-based right, and direct harm rather than indirect harm. This focus entails several consequences that are inimical to the full realization of Charter rights for the disadvantaged.

48. In order fully to understand the nature of the barriers to access that are imposed by a standing test based on direct individual harm, it is important to acknowledge that the circumstances of the disadvantaged include social, economic, and physical vulnerability, isolation, and fear of persons in authority or of sustained public visibility. Those conditions make it all the more difficult for them to think of confronting in litigation a governmental authority upon whose goodwill they may depend for income, chances of improvement, or even (as in the case of refugees) their very lives. The ways in which people experience their disadvantage vary from person to person, depending on individual characteristics and circumstances, and on the number and range of disadvantaging characteristics to which each is subject. Yet to focus only on the individual may be to miss the fundamental systemic problems that affect all: to "privatize" systemic disadvantage, locating it in each individual and her or his ability to cope with disadvantaging conditions, may well be to put that systemic disadvantage beyond detection and cure.

49. These characteristics of the disadvantaged make individual standing, based on direct harm, particularly inappropriate as the sole approach to the determination of as-of-right standing in Charter cases, as is illustrated by the following points.

50. In order to obtain standing under the "private rights" test as presently interpreted, it is necessary for the individual to show that he or she possesses the characteristic of disadvantage relied upon. Self-identification, in itself, may pose significant risks. As

well, individual members of disadvantaged groups who advance equality claims on behalf of the group may be subject to backlash based on bigotry toward the group as a whole. Group standing to reinforce the equality rights of the disadvantaged would reduce individual members' visibility and vulnerability to reprisal and would offer at the same time the support of others who share the same risks and collective interests. In this fashion, the sharing of the disadvantage and the action taken together about that disadvantage can provide a positive, empowering experience. It includes the individual rather than excludes her.

Action Travail des Femmes, supra.

51. Even where an individual is prepared to come forward initially, the nature of the power relations in equality litigation suggests that the action may not proceed to the stage where there is a final articulation of principle grounded in the group-based nature of systemic inequality. Many Charter litigants may find the advantages of an individual settlement overwhelming and irresistible, given the precariousness of their social position. The government may find strong inducement to compromise an individual case in order to save the cost of litigation and avoid the determination of a constitutional issue. The discretionary nature of government action may allow it to compromise many individual cases in this manner without establishing a new norm or constitutional precedent.

Quebec Multi-Ethnic Association for the Integration of Handicapped People, Minorité Invisible Minority (1990, vol. 1, no. 4), at 5-12 and 14-15.

"Equality Rights: Three Years Later," Annual Report of the Court Challenge Program, 1987-88, at 19-20.

52. An individual's case, pursued by an individual, may preclude the complex texture of the systemic harm that affects many individuals from being fully described to the court. While a court may be prepared to receive systemic arguments on the part of an individual, that person may not have the resources to make them, even if she sees the need to do so. Where a case is lost because the systemic arguments are not made, the loss affects all the disadvantaged, not just that individual. Even where an individual wins her own case on an individual basis, inattention to the systemic arguments may produce a decision that actually has a negative effect on the group.

53. Even a series of individual actions may fail to reflect all of the different ways in which a limitation or exclusion can disadvantage a group. Persons with different disabilities, or multiple disabilities, may be affected differently by any given instance of discrimination. For example, people who are blind and people who are deaf or hard of hearing experience differently their lack of access to government information services. Who can best address the barriers, an individual with a particular disability or a group of persons with various disabilities?

54. Persons identified by more than one of the grounds enumerated in section 15 or closely akin grounds (e.g., poverty) may suffer differential effects. It will be necessary for the court to consider what Razack calls "the indivisibility and simultaneity of disadvantages" (supra, paragraph 27).

55. Similarly, in terms of remedy, an individual action may fall short of addressing the real harm. An individual challenging a prohibition or limitation based on disability, for example, may be able to argue that the limitation should not apply to her individual circumstances rather than arguing that the limitation should be struck down because it discriminates generally against the group to which she belongs. The exceptional individual with a disability, who can bring herself very close to the norm of ability set out in the rule, thus achieves a remedy confined to exceptional circumstances. Even a series of such individual cases, producing solutions for exceptional individuals, would not address the general exclusion of disabled persons embodied in the law.

56. In any particular case, the identity and interest of the plaintiff may determine which of these approaches will be taken. In *Clark v. Clark*, for example, the father of a man with a mental disability sought a guardianship order to prevent his son from deciding where to live. Justin Clark resisted the application for guardianship by successfully demonstrating his own capacity to make decisions. While no Charter arguments were advanced, the case demonstrates how an individual approach may promote that person's interests while, at the same time, ignore a more general challenge to guardianship provisions that remove decision making capacity from all those with mental disability and are thus discriminatory. Who can initiate a case regarding the rights of people with mental disabilities can thus be seen to have a powerful impact on the way the issues are framed, and on the outcome.

Clark v. Clark (1982), 40 OR (2d) 383 (Co. Ct.).

57. For all these reasons, LEAF and CDRC outline below, at paragraphs 73 to 80, an approach that would extend as-of-right standing to groups as well as to individuals. This approach would acknowledge as an appropriate basis for standing not just direct harms, but also the extended or systemic effects of action or legislation. It is submitted that to encompass the more diffuse causality characteristic of discrimination is appropriate in light of this Honourable Court's decision in *Andrews*.

Public-Interest Standing

58. The three criteria for public-interest standing are that (1) there must be a serious issue; (2) the plaintiff must have a genuine interest as a citizen in the validity of the legislation; and (3) there must be no other reasonable and effective manner in which this issue may be brought before the court. In Canadian Council of Churches, Mr. Justice MacGuigan observes that the first two of these criteria address policy concerns about allocation of scarce judicial resources and the need to screen out the mere busybody. The third criterion attends to the need to ensure that "the court should have the benefit of the contending points of view of those most directly affected" by the laws at issue. The policy consideration said to underlie all of the standing requirements is the maintenance of an appropriate role for the courts and their relationship to other branches of government—the issue of justiciability. Mr. Justice McGuigan did not regard justiciability as being at issue in this case, and indeed remarked that it is seldom in issue in constitutional cases.

Supra, paragraph 12.

Canadian Council of Churches, supra, at 542.

59. LEAF and CDRC urge that courts avoid the perspective of the advantaged when interpreting the requirement that there be a serious issue. The disadvantaged cannot take for granted that their citizenship and dignity will be respected; they are subject to deprivations of both that would seldom come to the notice of a person in a more advantaged position. For Michael Huck the ability to choose the place in the theatre from which he could view a movie in his wheelchair had an important bearing on his dignity and autonomy. As this Honourable Court has recognized, this respect for the disadvantaged would mean that the negative effects of hate propaganda, for example, would not be characterized as mere "psychological pinpricks," that exclusions of Roman Catholics and Jews from opportunities would not be described as "unamiable" and "undesirable" but not contrary with public policy, and that sexual assault would not be compared with "stealing a goodnight kiss."

Canadian Odeon Theatres Ltd. v. Saskatchewan Human Rights Commission and Huck, [1985] 3 WWR 717 (Sask. CA), leave to appeal denied June 3, 1985, 60 NR 240 (SCC), at 744-45.

R v. Keegstra (1988), 87 AR 177 (CA), at 193, reversed at [1991] 2 WWR 1.

The Canada Trust Company (Leonard Foundation) v. OHRC (1987), 61 OR (2d) 75 (HC), at 93.

R v. Chase, [1987] 2 SCR 293.

60. The application of the requirement to demonstrate that there is "no other reasonable and effective manner" in which the issue may be brought before the court is a major barrier to access to the courts on behalf of groups animated by the interests of the disadvantaged.

61. Application of this standard has involved a review of the impugned legislation to determine whose interests are affected by it. Those interests are then, notionally, arranged in concentric circles, at the centre of which are the interests that would give rise to private standing—namely, direct harm to traditional interests. Radiating outward are interests that progressively decline in the degree to which they approximate the traditional test for as-of-right standing. A claimant to public-interest standing located in one of the outer rings will fail if the court regards it as more appropriate, or possible, for one in an inner ring to prosecute the case, even if there is no evidence that such a case will come forward at the instigation of the preferred plaintiff.

62. This whole assessment is predicated on "the direct harm" model described above at paragraphs 8 to 11. It favours those whose claim to standing relies most clearly on direct harm in the sense of injuries of the sort traditionally acknowledged in the legal system—namely, harm to property, risk of criminal prosecution, or deprivation of procedural legal rights. Those relying on more extended or complex causality of harm or on interests, however direct, more recently brought within the purview of legal analysis will fail to achieve public-interest standing if a candidate with a more traditional profile is present, or can be envisioned. Whether such a preferred candidate will even be able to prosecute his or her case to a conclusion, and what arguments she or he is equipped to make concerning group aspects of the disadvantage, do not typically figure in the analysis.

63. Application of this approach works a hardship on the disadvantaged. For example, it has meant that a well-respected group with a long history of advocating women's procreative choice was denied standing to challenge provincial restrictions on the availability of abortion. Even though the majority of the Court acknowledged that CARAL had an "unquestioned direct interest" in the subject matter of the litigation, it concluded that litigation by an individual physician facing personal sanctions under the law would be a more "reasonable and effective manner" of bringing the constitutional challenge. This decision subsumed the adverse systemic effects on all women's equality of restrictions on access to abortion under an individual male accused's conception of the constitutional interests at stake. It thereby not only affirmed the traditional unequal power relations, often paternalistic, between a doctor (usually male) and patients or potential patients (in this case female), but also legitimated that paternalism by which the privileged have so long presumed and been accorded standing to speak on behalf of the disadvantaged.

Canadian Abortion Rights Action League (CARAL) v. AG Nova Scotia (1990), 69 DLR (4th) 241 (NS CA), at 251.

64. In discounting the readiness and appropriateness of ensuring access of the disadvantaged to articulate and pursue their constitutional interests themselves, the Court failed to recognize and give effect to the democratic principles of self-determination that so many Charter guarantees promise to protect and promote. Relegating to the constitutional sidelines a group particularly well-situated to inform judicial decision making with the experience-based perspective of the disadvantaged not only undermines the community-building and autonomy interests essential to full equality before and under the law, it also deprives the Court of the most reasonable and effective voice and evidentiary basis for determining substantive equality claims.

65. It is important that the courts be aware of those factors that might keep disadvantaged individuals from initiating a case. While the court should show appropriate respect for the position of those disadvantaged who have a real capacity to pursue their rights in court, whether because of private means or group organization, it should not displace an appropriate claimant to public-interest standing simply on the basis of assumptions or speculation concerning the ability of another individual or group to proceed.

66. In the *CARAL* case, the physician was at least prepared to bring the challenge for which the court had notionally given him responsibility. In the instant case, the Federal Court of Appeal has assigned to imaginary individual refugees (or to a "group" of refugee claimants it seems to assume exists but never describes) the responsibility for challenging most of the refugee provisions of the Immigration Act. It has done so without regard to any showing of their ability or readiness to do so, and on the assumption that a series of randomly timed challenges to various provisions can effectively put before the Court the issues proposed to be canvassed by the Council, with a comparable evidentiary base. The Court's observation that there are challenges to certain (unspecified) provisions coming forward daily (at various unspecified stages of the review process) is no assurance that the cases will ever reach adjudication. LEAF and CDRC submit

that it is unlikely that a vulnerable refugee claimant would refuse a settlement offered by the government simply in order to pursue the point of public law underlying the claim.

Canadian Council of Churches, supra, at 552-53.

67. In his dissenting reasons in *CARAL*, the Chief Justice of Nova Scotia offers very important insights into why it is unsatisfactory to assume that the voice of the accused will invariably be the "reasonable and effective" way of bringing forward constitutional issues:

> Mr. Justice Matthews has placed much emphasis on the fact that between the decision in this matter, in chambers, and the hearing of this appeal, Dr. Morgentaler has been charged with contravening the Act. He is persuaded that Dr. Morgentaler is more directly affected by the legislation and that issues, identical to those that the appellant seeks to have decided, will be brought before the court. That the action against Dr. Morgentaler will not proceed is, in his opinion, a matter of pure speculation. With respect, I am unable to agree. There is always the possibility that Dr. Morgentaler will lose his interest in the abortion issue and plead guilty. It is possible that the Crown may not proceed with its case. It is possible that Dr. Morgentaler may die before the proceedings wind their way through the court system. It is possible that there may be a change of counsel so that no longer will there be the same counsel representing both CARAL and Dr. Morgentaler. If any of these events should come to pass, CARAL will be denied access, unnecessarily, to the judicial system.

CARAL, supra, at 245-46.

68. Nor does the usual way of applying the "no other reasonable and effective manner" test take adequate account of the fact that different potential claimants to standing may have interests that are opposed to one another. In the *Borowski* case, for example, Mr. Justice Martland stated that a doctor "protected" by section 251 and a woman desirous of obtaining an abortion would have no reason to attack the protections against criminal liability that Mr. Borowski sought to impugn. Yet a doctor, or a woman, may well have wished to challenge the protections for different reasons than those advanced by Mr. Borowski—namely, because they were too restrictive.

Borowski, supra, at 596-97 (per Martland J).

69. The overall effect of a restrictive approach to public-interest standing may be to extend the tenure of laws, or of aspects of laws, that are unconstitutional. In the instant case, for example, the sections of the Immigration Act that are left to be challenged by individual refugee claimants will endure until they are successfully challenged. There is no mechanism in our law for redressing the wrongs of those who suffer adverse consequences because of those laws in the meantime. The refugee case is a particularly serious example of this common problem, since unsuccessful refugee claimants will likely be lost to view once they are expelled from Canada. Nor, given the effective exclusion of the disadvantaged from representation in legislatures, is there a realistic hope of redressing denials of rights through the legislative approach.

70. A strict interpretation of public-interest standing has proceeded, in large part, from the view that the Attorney General is the appropriate guardian of public rights. This view originates in the law with respect to public nuisance and analogous areas. In the

Charter context, this assumption is inappropriate, since the Attorney General as a member of Cabinet is representative of majoritarian interests and is generally likely to uphold the legislation being challenged. The Attorney General may not always have an interest directly opposed to that of equality-seekers; in some cases Attorneys General, while not bound to do so, may defend equality-promoting legislation. However, it cannot be said that there will necessarily be an identity of interest between the Attorney General and the equality-seeker.

Ontario Law Reform Commission, *Report on the Law of Standing* (Toronto, 1989), at 39-51.

71. Charter cases differ as well from division of powers cases, in which all the rights at issue are governmental rights distributed by sections 91 and 92 of the Constitution Act, 1867 and comparable provisions. In that context, rights for individuals (or groups) arise derivatively, usually because the wrong level of government has purported to act in a particular situation or because no government is entitled to act. When dealing in this way with rights that are essentially governmental, it may be appropriate to canvass whether a government could, or should, be required to act before considering whether other interests may come forward. In the Charter context, it is not appropriate always to give priority to the possibility of governmental action, because the impugned legislation will likely represent an act of the state against the rights of the individual, or the attempt by the state to reconcile or compromise the competing rights of different groups. The only state interest that can be said to be at issue is the state's ability under section 1 of the Charter to limit or to balance rights. It cannot be expected that the state will have the same interest in the vindication of any particular Charter right as will the parties asserting that right.

Hogg, supra, at 635-38.
Irwin Toy, supra, at 993-94.

A New Approach to the Law of Standing in Constitutional Cases

72. LEAF and CDRC submit that the shortcomings of the traditional tests for both as-of-right and public-interest standing do not survive scrutiny under the equality guarantees of the Charter and the equality principles inherent in the rules of law in a democratic society. The following new approaches are proposed.

As-of-Right Standing

73. As outlined above at paragraph 57, LEAF and CDRC propose that as-of-right standing to challenge violations of the Charter should be available to groups of disadvantaged persons on their collective representatives for remedies to address both the direct and more far-reaching systemic effects of legislation. In this way, access to the Charter for the disadvantaged would parallel access to the human rights codes with which the equality guarantees of the Charter are so closely allied. This approach to as-of-right standing would also recognize the demonstrated capacity of such groups to mediate, mobilize, and give voice to the concerns of the disadvantaged themselves.

Andrews, supra, at 175.

Equality Rights Three Years Later, at 14-15.

74. Under this approach, disadvantaged persons could sue on a group basis or through a collective representative to vindicate rights under the equality guarantees and other sections of the Charter. The intervenors submit that existing case law concerning the standing of non-profit corporations in the context of the "public-interest" standing test suggests that such group-oriented actions should be permitted to non-profit corporations established by the disadvantaged, as well as to unincorporated entities or groups of plaintiffs.

Energy Probe v. AG Canada (1989), 68 OR (2d) 449 (CA).

Canadian Council of Churches, supra.

CARAL, supra, 244-45.

Federated Anti-Poverty Groups of BC, Karen Farrell et al. v. Attorney-General of BC (unreported, BC SC—07/13/91), May 31, 1991, at 31-36, per Parrett J.

75. This approach would mean that a group of disadvantaged persons, or a non-profit corporation established by such a group, could proceed on the same footing vis-à-vis standing to sue as could an individual who is adversely affected, directly or indirectly, by a denial of equality or other Charter violation. In order to have such standing, the group would have to comprise primarily those characterized by historic and continuing social disadvantage, and have among its objects the promotion of their equality. In any particular case, the group must demonstrate a proximity of connection between the issues raised and the disadvantage(s) characterizing those for whom it speaks. This standard, which addresses the requirement of concreteness, would mean that those whose lives would, or could, be affected by the outcome of the litigation would secure standing as of right, while those with primarily an abstract, academic, or general interest in an issue would require an exercise of judicial discretion to grant them standing.

76. A group approach to standing raises the question of whether, or how, to examine the question of whether the harm alleged is "speculative." The Federal Court of Appeal in this case refused to allow the plaintiff to proceed with several claims it regarded as too speculative. While respecting, and indeed proposing, a concreteness requirement in the context of actions to enforce equality rights, LEAF and CDRC point out that the issue of speculative harm poses special problems in this context. A requirement that all persons in the group have present damage, or (as in class actions) exactly the same damage, would prevent the court from being able to grasp the true dimensions of the inequality. A requirement that only those in present danger may bring actions fails to recognize that this immediate peril may be affecting someone already so vulnerable that she or he simply does not have the resources to mount an emergency court action, with its short deadlines, procedural difficulties and high resource demands.

Brooks, supra, at 1248-49.

Tremblay v. Daigle, [1989] 2 SCR 530, at 537-38.

77. In some cases now arising under the Charter, courts have recognized that there is no need for an applicant to await the actual violation of her or his Charter rights before taking action to protect them. Such an approach is particularly appropriate where legislation can have short- and long-term consequences that manifest its discriminatory effect in different ways, and where the persisting disadvantage of second-class status is embedded in legislation in a way that makes it a concomitant of daily life at all times, not just when acute threat (e.g., deportation) presents itself. Only when the various effects of legislation may be encompassed in one action is it possible to access the depth and extent of the Charter violation. Only a matter brought in advance of imminent peril may afford an opportunity for the reflection and comprehensiveness needed to address the true nature of the violation.

R v. Vermette, [1988] 1 SCR 985, at 992.

Operation Dismantle Inc. et al. v. The Queen et al., [1985] 1 SCR 441.

Re Praisoody (1990), 1 OR (3d) 606 (Gen. Div.), at 623-25.

Tyler v. MNR (1990), 91 DTC 5022 (FCA), at 5028-29.

Black and Smith, supra, at 565-67.

O'Malley, supra.

Huck, supra.

78. The case of *Evans v. The Queen* illustrates well the problems for the individual that arise when systemic inequality is left to manifest itself, and be challenged, in an individual case. The appellant, a young man with a mental disability, was arrested on a narcotics charge, denied his right to counsel, and interviewed at length about the circumstances of two murders. During the interrogation, the police falsely suggested to him that evidence linking him to one of the murders had been found at the site. Although he had initially told the officers he could not understand the warning about his rights, and protested his innocence on several occasions, he ultimately signed a confession because "they wouldn't give me a rest until I confessed." The confession was the sole basis of his conviction. Incarcerated for several years, he was ultimately successful in having the conviction overturned by this Honourable Court. A prospective challenge to such discriminatory treatment of accused persons with mental disabilities might have spared this accused, and others, such an ordeal.

Evans v. The Queen, unreported, SCC, April 18, 1991 (Reasons of Madam Justice McLachlin).

79. It is important to the disadvantaged to be able to challenge such a law prospectively, before all of its potential harms have materialized. Any requirement to accumulate a record of abuses would work a terrible hardship on those whose experiences would form part of that record but who, because of legal and practical barriers, could never receive retroactive redress for the harm they have endured. This Court has recognized that a person or corporation charged with an offence may raise as a defence the constitutionality of the legislation, whether or not any of its interests are, or could be, directly harmed by the alleged constitutional violation. The intervenors submit that the

systemic concerns for the constitutionality of legislation that underlie this principle also direct that not all potential harms of a piece of legislation need have materialized before they can be involved in a challenge to the constitutional validity of such legislation.

R v. Big M Drug Mart, [1985] 1 SCR 295.

80. Recognizing this new type of as-of-right standing in relation to Charter actions would have several consequences of benefit to the litigation process itself. For courts, group claims, by consolidating or supplanting piecemeal and discrete individual claims, would more efficiently allocate scarce judicial resources. Equally, consolidation would be less taxing on the scarce human and financial resources of equality-seeking groups who simply cannot afford to sponsor multiple individual claims. Finally, group claims would spare individual counsel "reinventing the wheel" for individual clients where resources have already been developed by groups advancing group claims.

"Public-Interest" Standing

81. Broadening the approach to as-of-right standing in this fashion would ensure that groups advancing the claims of the disadvantaged would have more secure access to the courts; they would less frequently have to rely on judicial discretion for their standing to sue under the Charter.

82. It is, nonetheless, necessary to re-examine the approach to "public-interest" standing. There may well be groups or individuals who cannot satisfy the criteria set out above at paragraphs 73 to 75 for as-of-right standing. These will be advancing claims for public-interest standing. If this Honourable Court declines to broaden direct access to court on behalf of the disadvantaged, the re-examination of the so-called public-interest standing test becomes all the more important. In this context, in particular, it is crucial to bear in mind that there is a significant public interest, in the truest sense of that phrase, in promoting access to courts, and thus to the means to enforce their constitutional rights, on behalf of the disadvantaged. Without an avenue to seek judicial redress for violation of their rights, the disadvantaged have only paper rights, without remedy, a situation fundamentally at odds with our sense of justice.

83. It is accordingly submitted that this Honourable Court should take the following view of "public-interest" standing. First, it should include at the centre of its analysis not only the traditional private rights that may be claimed by individuals in the context of criminal or property law, but also the group rights concept elaborated above at paragraphs 74 to 79. In analyzing the standing of public-interest claimants, the Court should examine the seriousness of the issues raised and the degree of connection between the issues raised by the group and the grounds of its disadvantage, as outlined in paragraph 75. However, the third branch of the test should address, not the question of "no other reasonable and effective alternative" as that is presently dealt with, but rather the policy issue said to underlie that question—namely, would the proposed standing ensure that the court has the benefit of the views of those affected by the law. In this connection, as in the area of "private" standing, we submit that the requirement of direct effect is too narrow; a public-interest standing test should also take account of the systemic and less direct effects of legislation.

84. In applying the third branch of the test, this Court should consider the extent to which the claimant to public-interest standing is animated by the concerns of the disadvantaged to advance their own interests, and the likelihood that the serious questions raised by the proposed litigation would be addressed, at all, or as well, by any other possible or present claimant. Where inquiry discloses that there is not at this point any other person or party realistically able, willing, or present to proceed with the litigation, concern for the material likelihood that the serious questions raised will be addressed at all should incline the Court to the granting of standing, in view of the harm that could be done by prolongation of unconstitutional behaviour. In assessing whether it is realistic to expect alternative litigants, the limitations of individual litigants described above should be borne in mind. In this context, as in the case of our proposals for direct standing, the Court should exhibit reasonable tolerance for "speculative" issues as long as the stake in the outcome of the person advancing them is more than academic.

Diversity

85. In its reasons, the Federal Court of Appeal addressed the plaintiff's argument that its statement of claim constituted an "internally integrated attack on the legislation such as none of the directly affected parties would be able to mount," particularly since it is able to proceed by action rather than by administrative review and thus build a factual base for its assertions. The Court rejected the argument on the basis of a point-by-point examination of the statement of claim, holding that "far from being a tightly woven case of meritorious argument," the statement of claim was a "loosely assembled congeries of separate assertions, many entirely lacking in merit."

Canadian Council of Churches, supra, at 553 and 556.

86. The intervenors submit that any attempt to describe the effects of disadvantage will, of necessity, address different circumstances and situations, because legislation affects different disadvantaged persons in different ways depending on their circumstances. This was recognized by this Court in its landmark *Andrews* decision, and again in *Brooks* and *Janzen*, when it held that it was not necessary for all women to be affected in order to characterize something as sex discrimination. In assessing the validity of a claim to standing on either a group-based "private" basis, or a "public-interest" basis, then, the court should recognize this diversity.

Conclusion

87. On the systemic level, the existing legal model of standing tacitly presupposes that interest groups will emerge, organize, articulate all valid interests, and balance each other, creating by their interplay the "public interest." Experience has shown that this dynamic often magnifies the power of powerful and established interests, exaggerates the voice of the advantaged in agenda-setting and policy formulation, and thwarts the development of responsive law. The rectification of the role of standing proposed herein mobilizes emerging Charter values—with emphasis on equality before the law under this Court's substantive interpretation of section 15 with the aim of increasing the democratic accountability of government and enhancing the rule of law.

PART IV: NATURE OF ORDER SOUGHT

88. LEAF and CDRC respectfully request that the order of the learned motions judge granting standing to the Canadian Council of Churches be restored, as that order is consistent both with the approach to as-of-right standing articulated above, and the view taken herein concerning public-interest standing.

All of which is respectfully submitted.

THE OUTCOME

Head Notes—Canadian Council of Churches v. The Queen

Held: The appeal should be dismissed; the cross-appeal should be allowed.

Recognition of the need to grant public-interest standing, whether because of the importance of public rights or the need to conform with the Constitution Act, 1982, in some circumstances does not amount to a blanket approval to grant standing to all who wish to litigate an issue. A balance must be struck between ensuring access to the courts and preserving judicial resources. The courts must not be allowed to become hopelessly overburdened as a result of the unnecessary proliferation of marginal or redundant suits brought by well-meaning organizations pursuing their own particular cases.

Status has been granted to prevent the immunization of legislation or public acts from any challenge. Public-interest standing, however, is not required when it can be shown on a balance of probabilities that the measure will be subject to attack by a private litigant. The principles for granting public standing set forth by this Court, while they should be given a liberal and generous interpretation, need not and should not be expanded.

Three aspects of the claim must be considered when public-interest standing is sought. First, is there a serious issue raised as to the invalidity of legislation in question? Second, has it been established that the plaintiff is directly affected by the legislation or, if not, does the plaintiff have a genuine interest in its validity? Third, is there another reasonable and effective way to bring the issue before the Court?

Although the claim at issue made a sweeping attack on most of the many amendments to the Act, some serious issues as to the validity of the legislation were raised. Appellant had a genuine interest in this field. Each refugee claimant, however, has standing to initiate a constitutional challenge to secure his or her own rights under the Charter and the disadvantages faced by refugees as a group do not preclude their effective access to the court. Many refugee claimants can and have appealed administrative decisions under the statute and each case presented a clear concrete factual background upon which the decision of the court could be based. The possibility of the imposition of a 72-hour removal order against refugee claimants does not undermine their ability to challenge the legislative scheme. The Federal Court has jurisdiction to grant injunctive relief against a removal order. Given the average length of time required for an ordinary case to reach the initial "credible basis" hearing, there is more than adequate time for a claimant to prepare to litigate the possible rejection of the claim.

[I]f the basis for granting status were significantly broadened, public-interest litigants would displace the private litigant. ... Public interest organizations are, as they should be, frequently granted intervener status. The views and submissions of intervenors on issues of public importance frequently provide great assistance to the courts. Yet that assistance is given against a background of established facts and in a time frame and context that is controlled by the courts. A proper balance between providing for the submissions of public-interest groups and preserving judicial resources is maintained. (p. 256)

IN THE SUPREME COURT OF CANADA

(ON APPEAL FROM THE APPEAL DIVISION OF THE SUPREME COURT OF NOVA SCOTIA)

BETWEEN:

HER MAJESTY THE QUEEN

Appellant

(Plaintiff)

AND:

M.L.M.

Respondent

(Defendant)

AND:

WOMEN'S LEGAL EDUCATION AND ACTION FUND (LEAF)

Intervenor

Factum of the Women's Legal Education and Action Fund (LEAF)

R v. M.L.M.

INTRODUCTION

M.L.M. was charged with the 1991 sexual assault of his sixteen-year-old step-daughter. At trial, the central issue was the complainant's credibility. Because M.L.M. denied any sex took place, the issue of consent was not raised, although the complainant did testify that, out of fear, she did not resist or react to M.L.M.'s approaches. M.L.M. was convicted. On appeal, the Nova Scotia Court of Appeal raised the question of whether the Crown had established beyond a reasonable doubt that the sexual acts were without the complainant's consent. As a result, supplementary written and oral arguments were allowed on this issue. The majority of the Court of Appeal set aside the conviction and acquitted M.L.M. on the basis that, because the complainant had not overtly objected to the sexual activity, lack of consent was not proved beyond a reasonable doubt. The Crown appealed to the Supreme Court. LEAF was the sole intervenor.

FACTUM

PART I: FACTS

1. The Intervenor, the Women's Legal Education and Action Fund (LEAF), is a national advocacy organization engaged in public education, research, and test case litigation. Its objective is to secure women's equality rights as guaranteed by the Canadian Charter of Rights and Freedoms. LEAF has developed extensive expertise regarding sexual violence against women and children and access to justice for sexual assault survivors.

2. LEAF was granted standing to intervene by this Honourable Court on November 9, 1993 on the basis that the issues raised in the appeal raise questions of national importance for women, and in particular for women who are the victims of sexual assault and abuse.

3. The Intervenor accepts the statement of facts as set out in the Factum of the Appellant, with the exception of paragraphs 1 and 3, adopts paragraph 1 of the Factum of the Respondent, and offers the following additional facts in order to clarify the historical and relational context in which the abuse of the Complainant is alleged to have been committed.

Facts of the Offence

4. The Complainant testified that the Respondent assaulted her on five separate occasions when he inserted his finger in her vagina and was "moving it around," performing cunnilingus and sucking her breasts. On none of these occasions did the Respondent speak to the Complainant before or during the sexual acts. The Complainant did not move to assist the Respondent in removing her clothes, nor did she say any words or make any movements. On three occasions: January 28th, January 29th, and the morning of January 30th, the Respondent perpetrated the acts upon the Complainant while she feigned sleep.

Testimony of Pamela Monk, Case on Appeal, at 113, l. 10; at 115, ll. 3 and 20; at 116, l. 4; at 117, l. 3; at 118, l. 17; at 163, l. 30; at 164, ll. 1 and 22; at 165, l. 7; 166, ll. 7 and 23; at 167, l. 32; at 173, l. 4; at 174, l. 3; at 175, l. 7; at 176, l. 36; and at 177, ll. 1 and 29.

5. The first assault, which involved digital penetration of the Complainant's vagina, occurred while the Complainant was in bed with the flu calling to her mother and the Respondent to remove her six-year-old sister from her room. The Complainant testified that the Respondent:

> came up and he was yelling at her [Felicia] to get out, and then all of a sudden, he started touching me.

Testimony of Pamela Monk, Case on Appeal, at 112, l. 32.

6. At the trial, when asked why she had not spoken out to the Respondent or called to her mother during the assaults, the Complainant testified on 13 separate occasions that she was "scared of him" and "scared to say anything":

> Q. Any reason why you didn't speak out to him when he was doing these things?
>
> A. I was too scared to.
>
> Q. What do you mean by that?
>
> A. I was scared of him. I was scared to say anything.

Testimony of Pamela Monk, Case on Appeal, at 124, ll. 12 and 14; see also: at 117, l. 25; at 124, ll. 12 and 14; at 146, ll. 10, 11, 13; at 174, l. 8; at 177, l. 33; at 178, l. 29; and at 185, ll. 20 and 24.

Historical Context of the Respondent's Sexual Acts

7. The Complainant testified that she had reported sexual abuse by the Respondent on two occasions prior to the January 28-30, 1991 incidents. The first report occurred sometime prior to February 1987, before she was 12 years old:

Q. Okay. Now, even before that, you made an allegation against Melvin of sexually abusing you by rubbing his foot against your private parts. Is that correct?

A. Yes.

Q. You told that to your mother.

A. Yes.

Q. You later told her that it wasn't true, correct? Is that a yes?

A. Yes. Because I was scared, because she just went up and … I don't know … I was just … I'm just scared of him period. And she went out and she talked to him about it and he said he didn't, and she came back and told me, and I was scared so I told her it wasn't true.

Testimony of Pamela Monk, Case on Appeal, at 146, l. 1.

8. In February 1987, the Complainant reported to the police that she had been sexually abused by the Respondent. The police explained to her that the Respondent could not be charged because there was no corroboration of her complaint. However, both the Complainant and her younger sister Felicia were removed from the Mason home by the Department of Community Services. Although Felicia was returned, the Complainant was made a permanent ward of the Crown in March of 1988, and remained in foster care, usually with relatives, for most of the period from February 1987 to June of 1990.

Testimony of Anne Pugh, Case on Appeal, at 92, l. 16; at 93, l. 23.

Testimony of Pamela Monk, Case on Appeal, at 142, l. 5.

9. As a consequence of these allegations of sexual abuse, a family court custody application ensued. The Complainant withdrew her allegations against the Respondent after two meetings with his lawyer. In her evidence, the Complainant explained that she had been coaxed by the Respondent and her mother to withdraw the allegations, and that the Respondent's lawyer had told her that, if she didn't change her story, her younger sister would be taken away and put in a foster home.

Testimony of Pamela Monk, Case on Appeal, at 186, l. 4.

10. The Respondent's defence throughout this case was that the Complainant had fabricated the allegations giving rise to the charges, motivated by her dislike for him. It was never the Respondent's position that the Complainant consented to the acts, nor that he honestly believed, on the basis of her behaviour, that she was consenting.

Summation by the Defence, Case on Appeal, at 218, l. 21.

11. On November 17, 1992, after the Respondent's conviction on the indictment, and prior to the hearing of his appeal by the Court of Appeal, the Complainant was interviewed by the police. For reasons not apparent in the Record, the Complainant had nowhere to live in late 1992 and returned to live in the Mason home. The Respondent and the Complainant's mother put pressure on her to tell the police that she had lied at trial and fabricated the allegations against the Respondent. They told her

that if she didn't change her story she could stay with the police instead of going home. However, she told the police that the evidence she had given at trial was true.

Statement of Pamela Monk, Exhibit B, Affidavit of Jane McClure, Case on Appeal, at 8.11-8.15.

Reasons for Judgment of the Trial Judge

12. The learned Trial Judge convicted the Respondent on the basis of the Complainant's evidence and found as follows:

> The young lady, Pamela Nicole Monk, tells a very simplistic story. If believed, it would constitute a sexual assault against the accused in this particular case.
>
> The defence would have the court believe the young lady is a conniving person, is lying, changing stories from time to time for her own basic ends. Quite frankly, I do not believe this. Basically, I believe the testimony of the young lady. I think she was truthful. I think she was straightforward.

Reasons for Judgment of Palmeter CJ, Case on Appeal, at 233, l. 8.

13. In arriving at his decision, the Trial Judge found that the Complainant was an immature and "troubled young lady":

> Now, I say younger person because, although this young lady is seventeen years of age, my interpretation, my assessment of her is that she is not a mature seventeen year old young lady.
>
> I think she has been a troubled young lady. I don't know whether she still is or not, but she has been a troubled young lady. The evidence of the social worker indicated that. It's not unusual for victims of sexual abuse. In many cases they are never believed—never believed by even members of their own family.

Reasons for Judgment of Palmeter CJ, Case on Appeal, at 233, l. 123; at 235, l. 12.

14. The Respondent appealed against his conviction on three grounds, all unrelated to the issue of consent.

Notice of Application for leave to Amend Notice of Appeal, Appendix A, Amended Grounds of Appeal, Case on Appeal, at 8.3.

Reasons for Judgment of the Nova Scotia Court of Appeal

15. The Nova Scotia Court of Appeal raised the issue of consent on its own motion during the course of argument on the appeal and asked the parties to make submissions.

Reasons for Judgment of Freeman JA, Case on Appeal, at 252.

16. The Court of Appeal allowed the appeal, set aside the conviction, and entered an acquittal, having found that: "a properly instructed jury, acting judicially, would have been left with a reasonable doubt on the essential element of consent."

Reasons for Judgment of Freeman JA, Case on Appeal, at 261.

17. In arriving at its judgment the Court of Appeal reviewed the evidence and found:

> There is no evidence of any objection by the complainant, either by word or gesture. On the one occasion when she objected, in the living room while her mother was out of the house, the appellant did not press matters. Without the complainant's silence, indeed, her apparent complicity, the incidents could not have happened as they did. She explained her silence by saying she was "scared" but it was not clear she was afraid of the appellant or anything he might do. There was no evidence of threats or fear of the application of further force. There was no evidence the complainant was so afraid of the appellant that she dared not say "no" or "stop." She might have moved aside or removed his hand or cried out; she might have run downstairs. She did nothing to indicate that the appellant's advances were unwelcome.
>
> In the absence of the four vitiating factors listed in section 265(3), the complainant must be shown to have offered some minimal word or gesture of objection. Otherwise submission or lack or resistance must be equated with consent.

Reasons for Judgment of Freeman JA, Case on Appeal, at 256 and 259.

18. The Court of Appeal held not only that the Complainant's conduct was "consistent with" consent within the meaning of section 265(1) of the Criminal Code, but that the Complainant was "complicit" in her own violation.

Reasons for Judgment of Freeman JA, Case on Appeal, at 256.

PART II: ISSUES

19. Whether the Nova Scotia Court of Appeal erred in law in holding that submission or lack of resistance must be equated with consent for the purposes of section 265(1) of the Criminal Code.

20. It is the position of the Intervenor that the Court of Appeal equation of submission or lack of resistance with consent:

(a) is wrong in law and is inconsistent with the legal history of section 265(1);

(b) is inconsistent with the legal history of section 265(3); and

(c) violates section 15 of the Canadian Charter of Rights and Freedoms on the basis that the interpretation:

(i) is rooted in sexually discriminatory rape mythology;

(ii) denies the personhood of victims of sexual assault, thus denying them equality before and under the criminal law; and

(iii) violates guarantees of equal protection and benefit of the law by providing the least protection from sexual assault to those most vulnerable to such assault, and the least likely to be able to resist their assailants or to have their resistance perceived as resistance, by assailants and the courts.

PART III: ARGUMENT

Section 265(1) of the Criminal Code

The Legal History of Section 265(1)

21. It is submitted that in this case, the difference between the Trial Judge's decision that the Crown had proven a sexual assault beyond a reasonable doubt, and the Court of Appeal's judgment that the Crown had not proven lack of consent, turns on the Nova Scotia Court of Appeal's interpretation of consent under section 265(1) of the Criminal Code.

22. It is submitted that the Nova Scotia Court of Appeal reversed 100 years of Canadian rape and sexual assault law and disregarded the jurisprudence on consent in finding that the Complainant: "must be shown to have offered some minimal word or gesture of objection" or be deemed to be consenting.

Reasons for Judgment of Freeman JA, Case on Appeal, at 259.

23. At common law, rape was defined as unlawful and carnal knowledge of a woman forcibly and against her will.

J. Crankshaw, *The Criminal Code of Canada and the Canadian Evidence Act*, 2d ed., 1902, at 275.

24. This definition of rape was adopted in Canada and interpreted as requiring the Crown to establish:

> that the woman has been quite overcome by force or terror, she resisting as much as she could, and resisting so as to make the prisoner see and know that she really was resisting to the utmost; and that if this degree of coercion by the prisoner, and or resistance by the prosecutrix, have not been proved, the crime of rape has not been committed.

C.B. Backhouse, "Nineteenth Century Canadian Rape Law" D.H. Flaherty, ed., in *Essays in the History of Canadian Law* (Toronto: Osgoode Society, 1981), 200, at 213-20.

R v. Fick (1866), 16 UCQB 379 (CA), at 383.

25. In 1892, the Criminal Code was first introduced in Canada. The Code's definition of rape replaced the "against her will" terminology of the common law with "without her consent." This definition remained substantially unaltered until 1982. Rape was defined as:

> the act of a man having carnal knowledge of a woman, who is not his wife without her consent, or with consent which has been extorted by threats or fear of bodily harm, or obtained by personating the woman's husband, or by false and fraudulent representations as to the nature and quality of the act.

The Criminal Code, 1892, 55-56 Vict., c. 29, s. 266.

26. When sexual assault was incorporated into the general assault provisions under section 265(1) of the Criminal Code, the "without consent" terminology was maintained.

It is therefore submitted that requiring complainants to offer words or gestures of objection or resistance, or be found to be consenting is a return to the "against her will" standard for rape that was in existence prior to 1892. Such a standard is not only inconsistent with the legal history of section 265(1), but is also inconsistent with judicial considerations of the relationship between consent and acquiescence or compliance.

The Legal Meaning of Consent Under Section 256(1)

27. The Ontario Court of Appeal has stated in the context of the constitutionally protected rights of the accused that:

> The danger to constitutionally protected individual rights implicit in the equating of consent with acquiescence or compliance is self-evident and does not require detailed elaboration. ... Otherwise consent becomes a euphemism for failure to object or resist.

Acquiescence and compliance signal only a failure to object; they do not constitute consent.

R v. Wills (1992), 7 OR (3d) 337 (CA), at 348.

28. The British Columbia Court of Appeal has stated in the context of assault that:

> A consent forced upon him in the presence of his adversaries and not freely made would amount only to a submission, an acceptance of what may have seemed to be inevitable.

R v. Stanley, [1977] 36 CCC (2d) 216 (BC CA), at 234, per McIntyre J.

29. It is submitted that, in order for consent to be valid in all other areas of law, it must be freely given with an appreciation of all the risks and that in determining whether consent exists, courts must examine all the circumstances surrounding the assault.

R v. Jobidon, [1992] 2 SCR 714.

Wills, supra, para. 27.

Stanley, supra, para. 28.

30. As well, in the context of civil sexual assault cases, this Court has recognized that the relative power and powerlessness of the parties will affect consent:

> In my opinion, the unequal power between the parties and the exploitative nature of the relationship removed the possibility of the appellant's providing meaningful consent to the sexual contact.

Norberg v. Wynrib, [1992] 2 SCR 226, at 261, per La Forest J.

31. It is submitted that had the Nova Scotia Court of Appeal scrutinized the trial record for facts consistent with lack of consent, rather than for facts demonstrating resistance, it would have found ample proof of the Complainant's non-consent.

32. According to the evidence introduced at trial and accepted on appeal, the Complainant did not utter one word of consent during the assaults. There was evidence that she made no bodily movements or gestures of consent; there was evidence that she made no sounds signifying consent and made no movements of assistance as the Respondent rearranged her clothes in order to access parts of her body. Furthermore, it is clear that no

inference of consent could be drawn from the history of relations between the Complainant and the Respondent, a history marked by fear and two prior reports of sexual abuse.

Testimony of Pamela Monk, supra, at paras. 3-10.

33. It is therefore submitted that the Crown, in examination-in-chief, and the Defence, in cross-examination, covered each and every possible way in which the Complainant could have consented, and that the evidence thereby adduced constituted clear evidence of non-consent.

34. It is also submitted that the Complainant's decision not to call out to her mother during the assaults, or to enlist her support does not constitute evidence of her consent, as implied by the Court of Appeal. The record clearly indicates that the Complainant's mother consistently sided with the Respondent in pressuring the Complainant to withdraw both officially reported charges of sexual abuse, and in choosing not to believe any of her allegations about the Respondent.

Testimony of Pamela Monk, supra, at paras. 7-9.

35. Furthermore, the equation of non-resistance with consent presumes that an assault victim's primary goal is, or should be, to avoid the sexual assault. This assumption ignores the possibility that a woman threatened by sexual assault may perceive resistance to be futile or dangerous, or may have an entirely different goal such as: staying alive; minimizing physical injury; avoiding more invasive, frightening, or unwanted sexual acts; or getting the assault over with as quickly as possible.

36. It is clear that there is no one correct response to sexual assault:

> Women know that there is no response on their part that will assure their safety. The experience and knowledge of women is borne out by the *Canadian Urban Victimization Study: Female Victims of Crime* (1985). At page 7 of the Report the authors note:
>
> > Sixty percent of those who tried reasoning with their attackers, and sixty percent of those who resisted actively by fighting or using a weapon were injured. Every sexual assault incident is unique and so many factors are unknown (physical size of victims and offenders, verbal or physical threats, etc.) that no single course of action can be recommended unqualifiedly.

R v. Seaboyer; R v. Gayme, [1991] 2 SCR 577, at 652, per L'Heureux-Dubé J, dissenting in part.

Section 265(3) of the Criminal Code

The Legal Meaning of Section 265(3)

37. The Court of Appeal reviewed the facts and characterized the Complainant's behaviour as submissive and showing a lack of resistance to the sexual acts of the Respondent. The Court of Appeal then held:

> In the absence of the four vitiating factors listed in section 265(3), the complainant must be shown to have offered some minimal word or gesture of objection. Otherwise submission or lack or resistance must be equated with consent.

Reasons for Judgment of Freeman JA, Case on Appeal, at 258.

38. It is submitted that the Court of Appeal erred in reading section 265(1) conjunctively with section 265(3) to mean that where none of the circumstances codified in section 265(3) exist, proof of non-consent requires proof of resistance. Such an interpretation disregards the legal history of section 265(3) of the Criminal Code and its predecessors.

The Legal History of Section 265(3)

39. From 1892 until 1982 when the offence of "rape" was replaced with the offence of "sexual assault," the Criminal Code consistently recognized two conceptually distinct means of establishing the *actus reus* of criminal assaults. Either the Crown must prove absence of consent on the facts, or it must prove circumstances that legally vitiate consent. Prior to 1982, the offences of "assault," "indecent assault on a female," and "rape" all maintained this conceptual distinction and were defined as follows:

s. 244. A person commits assault when

(a) without the consent of another person or with consent, where it is obtained by fraud, he applies force intentionally to the person of the other, directly or indirectly;

s. 149(2) An accused who is charged with an offence under subsection (1) may be convicted if the evidence establishes that the accused did anything to the female person with her consent that, but for her consent, would have been an indecent assault, if her consent was obtained by false and fraudulent representations as to the nature and quality of the act.

s. 143 A male person commits rape when he has sexual intercourse with a female person who is not his wife,

(a) without her consent, or

(b) with her consent if the consent

(i) is extorted by threats or fear of bodily harm,

(ii) is obtained by personating her husband, or

(iii) is obtained by false and fraudulent representations as to the nature and quality of the act.

Criminal Code, RSC 1970, c. 34; SC 1974-75-76, c. 93, s. 21; SC 1972, c. 13, s. 70.

40. Therefore it is submitted that following the reasoning in *Jobidon*, when Parliament consolidated most sexual offence provisions under one assault section, it maintained the law's historic distinction between lack of consent as a matter of fact, and consent which is legally ineffective because it is culpably induced.

41. As established by this Honourable Court's ruling in *Jobidon*, had there been facts consistent with consent, the Court of Appeal's interpretation of section 265(3) was plainly wrong in law. In *Jobidon*, this Court held that section 265(3) merely codifies four circumstances long recognized by the common law in which consent to an assault will be legally ineffective, and that these four circumstances are not exhaustive.

Jobidon, supra, para. 29, at 744, per Gonthier J.

42. It is further submitted that there was no evidence in the trial record of any consent on the part of the Complainant that required the Court of Appeal to resort to section 265(3) to render consent legally ineffective, or to apply *Jobidon* to recognize new circumstances vitiating consent.

The Canadian Charter of Rights and Freedoms

Introduction

43. The Canadian Charter of Rights and Freedoms is the supreme law of the land. The common law and statutes must be interpreted and applied in a manner that is consistent with the fundamental values enshrined in the Charter.

Retail, Wholesale & Department Store Union, Local 580 v. Dolphin Delivery Ltd., [1986] 2 SCR 573, per McIntyre J, at 593 and 600.

44. Where a statute can reasonably bear a meaning that would accord with Charter values, such an interpretation should be favoured. In interpreting legislation, "the values embodied in the Charter must be given preference over an interpretation which would be contrary to them."

Hills et al. v. AG Canada, [1988] 1 SCR 513, at 558, per L'Heureux-Dubé J.

45. This Court has identified equality as one of the fundamental values of our society, against which the objects of all legislation must be measured. This Court has also stated that section 15(1) is the broadest of all guarantees in the Charter.

Andrews v. Law Society of British Columbia, [1989] 1 SCR 143, at 185, per McIntyre J.

46. In its most definitive interpretation of section 15, this Court identified the remedial purposes of the guarantee variously as: "to ensure equality in the formulation and application of the law"; "to protect those groups who suffer social, political and legal disadvantage in society"; "to ensure law-made distinctions among citizens do not bring about or re-enforce group disadvantage"; and "to promote a society in which all are secure in the knowledge that they are recognized at law as human beings equally deserving of concern, respect and consideration."

Andrews, supra, at 171, per McIntyre J, at 154, per Wilson J.

47. This Court has recognized that in criminal proceedings, section 7 guarantees to life, liberty, and security of the person encompass broader societal interests than those of the accused. These interests include those of complainants who, as a class, are entitled to security of the person and to equal benefit of the law as guaranteed by sections 15 and 28 of the Charter.

> It has been suggested that section 7 should be viewed as concerned with the interests of complainants as a class to security of the person and to equal benefit of the law as guaranteed by sections 15 and 28 of the Charter ... Such an approach is consistent with the view that s. 7 reflects a variety of societal and individual interests.

Seaboyer, supra, para. 36, at 603-4, per McLachlin J.

48. It is submitted that the pervasiveness of sexual violence and the law's historically ineffective response to it have consistently undermined the social recognition, achievement and exercise of the incidents of full personhood of women, and in particular, their security of the person and right to equal benefit and protection of the law, and that the resistance standard of consent adopted by the Court of Appeal would perpetuate this social and legal history of inequality.

Sexual Violence as an Equality Issue

49. This Honourable Court has recognized the link between sexual assault and women's inequality.

It cannot be forgotten that a sexual assault is very different from other assaults. It is true that it, like all the other forms of assault, is an act of violence. Yet it is something more than a simple act of violence. Sexual assault is in the vast majority of cases gender based. It is an assault upon human dignity and constitutes a denial of any concept of equality for women.

The reality of the situation can be seen from the statistics which demonstrate that 99 percent of the offenders in sexual assault cases are men and 90 percent of the victims are women.

Osolin v. The Queen, [1993] 4 SCR 595.

50. It is submitted that women as a class are singled out for sexual assault because they occupy an inferior social status as females, including being socially defined as appropriate targets for forced sex. As a result of these perceptions, women are more vulnerable to sexual assault. Social inequalities are also directly related to the incidence of victimization. Studies show that two factors operate in the rapist's selection of a victim: availability and vulnerability. The more disadvantaged, dependent, or relatively powerless an individual, the more vulnerable to sexual exploitation and violation.

51. Moreover, the factors that make all women and children potential targets of sexual assault operate to place certain women and children at even greater risk. For instance:

(a) Older women, women living in poverty, women with disabilities, rural women, lesbians, women of official language minorities, women of colour, young women, immigrant and refugee women, Inuit women, and aboriginal women are particularly vulnerable to violence.

(b) Young women are especially vulnerable to sexual assault. 51 percent of all sexual assaults happen to women between the ages of 16 and 21. Most of the violence is perpetrated by men known to the women, particularly those adult men in positions of authority—for example, teachers, fathers, and employers.

The Canadian Panel on Violence Against Women, "Part Three: Experiencing Violence—Populations" in *Changing The Landscape: Ending Violence—Achieving Equality* (Final Report, 1993), at 59-99.

(c) Three in four victims of sexual assault are female children, one in four are male children. It is submitted that children are singled out for sexual assault because of their age and sex, that is because of their vulnerability, accessibility, powerlessness, and perceived lack of credibility.

The Canadian Report of the Committee on Sexual Offences Against Children and Youths, 1984 (Badgley Report), at 198.

52. It is therefore submitted that the adoption of a resistance standard for consent in sexual assault law not only fails to provide security of the person and equal protection and benefit of the law to women as a class, but compounds the inequality of the least powerful and most vulnerable groups of women and children within society.

Rape Myths as a Factor of Women's Inequality

53. In Anglo-American legal systems, laws, as well as their judicial interpretation, have played a unique role in maintaining and legitimating women's inequality to men. Laws relating to sexual assault were developed, promulgated, and administered exclusively by men, the perpetrator group, reflecting and enforcing their perspectives about male and female sexuality. Such laws operated without reference to or regard for the experience and perspectives of women and children, the victim group, without concern for the inequality of the sexes, and in the absence of equality guarantees, constitutional or statutory.

Backhouse, supra, para. 24, at 200-47.

C. Boyle, *Sexual Assault* (Toronto: Carswell, 1984), chapter 1, esp. at 4-16.

54. Many legal doctrines governing sexual assault were exceptions to general rules of evidence; rules requiring evidence of recent complaint and corroboration; rules governing the admissibility and probative value of the complainant's reputation for chastity; and the complainant's sexual history are infamous examples.

Backhouse, supra, at 220-26 and 233-35.

Boyle, supra, para. 53, at 6-7.

55. With its successive reforms in 1976, 1982, and 1992, it is submitted that Parliament sought to reduce or eliminate the scope and operation of such discriminatory rules of evidence in the prosecution of sexual assault charges.

Criminal Law Amendment Act, 1975, SC 1974-75-76, c. 93, s. 8.

The Act to Amend the Criminal Code in Relation to Sexual Offences and other Offences Against the Person and to Amend Certain Other Acts in Relation Thereto or in Consequence Thereof, SC 1980-81-82-83, c. 125.

Preamble, Bill C-49, An Act to Amend the Criminal Code (sexual assault), 3rd Sess., 34th Parliament, 40-41 Elizabeth II, 1991-92.

56. This Honourable Court has also rejected gender-biased rules of evidence and in doing so has recognized the role that groundless rape myths and fantasized stereotypes have historically played in sexual assault cases. This Court has discredited such myths when confronted with them:

> A number of rape myths have in the past improperly formed the background for considering evidentiary issues in sexual assault trials. These include the false concepts that: women cannot be raped against their will; only "bad girls" are raped; anyone not clearly of "good character" is more likely to have consented.

Osolin, supra, para. 49, per Cory J, at 19.

> These inferences were based not on facts, but on the myths that unchaste women were more likely to consent to intercourse in any event, were less worthy of belief. These twin myths are now discredited.

Seaboyer, supra, para. 36, per McLachlin J, at 604.

57. In her dissenting judgment in *Seaboyer*, Madam Justice L'Heureux-Dubé sets out the most common myths and stereotypes, the first of which is:

> 1. Struggle and Force: Woman as Defender of Her Honour.

There is a myth that a woman cannot be raped against her will, that if she really wants to prevent a rape she can.

The prosecution attempts to show that she did struggle, or had no opportunity to do so, while the defence attempts to show that she did not.

Seaboyer, supra, para. 36, at 651-52.

58. In the case on appeal, the defence strategy played on long-standing rape myths. Its primary object was to portray the Complainant as a conniving liar motivated by animosity toward the Respondent.

Summation by the Defence, Case on Appeal, at 213, 1.18.

59. The Court of Appeal, in overturning the conviction, appears to have played on other long-standing rape myths.

60. It is submitted that the Court of Appeal's equation of non-resistance with consent appears to be based on the myth that every woman will struggle to prevent a sexual assault, and that absent a struggle, the victim must have been consenting.

61. The concept of consent is rooted in a belief in the equality of all individuals and respect for their autonomy, agency, and free will. Where consent converts what would otherwise be an attack on one's body, mind, and dignity into a lawful act, the interpretation of consent must be one that respects the principles of individual autonomy and agency of the person whose lack of consent is at issue.

While it is necessary to avoid an overly broad approach to consent, it is also necessary to recognize that valid consents reinforce the principle of individual autonomy, which underlies the rights set out in the Charter.

Wills, supra, para. 27, at 349.

62. It is submitted that the logical consequence of equating silence with non-resistance, and non-resistance with consent, is to render all females presumptively available for the sexual use of any man, unless and until they perform affirmative acts of

resistance. Putting the burden on the targets of sexual violence to resist, undermines the right of women and children to be free from invasions upon their person, thereby undermining their entitlement to respect as autonomous persons.

63. It is further submitted that the effect of a presumption that silence equals non-resistance, and non-resistance equals consent, is to deprive women and children of the equal protection of the law of assault.

64. Were Canadian law to respect the right of women and children to physical and mental integrity, it would promote an understanding of consent as something a woman does, rather than something a man thinks about a woman, or a court presumes about her. It would analyze consent from her perspective, as her choice to participate, in the context of her situation. It would not uphold a paradigm of sexual contact where a inert young girl, pretending to be asleep while being digitally penetrated by a stepfather, is presumed to be engaged in consensual sexual relations.

65. Were Canadian law to respect the right of women and children to physical and mental integrity, it would insist that consent, in sexual assault law, as in other areas of law requires individual free agency, an informed choice freely acted upon by an autonomous individual.

66. It is LEAF's submission that so long as the law legitimates a view of sexual relations that allows an assailant or a court to presume any individual sexually accessible and willing until she fends off an assault, it will legalize the sexual violation of the relatively powerless. Those most likely to be sexually abused and least likely to resist their assailant will be declared by law to be consenting "partners" in their own violation.

PART IV: NATURE OF ORDER SOUGHT

67. Based on the principles outlined above, LEAF submits that this appeal should be allowed, the conviction of the Trial Judge restored and that a declaration be made that the majority's interpretation of consent in the Court of Appeal is unconstitutional.

All of which is respectfully submitted.

THE OUTCOME

Head Notes—R v. M.L.M.

The judgment of the Court was delivered orally by

Lamer CJ—The appeal is allowed, the order of the Court of Appeal is set aside and the conviction is restored. Mr. Justice Sopinka will give the reasons of the Court.

Sopinka J—The Court of Appeal allowed the appeal from conviction on the ground that the decision of the trial judge was unreasonable and could not be supported by the evidence. In our opinion, taking into account all of the circumstances including the evidence of the complainant which was accepted by the trial judge, we are of the view that there was evidence upon which a jury, properly instructed and acting judicially, could reasonably convict. The trial judge was in the same position. The majority of the Court of Appeal was in error in holding that a victim is required to offer some minimal word or gesture of objection and that lack of resistance must be equated with consent.

IN THE SUPREME COURT OF CANADA

(ON APPEAL FROM THE FEDERAL COURT OF APPEAL)

BETWEEN:

HER MAJESTY THE QUEEN AND

CANADA EMPLOYMENT AND IMMIGRATION COMMISSION

Appellants

(Defendants)

AND

SHALOM SCHACHTER

Respondent

(Plaintiff)

AND

WOMEN'S LEGAL EDUCATION AND ACTION FUND (LEAF)

Respondent

(Intervenor)

Factum of the Women's Legal Education and Action Fund (LEAF)

R v. Schachter

INTRODUCTION

After his wife gave birth to their second child in July of 1985, Shalom Schachter took an unpaid leave of absence from work. In August, he applied for benefits under sections 30 and 32 of the Unemployment Insurance Act. Sections 30 provides 15 weeks of maternity benefits to biological mothers. Section 32 provides 15 weeks of childcare benefits to adoptive parents who may divide the benefits among themselves. The Unemployment Insurance Commission rejected his application as he did not fall within either of the groups. After an unsuccessful internal appeal, Schachter launched an action in the Federal Court Trial Division for a declaration that the Unemployment Insurance Act discriminated against biological fathers contrary to section 15 of the Charter. LEAF successfully applied to be an added party to the case. LEAF's principal argument before the Federal Court was that any increase in benefits to biological fathers could not be made by trading off existing maternity benefits for the biological mother.

On June 7, 1988, the Trial Division held that the Unemployment Insurance Act did indeed unconstitutionally discriminate against biological fathers by denying them the same benefits that were provided to adoptive parents. The Court then turned to the question of the appropriate remedy. Strayer J ruled out striking down section 30 or 32, and also rejected splitting the maternity benefits in section 30 between mothers and fathers because he found that maternity benefits were different in kind from childcare benefits as the former were meant to compensate for the unique physical and psychological effects of childbearing. Instead, Strayer J held that the only remedy consistent with section 15 was to extend the childcare benefits conferred by section 32 to biological fathers.

The government appealed to the Federal Court of Appeal solely on the issue of remedy, and again LEAF participated as an added party. The government argued that Strayer J did not have the jurisdiction to fashion an extension remedy, particularly where it required an appropriation of public funds. The government submitted that the only available option was to strike down section 32 completely.

The Federal Court of Appeal rejected the government's argument and the case proceeded to the Supreme Court, again with LEAF as an added party. In the interim, the federal government introduced amendments to the Unemployment Insurance Act to provide 10 weeks of childcare benefits to both natural and adoptive parents. Nonetheless, the government proceeded with the appeal on the grounds that judicial extension of underinclusive legislation set an undesirable precedent. LEAF, on the other hand, took the position that courts should have the discretion to extend legislation since this was a critical tool to making legislation consistent with not only the letter but also the spirit of the Charter's equality guarantees.

Intervenors who opposed the broad remedy ordered in the case were the Attorneys General for Ontario, Quebec, New Brunswick, British Columbia, Saskatchewan, Alberta, and Newfoundland. The Minority Advocacy Rights Council intervened to support the extension remedy as consistent with the equality guarantees.

FACTUM

PART I: FACTS

1. The Women's Legal Education and Action Fund ("LEAF") accepts the statement of facts contained in the factum of the appellant and relies, in addition, upon the following facts.

The Claims in This Case

2. In his original statement of claim, Mr. Schachter challenged as unconstitutional the provisions of section 30 of the Unemployment Insurance Act (the "Act"), which provides for 15 weeks of paid leave for the biological mother of a child who meets the eligibility criteria, as well as section 32 of the Act, which provides for parental leave for an adoptive father or mother. In that challenge, he alleged that, as a biological father, he was similarly situate to the biological mother, and to adoptive parents, and he claimed that failure to accord him a comparable opportunity for leave violated his right to equality under section 15 of the Charter. He sought either to have the mother's leave struck out, or to require that the 15-week period be shared in some fashion with the father.

Unemployment Insurance Act, 1971, SC 1970-72-72, c. 48, s. 30 (RSC 1985, c. U-1, s. 18).

Statement of Claim, paras. 13-17, Appendix "B."

3. This claim about the biological mother's benefits relied on the "similarly situated" reasoning that in *Andrews* this Honourable Court refused to follow. However, even that reasoning should not have produced a result favourable to the plaintiff: although the mother and father have in common that they are biological parents, they experience pregnancy and birth very differently. The trial judge concluded that section 30 of the Act was structured to benefit "pregnant women and pregnant women only," and only "incidentally" assist the woman in "whatever care of the baby she is able to provide" before

expiry of the leave. In arriving at this view, he relied on expert evidence that "underlined the physical demands placed on pregnant women and new mothers, which demands of themselves justify a period of at least 15 weeks free from outside paid employment." These demands include the possibility of difficult labour (20% of the deliveries in Canada today are by caesarian section), physical and hormonal changes, loss of sleep, and the special role of breast feeding. In fact, the learned trial judge found that the 15-week period was actually insufficient to accommodate the needs of the biological mother. These findings of fact were not challenged on the appeal.

Reasons for Judgment of Strayer J, Case on Appeal, at 98-99.

Andrews v. Law Society of British Columbia, [1989] 1 SCR 143, at 178-83.

Affidavit of Karyn Kaufman and Murray Enkin sworn April 14, 1988.

Appeal Book, Federal Court of Appeal, vol. 11, at 1581.

4. The plaintiff later amended his statement of claim to claim benefits under the Act in respect of his newborn child on the same terms, at the same rate, and to the same extent as benefits are payable under section 32 of the Act to an eligible adoptive parent. What the biological father has in common with the adoptive parent (whether father or mother) is the desire to care for the child; none of these three undergoes the particular experience of childbearing, childbirth, and recovery from childbirth, or establishment of breast feeding, which is the domain of the biological mother.

Amended Statement of Claim, paras. 13-20, Case on Appeal, at 3-6.

5. This amended claim of the father revealed two ways in which the Act was underinclusive. As he pleaded, it did not include "childcare" or "parenting" leave to biological fathers (leaving them as the only ones of the four parents in the Act without leave of any sort in connection with the arrival of a child). However, the Act also failed to provide a period of parenting leave for biological mothers, an omission significant in view of the trial judge's finding that the purpose of the section 30 pregnancy leave was to accommodate the physiological needs of the woman, with provision of care to the child merely "incidental." The combined effect of these two instances of underinclusiveness was to deny parenting leave to the biological parents, while making it available to adoptive parents.

6. LEAF was granted leave to intervene as a party to the action by the order of the Federal Court Trial Division dated June 30, 1987 and this order was confirmed by an order of this Honourable Court dated March 14, 1991.

Order of Federal Court Trial Division, dated June 30,1987, Case on Appeal, at 15.

Order of SCC dated March 14, 1991, Case on Appeal, at 73.

7. At trial, Mr. Schachter and LEAF challenged both aspects of the Act's underinclusiveness described in paragraph 5 herein. As to section 15 of the Charter, the defendants argued unsuccessfully that the biological father and the adoptive parent were not in the same circumstances, but they did not put forward any argument of justification under section 1 of the Charter.

Reasons for Judgment of Strayer J, Case on Appeal, at 91.

Findings of Federal Court, Trial Division.

8. As stated above at paragraph 3, the trial judge found that the primary purpose of the section 30 benefit is to meet the physiological needs of the mother before, during, and after childbirth, with only incidental relevance to childcare. In fact, the trial judge found that the evidence suggested that 15 weeks are not sufficient for both maternity and infant care.

Reasons for Judgment of Strayer J, Case on Appeal, at 99-100.

9. Benefits are provided to adoptive parents under section 32 of the Act for a period of up to 15 weeks on the placement of a child in their home for the purpose of adoption where it is reasonable for one of them to remain at home. The trial judge found that the purpose of the benefits for adoptive parents is an opportunity for parents to establish a relationship with the child when it is first placed in their home, a rationale equally applicable to childcare leave for the biological parents. The trial judge found it to be "obvious" that section 32 had "nothing to do with the particular pre-natal or post-natal needs and role of the natural mother herself."

Unemployment Insurance Act, 1971, s. 32 (RSC 1985, c. U-1, s. 20).

Reasons for Judgment of Strayer J, Case on Appeal, at 94, 98-99.

10. The trial judge held that the adoptive leave provisions in section 32 of the Act are inconsistent with the guarantee of equality in section 15 of the Charter. He found that the Act discriminates against natural parents because, unlike adoptive parents, they are not given a choice as to which parent will stay home and receive benefits after the birth of a child; natural fathers have no right to benefits after the introduction of a new-born child into the home; and there is no recognition in the Act of the need for natural parents to establish a relationship with a new-born child apart from the recognition of the physiological demands of pregnancy for the natural mother.

Reasons for Judgment of Strayer J, Case on Appeal, at 98-99, 108.

11. It was found that this distinction violated the section 15(1) guarantee of equality without discrimination based on sex and based on the ground of differences between natural and adoptive parents. The distinctions in the Act were rooted in sexual stereotyping of the respective roles of the father and mother generally, and specifically in relation to their new-born biological child: "... this approach is predicated on the belief that, upon the birth of a baby, its natural mother is the natural and inevitable care-giver and that the father is the natural breadwinner."

Reasons for Judgment of Strayer J, Case on Appeal, at 92-93.

12. Having found that section 32 violated the Charter, the trial judge considered that the court could either declare section 32 to be invalid or declare that natural parents are entitled to benefits equal to those provided to adoptive parents.

Reasons for Judgment of Strayer J, Case on Appeal, at 101-2.

13. A declaration of invalidity was found not to be "appropriate and just in the circumstances" because it would deprive of adoption leave benefits those persons qualified to receive them under section 32. The trial judge considered that where a statute granting social service or income insurance benefits is inconsistent with the Charter because it does not extend those benefits far enough, the remedy of invalidating the underextensive provision would rarely, if ever, be just.

Reasons for Judgment of Strayer J, Case on Appeal, at 102-14.

14. A number of alternative remedies were considered, including striking out various sections of the existing provisions in order to extend childcare benefits to natural parents. However, the trial judge rejected these alternatives because none of them was an adequate remedy for the unequal provision of benefits under the legislation.

Reasons for Judgment of Strayer J, Case on Appeal, at 101-7.

15. The learned trial judge considered unsuitable a declaration that natural fathers should be entitled to share the section 30 pregnancy benefits under the Act, because the effect of such a declaration would be to deprive mothers of benefits, which, it had been found, answered the physiological needs of natural mothers and were not related to childcare.

Reasons for Judgment of Strayer J, Case on Appeal, at 105.

16. The learned trial judge also rejected the possibility of striking out certain words in section 32 to extend that section to natural parents. He held that while it was possible to strike out portions of a legislative provision so that the remainder would be consistent with the Charter, to do so in this case would not extend to natural parents the same benefits as adoptive parents because the word "placement" in section 32 could not be interpreted to mean the birth of a child.

Reasons for Judgment of Strayer J, Case on Appeal, at 104.

17. The learned trial judge also rejected the alternative of striking out the limiting words in the section 32.1 added to the Act in 1988 to provide benefits to natural fathers in extreme circumstances like maternal death or disability. This remedy would have extended benefits to natural fathers but would not have treated natural parents equally with adoptive parents.

Reasons for Judgment of Strayer J, Case on Appeal, at 105.

Act to Amend the Unemployment Insurance Act, 1971, SC 1988, c. 8, ss. 2 and 3.

18. Having considered the possible remedies, the trial judge concluded that under section 24 of the Charter the only remedy that was "appropriate and just in the circumstances" and that would adequately protect the right to equality in section 15(1) of the Charter was the extension to natural parents of the childcare benefits in section 32, and he therefore issued a declaration that a natural father or mother of a new-born child was entitled to benefits under the Act on the same terms and conditions as adoptive parents.

Reasons for Judgment of Strayer J, Case on Appeal, at 104.

19. Section 22(3)(a) of the Act provides that the total benefit period for reasons of pregnancy, placement of a child or children for the purpose of adoption, prescribed illness, injury or quarantine, or for any combination of these reasons may not exceed 15 weeks. The trial judge held that these provisions should not preclude the natural mother from receiving benefits during the parenting leave period, even though she had received benefits during the pregnancy leave period, because of his finding that section 30 benefits are essentially for pregnancy and cannot be regarded as of more than incidental use for childcare purposes.

Unemployment Insurance Act, 1971, s. 22(3); RSC 1985, c. U-1, s. 11(3).

Reasons for Judgment of Strayer J, Case on Appeal, at 103-4.

20. Although the learned trial judge issued a declaration that the biological parents were entitled to benefits under the Act, he also ordered that the judgment be suspended until the time provided for appeal and, if an appeal were taken, until the final determination of the appeal. Such a suspensive order was consistent with his use of the declaratory power, which he described as follows:

> ... I consider it appropriate and just to make a declaration as to the entitlement of others to the same benefits and leave it to Parliament to remedy the situation in accordance with the Charter, either by extending similar benefits to natural parents, or by eliminating the benefits given to adoptive parents, or by some provision of more limited benefits on an equal basis to both adoptive and natural parents in respect of child-care. I am not in effect telling Parliament that it must follow one route or the other: all I am determining is that if it is going to provide such benefits it must provide them on a non-discriminatory basis. I am prepared to assume at this stage that Parliament will take the necessary action to render equal a system of benefits found by this Court to be unequal.

Judgment of Strayer J, Case on Appeal, at 110.

Reasons of Strayer J, Case on Appeal, at 102.

Finding of the Federal Court of Appeal.

21. On appeal to the Federal Court of Appeal, the appellants accepted the learned trial judge's finding that section 32 of the Act is inconsistent with section 15(1) of the Charter. As the appellant had not submitted at trial any justification under section 1 of the Charter for the legislative distinction, there were no substantive issues at stake on the appeal. Rather, the appeal dealt solely with the relief granted by the learned trial judge, with the justices noting the appellant's concession that, assuming a court had the jurisdiction to grant it, the remedy devised by the trial judge was just and appropriate in the circumstances.

Reasons for Judgment of Heald JA, Case on Appeal, at 114.

Reasons for Judgment of Mahoney JA, Case on Appeal, at 135.

22. The main issue raised on the appeal to the Federal Court of Appeal involved the question of whether the Court had jurisdiction under section 24(1) of the Charter to grant the remedy of extending the benefit in section 32 of the Act to natural parents or whether, having found that the legislation violated the Charter, the Court was bound to

declare it to be of no force and effect pursuant to section 52(1) of the Constitution Act, 1982. The appellants also raised the issue of whether the remedy constituted an improper amendment of legislation by the Court and whether it was impermissible because it resulted in an appropriation of public monies for a purpose not authorized by Parliament.

Reasons for Judgment of Heald JA, Case on Appeal, at 113.

Reasons for Judgment of Mahoney JA, Case on Appeal, at 134-35.

23. The majority of the appellate court dismissed the appeal and held that a remedy was available in these circumstances under section 24 of the Charter and that the appropriate and just remedy was to extend the benefits in section 32 of the Act to natural parents, as the learned trial judge had done.

Reasons for Judgment of Heald JA, Case on Appeal, at 132.

24. They held that where an individual's rights have been infringed by unconstitutional legislation a declaration of invalidity pursuant to section 52 is not the only remedy available. Rather, where the manner in which the substantive right was infringed makes it appropriate to do so, a court may grant a remedy under section 24.

Reasons for Judgment of Heald JA, Case on Appeal, at 114-16.

25. Moreover, they found that because what was omitted from section 32 of the Act (rather than what it contained) rendered it unconstitutional, it was permissible to grant a remedy under section 24, rather than declaring the section to be unconstitutional.

Reasons for Judgment of Heald JA, Case on Appeal, at 116.

26. The majority also held that the remedy under section 24 of the Charter should be one that adequately protects the Charter right that has been infringed. Where the right to equality in section 15 is infringed by underinclusive legislation, a mere declaration of invalidity is inadequate because it does not guarantee the positive right conferred by the section. The positive right could only be guaranteed by a positive remedy.

Reasons for Judgment of Heald J, Case on Appeal, at 121.

27. With respect to the Court's jurisdiction to grant a remedy that extends a benefit granted by legislation, the majority found that the Charter empowered the Court to grant such a remedy and that in doing so it does not in any way impinge on Parliament's prerogative to choose among constitutionally valid policy options in enacting legislation that conforms to the requirements of the Charter. Because the remedy is a temporary one, the Court is still leaving it to Parliament to extend similar benefits to natural parents or to eliminate the benefits altogether or to choose some other alternative to ensure that its legislation conforms with the Charter.

Reasons for Judgment of Heald JA, Case on Appeal, at 130-31.

28. The majority also held that section 24 of the Charter empowers the Court to extend benefits to groups aggrieved by an exclusion from benefits. Such an extension was found to be permissible even though the remedy granted results in an appropriation

of funds not authorized by Parliament. The Court held that this result had occurred in previous cases, and did not make the remedy granted by the trial judge impermissible.

Reasons for Judgment of Heald JA, Case on Appeal, at 132.

29. The Court concluded that the extension of benefits is the only remedy that respects the purposive nature of the Charter and gives effect to the equality rights enshrined in section 15 and therefore is the only remedy that is "appropriate and just."

Reasons for Judgment of Heald JA, Case on Appeal, at 132.

30. Mahoney JA, in his dissenting reasons, stated that the validity of the purposive approach to remedies is not open to question. He also accepted the "logic and force of the practical considerations," which he described as follows:

> Parliament can effectively act if it is not content with the remedy; a stay of the remedy can be ordered should the court consider it unduly disruptive, as in the Manitoba Language Right Reference, [1985] 1 SCR 721, and the remedy granted probably comes closer to the attainment of Parliament's real intentions than would a bare declaration of invalidity. They suggest that persons whose equality rights are violated by legislative underinclusion ought not be put in the "dog in the manger" position of seeking, as the only available remedy, to deprive others of some advantage and ask, if that is the necessary result, why any right-minded person would undertake such a Charter challenge. Persons ought not be deterred from asserting their rights. A declaration of invalidity does nothing to promote equality; equal access to nothing is not equality.

Reasons for Judgment of Mahoney JA, Case on Appeal, at 139.

31. He stated that if the learned trial judge had the power to grant the remedy he did, he would not disturb it, because:

> I do think that it does best fulfil a purposive approach to remedy; it does promote equality while a declaration of invalidity cannot, except in sterile formality.

Reasons for Judgment of Mahoney JA, Case on Appeal, at 139.

32. However, he stated that the constitution does not permit the remedy crafted by the learned trial judge. Section 52(1) does not provide a remedy in any real sense of that word, but "states a constitutional fact which no court can ignore." Moreover, whatever remedial scope section 24(1) might offer the court in circumstances that do not entail the appropriation of public monies, it does not authorize "a judicial appropriation of funds within the exclusive control of a sovereign Parliament or legislature."

Reasons for Judgment of Mahoney J, Case on Appeal, at 146.

33. This holding was, in turn, based on the learned justice's understanding that the remedy fashioned by the trial judge would offend the "firmly established," "fundamental" principle of the British constitution (originally expressed in the Bill of Rights of 1688 and incorporated into Canada by means of the preamble to the Constitution Act, 1867):

> That levying Money for or to the Use of the Crown, by Pretence of Prerogative, without Grant of Parliament, for longer Time, or in other Manner than the same is or shall be granted, is illegal.

Reasons for Judgment of Mahoney JA, Case on Appeal, at 144.

34. Citing the principle that "no money can be taken out of the Consolidated Revenue Fund ... excepting under a distinct authorization from Parliament itself," Mr. Justice Mahoney went on to say, "The appropriation of public monies by a court is as offensive to that principle as is its appropriation by prerogative."

Reasons for Judgment of Mahoney J, Case on Appeal, at 144-45.

PART II: ISSUES

35. LEAF submits that the issues on this appeal may be described as follows:

(a) What guidance can this Honourable Court offer with respect to the considerations that affect the determination of remedy where underinclusive legislation is found to violate an individual's rights?

(b) Does a court have jurisdiction under the Charter to make an order that extends the application of a law or results in an expenditure of public money?

36. In the context of this case, these issues might be simply described as:

(a) In what circumstances, for what reasons, and subject to what guidelines should the Court use what has been described as the remedy of "extension"?

(b) Does the Court have the authority under our constitution to use the extension remedy?

The questions are posed in this order because, LEAF submits, the answer to the first has a bearing on the interpretation of constitutional instruments that will answer the second. Consideration of the purpose and effects of a proposed extension may make it clear that it is institutionally appropriate for the courts to grant it within certain principled limits flowing from the Charter itself and the purpose of constitutional instruments like the Charter.

PART III: ARGUMENT

Considerations Affecting the Use of the Extension Remedy

Nature of the Right at Issue

37. A remedy under the Charter must be effective in light of the right in question and the manner in which it is infringed. As indicated by the topic headings within the Charter itself, it encompasses legal, political, and egalitarian rights. Where legal rights involving the freedom from government action are at stake, striking down is an effective remedy because it ensures individuals' freedom from government intrusion.

For example, *Hunter v. Southam Inc.*, [1984] 2 SCR 145, at 148.

R v. Big M Drug Mart Ltd., [1985] 1 SCR 295, at 313.

R v. Morgentaler, [1988] 1 SCR 30, at 80.

38. On the other hand, positive rights, including political and egalitarian rights, call for positive remedies. It would seriously undermine the practical value of constitutionally entrenched rights if the court's discretion regarding remedies under the Charter were

constrained in such a way as to mean that effective remedies are available only for one group of Charter rights. Where the right is an affirmative one, such as the right to vote or the right to equal benefit of the law, a remedy extending the benefit is particularly appropriate.

Hoogbruin and Raffa v. AG British Columbia (1985), 70 BCLR 1 (CA), at 6.

Marchand v. Simcoe County Board of Education (1986), 55 OR (2d) 638 (HCJ), at 661-63.

Mahe v. Alberta, [1990] 1 SCR 342, at 394-95.

The Purposive Approach to Remedies

39. It has been held that with respect to remedies, as well as substantive rights, the Charter should be given a generous and purposive interpretation. In selecting the appropriate remedy, the court should consider what best achieves the purpose of section 15(1) of the Charter, which has been found to be to promote equality and to alleviate the effects of disadvantage, not merely to create sameness or to eliminate distinctions. The structure of the Charter itself makes it clear that equality is to be promoted and disadvantage alleviated both by the Charter and in legislation. The trial judge and all justices of the Court of Appeal who heard this matter agreed with the purposive approach to Charter remedies.

Canadian Charter of Rights and Freedoms, Constitution Act, 1982, s. 32(2), as enacted by Canada Act 1981 (UK), 1982, c. 11.

R v. Gamble, [1988] 2 SCR 595, at 641.

Osborne et al. v. Canada (1991), 125 NR 252 (SCC), at 280.

Andrews v. Law Society of British Columbia, [1989] 1 SCR 143, at 170-72.

Brooks v. Canada Safeway Ltd., [1989] 1 SCR 1219, at 1238.

McKinney v. University of Guelph (1990), 76 DLR (4th) 545 (SCC), at 607-10, per Wilson J, dissenting on other grounds, and at 646, per La Forest J.

40. The court's approach to remedies should be consistent with the Supreme Court of Canada's recognition that the Charter should not be used as an instrument of better situated individuals to roll back legislation that has as its object the improvement of the condition of less-advantaged persons.

> In interpreting and applying the Charter, I believe that the courts must be cautious to ensure that it does not simply become an instrument of better situated individuals to roll back legislation that has as its object the improvement of the condition of less-advantaged persons.

Edwards Books and Art Ltd. v. The Queen, [1986] 2 SCR 713, at 779.

41. If the advantaged cannot use the Charter to roll back legislation intended to improve the condition of the disadvantaged, it follows that the courts should not devise an approach to remedies that means that genuine efforts by the disadvantaged to enforce their rights under the Charter would result in other (or the same) disadvantaged persons losing their rights under legislation.

42. Ensuring that groups or individuals have the same entitlement to no benefits is contrary to the purpose of the equality guarantee in section 15, and produces only sameness not equality. The majority in the Federal Court of Appeal agreed with the proposition put forward in oral argument by counsel for LEAF that such a result amounted to "equality with a vengeance" because of the punitive aspect of the result. The dissenting justice also accepted the logic and force of the "practical" consideration that "equal access to nothing is not equality."

Reasons for Judgment of Heald J, Case on Appeal, at 125.

Reasons for Judgment of Mahoney J, Case on Appeal, at 139.

43. The principle that equality cannot be achieved by reducing existing benefits has also been recognized in legislation.

Pay Equity Act, 1987, SO 1987, c. 34, s. 9(1).

Employment Standard Act, RSO 1980, c. 137, s. 33.

Canadian Human Rights Act, RSC 1985, c. H-6, s. 11.

British Columbia Human Rights Code, RSBC 1979, c. 186, s. 6.

Individual's Rights Protection Act, RSA 1980, c. I-2, s. 6.

Labour Standards Act, RSS 1978, c. L-l, s. 17.

Access to Charter Guarantees

44. If the only result of a challenge to underinclusive legislation is to deprive others of the benefits granted by the legislation, individuals who are members of disadvantaged minorities and others who fear this result will hesitate to enforce their rights under section 15 of the Charter. Such a chilling effect on equality litigation will exacerbate the trend, already documented, of the Charter being used primarily as an "instrument of better-situated individuals," a result that this Court sought to avoid in its interpretation of equality rights in *Andrews*. The logic and force of this consideration were recognized by Mahoney JA in his dissenting reasons in the Federal Court of Appeal.

Reasons for Judgment of Mahoney JA, Case on Appeal, at 139.

Brodsky and Day, *Canadian Charter Equality Rights for Women: One Step Forward or Two Steps Back* (Ottawa: Canadian Advisory Council on the Status of Women, 1989), at 56, 117-19 and 137-40.

45. Such a result would have the effect of inhibiting access by the disadvantaged to constitutional guarantees meant to alleviate their disadvantage. It would run counter to the strong interest in access to the Charter, which has been shown by this Honourable Court:

> Earlier sections of the Charter assure, in clear and specific terms, certain fundamental freedoms, democratic rights, mobility rights, legal rights and equality rights of utmost importance to each and every Canadian. And what happens if those rights or freedoms are denied? Section 24(1) provides the answer—any one whose rights or freedoms, as guaranteed by this Charter, have been infringed or denied may apply to a court of competent jurisdiction to obtain such remedy as the court considers appropriate and just

> in the circumstances. The rights and freedom are guaranteed by the Charter and the courts are directed to provide a remedy in the event of infringement ... it would be inconceivable that Parliament and the provinces should describe in such detail the rights and freedoms guaranteed by the Charter and should not first protect that which alone makes it in fact possible to benefit from such guarantee, that is, access to a court.

BCGEU v. AG British Columbia, [1982] 2 SCR 214, at 229.

These declarations emerged in a case dealing with lack of physical access to a court, but apply with equal, if not more, force to a case where the adverse results of attempts to enforce Charter guarantees have a chilling effect on future attempts at access.

Role of the Legislature and of the Court in Protecting the Disadvantaged

46. An important reason for judicial deference to Parliament is the belief that the legislature is the better forum for balancing different interests and making decisions about allocation of resources among contending policies. One of the reasons for this view is the belief that the legislature is a representative institution.

> When striking a balance between the claims of competing groups, the choice of means, like the choice of ends, frequently will require an assessment of conflicting scientific evidence and differing justified demands on scarce resources. Democratic institutions are meant to let us all share in the responsibility for these difficult choices. Thus, as courts review the results of the legislature's deliberations, particularly with respect to the protection of vulnerable groups, they must be mindful of the legislature's representative function. For example, when "regulating industry or business it is open to the legislature to restrict its legislative reforms to sectors in which there appear to be particularly urgent concerns or to constituencies that seem especially needy." (*Edwards Books and Art Ltd.*, supra)

Irwin Toy Ltd v. AG Quebec, [1989] 1 SCR 927, at 993-94.

47. However, it is now recognized that while legislatures may be "representative" institutions in the sense that they are popularly elected, they may not be representative in other important ways. Traditional ideas of who should be able to vote or to run for office, reflected in legislation, have meant that until comparatively recently, women, members of certain visible minority groups, aboriginal people, and persons with certain disabilities, were formally excluded from a role in our democracy. In spite of legislative or judicial alleviation of these exclusions, it cannot be said that these groups are now well-represented in democratic institutions. Their relationship to legislatures is still, most frequently, that of petitioners from outside, rather than full participants within.

Peter Hogg, *Constitutional Law of Canada*, 2d ed. (Toronto: Carswell, 1985), at 723.

Provincial Elections Act, SBC 1939, c. 16, ss. 2-5, as amended by SBC 1945, c. 26, s. 2 and SBC 1947, c. 28, ss. 5-14A.

Canadian Disability Rights Council (CDRC) v. Canada (1988), 21 FTR 268 (FCTD).

Sylvia B. Bashevkin, *Toeing the Lines: Women and Party Politics in English Canada* (Toronto: University of Toronto Press, 1986), at 70-79.

48. Indeed, the representativeness of the modern democratic state has been trenchantly criticized:

> What the system ... does *not* ensure is the effective protection of minorities whose interests differ from most of the rest of us. For if it is not the "many" who are being treated unreasonably but rather only some minority, the situation will not be so comfortably amenable to political correction. Indeed there may be political pressures to *encourage* our representatives to pass laws that treat the majority coalition on whose continual support they depend in one way, and one or more minorities whose backing they don't need less favourably. (Emphasis in original)

John Hart Ely, *Democracy and Distrust* (Cambridge: Harvard University Press, 1980), at 78.

49. Equality cases under section 15 of the Charter involve claims by the disadvantaged, members of "discrete and insular minorities." Their lack of influence on the legislative process has contributed to the historical disadvantage they have suffered. The purpose of section 15 is to overcome the effects of this disadvantage.

R v. Turpin et al., [1989] 1 SCR 1296, at 1332.

Ely, supra, at 151-53 and 160-61.

Andrews, supra, at 183.

50. A remedy that deprives such disadvantaged groups of existing benefits is likely to be particularly devastating because of their inability to mobilize the legislative process to restore what the Court has taken away in the name of someone else's rights. The Court should hesitate, then, to select a remedy that would leave the disadvantaged dependent on the actions of a majoritarian legislature to restore to them benefits that fulfil a constitutional purpose and are deficient only in that they are underinclusive.

51. The adoption of the phrase "discrete and insular minorities" from the *Caroline Products* case to describe those who may claim the benefit of section 15 of the Charter is instructive in considering the role of the court (as opposed to the legislature) in defending the interests of such minorities. Ely says, of the origins of the term, that its author (Justice Stone of the US Supreme Court) was referring:

> ... to the sort of "pluralist" wheeling and dealing by which the various minorities that make up our society typically interact to protect their interests, and [it] constituted an attempt to denote those minorities for which such a system of "mutual defense pacts" will prove recurrently unavailing.

Ely, supra, at 151.

52. Of this approach, he says:

> The whole point of the approach is to identify those groups in society to whose needs and wishes elected officials have no apparent interest in attending. If the approach makes sense, it would not make sense to assign its enforcement to anyone but the courts.

Ely, supra, at 151.

An Approach to the Extension Remedy

53. Because of the adverse consequences to the disadvantaged of having their court proceedings in search of equality result in the elimination of their statutory rights, or those of others equally or more disadvantaged, in circumstances where their powerlessness bodes ill for the prospects of restoring those rights through legislative action, LEAF proposes that a provision that itself promotes the equality of a disadvantaged group should not be struck down in the name of the equality of another disadvantaged group unless to do so would promote, or safeguard, the equality of both groups without resorting to further legislative action. Where it cannot be said that striking down would promote the substantive equality of both groups, then another alternative should be sought, and can be sought, given the provisions of section 24 of the Charter.

54. In considering which alternative to striking down it should implement, the court has several options: striking down with a suspensive provision, a mere declaration, various structural remedies, and extension.

> *Reference re Manitoba Language Rights*, [1985] 1 SCR 721 (striking down with a suspensive provision).
>
> *Philips and Lynch v. AG Nova Scotia* (1986), 27 DLR (4th) 156 (NS SCTD), affirmed (1986), 34 DLR (4th) 633 (NS CA) (mere declaration).
>
> *Marchand*, supra (structural remedy).

55. In selecting the remedy, the court should have regard to the principle enunciated in paragraph 52, namely, that the result should promote, or sustain, the equality of both the plaintiff (who has successfully established entitlement to Charter guarantees) and the group protected by the legislation. In fashioning the remedy, the court should also set against its traditional respect for legislative balancing of interests the realization that the Charter clearly mandates a role for the judiciary in safeguarding the interests of discrete and insular minorities. While the court may incline toward caution in reconciling its own role in vindicating minority interests with the role of Parliament in balancing a plurality of interests, LEAF submits that the Charter signals that such caution should not prevent performance of an appropriate judicial role. In particular, should Parliament itself consider that the court has gone too far in the protection of the disadvantaged, it may use the override provided in section 33 to reassert its majoritarian preferences.

56. Even though the biological father is not usually considered a disadvantaged person, LEAF submits that the principles outlined in paragraph 55 are relevant to the analysis of this case. The father here is challenging the stereotype that the mother should be the primary, if not exclusive, caregiver to infants and young children. Success of his argument could promote the equality of women by engaging the participation of fathers in childcare. If the remedy fashioned by the learned trial judge and approved by the majority of the Federal Court of Appeal were affirmed by this Court, the father's success in the section 15 argument would promote the equality of women (a disadvantaged group) by promoting the participation of fathers in childcare without sacrificing measures aimed at benefiting the adoptive parents. The remedy at trial also demonstrates

appropriate deference to the role of Parliament, and proceeds from a sophisticated analysis of a complete trial record, which judges are particularly well suited to perform.

57. The provision of leave to adoptive parents may itself be seen to further the equality-promoting purposes underlying section 15. Facilitating adoption is of benefit not only to those who do not have biological children, but also to the children who might not otherwise enjoy a stable family life and who obviously lack a political voice. Offering paid leave from work to adoptive parents may make adoption possible for families where both parents need to be in the paid labour force, thus keeping adoption from being a privilege afforded only to the well-to-do.

58. The option offered in the adoption context to either the mother or the father addresses the stereotype that only women do or should parent on a full-time basis. Women's traditional role as primary care-takers of children has been a barrier to their full participation in the work force and public sphere. Women have traditionally been disadvantaged by being required to bear a disproportionate burden of the costs associated with procreation. As the trial judge recognized, the benefits contained in the Act contribute, to some degree, to the amelioration of disadvantages historically suffered by women with respect to childbirth and childcare.

Judgment of Strayer J, Case on Appeal, at 92.

Brooks, supra, at 1237-39.

Mabel Penery French (1905), 37 NBR 359 (SC), at 365-66.

59. Striking down the adoptive leave provision in the interests of the biological father's equality would thus deprive adoptive parents of benefits that promote equality. It would also leave the father with no leave and create a situation where the only one of the four parents in this analysis with any leave at all would be the biological mother. Thus the "remedy" of striking down would reinforce the stereotypical position that, as between the biological mother and father, the biological mother should undertake childcare (doing it in a period which the Court held was primarily to attend to her physiological circumstances), and reinforcing the position that it is primarily couples who can afford to have one stay out of the work force altogether who are able to adopt children.

60. The remedy of extension in these circumstances preserves the equality-promoting benefit of the adoptive parents, and promotes the equality of both the biological parents. As Mr. Justice Strayer found, making parenting leave available to either biological parent would undercut the old stereotype that only the biological mother is a suitable caretaker for the child. By creating an environment where those biological fathers who are willing to depart from the stereotype are not penalized for doing so, and which recognizes the biological mother's unique interest in both physiological recovery and the possibility of choosing an extended parenting leave, the solution of extension realizes in this case the optimal expression of these parents' rights to equality on the basis of gender.

61. The evidentiary record before the trial court contained detailed evidence concerning the interest in parenting of all four kinds of parents affected by the decision, as well as the biological mother's unique physical circumstances; the trial judge commented on its high quality. The record also presented a full history of the legislation,

outlining not only the changes to the provisions at issue, but also the rationale for these changes; it emerged that the rationale underlying the present configuration of the benefits may have failed to take into account important evidence concerning the use to which the pregnancy benefits were put. Thus, in this case, as in perhaps few others, this Honourable Court may be able to conclude that the trial judge was making his remedial selection in adequate possession of the adjudicative and legislative facts bearing on the issue.

Deference to Parliament

62. The remedy selected by the learned trial judge is extension, with a form of suspensive provision: while setting out that the Charter requires extension rather than striking down, he also afforded to Parliament an opportunity to consider what action it wished to take in light of the constitutional principles he had laid down. In this respect, the remedy resembled that of this Court in the Manitoba Language Reference.

63. It is submitted that the remedy granted by the trial judge in this case does not interfere any more with Parliamentary authority than would a declaration striking down this section. To deprive adoptive parents of the childcare benefits granted to them pursuant to section 32 of the Act would be just as much a judicial amendment of the legislation enacted by Parliament as the extension of benefits granted by the trial judge. The remedy extending benefits does not impinge upon Parliament's prerogative to chose amongst constitutionally valid policy options by enacting new legislation.

Reasons for Judgment of Heald JA, Case on Appeal, at 130-31.

64. While setting out that the Charter requires extension rather than striking down, the trial judge's remedy affords Parliament an opportunity to act in accordance with the constitutional principles laid down in the judgment. The Court's remedy in effect establishes the state of the law pending such action by Parliament. Where a case involves benefits to a disadvantaged group protected by section 15, the court should avoid creating a legislative vacuum during this period. There is no certainty that Parliament will take any action. The group in question is disadvantaged in the sense that it has the least access to the legislative process. It is precisely in these circumstances that the court plays an important role in preserving and promoting equality in accordance with the Charter.

65. In the choice of remedy, the trial judge indicated his regard for the role of Parliament while at the same time attending to a problem that has a particularly harsh effect on the disadvantaged, although it is not confined to them: the problem of turning a court judgment into a practical reality. Mere declaratory relief requires follow-up either with the legislature, or program administrators, or both, that may simply be beyond the means of the disadvantaged. By providing a remedy in default of legislative action, the Court assisted the plaintiff and others in his situation in getting the legislature and administrators to take an interest in implementing constitutional behaviour.

66. It is submitted that this case does not raise questions of whether a court can legislate by proclaiming legislation in force in a province or determining the specific details of legislation. Those are the issues raised in the cases cited by the appellants as indicative of uncertainty with respect to the issue of the courts' power to legislate.

R v. Van Vliet (1988), 45 CCC (3d) 481 (BC CA), leave to appeal to SCC refused 56 CCC (3d) vi (SCC).

R v. Varga (1985), 48 CCC (3d) 281 (BC CA).

R v. Hamilton; R v. Asselin; R v. McCullagh (1986), 57 OR (2d) 412 (CA), leave to appeal to SCC refused (SCC, April 9, 1987).

R v. Paquette, [1988] 2 WWR 44 (Alta. CA), leave to appeal to SCC refused (1988), 85 AR 235n (SCC).

67. It is submitted that the remedy granted by the trial judge in the present case does not involve this type of legislative decision making because it merely extends an existing legislative benefit to a group required by the Charter to be covered.

68. Courts in the United States have considered that a remedy extending benefits constitutes a lesser interference with legislative intent than eliminating a valid and important policy clearly embodied in legislation. It is submitted that this approach does not involve a court in speculating as to Parliament's hypothetical intent.

Welsh v. United States, 398 US 333 (1970), at 354-56.

Califano v. Westcott, 443 US 76 (1979), at 90.

Consistency with Canadian and US Approaches to Remedy

69. It is submitted that in exercising the broad discretion granted to them by section 24(1) of the Charter, Canadian courts can properly look to the approach taken by courts in the United States in similar circumstances. A remedy extending benefits has been granted under the US Constitution where a law is found to be invalid not because its substance is impermissible but because it is underinclusive. This remedy has quite explicitly been adopted to extend benefits to fathers as a corrective to sex-discrimination patterns affecting women.

Weinberger v. Wiesenfeld, 420 US 636 (1975), at 641-42 and 651-53 (gender-based distinction in social security benefits contrary to Due Process Clause in Fifth Amendment).

Califano, supra (gender-based distinction in social security benefits violates Fifth and Fourteenth Amendments).

Heckler v. Mathews, 464 US 728 (1984) (pension benefits not extended equally contrary to Due Process Clause of Fifth Amendment).

Welsh, supra, at 361-65, per Harlan J, concurring in the result (exemption from military service found not to extend to conscientious objectors violated First Amendment).

70. The remedial route adopted by the trial judge is consistent with other cases where legislation has been found to be inconsistent with section 15(1) because benefits accorded to one group are denied to another and courts have granted remedies extending the benefit to both groups. Such an interpretation renders the legislation consistent with the Charter and avoids the necessity of striking down the legislation, thereby depriving everyone of the benefits.

See, for example, *Addy v. The Queen in Right of Canada* (1985), 22 DLR (4th) 52 (FCTD).

R v. Punch (1985), 22 CCC (3d) 289 (NWT SC).

R v. Hamilton; *R v. Asselin*; *R v. McCullagh* (1986), 57 OR (2d) 412 (CA), leave to appeal to SCC denied (1987), 59 OR (2d) 399n (SCC).

Tétrault-Gadoury v. Canadian Employment and Immigration Commission (1991), 126 NR 1 (SCC).

71. Courts interpreting section 15 of the Charter have granted remedies that have, in fact, extended benefits; this result has been achieved by striking out a provision that makes an exception to or an exclusion from the benefit of the law.

Re Blainey and Ontario Hockey Association (1986), 54 OR (2d) 513 (CA), at 531-33, leave to appeal to SCC denied 58 OR (2d) 274.

Silano v. British Columbia, [1987] 5 WWR 739 (BC SC), at 755.

Hebb v. R (1989), 69 CR (3d) 1 (NS SCTD), at 20-23.

72. It is submitted that the availability of such an extension of rights should not depend on whether the obstacle to extension is a specific limitation on the one hand or legislative silence on the other. Most legislation was drafted without the possibility of this effect in mind. As a result, there is no predictable pattern in statutory construction: sometimes a benefit is withheld by means of an explicit limitation and sometimes by silence. The availability of an effective remedy should not depend upon such accidents of drafting.

Hoogbruin and Raffa, supra, at 5-6.

Dixon v. AG British Columbia, [1989] 4 WWR 393 (BC SC), at 427-29.

Knodel v. British Columbia, unreported, August 30, 1991 (BC SC).

Does the Court Have the Power To Grant the Remedy of Extension?

Relationship of Section 24 of the Charter and Section 52 of the Constitution

73. Where Charter rights are infringed by legislation neither section 24 nor section 52 of the Constitution Act, 1982 provides the sole remedial route. Although legislation that is inconsistent with the Charter is of no force or effect pursuant to section 52, it is submitted that nothing in that section or in the constitution establishes that this is the exclusive remedy. An individual whose rights have been infringed is entitled to a remedy that is appropriate and just in the circumstances.

R v. Big M Drug Mart Ltd., [1985] 1 SCR 295, at 313.

Singh et al. v. Minister of Employment and Immigration, [1985] 1 SCR 177, at 221.

Jones v. The Queen, [1986] 2 SCR 284, at 323.

BCGEU v. AG British Columbia, supra, at 229.

Second Report of the Special Joint Committee of the Senate and House of Commons on the Constitution of Canada, 1978 ("Second Report"), reproduced in Bayefsky, *Canada's Constitution Act, 1982 and Amendments, a Documentary History*, vol. I, at 420-23.

74. It has been recognized that where, as here, legislation is inconsistent with the rights under the Charter not because of what it contains but because it fails to extend far enough, or because officials have failed to take the appropriate steps under it, the courts are not required to strike down the legislation under section 52 but, rather, should grant a remedy under section 24.

Mahe v. Alberta, [1990] 1 SCR 342, at 392.

75. Section 24(1) of the Charter grants to the courts a wide and unfettered discretion to fashion remedies that are appropriate and just in the circumstances of any particular case. In determining what remedy is most appropriate, a court should consider the right in question, the manner in which it was infringed, and the adequacy of any alternative remedies.

Mills v. The Queen, [1986] 1 SCR 863, at 965.

Big M Drug Mart Ltd., supra, at 313.

R v. Gamble, [1988] 2 SCR 595, at 641.

Rahey v. The Queen, [1987] 1 SCR 588, at 648.

Dixon, supra, at 427-28.

76. It has been held that the effect of the court's broad remedial power under section 24 is not merely that an appropriate remedy is available for the violation of a Charter right but that the court is able to grant a remedy which constitutes the "best possible solution." It is submitted that as the review of alternative remedies above indicates, the remedy granted by the trial division in this case is the "best possible" because it is the only one that effectively remedies the wrong and is consistent with the purpose of the right in question.

Re Kodellas et al. and Saskatchewan Human Rights Commission (1989), 60 DLR (4th) 143 (Sask. CA), at 201.

See paragraphs 13 to 18, above.

77. It is submitted that the legislative history of sections 24(1) and 52(1) does not support the conclusion that where a law is inconsistent with the Charter there is no role for section 24(1). The Special Joint Committee of the Senate and the House of Commons recommended in its "Second Report" (October 10, 1978) that the Constitutional Amendment Bill contain a provision clearly establishing the supremacy of the Charter over all other laws to ensure that the Charter would be interpreted as an overriding statute. Such a provision was, arguably, necessary to signal a clear departure from the principle of the supremacy of Parliament, and from the deference to that principle that had been embodied in the Canadian Bill of Rights.

"Second Report," reproduced in Bayefsky, supra.

Canadian Bill of Rights, RSC 1970, appendix III, s. 2.

78. The Committee also recommended that the Charter contain a provision by which effective remedies would be made available where rights were infringed. In effect, the courts should have the power to grant whatever remedy may be appropriate in the circumstances, including pecuniary damages, to enforce the protected rights and freedoms. ... Moreover, the courts should have the specific obligation placed upon them to grant an effective remedy where a denial of rights has occurred. They must not be allowed to decline to intervene.

"Second Report," reproduced in Bayefsky, supra, at 423.

79. Section 52 of the Charter is, to some extent, a legacy of the division of powers conflict that characterized constitutional law before the advent of the Charter. Invalidating *ultra vires* legislation, a solution to disputes between governments, can in many cases be suitably transposed to the context of a dispute under the Charter between an individual and one level of government. However, the Charter specifically contemplates that invalidation will not be a suitable remedy in all such cases. Section 24(1) of the Charter is based on the premise that the Charter gives rights to individuals, not governments, and that the creation of new rights for individuals vis-à-vis the state requires the creation of remedies over and above those which were developed to deal with the jurisdictional disputes of government actors.

80. Remedy has been defined to be a means of providing "reparation, redress, relief." In medicine, it is something that "alleviates pain and promotes restoration to good health." This plain English meaning of the term used in section 24 is inconsistent with the idea that violation of the Charter must in all or most cases result in invalidation under section 52, without more.

Shorter Oxford English Dictionary, 3rd ed., at 1791.

81. It is also clear that the new approach to defining substantive rights in the Charter (as distinct from the Canadian Bill of Rights) requires that section 24 be given the interpretation contended for by LEAF. For example, that the scope of the equality guarantees in section 15 was specifically intended to eliminate the problems of the old "equality before the law" definition has been recognized by this Court. The conceptual change wrought by the changed definition has already been signalled by this Court.

> It is readily apparent that the language of section 15 was deliberately chosen in order to remedy some of the perceived defects under the Canadian Bill of Rights.
>
> It is clear that the purpose of section 15 is to ensure equality in the formulation and application of the law. The promotion of equality entails the promotion of a society in which all are secure in the knowledge that they are recognized at law as human beings equally deserving of concern, respect, and consideration. It has a large remedial component.

Andrews, supra, at 170-71.

Brooks, supra, at 1243-45.

Bliss v. AG Canada, [1979] 1 SCR 183, at 191-92.

82. It is submitted that the language of section 24(1) clearly requires that a remedy be available where Charter rights have been infringed or denied, whether the infringement

arises because of a statute or because of the actions of government officials. It would seriously diminish the effectiveness of the Charter guarantees if courts were restricted under section 24 of the Charter to the remedial approach developed in relation to the division of powers under the constitution.

C. Rogerson, "The Judicial Search for Appropriate Remedies under the Charter: The Examples of Overbreadth and Vagueness" in R.J. Sharpe, ed., *Charter Litigation* (Toronto: Butterworths, 1986), at 285-87 and 305-6.

83. In the present case, the effect of imposing such a limitation on the scope of section 24(1) is to deny any remedy whatsoever to Mr. Schachter, to reaffirm that the task of childcare is primarily that of the biological mother and at the same time to eradicate the vested rights of others, which, because they are promoting equality, are consistent with the Charter's equality guarantees. Such a result is contrary to the clearly expressed intention in section 24 that a remedy should be available for an infringement of rights, and contrary to the purpose of the Charter's equality guarantees—which the Court has found, in a judgment not being appealed, to have been infringed by the legislation at issue here.

84. Finally, section 24 of the Charter accords to a trial court a wide discretion to grant an appropriate and just remedy. In the context of remedies under subsection 24(2) it has been held that an appeal court should not lightly interfere with the trial court's opinion. It is submitted that similar deference should be shown with respect to a trial court's exercise of the broad discretion under section 24(1) to fashion and remedy that is appropriate and just in the circumstances.

R v. Dugay, [1989]1 SCR 93, at 98.

Impact on the Spending Power

85. It is submitted that the remedy granted by the trial judge in this case does not constitute an improper interference with Parliament's authority over spending because that power is, like all exercises of governmental power, subject to the Charter. There is no basis in the constitution for finding that the Charter has a limited extent that does not reach to all exercises of government authority. The executive branch of government has been found to have a duty to act in accordance with the dictates of the Charter.

Operation Dismantle Inc. et al. v. The Queen et al., [1985] 1 SCR 441, at 463-64.

Retail, Wholesale & Department Store Union, Local 580 v. Dolphin Delivery Ltd., [1986] 2 SCR 573, at 598-99.

86. While the courts have recognized that, as a matter of constitutional law, they do not have authority to require a Minister of the Crown to make a specific expenditure, they have done so where there is no legislation requiring the expenditure and no other provisions of the constitution are involved.

Reference re Constitution Question Act (1991), 127 NR 161 (SCC), at 202-7.

Hamilton-Wentworth v. Ministry of Transportation (1991), 2 OR (3d) 716 (Div. Ct.), at 732.

87. In this case, the general language of both the Unemployment Insurance Act and the Financial Administration Act, referred to by Mahoney JA, is broad enough to include expenditures that might be required as a result of judicial consideration of the provisions of the Unemployment Insurance Act, whether pursuant to the Charter or to the Court's general power of construing statutes.

Judgment of Mahoney J, Case on Appeal, at 143-45.

McLeod v. Egan, [1975] 1 SCR 517, at 519.

88. In the Charter context, this Court has recognized that, although Parliament requires flexibility in choosing alternatives, it must comply with the Charter when granting benefits under the Unemployment Insurance Act, RSC 1985, c. U-1.

> Even allowing the government a healthy measure of flexibility in legislating in this area, the complete denial of unemployment benefits is not an acceptable method of achieving any of the government objectives. ...

Tétrault-Gadoury, supra, at 26.

89. The historical roots of Parliament's exclusive jurisdiction over spending are found in the context of restraints on arbitrary exercises of power by the executive branch of government. Parliamentary authority in this area was originally a countervail to the exercise of despotic power by the Crown.

90. Mahoney JA relies in his judgment on the long-standing principle of constitutional government that only Parliament (and not the executive) may authorize expenditures of public monies, and then purports to extend that principle to the relationship between the judiciary and Parliament.

Paragraphs 32 and 33, supra.

91. It is respectfully submitted that what Mahoney JA was referring to in his invocation of the Bill of Rights of 1688 and the long-standing principle concerning Parliamentary control over spending was a constitutional convention dealing with the relations between the two Houses of Parliament and between Parliament and the executive. In Canada, that convention is given expression, to a certain extent, in the provisions of sections 53 and 54 of the Constitution Act, 1867.

DeSmith and Brazier, *Constitutional and Administrative Law*, 6th ed. (Penguin Books, 1989), at 28.

92. It is further respectfully submitted that it is not appropriate to extend that convention, without more, to include the relationship of the judiciary to Parliament, as the learned justice purported to do in his reasons. The convention that has traditionally governed the relations between the judiciary and the legislature is that of Parliamentary sovereignty, which is the source of virtually complete judicial deference to legislative choices in a legal and political system that does not have entrenched guarantees of rights to which legislatures themselves are subject, and that are interpreted by the courts.

93. Accordingly, it is suggested that one must look not to the implications of the "spending" convention for guidance as to the appropriate role of the court in this

instance, but rather to the implications of the tradition of Parliamentary sovereignty and its modification by the fundamental guarantees of the Charter.

94. In the United Kingdom, the need to ensure that national law conforms with the law of the European Community has modified the doctrine of Parliamentary sovereignty. In the case of conflict between domestic law and the higher, or supreme, law of the Community, the doctrine of Parliamentary sovereignty must give way and Community law prevails.

R v. Secretary of State for Transport, ex. p. Factortame Ltd., [1990] 2 AC 85.

H.W.R. Wade, "Notes: What Has Happened to the Sovereignty of Parliament?" (1991), 107 LQR 1.

95. It is submitted that, similarly, in Canada, the constitution, the supreme law, takes precedence over other legislation. While this may be an incursion into the authority of Parliament, it is clearly called for by the Constitution Act, 1982.

Constitution Act, 1982, s. 52.

96. On the other hand, if this Honourable Court is of the view that the "spending" convention is relevant to the relations between Parliament and the courts, it is submitted that that convention is neither immutable nor the exclusive source of wisdom on the appropriate relationship between the two institutions.

DeSmith and Brazier, supra, at 43-44.

97. For example, Parliament itself has had to legislate in the area of control over money bills, in order to refresh its traditional supremacy vis-à-vis the House of Lords.

Parliament Act, 1911, 1 & 2 Geo. V, c. 13.

DeSmith and Brazier, supra, at 36.

98. It has been held by this Honourable Court that the purpose of constitutional conventions is "to ensure that the legal framework of the constitution will be operated in accordance with the prevailing constitutional values or principles of the period."

Re Resolution to Amend the Constitution, [1981] 1 SCR 753, at 880.

99. It would be inconsistent with this approach to allow a convention developed in the heyday of Parliamentary sovereignty (now limited by the Charter) to prevent judicial fashioning of remedies consistent with the Charter's equality guarantees.

DeSmith and Brazier, supra, at 35 and 37.

100. In determining both the force and applicability of a constitutional convention, the crucial questions must always be whether or not a particular class of action is likely to destroy respect for the established distribution of authority and whether or not it is likely to maintain respect for the constitutional system by changing (or sustaining) the distribution of authority. This distribution of authority implies the maintenance of limited monarchy, representative government, responsible government, and efficient government; it implies also that constitutional rules must be comparable with the realities of practical politics.

DeSmith and Brazier, supra, at 46.

101. On this test, it is suggested that the remedy of extension, granted in the circumstances above, actually fosters respect for basic constitutional values and representative institutions by providing for the protection of vulnerable minorities through the proper and effective interplay of court and legislature.

102. In fact, it is submitted that the entrenchment of rights and freedoms in the Charter, and the courts' role in ensuring that governments respect those rights, are in keeping with that spirit of resistance to arbitrary exercises of power by the dominant that is at the root of Parliament's original assertion of its authority over spending vis-à-vis the monarch.

103. It is also consistent with the relationship between reviewing courts and legislatures that has evolved over the years. For example, in non-Charter adjudication, the courts have traditionally made orders that affect, directly or indirectly, Parliament's authority over spending and the allocation of governmental resources. Where the Crown has been found liable for breach of trust and breach of fiduciary duty, for example, courts have made damage awards against the Crown. The Crown is not excused from paying such awards on the basis that they have not been authorized by Parliament.

Miller v. The King, [1950] SCR 168.

Guerin v. The Queen, [1984] 2 SCR 355.

104. In the development of the fairness doctrine in administrative law, it has been accepted that the courts' decisions would require resources to be allocated to provide the procedures necessary for fair process. These decisions involve the courts in their traditional role of developing the law and, although they may have had a significant impact on legislative or parliamentary decisions about spending, were not considered to usurp the spending power.

For example, *Re Nicholson and Haldimand-Norfolk Regional Board of Commissioners of Police*, [1979] 1 SCR 311.

105. In cases where legislation has been reviewed on federalism grounds, the courts have granted remedies that have the result of requiring an expenditure of public funds. While Parliament's power over revenues is constitutionally entrenched, its exercise of that power must comply with the constitution and is subject to review by the courts.

Reference re Employment and Social Insurance Act, 1935, [1937] 1 DLR 684 (PC).

106. In the case of *Prior v. Canada*, on which the applicants rely, by contrast, it was the very power to raise money through income taxes that was called into question. The Federal Court of Appeal in that case found that it did not have jurisdiction to interfere with that power. However, the court did not conclude that it would lack jurisdiction to determine whether or not the exercise of that power in a specific piece of legislation was in conformity with the Charter. Indeed, the courts have always taken jurisdiction to consider whether legislation regulating taxation was validly enacted pursuant to the powers in the constitution, and it has been stated in a decision of this Honourable Court that "action taken under the Constitution Act, 1867 is of course

subject to Charter review" in order "to supervise and on a proper occasion curtail the exercise of a power to legislate."

Prior v. Canada (1989), 101 NR 401 (FCA), at 404.

British Columbia Electric Railway v. The King, [1946] AC 527.

Simpson-Sears Ltd. v. New Brunswick (Provincial Secretary), [1978] 2 SCR 869.

Reference Re Bill 30, An Act to Amend the Education Act (Ont.), [1987] 2 SCR 1148, at 1206-7.

107. In cases decided under the Charter, expense has been held not to justify limitation on rights under section 1 of the Charter. As in the administrative law area, courts have made rulings regarding fair procedure that may have a significant effect on public spending and on the allocation of funds. It is submitted that just as financial consequences are not an obstacle to the courts' ability to fashion effective remedies for the right to trial within a reasonable time and the right to counsel, they should not prevent courts from granting effective remedies where equality rights are at stake.

Singh, supra, at 218.

Askov et al. v. The Queen, [1990] 2 SCR 1199.

108. It has also been held that a lack of funds or resources do not justify discrimination under section 15 of the Charter and cannot be used as a basis for rendering Charter rights meaningless.

Leroux v. Co-operators General Insurance Co. et al. (1990), 65 DLR (4th) 702 (Ont. HCJ), at 715-17, reversed on other grounds (unreported, September 16, 1991, Ont. CA).

R v. Rowbotham et al. (1988), 25 OAC 321 (CA).

109. Where a Charter right imposes a positive obligation on government, the court may order that public funds must be spent. Under section 23 of the Charter it has been held that the government must do whatever is necessary to discharge its obligation to provide minority language education, including providing public funding that is adequate for the purpose. The framers must be taken to have intended the foreseeable financial consequence of the enactment of the Constitution Act, 1982.

Mahe, supra, at 393-95.

Marchand, supra, at 661-62.

110. It is submitted that there is nothing in the Constitution Act precluding a court from granting a remedy that results in an expenditure of public funds not specifically authorized by Parliament where that remedy is appropriate and just in the circumstances. This is particularly noticeable in the case of section 15. Section 32(2), postponing the coming into force of section 15 for three years after proclamation of the Charter, was meant to give governments time to bring their legislation and practices into conformity with the equality guarantee. Had the framers of the Constitution Act, 1982 not wanted this compliance effort (or any other, future, compliance effort) to affect government spending priorities, they might have so specified.

"Proposed Resolution Respecting the Constitution of Canada, October 6, 1980," reproduced in Bayefsky, supra, at 751.

111. It is therefore submitted that the decision of the Federal Court of Appeal does not usurp the functions of Parliament, carve out a new legislative role for the courts, or interfere with Parliamentary authority over revenue and expenditures. On the contrary, the decision accurately applies the following well-established principles: it takes a purposive approach to Charter rights, it grants the remedy that is most appropriate and just in the circumstances and which is consistent with the purpose of the Charter, it carries out the purpose of alleviating disadvantage as opposed to rolling back the gains made in legislation, it respects the principle that administrative cost and inconvenience do not justify the infringement of rights and it does not interfere with Parliament's authority to choose among various policy options and enact legislation that conforms to the Charter.

112. It is further submitted that the decision of the Federal Court of Appeal is correct in holding that a remedy is available under section 24 of the Charter and that the remedy granted by the trial judge is the most appropriate and just in the circumstances.

PART IV: NATURE OF ORDER SOUGHT

113. It is respectfully requested that the appeal be dismissed.

All of which is respectfully submitted.

THE OUTCOME

Head Notes—R v. Schachter

Held: The appeal should be allowed.

The first constitutional question should be answered in the affirmative, leaving open the option of suspending the declaration of invalidity for a period of time to allow Parliament to amend the legislation in a way which meets its constitutional obligations. The second constitutional question should be answered in the negative. Section 24(1) of the Charter provides an individual remedy for actions taken under a law which violate an individual's Charter rights. A limited power to extend legislation is available to courts in appropriate circumstances by way of the power to read in derived from s. 52 of the Constitution Act, 1982.

Per Lamer CJ and Sopinka, Gonthier, Cory, and McLachlin JJ: Generally speaking, when only a part of a statute or provision violates the Constitution, only the offending portion should be declared to be of no force or effect. The doctrine of severance requires that a court define carefully the extent of the inconsistency between the statute in question and the requirements of the Constitution, and then declare inoperative (a) the inconsistent portion, and (b) such part of the remainder of which it cannot be safely assumed that the legislature would have enacted it without the inconsistent portion.

In the case of reading in, the inconsistency is defined as what the statute wrongly excludes rather than what it wrongly includes. Where the inconsistency is defined as what the statute excludes, the logical result of declaring inoperative that inconsistency may be to include the excluded group within the statutory scheme. The reach of the statute is effectively extended by way of reading in rather than reading down.

Section 52 of the Constitution Act, 1982 does not restrict the court to the verbal formula employed by the legislature in defining the inconsistency between a statute and the Constitution. Section 52 declares the law, and not the words expressing that law, to be of no force or effect to the extent of any inconsistency with the Constitution. The inconsistency can be defined as what is left out of the verbal formula as well as what is wrongly included.

The purpose of reading in is to be as faithful as possible within the requirements of the Constitution to the scheme enacted by the legislature. In some cases, of course, it will not be a safe assumption that the legislature would have enacted the constitutionally permissible part of its enactment without the impermissible part. There reading in would not be appropriate. Just as reading in is sometimes required in order to respect the purposes of the legislature, it is also sometimes required in order to respect the purposes of the Charter. Reading in therefore is a legitimate remedy akin to severance and should be available under s. 52 in cases where it is an appropriate technique to fulfil the purposes of the Charter and at the same time minimize the interference of the court with the parts of legislation that do not themselves violate the Charter.

The first step in choosing a remedial course under s. 52 is to define the extent of the inconsistency which must be struck down. Usually, the manner in which the law violates the Charter and the manner in which it fails to be justified under section 1 will be critical to this determination.

In some circumstances, s. 52(1) mandates defining the inconsistent portion which must be struck down very broadly. This will almost always be the case where the legislation or legislative provision does not meet the first part of the *Oakes* test, in that the purpose is not sufficiently pressing or substantial to warrant overriding a Charter right. Where the purpose of the legislation is itself unconstitutional, the legislation should almost always be struck down in its entirety.

Where the purpose of the legislation or legislative provision is deemed to be pressing and substantial, but the means used to achieve this objective are found not to be rationally connected to it, the inconsistency to be struck down will generally be the whole of the portion of the legislation which fails the rational connection test. It matters not how pressing or substantial the objective of the legislation may be; if the means used to achieve the objective are not rationally connected to it, the objective will not be furthered by somehow upholding the legislation as it stands. Where the second and/or third elements of the proportionality test are not met, there is more flexibility in defining the extent of the inconsistency. Striking down, severing or reading in may be appropriate in cases where the second and/or third elements of the proportionality test are not met.

Having determined the extent of the inconsistency the means of dealing with it, whether by way of severance, reading in, or striking down legislation in its entirety, must be considered.

One important distinction exists between severing and reading in. In the case of severance, the inconsistent part of the statutory provision can be defined with some precision on the basis of the requirements of the Constitution. This is not always the case with reading in. In cases where the question of how the statute ought to be extended in order to comply with the Constitution cannot be answered with a sufficient degree of precision on the basis of constitutional analysis, the legislature and not the courts must fill in the gaps.

In determining whether reading in is appropriate, the question is not whether courts can make decisions that impact on budgetary policy but rather to what degree they can appropriately do so. A remedy which entails an intrusion into this sphere so substantial as to change the nature of the legislative scheme in question is clearly inappropriate. The court should consider whether the significance of the part which would remain is substantially changed when the offending part is excised. The problem with striking down only the inconsistent portion is that the significance of the remaining portion may change so markedly without the inconsistent portion that the assumption that the legislature would have enacted it is unsafe.

In cases where the issue is whether to extend benefits to a group not included in the statute, the question of the change in significance of the remaining portion sometimes focuses on the relative size of the two relevant groups. The assumption that the legislature would have enacted the benefit is more often sound where the group to be added is smaller than the group originally benefitted. This assumption, however, is not necessarily safe when the group to be added is much larger than the group originally benefitted. This is not because of the numbers per se. Rather, the numbers may indicate that for budgetary reasons, or simply because it constitutes a marked change in the thrust of the original program, it cannot be assumed that the legislature would have passed the benefit without the exclusion.

It is sensible to consider the significance of the remaining portion when asking whether it is safe to assume that the legislature would have enacted the remaining portion. If the remaining portion is very significant, or of a long standing nature, it strengthens the assumption that it would have been enacted without the impermissible portion. The fact that the permissible part of a provision is encouraged by the purposes of the Constitution, even if not mandated by it, strengthens the assumption that the legislature would have enacted it without the impermissible portion.

The final step is to determine whether the declaration of invalidity of that portion should be temporarily suspended. A court may strike down legislation or a legislative provision but suspend the effect of that declaration until Parliament or the provincial legislature has had an opportunity to fill the void. The question of whether to delay the effect of a declaration is an entirely separate question from whether reading in or nullification is the appropriate route under s. 52 of the Constitution Act, 1982. Delayed declarations of nullity should not be seen as preferable to reading in cases where reading in is appropriate. The question whether to delay the application of a declaration of nullity should turn not on considerations of the role of the courts and the legislature but rather on considerations relating to the effect of an immediate declaration on the public.

Where s. 52 is not engaged, a remedy under s. 24(1) of the Charter may nonetheless be available. This will be the case where the statute or provision in question is not in and of itself unconstitutional, but some action taken under it infringes a person's Charter rights. Section 24(1) would there provide for an individual remedy for the person whose rights have been so infringed.

An individual remedy under s. 24(1) of the Charter, will rarely be available in conjunction with action under s. 52 of the Constitution Act, 1982. Ordinarily, where a provision is declared unconstitutional and immediately struck down pursuant to s. 52, that will be the end of the matter. No retroactive s. 24 remedy will be available.

The right which was determined to be violated here is a positive right: the right to equal benefit of the law.

Positive rights by their very nature tend to carry with them special considerations in the remedial context. It will be a rare occasion when a benefit conferring scheme is found to have an unconstitutional purpose. Cases involving positive rights are more likely to fall into the remedial classifications of reading down/reading in or striking down and suspending the operation of the declaration of invalidity. ... Indeed, if the benefit which is being conferred is itself constitutionally guaranteed ... reading in may be mandatory. [Even negative rights may have certain positive aspects]. ... [T]he equality right is neither purely positive nor purely negative. In some contexts it will be proper to characterize s. 15 as providing positive rights. (p. 721)

This benefit was monetary and not one which Parliament is constitutionally obliged to provide to the included group or the excluded group. What Parliament is obliged to do, by virtue of the conceded s. 15 violation, is to equalize the provision of that benefit if it is to be provided at all. The benefit itself is not constitutionally prohibited; it is simply underinclusive. Thus striking down the provision immediately would be inappropriate as such a course of action would deprive eligible persons of a benefit without providing any relief to the respondent. Such a situation demands, at the very least, that the operation of any declaration of invalidity be suspended to allow Parliament time to bring the provision into line with constitutional requirements.

Without a mandate based on a clear legislative objective, reading the excluded group into the legislation would be imprudent. A consideration of the benefit and size of the group and of the budgetary implications of such a course of action underlined this conclusion. The appropriate action was to declare the provision invalid and suspend that declaration to allow the legislative body in question to weigh all the relevant factors in amending the legislation to meet constitutional requirements. Significantly, Parliament did amend the impugned provision after this action was launched and the amendment was not the one that reading in would have imposed.

Per La Forest and L'Heureux-Dubé JJ: The legislation concerned concededly violates the Canadian Charter of Rights and Freedoms and does not fall within the very narrow type of cases where only a portion of the legislation may be read down or corrected by reading in material as being the obvious intention of the legislature. There is a long tradition of reading down legislation and, where it substantially amounts to the same thing, reading in is possible. These devices, however, should only be employed in the clearest of cases. In light of Parliament's subsequent action, there was no reason to declare the impugned legislation invalid and then suspend that declaration.

Further dimensions to the issue of reading in and reading down require qualifications to the propositions set down as guidelines by Lamer CJ. The process of reading down or reading in should not be closely tied with the checklist set forth in *R v. Oakes* because that might encourage a mechanistic approach rather than an examination of more fundamental issues going well beyond the factual context.

IN THE SUPREME COURT OF CANADA

(ON APPEAL FROM THE COURT OF APPEAL FOR MANITOBA)

BETWEEN:

ANDRZEJ MOGE

Appellant

AND:

ZOFIA MOGE

Respondent

AND:

WOMEN'S LEGAL EDUCATION AND ACTION FUND (LEAF)

Intervenor

Factum of the Women's Legal Education and Action Fund (LEAF)

Moge v. Moge

INTRODUCTION

The Moges were married in Poland in the 1950s and moved to Canada in 1960. Zofia Moge had a seventh grade education, poor English language skills, and no particular job training. During the marriage, she cared for the household, which included three children, and worked as a hotel cleaner. The Moges separated in 1973 and divorced in 1980. After the separation, Zofia Moge was awarded custody of the children and $150 a month child and spousal support. The support was eventually increased to $400 a month after she was laid off from her full-time job and suffered medical problems that prevented her from obtaining all but intermittent employment. At all material times, the husband was employed full time in the auto industry.

In 1989, Andrzej Moge obtained an order terminating support. The trial judge found that Zofia Moge had had time to become financially independent and that her former spouse had supported her as long as he could be required to. The Manitoba Court of Appeal set aside the judgment and awarded Zofia Moge spousal support in the amount of $150 a month for an indefinite period. Central to the court's decision was that, in assessing a spouse's ability to become self-sufficient, courts must be aware of all relevant circumstances, including whether the marriage itself may have had an adverse economic impact upon the spouse's earning potential.

The husband appealed to the Supreme Court. LEAF was the sole intervenor.

FACTUM

PART I: FACTS

1. The Women's Legal Education and Action Fund (LEAF) adopts the facts as set out in the Respondent's Factum.

PART II: ISSUES

2. This case raises issues of the interpretation of the spousal support provisions of the Divorce Act in a manner consistent with section 15 of the Charter, including:

(a) principles for assessment of economic disadvantages and advantages arising from marriage and marriage breakdown; and

(b) the nature of the obligation to become economically self-sufficient.

PART III: ARGUMENT

Women's Economic Disadvantage Flowing from Marriage and Marriage Breakdown Is a Sex Equality Issue

The Relationship Between Women's Economic Disadvantage and the Gender-Based Division of Labour Within Marriage

3. Separation and divorce are strongly associated with the economic disadvantage of women relative to men. Despite recent family law reforms in the direction of gender equality, including improved property laws, recent research shows that the poverty rate of divorced or separated women and children in their custody continues to be extremely high and far exceeds that of divorced or separated men.

Department of Justice, Canada, *Evaluation of the Divorce Act Phase II: Monitoring and Evaluation* (Ottawa: Dept. of Justice, Bureau of Review, May 1990), at 91-96.

Lenore Weitzman, *The Divorce Revolution: The Unexpected Social and Economic Consequences for Women and Children in America* (New York: The Free Press, 1985), at 36.

M. McCall, *Background Paper: Options for the Reform of the Law of Spousal Support Under the Divorce Act, 1985* (1991), prepared for the Dept. of Justice, Canada, at 56-61.

4. Forty-six percent of divorced women in a 1988 study had total incomes, including employment and support income, below the poverty line. In contrast, only 13% of men who paid support fell below the poverty line. The average income of male one-person households after marriage breakdown was $13,500 above the poverty line.

Department of Justice, supra, at 93-94.

5. A major factor contributing to women's economic disadvantage on separation and divorce, both historically and today, has been the differential work patterns of women as compared with men during and following marriage. Historically, women were almost exclusively responsible for the unpaid labour of caring for home and family during marriage, whether or not they were also employed in paid work. Men were largely responsible for the financial support of the family.

M. Gunderson, L. Muszinski, and J. Kleck, *Women and Labour Market Poverty* (Ottawa: Canadian Advisory Council on the Status of Women, 1990), at 13-14.

6. Despite significant increases in labour force participation, a greater diversity of marital relationships and gradually changing understandings and expectations of those entering marriage, women continue to be primarily responsible for the unpaid work of homemaking and childcare and encouraged or limited so as to make this work their first priority. Women also generally continue to be responsible for care of children on separation.

Gunderson et al., supra, at 20 and 24-27.

Statistics Canada, *Women in Canada: A Statistical Report*, 2d ed. (Ottawa: Supply and Services, 1990), at 10, 20, 74-75, and 80.

7. Canadian society continues to be organized around a gender-based division of labour during marriage. Childcare and domestic work are largely treated as a private responsibility. The work world is generally unresponsive to family needs, having been historically structured on the assumption of a wife at home.

R. Abella, *Equality in Employment: Royal Commission Report*, Royal Commission on Equality in Employment, 1984, at 28-29.

8. The gender-based division of household labour has been used to socially define women as secondary earners who are likely to limit their work force participation and is associated with the systemic economic devaluation of childcare, cleaning, and other domestic work. As a basis of societal organization, this division of labour has exacerbated the unequal position of women in the paid work force by contributing to the creation and perpetuation of systemic pay and employment inequity on the basis of sex. For individual married women who work outside the home, the "secondary earner" ideology and the devaluation of skills involved in domestic work frequently results in discrimination in employment.

Abella, supra, at 28-32.

9. At the same time, the division of labour during marriage is gender-based in large part because the overall sex segregation and stratification of the work force has meant that women are generally paid less, with the result that it has frequently been economically rational for the family that married women rather than men limit work force participation to address childcare and other family needs.

E.D. Pask and M.L. McCall, eds., *How Much and Why? Economic Implications of Marriage Breakdown: Spousal and Child Support* (Calgary: Canadian Research Institute for Law and the Family, 1989), at 56-60.

Abella, supra, at 62-69 and 245-247.

10. Although the increasing participation of married women in the paid labour force will often improve those women's economic possibilities on divorce, there are significant negative economic consequences to the accommodation of paid work to responsibilities for care of children and home, and to husbands' career needs.

The Dynamics and Implications of the Gender-Based Division of Labour Within Contemporary Marriages

11. Most married women who are employed, even those who work full time in non-traditional jobs, continue to bear prime responsibility for care of children and home, with the result that their total working hours are markedly greater than their husbands'.

Statistics Canada, *General Social Survey Analysis Series: Where Does Time Go?* (Ottawa: Min. of Industry, Trade and Technology, 1991), at 50-54 and 58-61.

Statistics Canada, *Women in Canada*, supra, at 13 and 26 (Table 20).

W. Michelson, *From Sun to Sun: Daily Obligations and Community Structure in the Lives of Employed Women and Their Families* (Totowa, New Jersey: Rowman & Allanheld, 1985), c. 5.

Gunderson et al., supra, at 24-26 and 34.

12. As a consequence of the conflicting physical and emotional demands of paid work and responsibilities for home and family, compounded by a lack of adequate childcare, women are often forced to make sacrifices affecting their paid work opportunities with which men are not confronted.

Pask and McCall, supra, at 56-72.

National Council of Welfare, *Women and Poverty Revisited* (Ottawa: Supply and Services, 1990), at 2, 42-53.

13. A significant majority of women with children continue to interrupt their careers because of matters relating to the home and family, whereas extremely few men do so.

T.K. Burch, *Family History Survey: Preliminary Findings* (Ottawa: Supply and Services, 1985), Statistics Canada Cat. no. 99-955, at 25-27.

P. Robinson, *Women's Work Interruptions: Results from the 1984 Family History Survey* (Ottawa: Supply and Services, 1985), Statistics Canada Cat. no. 99-962, at 27-29.

14. Work interruptions significantly harm women's present and future earning potential. Women who interrupt their employment experience losses in numerous employment related areas, including seniority, opportunity for advancement, development of job skills, opportunity to keep skills up-to-date, fringe benefits, and the ability to accumulate future benefits such as pensions and disability insurance.

Pask and McCall, supra, at 56-65.

15. Average lifetime earning power has been estimated to decline by 1.5% for every year out of the work force. For occupations requiring post-secondary education, the loss may be as high as 4.3% per year. The rate of depreciation rises the longer the period of absence.

E.S. Beninger and J.W. Smith, "Career Opportunity Costs: A Factor in Spousal Support Determination" (1982), 16 *Fam. LQ* 201, at 207.

16. The longer women spend outside the work force, the harder it is to return. The possibility of returning decreases with age.

D. Boothby, Economic Council of Canada, *Women Re-Entering the Labour Force* (Ottawa: Supply and Services, 1986), at 11.

17. Women make up the majority of part-time workers and the largest proportion is accounted for by married women with young children. Part-time jobs often pay only the minimum wage or little above that, and rarely involve private pension plan coverage or other benefits.

Statistics Canada, *Women in Canada*, supra, at 75-76 and 87-89.

McCall, supra, at 53-54.

18. Women's responsibilities for care of children also mean women forgo skills development, and employment and promotional opportunities involving overtime, a demanding work schedule, long hours, travel, or relocation.

P. Hudis, "Commitment to Work and Family: Marital Status Differences in Women's Earnings" (1976), 38 *J of Marriage and the Fam.* 267, at 269 and 276-77.

Pask and McCall, supra, at 59.

19. Married women are disproportionately concentrated in lower paying jobs that often lack fringe benefits like disability insurance and medical and dental benefits. Where pension plans exist, they tend to be calculated on a percentage of earnings resulting in the accumulation of low pensions.

Gunderson et al., supra, at 102-4.

Statistics Canada, *Women in Canada*, supra, at 99.

20. Those aspects of childcare that involve disruption of the workday fall most heavily on female parents. Women are more likely than their husbands to take time off work to deal with childcare crises, to stay home with a sick child, or to take children to medical or dental appointments.

Michelson, supra, at 69-70.

21. Married immigrant women have historically had high rates of labour force participation, but are concentrated in the lowest paying and least secure job sectors. For women with limited official language skills, the fewer opportunities to upgrade these skills compared with husbands mean that the negative economic consequences of giving priority to responsibility for care of home and family are particularly great.

S. Dutt, *The Social Reality of Immigrant Women: A Changing Demographic Perspective* (1989), A Report prepared for the Review of Demography and Its Implications for Economic and Social Policy (Multiculturalism Sector, Secretary of State, Canada), at 20-30 and 38-43.

A. Estable, *Immigrant Women in Canada: Current Issues* (Background paper prepared for the Canadian Advisory Council on the Status of Women, 1986), at 17-25 and 39-46.

22. While most of the economic disadvantage associated with marriage arises from childrearing responsibilities, it is by no means limited to that. Women often sacrifice their own career aspirations to help promote their husbands' careers, including relocation to accommodate their husbands' job requirements and goals. Next to childrearing, relocation as a result of their husbands' job has the most detrimental financial effect on women's employment earnings.

Pask and McCall, supra, at 59-60.

J. Mincer, "Family Migration Decisions" (1978), 86 *J of Political Economy* 749, at 771.

23. Consequences for women who have accommodated career to family responsibilities frequently include: lower education and skills; deteriorated skills and skills that are not up to date, as well as skills that are devalued or unrecognized; lower job level, income, and income potential; poorer employment benefits including pensions, disability insurance, and unemployment insurance entitlement; and poor job security and experience. Women in these circumstances are less able to cope with or overcome employment and pay inequity, high levels of unemployment, and other such barriers to self-sufficiency, as well as illness and disability.

National Council of Welfare, supra, at 2 and 38-56.

24. While most women are economically disadvantaged on the termination of marriage, marriage has significantly benefited most men. The division of labour in most homes has enabled husbands to expand their knowledge and experience in work-related areas, develop a higher income potential than their wives, and achieve more secure employment.

Beninger, supra, at 203.

The Role of Spousal Support in Valuing Unpaid Domestic Labour and Addressing Women's Economic Disadvantage Flowing from Marriage and Marriage Breakdown

25. Historically, entitlement to spousal support was made available to women only. When ordered, spousal support has provided some financial recognition of the impact that women's contributions to their marriage and society, through assumption of responsibility for care of children and other work in the home, have had on their economic status. As such, spousal support has advanced sex equality. However, even where support was available, women continued to be economically disadvantaged on separation and divorce relative to men.

C. Rogerson, "The Causal Connection Test in Spousal Support Law" (1989), 8 *Can. J of Fam. Law* 95, at 105-6.

26. Although support provisions are now expressed in gender-neutral terms, women almost exclusively continue to be in the position of needing spousal support.

Department of Justice, supra, at 75, fn. 70.

27. Spousal support awards, including those under the Divorce Act, are inadequate and have only a marginal impact on reducing women's poverty on separation. Reasons for inadequate spousal support awards include:

(a) a failure to recognize when, why, and to what extent women have been economically disadvantaged as a result of family responsibilities;

(b) a failure to recognize the financial advantages accruing to men from the assumption of family responsibilities by women; and

(c) unrealistic assumptions about the ability of women to become self-sufficient.

Department of Justice, supra, at 93-94 and 131.

C. Rogerson, "Judicial Interpretation of the Spousal and Child Support Provisions of the Divorce Act (Part I)" (1991), 7 *Canadian Family Law Q* 155, at 196 and 215-17.

28. LEAF submits that the availability of spousal support is an important mechanism for providing equal access to economic resources and relieving against the economic disadvantage of women, particularly in the absence of significant government initiatives concerning childcare, pay and employment inequity, and income security. Spousal support remains crucial in relieving against women's economic disadvantage in comparison to men related to marriage and marriage breakdown, and for adequately recognizing women's contributions to their marriage and society through childbearing, care of children, and other work in the home.

29. This Court unanimously held that it is unfair and contrary to the principles of equality when the costs of an activity by which society benefits are disproportionately placed upon women. In particular,

> [c]ombining paid work with motherhood and accommodating the childbearing needs of working women are ever increasing imperatives. That those who bear children and benefit society as a whole thereby should not be economically or socially disadvantaged seems to bespeak the obvious.

Brooks v. Canada Safeway Ltd., [1989] 1 SCR 1219, at 1238 and 1243.

30. LEAF submits that just as it is contrary to the principles of sex equality that the individual and systemic costs of having children be borne by women, it is inconsistent with sex equality principles that the costs of caring for children and maintaining family households fall primarily on women.

31. LEAF therefore submits that denial of effective relief against economic disadvantage related to women's contributions to their marriage and society through application of spousal support provisions under the Divorce Act is a denial of equal protection and benefit of the law.

Interpretation of the Spousal Support Provisions in the Divorce Act Must Be Guided by the Charter's Guarantees of Sex Equality

32. The Charter is the supreme law of Canada and, accordingly, statutes must be interpreted and applied in a manner consistent with the fundamental values enshrined in the Charter.

Hills et al. v. AG Canada, [1988] 1 SCR 513, at 558.

R v. Thompson, [1990] 2 SCR 1111, at 1158.

Retail, Wholesale & Department Store Union, Local 580 v. Dolphin Delivery Ltd., [1986] 2 SCR 573. at 603.

33. This Court has identified equality as one of the fundamental values of our society, against which the objects of all legislation must be measured. This Court has also stated that "the s. 15(1) guarantee is the broadest of all guarantees [in the Charter]. It applies to and supports all other rights guaranteed by the Charter."

Andrews v. Law Society of British Columbia, [1989] 1 SCR 143, at 185.

34. In this Court's developing jurisprudence, while section 15 does not itself guarantee social equality, equal law is seen as a means to attaining an equal society. Thus, the purpose of section 15 "is to ensure equality in the formulation and application of the law. The promotion of equality entails the promotion of a society in which all are secure in the knowledge that they are recognized at law as human beings equally deserving of concern, respect and consideration."

Andrews, supra, at 171.

35. This Court has acknowledged the importance of promoting the equality of disadvantaged groups. In the words of Madam Justice Wilson (as she then was), "... s. 15 is designed to protect those groups who suffer social, political and legal disadvantage in our society ... ."

Andrews, supra, at 154.

36. LEAF submits that the spousal support provisions in the Divorce Act must be interpreted and applied in a manner consistent with constitutional equality standards, and in particular, the equality standards articulated by this Court in *Andrews v. Law Society of British Columbia*.

37. Where a statute can reasonably bear a meaning that would accord with Charter values, such an interpretation should be favoured. In interpreting legislation, "the values embodied in the Charter must be given preference over an interpretation which would run contrary to them."

Hills, supra, at 558.

38. This Court has considered the social and economic context of women's lives to ensure its decisions develop legal doctrine in a manner that affords equality for Canadian women. It has considered that the specific reality of women's experience of social, economic, and sexual disadvantage must be appreciated in order to ensure that women are truly accorded equal protection and benefit of the law.

Brooks, supra.

Janzen and Govereau v. Platy Enterprises Ltd. et al., [1989] 1 SCR 1252.

R v. Lavallee, [1990] 1 SCR 852, at 874-75.

39. For example, in determining that pregnancy discrimination constituted discrimination on the basis of sex, this Court assessed and recognized the impact of women's

social and economic disadvantage in society associated with procreation, and stated that removal of such disadvantage is a key purpose of anti-discrimination legislation. This case also requires a contextual approach to elaboration of legal doctrine in light of the continuing significant poverty and other economic disadvantage of women flowing from marriage and marriage breakdown.

Brooks, supra, at 1238.

40. Spousal support law under the Divorce Act, by definition, is concerned with addressing the economic consequences of marital relationships, and in particular the roles of the spouses during cohabitation. Mr. Justice La Forest, in *Richardson v. Richardson*, recognized that it is largely women who are economically disadvantaged by marriage and its breakdown. The majority justices in the Court below recognized that principles for determination of spousal support under the Divorce Act are to be measured against their impact on achieving "true equality" for women.

Richardson v. Richardson, [1987] 1 SCR 857, at 877.

Moge v. Moge (1990), 25 RFL (3d) 396 (Man. CA), at 400 and 404.

41. In actions for spousal support, the Charter requires that principles for the determination of spousal support must not impose a detrimental burden on women as compared with men by virtue of the division of labour within marriage. It is respectfully submitted that the legal analyses adopted by the trial judge and the majority and dissenting justices in the Court of Appeal do not meet this requirement and are therefore discriminatory.

42. An interpretation of the law is discriminatory when it has the effect of imposing burdens and obligations or when it withholds or limits access to opportunities and benefits to historically disadvantaged groups. In formulating its approach to equality, this Court has ruled that the overriding concern is to increase the substantive equality of disempowered, disenfranchised, and socially excluded groups.

Andrews, supra, at 174.

Brooks, supra, at 1238.

R v. Turpin et al., [1989] 1 SCR 1296, at 1329.

43. Denial of adequate spousal support perpetuates the relative disadvantage of women, who are already disadvantaged in society.

44. LEAF submits that interpretation of the spousal support provisions of the Divorce Act consistent with the principles and values enshrined in the Charter would occur within a framework that recognizes the impact of the continuing gender-based division of labour during marriage and after separation on women's economic status and ability to become self-sufficient.

Interpretation of Sections 15 and 17 of the Divorce Act

45. Sections 15 and 17 of the Divorce Act were part of a trend to reform family law to recognize the terminability of the marital relationship and to address more directly and fully the economic consequences to the spouses of marriage and divorce.

46. These reforms were intended to promote sex equality. The framing of spousal support entitlement in terms of economic disadvantage and advantage was an important further shift toward valuing the functions of childcare and maintenance of the home, rather than presenting women's need for support in terms of a dependency on men. It countered stereotypical assumptions that most women's lives were or should be centred almost exclusively around the home, and it eliminated a fault-based entitlement to support with its entrenched sexist assumptions about the blameless wife.

Law Reform Commission of Canada, *Maintenance on Divorce*, Working Paper no. 12 (1975).

47. While marriage is increasingly understood as a relationship in which spouses can determine their own division of functions unconstrained by traditional legal preconceptions of gender roles, it was recognized that for the foreseeable future, at the termination of most marriages women will need spousal support as a result of a gender-based division of labour during marriage.

Law Reform Commission of Canada, supra, at 22.

Assessment of Economic Disadvantages and Advantages and the Causal Connection Test

48. As noted in the Appellant's factum at paragraphs 49-61, in the majority of decisions the support provisions in the Divorce Act have been interpreted so as to require that need for support following marriage breakdown be causally connected to the marriage or its breakdown.

49. The *Pelech*, *Richardson*, and *Caron* decisions (the "trilogy"), the jurisprudential source of the "causal connection test," were decided under the 1968 divorce legislation in the context of applications to vary final support agreements and without consideration of subsequent equality jurisprudence under human rights codes and section 15 of the Charter. Causal connection principles therefore cannot be readily transferred to the interpretation of the Divorce Act without closer examination.

Pelech v. Pelech, [1987] 1 SCR 801.

Caron v. Caron, [1987] 1 SCR 892.

Richardson, supra.

50. The fact of marriage itself does not justify an award of support to address financial need. In *Linton v. Linton*, the Ontario Court of Appeal found that the Divorce Act was designed to address financial need that arises from the economic consequences of the division of responsibilities within marriage. LEAF submits that an interpretation of the Divorce Act that bases support on addressing the economic disadvantages and advantages flowing from marriage and its breakdown, including the functions of the spouses, is consistent with the terms of the Act and section 15 of the Charter.

Linton v. Linton (1990), 1 OR (3d) 1 (CA), at 26.

Divorce Act, RSC 1985, c. 3 (2nd Supp.), ss. 15(5)(b), 15(7)(a) and (c), and 17(7)(a) and (c).

51. The causal connection test has excluded the legislative requirement to address economic advantages arising from marriage, including how the division of family responsibilities often increases the ability of one spouse to pursue income enhancing opportunities. It is also respectfully submitted that, while the concern to find a causal connection between need and the marriage can be applied to reflect the legislative policy of compensation spouses for any disadvantage suffered as a result of roles undertaken within marriage and other sacrifices made, it has not been interpreted and applied this way. The application of the test, including in the trilogy, has limited the availability of spousal support to women through the imposition of a narrow view of economic disadvantage.

Rogerson, "The Causal Connection Test," supra, at 104, 110-12, and 122-32.

52. For example, in *Richardson v. Richardson* the majority of this Court questioned whether there was any economic disadvantage flowing from the marriage where a former wife, who was a secretary during marriage, was unemployed on divorce after being out of the work force to care for the two children of the marriage for essentially five years prior to separation. Mr. Justice La Forest, in his dissent, noted that while the husband's career advanced, the wife's absence from the work force during marriage entailed a deterioration in skills, and loss of seniority and opportunity to keep skills up to date. His dissent also recognizes the practical difficulties for Mrs. Richardson in finding another job, particularly when combined with her post-separation responsibility for care of a child.

Richardson, supra, at 886-87.

Rogerson, "The Causal Connection Test," supra, at 124.

53. It is respectfully submitted that the reasoning of the majority in *Richardson* also ignores the likely impact of the division of family responsibilities on the wife's job choices. Recent cases have rejected the "once a secretary always a secretary" argument, and recognized that a spouse who has the same job after separation as she had prior to or during marriage may well have suffered significant economic disadvantage.

Linton, supra, at 28.

Mullin v. Mullin (1989), 24 RFL (3d) 1 (PEI CA), at 16.

54. LEAF submits that interpretation of sections 15(7) and 17(7) of the Divorce Act consistent with section 15 of the Charter would preclude judicial termination of support entitlement until:

(a) a spouse economically disadvantaged by marriage or its breakdown, including post-separation childcare responsibilities, has had a reasonable and sufficient opportunity or has in fact reached an adequate level of financial autonomy, where this is possible; and

(b) there has been adequate financial recognition of any economic advantages to a spouse arising from the marriage.

55. An approach to the Divorce Act that fully recognizes the economic advantages and disadvantages flowing from marriage and its breakdown would include recognition of the consequences of:

(a) the division of labour within the home during marriage, including the connection between current need and a traditional role during marriage for a woman who is ill, unemployed, or underemployed;

(b) the contributions to the other spouse's income-earning capacity and other contributions to the family not adequately compensated by the award or matrimonial property;

(c) detrimental reliance flowing from the assumption by one spouse of economic support of the family, with the resulting failure to pursue economic opportunities by the other spouse;

(d) giving up spousal support or pension benefits upon marriage, or a job in order to relocate;

(e) post-separation custodial responsibilities.

56. In recent cases, the future economic loss associated with career sacrifice, and gain associated with increased earning capacity, have been quantified by experts and used as the basis for awarding spousal support.

Ormerod v. Ormerod (1990), 27 RFL (3d) 225.

Keast v. Keast (1986), 1 RFL (3d) 401 (Ont. Dist. Ct), at 409.

57. In the case at bar, to accept the Appellant's argument that the Respondent's current need does not flow from the marriage fails to recognize:

(a) over a lengthy marriage Zofia Moge was primarily responsible for the care of the three children of the marriage as well as other work in the home;

(b) in addition she worked outside the home as a cleaner, tailoring her paid work to her family responsibilities;

(c) during marriage she relied on her husband's assumption of primary responsibility to support the family, affecting her work-related decisions;

(d) after the separation she had custodial responsibility for the three children of the marriage, one of whom remained dependent until very recently;

(e) the Moges separated at a time when family law did not provide for division of family property;

(f) Zofia Moge has a limited education and work experience, and has some health difficulties that restrict her employment options;

(g) she had no real opportunity to upgrade her earning potential, including improvement of her English language skills;

(h) the possibilities for enhancing earning capacity are limited for an immigrant woman in her 50s with limited English and job experience; and

(i) low levels of child and spousal support have affected her ability to acquire assets or save for retirement years. By way of contrast, the Appellant's financial position has steadily improved following separation.

58. LEAF submits that these factors associated with Zofia Moge's economic disadvantage, which are typical of Canadian women, are both inter-related, cumulative, and related to her marriage and its breakdown.

59. The Appellant's argument, like the case law upon which he relies, reflects an interpretation of section 17(7) of the Divorce Act that minimizes the economic consequences for both spouses of a gender-based division of labour during marriage so as to give priority to the legislative object of promoting self-sufficiency. LEAF submits that any rationales for emphasizing self-sufficiency in the context of a final separation agreement do not apply to other original and variation applications.

The Traditional–Modern Marriage Dichotomy

60. Courts recently have employed a categorization of marriages as either traditional or non-traditional for purposes of assessing support entitlement. The terminology has been used by courts as a short-form indicator of support entitlement. A classification as "traditional" provides the basis for holding that a woman's economic need, at least on separation, is related to or "causally connected" to her role in marriage.

Moge, supra, at 401-3.

Heinemann v. Heinemann (1989), 20 RFL (3d) 236 (NS CA), at 272-74.

Rogerson, "Judicial Interpretation," supra, at 179-96.

61. For those who are not considered to be in a "traditional" marriage, expeditious self-sufficiency "has become the rule." Support is seen as short term and transitional. Particularly for women more recently married, entitlement to support is assessed against false assumptions of women's equality within marriage, in employment and training, and under family property laws. The presumption is therefore that need is not related to marriage; instead, extrinsic factors to financial autonomy or individual choices are considered responsible unless there is strong and direct evidence to the contrary.

Moge, supra, at 400.

Heinemann, supra, at 272-274.

Rogerson, "Judicial Interpretation," supra, at 197-244.

62. The categorization of marriages as traditional or modern invites and in practice operates on the basis of inaccurate and often stereotypical views about the role of women in each type of marriage and women's economic possibilities on divorce.

63. Although it has been recognized that a wife could work outside the home for most of the marriage and yet be part of a traditional marriage, recognition of significant or long-term economic disadvantage becomes largely limited to a narrow female homemaker/male breadwinner model of household. This family occurs infrequently in Canadian society, even in marriages of longer duration.

Heinenmann, supra, at 272-74.

Gunderson et al., supra, at 14-15.

64. The debate in the case at bar about whether the Moge marriage was a traditional one demonstrates how the process of categorization becomes a subjective search for a stereotypical marriage, and shifts the focus away from a concrete examination of the economic disadvantages and advantages arising from all varieties of marriage. As such, it is an interpretative tool that is of little assistance in addressing the criteria in sections 15(7) and 17(7) of the Divorce Act, and superimposes criteria that the Divorce Act was designed to eliminate and that are inconsistent with section 15 of the Charter.

65. While increasingly marriages may appear to be non-traditional in the sense that women often work outside the home, even in non-traditional occupations, women's roles within marriage remain significantly unchanged. Women's continued disproportionate responsibility for childcare and household work within marriage means that in most recent marriages, women's poorer financial position on separation will be attributable, at least in part, to the marriage.

66. With the traditional–modern marriage categorization, a woman's paid employment during marriage is seen as the prime gauge for determining the existence or depth of economic disadvantage. LEAF submits that the more appropriate focus for determining economic disadvantage is the extent to which the marriage is characterized by a differential and/or inequitable division of labour.

Rogerson, "Judicial Interpretation," supra, at 206-9.

67. LEAF further submits that entitlement to spousal support should be based on an examination of the events and actual roles played by the parties in the marriage, and assessed within a framework that recognizes the significant negative economic consequences for women of all forms of a gender-based division of labour within marriage.

Economic Self-Sufficiency and the Clean Break Philosophy

68. The goal of economic self-sufficiency at sections 15(7)(d) and 17(7)(d) of the Divorce Act has been used as the legislative basis for an interpretation of the spousal support provisions where the priority is to cut the economic ties between the spouses as quickly as possible and allow spouses to go their separate ways. Spouses are declared self-sufficient and support terminated after a short period, regardless of any continuing economic disadvantage flowing from the marriage and a poor standard of living.

69. This "clean break philosophy," where circumstances are viewed through the lens of promotion of self-sufficiency and a narrow view is taken of economic disadvantage and advantage, is the model of support upon which the courts now frequently operate. LEAF submits that this approach is inconsistent with the terms of the Divorce Act and section 15 of the Charter.

Moge, supra, at 400.

Rogerson, "Judicial Interpretation," supra, at 162-63, 177-78, and 198-231.

Rogerson, "The Causal Connection Test," supra, at 115-18 and 122-27.

70. The objective of promoting economic self-sufficiency in the Divorce Act is carefully qualified and is only one of four objectives that a support order must address. There is no indication that Parliament intended that this provision be given priority over other objectives. LEAF submits that some legislative objectives will be more relevant to some marriages because of the variety of marriage situations that exist, but in each case all objectives must be addressed in assessing entitlement, quantum, and duration of support.

Linton, supra, at 26-27.

Thorsteinson v. Thorsteinson (1988), 52 Man. R (2d) 115 (QB Fam. Div.), at 118.

71. LEAF submits that to be consistent with and further section 15 of the Charter, the objective of promoting economic self-sufficiency through the spousal support provisions in the Divorce Act must be interpreted and applied so as to truly promote the economic and social equality of women following marriage breakdown.

72. While women are increasingly equal to men in legal status, *de facto* women remain disadvantaged on marriage breakdown. It would undermine women's equality to apply the legislative object of self-sufficiency in a manner that presumes women, whenever they were married, are on an equal social and economic footing with men on marriage breakdown when they are not. It would further undermine women's equality to assess the degree of women's economic disadvantage and the necessary steps and barriers to becoming self-sufficient according to a standard reflecting the life circumstances of men.

73. LEAF submits that an assessment of the ability of women to achieve economic self-sufficiency following marriage breakdown must take account of the ongoing nature of the economic disadvantage arising from the marriage.

74. Divorce does not provide women with a "clean break" from the consequences of the roles they play during marriage. The majority in the court below recognized that when women take low-paid relatively unskilled work during marriage, their ability to improve their earning capacity after marriage breakdown is diminished by their limited skills, training, and experience. Even when a woman has been employed during the marriage in a full-time occupation, she may never be able to compensate for all the opportunities she has lost or had to turn down because of her family responsibilities.

Moge, supra, at 402.

75. While the support provisions of the Divorce Act are not designed to address the disadvantage women experience due to extrinsic barriers to autonomy, assessment of the practicability of self-sufficiency or a reasonable time-frame in which to achieve same must include consideration of the reduced ability to overcome extrinsic barriers to self-sufficiency. For example, women will be more vulnerable to unemployment due to lack of seniority or limited job experience, as occurred in the case at bar.

76. Women's post separation responsibility for care of dependent children also frequently affects their ability to become self-sufficient. The Divorce Act recognizes that there are negative economic consequences to the custodial parent that are not addressed

by child support obligations. Primary responsibility for care of children on separation affects training and employment possibilities, often more so than during marriage, because of limited time and money, and a lack of adequate childcare.

Divorce Act, ss. 15(7)(b) and 17(7)(b).

Brockie v. Brockie (1987), 5 RFL (3d) 440 (Man. QB), at 446-47, affirmed (1987), 8 RFL (3d) 302 (Man. CA).

Rogerson, "Judicial Interpretation," supra, at 202-3.

77. In addition, low levels of child support, as in the case at bar, mean that a woman already economically disadvantaged by the marriage is unable to save for significant expenses and retirement, or cope with financial crises, because all her "extra" money has been required for the support of the children.

78. An approach to spousal support that ignores the interrelationship between the needs of former spouses as adults and their needs as parents leads to an inadequate resolution of the economic and custodial problems resulting from marriage breakdown. The custodial parent needs relief not only because of her status as former spouse, but by virtue of her role as parent, and in order to enable her to perform the ongoing function of the provision of childcare.

C. Rogerson, "Winning the Battle, Losing the War: The Plight of the Custodial Mother After Judgment" in M.E. Hughes and E.D. Pask, eds., *National Themes in Family Law* (Toronto: Carswell, 1988), 20, at 22 and 43-46.

79. The economic disadvantage experienced by women who have been primarily responsible for care of children and home during marriage often means, particularly in long-term marriages, that economic disadvantage is permanent and the ability to be self-supporting at an adequate level is limited. This is the case not only for women divorcing at age 50 or 60, but also for women in their 30s or 40s, especially when post-separation responsibility for dependent children continues for some time.

80. The greater the participation in the work force during marriage and the more time for unconstrained post-separation participation in the work force prior to retirement, the better a woman's relative income-earning possibilities will likely be in the years following divorce. Nevertheless, there may still be ongoing economic disadvantages and advantages to the spouses flowing from the marriage and its breakdown that require spousal support to bring her to an appropriate standard of living.

81. LEAF submits that the level of self-sufficiency, or living to which a divorced spouse is entitled, should be subjectively determined. The length of the marriage, the marital standard of living, the impact of roles assumed during marriage on earning capacity, the expectations of the parties, and the relative earnings of the spouses should be considered.

82. Concern to cut the economic ties has led some courts in recent years to set a glass ceiling as to the amount of income a spouse could earn before her right to support was terminated. Generally, a wife was self-sufficient if she earned approximately $20,000.00 per annum or if she was or could be employed full time.

Rogerson, "Judicial Interpretation," supra, at 207.

Cymbalisty v. Cymbalisty (1989), 56 Man. R (2d) 28 (QB), at 32.

83. Recently some courts have defined the post-divorce standard of living as a reasonable standard, which in the case of a long-term marriage should be assessed in the context of the marital standard of living.

Lynk v. Lynk (1989), 21 RFL (3d) 337 (NS SCCA), at 352.

Mullin v. Mullin (1989), 24 RFL (3d) 1 (PEI CA), at 18.

Linton, supra, at 27.

Row v. Row, unreported, August 22, 1991, Alta. QB, Judicial District of Edmonton, 4803 81175, at 2.

84. LEAF submits that to be consistent with section 15 of the Charter, the concept of need, and the determination of what constitutes economic self-sufficiency or the appropriate standard of living, should include recognition of economic advantages to a higher-income spouse arising from marriage as well as the consequences of ongoing economic disadvantages. The legislative objectives of spousal support should be read together such that a spouse, although able to meet her current expenses, may nevertheless be entitled to support to address other legislative concerns and thereby improve her standard of living. The longer the marriage and the greater the degree of economic interdependency of the spouses, including role differentiation, the stronger the claim to equal standards of living after marriage breakdown, or the marital standard where financially possible.

85. It is further submitted that the concept of economic self-sufficiency should address future as well as current needs. Recognition of the economic cycles of a family, involving the need to save for retirement years particularly for women who are separated in their forties, would be an important factor in alleviating the poverty of divorced elder women.

M. Grassby, "Women in Their Forties" (1991), 30 RFL (3d) 369.

PART IV: NATURE OF ORDER SOUGHT

86. Based on the principles of interpretation outlined above, LEAF submits that this appeal should be dismissed and the Respondent's entitlement to support should not be time limited.

All of which is respectfully submitted.

THE OUTCOME

Head Notes—Moge v. Moge

Held: The appeal should be dismissed.

Per La Forest, L'Heureux-Dubé, Gonthier, Cory and Iacobucci JJ: The husband's support obligation to his wife should be determined not on the basis of the reasoning in *Pelech*, *Caron*, and *Richardson*, but on the principles embodied in the 1985 Divorce Act. The principles articulated in the trilogy should not be applied to non-consensual situations. In the trilogy, this Court did not espouse a new model of support but rather showed respect for the wishes of persons who, in the presence of the statutory safeguards, decided to forgo litigation and settled their affairs by agreement under the 1970 Divorce Act. In paying deference to the freedom of individuals to contract, the Court did not intend to extend the principles articulated in the trilogy to all applications for relief between spouses. Such an extension would virtually eliminate the significance of the statutory criteria and, at the same time, close the door to the wise exercise of judicial discretion that can accommodate a diverse range of economic variables on marriage breakdown.

Under the 1985 Divorce Act, the "means and needs" test is no longer the exclusive criterion for support. All four of the objectives defined in ss. 15(7) and 17(7) of the Act must be taken into account when spousal support is claimed or an order for spousal support is sought to be varied. No single objective is paramount. With these objectives, Parliament intended that support reflect the diverse dynamics of many unique marital relationships. The objective of self-sufficiency is only one of the objectives enumerated in the sections and there is no indication that it should be given priority in determining the right to, quantum and duration of spousal support. The Act clearly indicates that this objective is to be made a goal only "in so far as is practicable." To elevate economic self-sufficiency to the pre-eminent objective would be inconsistent not only with the proper principles of statutory interpretation, but also with the social context in which support orders are made.

In Canada, the feminization of poverty is an entrenched social phenomenon. (p. 853) Given the multiplicity of economic barriers women face in society, decline into poverty cannot be attributed entirely to the financial burdens arising from the dissolution of marriage. ... However, there is no doubt that divorce and its economic effects are playing a role. (p. 854) It is apparent that support payments, even assuming they are paid, are making only a marginal contribution to reducing economic hardship among women following divorce. (p. 855)

It would thus be perverse in the extreme to assume that Parliament's intention in enacting the Act was to penalize women in this country financially.

The support provisions of the 1985 Divorce Act are intended to deal with the economic consequences, for both parties, of the marriage or its breakdown. What the Act requires is a fair and equitable distribution of resources to alleviate these consequences regardless of gender. Under this approach, the distinction between traditional and modern marriages may not be as useful as courts have indicated so far. The doctrine of equitable sharing of the economic consequences of the marriage or its breakdown, which the Act promotes, recognizes and accounts for the economic disadvantages or advantages flowing from the role adopted by the spouses in the marriage.

[T]his analysis applies equally to both spouses, depending upon how the division of labour is exercised in a particular marriage. ... The reality, however, is that in many if not most marriages, the wife still remains the economically disadvantaged partner. (pp. 849-50)

Studies indicate that women have tended to suffer economic disadvantages and hardships from marriage or its breakdown because of the traditional division of labour within that institution.

Historically ... the contributions made by women to the marital partnership were non-monetary and came in the form of work at home. ... Today, though more and more women are working outside the home, such employment continues to play a secondary role and sacrifices continue to be made for the sake of domestic considerations. These sacrifices often impair the ability of the partner who makes them (usually the wife) to maximize her earning potential because she may tend to forgo educational and career advancement opportunities. These same sacrifices may also enhance the earning potential of the other spouse (usually the husband) who, because his wife is tending to such matters, is free to pursue economic goals. (p. 861) In effect, she is left with a diminished earning capacity and may have conferred upon her husband an embellished one. (p. 862) Often difficulties are exacerbated by the enduring responsibility for children of the marriage. (p. 863)

The Act now recognizes that work within the home has undeniable value and transforms the notion of equality from the rhetorical status to which it was relegated under a deemed self-sufficiency model to a substantive imperative. It seeks to put the remainder of the family in as close a position as possible to the household before the marriage breakdown. Legislative support for the principles of compensation is to be found in ss. 15(7)(a) to (c) and ss. 17(7)(a) to (c) which are extremely broad in scope. The promotion of self-sufficiency remains relevant, but it does not deserve unwarranted pre-eminence. While spouses would still have an obligation after the marriage breakdown to contribute to their own support in a manner commensurate with their abilities, the ultimate goal is to alleviate the disadvantaged spouse's economic losses as completely as possible, taking into account all the circumstances of the parties, including the advantages conferred on the other spouse during the marriage. Marriage per se does not, however, automatically entitle a spouse to support. In rare cases, the spouses are able to make a clean break. But in most marriages in which both partners make economic sacrifices and share domestic responsibilities, or where one spouse has suffered economic losses in order to enable the other spouse to further a career, their roles should be considered in the spousal support order. As the Act is not exclusively compensatory in nature, an equitable sharing of the economic consequences of marriage does not exclude other considerations, particularly when dealing with sick or disabled spouses. In the final analysis, courts have an overriding discretion and the exercise of such discretion will depend on the particular facts of each case, having regard to the factors and objectives designated in the Act.

The exercise of judicial discretion in ordering support requires an examination of all four objectives set out in s. 17(7) of the Act in order to achieve equitable sharing of the economic consequences of marriage or its breakdown. In the proper exercise of their discretion, courts must be alert to a wide variety of factors and decisions made in the family interest during the marriage which have the effect of disadvantaging one spouse or benefiting the other upon its dissolution. While the most significant economic consequence of marriage or marriage breakdown usually arises from the birth of children, exacerbated by the need to accommodate and integrate those demands with the requirements of paid employment, the financial consequences of the end of a marriage extend well beyond the simple loss of future earning power or losses directly related to the care of children. Further, families need not fall strictly within a particular marriage model in order for one spouse to suffer disadvantages. Although spousal support orders still remain essentially a function of the evidence led in each particular case, to require expert evidence to present an accurate picture of the economic consequences of the marriage breakdown would not be practical or possible for many parties. The general economic impact of divorce on women, however, is a phenomenon the existence of which cannot reasonably be questioned and should be amenable to judicial notice. In any event, whether judicial notice of the circumstances generally encountered by spouses at the dissolution of a marriage is to be a formal part of the trial process or whether such circumstances merely provide the necessary background information, it is important that judges be aware of the social reality in which support decisions are experienced when engaging in the examination of the objectives of the Act.

Under s. 21(5) of the 1985 Divorce Act, a court of appeal should only interfere with the trial judge's decision where it is persuaded that his reasons disclosed material error. This section does not give a court of appeal an independent discretion to decide a case afresh. Here, the trial judge committed an error in principle in engaging in an analysis premised upon a model of spousal support which is not sustainable on the wording of the Act. The trial judge focused on "financial independence" and failed to consider the disparity between the earning ability of each former spouse and to have regard to the fact that the wife was disadvantaged by the marriage. Correcting such an error fell within the scope of review of the Court of Appeal. Continuing support is in order in this case since the four objectives set out in s. 17(7) are met: (1) the wife has sustained a substantial economic disadvantage "from the marriage or its breakdown" (s. 17(7)(a)); (2) the wife's long-term responsibility for the upbringing of the children of the marriage after the spousal separation in 1973 has had an impact on her ability to earn an income (s. 17(7)(b)); (3) the wife continues to suffer economic hardship as a result of the "breakdown of her marriage" (s. 17(7)(c)); and (4) the wife has failed to become economically self-sufficient notwithstanding her conscientious efforts (s. 17(7)(d)). These findings are irrefutable even in the absence of expert evidence relating to the appropriate quantification of spousal support.

Per Gonthier and McLachlin JJ: In the 1985 Divorce Act, Parliament has enacted that judges considering applications for variation of support must consider the four factors set out in s. 17(7). The judge's task under that section is to make an order which provides compensation for marital contributions and sacrifices (s. 17(7)(a)), which takes into account financial consequences of looking after the children either before or after the separation (s. 17(7)(b)), which relieves against need induced by the separation (s. 17(7)(c)), and, to the extent it may be "practicable," promotes the economic self-sufficiency of each spouse (s. 17(7)(d)). The need to consider all four factors set out in s. 17(7) rules out the strict self-sufficiency model. The trial judge thus erred in giving no weight to the first three factors of s. 17(7) and in imposing a categorical requirement of self-sufficiency. The majority of the Court of Appeal was correct in rejecting the view that there is an absolute obligation for a spouse to become self-sufficient and that there is a time after which one spouse should no longer have to support another. They placed considerable emphasis on the need to compensate the wife for her contributions to the marriage and on the permanent economic disadvantage she suffered as a consequence. They then concluded that she was entitled to an order of maintenance to supplement her own income because her earning potential had been diminished. This conclusion represented a proper application of s. 17(7) of the Act.

Sections 17(7)(a) and 17(7)(c) raise the requirement of causation by the marriage or its breakdown. The question under s. 17(7)(a) is whether a party was disadvantaged or gained advantages from the marriage, as a matter of fact; under s. 17(7)(c) whether the marriage breakdown in fact led to economic hardship for one of the spouses. Hypothetical arguments after the fact about different choices people could have made which might have produced different results are irrelevant, unless the parties acted unreasonably or unfairly. In the context of s. 17(7), what is required is a common-sense, non-technical view of causation. The legal or ultimate burden remains with the plaintiff, but in the absence of evidence to the contrary adduced by the defendant, an inference of causation may be drawn although positive or scientific proof of causation has not been adduced.

Although evidence of the spouses' respective contributions and gains from the marriage is necessary under s. 17(7)(a) of the Act, the evidence need not be detailed, in the sense of a year-by-year chronology of sacrifices and gains. In most cases it will suffice if the parties tell the judge in a general way what each did. That will allow the judge to get very quickly an accurate picture of the sacrifices, contributions and advantages relevant to determining compensation under s. 17(7)(a), making detailed quantification and expert evidence unnecessary.

IN THE SUPREME COURT OF CANADA
(ON APPEAL FROM THE FEDERAL COURT OF APPEAL)

BETWEEN:

PHILIP CONWAY

Appellant

AND:

HER MAJESTY THE QUEEN

Respondent

AND:

THE ATTORNEY GENERAL OF QUEBEC
THE ATTORNEY GENERAL OF ONTARIO
THE ATTORNEY GENERAL OF BRITISH COLUMBIA
WOMEN'S LEGAL EDUCATION AND ACTION FUND
MINORITY ADVOCACY AND RIGHTS COUNCIL
COALITION OF PROVINCIAL ORGANIZATIONS OF THE HANDICAPPED

Intervenors

Factum of the Women's Legal Education and Action Fund (LEAF)

Conway v. The Queen (also known as Weatherall v. The Queen)

INTRODUCTION

In 1986, Phillip Conway, an inmate at Collins Bay Penitentiary in Kingston, began a court action to prevent women guards from performing frisk searches and cell patrols in male prisons. The frisk search consisted of a hand search of a clothed inmate from head to foot, while the surveillance patrols involved regular scheduled cell patrols ("counts") and unannounced patrols ("winds") conducted at random times every hour. Conway objected to the cross-gender touching that occurs during a frisk search and to the possibility that women might view him undressed during the counts and winds. He alleged that the performance of these duties by women violated his rights to security of the person, privacy, and equality as guaranteed by sections 7, 8, and 15 of the Charter.

The Federal Court Trial Division held that the frisk searches did not violate sections 7, 8, and 15 of the Charter but that the winds conducted by women were an invasion of male inmates' privacy and, therefore, violated section 8. The Federal Court of Appeal set aside the judgment, and held that neither the cross-gender frisk searches nor the cross-gender winds were unconstitutional in any way. Conway appealed to the Supreme Court. LEAF intervened to address the particular equality issues for women. Because the court challenge was initiated pursuant to initiatives to employ more women as correctional officers, the case potentially raised significant issues concerning section 15(2) of the Charter and its relation to other Charter guarantees. The Attorneys General of Quebec, Ontario, and British Columbia and the Minority Advocacy and Rights Council intervened to address this issue. The Coalition of Provincial Organizations of the Handicapped intervened to address the implications of the case with respect to the privacy and dignity rights of persons with disabilities.

FACTUM

PART I: FACTS

1. The Intervenor, the Women's Legal Education and Action Fund ("LEAF") is a national, federally incorporated, not-for-profit organization founded in April 1985 to secure equal rights for Canadian women as guaranteed by the Canadian Charter of Rights and Freedoms. To this end, it engages in test case litigation, research, and public education.

2. LEAF adopts the facts as set out in the Factum of the Respondent, and relies on the following additional facts.

3. The issue raised by this case relates to two particular forms of routine surveillance conducted by correctional officers in federal penal institutions: pat-down frisk searches and "winds." The term "winds" refers to the random viewing of prisoners in their cells.

4. Prison cells are checked on a regular basis to ensure that inmates are alive and not engaging in prohibited conduct.

Transcript of Payne, Case on Appeal, vol. VIII, at 1069, l. 15-1070, l. 3.

5. The evidence establishes the following facts with respect to the attitude of male prisoners to the surveillance activities in this case:

(a) They have concerns about invasions of privacy arising from searches and other forms of surveillance, regardless of the gender of the guards involved.

Transcript of Spearman, Case on Appeal, vol. V, at 704, ll. 11-16.

Transcript of Payne, Case on Appeal, vol. VII, at 1055, l. 27; at 1056, l. 14.

Transcript of Mainwaring, Case on Appeal, vol. VI, at 839, ll. 6-14.

Transcript of Shawver, Case on Appeal, vol. VIII, at 1270, ll. 16-20; at 1299, ll. 12-24.

Transcript of Beliveau, Case on Appeal, vol. IX, at 1445, ll. 17-24.

(b) There have been very few complaints relating to gender, compared with the volume of complaints relating to search/privacy issues as a whole.

Transcript of Mainwaring, Case on Appeal, vol. VI, at 838, l. 19; at 839, l. 14.

Transcript of MacDonald, Case on Appeal, vol. VII, at 958, l. 20; at 959, l. 4.

Transcript of Payne, Case on Appeal, vol. VII, at 1060, l. 21; at 1061, l. 20.

Transcript of Serin, Case on Appeal, vol. VII, at 1104, ll. 10-19.

(c) Many male prisoners express a preference for female guards in the conduct of pat-down frisks because they perceive that women guards perform these duties in a more sensitive fashion.

Transcript of Ostiguy, Case on Appeal, vol. VIII, at 1156, ll. 17-25.

(d) The integration of women guards into men's prisons has generally ameliorated conditions of incarceration for male inmates.

Transcript of Payne, Case on Appeal, vol. VII, at 1062, ll. 23-28.

Transcript of Serin, Case on Appeal, vol. VII, at 1108, l. 19; at 1109, l. 4.

Transcript of Ostiguy, Case on Appeal, vol. VIII, at 1158, l. 18; at 1159, l. 20.

Transcript of Shawver, Case on Appeal, vol. VIII, at 1272, ll. 7-22.

Transcript of Beliveau, Case on Appeal, vol. IX, at 1427, ll. 11-27; at 1428, l. 27; at 1429, l. 12; at 1432, l. 14; at 1434, l. 24.

E. Szcokyj, "Working in a Man's World: Women Correctional Officers in an Institution for Men" (July 1989), *Canadian Journal of Criminology* 319, at 320-21.

6. The reasons given by the Appellant for objecting to frisks being conducted by women correctional officers were that his girl friend objected to it and that it "feels wrong." With respect to "winds," the Appellant testified that he objected to women's employment on the cell blocks because he considered it "an invasion of privacy, natural privacy."

Transcript of Conway, Case on Appeal, vol. V, at 631, ll. 5-12; at 634, l. 15; at 635, l. 3; at 659, l. 8; at 660, l. 11.

7. Many of the reasons given through the evidence of John Hill for complaints by male prisoners about the presence and activities of women guards reflect discriminatory attitudes to the very presence of women. They include:

(a) female guards cause most of the tension between guards and inmates;

(b) the presence of female guards puts the inmates' lives in danger;

(c) female guards are more likely to be taken hostage and raped;

(d) there has been nothing but trouble since the day female guards came into men's prisons;

(e) male guards dislike having to work with women and take their frustrations out on the inmates;

(f) women cause disruption between inmates and staff because the male guards try to impress the female guards; and

(g) male prisoners resent the presence of female staff because they do not have "access" to them.

Exhibit D-28, Case on Appeal, vol. IV, at 479-483 and 489-91.

Several of the inmates indicated that the solution would be the removal of women guards from men's institutions.

Exhibit D-28, Case on Appeal, at 479, 482, 483, and 487.

Transcript of Weatherall, Case on Appeal, vol. V, at 749, ll. 22-24.

8. Women first entered male correctional facilities as correctional officers as a result of the repeal of certain exclusionary directives that were recognized as discriminatory. Their entry, therefore, was not the result of "affirmative action." The affirmative action program referred to in para. 6 of the Respondent's Factum has been directed toward increasing the number of women entering these facilities as correctional officers.

Transcript of Trepanier, Case on Appeal, vol. VI, at 890, l. 9; at 891, l. 15.

9. Reactions to being viewed in the nude and performing private bodily functions vary with social, cultural, and historical context, as well as individual and group "socialization" and social situation. Reactions to being seen by members of the opposite sex in these situations vary according to the same factors.

Transcript of Shawver, Case on Appeal, vol. VIII, at 1265, l. 23; at 1267, l. 23; at 1286, l. 15; at 1287, l. 5; at 1292, l. 27; at 1296, l. 18.

10. The evidence establishes that the privacy needs of male prisoners in this case could be respected by various modifications to the physical environment, such as privacy screens, and by the training of male and female staff to deal with inmates in their living quarters and elsewhere with sensitivity, all without compromising security. Difficulties experienced in providing for prisoners' privacy needs vary with the age and layout of specific correctional facilities, but are not insurmountable in Collins Bay.

Transcript of Braun, Case on Appeal, vol. VI, at 883, ll. 3-25.

Transcript of MacDonald, Case on Appeal, vol. VII, at 944, l. 4; at 946, l. 6; at 1014, l. 24; at 1015, l. 3.

Transcript of Payne, Case on Appeal, vol. VII, at 1029, l. 25; at 1030, l. 1; at 1054, l. 18; at 1056, l. 30.

Transcript of Ostiguy, Case on Appeal, vol. VIII, at 1157, l. 22; at 1158, l. 18.

Transcript of Carson, Case on Appeal, vol. VIII, at 1197, ll. 12-14.

11. Expert evidence confirms that privacy needs can be addressed by physically modifying prison conditions. Furthermore, concerns about gender can be significantly reduced, indeed eliminated, by training and sensitive introduction of innovation into the prison system.

Transcript of Shawver, Case on Appeal, vol. VIII, at 1273, ll. 10-15; at 1305, l. 23; at 1306, l. 18.

Transcript of Beliveau, Case on Appeal, vol. IX, at 1435, l. 24; at 1436, l. 13; at 1461, l. 14; at 1462, l. 19.

Szcokyj, supra, at 324-25.

12. The evidence establishes that while it might be possible to "roster" staff at its current gender composition in such a way as to assign women to positions in which they would not be called upon to perform frisk searches or "winds," such reorganization would have the following implications for women's employment in men's prisons:

(a) Limiting the duties performed by women guards could result in the positions held by them being reclassified to a lower classification and, as a result, being paid at a lower salary.

Transcript of Mainwaring, Case on Appeal, vol. VI, at 834, 14-21.

(b) Male guards would perceive female guards as being paid the same salary but not doing the same job.

Transcript of MacDonald, Case on Appeal, vol. VII, at 955, l. 5; at 956, l. 25.

Transcript of Payne, Case on Appeal, vol. VII, at 1050, ll. 6-13.

(c) It could cause resentment between male and female guards because female guards would be perceived as getting the less stressful assignments.

Transcript of Mainwaring, Case on Appeal, vol. VI, at 834, l. 22; at 835, l. 9.

(d) It could compromise women's chances for promotion by limiting their opportunities to gain experience in important correctional functions.

Transcript of Mainwaring, Case on Appeal, vol. VI, at 834, ll. 5-14.

Transcript of MacDonald, Case on Appeal, vol. VII, at 956, l. 26; at 957, l. 7.

Transcript of Payne, Case on Appeal, vol. VII, at 1048, ll. 4-9; at 1075, l. 22; at 1076, l. 3; and at 1077, l. 27; at 1078, l. 8.

PART II: ISSUES

13. The issue raised by this case is whether certain forms of surveillance (frisks and "winds"), which are routine in the prison context, violate the Appellant's Charter rights when performed by women.

14. LEAF submits that the following principles are central to the proper analysis of this issue:

(a) This issue must be approached with due regard to the fundamental value this Court has attached to equality rights in Canadian society.

Andrews v. Law Society of British Columbia, [1989] 1 SCR 143, at 185, per McIntyre J.

(b) Equality in employment is fundamental as a pre-condition for social equality for women in Canadian society.

(c) "The idea of human dignity finds expression in almost every right and freedom guaranteed in the Charter."

R v. Morgentaler, [1988] 1 SCR 30, at 166.

(d) Charter rights should be analyzed not in the abstract, but in their social context.

Edmonton Journal v. AG Alberta, [1989] 2 SCR 1326, at 1352-53, per Wilson J.

15. LEAF submits that in adopting the necessary concrete and contextual approach to this case, this Court is required to address the problem of protecting the privacy and dignity of individual inmates while taking into account, in addition to the security needs of the prison system:

(a) The fact that men and women are unequally situated in society in relation to their access to power, their equality of opportunity in employment, and their experience of sexual violence and sexual exploitation.

(b) The fact that the integration of women guards into men's penal institutions has demonstrably improved conditions of incarceration for male inmates as a whole, thereby promoting their dignity.

16. In resolving this issue, this Court must be mindful of the fact that this case is the Appeal of an individual inmate in a single penal institution concerning two particular forms of search in the prison context. Furthermore, this Court must be mindful of the fact that this matter was tried without representation from women prison guards or women prisoners, without the benefit of the collective views of inmates whose privacy and dignity interests may be adversely affected by a remedy that would restrict the role of women guards in men's prisons, and without regard for the social diversity of the inmate population.

PART III: ARGUMENT

Privacy Claims of Appellant

17. LEAF submits that the state has a constitutional obligation to respect and protect the dignity of the socially powerless within the confines of the Charter. LEAF submits that this obligation is imposed by a number of Charter provisions, including sections 7, 8, and 15.

18. LEAF submits that prisoners are a powerless group in society and therefore have such a claim on the state. LEAF submits that privacy and dignity concerns arising in the prison context require special consideration given the degree of intrusion to which inmates have historically been subjected.

19. LEAF further submits that many prisoners experience multiple disadvantages on the basis of race, aboriginal status, disability, socio-economic circumstances, and other factors that increase their vulnerability and impose an enhanced obligation on the state and the courts to promote and protect their Charter rights.

20. LEAF submits that surveillance functions that exceed the minimum requirements for maintenance of security within a penal institution arguably violate sections 7 and 8 of the Charter. LEAF submits that much of the surveillance revealed in the evidence in this case as a routine aspect of prison life should be re-examined in the context of the Charter's commitment to human dignity.

21. LEAF submits, however, that the Appellant has not put forward grounds for objecting to the participation of female guards in frisk searches and "winds" that provide

a constitutional basis for distinguishing between these activities when performed by female and male guards.

22. LEAF submits that the trial judge grounded his findings of Charter violation with respect to "winds" not on the specific facts of the Appellant's case but on an implicit presumption that public decency demands the protection of males from being viewed or touched by women in the circumstances involved in this case.

Reasons for Judgment of Strayer J, Case on Appeal, vol. IV, at 549-50.

23. LEAF submits that in contexts in which women are perceived as functioning in their proper sphere and performing roles socially constructed as "women's work," such as nursing and other occupations characterized as "care-giving," contact such as that at issue in this case (touching clothed males and infrequent viewing of unclothed males) is generally not seen as remarkable or per se violative of standards of decency.

24. LEAF submits that, given that concepts of public decency are highly socialized, culturally specific and temporally variable, it is not possible to develop or articulate a general "public decency" standard, nor is it appropriate to make the attempt in response to an individual claim. This difficulty is highlighted in the context of this case by the fact that many male inmates recognize and value the changes brought about in prison conditions and administration by the presence of women guards.

See paras. 5(d) and 9, supra.

25. The Charter has been found by this Court to protect "a reasonable expectation of privacy."

Hunter v. Southam Inc., [1984] 2 SCR 145, at 159.

26. LEAF submits that in determining what is a "reasonable expectation," care must be taken to scrutinize the factual and conceptual basis of such claims to determine whether they conflate "reasonableness" with stereotypical views about the "unnaturalness" or inappropriateness of women in certain social contexts such as non-traditional work.

Appellant's Equality Rights Claim

Substantive Equality Under the Charter

27. In defining an approach to the interpretation of section 15(1) of the Charter, this Court has held that the objective of the equality guarantees is not to provide "same treatment" for individuals but to remedy social disadvantage. The purpose of section 15(1) is not to eliminate all distinctions but only discriminatory distinctions. A distinction is discriminatory only if it functions to cause or to reinforce social disadvantage.

Andrews, supra, at 165-76, per McIntyre and 152-54, per Wilson J.

R v. Turpin et al., [1989] 1 SCR 1296, at 1331-32.

McKinney v. University of Guelph, [1990] 3 SCR 229, at 390, per Wilson J.

28. This Court has explicitly recognized that "same treatment" may in fact exacerbate social disadvantage. In many cases, inequality will only be remedied by a recognition

that groups socially, politically, and/or economically unequal may require different treatment in order to achieve equality of results.

Andrews, supra, at 169 and 171, per McIntyre J.

29. LEAF submits that the section 15 equality guarantees embodied in sections 15(1) and (2) have the same purpose—namely, the promotion of substantive, not formal, equality. LEAF submits that section 15(2) must always be considered together with section 15(1), both in examining the substantive content of equality and other Charter rights and in applying equality values to an assessment of the application of section 1 in any case in which a Charter challenge arises in connection with programs designed to promote the equality of members of disadvantaged groups.

30. LEAF submits that the promotion of equality includes, and may require, the adoption of positive measures. Positive measures have been recognized as essential components of a public policy directed toward the amelioration of the social and economic inequality of disadvantaged groups in our society.

Action Travail des Femmes v. Canadian National Railway Company, [1987] 1 SCR 1114, at 1139.

Judge R.S. Abella, *Report of the Commission on Equality in Employment* (Ottawa, 1984), at 9-10.

31. LEAF submits that positive measures aimed at remedying social disadvantage are integral to Charter equality guarantees. As such, positive ameliorative measures contemplated by section 15(2) should not be treated as contingent favours that are to be fitted around or subordinated to other Charter rights.

Differential Rules for Women Prisoners

32. The Appellant alleges that his sex equality rights are violated by the existence of directives and policies with respect to the Prison for Women, which provide that surveillance and searches of women prisoners of the type at issue in this case will be carried out only by women guards. He characterizes the asymmetrical rules with respect to cross-gender surveillance of male and female prisoners as conferring on female prisoners a benefit denied to male prisoners on the basis of sex.

33. The constitutional validity of the rules providing for same-sex surveillance in women's prisons is not an issue in this case and the Appellant has not sought to have these rules struck down or altered in any way.

34. LEAF submits that for the Appellant to make out a sex equality violation, he would have to demonstrate that male inmates suffer discrimination within the meaning of section 15(1) of the Charter by virtue of the fact that women inmates are frisked and viewed only by women guards.

35. LEAF submits that the evidence does not establish such discrimination. There is no evidence that male inmates are affected in any way by the conditions of incarceration of female inmates.

36. LEAF further submits that limitations on the range of duties performed by male guards in women's prisons do not implicate the sex equality rights of male prisoners.

37. LEAF submits that if a challenge had been made to the rules in women's prisons, the Court would have had to examine the question of whether substantive equality principles justify or require such rules in women's prisons. In addressing that question, the Court would have to consider factors like:

(a) Women's bodies and female nudity are sexualized in our society in a manner and degree that is not paralleled for men.

C. Smart, *Feminism and the Power of Law* (London and New York: Routledge, 1989), at 38-43.

N. Wolf, *The Beauty Myth* (Toronto: Vintage Books, 1991), at 138-39 and 153-54.

b. hooks, *Black Looks: Race and Representation* (Boston: South End Press, 1992), at 61-77.

(b) The majority of women prison inmates have histories of childhood and adult sexual abuse at the hands of men.

Creating Choices: Report of the Task Force on Federally Sentenced Women (Correctional Services Canada, 1990), at 106-7.

(c) Women justifiably fear sexual violence at the hands of men, particularly men in positions of power.

Solicitor General Canada, *Canadian Urban Victimization Study: Female Victims of Crime Bulletin* 4 (1985).

C. MacKinnon, *Toward a Feminist Theory of the State* (Cambridge: Harvard University Press, 1989), at 126-54.

E.A. Stanko, *Intimate Intrusions: Women's Experience of Male Violence* (London and New York: Routledge & Kegan Paul, 1985), at 1-5 and 70-82.

M.(K.) v. M.(H.), [1992] 3 SCR 6.

Norberg v. Wynrib, [1992] 2 SCR 318.

(d) The imbalance of power resulting from the authority that men guards would have over women inmates compounds the normal imbalance of power produced by gender relations in our society.

Janzen and Govereau v. Platy Enterprises Ltd. et al., [1989] 1 SCR 1252, at 1281 and 1284-85.

(e) Canada is bound by an International Covenant requiring it to recognize and respect these concerns as they affect women inmates.

United Nations, Standard Minimum Rules for the Treatment of Prisoners, article 53.

38. LEAF submits that in this context the social meaning of cross-gender surveillance is different and more threatening for women than for men.

39. LEAF submits that women prisoners have an interest in being free of cross-gender surveillance that does not relate to formalistic notions of public decency, but to a compelling interest in security of the person in the context of a sex unequal society and prison subculture.

40. LEAF submits that if examined from this perspective, any difference in treatment between women inmates and men inmates would be recognized as a positive measure aimed at reducing the substantive disadvantage of women prisoners rather than as a "benefit" to which male prisoners are *a priori* entitled.

41. The trial judge expressed concerns that arguments in support of a differential rule based on apprehensions about male violence were arguments "against the male gender" and constituted "stereotyping" of the type that section 15(1) of the Charter was designed to preclude.

Reasons for Judgment of Strayer J, Case on Appeal, vol. IV, at 564.

42. LEAF submits that it is a formalistic error potentially devastating to the goal of promoting substantive equality to confuse the study and analysis of patterns of social disadvantage and the development of measures for remedying disadvantage on the basis of the objective facts of women's lives with "stereotyping." LEAF submits that it is not stereotyping to describe the realities of women's lives and to rely on that description as a basis for promoting women's equality.

Section 15(2)

43. LEAF submits that this Court, in giving meaning to section 15(1) and section 15 as a whole, has suggested that section 15(2) functions both as an interpretative principle for section 15(1) equality rights and as a "saving provision" in certain circumstances in which equality-promoting measures may prima facie violate section 15(1).

Andrews, supra, at 171, 175-76, and 182, per McIntyre J.

44. LEAF submits that the question of giving section 15(2) independent force as a "saving provision" does not arise on the facts of this case. Section 15(2) could have application only to "save" the instrument alleged to have created the inequality. In this case that instrument—one that was not challenged by the Appellant—would be the differential rule for female prisoners. LEAF submits that substantive equality analysis requires that the question of whether that rule is an ameliorative measure is one properly addressed at the stage of determining whether or not it violates any right of the Appellant pursuant to section 15(1).

45. LEAF submits that while section 15(2) may function to "save" *prima facie* violations of Charter rights guaranteed by section 15(1) in appropriate cases, it cannot function in this way with respect to other Charter rights. Equality considerations must, of course, inform any examination of the content of other Charter rights and of section 1.

Equality Rights of Women Correctional Officers

46. Women in Canadian society are disadvantaged in employment. One of the important factors contributing to their disadvantage in employment is occupational segregation.

Judge R.S. Abella, *Report of the Commission on Equality in Employment*, at 19 and 62-70.

M Gunderson, L. Muszynski, and J. Keck, *Women and Labour Market Poverty* (Ottawa: Canadian Advisory Council on the Status of Women, 1990), at 43-45 and 92-97.

47. Women are disadvantaged by their historical exclusion from and under-representation in positions as correctional officers in the federal penal system.

See Respondent's Factum, paras. 4-7.

48. LEAF submits that this Court must guard against approaching the issue of women's employment in men's prisons from any presumption that women are alien to this workplace and should only be admitted on appropriate terms.

49. What the Appellant objects to in this case is the presence of women guards performing the full range of routine duties of prison guards. In other words, he complains that women correctional officers have not been limited in their roles and assignments.

50. The trial judge characterized the introduction of women guards into Collins Bay as part of an affirmative action program. After finding that "winds" by women infringed the Appellant's section 8 Charter rights, he asked himself whether assigning such duties to women was necessary to the affirmative action program. He found that it was not.

Reasons for Judgment of Strayer J, Case on Appeal, vol. IV, at 563.

51. The presence of women as guards in the Collins Bay Penitentiary is not a consequence of the federal affirmative action program, but the result of the repeal of previous exclusionary policies. LEAF therefore submits that it is incorrect to characterize the issue in this case as one of weighing the benefits of "affirmative action" for women employees against the privacy rights of men prisoners.

See para. 8, supra.

52. LEAF submits that the trial judge's approach to the issue characterizes the presence of women guards at Collins Bay as simply a matter of beneficent federal policy, and not as a matter of right on the part of women guards. "Fixing" the inmate's problem, therefore, becomes a simple matter of modifying the affirmative action policy, or altering the terms on which women will be permitted to enter and function within what is presumptively and "naturally" a male domain.

53. LEAF submits that a resolution to this case that dictates that women be given more limited roles and assignments as correctional officers will have negative impact on

their opportunities for equal pay, equal opportunity for advancement, and equal respect and dignity in the workplace.

See para. 12, supra.

J. Belknap, "Women in Conflict: An Analysis of Women Correctional Officers" (1991), 2 *Women and Criminal Justice* 89, at 99-100.

Section 1

54. This Court has described section 1 as the locus in which "the fundamental values and aspirations of Canadian society" are brought together. In particular, this Court has held that the principles underlying section 15 are integral to the section 1 analysis.

R v. Keegstra, [1990] 3 SCR 697, at 735-36 and 756.

55. This Court has held that where Charter challenges involve mediating the claims of different groups, the analysis under section 1 involves different considerations than where the conflict is strictly between an individual and the state as "singular antagonist."

Irwin Toy Ltd. v. AG Quebec, [1989] 1 SCR 927, at 993-94.

United States of America v. Cotroni, [1989] 1 SCR 1469, at 1489-90.

56. LEAF submits that if this Court finds that the assignment of women to the contested functions *prima facie* violates the Appellant's Charter rights, the proper constitutional question is not whether the assignment of women to these functions is necessary to affirmative action, but whether any limitation on women's equality of opportunity is necessary to remedy the Appellant's claim.

57. LEAF submits that in examining the question of whether measures designed to promote equality can function as limits "prescribed by law" on other Charter rights, this Court should be guided by its recognition that the word "law" in section 15(1) should not be restricted to "laws," even broadly construed, but should be generously interpreted to include all measures that implicate equality rights.

McKinney, supra, at 276-78, per La Forest J, and 382-85, per Wilson J.

Remedies

58. LEAF submits that if this Court determines that the measures complained of in this case limit the Appellant's Charter rights and are not justified by section 1, the considerations urged above for section 1 analysis should inform the Court's consideration of appropriate remedies.

59. The remedy sought by the Appellant, the prohibition against women guards participating in frisk searches and "winds" at Collins Bay Penitentiary, is one that would impact fundamentally on equal employment conditions and opportunities for women, and thus on their equality rights.

60. LEAF therefore submits that any remedy that would extend the rule in women's prisons to men's prisons simply on the basis of asymmetry cannot be justified in view of its impact on women's employment in men's prisons.

61. LEAF submits that any declaration that might be granted to protect the Appellant's Charter rights should expressly require that its implementation have no detrimental impact on women's equality rights.

62. It is submitted that a number of remedies that would have no such detrimental impact would be available in this case. These remedies would include:

(a) Modifying the physical environment of the prison so that the prisoners were not exposed to the view of guards while nude or when performing intimate personal functions, thereby addressing the issue of inmate dignity and privacy.

(b) Providing proper training and supervision to guards so that surveillance is performed with respect for privacy and dignity.

(c) Providing avenues to allow inmates to grieve and guards to be disciplined for abuse of surveillance powers.

63. LEAF submits that there is no constitutional justification for the Respondent to refuse to incur any additional cost that might be associated with providing of these alternative remedies. LEAF submits that these alternative remedies are not only consistent with but required by the Respondent's obligation and recognized commitment to promote equal employment opportunities for women correctional officers.

Singh et al. v. Minister of Employment and Immigration, [1985] 1 SCR 177, at 218-20.

R v. Schachter, [1992] 2 SCR 679, at 709-12.

Respondent's Factum, para. 52.

64. LEAF further submits that courts should be extremely reluctant to grant a Charter remedy that would result in a violation of the Charter rights of others. LEAF submits that where the only option available to the Court in granting a Charter remedy would result in a violation of the Charter rights of others, the Court should suspend the implementation of the remedy in order to allow the affected parties the opportunity to address the issue in a manner that would not result in such a violation.

Schachter, supra, at 719.

PART IV: NATURE OF ORDER SOUGHT

65. LEAF respectfully requests that the Appellant's appeal be dismissed.

All of which is respectfully submitted.

THE OUTCOME

Head Notes—Conway v. The Queen

Held: The appeal should be dismissed.

The frisk search, the count and the wind are all practices necessary in a prison for the security of the institution, the public and the prisoners themselves. The possible inappropriate effects of these practices are minimized by the provision of special training to ensure they are professionally executed with due regard for the dignity of the inmate. A substantially reduced level of privacy is present in prison—a prison cell is expected to be exposed and to require observation—and a prisoner thus cannot hold a reasonable expectation of privacy with respect to these practices. This conclusion is unaffected by the fact that the practices at times may be conducted by female guards. There being no reasonable expectation of privacy, s. 8 of the Charter is not called into play; nor is s. 7 implicated.

It does not follow from the fact that female prison inmates are not subject to cross-gender frisk searches and surveillance that these practices result in discriminatory treatment of male inmates. Equality under s. 15(1) of the Charter does not necessarily connote identical treatment; in fact, different treatment may be called for in certain cases to promote equality. Equality, in the present context, does not demand that practices which are forbidden where male officers guard female inmates must also be banned where female officers guard male inmates.

The reality of the relationship between the sexes is such that the historical trend of violence perpetrated by men against women is not marched by a comparable trend pursuant to which men are the victims and women the aggressors. Biologically, a frisk search or surveillance of a man's chest area conducted by a female guard does not implicate the same concerns as the same practice by a male guard in relation to a female inmate. Moreover, women generally occupy a disadvantaged position in society in relation to men. (p. 877)

Given the historical, biological and sociological differences between men and women, it is clear that the effect of cross-gender searching is different and more threatening for women than for men.

The different treatment to which the appellant objects thus may not be discrimination at all. (p. 878)

In any event, even if this different treatment amounts to a breach of s. 15(1), the practices are saved by s. 1 of the Charter. The important government objectives of inmate rehabilitation and security of the institution are promoted as a result of the humanizing effect of having women in these positions. Moreover, Parliament's ideal of achieving employment equity is given a material application by way of this initiative. The proportionality of the means used to the importance of these ends would thus justify the breach of s. 15(1), if any.

IN THE SUPREME COURT OF CANADA

(ON APPEAL FROM THE COURT OF APPEAL FOR ONTARIO)

BETWEEN:

M.(K.)

Appellant

(Plaintiff)

AND:

M.(H.)

Respondent

(Defendant)

AND:

WOMEN'S LEGAL EDUCATION AND ACTION FUND (LEAF)

Intervenor

Factum of the Women's Legal Education and Action Fund (LEAF)

M.(K.) v. M.(H.)

INTRODUCTION

Between the ages of 8 and 16, K.M. was sexually abused by her father. Although she never forgot the abuse, it was not until she had undergone counselling for psychological problems in her adult life that she realized the extent of the damage she had suffered as a result. When she was 28, K.M. commenced a civil suit against her father. A jury assessed damages at $50,000 but the trial judge ruled that the award was barred by section 45 of the Ontario Limitations Act, which set a limitation of four years for actions founded in "assault, battery, wounding or imprisonment." The limitation period commenced upon the plaintiff's reaching the age of majority and becoming aware of the assault. K.M. appealed on several grounds that included: incest is a separate and distinct tort that should not be subject to any limitation period; and if a limitation period does apply, it cannot start to run until the incest survivor makes the link between the incest and her full injuries, which is often delayed until the survivor is in therapy. After the Ontario Court of Appeal dismissed the case, K.M. appealed further to the Supreme Court. LEAF was the sole intervenor.

FACTUM

PART I: FACTS

1. The Intervenor, the Women's Legal Education and Action Fund (LEAF), is a national advocacy organization engaged in public education, research, and test case litigation. Its objective is to secure women's equality rights as guaranteed by the Canadian Charter of Rights and Freedoms. LEAF has developed extensive expertise regarding sexual violence against women and children and access to justice for sexual assault survivors.

2. The Intervenor adopts the facts as set out in the Appellant's Factum.

PART II: ISSUES

3. The Intervenor submits that the limitation of actions by victims of childhood sexual assault entails issues of both sex and age equality and, accordingly, the interpretation and application of limitations law to such actions must be consistent with the principles and values enshrined in section 15 of the Charter of Rights and Freedoms.

4. LEAF submits that an interpretation of limitations law that is consistent with constitutionally protected sex and age equality rights would preserve actions for childhood sexual assault by:

(a) an application of the doctrine of delayed discovery that recognizes the dynamics of childhood sexual assault;

(b) an application of equitable principles that would prevent a perpetrator from relying on his own misconduct to escape liability by raising the statute of limitations as a defence; and

(c) recognizing that a parent owes a fiduciary duty to his child and that childhood sexual assault by a parent constitutes a breach of that duty, an action for which there is no statutory limitation period.

PART III: ARGUMENT

Childhood Sexual Assault Is an Equality Issue

5. Child sexual abuse is a largely hidden yet pervasive problem that has damaged the lives of tens of thousands of Canadian children. The most comprehensive Canadian study reveals the following findings:

(a) At some time during their lives, about one in two females and one in three males have been victims of one or more unwanted sexual acts.

(b) About four in five of these unwanted sexual acts had been first committed against these persons when they were children or youths.

(c) Four in one hundred of young females have been raped.

(d) About three in four persons who have been sexually assaulted for the first time as children were females (71.8 percent) and about one in four (28.2 percent) was a male.

(e) About one in four assailants is a family member or a person in a position of trust.

(f) At least one in eleven children under the age of seven is sexually assaulted by someone in a position of parental authority.

(g) Virtually all assailants are males; one in one hundred is female.

(h) About 90 percent of the victims of child sexual assault are female.

Report of the Committee on Sexual Offences Against Children and Youth: Sexual Offences Against Children, vol. I (Ottawa: Canadian Government Publishing Centre, 1984) (Badgley Report), at 1-2, 196-98, and 213-15.

6. Other Canadian authorities confirm that the targets of child sexual abuse are predominantly female while men make up the overwhelming majority of the perpetrators.

K. Finkel, "Sexual Abuse of Children in Canada" (1984), 130 *The Canadian Medical Association Journal*, 345, at 345 and 348.

Report of the Manitoba Advisory Council on the Status of Women: The "System's" Response to Victims of Incest in Manitoba (Manitoba, 1985), at 2-4.

Report of the Special Adviser to the Minister of National Health and Welfare on Child Sexual Abuse in Canada: Reaching for Solutions (Ottawa: Supply and Services, 1990) (Rogers Report), at 17 and 22.

7. Women are socially defined as inferior and as appropriate targets for forced sex. As a result of these perceptions, women are made vulnerable to sexual assault. Not only are women targeted for sexual assault, their accusations of sexual assault and their claims of injury are systematically disbelieved because of their gender. Children are targeted for sexual assault because of age and sex, that is, because of their vulnerability, accessibility, powerlessness, and lack of credibility.

Rogers Report, supra, at 17-18.

8. Just as women are sexually harassed based on their sex, women are sexually assaulted based on their sex. This Court has quoted with approval a scholar's argument that sexual harassment is used in a sexist society to "underscore women's difference from, and by implication, inferiority with respect to the dominant male group" and to "remind women of their inferior ascribed status." The same is true of sexual assault.

Janzen and Govereau v. Platy Enterprises Ltd. et al., [1989] 1 SCR 1252.

9. Sexual assault is categorical and group-based. Just as "no man would have been subjected to [sexual harassment]," men are not under most circumstances subjected to sexual assault by women; nor are adult men treated in the way children of both sexes are treated by those who sexually assault them. Just as "[a]ny female considering employment at the ... [r]estaurant was a potential victim ... and as such was disadvantaged because of her sex," any woman and child in an unequal society is a potential victim of sexual assault and as such is disadvantaged because of age and sex.

Janzen and Govereau, supra, at 1288-90.

10. It is submitted that childhood sexual assault constitutes discrimination on the basis of sex and age. Its treatment by the legal system therefore implicates the equality rights of women and children. For purposes of the laws concerning sexual assault, women and children are groups disadvantaged by social inequality within the meaning of section 15 of the Charter of Rights and Freedoms.

11. The appellant's gender and age made her vulnerable to abuse of power by someone already powerful in the relationship by virtue of his parental status. On the basis of sex, the appellant suffered "the unwanted imposition of a sexual requirement in the context of unequal power." That power imbalance, and the previous abuse of that power, affected her ability to bring a civil action against her father.

Janzen and Govereau, supra, at 1280.

12. LEAF therefore submits that the denial of effective civil redress for this plaintiff and for victims of childhood sexual assault generally is a denial of equal protection and equal benefit of the law.

The Charter as an Interpretive Aid to Limitations Law

13. The Charter is the supreme law of the land and, accordingly, the common law and statutes must be interpreted and applied in a manner that is consistent with the fundamental values enshrined in the Charter. LEAF submits that this Court has jurisdiction to consider Charter arguments in this case even though they were not raised at trial or on appeal.

Corporation Professionnelle des Médecins du Québec v. Thibault, [1988] 1 SCR 1033, at 1039.

Hills et al. v. AG Canada, [1988] 1 SCR 513, at 558.

R v. Thompson, [1990] 2 SCR 1111, at 1158.

Retail, Wholesale & Department Store Union, Local 580 v. Dolphin Delivery Ltd., [1986] 2 SCR 573, at 592-93 and 603.

R v. Swain, [1991] 1 SCR 933.

15. In this Court's developing jurisprudence, while section 15 does not itself guarantee social equality, equality law is seen as a means to attaining an equal society. Thus, the purpose of section 15 "is to ensure equality in the formulation and application of the law. The promotion of equality entails the promotion of a society in which all are secure in the knowledge that they are recognized at law as human beings equally deserving of concern, respect and consideration."

Andrews v. Law Society of British Columbia, [1989] 1 SCR 143, at 171.

16. This Court has acknowledged the importance of promoting the equality of disadvantaged groups. In the words of Madam Justice Wilson (as she then was), "... s. 15 is designed to protect those groups who suffer social, political and legal disadvantage in our society ... ."

Andrews, supra, at 154.

17. LEAF submits that limitations law including the doctrines of reasonable discoverability and fraudulent concealment, where it impacts on equality rights, must be interpreted and applied in a manner consistent with the rights and values enshrined in the Charter, and in particular, the equality standards articulated by the Court.

18. Where a statute can reasonably bear a meaning that would accord with Charter values, such an interpretation should be favoured. In interpreting legislation, "the values embodied in the Charter must be given preference over an interpretation which would run contrary to them."

Hills, supra, at 558.

19. Common law rules should be formulated and developed on the basis of the rights and values guaranteed by the Charter.

Dolphin Delivery, supra, at 603.

Swain, supra, at 8.

20. This Court now considers the social and economic context in which women live their lives to ensure its decisions afford true equality for Canadian women. It has recognized that the specific reality of women's experience of social and sexual subordination must be appreciated in order to ensure that women are truly accorded equal protection and benefit of the law. For example, the "Battered Wife Syndrome" was recently recognized as a valid defence to a charge of murder. This entails an appreciation that it is predominantly women who experience spousal assault and that, in the interests of equality, legal doctrine must be responsive to women's experience. The issue of whether the accused's apprehension of death or grievous bodily harm was reasonable was assessed in light of her particular circumstances, as elucidated by expert opinion on the "Battered Woman Syndrome." Similarly, the reasonableness of a sexual assault victim's delay in commencing suit must be assessed in light of her particular circumstances and expert opinion on "Post-Traumatic Stress Disorder" or the "Post-Incest Syndrome" experienced by sexual assault victims.

R v. Lavallee, [1990] 1 SCR 852, at 877.

21. In determining that pregnancy discrimination and the abuse of sexual and economic power in the workplace constituted discrimination on the basis of sex, this Court assessed and recognized the impact of women's social, sexual and economic disadvantage in society. This case also commands a fresh approach in light of the reality of sexual assault in the lives of children, the majority of whose victims are female.

Brooks v. Canada Safeway Ltd., [1989] 1 SCR 1219, at 1238.

Janzen and Govereau, supra.

22. Limitations law is, by its very nature, a balancing of the interests between plaintiffs who wish to pursue legal action for recovery of damages and defendants who expect to be free of stale claims. In actions arising from childhood sexual assault, the Charter requires that this balancing of interests must be done in a manner that does not impose a disproportionately detrimental burden on women and children as compared with men. It is submitted that the legal analysis adopted by the trial judge does not meet this requirement and is therefore discriminatory.

23. An interpretation of the law is discriminatory when it has the effect of imposing burdens, obligations, or disadvantages or when it withholds or limits access to opportunities, benefits, and advantages available to others. In formulating its approach to equality,

this Court has ruled that the overriding concern is to increase the substantive equality of those groups previously excluded from power and full participation.

Andrews, supra, at 174.

Brooks, supra, at 1238.

R v. Turpin et al., [1989] 1 SCR 1296, at 1329.

24. Denial of the right to seek a civil remedy for childhood sexual assault creates and perpetuates the relative powerlessness of women and children, who are already disadvantaged in society. It does so to the advantage of men who wield their power to sexually exploit and abuse women and children.

25. LEAF submits that the interpretation of limitations law in childhood sexual abuse cases that is consistent with the principles and values enshrined in the Charter would:

(a) toll any applicable limitations period until:

(i) the injuries resulting from the sexual assault or assaults are substantially manifested, and

(ii) the plaintiff knows or ought reasonably to have known that the injuries are attributable to sexual assault, and

(iii) a reasonable person, in the particular circumstances of the plaintiff, ought to be able to bring an action without harm to his or her own interests and without aggravating the injuries of the sort pleaded in the statement of claim;

(b) disentitle a defendant from relying on a limitation period to bar childhood sexual assault where it would be inequitable to do so; and

(c) where there exists a dependency relationship between the plaintiff and defendant permit a victim to recover damages for childhood sexual assault through an action for breach of fiduciary duty.

26. It is submitted that such an interpretation is consistent not only with the principles and values enshrined in the Charter, but also with pre-Charter principles and policies of common law; an interpretation of common law made through the filter of Charter values magnifies the aptness of such an approach. Such an interpretation can be reached through an application of the existing principles with consideration of the following:

(a) the unique dynamics of the childhood sexual assault;

(b) the policy and principles both of limitations law and the law of tort; and

(c) principles of equity.

27. It is submitted that the Intervenor is not seeking a retrospective application of the Charter for the following reasons:

(a) The Charter is being relied upon, not to strike down the statute of limitations, but as an aid to its interpretation. Because the action was commenced after section 15 came into effect, a proper legal analysis of the limitations defence, which raises equality issues, must take into account the principles and values of the Charter.

(b) The Ontario limitations statute does not operate to extinguish personal causes of action. Therefore LEAF submits the issue of statutory interpretation does not arise until the statue of limitations is pleaded as a defence.

(c) Reliance on a statute of limitations to bar the plaintiff's action constitutes a continuing and current violation of her right to equal protection and benefit of the law. The continuing discrimination lies in the ongoing protection afforded primarily male defendants in sexual assault cases from otherwise recoverable damages flowing from their wrongful acts compared with the denial to primarily female/infant plaintiffs to access to damages through civil action.

(d) Alternatively, the Intervenor submits that the respondent's arguments on retrospectivity do not apply to a Charter analysis of a cause of action for breach of fiduciary duty given the absence of a statutory limitation period for such an action.

Corporation Professionelle des Médecins du Quebec v. Thibault, supra, at 1046-47.

Dubois v. The Queen, [1985] 2 SCR 350, at 359-60.

Limitations Act, RSO 1980, c. 240, as amended, ss. 15 and 245.

R v. Gamble, [1988] 2 SCR 595.

Whittman et al. v. Emmott et al. (1991), 77 DLR (4th) 77 (BC CA).

The Dynamics of Childhood Sexual Assault

28. The particular injuries caused by childhood sexual assault arise from the fact that the sexual abuse occurs within the context of a relationship of trust and dependency. Adult authority or parental power is exercised not only to perpetrate the sexual exploitation of the dependent, innocent child but to prevent recognition and revelation of the abuse.

Case on Appeal, vol. I, at 279, lines 23-30.

D. Finklehor and A. Brown, "The Traumatic Impact of Child Sexual Abuse: A Conceptualization" (1985), 55(4) *American Orthopsychiatric Association Inc.* 531, at 532-33.

R.C. Summit, "The Child Sexual Abuse Accommodation Syndrome" (1983), 7 *Child Abuse and Neglect* 177, at 182-84.

29. The abuser wields his power to secure silence about the incestuous relationship through threats of physical harm or more subtle means, such as inducements or promises. The adult may convince the child that disclosure will lead to the disintegration of the family, the child's removal from the home, or that the child will be disbelieved and rejected.

Case on Appeal, vol. I, at 59, 60, 64, 67, 68, 71, 74-75, 110, 135-36, 137, and 141-42.

Margaret J. Allen, "Tort Remedies for Incestuous Abuse" (1983), 13 *Golden Gate University Law Rev.* 609, at 630.

Finklehor and Brown, supra, at 532.

B. Handler, "Civil Claims of Adults Molested as Children: Maturation of Harm and the Statute of Limitations Hurdle" (1987), 15 *Fordham Urban Law Journal* 709, at 715-17.

Melissa G. Salten,"Statutes of Limitations in Civil Incest Actions: Preserving the Victims Remedy" (1984), 7 *Harvard Women's Law Journal* 206, at 196-97.

30. Silencing is particularly powerful and effective within the parent-child relationship. The thought of "betraying" the person on whom the child is entirely dependent for all the necessities of life may evoke feelings of guilt and disloyalty and precipitate terrible uncertainty about the consequences for herself and her family. Victims often maintain their silence in the hope of protecting a sibling, or preserving the integrity of the family unit.

Case on Appeal, vol. I, at 67, lines 28-29; at 220, lines 3-6.

Allen, supra, at 615.

Salten, supra, at 197.

Summit, supra, at 181-82.

31. A child's involuntary participation in the "conspiracy of silence" will foster feelings of guilt and shame. The abuser may, as he did in this case, construct the sexual encounters in such a way that she is made to feel she instigated the sexual contact. She will come to perceive herself as an accomplice in her own exploitation. Thus victims lose their nascent ability to determine right from wrong and real from unreal, as they become entrapped in the abuser's definition of what he is doing to them.

Case on Appeal, vol. I, at 66, lines 26-32; at 95, lines 6-11; at 107, lines 28-30; at 217, lines 27-28; at 218, lines 3-6; at 277, lines 24-30; at 306, lines 12-20; and at 327, lines 23-28.

Allen, supra, at 616.

Salten, supra, at 197-99.

32. Child victims develop an array of defensive mechanisms in order to accommodate or survive the reality of ongoing sexual molestation. These include dissociation, repression and denial. Their particular constellation is peculiar to childhood sexual assault and has been coined "Post-Traumatic Stress Disorder" or "Post-Incest Syndrome."

Case on Appeal, vol. I, at 66, lines 3-6; at 101, lines 9-12; at 193, lines 18-32; at 196, lines 9-10; at 207, lines 21-28; at 208, lines 26-32; at 209, lines 3-23; at 225, lines 15-30; and at 304, lines 7-19.

Handler, supra, at 716-19.

J. Lamm, "Easing Access to the Courts for Incest Victims: Towards an Equitable Application of the Delayed Discovery Rule" (1991), 100 *Yale Law Journal* 2187, at 2198.

A. Rosenfeld, "The Statute of Limitations Barrier in Childhood Sexual Abuse Cases: The Equitable Estoppel Remedy," [1989] 12 *Harvard Women's Law Journal* 206, at 208-10.

Summit, supra, at 184-86.

33. Victims of childhood abuse often experience a sense of powerlessness, particularly relative to the perpetrator, a loss of self-esteem, and a loss of confidence of those traditionally in a position of trust or authority.

Case on Appeal, vol. I, at 105, lines 27-32; vol. II, at 410, lines 7-8.

Finklehor and Brown, supra, at 532.

Salten, supra, at 200-201.

34. Despite the operation of these overwhelming psychodynamics, some victims disclose their abuse while it is still occurring. The response to the disclosure is critical. If the child's disclosure is validated and she receives appropriate professional intervention, her chance of proceeding onto a path of recovery is good. If family members pressure her to suppress or retract her story or if her disclosure is met with disbelief or lack of understanding, her victimization will become intensified. She will likely recant and repress the abuse.

Case on Appeal, vol. I, at 74, lines 2-33; at 75, lines 4-9; at 134, lines 8-32; at 135, lines 3-8 and 14-32; at 136, lines 3-32; at 234, lines 7-23; at 280, lines 20-22; and at 306, lines 27-30.

Summit, supra, at 186-88.

35. Until recently few professionals had the knowledge or skill to handle a disclosure effectively. Some even held the view that disclosure was apt to be a lie or fantasy as it was to be the painful revelation of a terrible truth.

Case on Appeal, vol. I, at 211, lines 8-32; at 212, lines 3-29; at 204, lines 2-32; at 235, lines 23-28; vol. II, at 476, lines 25-30.

Summit, supra, at 190.

36. Disclosure of the sexual abuse by a victim does not mean she understands that it is wrong or appreciates the injuries. There is a difference between a child feeling the acts are unwanted and invasive and knowing that her father is wrongfully abusing his parental power. It is yet a further step to understanding that wrongful abuse gives rise to legal redress.

Case on Appeal, vol. I, at 132, lines 24-32.

Salten, supra, at 199.

37. The injuries of childhood sexual assault are extremely complex and many of them do not manifest themselves until many years after the abuse ceases. In addition to the loss of self-esteem, self-respect, confidence, and trust in others is the experience of extreme fear and phobias. Sexual permissiveness or promiscuity is a common reaction. Childhood sexual assault victims frequently encounter difficulties in intimate relations,

including sexual intimacy. They may experience a variety of psychosomatic problems, such as nightmares, insomnia, headaches, gastro-intestinal problems, or numbness. They commonly suffer from addictive behaviour, depression, suicidal periods, self-mutilation, and anxiety.

Case on Appeal, vol. I, at 86, lines 3-16; at 87, lines 16-18; at 88, lines 12-32; at 90, lines 3-11; at 98, lines 21-27; at 103, lines 3-32; and at 104, lines 21-32.

Case on Appeal, vol. II, at 311, lines 18-23; at 317, lines 30-32; at 318, lines 3-11, at 409; lines 17-18, at 410; lines 7-8 and 10; and at 411, line 13.

D. Gelinas, "The Persisting Negative Effects of Incest" (1983), 46 *Psychiatry* 312, at 315-23.

Lamm, supra, at 2192-95.

38. A mishandled disclosure reinforces the conditioned silencing by the perpetrator and results in further psychological repression and damage. It also reinforces the victim's view that she is to blame.

Case on Appeal, vol. I, at 326, lines 7-28; at 329, lines 22-32; and at 330, lines 3-22.

39. It is submitted that the dynamics of childhood sexual assault as described above prevent the victim from perceiving and discovering her injuries until mature adulthood, for the following reasons:

(a) The very nature of the injuries and their latent manifestations render them inherently imperceptible.

(b) She has been subjected to years of conditioning by her perpetrator to remain silent about the abusive relationship.

(c) If she has attempted to disclose the abuse and this disclosure was accompanied by family pressure to recant or inappropriate professional advice, the pressure to remain silent will be reinforced.

(d) As a result of the abuse and any outside reaction to it, she has developed deep mistrust of authority figures and has been conditioned to believe any further revelation of the abuse will be met with disbelief.

(e) In order to survive psychologically she is actively engaged in ways to repress, forget, minimize, or deny the realities of the abuse.

(f) She feels guilty and complicit about the abuse and therefore does not identify the perpetrator as the wrongdoer.

(g) Society has yet to fully recognize, understand, and be receptive to the problem.

40. As a result of these factors, and because the injuries do not manifest themselves until much later in life, victims of childhood sexual assault do not appreciate the nexus between their injuries and the sexual assault. It is necessary for a victim to make the causal connection between the assault and her injuries, for her to identify the perpetrator as the wrongdoer or potential defendant.

Case on Appeal, vol. I, at 100, lines 4-24; at 101, lines 9-32; at 107, lines 2-32; at 108, lines 3-8; at 215, lines 7-17; at 218, lines 19-23; at 219, lines 3-16; at 222, line 29; at 307, lines 3-5; at 313, lines 8-10; at 314, lines 23-25; at 319, lines 20-24; at 320, lines 14-18; at 330, lines 11-32; at 338, lines 26-30; and at 335, lines 3-22.

41. Victims often require appropriate professional intervention before they are able to realize that they are innocent victims and shift the blame to where it belongs. Appropriate therapy assists victims in appreciating the cause of their injuries and in overcoming their overwhelming sense of powerlessness in order to do something about it.

Case on Appeal, vol. II, at 285, lines 16-21; at 328, lines 11-26; at 331, lines 3-9; at 340, lines 14-16; at 367, lines 18-21; at 386, lines 16-29; and at 389, lines 6-23.

42. Professionals with experience or expertise in childhood sexual abuse realize that even when a victim discloses abuse she may be psychologically unready to relate the details or deal with it. Until she is ready, it would be inappropriate, and perhaps negligent, to insist that she explore the issue in her therapy.

Case on Appeal, vol. I, at 261, lines 5-30.

43. LEAF submits that in light of these dynamics, a victim of childhood sexual abuse should not be expected to commence suit until:

(a) there is a substantial manifestation of her injuries;

(b) she appreciates that the conduct of the perpetrator is wrongful;

(c) she causally connects the tortious act with her injuries; and

(d) having regard to all the particular circumstances, it would be reasonable for her to do so.

To bar a victim of sexual assault from legal action against the perpetrator before these conditions are met would fail to provide her with equal protection and benefit of the law.

Limitation Law as a Barrier to Civil Redress

44. Limitation periods have been framed to embrace the interests of individual litigants as well as broader societal interests, with the particular rationale of limitation periods being identified as follows:

(a) the desirability of having an assessment of the evidence while the memories of witnesses are relatively fresh and reliable;

(b) a concern for potential defendants in granting them a period of repose in which they need no longer be concerned about potential lawsuits;

(c) a need for diligence on the part of potential claimants to ensure that the resources of the judicial system are directed toward current problems. The imposition of limitation periods is thought to prompt early settlement thereby minimizing the disruptive effects of unsettled claims on commercial intercourse.

Handler, supra, at 719-21.

E. Hartnett, "Use of Massachusetts Discovery Rule by Adult Survivors of Father-Daughter Incest" (1990), 24 *New England Law Review* 1243, at 1253.

Rosenfeld, supra, at 211-12.

45. An application of the rationale for limitation periods to childhood sexual assault does not disclose a need for a strict interpretation in that:

(a) Due to statutory tolling of limitation periods until the age of majority, evidence in these cases is inevitably stale in any event;

(b) There is no equitable rationale for allowing perpetrators of this intentional tort to move on with their lives without liability or worry while their victims suffer the consequences for the rest of their lives;

(c) Failure to initiate early action results not from lack of diligence on the part of victims but rather from an inability that is a direct result of the tortious act.

W.K.L. v. The Queen (unreported May 16, 1991, SCC). Reasons for Judgment by McLachlin J, at 11.

Lamm, supra, at 2198.

46. In recognition of the principles and policies on which it is founded, the law of limitations allows for an extension beyond strict time frames in order to preserve actions in appropriate circumstances. This is achieved through statutory extensions in cases of minority or unsoundness of mind. Additionally, through the application of the doctrine of reasonable discoverability courts have tolled the application of a limitation period until the plaintiff discovers, or ought to have discovered by exercise of reasonable diligence, the material facts on which the cause of action is based. Furthermore, the courts have applied the principle of fraudulent concealment to extend limitation periods in circumstances where it would be inequitable to allow the defendant to assert such a bar.

Limitations Act, RSO 1980, c. 240, s. 47, as amended.

Central Trust Company v. Rafuse, [1986] 2 SCR 147.

Guerin v. The Queen, [1984] 2 SCR 355.

47. Courts have recognized that limitation periods should be interpreted liberally in order to satisfy the objective of securing an opportunity for a plaintiff to seek redress for wrongdoing. "Where two interpretations of the statute are possible, reason favours the one which enables the plaintiff to bring his action."

Papamonolopoulos v. Board of Education for the City of Toronto (1986), 56 OR (2d) 1 (CA), at 7.

48. It is submitted that the circumstances of childhood sexual abuse demand an accommodation of limitations law so as not to deny recovery to victims whose delay in bringing an action is not a result of their own lack of diligence but is generally the result of the very attributes for which they were targeted by the abuser.

49. LEAF submits that an expansive interpretation of limitations law as applied to childhood sexual assault would also be consistent with the purposes and policies of tort law. While the principal purpose of tort law is to compensate the plaintiff for damages, deterrence is also recognized as one of its fundamental purposes. This is particularly so for torts of intention.

Allen M. Linden, *Studies in Canadian Tort Law* (Toronto: Butterworths, 1982), at 6 and 23.

Granville Williams, "The Aim of Tort Law" (1951), *Current Legal Problem* 137, at 144 and 172.

50. The suit of a victim of childhood sexual assault should be preserved in order to ensure that both policy objectives of tort law are achieved. The ongoing and insidious nature of the injuries resulting from childhood sexual assault can result not only in significant ongoing expense for the individual plaintiff, but can constitute a drain on the public's resources required to rehabilitate plaintiffs. Public policy would dictate a shifting of these financial burdens to the perpetrator of the injuries.

51. Similarly, the concern for deterrence demands an expansive interpretation of limitations law. The intentional tort of childhood sexual abuse is an egregious wrong, the deterrence of which is of greater social importance than the individual right of a sexual offender to escape liability by the operation of a limitation period. This balance can only be achieved if the defendant is prevented from relying on a delay that, in many cases, his own conduct has created.

52. In holding that a sexual assault case pending before the criminal court should proceed, notwithstanding delay, this Court confirmed that delay in reporting sexual abuse is understandable and affirmed that a "judicial statute of limitations would mean sexual abusers would be able to take advantage of the failure to report which they themselves, in many cases caused." This principle is equally germaine to the civil context.

W.K.L., supra, at 10-11.

The Doctrine of Reasonable Discoverability as Applied to Childhood Sexual Assault

53. The traditional limitations rule that the date of accrual of a cause of action is the date of the wrongful act giving rise to the claim, "developed against the relatively unsophisticated backdrop of barroom brawls, intersection collisions, and slips and falls … ." In many contexts, including assault, this rule is not unreasonable as the connection between the defendant's act and the plaintiff's injuries is usually apparent at the time. For example, it is not unreasonable to expect the victim of a car accident to realize that injury has resulted or will likely result.

Martinez-Perrer v. Richardson-Merrell, Inc., App. 164, 105 Cal. Rptr. 591 (Cal. CA, 1980), at 595.

54. Canadian courts have recognized circumstances where this connection is not readily apparent. Courts have held that it would be an injustice to bar a plaintiff from

bringing a claim if she was unaware of its existence, even if a lengthy delay has passed. This Court has held that a cause of action in tort could not accrue until the plaintiff had discovered or ought reasonably to have discovered by the exercise of reasonable diligence the material facts on which to base a claim. While this could lead to greater exposure for defendants, it would be a greater injustice to deny relief to the plaintiff.

Central Trust Co., supra, at 223-24.

City of Kamloops v. Nielson, [1984] 2 SCR 2, at 40.

Consumers Glass Co. Ltd. v. Foundation of Canada Ltd. (1985), 51 OR (2d) 385 (CA), at 399-400.

55. The term "injury" is not synonymous with "wrongful act" but is a separate legal concept referring to the damages caused by the wrongful act. Thus, discovery of "injury" means discovery of the damaging effects of the wrongful acts, not discovery or knowledge of the acts themselves. The discovery rule will apply in cases where the defendant's act would not serve to put the reasonable plaintiff on notice that injury will ensue from that act.

Central Trust Co., supra, at 223-24.

Consumers Glass Co. Ltd., supra, at 399-400.

56. In actions for personal injury or professional negligence, the running of the limitation periods pursuant to the British Columbia limitation statute is postponed until such time as a reasonable person acquires appropriate advice. The law recognizes that it may be difficult, even impossible, for persons to ascertain the casual connection between a wrongful act and a subsequent injury without such advice. The statute also directs the court to consider the plaintiff's own interests and circumstance in determining when the plaintiff ought to be able to bring an action. Accordingly, circumstances such as the relationship of the plaintiff to the defendant (for example, an employee-employer relationship) and the availability of appropriate advice would be circumstances relevant to the determination of the date the limitation period commences.

Evans v. Vancouver Port Corporation (1989), 42 BCLR (2d) 174 (CA), at 183.

Limitations Act, RSBC 1979, c. 236, s. 6.

57. Even in the absence of specific statutory language, American courts have adopted a similar approach in products liability actions. Until a plaintiff receives the relevant medical diagnosis that connects the symptomatology to the noxious substance or device, the limitation period is postponed.

Allied Resin Corp. et al. v. Barry J. Waltz, 559 NE 2d 390, at 393 (Ind. App. 1 Dist., 1990).

Hando v. P.P.G. Industries Inc., 881 P.2d 956 (Mont., 1989), at 961-62.

58. In medical malpractice suits, the cause of action accrues when the plaintiff becomes aware of his or her injury and when he or she discovers the causal relationship between the harm and the defendant's misconduct, an awareness that almost invariably requires medical or professional knowledge.

Gaudet et al. v. Levy et al. (1984), 47 OR (2d) 577 (HC), at 582-83.

Raymond v. Eli Lilly & Co., 371 A.2d 170 (New Hampshire SC, 1977), at 172-74.

59. In all of the aforementioned authorities, the date for determining when the limitation period starts running depended upon the nature of the harm and how that harm could reasonably be ascertained. Since the injuries occasioned by childhood sexual assault are primarily psychological and extremely complex, and because long-standing blocking mechanisms have to be overcome, survivors often require professional assistance to recognize the connection between the sexual acts and the resulting emotional, psychological, and social damage they have suffered. Generally, it is only when a survivor enters therapy that any meaningful understanding of her injuries can be developed. Accordingly, a reasonableness standard for the harms caused by sexual assault would postpone the limitation period until a plaintiff, acting diligently, receives appropriate professional advice.

Case on Appeal, vol. I, at 97, lines 8-32; at 101, lines 11-30; and at 207, lines 18-28.

Salten, supra, at 202.

60. Delayed discovery must also be understood within the context of a society in which childhood sexual assault, until very recently, was never publicly acknowledged or very well understood. Survivors have been powerfully silenced by the social unwillingness to deal with the problem and by the stigmatization of those survivors who dared to name the harm. Such an atmosphere impeded survivors like the Appellant, and thousands like her, from uncovering the link between their injuries and the abuse they suffered as children. Instead, it contributed to keeping the connection obscured. Precisely because childhood sexual assault is poorly understood and its manifestations are primarily psychological, professional intervention is usually required before the victim can discover her injuries and their cause.

Allen, supra, at 630-31.

61. Childhood sexual assault causes deep-rooted injuries that are more subtle and complex than those caused by other tortious acts. Their latent manifestation makes them more analogous to injuries caused by toxic exposure, than to injuries caused by a car crash or simple assault. While there is no Canadian case law directly on point, courts in the United States have carefully considered the particular dynamics of incest in applying the delayed discovery doctrine.

Evans et al. v. Eckelman et al., 265 Cal. Rptr. 605 (Cal. App. 1 Dist., 1990).

Hammer v. Hammer, 418 NW 2d 23 (Wis. App., 1987).

Hildebrand v. Hildebrand, 736 F. Supp. 1512 (SD Ind., 1990).

Johnson v. Johnson and Johnson, 701 F. Supp. 1316 (ND Ill., 1988).

Lindabury v. Lindabury, 552 SO 2d 1117 (Fla. App. 3 Dist., 1989).

Osland v. Osland, 442 NW 2d 907 (ND, 1989).

Petersen v. Bruen, 792 P.2d 18 (Nev., 1990).

62. A recent decision in the English Court of Appeal recognizes that delayed discovery must be applied in a manner that is responsive to the unique dynamics of childhood sexual assault and, further, in a way that recognizes that the delay is a direct result of the wrongdoing of the abuser. While interpreting a different statutory regime that Court held that the limitations period was tolled until the plaintiff:

(a) knew that her injuries were "serious" and sufficiently serious to institute proceedings; and

(b) knew or ought reasonably to have known that the injuries were attributable in whole or part to the actions of the defendant.

In assessing the later criteria, the Court took into account the nature of the injuries, the impact of those injuries, and the lack of public awareness concerning child abuse.

Stubbings v. Webb (1991), 3 WWR 383 (Eng. CA).

Fraudulent Concealment as Applied to Childhood Sexual Assault

63. The principle of fraudulent concealment has been applied to temper the strict application of limitation periods in circumstances where it would be inequitable for the defendant to rely on such a defence. Fraud, in this context, is used in the broadest sense to include not only common law fraud but other intentional wrongdoing, where it would be against conscience to allow the defendant to avail himself of the lapse of time.

64. The statutory limitation period will be tolled, as a result of concealed fraud, until the plaintiff discovers the fraud or with reasonable diligence ought to have discovered it.

Archer v. Moss, [1971] 1 All ER 746 (Eng. CA), at 750.

Massie & Renwick Ltd. v. Underwriters' Survey Bureau Ltd. et al., [1940] SCR 218, at 244.

Nesbitt, Thompson & Co. v. Pigott, [1941] SCR 520, at 530.

Pigott et al v. Nesbitt Thompson & Co. Ltd., [1939] OR 66 (CA), at 82-83.

Underwriters' Survey Bureau Ltd. et al. v. Massie & Renwick Ltd., [1937] Ex. CR 103, at 126-28.

65. The classic definition of equitable fraud adopted in fraudulent concealment jurisprudence is as stated by Lord Evershed:

> It is, I think, clear that the phrase covers conduct which, having regard to some special circumstances between the parties concerned it is an unconscionable thing for one to do towards the other.

Kitchen v. Royal Air Forces Ass'n et al., [1958] 2 All ER 241 (Eng. CA), at 246.

66. While the finding of equitable fraud has not been restricted to circumstances where some duty is owed by the defendant to the plaintiff, the nature of their relationship is taken into account in determining whether equity should intervene on behalf of the plaintiff to relieve against a statutory limitation period.

Guerin, supra, at 389-90.

Kitchen, supra, at 246.

Phototinopoulos v. Phototinopoulos et al. (1989), 31 CPC (2d) 267 (Alta. CA), at 273-75.

Public Trustee v. Mortimer et al. (1985), 49 OR (2d) 741 (HC), at 753-54.

67. For an application of the doctrine of fraudulent concealment, it is not necessary for the wrongdoer to take active measures to prevent detection. By saying nothing the tortfeasor keeps it secret. In an assault action where the nature of the assault is "furtive and secret" the doctrine will be involved to the benefit of the plaintiff.

Guerin, supra, at 389-90.

Kitchen, supra.

Massie & Renwick Ltd., supra, at 241.

Nesbitt, Thompson & Co., supra, at 530.

Phototinopoulos, supra, at 273-75.

68. LEAF submits that, in the context of childhood sexual abuse, the concept of fraudulent concealment arises because the perpetrator's conduct is both willful and secret. In many cases, the perpetrator goes further and takes active steps to ensure that his victim does not disclose the abusive relationship to either members of the family, outsiders or both. A perpetrator can conceal the relationship and his wrongdoing through one or more of the following ways:

(a) by applying subtle intimidation through the use of authority over the child;

(b) by creating a context of physical punishment or domination;

(c) by threatening the victim about what might happen to her or the family if she were to disclose;

(d) by the use of rewards or inducements aimed at soliciting compliance with the unwanted sexual contact and at maintaining the silence; and

(e) by placing pressure on the victim and the family if the victim discloses to outsiders.

Handler, supra, at 715-17.

Salten, supra, at 196-99.

Summit, supra, at 181-84.

69. It is submitted that the reliance on equitable principles is particularly compelling to relieve against antiquated limitation periods that were developed without consideration for the vulnerabilities of certain groups such as women and children and that are out of touch with modern conditions.

Public Trustee, supra, at 753-54.

70. To the extent that the Ontario statute of limitations may bar actions such as this one it is submitted that it was formulated in an era when professional and public

awareness did not appreciate the dynamics and extent of childhood sexual assault and is neither reflective of nor responsive to a contemporary analysis of the problem.

Ontario Ministry of the Attorney General, *Report of the Limitations Act Consultation Group: Recommendations for a New Limitations Act*, March 1991.

71. It is submitted that in recognition of the equality rights of both women and children under the Charter, equitable doctrines such as fraudulent concealment should prevail over a narrow application of limitations law.

72. LEAF submits that this Court should give consideration to the application of fraudulent concealment in this case notwithstanding the lack of specific reference to the doctrine as a reply to the limitations defence in the pleadings or in argument at trial.

73. An appellate court will consider an issue on appeal that was not pleaded, proceeded with, nor argued at trial, if it is satisfied beyond doubt, that it has before it all the facts bearing upon the new contention, as completely as would have been the case if the controversy has arisen at the trial. Accordingly, a new issue will not be allowed if there is no evidentiary basis at trial or if the opposing party has missed an opportunity for rebuttal.

Canadiana Towers Ltd. v. Fawcett et al. (1978), 21 OR (2d) 554 (CA), at 563-64.

Connecticut Fire Insurance Company v. Kavanaugh, [1982] AC 473 (Eng. HL), at 480.

K.M. v. H.M. (unreported decision of Ont. CA, November 14, 1989). Reasons for Judgment by Howland CJO.

Lamb and Miller v. Kincaid and Krober, [1907] 38 SCR 516, at 539.

Scarborough Golf & Country Club Ltd. v. City of Scarborough et al. (1988), 66 OR (2d) 257 (CA), at 269.

Shaver Hospital for Chest Diseases v. Slesar et al. (1979), 27 OR (2d) 383 (CA), at 386.

Thomson v. Lambert and Lambert, [1938] SCR 253, at 269.

74. It is submitted that all evidentiary aspects of fraudulent concealment, including the nature of the unconscionable act, the relationship between the parties, the role of the defendant in concealing the wrongdoing and the "discoverability" of the cause of action by the plaintiff were all fully canvassed, both in the pleadings and the evidence at trial. Although fraudulent concealment is a new legal formulation of the plaintiff's case it raises the identical evidentiary issues as do the issues of fiduciary duty, unsoundness of mind and reasonable discoverability, all of which issues were raised in response to the limitations defence.

Case on Appeal, vol. I, Statement of Claim, at 1-13.

Statement of Defence of the Defendant Herbert Metzger, at 15-22.

75. The issue of whether the plaintiff discovered or ought reasonably to have discovered her cause of action was central to the theory of the case as litigated at trial. As

such, a substantial portion of the trial entailed evidence regarding her ability to discover her cause of action and injuries.

Case on Appeal, vol. I; Preliminary Objection at 47; vol. VI, Ruling of the Honourable Mr. Justice Maloney, dated January 22, 1988, at 1133-36.

76. Extensive questioning of the appellant, the respondent, and numerous experts at trial was specifically directed at the perpetrator's attempts to conceal the abusive relationship to demonstrate to the court the unique dynamics of childhood sexual assault and, in particular, to convey to the court how this conditioned silencing affected the plaintiff's ability to discover her injuries.

77. Considerable evidence was tendered at trial on the respondent's use of rewards and inducements, physical punishment, direct threats, and other attempts to ensure the appellant's silence and later recantation once she had disclosed the sexual activity to outsiders.

Case on Appeal, vol. I, Karen Marciano, examination-in-chief, at 59, 60, 64, 67, 68, 71, 74, and 75; Karen Marciano, cross-examination, at 110, 135, 136, 137, 141, and 142; Barbara Pressman, examination-in-chief, at 213, 214, 219, 220, and 224; Barbara Pressman, cross-examination, at 233 and 234.

Vol. II, Dr. Lionel Mausberg, examination-in-chief, at 326 and 329.

Vol. III, Herbert Metzger, examination-in-chief, at 650, 659, 662, 680, and 682.

Vol. IV, Herbert Metzger, cross-examination, at 737, 741, 742, 743, 744, 745, 746, 747; Dr. Ronald Langevine, examination-in-chief, at 847, 850, and 851.

Vol. V, Dr. Ronald Langevine, cross-examination, at 911 and 913.

78. It is respectfully submitted that the appellant placed in issue at trial her father's attempts to conceal his conduct and secure her silence. The respondent had ample opportunity to cross-examine the appellant on this issue and did so.

Case on Appeal, vol. I, Karen Marciano, examination-chief, at 59, 60, 64, 67, 68, 71, 74, and 75; Karen Marciano, cross-examination, at 110, 135, 136, 137, 141, and 142

79. The respondent was also questioned by his counsel and subjected to cross-examination on these allegations. He had ample opportunity to provide explanation regarding his alleged concealment while in the witness box.

Case on Appeal, vol. III, Herbert Metzger, examination-in-chief, at 650, 659, 662, 680, 681, 682;

Vol. IV, Herbert Metzger, cross-examination, at 737, 741, 742, 743, 744, 745, 746, and 747.

80. The fact that a perpetrator must conceal the abusive relationship in order to ensure his victim's sexual accessibility was discussed by many of the experts at trial. Evidence was tendered by these experts both in relation to the appellant's allegations that the perpetrator attempted to conceal his conduct and in the larger context of how

this conspiracy of silence affects victims of sexual abuse. The respondent had ample opportunity to cross-examine the experts on this evidence and in fact did so.

Case on Appeal, vol. I, Barbara Pressman, cross-examination, at 233 and 234.

Vol. II, Dr. Lionel Mausberg, examination-in-chief, at 326 and 329.

Vol. IV, Dr. Ronald Langevine, examination-in-chief, at 847, 850, and 851.

Vol. V, Dr. Ronald Langevine, cross-examination, at 911 and 913.

81. LEAF submits that the facts bearing on the issue of the respondent's attempt to secure the appellant's silence, thereby concealing his conduct, were all included in the extensive examination-in-chief and cross-examination of numerous witnesses. Therefore, it is respectfully submitted that the court had before it all the facts bearing upon this new issue of fraudulent concealment as completely as would be the case had it been pleaded and argued at trial.

82. A perpetrator's concealment of the abusive relationship, commonly referred to in the social science literature, case law, and scholarly articles as his "silencing," is a key factor in understanding the dynamics of childhood sexual abuse and its impact on the victim.

Handler, supra, at 715-17.

Salten, supra, at 196-99.

Summit, supra, at 1281-84.

83. Having regard to the special relationship between the plaintiff and the defendant, particularly in cases of childhood sexual assault, LEAF submits that equity compels relief against any applicable limitation period that works to the benefit of a defendant. It is submitted that fraudulent concealment is an appropriate legal characterization of an abuser's "silencing" behaviour.

84. The applicability of the doctrine of fraudulent concealment or equitable fraud to cases of childhood sexual assault has been advanced by several legal scholars and, it is submitted, ought to be considered by this Court.

D. De Rose, "Adult Incest Survivors and the Statute of Limitations: The Delayed Discovery Rule and Long-Term Damages" (1985), 25 *Santa Clara Law Review* 191, at 197-99.

Handler, supra, at 722-29.

Rosenfeld, supra, at 216-19.

Salten, supra, at 208-11.

85. The Intervenor submits that this Court ought to consider the application of the principle of fraudulent concealment because:

(a) the factual basis for it was pleaded in the Statement of Claim and elaborated in evidence at trial;

(b) all of the facts bearing upon this argument are as completely before this Court as they would be had the argument been advanced at trial; and

(c) the legal analysis adopted by this Court in this case will have a significant impact on the sex equality rights of many Canadian women and children and, therefore, this Court ought to consider every applicable argument; the correct legal characterization of an abuser's "silencing" conduct is key to this analysis.

Childhood Sexual Assault Is a Breach of Fiduciary Duty

86. It is respectfully submitted that a parent stands in a fiduciary relationship to his or her child and therefore owes a duty to that child, a breach of which will give rise to a cause of action for which there is no statutory limitation period. The equitable defence of laches may, however, be invoked to limit an action for breach of fiduciary duty in appropriate circumstances.

87. Although the parent-child relationship does not fall within the traditional categories in which fiduciary obligations have been imposed, it possesses the three general characteristics, which if present, should attract the imposition of a fiduciary obligation. The categories of fiduciary relationships are not closed and should be found to exist where the recognized characteristics exist. These are:

(a) The fiduciary has scope for the exercise of some discretion or power.

(b) The fiduciary can unilaterally exercise that power of discretion so as to affect the beneficiary's legal or practical interests.

(c) The beneficiary is particularly vulnerable to or at the mercy of the fiduciary holding the discretion or power.

Frame v. Smith and Smith, [1987] 2 SCR 99, at 134 and 136.

Guerin, supra, at 384.

Lac Minerals v. International Corona Resources, [1989] 2 SCR 574, at 599 and 645-46.

88. A parent has considerable scope for the exercise of power and discretion over his or her child. Parental power includes the ability to make decisions regarding a child's health, education and spiritual or religious upbringing. Parents have the authority to seek compliance with certain rules and to impose a system of discipline involving a variety of measures such as physical punishment, the deprivation of social contact, the withdrawal of privileges or the giving of benefits and rewards. A parent has power or discretion over virtually every aspect of a child's life.

89. Furthermore, the parent is able to unilaterally exercise the power or discretion so as to affect the child's legal or practical interests. A child is essentially powerless to control or consent to the exercise of parental power and, accordingly, the parent-fiduciary is able to exercise his or her discretion unilaterally. In the context of incest, this is often achieved by misrepresenting the nature of the perpetrator's actions to the victim; he may define the abuse as sex education, a game, or natural.

90. The exercise of parental power or discretion affects the interests of the child as beneficiary in both the legal and practical sense. Only a parent or legal guardian has the authority, in law, to consent to medical treatment on behalf of the child, to register the

child in an educational institution, to obtain a passport for the child, to change the child's name. It is assumed that in exercising this authority a parent will act in the child's best interests. The exercise of parental power or discretion also affects the practical interests of the child, in so far as a child's social and material realities are largely created by parental choices, decisions, and means.

91. Madam Justice Wilson (as she then was) comments in dissent that "[t]o deny relief because of the nature of the interest involved, to afford protection to material interests but not to human and personal interests would, it seems to me, be arbitrary in the extreme ... non-economic interests should also be capable of protection in equity through the imposition of a fiduciary duty." A child's interest in his or her physical or psychological integrity should be afforded equitable protection through the imposition of a fiduciary duty upon his or her parent.

Frame, supra, at 143.

92. The final feature, namely, that the beneficiary is peculiarly vulnerable to the fiduciary holding the discretion, is considered by Mr. Justice Sopinka to be "indispensable to the existence of the relationship."

Lac Minerals, supra, at 599.

93. The hallmark of a fiduciary relation is one in which there is implicit dependency, where one party is in a position of disadvantage or where one party is at the mercy of another's discretion.

Lac Minerals, supra, at 599-600.

94. Relying upon the *Oxford English Dictionary* definition of "vulnerable," this Court stated that "Persons are vulnerable if they are susceptible to harm, or open to injury. They are vulnerable at the hands of a fiduciary if the fiduciary is the one who can inflict harm."

Lac Minerals, supra, at 662-63.

95. A child is dependent upon his or her parent not only for physical survival but for his or her social, psychological, emotional, intellectual, and spiritual development and well-being. A child's vulnerability or susceptibility to harm at the hands of a parent cannot be compared with any other relationship. A child's peculiar vulnerability is recognized in law. Family service agencies are vested with statutory authority to apprehend children in need of protection. Parental failure to provide the necessaries of life for a child under the age of 16 years is specifically recognized as a criminal offence.

Criminal Code, RSC 1970, c. C-34, ss. 214 and 215.

96. LEAF submits that all of the essential elements of a fiduciary relationship exist between a parent and his or her child. It is further submitted that sexual interference, sexual exploitation, sexual assault, or incest perpetrated by a parent against his own child is a breach of a parent's fiduciary obligation to act loyally and in the child's best interests.

97. Canadian courts have specifically referred to the parent-child relationship as an example of a fiduciary relationship. Legal scholars confirm that the parent-child relationship fits within the fiduciary principle.

Follis v. Albemaste TP et al., [1941] 1 DCR 178.

Henderson et al. v. Johnson et al., [1956] 5 DCR (2d) 524, at 533.

Lac Minerals, supra, at 606.

C.J. Shepherd, "Fiduciary Classifications" (1936), *The Law of Fiduciaries* 21, at 30.

98. When the same conduct gives rise to alternative causes of action, a court ought to permit the action to be framed so as to afford the appropriate remedy.

Frame, supra, at 149-50.

Lac Minerals, supra, at 631.

99. Further, if a cause of action at common law is statute barred by a limitation period but the facts also give rise to an equitable claim to which the limitations period does not apply, the court ought to permit the claim in equity and provide equitable relief.

Nocturn v. Lord Ashburton, [1914] AC 932 (HL), at 957.

100. It is respectfully submitted that this Court ought to permit sexual assault survivors to frame their causes of action in equity to escape the effect of any statutory limitation period, so as to ensure their access to justice.

101. This Court held that "[t]he essence of the imposition of fiduciary obligation is its utility in the promotion and preservation of desired social behaviour and institutions. ... The imposition of a remedy which restores an asset to the party who would have acquired it but for a breach of fiduciary duties or duties of confidence acts as a deterrent to the breach of duty and strengthens the social fabric those duties are imposed to protect."

Lac Minerals, supra, at 672-73.

102. It is submitted that the imposition of a remedy on incestuous parents will act as a deterrent to the breach of parental duties, will promote healthier familial relations and will afford child victims the protection from sexual assault they currently lack.

PART IV: NATURE OF ORDER SOUGHT

103. It is submitted that the Judgment of the Honourable Mr. Justice Maloney, dated January 22, 1988 be set aside either to let the jury verdict stand or so that the defendant can be found liable to damages for breach of his fiduciary duty.

All of which is respectfully submitted.

THE OUTCOME

Head Notes—M.(K). v. M.(H.)

Held: The appeal should be allowed.

Per La Forest, Gonthier, Cory, and Iacobucci JJ: Incest is both a tortious assault and a breach of fiduciary duty. The tort claim, although subject to limitations legislation, does not accrue until the plaintiff is reasonably capable of discovering the wrongful nature of the defendant's acts and the nexus between those acts and the plaintiff's injuries. In this case, that discovery occurred only when the appellant entered therapy, and the lawsuit was commenced promptly thereafter. The time for bringing a claim for breach of a fiduciary duty is not limited by statute in Ontario, and this breach therefore stands along with the tort claim as a basis for recovery by the appellant. Incest does not constitute a distinct tort, separate and apart from the intentional tort of assault and battery, and the continuous nature of the tort need not be decided here.

Incest unquestionably constitutes an assault and battery, and based on the jury's verdict, all of the requisite elements of the test were proved. Assault and battery, however, can only serve as a crude legal description of incest; the law must also take account of the unique and complex nature of incestuous abuse and its consequential harms. Various psychological and emotional harms immediately beset the victim of incest, but much of the damage is latent and extremely debilitating. When the damages begin to become apparent, the causal connection between the incestuous activity and present psychological injuries is often unknown to the victim. A statute of limitations provides little incentive for an incest victim to prosecute his or her action in a timely fashion if the victim has been rendered psychologically incapable of recognizing that a cause of action exists.

The reasonable discoverability rule, as developed in previous decisions of this Court, should be applied and the limitations period should begin to run only when the plaintiff has a substantial awareness of the harm and its likely cause. The causal link between fault and damage is an important fact, essential to the formulation of the right of action, that is often missing in cases of incest. In making this link, the plaintiff must have an awareness of the wrongfulness of the defendant's incestuous conduct. Battery consists of wrongful touching, and the plaintiff must discover the wrongfulness of the contact and its consequential effects before the cause of action accrues. The issue properly turns on the question of when the victim becomes fully cognizant of who bears the responsibility for his or her childhood abuse, for it is then that the victim realizes the nature of the wrong suffered. As such, responsibility plays a pivotal role in both the genesis and the cessation of the harms caused by incestuous abuse.

The close connection between therapy and the shifting of responsibility is typical in incest cases and creates a presumption that incest victims only discover the necessary connection between their injuries and the wrong done to them (thus discovering their cause of action) during some form of psychotherapy. If the evidence in a particular case is consistent with the typical features of "post-incest" syndrome, then the presumption will arise. The defendant can refute the presumption by leading evidence showing that the plaintiff appreciated the causal link between the harm and its origin without the benefit of therapy.

In this case, the trial judge did not address the critical issue of when appellant discovered her cause of action, in the sense of having a substantial awareness of the harm and its likely cause, and made no finding that appellant had made the necessary connection at any time before entering therapy. Moreover, the presumption outlined above should be applied here. Appellant was a typical incest survivor, and both presumptively and in fact did not make the causative link between her injuries and childhood history until she received therapeutic assistance. Evidence to the contrary was entirely speculative. In the result, the limitations period did not begin to run against her until she received therapy, and this action was commenced before that period expired.

Appellant argued that the limitation period was also tolled by respondent's fraudulent concealment of her cause of action. This point need not be decided, but some comment on the law of fraudulent concealment is provided for the sake of clarity. Fraudulent concealment (when applicable) will toll the limitation of both common law and equitable claims until the time the plaintiff can reasonably discover her cause of action. Incest cases may be amenable to the application of fraudulent concealment as an answer to a limitations defence; incest takes place in a climate of secrecy, and the victim's silence is attained through various insidious measures which condition the victim to conceal the wrong from herself. The fact that the abuser is a trusted family authority figure in and of itself masks the wrongfulness of the conduct in the child's eyes, thus fraudulently concealing the cause of action.

Incest also constitutes a breach of the fiduciary relationship between parent and child. Ontario's Limitations Act does not limit actions against a fiduciary, although certain equitable doctrines may bar a claim because of delay. The courts below did not consider appellant's claim in equity, but the issue should now be addressed; a breach of fiduciary duty cannot be automatically overlooked in favour of concurrent common law claims. The relationship between parent and child is fiduciary in nature, and the sexual assault of one's child is a grievous breach of the obligations arising from that relationship. Equity has imposed fiduciary obligations on parents in contexts other than incest, and a duty to refrain from incestuous assaults on one's child is an obvious addition to this category. The three indicia of a fiduciary relationship are all evident in this case, and the non-economic interests of an incest victim are particularly susceptible to protection from the law of equity.

The plaintiff's delay in bringing her claim for breach of fiduciary duty raises three potential hurdles that may bar her claim: limitations legislation, the application of that legislation by analogy, and the equitable doctrine of laches. All of these hurdles, however, are overcome in this case. First Ontario's Limitations Act applies only to a closed list of enumerated causes of action which does not include fiduciary obligations. Equity in some cases will operate by analogy and adopt a statutory limitation period that does not otherwise expressly apply, but this is not such a case. Equity has rarely limited a claim by analogy when the action falls within its exclusive jurisdiction, as in this claim for breach of fiduciary duty. Moreover, even if it is appropriate to draw an analogy to a common law action, the analogy will be governed by the parameters of the equitable doctrine of laches. Finally, any analogy would be nullified by the doctrine of fraudulent concealment. Even if an analogy could be drawn, it would not be fatal to appellant's claim: as with the limitation in tort, a limitation by analogy would be tolled by the operation of the reasonable discoverability principle.

For the respondent to benefit from the defence of laches, acquiescence on the part of the appellant must be demonstrated. Acquiescence in this context consists of delay by a plaintiff despite knowledge that her rights have been violated. Such a delay gives rise to an inference that the plaintiff's rights have been waived. A plaintiff's conduct will be measured objectively: was it reasonable for the plaintiff to have remained ignorant of her legal rights given her knowledge of the facts relevant to a legal claim? In this case, because the appellant mistakenly blamed herself for the incest, it was entirely reasonable for her to have been incapable of appreciating that her rights in equity or in law had been violated. As such, she could not have acquiesced to the respondent's conduct. The doctrine of acquiescence bears a marked similarity to the common law discoverability principle. They share the common requirement of knowledge on the part of the plaintiff. The point of distinction is a residual inquiry in equity: in light of the plaintiff's knowledge, can it reasonably be inferred that the plaintiff has acquiesced to the defendant's conduct? The answer to that question depends on the circumstances of each case, but it would require particularly compelling evidence to demonstrate that an incest victim had "acquiesced" to the sexual assaults made against her.

As for the remedy in this case, the jury has assessed damages in tort, and this award should not be disturbed. An additional remedy in equity should not be awarded in this case, as the policy objectives animating the remedy for this breach of a parent's fiduciary duty are the same as those underlying incestuous sexual assault. Both seek to compensate the victim for her injuries and to punish the wrongdoer.

Per L'Heureux-Dubé J: The reasons and result of La Forest J and the comments of McLachlin J on the nature and quantum of damages associated with a breach of fiduciary duty, as opposed to those underlying the torts of battery and assault, were agreed with.

Per Sopinka J: The reasons and result of La Forest J were agreed with except with respect to the creation of a presumption and the shifting of the legal burden of proof.

Resort should not be had to a presumption that a plaintiff typical of the syndrome is unaware of the injury done to her until she undergoes therapy. Firstly, the legal effect of presumptions is varied and uncertain as to its evidentiary effect. Secondly, this presumption will create difficulties for the trial judge and the litigants in that it will reverse the ordinary burden of proof without any justification. It is not clear whether the presumption, which would require determination on a prima facie basis, would create merely an evidentiary burden or a legal burden. The former could be blunted by the defendant's leading some evidence restoring the legal burden of proof to the plaintiff. The latter would reverse the legal burden of proof so that the defendant would bear the risk of non persuasion and is the probable result intended because of the use of the term "refute."

There was no reason to reverse the traditional burden of proof. The basic criteria for the allocation of the burden of proof apply to justify maintaining the legal burden of proof with respect to reasonable discoverability on the plaintiff. It is the plaintiff who is seeking an exemption from the normal operation of the statute of limitations asserting that she was not aware of her cause of action for many years after the statutory period would otherwise have commenced to run. Moreover the plaintiff is in the best position to adduce evidence of her lack of awareness and the defendant is not. The appeal should be disposed of as proposed by La Forest J.

Per McLachlin J: Agreement with the reasons of La Forest J was qualified.

A presumption that the plaintiff discovers the cause of action when a therapeutic relationship begins is not necessary. The question is a matter of fact to be determined in all the circumstances. A presumption is appropriate in special circumstances, as where the facts are largely in the possession of the opposing party on an issue, but there were no such circumstances here. Further, there was no magic in the commencement of a therapeutic relationship. The commencement of the relationship is only one of a number of factors which should be considered in determining when the limitation period begins to run.

The award which the jury made was not adequate. The jury assessed damages for the tort of battery and assault, as requested, and the appellant did not appeal from that award and only asked that the jury's award be reinstated. The question of whether the award was appropriate or not did not arise here.

The measure of damages for assault and battery would not necessarily be the same as compensation for breach of fiduciary duty. The wrong encompassed by the torts of battery and assault may be different from the wrong encompassed by the action for a breach of fiduciary duty. Trustees have always been held to highest account in a manner stricter than that applicable to tortfeasors. While agreeing with La Forest J that where the same policy objectives underlie two different causes of action similar measures of compensation may be appropriate. The policy objectives or the wrong involved in breach of fiduciary duty of this nature are not necessarily the same as those which underlie the torts of battery and assault.

IN THE SUPREME COURT OF CANADA

(ON APPEAL FROM THE FEDERAL COURT OF APPEAL)

BETWEEN:

HER MAJESTY THE QUEEN

Appellant

(Respondent)

AND:

SUZANNE THIBAUDEAU

Respondent

(Appellant)

AND:

SUPPORT AND CUSTODY ORDERS FOR
PRIORITY ENFORCEMENT (SCOPE)

Intervenor

(Intervenor)

AND:

CHARTER COMMITTEE ON POVERTY ISSUES, FEDERATED ANTI-POVERTY GROUPS OF BC, NATIONAL ACTION COMMITTEE ON THE STATUS OF WOMEN, AND WOMEN'S LEGAL EDUCATION AND ACTION FUND ("THE COALITION")

Intervenor

AND:

ATTORNEY GENERAL OF QUEBEC

Intervenor

Factum of the Coalition

R v. Thibaudeau

INTRODUCTION

Suzanne Thibaudeau, a divorced mother of two living in Quebec, received $1,150 per month in child support payments directed solely to the maintenance of her children. Under section 56(1)(b) of the Income Tax Act, she was obliged to include these payments as taxable income. Her former spouse, on the other hand, was able to claim a deduction for these payments under section 60. Sections 56(1)(b) and 60(b) of the Income Tax Act comprise what is known as the "inclusion-deduction" system. Unlike all other provisions of the Act that are directed at individuals, the inclusion-deduction scheme is directed at separated couples as a means of enabling them to split their income in a manner that favours their respective levels of taxability. The scheme was first implemented in 1944 to encourage payment of alimony and increase benefits to the children of divorced families.

In her 1989 tax return, Thibaudeau excluded the income tax payable on the child support payments, and argued that she should not be required to pay the tax because the income was not intended for her personal use and payment of the tax reduced the amount of income available for her children.

After Revenue Canada rejected her tax return, Thibaudeau challenged its decision in the Federal Tax Court in August 1992. Thibaudeau argued that paragraph 56(1)(b) discriminated against her on the grounds of civil and social status, and sex contrary to section 15 of the Charter. The trial judge found that the inclusion-deduction system did subject Thibaudeau to a tax burden. Nonetheless, he dismissed her application on the grounds that her alimony payments had been grossed up to take account of the tax burden and she therefore had had an opportunity to address the burden both when the separation agreement was drafted, and through subsequent variation orders.

Thibaudeau appealed to the Federal Court of Appeal. Her section 15 argument concentrated on her status as a custodial parent, which Thibaudeau argued was a ground of discrimination analogous to those enumerated in section 15. By contrast, the intervenor Support and Custody Orders for Priority Enforcement (SCOPE) argued that the inclusion-deduction system discriminated on the basis of sex because the vast majority of custodial parents are women.

The Court dealt first with the SCOPE claim. Both the majority and minority rejected SCOPE's argument that the Act discriminated on the basis of sex. First, the Court noted that the Act, on its face, did not distinguish between male and female custodial parents. Second, the Court held that section 56(1)(b) did not lead to indirect discrimination against custodial mothers because the negative effect was felt equally whether the custodial parent was a man or a woman. The numbers of women involved were, to the Court of Appeal, irrelevant.

Turning to Thibaudeau's argument, the majority of the Court, in an opinion written by Hugessen JA, agreed that she had been discriminated against as a custodial parent. Hugessen JA further found that section 56(1)(b) was not a justifiable limit under section 1. Accordingly, section 56(1)(b) was struck down in its entirety.

The government immediately appealed the decision to the Supreme Court. LEAF was granted intervenor status in coalition with the Charter Committee on Poverty Issues, the Federated Anti-Poverty Groups of British Columbia, and the National Action Committee on the Status of Women. SCOPE also intervened.

FACTUM

PART I: FACTS

1. Section 56(1)(b) of the Income Tax Act, SC 1970-71-72, c. 63, required the Respondent to include in her 1989 taxable income the child support payments made that year by her ex-husband.

2. Women as a group are economically disadvantaged relative to men. Women earn incomes far below that of men, and experience higher rates of poverty. Most women are economically disadvantaged upon divorce and separation.

Case on Appeal, vol. 3, 442, at 443-48.

Case on Appeal, vol. 3, 513, at 542-43.

Case on Appeal, vol. 3, 566, at 581-82.

Case on Appeal, vol. 4, 682, at 685.

Case on Appeal, vol. 5, 937, at 955 and 966.

Case on Appeal, vol. 6, 1037, at 1039 and 1058-62.

Case on Appeal, vol. 6, 1076, at 1076-80.

3. Ninety-eight per cent of those parents who receive child support are women. A large majority of these women are single parents who, as a group, are particularly vulnerable to poverty.

Case on Appeal, vol. 6, 1033, at 1035-36.

Case on Appeal, vol. 7, 1273, at 1275.

Case on Appeal, vol. 9, 1495, at 1506.

Supplementary Case on Appeal, vol. 2, 179, at 185.

PART II: ISSUES

4. Does section 56(1)(b) of the Income Tax Act, SC 1970-71-72, c. 63, violate section 15 of the Canadian Charter of Rights and Freedoms (the "Charter")?

5. If so, is section 56(1)(b) justified under section 1 of the Charter?

PART III: ARGUMENT

Summary of the Coalition's Position

6. The Coalition submits that the Court of Appeal erred in employing a formalistic approach that restricted the equality analysis to section 56(1)(b)'s impact on separated custodial parents on the ground of family status. Section 56(1)(b) also has a discriminatory impact on women that constitutes a violation of the sex equality guarantee in section 15 of the Charter.

7. The Coalition submits that the interpretive approach developed by this Court demands an equality analysis on the basis of the intersection of grounds of discrimination. Section 56(1)(b) discriminates against separated custodial parents and, in particular, against single mothers, especially those living in poverty. Section 56(1)(b) violates section 15 of the Charter on the grounds of sex and family status together.

8. The Coalition agrees with the Court of Appeal's conclusion that the section 15 violation cannot be justified pursuant to section 1 of the Charter. The Coalition makes no additional submissions on this issue.

The Equality Guarantees in Section 15 of the Charter

The Purpose of Section 15 of the Charter

9. This Court has identified equality as one of the fundamental values of our society, against which the objects of all legislation must be measured. This Court has also stated that "the s. 15(1) guarantee is the broadest of all guarantees [in the Charter]. It applies to and supports all other rights guaranteed by the Charter."

> *Andrews v. Law Society of British Columbia*, [1989] 1 SCR 143, at 185, per McIntyre J.

10. In its developing jurisprudence, this Court has acknowledged the importance of promoting the equality of disadvantaged groups. As Madam Justice Wilson stated, "s. 15 is designed to protect those groups who suffer social, political and legal disadvantage in our society." Similarly, Lamer CJ recognized that the purpose of section 15 is "to remedy or prevent discrimination against groups subject to stereotyping, historical disadvantage and political and social prejudice in Canadian society."

> *Andrews*, supra, at 154, per Wilson J.
>
> *R v. Swain*, [1991] 1 SCR 933, at 992, per Lamer CJ.
>
> *R v. Turpin et al.*, [1989] 1 SCR 1296, at 1333, per Wilson J.

11. In employing a purposive approach, this Court has recognized women's experiences of social and economic disadvantage. This Court has also ruled that section 15 applies to claims of inequality in social and economic legislation.

Brooks v. Canada Safeway Ltd., [1989] 1 SCR 1219, at 1242-44, per Dickson CJ.

Janzen and Govereau v. Platy Enterprises Ltd. et al., [1989] 1 SCR 1252, at 1290, per Dickson CJ.

Symes v. Canada, [1993] 4 SCR 695, at 756 and 753, per Iacobucci J.

12. This purposive approach to equality has enabled Canadian courts and human rights tribunals to recognize and remedy the various manifestations of discrimination that arise from complex and changing social relations and, therefore, to promote "a society in which all are secure in the knowledge that they are recognized at law as human beings equally deserving of concern, respect and consideration."

Andrews, supra, at 171, per McIntyre J.

Charter Values and International Law

13. In interpreting the content of Charter rights, attention should be paid to the values that underlie the Charter and to Canada's international human rights obligations. This Court has determined that section 15 embodies "a broad range of values" including "respect for the inherent dignity of the human person" and "commitment to social justice and equality."

Andrews, supra, at 171, per McIntyre J, and at 197, La Forest J.

R v. Oakes, [1986] 1 SCR 103, at 136.

Reference re Public Service Employee Relations Act (Alta.), [1987] 1 SCR 313, at 349, per Dickson CJ.

14. In *Slaight Communications*, this Court recognized that Canada's international human rights obligations are both "relevant and persuasive source(s)" for the interpretation of the Charter's provisions. The Court also confirmed its earlier recognition in *Reference re Public Service Employee Relations Act (Alta.)* that "the Charter should generally be presumed to provide protection at least as great as that afforded by similar provisions in international human rights documents which Canada has ratified."

Slaight Communications v. Davidson, [1989] 1 SCR 1038, at 1056, per Dickson CJ.

Reference re Public Service Employee Relations Act (Alta.), supra, at 349-50.

15. The interpretive principle adopted by this Court is consistent with the international law principle that domestic law must be interpreted in a manner consistent with a state's international obligations.

J. Claydon, "The Use of International Human Rights Law to Interpret Canada's Charter of Rights and Freedoms" (1987), 2 *Connecticut Journal of International Law* 349, at 353.

P. Alston and G. Quinn, "The Nature and Scope of States Parties' Obligations under the International Covenant on Economic, Social and Cultural Rights" (1987), 9 *Human Rights Quarterly* 156, at 171.

16. In *Slaight Communications*, this Court considered Canada's ratification of the International Covenant on Economic, Social and Cultural Rights. The Covenant is also relevant to the present Appeal. Article 11 of the Covenant recognizes the right to an adequate standard of living including food, clothing, and housing. Article 10 requires the "widest possible care and assistance be accorded to the family while it is responsible for the care and education of dependent children."

International Covenant on Economic, Social and Cultural Rights, GA Res. 2200 A (XXI), 21 UN GAOR, Supp. (no. 16) 49, Doc. A/6316 UN (1966), s. 6.

The Analysis Under Section 15 of the Charter

17. This Court has made it clear that the section 15 analysis "should not become a mechanical and sterile categorization process conducted entirely within the four corners of the impugned legislation." Rather, the section 15 analysis should proceed within the broader context of the entire social, political and legal fabric of our society.

Turpin et al., supra, at 1331-32.

Andrews, supra, at 152, per Wilson J.

18. The Coalition therefore submits that under the section 15 analysis, the Court must consider the following questions:

(a) Which group or groups are affected by the impugned provision?

(b) Does the impugned law discriminate on the basis of group-characteristics recognized as enumerated or analogous grounds of discrimination?

19. With respect to the first question, it is not sufficient to simply reiterate the language of the impugned provision. Rather, there must be an assessment of the impact of the law on disadvantaged groups in order to identify group characteristics that may constitute grounds of discrimination within the meaning of section 15. In conducting this inquiry, there must be an appreciation that the affected group is likely to be diverse in that not all members of the group will share all group characteristics. This approach to identifying affected groups incorporates the concept of adverse effect discrimination in the section 15 analysis as this Court has directed.

Brooks, supra, at 1239 and 1247.

Janzen and Govereau, supra, at 1289-90.

Symes, supra, at 769, per Iacobucci J.

20. Similarly, there must be an appreciation of the complexity of the group, in particular, that some members of the group will be identified by multiple characteristics. This recognition is of particular relevance to the second question. The Coalition submits that when considering the second question, the Court must consider not only whether

there is discrimination on each of the grounds claimed, but also whether the discrimination arises out of the intersection of group characteristics. This inquiry recognizes that discrimination does not occur in discrete categories. Various forms of discrimination are inter-related, mutually reinforcing, and can operate together.

K. Crenshaw, "Demarginalizing the Intersection of Race and Sex: A Black Feminist Critique of Anti-Discrimination Doctrine, Feminist Theory and Antiracist Politics" (1989), *University of Chicago Legal Forum* 139.

N. Duclos, "Disappearing Women: Racial Minority Women in Human Rights Cases" (1993), 6 *CJWL* 25, at 40-51.

N. Iyer, "Categorical Denials: Equality Rights and the Shaping of Social Identity" (1993), 19 *Queen's Law Journal* 179, at 191-94.

L. Philipps and M. Young, "Sex, Tax, and the Charter: A Review of Thibaudeau v. The Queen" (1995), 2 *Review of Constitutional Studies*, at 31-38.

21. A disjunctive approach to grounds of discrimination fragments the experience of equality seekers and distorts the nature of their equality claims. As an Ontario Board of Inquiry explained:

> An example might occur should a woman of colour claim that she has been discriminated against by a refusal to hire her. How should she frame her claim?
>
> Both "race" and "sex" are prohibited grounds of discrimination. Under a disjunctive approach, the claim would be analyzed as being *either* race discrimination or sex discrimination. This would not only fragment her experience and existence; it may also defeat her claim. If the employer could show that it hires men of colour, it might resist the claim of race discrimination; if it could show that it hires white women, it might resist the claim of gender discrimination.

Leshner v. The Queen (1992), 16 CHRR D/184, per Dawson at D/213-14 (emphasis in original).

Application of Section 15 of the Charter to the Case at Bar

Introduction

22. On its face, section 56(1)(b) draws a distinction between separated custodial parents and parents who have not separated. Persons raising children in two-parent families are each liable for tax on that portion of their incomes used to provide for their children, and transfers of income between persons within such families are not subject to tax. Following separation, section 56(1)(b) imposes an additional tax liability on custodial parents by requiring that child support payments made by the non-custodial parent be included in the custodial parent's taxable income.

Case on Appeal, vol. 3, 442, at 452.

Case on Appeal, vol. 3, 513, at 540.

23. Section 56(1)(b) draws a further distinction on its face between separated custodial and non-custodial parents. By virtue of section 60(b) of the Income Tax Act,

non-custodial parents are not liable for tax on that portion of their incomes used to provide for their children through the payment of child support. Section 56(1)(b) therefore transfers liability from the non-custodial parent to the custodial parent.

The Larger Social and Economic Context

24. Underlying much social and economic policy in Canadian society is the assumption that child-rearing work is the responsibility of women. Although not all women perform child-rearing work, and some men do, child-rearing has been seen traditionally as a female role within a two-parent heterosexual family. Women are stereotyped as secondary earners. Such discriminatory notions about women's status in society reinforce the social and economic devaluation of child-rearing work and are used to justify the lack of social resources available to those with primary responsibility for child-rearing.

M. Gunderson, L. Muszynski, and J. Keck, *Women and Labour Market Poverty* (Ottawa: Canadian Advisory Council on the Status of Women, 1990), at 13.

M. Eichler, "Lone-parent Families: An Instable Category in Search of Stable Policies" in J. Hudson and B. Galaway, eds., *Single Parent Families: Perspectives on Research and Policy* (Toronto: Thompson Educational Publishing, Inc., 1993), 139 at 144-52.

E. Zweibel, "Child Support Policy and Child Support Guidelines: Broadening the Agenda" (1993), 6 *CJWL* 371, at 389-90.

S.A. McDaniel, "Single Parenthood: Policy Apartheid in Canada" in Hudson and Galaway, supra, 203, at 205-6.

Philipps and Young, supra, at 45-49.

25. While the costs of child-rearing are high, those with responsibility for childcare work also experience a restricted ability to earn an adequate living. The lack of social resources, including adequate childcare programs, creates a further obstacle to market earnings. The inadequacy of social resources for those performing childcare work is most acutely felt by single parents who experience a dramatic increase in the direct and indirect costs and income earning limitations linked to responsibility for child-rearing.

Case on Appeal, vol. 4, 586, at 599.

Zweibel, supra, at 392-94.

Statistics Canada, *Lone-Parent Families in Canada* (Ottawa: Minister of Industry, Science and Technology, 1992), at 21-26 and 35-38.

Gunderson et al., supra, at 18-19 and 28-29.

26. Women disproportionately experience the disadvantages resulting from the stereotyping of child-rearing as gendered work and from the reality that it is unpaid work. Despite significant increases in labour force participation, and a greater diversity of domestic relationships, women continue to be primarily responsible for the unpaid work of home-making and childcare. Child-rearing responsibilities are strongly associated with the economic disadvantage of women relative to men. The lack of adequate

social resources often forces women to make sacrifices affecting their paid-work opportunities that men do not have to make.

Case on Appeal, vol. 3, 442, at 444.

National Council of Welfare, *Women and Poverty Revisited* (Ottawa: Minister of Supply and Services, 1990), at 20-23.

Gunderson et al., supra, at 9, 13-17, and 24-27.

27. As this Court has recognized, women experience an unfair disadvantage as a result of bearing the disproportionate share of the social costs of both child-bearing and child-rearing. This disadvantage is exacerbated upon separation or divorce because women generally continue to be responsible for the care of children. Many women experience a severe decline in their standard of living following separation.

Brooks, supra, at 1238.

Moge v. Moge, [1992] 3 SCR 813, per L'Heureux-Dubé J, at 849-50, 854-56, 861-63, and 867-68.

Symes, supra, per Iacobucci J, at 762-63.

Gunderson et al., supra, at 20.

28. Single mother-led families experience the highest incidence of family poverty in Canada. In 1992, 58.4 percent of single mother-led families lived in poverty. In addition to experiencing the material restrictions of poverty such as substandard housing, inadequate diet, and reduced health, the stresses and stigma associated with poverty are magnified for low-income women caring for children. Discriminatory views about single mothers living in poverty include the belief that single mothers are long-term welfare recipients who have too many children.

National Council of Welfare, supra, at 58.

National Council of Welfare, *Poverty Profile 1992* (Ottawa: Supply and Services, 1994), at 14.

National Council of Welfare, *In the Best Interests of the Child* (Ottawa: Queen's Printer, 1979), at 4-8.

Social Assistance Review Committee, *Transitions* (Toronto: Queen's Printer, 1988), at 29-32.

Gunderson et al., supra, at 21.

29. The Coalition submits that the devaluation of women and of work done by women and the assumption that child-rearing is performed by women in the heterosexual two-parent family have resulted in the social and economic penalization of those persons with primary responsibility for child-rearing and, in particular, of single mothers.

The Groups Affected by Section 56(1)(b) of the Income Tax Act

30. On its face, section 56(1)(b) affects persons with custody of a child following separation. The affected group can therefore be distinguished on the basis of family

status alone. When the impact of the law is assessed in the larger social and economic context, however, it becomes clear that the vast majority of the affected group are women. Moreover, many members of this group are poor single mothers. Thus, the characteristics of the affected group include sex and poverty in addition to family status.

Impact on the Basis of Sex

31. The Court of Appeal found that section 56(1)(b) creates a distinction based on the applicant's status as a separated custodial parent, and that the relevant ground of discrimination is "family status." It held that section 56(1)(b) does not discriminate on the basis of sex because the impugned provision:

(a) does not directly delineate women or men as a targeted group;

(b) affects some men although the vast majority of those affected are women; and

(c) on its face, appears to affect individual women and individual men in the same way.

32. Under the Court of Appeal's approach, the section 15 analysis is reduced to a question of direct discrimination because the only violation of equality guarantees recognized is that related to the group characteristic delineated by the impugned law. Such an approach ignores the contextual and purposive analysis developed by this Court in *Andrews* and *Turpin* that demands a consideration of broader social and historical inequities within which the legislation operates, and that may be reinforced by the legislation.

Andrews, supra, per Wilson J, at 152.

Turpin et al., supra, at 1331-32.

33. The result of the Court of Appeal's approach is reminiscent of *Bliss*. In that case, the impugned provision expressly differentiated on the basis of pregnancy and not sex. The Court described Stella Bliss as a pregnant person rather than as a woman, and found that there was no sex discrimination. Similarly, by assigning those women affected by section 56(1)(b) to the class "separated custodial parents," the Court of Appeal applied a rigid categorical approach to the interpretation of equality guarantees that is at odds with the contemporary jurisprudence of this Court.

Bliss v. AG Canada, [1979] 1 SCR 183.

34. In *Brooks*, this Court held that pregnancy discrimination constitutes discrimination on the basis of sex. In reaching this conclusion, this Court assessed and recognized the social and economic disadvantage associated with procreation experienced by women, and the Court stated that removal of such a disadvantage is a key purpose of anti-discrimination legislation.

Brooks, supra, at 1238.

35. The impact of section 56(1)(b) must be assessed in light of the larger context of women's inequality. This assessment should not be precluded by the fact that some men are also affected by the impugned provision. As this Court has recognized, sexual har-

assment is appropriately characterized as sex discrimination even though some victims of sexual harassment are men. Sexual harassment is a gendered abuse of power when considered in the context of a society in which women as a group are particularly vulnerable to harassment because of their ascribed inferior status. Similarly, the gendered role of custodial parents requires that a sex equality analysis be undertaken.

Janzen and Govereau, supra, at 1289-90.

36. The Federal Court of Appeal's conclusion that the impugned provision could not discriminate on the basis of sex because on its face it affects individual women and men in the same way is the result of a formalistic approach to equality analysis that has been rejected by this Court. The Court of Appeal's approach denies recognition of the social forces that place women, almost exclusively, in the position of needing and receiving child support. The disproportionate impact of section 56(1)(b) on women is a clear signal that the provision may reinforce the disadvantage experienced by women on the basis of sex.

Action Travail des Femmes v. Canadian National Railway Company, [1987] 1 SCR 1114, at 1139.

Brooks, supra, at 1234.

Janzen and Govereau, supra, at 1279.

Symes, supra, per Iacobucci J, at 762.

Intersection of Sex, Family Status, and Poverty

37. A consideration of the larger social and economic context within which child-rearing work is performed reveals that section 56(1)(b) imposes a tax liability on those performing the traditionally female role of primary care giver for children after separation of the two-parent family. Section 56(1)(b) therefore affects the group concerned on the basis of a socially gendered role related to sex and family status.

38. The Coalition submits that section 56(1)(b) implicates the group characteristics of sex and family status in a second way. The large majority of those affected by section 56(1)(b) are single mothers. Thus, section 56(1)(b) has a numerically disproportionate impact on single mothers on the basis of sex and family status. Furthermore, the Coalition submits that the imposition of an additional tax liability on single mothers who are poor exacerbates their social and economic disadvantage on the basis of their sex, family status, and poverty.

39. Other courts have addressed the inequities facing low-income single parents and have recognized the role of enumerated grounds such as race and sex while also recognizing analogous grounds such as poverty, social condition and family status. Recognizing family status as an analogous ground under section 15 should not mean, as it did for the Court below, that a court cannot also recognize as a sex equality issue the inequities experienced by custodial parents that flow from an undervaluing of child-rearing work.

Dartmouth/Halifax County Regional Housing v. Sparks (1993), 101 DLR (4th) 224 (NS SC App. Div.).

R v. Rehberg (1994), 111 DLR (4th) 336 (NS SC).

Federated Anti-Poverty Groups of British Columbia v. AG British Columbia (1992), 70 BCLR (2d) 325 (SC).

40. Similarly, the Coalition submits that recognizing the prevalence of poverty among women, and in particular among single mothers, ought to reinforce sex equality claims. It would be ironic if the courts were to adopt an approach to the grounds of discrimination that resulted in a failure to recognize the impact of poverty on the situation of single mothers. As an academic commentator recently wrote, commenting on the Court of Appeal's decision:

> In short, the courts must be careful to ensure that the most vulnerable members of Canadian society—those who are subject to multiple forms of discrimination including on the basis of poverty, are not disentitled to remedial action because of the complex and intersecting nature of their claims.

M. Jackman, "Constitutional Contact with the Disparities in the World: Poverty as a Prohibited Ground of Discrimination under the Canadian Charter and Human Rights Law" (1994), 2 *Review of Constitutional Studies* 77, at 110.

Section 56(1)(b) of the Income Tax Act Discriminates on the Grounds of Sex and Family Status

41. The Coalition submits that section 56(1)(b) discriminates on the ground of sex. Because of socially assigned roles, those affected by section 56(1)(b) are most often women. Section 56(1)(b) therefore imposes an additional obligation that falls disproportionately on a group in society that already shoulders a disproportionate share of the child-rearing costs, and that already experiences high rates of poverty. Section 56(1)(b) furthers women's inequality by increasing the costs of child-rearing. Section 56(1)(b) operates to reinforce women's existing social and economic disadvantage.

42. The Coalition submits that a more comprehensive recognition of the impact of section 56(1)(b) must take into account the intersection of sex and family status as well as the conditions of poverty and economic disadvantage experienced by the group defined by this intersection. Further, the Court must recognize the compounding effect that poverty and economic disadvantage has in disadvantaging this group.

43. An examination of the social reality of single parents and single mothers in particular, as referred to in paragraphs 24 to 29 above, reveals "indicia of discrimination such as stereotyping, historical disadvantage or vulnerability to political and social prejudice." The Coalition therefore submits that family status should be recognized as an analogous ground of discrimination under section 15 of the Charter in order to give effect to the Charter's equality guarantees in the present case.

Turpin et al., supra, per Wilson J, at 1333.

44. A number of courts have held that poverty is an analogous ground of discrimination under section 15. The Coalition supports this view. However, the issue of whether poverty is an analogous ground has not been placed before this Court in this case. In this

case, the Coalition submits that vulnerability to poverty is a condition integrally linked to the social and historical experience of women and single mothers in society. Stereotyping and discrimination faced by single mothers is also integrally related to stereotyping and discrimination on the basis of poverty. Poverty, therefore, is a condition of the group that is directly pertinent to the impact of section 56(1)(b) and, as such, must be considered a key element of the context to be considered.

45. The Coalition submits that section 56(1)(b) creates a burden that results in discrimination on the grounds of sex and family status through the imposition of an additional tax liability on persons fulfilling the role of child-rearing outside of the two-parent family. In two-parent families, each parent is liable only for the tax cost on that portion of his or her income used to support the couple's children. By contrast, under section 60(b), non-custodial parents have the benefit of no tax liability for that portion of their income used for child support payments.

46. Section 56(1)(b) operates to reduce the already limited societal support for single parents. However, section 56(1)(b) treats the non-custodial parent's child support payments as income in the hands of the custodial parent as though it were a payment for child-rearing work, rather than a contribution toward the support of the non-custodial parent's children. Section 56(1)(b) reflects and reinforces the stereotypical notion that those fulfilling the traditionally "female" role of child-rearing provide these services for the benefit of those in the traditionally "male" role of provider.

47. Moreover, the discriminatory impact falls disproportionately on single mothers on the basis of sex and family status. For those single mothers who are poor, section 56(1)(b) increases the obstacles to improving the well-being of their families. Because section 56(1)(b) increases taxable income, it increases the effective rate of tax on income earned in the market. For those single mothers attempting to make a transition from income assistance to market income, the higher tax rate on market income makes the transition even more difficult.

48. For the single mother living in poverty who makes a transition to employment, section 56(1)(b) deepens her poverty. The tax depletes already inadequate resources needed to provide for her children's well-being. By compromising the ability of single mothers to provide for their children, the additional tax liability increases the risks associated with poverty such as poor health, and exacerbates the stresses and stigma associated with the poverty of single mothers.

49. The approach of the Court below overlooks the essence of a disproportionate impact claim that is to challenge a rule or practice that reinforces a group's pre-existing disadvantage. If left unrecognized and unremedied, the discriminatory effect of the rule or practice "fosters the belief, both within and outside the group, that the exclusion is the result of 'natural' forces," rather than the result of social and historical inequities reinforced by the rule or practice.

Action Travail, supra, at 1139.

See also Philipps and Young, supra, at 13-31.

50. In reviewing Canada's level of compliance with its international human rights obligations, the United Nations Committee on Economic, Social and Cultural Rights expressed particular concern that over half of single mothers in Canada live in poverty. The Committee encouraged Canadian courts to interpret the Charter and human rights legislation so as to provide appropriate remedies for violations of social and economic rights.

UN ESC, Committee on Economic, Social and Cultural Rights, Concluding Observations of the Committee on Economic, Social and Cultural Rights on a Report Submitted by Canada, Geneva, 20 June 1993, E/C. 12/1993/5, (1994), 20 CHRR C/1.

See also Jackman, supra, at 118-21.

51. The Coalition submits that section 15 of the Charter should be interpreted in the present case in a manner that is consistent with Canada's obligations under international law. A finding that tax provisions that exacerbate the economic disadvantage of single mothers contravene section 15 of the Charter on the basis of sex and family status is, in the Coalition's view, the only conclusion that is consistent with such an interpretation and with a purposive and substantive approach to equality rights.

PART IV: NATURE OF ORDER SOUGHT

52. The Coalition requests that the Appeal be dismissed on the basis that section 56(1)(b) of the Income Tax Act violates section 15 of the Charter on the grounds of sex and family status, and that section 56(1)(b) is not justified pursuant to section 1 of the Charter.

All of which is respectfully submitted.

THE OUTCOME

Head Notes—R v. Thibaudeau

Held (L'Heureux-Dubé and McLachlin JJ dissenting): The appeal should be allowed. Section 56(1)(b) ITA does not infringe the equality rights guaranteed by s. 15(1) of the Charter.

Per La Forest and Sopinka JJ: There is agreement with Cory and Iacobucci JJ and with Gonthier J that s. 56(1)(b) ITA does not impose a burden or withhold a benefit so as to attract the application of section 15(1) of the Charter.

Per Cory and Iacobucci JJ: Section 56(1)(b) ITA does not violate s. 15(1) of the Charter.

[W]e cannot support Gonthier J's approach to s. 15 [becuase his analysis] imports into [the section] the justificatory analysis which properly belongs under s. 1 [thereby depriving] the s. 1 analysis of much of its substantive role. As well, it places an additional and erroneous onus on the claimant. ... [T]he claimaint bears only the burden of

proving that the impugned legislation is discriminatory[; ...] the goverment ... bears the onus of justifying that discrimination. (para. 154)

The purpose of s. 15(1) is to protect human dignity by ensuring that all individuals are recognized at law as being equally deserving of concern, respect and consideration. Consequently, it is the effect that an impugned distinction has upon a claimant which is the prime concern under s. 15(1). Here, the group of single custodial parents receiving child support payments is not placed under a burden by the inclusion/deduction regime. Although there may be some cases in which the gross-up calculations shift a portion of the payer's tax liability upon the recipient spouse, one cannot necessarily extrapolate from this that a "burden" has been created, at least not for the purposes of s. 15(1). Sections 56(1)(b) and 60(b) operate at the level of the couple and are designed to minimize the tax consequences of support payments, thereby promoting the best interests of the children by ensuring that more money is available to provide for their care. If anything, the inclusion/deduction regime confers a benefit on the post-divorce "family unit." The fact that one member of the unit might derive a greater benefit from the legislation than the other does not, in and of itself, trigger a s. 15(1) violation, nor does it lead to a finding that the distinction in any way amounts to a denial of equal benefit or protection of the law. Sections 56(1)(b) and 60(b), which incorporate federal and provincial statutes under which child support orders are issued, must be examined in conjunction with those statutes in order to assess the effect of ss. 56(1)(b) and 60(b) upon the claimant. The amount of income taxable under ss. 56(1)(b) and 60(b) is determined by the family law system and, unless it operates in a defective manner, the amount of child support will include grossing-up calculations to account for the tax liability that the recipient ex-spouse will incur on the income. If there has been an error, the system provides avenues to revisit the support order to correct the situation. Any disproportionate displacement of the tax liability between the former spouses lies in the family law system, not in the ITA. Therefore, in light of the interaction between the ITA and the family law statutes, s. 56(1)(b) does not impose a burden upon the respondent within the meaning of s. 15(1).

The disagreement with McLachlin J's conclusion that ss. 56(1)(b) and 60(b) occasion a burden is limited to an application of her approach to the facts of this case, not with her methodology per se, which is endorsed. By corollary, the concurrence with Gonthier J in the disposition of this appeal is one of result, not of method.

Per Gonthier J: The special nature of the ITA is a significant factor that must be taken into account in defining the scope of the right "to the equal benefit of the law" provided for in s. 15(1) of the Charter. It is of the very essence of the ITA to make distinctions, so as to generate revenue for the government while equitably reconciling a range of necessarily divergent interests. In view of this, the right to the equal benefit of the law does not mean that each taxpayer has an equal right to receive the same amounts, deductions or benefits, but merely that he or she has a right to be equally governed by the law. The concept of fiscal equity should not be confused with the concept of the right to equality. There is discrimination under s. 15(1) when the impugned provision creates a prejudicial distinction affecting the complainant as a member of a group, based on an irrelevant personal characteristic shared by the group.

The first stage in the method of analysis under s. 15(1) involves determining whether the provision in question creates a distinction between the individual, as a member of a group, and others. The inclusion/deduction system, adopted to deal with the unfavourable economic consequences resulting from the breakup of the family unit, creates a distinction since it applies only to separated or divorced spouses, where one parent is paying alimony to the other under a judgment or agreement. The system exceptionally permits income splitting between the latter in order to increase their available resources. This group of separated or divorced couples clearly cannot be subdivided by income level, as income level is not a characteristic attaching to the individual *[and because the provisions of the ITA at issue] have to do with the distribution of the obligation to pay taxes within the couple. (para. 122)*

The second stage involves determining whether this distinction creates prejudice in respect of the group in question. A comparison between the treatment of couples subject to the general taxation system and that applicable to separated or divorced couples subject to ss. 56(1)(b) and 60(b) indicates that the inclusion/deduction system does not produce a prejudicial effect on the latter group. The general rule is that the income of parents used for the maintenance of their children shall be taxed in the hands of the parents. The special system applicable to separated or divorced parents maintains this rule, but taxes the income in the hands of the parent who ultimately receives it rather than in the hands of the parent who earned it. Imposing the tax on the person who can dispose of the income is not a prejudicial measure in itself. Further, this comparison indicates that the parents to whom the special inclusion/deduction system applies enjoy an overall lessening of their tax burden. In fact, although the tax savings generated by the inclusion/deduction system depend on a variable—the difference between the tax rates of the members of the couple—it was shown that on the whole members of the group derive a benefit from it since most of the parents receiving alimony for the children are subject to a marginal tax rate lower than that of the parents paying the maintenance. It can thus be said that the purposes for which the system was created have been to a large extent achieved. In view of the substantial savings generated by the inclusion/deduction system, the group of separated or divorced parents cannot as a whole claim to suffer prejudice associated with the very existence of the system in question.

Even accepting that a comparison should be made between those who receive and those who pay the maintenance, it was not shown that in the context at issue here the distinction created by the ITA in making the maintenance taxable in the hands of the recipient alone entails a disadvantage. The tax burden of the couple is reduced and this has the result of increasing the available resources that can be used for the benefit of the children, in satisfaction of their parents' obligation to support them.

The question of the distribution of the resources available for the benefit of the children is important in assessing the prejudice alleged by the respondent. This question is governed by the rules of family law which are incorporated into ss. 56(1)(b) and 60(b) by reference. As the fiscal impact resulting from the obligation of inclusion is one of the factors to be taken into account in computing the alimony, the very way in which that impact is distributed between the parents for the ultimate benefit of the child must still be subject to the fundamental criterion of the latter's best interests. That criterion expresses a fundamental value of our society. Since it is governed by that criterion the distribution of the fiscal impact is therefore not open to challenge under the Charter. The fact that the tax saving resulting from the inclusion/deduction system does not benefit both parents in equal proportion therefore does not infringe the equality rights protected by the Charter. Additionally, there is no evidence to show that the recipient parent or the children would benefit by taxation in the hands of the payer of the alimony. In short, the fact that the support may not be increased by an amount equal to the payer's tax relief or the recipient's tax increase does not as such place the latter at a disadvantage since in principle the distribution takes place in accordance with family law, which is incorporated into the tax system by reference and the aims of which are promoted by contributing to an alleviation of the tax burden. Additionally, such results, if any, depend primarily on the individual case. They do not establish a disadvantage for the group.

Finally, a review of the principal provisions of the ITA dealing with tax credits which the respondent could claim (ss. 118(1)(b) and (d) and 122.2) does not alter the conclusion that there is no prejudicial effect. That review indicates that these credits are independent of the inclusion/deduction system and do not depend on receipt of alimony. In enacting these provisions it would appear that the legislature instead intended to alleviate the tax burden of a wide range of persons whose only common denominator is having dependents. This arrangement is not de facto contrary to the custodial parent in a separation situation generally being the one able to claim such credits.

As no prejudice exists, there is no need to go on to the third step.

[I]n the third state it must be determined whether the distinction created is based on an irrelevant personal characteristic which is an enumerated or analogous ground under s. 15(1). ... Relevant is to be determined in light of the underlying objectives of the legislation. As no prejudice exists. (para. 106)

Section 56(1)(b) ITA does not infringe the equality rights guaranteed by s. 15(1) of the Charter.

Per McLachlin J (dissenting): An analysis under s. 15(1) of the Charter involves two stages: (1) the claimant must show that the impugned legislation treats him or her differently by imposing a burden not imposed on others or denying a benefit granted to others; and (2) the claimant must show that this unequal treatment is discriminatory. In the great majority of cases the existence of prejudicial treatment based on an enumerated or analogous ground leads to a conclusion that s. 15(1) has been infringed.

Section 56(1)(b) ITA imposes on one member of the separated or divorced couple a burden which does not affect the other member of that couple. This section requires the separated or divorced custodial parent to include child support payments, while the non-custodial parent may deduct these payments from his taxable income, under s. 60(b) ITA. This inequality between the custodial and non-custodial spouse is exacerbated by the fact that the latter enjoys an automatic and absolute right of deduction of support payments from personal income, while the former's ability to offset the increase in her taxes by obtaining an adjustment of support is unpredictable. Further, one of the premises on which the deduction/inclusion scheme rests—namely that custodial parents (the great majority of whom are women) are generally subject to a lower tax rate than non-custodial parents—is less and less in accord with present reality and undermines the importance our society places on women attaining financial self-sufficiency.

Such a mechanism not only does not encourage women to attain financial self-sufficiency, it seems designed in some cases to discourage them from increasing their income. (para. 182)

Furthermore, the deduction/inclusion scheme overlooks the custodial parent's financial contribution to the support of the children. The custodial parent not only cannot deduct amounts she spends on maintaining the children, but must also pay the tax that the non-custodial parent would ordinarily have had to pay on the income devoted to child support. Apart from s. 56(1)(b) ITA, child support is not included in the taxable income of other persons in situations similar to that of the custodial parent. The general principle of individual taxation applies, and the person having custody is not taxed on amounts which do not personally belong to him or her. In short, the requirement of s. 56(1)(b) ITA that separated or divorced custodial parents include child support in their taxable income imposes obligations on separated or divorced custodial parents that do not apply to others in similar situations and denies benefits which the law accords to others. The fact that the deduction/inclusion scheme confers a benefit on the majority of divorced or separated couples as compared with other couples is no bar to concluding that the same system imposes prejudicial treatment within the couple by imposing on one of its members a burden not imposed on the other.

Even if the legislation is viewed from the perspective of the couple, however, the deduction/inclusion scheme works significant inequality. When the custodial parent's marginal tax rate is greater than that of the non-custodial parent, the scheme has the effect of increasing the total tax paid by both parents. From the outset, the deduction/inclusion scheme imposes prejudicial treatment on separated or divorced couples in about 30 percent of cases. Moreover, where the scheme constitutes a benefit for the couple, the tax savings it generates often benefit only the non-custodial parent since the legislation contains nothing to encourage an equitable division between family members of any benefits that may result from tax savings granted to the non-custodial parent by means of the deduction.

The family law regime does not in practice succeed in rectifying the inequality created by the deduction/inclusion scheme. The tax impact of support payments is not always considered by the courts and, when it is, the adjustment is often insufficient to cover the additional tax which the custodial parent must pay as a result of being subject to the scheme. The amount of child support is determined in light of several factors and thus leaves room for the exercise of a very wide discretionary judicial power which precludes, in many cases, complete neutralization of the negative effects that may result from the inclusion requirement provided for in s. 56(1)(b). The legality of the system is not preserved by the fact that the custodial parent can appeal a judgment which does not adequately take the tax impact into account or obtain an increase in child support when new circumstances increase the additional tax burden she must bear as a result of including child support in her taxable income.

While the status of separated or divorced custodial parent is not one of the grounds enumerated in s. 15(l), it constitutes an analogous ground of discrimination. This conclusion results from the following considerations: (1) the imposition of prejudicial treatment solely on the basis of this status may violate the dignity of an individual and his or her personal worth to a degree affecting the individual's personal, social or economic development; (2) separated or divorced custodial parents considered as a group have historically been subject to disadvantageous treatment; (3) the special difficulties with which separated or divorced custodial parents must live and their minority position as compared with Canadian families as a whole justifies viewing them as a discrete and insular minority; (4) classification as a separated or divorced custodial parent may give rise to adverse distinctions on the basis of immutable personal characteristics in the broad sense of the term, rather than on the merit and actual circumstances of a particular individual; and (5) the status of separated or divorced custodial parents is linked to the enumerated ground of sex given that the great majority of the members of this group are women. The distinction in s. 56(1)(b), based on the status of separated or divorced custodial parent, is discriminatory and infringes s. 15(1) since it runs directly counter to the values underlying it.

Section 56(1)(b) cannot be justified under s. 1 of the Charter. The objective of the inclusion/deduction scheme is to increase the resources of the family as a unit in order to increase child support and ease the discharge of the non-custodial parent's obligations. This legislative objective is of sufficient importance to justify an infringement of a constitutional right, but s. 56(1)(b) does not meet the proportionality test. Even in the absence of mechanisms for dividing the tax saving, there is a tenuous rational connection between the means chosen by Parliament and the objective pursued. However, while Parliament does not have to choose the least intrusive means of all to meet its objective, it did not select one of a range of choices so as to impair a constitutional right as little as possible. The inclusion/deduction scheme does not reasonably minimize the impairment of the equality rights of the respondent and persons in her situation. Alternatives less intrusive of that right protected by the Charter may be readily envisaged. The tax credits provided by the ITA do not attenuate any inequality which the inclusion requirement may work on the custodial parent. Finally, the inclusion/deduction scheme does not meet the proportionality of effects test. The harmful effects of the scheme are disproportionate to the benefits it may produce. While the scheme seems, in the majority of cases, to produce tax savings for the broken family as a whole, in view of the importance of the interest at stake, an adverse tax impact in more than 30 percent of cases is unacceptable. The deduction/inclusion scheme exacerbates the significant financial difficulties encountered by custodial parents and children upon the breakup of the family.

Section 56(1)(b) thus infringes the equality rights guaranteed by s. 15(1) in an unjustifiable manner insofar as it applies to amounts paid between separated or divorced parents for child support. Although the inclusion/deduction scheme is designed to improve the situation of the family as a whole and in many cases succeeds in achieving this objective, it does so at the cost of imposing an unequal and unjustifiable tax burden on custodial parents in the respondent's situation. Therefore, a reading down of s. 56(1)(b) to exclude child support payments appears appropriate. Since the issue turned essentially on s. 56(1)(b), there should be no ruling on the constitutionality of s. 60(b) ITA. Except as regards the respondent, the effects of the declaration of unconstitutionality respecting s. 56(1)(b) should be suspended for a period of one year from the date of the judgment.

Per L'Heureux-Dubé J (dissenting): In an analysis under s. 15(1) of the Charter, it is preferable to focus on the group adversely affected by the distinction as well as on the nature of the interest affected, rather than on the grounds of the impugned distinction. A claimant under that section must establish that: (1) there is a legislative distinction; (2) this distinction results in a denial of one of the four equality rights on the basis of the claimant's membership in an identifiable group; and (3) this distinction is "discriminatory" within the meaning of s. 15(1).

[O]ne should exercise extreme caution before defining one's unit of comparison in such a way as to raise certain types of distinction above Charter scrutiny. Defining the unit of analysis as the "couple" is ... inconsistent with the purpose and spirit of s. 15. (para. 10)

Section 56(1)(b) ITA makes distinctions and these distinctions have the effect of imposing a burden unequally on the basis of one's membership in an identifiable group—separated or divorced custodial parents. Although the inclusion/deduction regime confers a net tax saving upon a majority of divorced or separated couples, its effect is not experienced equally by both members of the couple. The regime imposes at the outset a tax burden uniquely on custodial spouses, and confers a tax benefit uniquely on non-custodial spouses. As a practical matter, the family law system is incapable of remedying the initial unequal distribution effectuated by the inclusion/deduction regime. It does not address to any meaningful extent the inequalities flowing from the burden imposed upon custodial spouses of an imperfect "gross-up" of the support award to account for tax payable, as well as from the benefits accruing to non-custodial spouses as a result of the "upside-down subsidy" that occurs when custodial spouses are in a lower marginal tax bracket. Even if the family law system were to operate perfectly, it could not completely offset the redistributive effects of the inclusion/deduction regime. Thus, whereas the family law system perpetuates an inequality, the regime is undoubtedly the source of this inequality. A denial of equality does not necessarily require that all members of a group be adversely affected by the distinction. It suffices that a particular group is significantly more likely to suffer an adverse effect as a result of a legislative distinction than any other group.

Here, the inclusion/deduction regime is, on the whole, very likely to disadvantage custodial spouses and, concomitantly, very likely to advantage non-custodial spouses. A regime that materially increases the vulnerability of a particular group imposes a burden on that group which violates one of the four equality rights under s. 15. As such, the inclusion/deduction regime imposes upon separated or divorced custodial spouses an unequal burden of the law and denies them the equal benefit of the law.

The distinction made by s. 56(1)(b) is discriminatory within the meaning of s. 15(1) of the Charter. Separated or divorced custodial spouses, the vast majority of whom are women, are, on the whole, an economically and socially vulnerable group, bound together by traits that are personal, though not necessarily wholly immutable. Adverse legislative distinctions on the basis of membership in this group are likely to be reasonably perceived to have a discriminatory impact by members of this group, and are capable of touching upon essential aspects of personal self-worth and dignity. The interest most directly and adversely affected by s. 56(1)(b) is the economic situation of separated or divorced custodial parents and their children—an important societal interest. The impugned distinction may visit significant economic hardship upon this group. In view of the nature of the group and the interest affected, the distinctions drawn in the inclusion/deduction regime, and in particular in s. 56(1)(b), are reasonably capable of having a material discriminatory impact on separated or divorced custodial parents. The fact that some isolated individuals within this group may not be adversely affected does not alter the general validity of this conclusion. Section 56(1)(b) therefore violates s. 15(1) of the Charter, since it is capable of either promoting or perpetuating the view that separated custodial parents are less capable, or less worthy of recognition or value as human beings or as members of Canadian society, equally deserving of concern, respect, and consideration.

Section 56(1)(b) cannot be saved under s. 1 of the Charter. The modern purpose of the inclusion/deduction regime—to place more money in the hands of the separated or divorced "couple" for the purposes of raising the level of child support—is a pressing and substantial objective, but the regime does not achieve this objective in a proportionate manner. While the regime is rationally connected to its objective, it lies outside the reasonable range of minimally intrusive alternatives available to the government. The government has not demonstrated that the benefit accruing to the separated or divorced "couple" is fairly and equitably shared between the two individuals. The initial unequal distribution will only be equally divided by the good graces of the non-custodial spouse or in the unlikely event that the family law system fully understands, anticipates, and applies the principles of tax expenditure analysis. Other alternatives could more effectively achieve the objective. Further, the deleterious effects of the impugned distinction outweigh its salutary effects. The fact that the regime often imposes a very real disadvantage upon the very group it is intended to help is not outweighed by the net tax savings to couples that it frequently occasions. Accordingly, s. 56(1)(b) should be declared invalid in respect of child support payments. The declaration of invalidity should be suspended for a 12-month period to enable Parliament to implement a less discriminatory alternative. No pronouncement is made on the constitutionality of s. 60(b) ITA.

IN THE SUPREME COURT OF CANADA
(ON APPEAL FROM THE COURT OF APPEAL FOR ONTARIO)

BETWEEN:

PERCIVAL WHITLEY

AND:

TIMOTHY MOWERS

Appellants

AND:

HER MAJESTY THE QUEEN

Respondent

AND:

WOMEN'S LEGAL EDUCATION AND ACTION FUND (LEAF)

Intervenor

Factum of the Women's Legal Education and Action Fund (LEAF)

Whitley and Mowers v. The Queen

INTRODUCTION

In 1992, Whitley and Mowers were convicted of sexual assault. (A third accused, Rickard, was also convicted but did not participate in the appeal to the Supreme Court of Canada.) At trial, they argued that the complainant had consented, and in the alternative, they honestly believed that she had. The trial judge did not put the mistaken belief in consent defence to the jury as he thought insufficient evidence had been offered to give it any air of reality. On the issue of consent, he instructed the jury that for consent to be genuine it must be given "without mental reservation." Whitley and Mowers appealed their convictions to the Ontario Court of Appeal on the basis that the trial judge erred in not putting the defence of mistaken belief in consent to the jury and that the trial judge misdirected the jury on the nature of consent. The Court of Appeal upheld the convictions although it did reduce the sentences. Whitley and Mowers appealed further to the Supreme Court of Canada. LEAF intervened in order to address some of the equality issues for women that arise when the defence of honest but mistaken belief in consent is raised by an accused in a sexual assault trial.

FACTUM

PART I: FACTS

1. The Intervenor, the Women's Legal Education Action Fund (LEAF), is a national, not-for-profit advocacy organization that promotes the right of women to equal treatment before and under the law. LEAF has developed considerable expertise relating to sexual violence against women through its involvement in test case litigation, research and public education.

2. The Appellants, Timothy Mowers and Percival Whitley ("Mowers" and "Whitley"), seek to overturn their convictions on charges of sexual assault. William Rickard, a third man found guilty of the sexual assault, is not appealing his conviction to this Court.

3. LEAF accepts the facts set out in Part I of the Respondent's factum. LEAF rejects paragraphs 51 and 52 of Whitley's factum and paragraphs 75 and 76 of Mowers's factum to the extent that they distort or misrepresent the evidence given at trial.

4. Contrary to paragraphs 51(vi) and 51(ix) in Whitley's factum and paragraph 75(j) in Mowers's factum, the complainant never testified that she was aware that Whitley was in the bedroom during the initial kissing and touching by Mowers alone. Rather, the complainant maintained throughout her evidence in chief and in cross-examination by three counsel that she did not think anyone else was in the room; she assumed no one else was in the room because people do not watch other people in such circumstances; she assumed that the other two accused were in the other room; she heard voices in the other room, and those voices "didn't sound close."

Appellant Whitley's factum, paragraphs 51(vi) and (ix).

Appellant Mowers's factum, paragraphs 8 and 75(j).

Case on Appeal, vol. 1, Holt, at 115, at 118, ll. 20-30, and at 119, ll. 1-30.

5. Both Appellants testified that the complainant actively participated in the prolonged sexual activity with the three accused. For instance, Mowers maintained that the complainant helped rub lotion onto her own body, gave "confirming moans," opened her own mouth to accept his penis, spread her legs for him and, generally, acted with "just the same equality" as during the "surprisingly passionate kissing" that occurred prior to Whitley touching her. Whitley, too, maintained that the complainant laid down and opened her legs for him, smiled, whispered to Mowers and rubbed lotion onto her skin along with the accused. Rickard, on the other hand, did not depict the complainant as an active participant. Rather, he admitted that he thought he could touch the complainant in the first instance "because she was letting Percy do it." He noted that she was "already with two guys, so I just went in with them too" and when she "did nothing" throughout the assault, "I thought she was a party girl when she didn't resist. I honestly thought she's saying it was okay."

Case on Appeal, vol. 2, Whitley, at 310, l. 30, at 311, ll. 10-35, at 314, ll. 15-30, at 323, ll. 15-30, at 354, l. 30 to 355, l. 20; Mowers, at 393, l. 20 to 394, l. 20, at 395, ll. 1-10, at 396, ll. 15-40, at 399, ll. 1-40, at 434, ll. 22-25, at 439, ll. 20-21, at 440, ll. 7-11, at 441, ll. 8-33, at 443, ll. 20-28, at 448, l. 30 to 449, l. 40; vol. 3, Rickard, at 505, l. 30 to 507, l. 30.

6. By its verdict, the jury clearly rejected the Appellants' evidence that the complainant actively participated in "group sex."

7. As an alternative defence after the close of their evidence and, now, on appeal, the Appellants seek to rely on what they describe as the complainant's non-objection and absence of physical resistance as the basis for an alleged "mistaken belief in consent" defence, despite the fact that absence of physical resistance and/or non-objection do not constitute legal consent.

PART II: ISSUES

8. LEAF will address the issue of whether the learned Trial Judge erred in refusing to put the defence of mistaken belief in consent to the jury.

9. It is the position of LEAF that as a matter of law and, in particular, as a matter of constitutional law, the Court of Appeal for Ontario was correct in ruling that the defence of a mistaken belief in consent was not available in this case. In particular, it is LEAF's position that:

(a) the "mistaken belief in consent defence" is not available as a defence where the belief is based on a mistake about the legal definition of consent, or on a misapplication of the legal definition of consent to the facts that are legally material;

(b) mistakes that are mistakes of law are not a defence to sexual assault and therefore the air of reality test has no application; and

(c) the test of whether the defence of mistake of fact in sexual assault cases should be put to the jury is whether the jury, having rejected the consent defence, could still harbour a reasonable doubt based on the remaining evidence in toto.

PART III: ARGUMENT

The Canadian Charter of Rights and Freedoms

10. The Canadian Charter of Rights and Freedoms is the supreme law of the land. Common law rules and statutes must be interpreted in a manner consistent with the fundamental values enshrined in the Charter.

Retail, Wholesale & Department Store Union, Local 580 v. Dolphin Delivery Ltd., [1986] 2 SCR 573.

11. Section 15(1) is the broadest of all guarantees in the Charter. It is designed to "protect those groups who suffer social, political and legal disadvantage in our society." This Court has identified the remedial purposes of section 15(1) guarantees variously as: "to ensure equality in the formulation and application of the law"; "to ensure law made distinctions among citizens do not bring about or reinforce group disadvantage"; and "to promote a society in which all are secure in the knowledge that they are recognised at law as human beings equally deserving of concern, respect, and consideration."

Andrews v. Law Society of British Columbia, [1989] 1 SCR 143, at 154, per Wilson J, and at 171, per McIntyre J.

12. As this Honourable Court has recognized:

Sexual assault is, in the vast majority of cases, gender based. It is an assault upon human dignity and constitutes a denial of any concept of equality for women. The reality of the situation can be seen from the statistics that demonstrate that 99 percent of the offenders in sexual assault cases are men and 90 percent of the victims are women.

Osolin v. The Queen, [1993] 4 SCR 595, at 669, per Cory J.

13. Studies show that two factors operate in the rapist's selection of a victim: availability and vulnerability. The more disadvantaged, dependent, or relatively powerless an individual, the more she is vulnerable to sexual exploitation and violation.

Ministry of the Solicitor General, Canadian Urban Victimization Survey, "Female Victims of Crime" (Ottawa: Supply and Services, 1985), at 2.

Report of the Committee on Sexual Offences Against Children and Youth (Badgley Report), *Sexual Offences Against Children and Youth*, vol. 1 (Ottawa: Supply and Services, 1984) (Chair: R.F. Badgley), at 196-98.

14. Some women are more vulnerable than others:

(a) Older women, women living in poverty, women with disabilities, rural women, lesbians, women of official language minorities, women of colour, young women, immigrant and refugee women, Inuit women and aboriginal women are particularly vulnerable to violence.

Final Report of the Canadian Panel on Violence Against Women, *Changing the Landscape: Ending Violence—Achieving Equality* (Ottawa: Supply and Services, 1993).

(b) People with disabilities are at least 150% as vulnerable to sexual abuse as individuals of the same age and sex who are not disabled.

D. Sobsey, "Sexual Offenses and Disabled Victims: Research and Practical Implications" (1988), 6:4 *Vis-à-vis: A National Newletter on Family Violence*, Canadian Council on Social Development, at 1.

(c) Since racism and sexism are root causes of violence, women of colour in Canada are extremely vulnerable as they are subjected daily to both forms of harassment on an individual and systemic level.

Final Report of the Canadian Panel on Violence Against Women, supra, at 80.

15. Young women are at the greatest risk of being sexually assaulted. Sixty eight percent of all sexual assaults happen to women between the ages of 16 and 25. Four out of five victims of sexual assault reported to the police were attacked by someone known to them. A third of all college men say they would rape women if they could be assured they would not get caught.

Solicitor General, supra, para. 13, at 2-3.

The Daily, "The Violence Against Women Survey" (Ottawa: Statistics Canada, November 18, 1993).

S. Ward et al., "Acquaintance Rape and the College Social Scene" (1991), *Family Relations* 65.

R. Gunn and C. Minch, *Sexual Assault: The Dilemma of Disclosure. The Question of Conviction* (Winnipeg: U. of Manitoba, 1988), at 3-13 and 44-46.

N. Malamuth, "Rape Proclivity Among Males" (1981), 37:4 *Journal of Social Issues* 138, at 140.

16. It is respectfully submitted that the factors that have made members of disempowered groups more vulnerable to sexual assault have also historically placed them at a disadvantage at each stage of the criminal justice system, which results in part because of stereotypical and unfounded assumptions about women and sexual assault.

The Law of Consent

17. Even before Parliament provided specific statutory guidance by enacting section 273.1 of the Criminal Code, Courts and Parliament developed the definition of consent. As Mr. Justice Gonthier, for the majority, stated in *R v. Jobidon*:

> Just as the common law has built up a rich jurisprudence around the concepts of agreement in contract law, and *volenti non fit injuriain* the law of negligence, it has also generated a body of law to illuminate the meaning of consent and to place certain limitations on its legal effectiveness in the criminal law. It has done this in respect of assault. ...

R v. Jobidon, [1991] 2 SCR 714, at 735, per Gonthier J.

Criminal Code, RSC 1985, c. C-46, ss. 273.1(1) and (3).

18. The definition of consent includes the expression of voluntary agreement to the act in question by the complainant. Consent that is obtained by fear of the application of force or the application of actual force is not valid consent.

Criminal Code, supra, ss. 265(3) and 273.1.

19. In the recent sexual assault case of *R v. M.L.M.* this Honourable Court unanimously held that:

> The majority of the Court of Appeal was in error in holding that the victim is required to offer some minimal word or gesture of objection and that lack of resistance must be equated with consent.

R v. M.L.M., [1994] 2 SCR 3, at 4.

20. In *R v. Wills*, the Ontario Court of Appeal found that in order to assert that an individual consented to giving up a constitutionally protected right, which would include a woman's right to bodily security, the Crown must prove: (1) there was consent; (2) the giver of the consent had the authority to give the consent; (3) the consent was voluntary and not the product of coercion or other conduct that influenced the accused's choice; (4) the giver of the consent was aware of the nature of the conduct to which she was being asked to consent; (5) the giver of the consent was aware of her right to refuse to consent; and (6) the giver of the consent was aware of the potential consequences of giving the consent.

R v. Wills (1992), 7 OR (3d) 337 (CA), at 348-54.

R v. Morgentaler, [1988] 1 SCR 30, at 171 and 173, per Wilson J.

Mistake of Law Versus Mistake of Fact

21. In full *mens rea* offences, mistakes based on a belief in the existence of facts regarding the external circumstances of the offence which, if true, would render the

accused's acts innocent, will exonerate the accused. On the other hand, mistakes based on the meaning, scope or application of a law do not exonerate, nor do honest mistakes about the legal consequences of one's actions.

Criminal Code, supra, s. 19.

G. Williams, *Criminal Law*, The General Part, 2d ed. (London: Stevens & Sons, 1961), at 287-93.

E. Mureinik, "The Application of Rules: Law or Fact" (1982), 98 *The Law Quarterly Review* 587.

L. Hall and S. Seligman, "Mistake of Law and Mens Rea" (1940-41), 8 *University of Chicago Law Review* 641.

22. In *Molis v. The Queen*, this Honourable Court held that section 19 of the Criminal Code refers not just to ignorance of the existence of law but also to mistakes as to its meaning, scope, or application. Further, this Court has consistently recognized that an honest mistake about the legal consequences of one's actions is no defence to a criminal charge. Every individual in Canada has the duty to understand and know the criminal law even with respect to points of interpretation over which judges may differ.

Molis v. The Queen, [1980] 2 SCR 356.

R v. Forster, [1992] 1 SCR 339.

Jones v. The Queen, [1991] 3 SCR 110.

L. Vandervort, "Mistake of Law and Sexual Assault: Consent and Mens Rea" (1987-88), 2 *Canadian Journal of Women and the Law* 233, at 233-56.

Williams, supra, para. 21, at 288-89.

23. Many provincial appellate courts have also identified various situations in which mistakes of law will not exculpate. In all of these cases, the accused was aware of the empirical or socio-factual elements that constituted the offence, but he was mistaken about or misapprehended the legal status, description, or consequences of his actions.

R v. Rio Algoma (1988), 46 CCC (3d) 242 (Ont. CA).

R v. Baxter (1982), 6 CCC (3d) 447 (Alta. CA).

R v. MacDonald (1983), 3 CCC (3d) 419 (Alta. CA).

Vandervort, supra, at 247-56.

24. One rationale for the rule that mistakes of law do not exculpate has been stated as follows:

> To permit an individual to plead successfully that he had a different opinion or interpretation of the law would contradict postulates of a legal order. For there is a basic incompatibility between asserting that the law is what certain officials declare it to be after a prescribed analysis, and asserting, also, that those officials must declare it to be, i.e. that the law is, what defendants or their lawyers believed it to be. A legal order implies the rejection of such contradiction. It opposes objectivity to subjectivity, judicial process to individual opinion, official to lay, and authoritative to non-authoritative declarations of what the law is.

J. Hall, *General Principles of Criminal Law*, 2d ed. (Indianapolis: Bobbs-Merrill, 1960), at 383.

25. In the area of sexual violence, the distinction between mistakes of fact and mistakes of law has long been blurred. Notwithstanding that consent is defined as a matter of law, Canadian courts since *Pappajohn v. The Queen*, [1980] 2 SCR 120 have assumed that consent involves a pure question of fact to be resolved by the accused alone. A full critical analysis of the distinction between mistakes of law and mistakes of fact in the sexual assault context has never been undertaken by this Court.

Vandervort, supra.

26. It is submitted that ignorance, misinterpretation and misapplication of the legal definition of consent in sexual assault cases constitute mistakes of law and do not operate as a defence. An accused's belief cannot render non-consensual sex legally blameless if that belief is based on a misapprehension of what constitutes sexual consent as a matter of law. The defence of mistaken belief in consent is not available in cases where the accused had no mistaken belief in a false set of facts bearing on the presence of consent, but merely failed to appreciate, or was indifferent to, the legal significance of facts of which he was well aware.

Vandervort, supra, at 233-309.

27. The criminal law, rather than commonly held inaccurate myths, or personally held myths, must define the extent to which an individual's right to sexual integrity is protected. When an offender chooses to act as if his behaviour is subject only to the norms of commonly held myths or those of his personal world, rather than those of Canadian law in the 1990s, he does not make an exculpatory mistake of fact, but rather, he has chosen to defy the law and to run the risk of arrest and conviction.

Vandervort, supra, at 295-305.

R v. Barrow (1984), 14 CCC (3d) 471 (NS CA).

28. Bringing the law of mistake in sexual assault cases into line with the rest of the criminal law does not exclude the possibility that a mistake of fact can exonerate an accused charged with sexual assault. However, to provide a defence to an accused for the commission of the offence of sexual assault, the exculpatory belief must be such that if the facts were as the accused claims to have believed them to be, the actions would not have violated the law. It is submitted that such mistakes can occur when there is some evidence that the accused misperceived the verbal or non-verbal behaviour of the complainant.

Vandervort, supra.

See infra, paras. 38 to 45.

29. The Appellants allege that the complainant actively participated after the group sex began. On the other hand, the complainant gave evidence of active resistance, which was both verbal and physical. As the Court of Appeal properly held: "By its verdict the jury has held that the appellants' acts were without the complainant's consent and that each of the appellants knew it." It is submitted, on that basis alone, this Court ought to

dismiss the appeal. Nonetheless, the Appellants go on to assert that there is an evidentiary basis for the mistaken belief in consent defence.

30. In advancing the mistaken belief in consent defence, the Appellants seek to rely on the alleged non-resistance of the complainant who, according to them, "voiced no objection" to the actions performed on her body. It is submitted that any "mistake" based on a belief that non-resistance is consent, is an error of law and does not exculpate an accused.

M.L.M., supra.

31. It is further submitted that the Appellants' assertion that the complainant must have consented because she did not resist and suffered no injuries is based on the myth that women will necessarily struggle or offer overt physical resistance to prevent a sexual assault and that, absent a struggle, the complainant must be consenting. This myth has been discredited by this Court in *Seaboyer*.

R v. Seaboyer; R v. Gayme, [1991] 2 SCR 577, at 651, per L'Heureux-Dubé J.

32. There is no one correct response to sexual assault. As Madam Justice L'Heureux-Dubé noted in *Seaboyer*:

> Women know that there is no response on their part that will assure their safety. The experience and knowledge of women is born out by the Canadian Urban Victimization Study. …
>
> Sixty percent of those who tried reasoning with their attackers, and sixty percent of those who resisted by actively fighting or using a weapon were injured. …

Seaboyer, supra, at 652, per L'Heureux-Dubé J.

M.L.M., supra.

33. Mowers claims that he is in a "unique situation among the three accused," since he was involved in the initial consensual activity with the complainant. However, the granting of consent to Mowers in the activity of kissing and touching cannot legally be equated with consent to do more. The nature of the activity changed, even from Mowers's perspective, the moment the complainant felt "too many sets of hands on [her]." If Mowers truly believed that consent to kiss and touch the complainant was equivalent to consent to engage in group sex, he made a mistake of law that will not exculpate him.

34. Whitley argues that because Mowers was touching the complainant, she was consenting to let Whitley perform sexual acts on her body. As a matter of law, consent to A cannot found legally valid consent to B or C. If Whitley truly believed that consent to Mowers meant he had consent to touch the complainant, he made an error of law that will not exculpate him.

35. Whitley suggests that because Mowers "invited" him to touch the complainant he believed that the complainant was consenting. Any belief that the complainant consented because Mowers, in essence, consented for her, is a mistake of law and will not exculpate him.

Air of Reality

Mistakes of Law and "Air of Reality"

36. The "air of reality" test is the test used to determine when any defence may be put before the trier of fact for consideration.

Osolin, supra, at 676, per Cory J.

37. It is submitted that the Appellants' claims to have made the mistakes outlined in paragraphs 51 and 52 of Whitley's factum and paragraphs 75 and 76 of Mowers's factum are, as mistakes of law, barred as defences by section 19 of the Criminal Code of Canada. Hence the "air of reality" test has no application to these specific claims.

Mistakes of Fact and "Air of Reality"

38. This Honourable Court has consistently held that the defence of mistake of fact regarding consent to a charge of sexual assault must meet the "air of reality" test before it can be considered by the trier of fact.

Pappajohn, supra.

R v. Robertson, [1987] 1 SCR 918.

Reddick v. The Queen, [1991] 1 SCR 1086.

Osolin, supra.

39. "In order to give an air of reality to the defence of honest but mistaken belief, there must be: (1) evidence of lack of consent to the sexual acts; and (2) evidence that notwithstanding the actual refusal, the accused honestly but mistakenly believed that the complainant was consenting."

Osolin, supra, at 648, per McLachlin J.

40. It is submitted that the decisions of this Honourable Court have in fact used a consistent approach in the cases where the Court has found that there is no "air of reality" to a proposed defence of mistake regarding consent: there is no "air of reality" to a mistake defence unless the trier of fact, having accepted that the victim did not consent, could still harbour a reasonable doubt about the accused's awareness of the risk of non-consent based on the remaining evidence in toto.

Pappajohn, supra, at 500-1, per McIntyre J.

Robertson, supra, at 938-39, per Wilson J.

Reddick, supra, at 1088, per McLachlin J.

Osolin, supra, at 609, per L'Heureux-Dubé J, at 648-49, per McLachlin J, and at 682-83 per Cory J.

C. Boyle, *Sexual Assault* (Toronto: Carswell, 1984), at 166.

41. An accused who argues that the complainant consented is advancing an *actus reus* argument. Accused, such as the Appellants in the instant case, will often allege that the complainant overtly agreed to, by words and actions, and in fact enjoyed, the sexual

contact that is the subject of the criminal charge. In the case at hand, the accuseds' evidence as to such consent was rejected by the trier of fact.

42. An accused who advances a mistake defence is advancing a *mens rea* argument. It is submitted that an accused who asserts that he shot a person, mistakenly believing that it was a deer, or who asserts that he mistakenly believed a small, cellophane-wrapped packet of cocaine to be sugar, will need some other evidence to give an "air of reality" to the proposed defence of mistake. Given that the accused is conceding the *actus reus* of the offence but alleging perceptual error, that other evidence must go to the issue of the accused's perception.

43. The Appellants, by advancing an alternative defence of mistake regarding consent that includes acknowledgment that consent was absent, must, from the remaining evidence point to something in support of their assertion that they misperceived the complainant to have overtly communicated her agreement. To give an "air of reality" to this *mens rea* argument, the Appellants must identify circumstances that interfered with their ability to perceive accurately the facts.

44. The Appellants do not point to any evidence that supports a theory that they genuinely misperceived the complainant to have willingly spread her legs, that they misperceived her to have embraced the Appellants, that they misperceived her to have willingly fondled their penises, or that they misperceived her to have performed fellatio. To instruct the trier of fact to consider the defence in the absence of any evidentiary support for the alleged misperception is to invite speculation.

45. It is therefore submitted that the learned trial judge was correct in law in ruling that the defence of mistake of fact was unavailable to the Appellants on the basis of the "air of reality" test.

Conclusion

46. LEAF submits that to permit an accused to rely on his own interpretation of the law of consent is to permit the accused in sexual assault cases to raise a defence that is not available to persons accused of other types of offences.

47. LEAF submits that where courts permit an accused to rely on his own interpretation of consent, they are permitting the accused to rely on a defence based on myths and stereotypes about women and sexual assault.

48. LEAF further submits that given the gendered nature of sexual assault, to allow those accused of sexual assault to rely on groundless myths and stereotypes about women and sexual assault is to discriminate directly against women, and in particular those women who are especially vulnerable because of their age, race, and/or ability, contrary to sections 7, 15, and 28 of the Charter.

49. In a sex unequal society, jury members are also influenced by stereotypes about women and sexual assault. LEAF submits that for the same reason that judges are required to give careful limiting instructions when sexual history evidence is admitted, so too must judges strictly prohibit juries from relying on "defences" based on myth and stereotype.

50. It is respectfully submitted that this Honourable Court must acknowledge mistakes of law for what they are in sexual assault cases. To fail to do so will deny women effective protection of sexual assault laws and perpetuate women's social and legal inequality in Canada.

PART IV: NATURE OF ORDER SOUGHT

51. It is respectfully submitted that this Honourable Court ought to dismiss this appeal and uphold the convictions of the Appellants.

All of which is respectfully submitted.

THE OUTCOME

Head Notes—Whitley and Mowers v. The Queen

The judgment of the Court was delivered orally by

Lamer CJ—Assuming without deciding that on the evidence adduced in this case, the defence of honest but mistaken belief in consent should have been put to the jury, we are all of the view that, having regard to the manner in which the issue of knowledge of absence of consent was put to the jury, the jury's conviction negatived that defence. Therefore the failure, if any, to specifically frame the matter as a defence, did not occasion a substantial miscarriage of justice. With respect to the argument that the trial judge misdirected the jury on the issue of consent, we agree with the Ontario Court of Appeal.

Both appeals are accordingly dismissed.

IN THE SUPREME COURT OF CANADA

(ON APPEAL FROM THE COURT OF APPEAL FOR BRITISH COLUMBIA)

BETWEEN:

HUBERT PATRICK O'CONNOR

Appellant

AND:

HER MAJESTY THE QUEEN

Respondent

AND:

THE ABORIGINAL WOMEN'S COUNCIL; THE DISABLED WOMEN'S NETWORK OF CANADA; CANADIAN ASSOCIATION OF SEXUAL ASSAULT CENTRES; AND THE WOMEN'S LEGAL EDUCATION AND ACTION FUND

Intervenors

AND:

CANADIAN MENTAL HEALTH ASSOCIATION

Intervenors

Factum of the Aboriginal Women's Council et al.

O'Connor v. The Queen

INTRODUCTION

In February 1991, Hubert Patrick O'Connor, a Roman Catholic bishop, was charged with committing sexual assault, indecent assault, and gross indecency against four Aboriginal women.

The women had attended the St. Joseph's Mission School in Williams Lake, British Columbia when they were between the ages of eight and sixteen; O'Connor was their priest and principal. Upon completion of their schooling they remained as employees under the supervision of O'Connor, who continued to be their priest. It was during this later period that the assaults that were the subject matter of the charges occurred. The charges against O'Connor were laid some twenty-five years later. O'Connor did not deny engaging in sexual intercourse with two of the women, but claimed that the intercourse was consensual. However, the pivotal issue became defence counsel's request for the complainants' medical, therapeutic, education, and employment records. Some of these records were in possession of the Crown; some were not. The Crown was ordered to produce all of them to the defence.

In November 1992, the trial judge stayed the proceedings because he found that the Crown's delay in complying with the disclosure order had irreparably damaged the integrity of the trial. The Crown appealed both the stay of proceedings and the original disclosure order. LEAF—in coalition with the Aboriginal Women's Council, the Canadian Association of Sexual Assault Centres, the DisAbled Women's Network of Canada, obtained leave to intervene in the appeal.

On March 30, 1994, the British Columbia Court of Appeal dissolved the stay and ordered the case back for trial. On May 16, 1994, the Court issued a second decision in which it set out a two-stage test for determining how and when complainants' records ought to be released to the defence. O'Connor appealed the March 30 ruling to the Supreme Court. The Coalition of women's groups, including LEAF, again obtained intervenor status. Other intervenors were the Attorneys General for Canada and Ontario, the Canadian Mental Health Association, and the Canadian Foundation for Children, Youth and the Law. All of the intervenors made arguments respecting the appropriate test for disclosure of the complainants' records. Only the Coalition addressed the equality issues for women. The case was heard on February 1, 1995.

FACTUM

PART I: FACTS

1. The Intervenor Coalition (the "Coalition"), composed of the Aboriginal Women's Council, the Canadian Association of Sexual Assault Centres, the DisAbled Women's Network of Canada, and the Women's Legal Education and Action Fund, brings to this appeal extensive expertise in the following areas:

(a) sexual violence against women and children;

(b) the life circumstances of First Nations women and of women with disabilities;

(c) the relationships among inequalities based on sex, race, and disability alone or in combination, vulnerability to sexual violence and diminished access to justice; and

(d) constitutional law and equality jurisprudence.

2. On the basis of this collective expertise, the Coalition intervenes in this appeal to ensure that the fundamental constitutional equality implications of pre-trial disclosure in criminal cases involving sexual violence are fully recognized and addressed by this Court.

PART II: ISSUES

3. The Coalition takes no position on the correctness of the British Columbia Court of Appeal's doctrinal analysis of the threshold for a stay of proceedings for common law abuse of process or as a remedy for breach of an accused's constitutional rights.

4. The Coalition submits, however, that while it would be open to this court to dismiss the appeal without addressing the disclosure order sought by the defence, ordered by the Associate Chief Justice and ultimately complied with by the Crown in this case, it would not be open to this Court to consider reinstating the stay of proceedings entered at trial without analyzing the constitutional propriety of that disclosure order.

5. The Coalition submits that the ultimate object of an order of a stay of proceedings—the maintenance of public confidence in the legal and judicial process—would be undermined by the issuance of a stay that is related in any way to this disclosure order that was found by the BC Court of Appeal to have been procedurally and substantively flawed and which, in our submission, violates the constitutional rights of the complainants.

6. The Coalition submits that the constitutional rights of the victims of sexual violence to security of the person without discrimination based on sex, race or disability and to equal protection and benefit of the law cannot be fully recognized or vindicated in this appeal or in criminal law and procedure more generally unless courts take cognizance of

the social, historical, political and legal conditions of inequality in which sexual violence occurs; out of which legal principles and legal practices emerge; and under which records sought to be disclosed are generated.

PART III: ARGUMENT

Equality Guarantees Must Be Applied to Disclosure Principles and Practice

7. The Coalition submits that the maintenance of public confidence in the integrity of legal and judicial processes requires not only scrupulous protection of the fair trial rights of accused persons but also judicial recognition and censure of:

(a) the degree to which rape myths and sexual and other discriminatory stereotypes presently animate disclosure requests and rationalize disclosure orders;

(b) the degree to which overbroad, unjustifiably invasive and prejudicial disclosure requests and orders are but the latest manifestation of law's lengthy history of discrimination against victims of sexual violence who wish to hold their abusers criminally accountable; and

(c) the degree to which defence counsels' increasingly aggressive and expansive pursuit of complainants' personal records serves by design or effect to counteract initiatives by Parliament and the courts that have attempted to reduce the operation of discriminatory assumptions, logic, and outcomes in sexual offence law.

8. None of the courts in the record below and no reported case reviewed by the Coalition concerning disclosure of complainants' personal records in sexual offence proceedings explicitly refers to complainants' section 15 Charter rights when addressing disclosure requests.

9. In the Coalition's submission, evolving contemporary disclosure jurisprudence reflects, exploits and reinforces discriminatory stereotypes about women, children, and their sexuality that are little different in their genesis or substance from the evidentiary rules abrogated by Parliament in 1983, and from the rape myths discredited by this Court in *R v. Seaboyer*.

Criminal Law Amendment Act, SC 1980-81-82-83, c. 125.

R v. Seaboyer; R v. Gayme, [1991] 2 SCR 577.

10. Courts have been applying disclosure law, it is submitted, as if constitutional guarantees protecting accuseds' fair trial rights eclipse the section 7 and section 15 rights of complainants. It is submitted, however, that this is not the correct approach: "a hierarchical approach to rights, which places some over others, must be avoided, both when interpreting the Charter and when developing the common law."

Dagenais v. Canadian Broadcasting Corp., [1994] 3 SCR 835, at 877, per Lamer CJ.

11. Like past evidentiary rules now recognized as discriminatory, evolving contemporary disclosure practices indulge the groundless suspicion that women's and children's

reports of sexual violence are uniquely likely to be fabricated, and therefore subject complainants to exhaustive and oppressive credibility testing to prove them worthy of the law's protection. In the result, complainants' access to law's protection is conditioned on legally sanctioned access to their private lives and disregard for their dignity and autonomy to a degree unparalleled in other criminal proceedings where credibility is at issue.

Osolin v. The Queen, [1993] 4 SCR 595, at 624-25, per L'Heureux-Dubé J.

R v. K.A.D., [1994] OJ no. 1837 (Ont. CJ Prov. Div.).

R v. Darby, unreported, February 24, 1994 (BC Prov. Ct.).

12. A legal system that not only tolerates but, in the name of fair trial rights, presumes the uncreditworthiness of individual members of the disadvantaged groups most targeted for sexual violence, does not reflect, far less promote, "a society in which all are secure in the knowledge they are recognized at law as human beings equally deserving of concern, respect and consideration." Such a system, it is submitted, overtly violates section 15.

Andrews v. Law Society of British Columbia, [1989] 1 SCR 143, at 171, per McIntyre J.

13. That so inegalitarian a legal system cannot and does not command public confidence in its fairness, decency, and integrity is evident in the fact that sexual assault has long been and remains one of the most under-reported of serious crimes.

Canadian Newspapers Co. v. AG Canada, [1988] 2 SCR 122, at 131-32, per Lamer CJ.

Seaboyer, supra, at 649, per L'Heureux-Dubé J.

Disclosure Practices Reinforce Existing Inequality

14. This Court has described section 15 as "the broadest of all [Charter] guarantees," one that "applies to and supports all other rights guaranteed by the Charter." Its purpose is "to ensure equality in the formulation and application of the law" and "to remedy or prevent discrimination against groups subject to stereotyping, historical disadvantage and political and social prejudice in Canadian Society."

Andrews, supra, at 171, per McIntyre J.

R v. Swain, [1991] 1 SCR 933, at 992, per Lamer CJ.

15. To apply disclosure legal rules and norms as if the conditions of systemic inequality under which they were framed and in which they operate were immaterial to the fairness of legal processes or to the integrity of the justice system perpetuates systemic inequality in and through law.

16. Studies show that two factors operate in a rapist's selection of a victim: vulnerability and availability. The more disadvantaged, dependent, or relatively powerless an individual, the more she or he is vulnerable to sexual exploitation and violation, particularly by individuals she or he knows. Contrary to rape mythology, only a minority of sexual assaults are committed by strangers.

Ministry of the Solicitor General, Canadian Urban Victimization Survey, "Female Victims of Crime" (Ottawa: Supply and Services, 1985), at 2.

Report of the Committee on Sexual Offences Against Children and Youth (Badgley Report), *Sexual Offences Against Children and Youth*, Vol. 1 (Ottawa: Supply and Services, 1984), at 196-98.

M. Burt, "Rape Myths and Acquaintance Rape" in Parrot and Bechhofer, eds., *Acquaintance Rape* (New York: Wiley, 1991).

17. According to Statistics Canada's national Violence Against Women survey, 39% of all Canadian women have experienced at least one incident of sexual assault since the age of 16, and over half of those had experienced more than one incident. Of the incidents of sexual assault reported to Statistics Canada, only 6% were reported to the police. Fear of the attitudes likely to be shown by the police and the courts toward complainants continues to deter significant numbers of women from reporting.

J. Roberts, "Criminal Justice Processing of Sexual Assault Cases" (March 1994), *Juristat*, vol. 14, no. 7, at 3-6.

Final Report of the Canadian Panel on Violence Against Women, *Changing the Landscape: Ending Violence—Achieving Equality* (Ottawa: Supply and Services, 1993), at 28-29.

18. People with disabilities are at least 150% as vulnerable to sexual abuse as individuals of the same age and sex who are not disabled. One recent survey determined that approximately one-third of the abusers reported were disability service providers like personal care attendants, psychiatrists, residential care staff, and special transit staff. Subsequent to their assaults, most disabled people seek counselling, support from current caregivers, and medical services.

D. Sobsey, "Patterns of Sexual Abuse and Assault" (1991), 9 *Sexuality and Disability* 243, at 248-49.

D. Sobsey, "Sexual Offences and Disabled Victims: Research and Practical Implications" (1988), 6:4 *Vis-à-vis: A National Newsletter on Family Violence*, Canadian Council on Social Development, at 1.

19. Several studies have determined that between 50 and 80% of women institutionalized for psychiatric disorders have prior histories of sexual abuse.

T. Firsten, "An Exploration of the Role of Physical and Sexual Abuse for Psychiatrically Institutionalized Women" (1990), unreported research paper, available from Ontario Women's Directorate.

20. It is submitted that disclosure rules or practices that make mental health or medical records routinely accessible in sexual offence proceedings will have disproportionately invasive consequences for women with disabilities whether their disability is exploited by abusers or their disability follows from a prior history of sexual abuse.

Osolin, supra, at 622 and 631, per L'Heureux-Dubé J.

21. First Nations women and children are particularly vulnerable to male sexual violence. As many as 8 out of 10 First Nations women have been sexually abused or assaulted in their lives, usually on more than one occasion. The breakdown of family structures caused by the residential school system as well as the modelling of corporal discipline, has been directly linked with violence against women in aboriginal communities.

Ontario Native Women's Association, *Breaking Free: A Proposal for Change to Aboriginal Family Violence* (December 1989).

A.C. Hamilton and C.M. Sinclair, Report of the Aboriginal Justice Inquiry of Manitoba, vol. 1, *The Justice System and Aboriginal People* (1991), at 478 and 481-82.

22. Aboriginal women are also highly vulnerable to sexual violence perpetrated by white men steeped in degrading and dehumanizing stereotypes of "Indians":

> The portrayal of the squaw is one of the most degraded, most despised and most dehumanized anywhere in the world. The "squaw" is the female counterpart to the Indian male "savage" and as such she has no human face; she is lustful, immoral, unfeeling and dirty. Such grotesque dehumanization has rendered all Native women and girls vulnerable to gross physical, psychological and sexual violence. ... I believe, for example, that Helen Betty Osborne was murdered in 1972 by four young men from The Pas because these youths grew up with twisted notions of "Indian girls" as "squaws." ... Osborne's attempts to fight off these men's sexual advances challenged their racist expectations that an "Indian squaw" should show subservience ... [causing] the whites ... to go into a rage and proceed to brutalize the victim.
>
> It is evident that the men who abducted Osborne believed that young aboriginal women were objects with no human value beyond sexual gratification.

Excerpt from written brief of Emma LaRocque to Aboriginal Justice Inquiry, quoted in vol. 1, at 479.

Aboriginal Justice Inquiry, vol. 2, *The Deaths of Helen Betty Osborne and John Joseph Harper*, at 52.

23. The legal system has too often treated the high incidence of abuse of aboriginal women as reason to discount the injury caused them by sexual assault. Racist stereotyping has also been shown to infiltrate sexual assault proceedings involving aboriginal complainants.

T. Nahanee, "Sexual Assault of Inuit Females: A Comment on 'Cultural Bias' " in J.V. Roberts and R.M. Mohr, eds., *Confronting Sexual Assault* (Toronto: University of Toronto Press, 1994), 192.

M. Nightengale, "Judicial Attitudes and Differential Treatment: Native Women in Sexual Assault Cases" (1991), 23 *Ottawa Law Review* 71.

Aboriginal Justice Inquiry, vol. 2, supra, at 52 and 91.

24. Comparable findings exist linking the heightened vulnerability of Black women to male sexual violence with racist stereotypes of Black women as promiscuous (hence

discreditable), and linking such racist stereotypes to low prosecution and conviction rates of those who sexually abuse or assault Black women.

K. Crenshaw, "Whose Story Is It Anyway?" in Morrison, ed., *Race-ing Justice En-Gendering Power: Essays on Anita Hill, Clarence Thomas and the Construction of Social Reality* (New York: Pantheon, 1992), 402, at 412-14.

L. Schafran, "Writing and Reading about Rape: A Primer" (1993), 66 *St. John's L Rev.* 979, at 1004.

M. Torrey, "When Will We Be Believed? Rape Myths and the Idea of a Fair Trial in Rape Prosecutions" (1991), 24 *U Calif. Davis L Rev.* 1011, at 1053.

25. Women who are particularly vulnerable to sexual violence are also especially likely to be subject to extensive documentation: the nature of their vulnerabilities and socio-economic disadvantages is such that they are likely to have extensive medical, social service and institutional, immigration or other records. Reinstatement through disclosure practices of extraordinary credibility testing of sexual offence victims will disadvantage through law individuals already disadvantaged in society by subjecting them to invasions of their privacy not suffered by less-documented individuals or individuals victimized by non-sexual crimes. Such a result would violate section 15 of the Charter.

26. A justice system animated by equality principles would recognize that sexual assault law has never worked effectively or equitably for victims of male violence, not least because in our inegalitarian society credibility no less than propensity to perpetrate sexual abuse has always been wedded to power. Accordingly, an equality-respecting justice system would treat individual complainants as individuals not as types. It would view such individuals' history of mental health treatment or of sexual violence not as justification for extra-invasive disclosure, but as reason for caution, sensitivity, and heightened vigilance about the purpose and effects of records disclosure.

Disclosure Practices Draw Upon and Perpetuate Discriminatory Rape Myths

27. This Court has recognized that there is a relationship between sexual violence against women and inequality between the sexes. In particular, it has recognized that: sexual assault is a gender-based crime insofar as 99 percent of the offenders are men and 90 percent of the victims are women; sexual assault is an attack upon human dignity that constitutes a denial of any concept of equality for women; and that in a sexually unequal society, workplace sexual coercion is an abuse of both sexual and economic power used to underscore women's ascribed inferiority to men.

Conway v. The Queen, [1993] 2 SCR 872, at 877, per La Forest J.

Osolin, supra, at 669, per Cory J.

Janzen and Govereau v. Platy Enterprises Ltd. et al., [1989] 1 SCR 1252, at 1284, per Dickson CJ.

28. Historically, both the common law and the Criminal Code permitted, and even mandated, sexually discriminatory evidentiary practices that were calculated to mislead

the jury and that were premised on what this Court has acknowledged are "groundless myths and fantasized stereotypes" about rape and about male and female sexuality.

Seaboyer, supra, at 604, per McLaughlin J.

Osolin, supra, at 670-71, per Cory J.

29. Most formally discriminatory rules of evidence were eliminated from the Criminal Code in 1983. Additionally, this Court has discredited the most transparently groundless rape myths—that is, the myth that a virtuous woman cannot be raped against her will; the myth that lack of resistance indicates willing consent; the prompt hue-and-cry myth that underlay "recent complaint" doctrine; and the myth that sexually active women are more likely to consent to sex with any man and, in any event, are more likely to be liars generally or, at least, to lie about sex.

Criminal Law Amendment Act, supra.

Seaboyer, supra, at 604 and 630, per McLachlin J.

R v. Mason, [1994] 2 SCR 3.

R v. W.(R), [1992] 2 SCR 122, at 136, per McLachlin J.

30. No legislated reforms or judicial dicta, however, have yet addressed, far less contradicted, the tenacious, demonstrably groundless and misogynist myth underpinning virtually all these now-abrogated or discredited evidentiary rules and practices. That foundational myth is that women are uniquely prone to lie about rape and to fabricate rape charges that place innocent men at risk.

Burt, supra, at 28.

Torrey, supra, at 1027.

H. Galvin, "Shielding Rape Victims in the State and Federal Courts: A Proposal for the Second Decade" (1986), 70 *Minn. L Rev.* 763, at 792-93.

31. Four hundred years ago, Lord Matthew Hale asserted that "rape is an accusation easily to be made and hard to prove, and harder to be defended by the party accused, tho' never so innocent."

Hale, *Pleas of the Crown*, vol. 1, 1678, at *635.

32. Hale's often-cited claim has governed the legal imagination ever since, notwithstanding its inaccuracy on every point. Rape accusations are, in fact, not easily made: rape remains one of the most under-reported serious crimes. If reported, and if deemed "founded" by the police, and if prosecuted and tried, rape has always been harder to prove than to defend against.

Julian Roberts and Michelle Grossman, "Changing Definitions of Sexual Assault: An Analysis of Police Statistics" in Roberts and Mohr, eds., *Confronting Sexual Assault: A Decade of Legal and Social Change* (Toronto: University of Toronto Press, 1991), 57, at 59-60.

Richard Andrias, "Rape Myths: A Persistent Problem in Defining and Prosecuting Rape" (1992), *Criminal Justice* 2, at 3-4.

33. The foundational myth that women have a propensity to fabricate rape charges, in turn, has spawned a host of subsidiary myths purporting to account for women's lies about rape; for instance, that women lie to protect their sexual reputations or out of vindictiveness toward the accused or from sheer maliciousness; that women fantasize they were raped and children fantasize that they were abused or that complainants suffer from sexual delusions.

Burt, supra, at 28-32.

Seaboyer, supra, at 651-55, per L'Heureux-Dubé J.

34. Wigmore is still cited as an authority on evidence, notwithstanding the discredited science behind his view that:

> (1) Modern psychiatrists have amply studied the behaviour of errant young girls and women coming before the court in all sorts of cases. Their psychic complexes are multifarious, distorted partly by inherent defects, partly by diseased derangements or abnormal instinct, partly by bad social environment, partly by temporary physiological or emotional condition. One form taken by these complexes is that of contriving false charges of sexual offenses by men.
>
> (2) No judge should ever let a sex offence charge go to the jury unless the female complainant's social history and mental makeup, have been examined and testified to by a qualified physician.

J.J. Wigmore, *Evidence in Trials at Common Law*, vol. 3A, s. 924, Chadbourne Rev. Ed. 1970, at 736-37.

L. Bienen, "A Question of Credibility: John Henry Wigmore's Use of Scientific Authority" (1983), 19 *Cal. Western L Rev.* 235.

35. In the 1990s, Wigmore's view that it was necessary for a "female complainant's social history and mental makeup" to be examined by a qualified physician pre-trial has emerged in a new form: defence arguments that a fair trial cannot be held unless the defence has access to the witness's medical, therapeutic or other institutional records. A variation is that a fair trial cannot be held if such records do not or no longer exist.

B. Spencer, "Medical health records of complainants are valuable tool in sexual assault cases," *The Lawyer's Weekly* 14:29, December 2, 1994, at 10.

The Disclosure Order Underlying this Appeal

36. On June 4, 1992, Associate Chief Justice Campbell issued a disclosure order of extraordinary scope and invasiveness requiring:

> a) The Crown to produce names, addresses and telephone numbers of therapists, counsellors, psychologists or psychiatrists whom [*sic*] have treated any of the complainants with respect to allegations of sexual assault or sexual abuse;
>
> b) The complainants authorize all therapists, counsellors, psychologists and psychiatrists whom [*sic*] have treated any of them with respect to allegations of sexual assault or sexual abuse, to produce to the Crown copies of their complete file contents and

any other related material including all documents, notes, records, reports of tape recordings and videotapes, and the Crown to provide copies of all this material to counsel for the accused forthwith;

c) The complainants authorize the Crown to obtain all school and employment records while they were in attendance at St. Joseph's Mission School and that the Crown provide those records to counsel for the accused forthwith;

d) The complainants authorize the production of all medical records from the period of time when they were resident at St. Joseph's Mission School as either students or employees.

R v. O'Connor (No. 1) (1994), 29 CR (4th) 40 (BC CA), at 48.

37. This order for pre-trial disclosure required the Crown: (a) to produce records not in its possession; (b) to compel the complainants to consent to disclosure of their personal records; (c) to secure access to records generated by a church-run residential school that was premised on a perception of aboriginal people as less than fully human; and (d) to secure mental health and counselling records relating to any and all allegations by any of the four complainants of sexual assault or sexual abuse, without limit as to time or context.

38. As emphasized by the Court of Appeal, the order was procedurally flawed by reason that it compelled third-party disclosure of confidential records made without notice to the third parties and it established no safeguards protecting the complainants' privacy rights. More importantly, the Court found the order was based on no inquiry into the relevance or materiality of the records sought.

O'Connor (No. 1), supra, at 61-62.

39. Submissions in support of access to the Mission School records were minimal. Their general importance was described as "self-evident" by defence counsel, and only the possible relevance of the medical records was sketched. In support of his request for the other records, defence counsel argued:

> [T]he importance of psychiatric and psychological counselling records with respect to accused persons' ability to defend themselves is evident—self-evident. It is for the purpose of testing the credibility of the complainants, determining issues such as recent complaint, corroboration, contradictory statements, et cetera.

None of these reasons for access to the complainants' medical and therapy records survived scrutiny by the BC Court of Appeal.

Appellant's Book of Evidence, vol. 1, at 66.

O'Connor (No. 1), supra, at 49.

R v. O'Connor (No. 2) (1994), 30 CR (4th) 55 (BC CA), at 63-65.

40. It is submitted that in a culture not steeped in rape myths shaped by systemic race and sex inequality, this disclosure order would not have been made:

(a) the minimalist rationales offered by the defence for the records sought would have been recognized as inadequate and rooted in discredited or discreditable rape mythology;

(b) biases inherent in the records would have been considered;

(c) the section 7, 15, and 28 rights of the complainants not only would have been adverted to, but would have been affirmed as an essential component of the conduct of a "fair" trial; and

(d) the privacy interests of the complainants would have been vindicated before, not after, a court-sanctioned intrusion occurred.

The Order's Oppressiveness on Its Face

41. As early as 1857, it was government policy to "civilize" and "Christianize" First Nations people to the end that they would abandon their distinctive cultural, social, political, and spiritual traditions and assimilate Anglo-Canadian values.

An Act for the Gradual Civilization of the Indian Tribes in the Canadas, SC 1857, 20 Victoria, c. 6.

42. For almost 100 years, starting with the 1884 Indian Act, residential schools served as the state's primary vehicle of forced assimilation. Under threat of fine or imprisonment, Indian parents residing on reserves were compelled to send their children aged 7 to 16 to schools designated by the Minister. Children absent from school could be taken from their families by truant officers "using as much force as the circumstances require." Children expelled or suspended from school or who failed to attend school regularly were deemed juvenile delinquents within the meaning of relevant juvenile delinquent legislation.

Indian Act, SC 1884, c. 27, ss. 10 and 74(7).

Indian Act, SC 1886, c. 43, s. 138.

Indian Act, RSC 1951, c. 29, ss. 113-122.

Davin, *Report on Industrial and Residential Schools for Indians and Halfbreeds*, Ottawa: 14 March 1879, PABC RG 10 vol. 6001 File 1-1-1, Part 1.

43. The residential school system was premised on the belief that removing aboriginal children from the "disruptive" influence of their parents and community traditions was the only way to "civilize" aboriginal people. Separated from their families for 9-10 months a year over an 8-year period, aboriginal children were not only instructed in "every aspect of European life, from dress and behaviour to religion and language," but taught to devalue their social, political, and spiritual traditions.

Aboriginal Justice Inquiry, vol. 1, at 62-68, 478, and 512-15.

Assembly of First Nations, *Breaking the Silence: An Interpretive Study of Residential School Impact and Healing as Illustrated by the Stories of First Nations Individuals*, 1994, at 1-16 and 167.

44. Evidence is now emerging that sexual and physical abuse of aboriginal students was widespread in the residential schools.

Breaking the Silence, supra, at 37-62.

45. Punished for speaking their language and either abused by persons in positions of trust and power or witness to such abuse, children who attended residential schools developed a number of survival strategies. As a way of coping with the trauma of their experience, some adopted silence and isolation well into adulthood; some ran away only to be forcibly returned. Whichever strategy was adopted, records covering their years of schooling are liable to be misleading; their silence would obscure their trauma or their resistance would brand them delinquents.

Breaking the Silence, supra, at 87 and 93.

C. Haig-Brown, *Resistance & Renewal: Surviving the Indian Residential School* (Vancouver: Tillacum Library, 1988), at 88-103.

46. The four complainants in this case are aboriginal women who attended St. Joseph's Mission School, a residential school, from age 8 to 16. All four continued to reside at the school as employees after they ceased to be students. The rapes and indecent assaults that are the subject of the charges in this case are alleged to have taken place while they were employees at the school.

Appellant's Book of Evidence, vol. 1, at 14.

47. The accused, now a bishop of the Roman Catholic Church, was the complainants' pastor and principal while they were students at the school and their pastor and employer at the time the alleged assaults took place. He does not deny having sexual intercourse with two of the four complainants; he denies the intercourse was non-consensual.

Appellant's Book of Evidence, vol. 1, at 65.

O'Connor (No. 1), supra, at 46.

48. The relation between the accused and the four complainants was one characterized by multiple inequalities of institutional and social power. Inherent in the teacher/student, employer/employee, and priest/penitent relation between the accused and the complainants were a number of power inequalities any one of which standing alone might constitute the kind of sexually exploitable "power dependency" relationship discussed by La Forest J in *Norberg v. Wynrib,* [1992] 2 SCR 226, at 252-56, and any one of which could have counselled silence on the basis of the relative credibility of the powerful and the powerless.

49. A justice system animated by equality principles would not have allowed records generated by state policies designed to eradicate an entire culture to be canvassed for potential information discreditable to survivors of such policies. Nor would it have authorized virtually unlimited access by the accused to the complainants' entire history of sexual abuse and their attempts to recover therefrom as the purchase price of access to white justice.

The Order's Oppressiveness in the Larger Legal Context

50. As L'Heureux-Dubé J predicted in dissent in *Osolin*, records are now being sought and experts are being called in sexual assault proceedings that defence counsel

would not pursue in other criminal proceedings. Some of these records seek to do indirectly what *Seaboyer* and Parliament prohibit when done directly.

Osolin, supra, at 624.

An Act to Amend the Criminal Code (sexual assault), SC 1992, c. 38, s. 276(3).

51. Some defence counsel pursue the strategy of searching out personal records of complainants in sexual violence cases as a way of counteracting sexual assault law reforms.

Cristin Schmitz, " 'Whack' sexual assault complainant at preliminary hearing," *The Lawyers Weekly*, May 27, 1988, at 22.

R v. Darby, unreported decision, February 24, 1994 (BC Prov. Ct.).

52. In the last 12 months, virtually every defence request for disclosure of a Crown witness's personal records in a criminal proceeding was a case involving sexual violence. In terms of their violation of complainants' privacy, many of the disclosures sought and obtained significantly exceed that previously achieved through sexual history evidence alone.

Appendix I.

53. In *R v. Stinchcombe*, this Court ruled that the Crown must make pre-trial disclosure of all materials gathered in the course of its investigation that are relevant to the issues in the case. The Crown's discretion to screen for relevance is limited: "[w]hile the Crown must err on the side of inclusion, it need not produce what is clearly irrelevant."

R v. Stinchcombe, [1991] 3 SCR 326, at 339, per Sopinka J.

54. Since *Stinchcombe*, lower courts have interpreted this "not clearly irrelevant" threshold to promote or require disclosure of virtually all materials sought by the defence even where the materials are not in the Crown's possession and/or even where a statutory or other privilege may be claimed for them at trial.

R v. Bhaye, unreported decision, September 22, 1994, no. 21198585 P10101 (Alta. PC (Crim. Div.)).

R v. Rockey, unreported decision, February 9, 1993, Ont. GD.

55. Some courts have held no foundation for materiality need be laid for disclosure:

> [I]t has not been conclusively laid down in the jurisprudence, that there exists any "threshold test" which must be overcome by the defence, demonstrating the likelihood of the existence of material evidence in the records, before access may be gained nor any judicial preview be made of requested documents before they are turned over to the defence:
>
>> [Such review would] deprive the defence of its inherent right to decide what is or is not of value to its own case. The trial judge does not know what defence might be advanced, so it must be left to the defence to assess and decide what, if anything, among the records, is material to its case.

R v. Kelly (1994), 31 CR (4th) 354 (Ont. CJ Prov. Div.), at 356 and 360.

56. Types of records sought through disclosure in the last 12 months include: abortion records; adoption records; alcohol or drug treatment records, child and family service records; birth control centre records; diaries; employment records; family correspondence; group home records; medical, mental health, and therapy records; rape crisis centre records; school records; victim assistance communications; and a variety of institution or agency records concerning prior sexual abuse complaints.

Appendix I.

57. One court on reviewing recent disclosure caselaw concluded:

> (1) trial judges are unwilling to become involved in examining records in order to determine if there is any relevant information in them; (2) as a consequence of that ... courts disclose either all or nothing of the records; (3) other than the general statement that relevancy must be shown, there is little discussion of the criteria to be applied or the factors to be considered; (4) the interests of the complainant/witness are rarely if ever represented at the hearing of such applications; (5) there is no satisfactory procedure governing such applications.

K.A.D., supra, at para. 19.

58. In *R v. Seaboyer*, supra, this Court held that evidence of the sexual history of sexual assault complainants, while not relevant per se to the issue of credibility or consent, may, in exceptional cases, be relevant to other issues.

59. In *Osolin v. The Queen*, supra, this Court decided that a statement by a sexual assault complainant recorded in psychiatric records admitted at trial for purposes of determining the competency of the complainant to testify could be used in cross-examination to assess her credibility, notwithstanding that defence counsel had sought to follow this line of questioning for purposes clearly rooted in unconstitutionally discriminatory stereotypes.

60. In light of decisions like these, the Coalition submits that Crowns would screen out information from personal records of complainants at their extreme peril, regardless of how tenuously, if at all, such information is connected with any material issue in the case or of how prejudicial such information is to the constitutional rights of complainants or to the administration of justice.

61. In *Seaboyer* this Court recognized the pressing and substantial importance of the four governmental objectives that led to the statutory evidentiary exclusions at issue in that appeal: to eliminate sex discrimination from sexual assault law; to encourage reporting, to eliminate distortions in the fact finding process and to protect complainants' privacy. The Coalition submits that each of these four objectives is being undermined by present disclosure rules and practices.

Seaboyer, supra, at 604-6 and 626.

62. Where Crowns, fearful of a stay of proceedings, or courts exercising the broad discretion left them by *Seaboyer* and *Osolin*, err on the side of overdisclosure, they typically err on the side of inequality.

63. The Coalition submits that guidelines along the lines set out by this Court in *Seaboyer* or by the BC Court of Appeal in *O'Connor* will never adequately protect complainants' section 7 and section 15 rights, even were this Court, for the first time, to direct lower courts explicitly to exercise their discretion in a manner that fully respects those Charter guarantees.

64. It is submitted that the targets of sexual violence will not receive equal justice until the legal system, including the courts, squarely confront the relationship between a society that systematically disadvantages and then devalues women and children, and laws that systematically devalue the word of women and children and then license violations of their integrity.

65. The Coalition submits, therefore, that until the devaluation of women and children, their word, and their integrity are addressed instead of reinforced by law, this Court should hold that disclosure of complainants' personal records is so likely to reinstate sexism in the administration of criminal law, to deter reporting, to distort the fact finding process and to violate victims' integrity that affirmation of complainants' constitutional rights, no less than of the integrity of the justice system, requires that no personal records be disclosed in any sexual offence proceeding.

PART IV: NATURE OF ORDER SOUGHT

66. The coalition respectfully submits that the appeal should be dismissed.

All of which is respectfully submitted.

THE OUTCOME

Head Notes—O'Connor v. The Queen

The O'Connor appeal was decided on two main issues: whether the stay of proceedings granted to O'Connor by the trial judge was appropriate, and what was the correct test for production of a complainant's personal records to the defence. The Coalition and LEAF did not present argument on the first issue; consequently the headnote will not deal with this in any detail. With respect to the records issue, the facts of the case were clearly restricted to those records in the possession of third parties—not the Crown—and the Coalition only addressed that situation. However, some members of the Court dealt as well with records in the possession of the Crown. This head note includes their comments because they are relevant to those Justices' analysis generally.

First Issue: The Stay of Proceedings

The Court ruled (Lamer, Sopinka, and Major JJ dissenting) that the stay was not merited by the facts of the case.

Second Issue: Production of Records in Possession of the Crown

Per Lamer CJ and Sopinka J (Cory, Iacobucci, and Major JJ concurring): The Crown's disclosure obligations established in *Stinchcombe* are unaffected by the confidential nature of therapeutic records when the records are in the possession of the Crown. The complainant's privacy interests in therapeutic records need not be balanced against the right of the accused to make full answer and defence in the context of disclosure, since concerns relating to privacy or privilege disappear where the documents in question have fallen into the Crown's possession. The complainant's lack of a privacy interest in records that are possessed by the Crown counsels against a finding of privilege in such records. Fairness must require that if the complainant is willing to release this information in order to further the criminal prosecution, then the accused should be entitled to use the information in the preparation of his or her defence. Moreover, any form of privilege may be forced to yield where such a privilege would preclude the accused's right to make full answer and defence. Information in the possession of the Crown which is clearly relevant and important to the ability of the accused to raise a defence must be disclosed to the accused, regardless of any potential claim of privilege that might arise. While the mere existence of therapeutic records is insufficient to establish the relevance of those records to the defence, their relevance must be presumed where the records are in the Crown's possession.

Per La Forest, L'Heureux-Dubé, Gonthier, and McLachlin JJ: This appeal does not concern the extent of the Crown's obligation to disclose private records in its possession, or the question whether privacy and equality interests may militate against such disclosure by the Crown. These issues do not arise in this appeal and were not argued before the Court. Any comment on these questions would be strictly obiter.

Third Issue: Production of Records in Possession of Third Parties

Per Lamer CJ and Sopinka J (Cory, Iacobucci, and Major JJ concurring): When the defence seeks information in the hands of a third party (as compared to the state), the onus should be on the accused to satisfy a judge that the information is likely to be relevant. In order to initiate the production procedure, the accused must bring a formal written application supported by an affidavit setting out the specific grounds for production. However, the court should be able, in the interests of justice, to waive the need for a formal application in some cases. In either event, notice must be given to third parties in possession of the documents as well as to those persons who have a privacy interest in the records. The accused must also ensure that the custodian and the records are subpoenaed to ensure their attendance in the court. The initial application for disclosure should be made to the judge seized of the trial, but may be brought before the trial judge prior to the empanelling of the jury, at the same time that other motions are heard. In the disclosure context, the meaning of "relevance" is expressed in terms of whether the information may be useful to the defence. In the context of production, the test of relevance should be higher: the presiding judge must be satisfied that there is a reasonable possibility that the information is logically probative to an issue at trial or the competence of a witness to testify. While "likely relevance" is the appropriate threshold for the first stage of the two-step procedure, it should not be interpreted as an onerous burden upon the accused. A relevance threshold, at this stage, is simply a requirement to prevent the defence from engaging in speculative, fanciful, disruptive, unmeritorious, obstructive and time-consuming requests for production.

When we speak of relevance to "an issue at trial," we are referring not only to evidence that may be probative to the material issues in the case (i.e. the unfolding of events) but also to evidence relating to the credibility of witnesses and to the reliability of other evidence in the case. There is a possibility of materiality where there is a "reasonably close temporal connection between" the creation of the records and the date of the alleged commission of the offence or in cases of historical events, as in this case, a close temporal connection between the creation of the records and the decision to bring charges against the accused. By way of illustration only, we are of the view that there are a number of ways in which information contained in third party records may be relevant, for example, in sexual assault cases:

1. they may contain information concerning the unfolding of events underlying the criminal complainant.

2. they may reveal the use of a therapy which influenced the complainant's memory of the alleged events.

3. they may contain information that bears on the complainant's "credibility, including testimonial factors such as the quality of their perception of events at the time of the offence, and their memory since."

As a result, we disagree with L'Heureux-Dubé J's assertion that therapeutic records will only be relevant to the defence in rare cases. The sheer number of decisions in which such evidence has been produced supports the potential relevance of therapeutic records. (p. 176 [1996] 2 WWR 153)

Upon their production to the court, the judge should examine the records to determine whether, and to what extent, they should be produced to the accused. In making that determination, the judge must examine and weigh the salutary and deleterious effects of a production order and determine whether a non-production order would constitute a reasonable limit on the ability of the accused to make full answer and defence. In balancing the competing rights in question, the following factors should be considered: (1) the extent to which the record is necessary for the accused to make full answer and defence; (2) the probative value of the record; (3) the nature and extent of the reasonable expectation of privacy vested in the record; (4) whether production of the record would be premised upon any discriminatory belief or bias; and (5) the potential prejudice to the complainant's dignity, privacy or security of the person that would be occasioned by production of the record. The effect on the integrity of the trial process of producing, or failing to produce, the record, having in mind the need to maintain consideration in the outcome, is more appropriately dealt with at the admissibility stage and not in deciding whether the information should be produced. As for society's interest in the reporting of sexual crimes, there are other avenues available to the judge to ensure that production does not frustrate the societal interests that may be implicated by the production of the records to the defence. In applying these factors, it is also appropriate to bear in mind that production of third party records is always available to the Crown provided it can obtain a search warrant. (p. 157 [1996] 2 WWR 153)

Per La Forest, L'Heureux-Dubé, and Gonthier JJ (dissenting on this issue) (McLachlin J concurring): Private records, or records in which a reasonable expectation of privacy lies, may include medical or therapeutic records, school records, private diaries and social worker activity logs. When deciding whether to order production of private records, the court must exercise its discretion in a manner that is respectful of Charter values. The constitutional values involved here are the right to full answer and defence, the right to privacy, and the right to equality without discrimination.

Witnesses have a right to privacy in relation to private documents and records which are not part of the Crown's "case to meet" against the accused. They are entitled not to be deprived of their reasonable expectation of privacy except in accordance with the principles of fundamental justice. Since an applicant seeking production of private records from third parties is seeking to invoke the power of the State to violate the privacy rights of other individuals, the applicant must show that the use of the State power to compel production is justified in a free and democratic society.

Unlike virtually every other offence in the Criminal Code, sexual assault is a crime which overwhelmingly affects women, children and the disabled. Ninety percent of all victims of sexual assault are female. It is a common phenomenon in this day and age for one who has been sexually victimized to seek counselling or therapy in relation to this occurrence. It therefore stands to reason that disclosure rules or practices which make mental health or medical records routinely accessible in sexual offence proceedings will have disproportionately invasive consequences for women, particularly those with disabilities, and children. (p. 210 [1996] 2 WWR 153)

The use of State power to compel production of private records will be justified in a free and democratic society when the following criteria are met: (1) it is shown that the accused cannot obtain the information sought by any other reasonable means; (2) production that infringes privacy must be as limited as reasonably possible to fulfil the right to make full answer and defence; (3) the arguments urging production rest on permissible chains of reasoning, rather than upon discriminatory assumptions and stereotypes; and (4) there is proportionality between the salutary and deleterious effects of production. The measure of proportionality must reflect the extent to which a reasonable expectation of privacy vests in the particular records, on the one hand, and the importance of the issue to which the evidence relates, on the other. Moreover, courts must remain alive to the fact that, in certain cases, the deleterious effects of production may demonstrably include negative effects on the complainant's course of therapy, threatening psychological harm to the individual concerned and thereby resulting in a concomitant deprivation of the individual's security of the person.

The first step for an accused who seeks production of private records held by a third party is to obtain and serve on the third party a subpoena duces tecum. When the subpoena is served, the accused should notify the Crown, the subject of the records, and any other person with an interest in the confidentiality of the records that the accused will ask the trial judge for an order for their production. Then, at the trial, the accused must bring an application supported by appropriate affidavit evidence showing that the records are likely to be relevant either to an issue in the trial or to the competence to testify of the subject of the records. If the records are relevant, the court must balance the salutary and deleterious effects of ordering that the records be produced to determine whether, and to what extent, production should be ordered.

The records at issue here are not within the possession or control of the Crown, do not form part of the Crown's "case to meet," and were created by a third party for a purpose unrelated to the investigation or prosecution of the offence. It cannot be assumed that such records are likely to be relevant, and if the accused is unable to show that they are, then the application for production must be rejected as it amounts to nothing more than a fishing expedition. The burden on an accused to demonstrate likely relevance is a significant one. It would be insufficient for the accused to demand production simply on the basis of a bare, unsupported assertion that the records might impact on "recent complaint" or the "kind of person" the witness is. Similarly, the applicant cannot simply invoke credibility "at large," but must rather provide some basis to show that there is likely to be information in the impugned records which would relate to the complainant's credibility on a particular, material issue at trial. Equally inadequate is a bare, unsupported assertion that a prior inconsistent statement might be revealed, or that the defence wishes to explore the records for "allegations of sexual abuse by other people." Similarly, the mere fact that a witness has a medical or psychiatric record cannot be taken as indicative of the potential unreliability of the evidence. Any suggestion that a particular treatment, therapy, illness, or disability implies unreliability must be informed by cogent evidence, rather than stereotype, myth or prejudice. Finally, it must not be presumed that the mere fact that a witness received treatment or counselling after a sexual assault indicates that the records will contain information that is relevant to the defence. The focus of therapy is vastly different from that of an investigation or other process undertaken for the purposes of the trial. While investigations and witness testimony are oriented toward ascertaining historical truth, therapy generally focuses on exploring the complainant's emotional and psychological responses to certain events, after the alleged assault has taken place.

If the trial judge decides that the records are likely to be relevant, then the analysis proceeds to the second stage, which has two parts. First, the trial judge must balance the salutary and deleterious effects of ordering the production of the records to the court for inspection, having regard to the accused's right to make full answer and defence, and the effect of such production on the privacy and equality rights of the subject of the records. If the judge concludes that production to the court is warranted, he or she should so order. Next, upon their production to the court, the judge should examine the records to determine whether, and to what extent, they should be produced to the accused. Production should only be ordered in respect of those records, or parts of records, that have significant probative value that is not substantially outweighed by the danger of prejudice to the proper administration of justice or by the harm to the privacy rights of the witness or to the privileged relation. The following factors should be considered in this determination: (1) the extent to which the record is necessary for the accused to make full answer and defence; (2) the probative value of the record; (3) the nature and extent of the reasonable expectation of privacy vested in the record; (4) whether production of the record would be premised upon any discriminatory belief or bias; (5) the potential prejudice to the complainant's dignity, privacy or security of the person that would be occasioned by production of the record; (6) the extent to which production of records of this nature would frustrate society's interest in encouraging the reporting of sexual offences and the acquisition of treatment by victims; and (7) the effect on the integrity of the trial process of producing, or failing to produce, the record, having in mind the need to maintain consideration in the outcome. Where a court concludes that production is warranted, it should only be made in the manner and to the extent necessary to achieve that objective.

A preliminary inquiry judge is without jurisdiction to order the production of private records held by third parties. The disclosure order in the present case did not emanate from a preliminary inquiry judge, but was issued in response to a pre-trial application by the defence. Even a superior court judge, however, should not, in advance of the trial, entertain an application for production of private third party records. Such applications should be heard by the judge seized of the trial, rather than a pre-trial judge. In addition, it is desirable for the judge hearing an application for production to have had the benefit of hearing, and pronouncing upon, the defence's earlier applications, so as to minimize the possibility of inconsistency in the treatment of two similar applications. More generally, applications for production of third party records should not be entertained before the commencement of the trial, even by the judge who is seized of the trial. First, the concept of pre-trial applications for production of documents held by third parties is alien to criminal proceedings. Second, if pre-trial applications for production from third parties were permitted, it would invite fishing expeditions, create unnecessary delays, and inconvenience witnesses by requiring them to attend court on multiple occasions. Moreover, a judge is not in a position, before the beginning of the trial, to determine whether the records in question are relevant, much less whether they are admissible, and will be unable to balance effectively the constitutional rights affected by a production order.

Since the right of the accused to a fair trial has not been balanced with the competing rights of the complainant to privacy and to equality without discrimination in this case, a new trial should be ordered.

IN THE SUPREME COURT OF CANADA

(ON APPEAL FROM THE ONTARIO COURT (GENERAL DIVISION))

BETWEEN:

L.L.A., THE SEXUAL ASSAULT CARE CENTRE OF THE PLUMMER MEMORIAL PUBLIC HOSPITAL AND WOMEN IN CRISIS (ALGOMA) INC. OPERATING AS "WOMEN'S OUTREACH"

Appellants

(Respondents)

AND:

ARDEN BEHARRIELL

Respondent

(Applicant)

AND:

HER MAJESTY THE QUEEN

Respondent

(Respondent)

AND:

ATTORNEY GENERAL OF CANADA

Intervenor

ABORIGINAL WOMEN'S COUNCIL, CANADIAN ASSOCIATION OF SEXUAL ASSAULT CENTRES, DISABLED WOMEN'S NETWORK ONTARIO AND WOMEN'S LEGAL EDUCATION AND ACTION FUND

Intervenors

AND:

CANADIAN FOUNDATION FOR CHILDREN, YOUTH AND THE LAW

Intervenor

AND:

CRIMINAL LAWYERS' ASSOCIATION

Intervenor

AND:

ATTORNEY GENERAL OF MANITOBA

Intervenor

Factum of the Aboriginal Women's Council et al.

A.(L.L.) v. Beharriell

INTRODUCTION

Beharriell was accused of sexually assaulting L.L.A. in Sault Ste. Marie between February and December of 1980 when L.L.A. was five years old. For many reasons, among them fear of Beharriell who was a close family friend, L.L.A. did not report the assault to police until 15 years later. Prior to trial, defence counsel obtained two subpoenas for L.L.A.'s counselling records held by two organizations: the Sexual Assault Care Centre of the Plummer Memorial Hospital and Women in Crisis (Algoma) Inc. L.L.A. and the two organizations were permitted to make arguments as to why the files should not be called into evidence. However, the trial judge found for the defence and ordered the majority of the documents to be produced. L.L.A. and the two organizations then appealed to the Ontario Court of Appeal. The Court quashed the appeals on a procedural matter; it held that there was no right in law to appeal a criminal interlocutory order. The appellants then sought and obtained leave to appeal directly to the Supreme Court.

LEAF intervened in coalition with the Aboriginal Women's Council, the Canadian Association of Sexual Assault Centres, the DisAbled Women's Network of Canada. This same coalition had appeared before the Supreme Court in *O'Connor*, which was heard only four months earlier. One of the Coalition's main goals was to distinguish *A.(L.L.)* from *O'Connor* and try to persuade the Supreme Court that in both cases the disclosure of complainants' records was at issue. Other intervenors were the Attorneys General of Canada and Manitoba, the Canadian Foundation for Children, Youth and the Law, and the Criminal Lawyers' Association, who each made submissions regarding the appropriate test for disclosure of complainants' records. *A.(L.L.) v. Beharriell* was heard on June 16, 1995 and at the time of this writing the decision was reserved.

FACTUM

PART I: FACTS

1. The Intervenor Coalition (the "Coalition"), constituted by the Aboriginal Women's Council, the Canadian Association of Sexual Assault Centres, the DisAbled

Women's Network Ontario, and the Women's Legal Education and Action Fund, brings to this appeal extensive expertise in the areas of sexual violence against women and children, the intersection of inequalities based on sex, race, and disability and vulnerability to sexual violence, the lived experiences of Aboriginal women and women with disabilities including the reality of their limited access to justice, and the application of constitutional law and equality jurisprudence to these contexts.

2. Members of the Coalition in this appeal brought this expertise to bear in written and oral argument in *R v. O'Connor*. The issues addressed by the Coalition members in that appeal concerned production of the confidential records of complainants in sexual assault cases, in the context of different facts. In *O'Connor*, the complainants are Aboriginal women and the accused is a white man who was their priest, employer, and principal. The incidents giving rise to the charges occurred 25 to 30 years ago when the four complainants were adults and the personal records being sought by the accused included inherently unreliable documents, both historic and contemporary in origin. In the present appeal, the complainant and the accused, who was a close family friend and neighbour, are white, the alleged assault occurred when the complainant was a child and the personal records are counselling records produced relatively recently.

3. The *O'Connor* case illustrates that Defence Applications for production implicate a broad range of personal records, including coercive institutional records made by, and in the control of, alleged perpetrators. The extensive range of records sought in *O'Connor* and other cases (see Appendix I) is not raised by this appeal however: what is being sought by the Respondent here are the counselling records of the Appellant generated by counsellors at a hospital-based sexual assault counselling centre and a community-based women's counselling centre. It is therefore counselling records that are the context in this appeal.

4. The Coalition is intervening in this appeal, as it did in *O'Connor* to ensure that the equality guarantees in the Charter animated by applications for production of counselling records in criminal cases involving sexual violence are fully recognized and addressed by this Court in its treatment of the issues arising in this case. This case is distinctly different on its facts from *O'Connor* and as a consequence, a different range of equality considerations are implicated. It is the submission of the Coalition that the issues raised by the *O'Connor* appeal cannot be subsumed in this appeal and require independent determination by this Court.

5. The equality guarantees that are fundamental to the issue of production of complainants' counselling records in sexual assault cases were not addressed by the trial Court whose decision to order production of the Appellant's records has been appealed to this Court. Indeed, in no reported Canadian case to date dealing with this issue have these constitutional imperatives been addressed.

6. In the Coalition's submission, the production of the counselling records of complainants in sexual assault cases is a practice of gendered inequality, like sexual assault itself. As will be argued below, production of such records denies women's equality and equal right to security of the person, and distorts and undermines the criminal justice process: it therefore cannot be permitted in any sexual assault prosecution.

PART II: ISSUES

7. In keeping with its position in *O'Connor*, the Coalition submits that the constitutional rights of the female victims of sexual violence to security of the person without discrimination based on sex, race, disability or sexual orientation and to equal protection and benefit of the law cannot be fully recognized or vindicated in this appeal, or in criminal law and procedure more generally, unless courts acknowledge the social, historical, political, and legal conditions of inequality in which sexual violence occurs and out of which legal principles and legal practices emerge, including those that govern Defence applications for production of personal records.

8. The Coalition does not take a position on other issues raised in this appeal.

PART III: ARGUMENT

Sexual Assault as a Practice of Sex Inequality

9. This Court has recognized that there is a relationship between sexual violence against women and inequality between the sexes. In particular, it has recognized that sexual assault is a gender-based crime insofar as 99 percent of the offenders are men and 90 percent of the victims are women; sexual assault is an attack on human dignity that constitutes a denial of any concept of equality for women; and that, in a sexually unequal society, institutional-based sexual coercion, such as that in the workplace, family, and medical profession is an abuse of both sexual and social power used to underscore women's ascribed inferiority to men.

Conway v. The Queen, [1993] 2 SCR 872, at 877, per La Forest J.

Osolin v. The Queen, [1993] 4 SCR 595, at 669, per Cory J.

Janzen and Govereau v. Platy Enterprises Ltd. et al., [1989] 1 SCR 1254, at 1284, per Dickson CJ.

Norberg v. Wynrib, [1992] 2 SCR 226, at 261-62 and 264, per La Forest J, and at 275 and 278-79, per McLachlin J.

M.(K.) v. M.(H.), [1992] 3 SCR 6, at 27, 32, and 56, per La Forest J.

10. This Court has recognized sexual assault as a gendered crime that is overwhelmingly perpetrated by men against women.

R v. Seaboyer; R v. Gayme, [1991] 2 SCR 577, at 648, per L'Heureux-Dubé J.

Osolin, supra, at 669, per Cory J.

11. While sexual assault has been de-gendered in law, it has not been de-gendered in fact. Women are targeted for sexual violence because they are women and all women are subordinated to the fear of sexual assault, irrespective of who they are.

S. Martin, "Some Constitutional Considerations on Sexual Violence Against Women" (1994), 32 *Alta. L. Rev.* no. 3, 535, at 544.

Preamble to Bill C-49, An Act to amend the Criminal Code (sexual assault), 3d Sess., 34th Parl., 1991.

12. The Coalition submits that there is a correlation between vulnerability to sexual violence and disadvantage: women and girls experiencing compounded inequalities are most at risk of sexual assault that may be directly motivated by these inequalities.

E.J. Shilton and A.S. Derrick, "Sex Equality and Sexual Assault: In the Aftermath of Seaboyer"(1991), 11 *Windsor YB Access Just.* 107, at 123.

13. The particular vulnerability to sexual assault that is experienced by women who are Aboriginal, disabled, or Black was discussed by the Coalition in its factum in *O'Connor* (paragraphs 17 to 24). Other cases will expose the particular operation and intersection of more inequalities that continue not to be acknowledged or challenged by a legal system that fails to invoke the guarantees of section 15. It is material to acknowledge that neither the *O'Connor* case nor the present appeal represent all the dynamics of power and institutionalized oppression to which women are subject.

14. Studies show that two factors operate in a rapist's selection of a victim: vulnerability and availability. The more disadvantaged, dependent or relatively powerless a woman, the more she is vulnerable to sexual exploitation and violation by men, particularly by men she knows. Contrary to rape mythology, only a minority of sexual assaults are committed by strangers.

Ministry of the Solicitor General, Canadian Urban Victimization Survey, *Female Victims of Crime* (Ottawa: Supply and Services, 1985), at 2.

Report of the Committee on Sexual Offences Against Children and Youth (Badgley Report), *Sexual Offences Against Children and Youth*, vol. 1 (Ottawa: Supply and Services, 1984), at 196-98.

M. Burt, "Rape Myths and Acquaintance Rape" in A. Parrot and L. Bechhofer, eds., *Acquaintance Rape: The Hidden Crime* (New York: Wiley, 1991).

15. According to Statistics Canada's National Violence Against Women survey, children are especially vulnerable to sexual assault: in 1993, 63 percent of the victims of sexual assault were children or teenagers.

J. Roberts, "Criminal Justice Processing of Sexual Assault Cases" (March 1994), *Juristat*, vol. 14, no. 7, at 6-7.

Final Report of the Canadian Panel on Violence Against Women, *Changing the Landscape: Ending Violence—Achieving Equality* (Ottawa: Supply and Services, 1993), at 28-29.

16. The inequality of children and the dominance and power that adults exercise over them has also been recognized by this Court. This inequality is reflected by the fact that children, predominantly girls, are most often sexually abused by an adult, almost always male, who occupies a relationship of power or trust.

R v. L.(D.O.), [1993] 4 SCR 419, at 428-29, per Lamer J, and at 439-41, per L'Heureux-Dubé J.

17. It is submitted that as fathers, brothers, grandfathers, uncles, neighbours, and family friends, men have access to, and can sexually exploit the vulnerability of, girls.

As adults they are imbued with power and social status denied children and are regarded as more credible than their young victims, because of the privilege accorded them by their age and their gender. These dynamics operate effectively to immunize adult men from prosecution and conviction for sexual offences against children.

L.(D.O.), supra, at 439-41, per L'Heureux-Dubé J.

18. In the Coalition's submission, the more socially powerless or stigmatized women and girls are, the more easily discredited and discreditable. The correlation between social status and credibility enhances perpetrators' expectations that their socially unequal victims will never report them or be credited if they do. To the extent law permits and even facilitates the stereotype-based discrediting of women, law colludes in immunizing those who exploit and then trade on status-based credibility and discreditation. In the result, and contrary to the Charter, the legal system directly reinforces the inequality of women.

Sexual Assault Law as a Practice of Sex Inequality

19. The principles grounding our system of criminal justice have been characterized by this Court as designed to avoid unprobative and misleading evidence, encourage the reporting of crimes and protect the security and privacy of the witnesses, all of which conform to fundamental conceptions of justice.

Seaboyer, supra, at 604-6 and 626, per McLachlin J.

20. Notwithstanding these principles, all of which operate to uphold the integrity of the criminal justice system, equality remains more an elusive and abstract concept than a part of the reality of women and girls who participate in the prosecution of crimes of sexual violence against them.

C. Boyle and M. McCrimmon, "R v. Seaboyer: A Lost Cause?" (1992), 7 CR (4th) 225.

21. The history of sexual assault law and the legal practices that govern the prosecution of sexual assault offences is a history that reflects the social, political, and legal disadvantage suffered by women. The substantive laws relating to rape and other sexual offences against women, and the evidentiary laws that governed the prosecution of crimes of sexual violence were promulgated in accordance with discriminatory myths and stereotypes about women and without regard for sex equality values.

Seaboyer, supra, at 665-74, per L'Heureux-Dubé J.

22. Discriminatory myths and stereotypes about women and children have been exploited in sexual assault cases to good effect by Defence counsel. It is submitted that efforts to reform the law of sexual assault have not achieved real equality for women and girls.

E. Sheehy, "Canadian Judges and the Law of Rape: Should the Charter Insulate Bias?" (1989), 21 *Ottawa L Rev.* 741, at 774 and 776.

23. It remains a fact that of the most serious crimes, sexual assault is one of the most unreported, the reasons for this being fear of treatment by police or prosecutors, fear of trial procedures, and fear of publicity, embarrassment, and retribution.

Canadian Newspapers Co. v. AG Canada, [1988] 2 SCR 122, at 131-32, per Lamer CJ.

Seaboyer, supra, at 649, per L'Heureux-Dubé J.

L.(D.O.), supra, at 441-42, per L'Heureux-Dubé J.

Case on Appeal, Affidavit of L.L.A., at 85-6, para. 4.

24. Of the incidents of sexual assault reported to Statistics Canada in 1993, only 6% were reported to police. Fear of the attitudes likely to be shown by the police and the courts toward complainants continues to deter significant numbers of women from reporting.

Roberts, supra, at 6-7.

25. This general lack of public confidence in the fair administration of justice in sexual assault cases was expressed by the Appellant in this case who deposed to the fact that had she been advised her counselling records could be subject to public scrutiny by way of disclosure she would not have laid criminal charges in relation to the sexual assault. The counsellor with the Women's Outreach Centre described that in the two and a half years of her employment with the Centre during which time she has counselled "well over 120 people" only two clients "have made a report to the police about the abuse they have suffered." The personal intrusiveness and the humiliation associated with the criminal process of reporting and prosecution were cited as significant reasons for not coming forward.

Case on Appeal, Affidavit of L.L.A., at 86, para. 8.

Case on Appeal, Affidavit of Sherrie Baic, at 72-73, para. 10.

26. The Appellant's decision not to report the incident until she was an adult was driven by fears of humiliation and her anxiety about being accessible to the Respondent, whom she was afraid might harm her. Throughout the Appellant's childhood and adolescence, which the Appellant experienced as the child of a single parent after the tragic death of her father when she was six, the Respondent was a proximate presence in her life. He was not only a very close friend of the Appellant's brother "for a very long time," the friend with whom she played was the Respondent's daughter. The Appellant's sister lived in the Respondent's building and the older siblings would take the Appellant with them to visit the Respondent at his apartment.

Case on Appeal, Preliminary Inquiry Evidence of L.L.A., at 39, 40, 43, 46, and 64.

Case on Appeal, Affidavit of L.L.A., at 86, para. 4.

27. That minority of women, like the Appellant, who have reported the sexual assaults against them have had their experience with respect to the prosecuting of these crimes distorted by the embedded discriminatory attitudes held by all participants in the criminal justice system: police, prosecutors, defence lawyers, jurors, and judges.

Seaboyer, supra, at 654-57 and 660-65, per L'Heureux-Dubé J.

C. Schmitz, " 'Whack' sexual assault complainant at preliminary hearing," *The Lawyers Weekly*, May 27, 1988, at 22.

28. Myths about women's proclivities to invent or fabricate allegations of sexual assault operate to distort the criminal justice process, directly contributing to lower conviction rates for sexual assault than for other offences.

Osolin, supra, at 625, per L'Heureux-Dubé J.

Seaboyer, supra, at 654, per L'Heureux-Dubé J.

L.(D.O.), supra, at 443, per L'Heureux-Dubé J.

29. The special and problematic nature of the treatment of complainants in sexual assault trials has been recognized by this Court. It is acknowledged in *Seaboyer* and *Osolin* that "groundless myths and fantasized stereotypes" about rape victims have improperly informed the determination of evidentiary issues in sexual assault trials, undermining the administration of justice and the role of the trier of fact. A recurring stereotype about women involves the assertion that women fantasize sexual assault: "Females are assumed to make up stories that sex occurred when in fact nothing happened. ..."

Seaboyer, supra, at 604, per McLachlin J, and at 653, per L'Heureux-Dubé J.

Osolin, supra, at 670-71, per Cory J.

30. The *"false* concepts" and unjust assumptions that have been discredited by this Court include: women cannot be raped against their will; lack of resistance indicates consent; sexually active women are more likely to consent and more likely to lie about sex, and children are inherently less reliable than adults.

Osolin, supra, at 670, per Cory J.

Seaboyer, supra, at 604 and 630, per McLachlin J.

R v. M.L.M., [1994] 2 SCR 3.

R v. W.(R), [1992] 2 SCR 122, at 132-34 and 136, per McLachlin J.

31. The stereotypes described in *Seaboyer* and *Osolin*, and characterized by this Court in *L.(D.O.)* as equally applicable to sexually assaulted girls, do not represent an exhaustive inventory of the operative biases that stigmatize and de-humanize women and girls.

L.(D.O.), supra, at 441-42, per L'Heureux-Dubé J.

Seaboyer, supra, at 654, per L'Heureux-Dubé J.

32. As described by the Coalition in *O'Connor*, the foundational myth about women and sexual assault is the fabrication myth that advances the proposition that women are uniquely likely to fabricate sexual assault allegations, placing innocent men at risk of prosecution and wrongful conviction.

Burt, supra, at 28.

M. Torrey, "When Will We Be Believed? Rape Myths and the Idea of a Fair Trial in Rape Prosecutions" (1991), 24 *U Calif Davis L Rev.* 1013, at 1027.

H. Galvin, "Shielding Rape Victims in the State and Federal Courts: A Proposal for the Second Decade" (1986), 70 *Minn. L Rev.* 763, at 792-93.

S. Bond, "Psychiatric Evidence of Sexual Assault Victims: The Need for Fundamental Change in the Determination of Relevance" (1993), 16 *Dalhousie LJ* 416, at 420 et seq.

33. The foundational myth that women have a propensity to fabricate rape charges, in turn has spawned a host of subsidiary myths: that women can prevent rape if they really want to; that "good" women do not get raped, only "bad" ones do and they "deserve" it; that women are inherently malicious and fickle, and that for reasons of maliciousness and pathology, they fabricate sexual assault allegations.

Burt, supra, at 28-32.

Seaboyer, supra, at 651-55, per L'Heureux-Dubé J.

34. The mendacious, maliciously motivated or pathologically mistaken woman-as-complainant is a discriminatory characterization not supported by the social science literature, which reports sexual assault complaints as no more likely to be false than reports of other crimes.

Torrey, supra, at 1028.

35. Children are similarly objectified by myths and stereotypes and are presumed to have fantasized about and fabricated sexual abuse, notwithstanding the repudiation of these assumptions by social-scientific research.

A. Young, "Child Sexual Abuse and the Law of Evidence: Some Current Canadian Issues" (1992), 2 *Can. J Fam. L* 11, at 19.

36. As observed by this Court, "[Y]oung children ... are generally not adept at reasoned reflection or at fabricating tales of sexual perversion. They, manifestly, are unlikely to use their reflective powers to concoct a deliberate untruth, and particularly one about a sexual act which in all probability is beyond their ken."

R v. Khan, [1990] 2 SCR 531, at 542, per McLachlin J.

37. Certain stereotypes are constructed around women who report sex crimes committed against them as children. The power differential between children and adults that makes children vulnerable to sexual abuse by adults also serves to silence child victims, often for years. The inability of children until adulthood to recognize the harm occasioned to them by the sexual abuse of an adult is a testament to the vulnerability of children and the effectiveness of adult exploitation of their inequality.

M.(K.) v. M.(H.), supra, at 31, 47, and 56, per La Forest J.

38. As acknowledged by this Court, children may not be able to report their sexual abuse until, through the marshalling of courage and emotional strength, they are "psychologically prepared for the consequences of that reporting."

R v. L.(W.K.), [1991] 1 SCR 1091, at 1101, per Stevenson J.

39. The discrediting by this Court of the discriminatory myths described above does not mean that they have simply ceased to exist. Their presence and influence continues to distort the experience of women and girls who bring charges of sexual assault.

Osolin, supra, at 621, per L'Heureux-Dubé J.

D. Majury, "Seaboyer and Gayme: A Study in Inequality" in *Confronting Sexual Assault: A Decade of Legal and Social Change* (Toronto: University of Toronto Press, 1994), 268, at 281.

40. In the present appeal, the Respondent invoked a series of stereotypes with respect to the Appellant to justify the Applications for production of her counselling records: that she may have imagined the assault or "made it up," that she may have a pattern of making sexual assault allegations (a stereotype that operates in conjunction with the flawed presumption that such allegations, if made, would have been made in relation to innocent men), that she is highly suggestible which may have resulted in her concocting a false story, that her "late" complaint indicates itself that the accusation is unreliable, that she lied about being assaulted.

Case on Appeal, Defence Submissions on Motion, at 118, 141, 143, and 145.

41. These myths, which deny the Appellant's agency and autonomy, are undercut by an equality analysis and the facts. The Appellant, as early as the third grade, disclosed the assault to friends. The Appellant as an adult, at her own initiative and not at the suggestion of her counsellors, reported the assault against her because she had heard that the Respondent had assaulted someone else. In describing her decision, the Appellant noted that she had a six-year old niece, and referred to her concerns that the Respondent not be able to do to someone else what he did to her.

Case on Appeal, Preliminary Inquiry Evidence of L.L.A., at 43, 44-45, 51, and 56.

42. The Appellant's inability to connect, for some time, the effects of the assault to other difficulties she was experiencing in her life is a feature of childhood sexual abuse recognized by this Court.

Case on Appeal, Preliminary Inquiry Evidence of L.L.A., at 43-44.

M.(K.) v. M.(H.), supra, at 28-29, per La Forest J.

L.(W.K.), supra.

Production of Records as a Practice of Sex Inequality

43. Women are the predominant victims of sexual violence, perpetrated principally by men. It is women therefore who participate in counselling and it is women's counselling records that are the subject of production applications brought by the men they prosecute for sex crimes. Production of counselling records, like sexual assault itself, is gendered, and as a consequence, an equality issue, implicating women's rights to equality and equal security of the person as guaranteed by the Charter.

44. In order for the law to give full recognition to equality it must be grounded in a theory of inequality. This formulation of equality theory and practice requires that practices, such as applications to produce personal records in sexual assault cases, be assessed in terms of whether they contribute to women's real inequality and whether the elimination of such practices will advance equality for women.

K. Lahey, "Feminist Theories of (In) Equality" in *Equality and Judicial Neutrality* (Toronto: Carswell, 1987), at 83.

45. When the counselling records of complainants are pursued or produced, complainants do not receive equal access to justice. The production of such records, or the potential for such production, deny their right to the equal benefit and protection of the law. Applications for production rely upon and reinforce biased attitudes about women that are rooted in faulty stereotypes. By so doing, such applications constitute a discriminatory practice that violates the equality guarantees of the Charter.

Egan v. Canada, [1995] SCJ 43 no. 43, at para. 180, per Cory J.

46. It is submitted that the production of complainants' counselling records operates to aggravate and perpetuate the disadvantage to which female sexual assault victims have historically been subject and as such constitute a violation of the Charter's equality guarantees. Equality requires the elimination of distinctions that "... treat certain people as second-class citizens, that demean them, that treat them as less capable for no good reason, or that otherwise offend fundamental human dignity."

Egan, supra, at para. 36, per L'Heureux-Dubé J.

47. In applications for production of complainants' counselling records, it is not merely the sensibilities of complainants that are at stake, it is their equal human status in court and in society. The issue is not merely, or even principally, one of privacy, but one of equality. Where does production, or even just the threat of it, leave women who have disclosed intimate details of their histories to counsellors? Like the now discredited use of a woman's past sexual history, will such records be used to improperly imply that such women are less believable or more likely to have consented? Will such records be de-contextualized and used to pathologize and stigmatize women who have counselling "histories"? In the Coalition's submission, the Courts, short of absolutely prohibiting production of such records, cannot prevent complainants' records being exploited for these and other real inequality-producing purposes.

48. Like past evidentiary rules now recognized as discriminatory, contemporary applications for production promote the groundless suspicion that women's reports of sexual violence are uniquely likely to be fabricated, and therefore complainants are subjected to exhaustive and oppressive credibility testing to prove them worthy of the law's protection. In the result, complainants' access to the law's protection is conditioned on legally sanctioned access to their private lives and disregard for their autonomy and dignity to a degree unparalleled in other criminal proceedings where credibility is at issue.

Osolin, supra, per L'Heureux-Dubé J, at 624-25.

R v. K.A.D., [1994] OJ no. 1837 (Ont. CJ Prov. Div.).

R v. Darby, unreported, February 24, 1994 (BC Prov. Ct.).

M. McCrimmon, "Developments in the Law of Evidence: The 1991-92 Term Truth, Fairness and Equality" (1993), 4 *Sup. Ct. Law Rev.* 225, at 272.

49. The constitutional guarantees of equality and equal security of the person require that the victims of sexual violence be protected from the discriminatory treatment

that accrues from the production to Defence of counselling records. This Court has acknowledged the importance of promoting the equality of disadvantaged groups, describing section 15 as the broadest of all Charter guarantees, one that applies to and supports all other rights guaranteed by the Charter. Its purpose is "to ensure equality in the formulation and application of the law" and "to remedy or prevent discrimination against groups subject to stereotyping, historical disadvantage and political and social prejudice in Canadian society."

Andrews v. Law Society of British Columbia, [1989] 1 SCR 143, at 171, per McIntrye J.

R v. Swain, [1991] 1 SCR 933, at 992, per Lamer CJ.

Egan, supra, at para. 38, per L'Heureux-Dubé J.

50. Section 15 is designed to protect those groups who suffer social, political and legal disadvantage in our society. It, more than any other section of the Charter, "... recognizes and cherishes the innate human dignity of every individual."

Andrews, supra, per Wilson J, at 154.

R v. Turpin et al., [1989] 1 SCR 1296, at 1332-33, per Wilson J.

Egan, supra, at para. 128, per Cory J.

51. It is submitted that female sexual assault victims constitute a group who suffer social, political and legal disadvantage in our society and for whom the protection of equality rights under section 15 were designed. As asserted by the Coalition in *O'Connor*, a legal practice that, in the name of fair trial rights, is premised on individual members of disadvantaged groups most targeted for sexual violence not being worthy of credit on the basis of discriminatory assumptions, does not reflect, far less promote, "a society in which all are secure in the knowledge they are recognized at law as human beings equally deserving of concern, respect and consideration." Such a practice, it is submitted, overtly violates section 15.

Andrews, supra, at 171, per McIntyre J.

52. It is the submission of the Coalition that judicial treatment of applications to produce complainants' personal records in sexual assault cases have reflected, exploited, and reinforced the same discriminatory stereotypes about women, children, and their sexuality that Parliament and this Court have endeavored to displace.

Criminal Law Amendment Act, SC 1980-81-82-83, c. 125.

Seaboyer, supra.

An Act to Amend the Criminal Code (sexual assault), SC 1992, c. 38, s. 276(3).

53. In the Coalition's submission, the escalating pursuit and production of complainants' personal records is but the latest manifestation of the operation of gender bias in sexual offence proceedings and is coincident with these equality-driven reforms. The burgeoning case law on production applications in sexual offence proceedings confirms that these applications rely upon and evoke discriminatory myths and stereotypes about women and sexual assault.

54. It is submitted that the increasing frequency and scope of applications and orders for production of personal records of complainants in sexual assault prosecutions, as well as the rationales offered for seeking records such as those being sought in this appeal, have no counterpart elsewhere in criminal law.

55. As noted by the Coalition in *O'Connor*, and updated for the purpose of this appeal, in the last 18 months virtually every request for disclosure of a Crown witness's personal records in a criminal proceeding arose in a case involving sexual violence. In terms of the violation of complainants' privacy, many of the disclosures sought and obtained significantly exceed that previously achieved through sexual history evidence alone.

Appendix I.

56. The issue of production of complainant's counselling records in sexual assault cases is reflexively framed in Defence arguments as a fair trial right: The premise is: no records, no fair trial.

B. Spencer, "Medical health records of complainants are valuable tool in sexual assault cases," *The Lawyers Weekly*, December 2, 1994, at 10.

Case on Appeal, Submissions of Defence on Motion, at 114.

57. The purpose of the criminal trial process is the attainment of truth. The principles of fundamental justice enshrined in section 7 of the Charter require the truth-seeking process to be a fair one. The process must enable the trier of fact to "get at the truth and properly and fairly dispose of the case" while at the same time providing the accused with the opportunity to make a full defence.

Seaboyer, supra.

58. Production of records in a sex unequal criminal justice system and culture will not assist "getting at the truth." The constitutional guarantee of a fair trial and the entitlement to make full answer and defence does not provide any right to promote and reinforce discriminatory assumptions about women and children. Nor do the fair trial rights of accused persons operate to "trump" the security of the person and equality rights of complainants. This Court has rejected a hierarchical approach to rights and has established that: "When the protected rights of two individuals come into conflict … Charter principles require a balance to be achieved that fully respects the importance of both sets of rights."

Dagenais v. Canadian Broadcasting Corp., [1994] 3 SCR 835, at 877, per Lamer CJ.

59. The principles governing our criminal justice system and the rules that apply, including the rules of evidence, recognize the interests not only of accused persons but also those of complainants. Equality of fairness to complainants as well as accused persons is a fundamental tenet of the criminal justice process.

R v. Corbett, [1988] 1 SCR 670, at 745-46, per La Forest J.

Seaboyer, supra.

R v. E.(A. W.), [1993] 3 SCR 155, at 198, per Cory J.

R v. Levogiannis, [1993] 4 SCR 475, at 485, per L'Heureux-Dubé J.

An Act to Amend the Criminal Code (sexual assault), SC 1992, c. 38, s. 276(3).

Preamble to Bill C-49, An Act to amend the Criminal Code (sexual assault), 3d Sess., 34th Parl., 1991.

60. Parliament's concerns for the fair trial rights of complainants in sexual assault cases are anchored in a long-established history of reformulating sexual assault laws to ensure greater fairness and access to justice for women. Parliament's grave concerns about the incidence of sexual violence and its interest in ensuring that such crimes are reported must be satisfied by denying production to Defence of women's personal histories as production denies women's equality rights and distorts the trial process.

61. Production and the threat of production will lead into the thicket of discriminatory myths and stereotypes that falsely define women and girls and the acts of sexual violence against them. Production applications will turn sexual assault trials into the "second rape."

Bond, supra, at 420 et seq.

62. In the Coalition's submission, production of records operates to deny women's real equality. It is a practice that like hate speech against identifiable groups, sends a message that the lives and experiences of some individuals—women—are not worth as much as the lives and experiences of others—men. Such a message is antithetical to the essential democratic values that venerate the equality, humanity, and dignity of all persons.

R v. Keegstra, [1990] 3 SCR 697, at 756, per Dickson CJ.

63. Law exerts a powerful influence on societal attitudes: the exploitation in the criminal process of discriminatory stereotypes to oppress women by effect or by design, communicates the law's acceptance of such stereotypes and acts to maintain their de facto and de jure inequality.

S. Murthy, "Rejecting Unreasonable Expectations: Limits on Using a Rape Victim's Sexual History To Show the Defendant's Mistaken Belief in Consent" (1991), 79 *California Law Rev.* 541, at 568.

64. It is submitted that the practice of production of counselling records in sexual offence proceedings has the effect of requiring certain complainants, those with a counselling history, to overcome the discriminatory presumptions that construct a relationship between the existence of such records and the complainants' credibility as witnesses. Other witnesses are not required to displace such presumptions in order to qualify for equal justice.

Osolin, supra, at 622, per L'Heureux-Dubé J.

65. Production of personal records will disadvantage most the women who, because of their disadvantaged status, have been most documented—women such as immigrant women, institutionalized women, poor women. The *O'Connor* case is a powerful illustration of this point: the breadth of records concerning the complainants in that case is a direct consequence of their being poor Aboriginal women subjugated to the residential

school system. The more a woman has been subject to the power and authority of the state, often because of her disadvantaged status, the greater the number of records that will be available for the Defence to pursue.

66. In the Coalition's submission, some women will simply choose not to report the sexual violence committed against them, or will not obtain counselling. The present appeal represents this inequality at work: the Appellant has asserted that had she known her records could be ordered produced, she would not have sought counselling and she would not have reported. It is submitted that production applications will operate to deny women who have been sexually assaulted the right to both seek counselling and pursue a prosecution of the offence against them. Women will therefore be forced into making choices unrelated to their best interests in order to avoid re-victimization in the court process.

Case on Appeal, Affidavit of L.L.A., at 86, para. 8.

67. All women whose counselling records are implicated by Defence applications to produce are denied a fair trial, the full protection and benefit of the law, and equal security of the person. The effect of production applications—on reporting, on women's decisions to seek counselling, on the prosecution process itself—denies women the equality rights promised to them under the Charter.

The Order for Production Underlying this Appeal

68. On February 15, 1994, Mr. Justice Loukidelis issued a production order requiring the Sexual Assault Care Centre of the Plummer Memorial Public Hospital and Women in Crisis (Agoma) Inc. ("the Record Holders") to produce to the Defence all records in their possession relating to the Appellant, L.L.A. for cross-examination purposes, limiting cross-examination to questions concerning possible contradictory statements found in the records with preliminary inquiry or trial testimony.

Case on Appeal: Reasons of Loukidelis J, at 191 and 197-207.

69. In the Coalition's submissions such limitations, even if enforced, do nothing to remedy the egregious injustice done to complainants in sexual assault cases whose personal histories become a focus of the judicial fact-finding process. Production of counselling records, irrespective of any restrictions placed on the extent or the use of the records, operates without exception to perpetuate the systemic and pernicious disadvantaging of women in the criminal justice process.

70. The rationale advanced by Defence in support of production of the records was related to the credibility of the Appellant and the unsubstantiated possibility that the allegations had been manufactured in the course of counselling. Defence counsel submitted that the records would have to be reviewed in order to determine:

> ... what if any statement [the complainant] has made in the past with respect to the incident; whether there have been allegations of sexual abuse to other people about other people; and what was the method of extracting the information from her during the 14 months she underwent sessions prior to going to see the police.

Case on Appeal: Defence Submissions on Motion, at 141.

71. The production order was made in this case notwithstanding there being no evidence that information concerning the assault was "extracted" by counsellors from the Appellant. To the contrary, the Appellant's evidence is that she brought up the issue of reporting the assault to the police, a decision she came to once she developed the strength to do so and the insight to realize that the assault was not her fault. The purpose for which the records were made and the circumstances in which their making occurred were also never analyzed by the Court below. At Women's Outreach the records were prepared as "a tool [for the counsellor] to help the client" and were not intended to be scrutinized as part of adversarial legal proceedings.

Case on Appeal, Preliminary Inquiry Evidence of L.L.A., at DD.44.56.

Case on Appeal, Affidavit of Sherrie Baic, at 73, para. 11.

72. The purpose of counselling as empowerment for women who have experienced sexual violence is apparent from the Appellant's testimony. Counselling relationships that ensure and maintain the woman's safety and trust operate to enable women to develop confidence and self-esteem and regain their autonomy and control.

Case on Appeal, Affidavit of Sherrie Baic, at 72, paras. 6, 7, and 9.

Case on Appeal, Affidavit of L.L.A., at 87, para. 10.

Case on Appeal, Preliminary Inquiry Evidence of L.L.A., at 44.

73. The fear that the records will be produced causes them to be kept in ways that do not always serve the clients' best interests or her recovery from the effects of the sexual assault. Production will operate to isolate women and deny them the right to empowerment and equality.

Case on Appeal, Affidavit of Bryna Coppel-Park, at 83, para. 4.

Case on Appeal, Affidavit of Sherrie Baic, at 73, para. 14.

74. As submitted by the Coalition in *O'Connor* in a legal and social culture not constructed in accordance with principles of systemic inequality and discriminatory stereotypes, the order for production of the Appellant's counselling records would not have been made. Sex equality would have repudiated the illegitimate grounds for the application and affirmed the essential character and role of the Appellant's sections 7, 15, and 28 rights.

75. The significance of this appeal is revealed as much by what the appeal does not concern as by what it does concern. This appeal does not engage the controversy of "false memory syndrome" as the evidence discloses that the Appellant never lost the memory of the incident. It is an appeal that does not concern the range of records or compounded inequalities raised by *O'Connor*. It is an appeal about confidential counselling for adult women survivors of childhood sexual abuse and their equality-driven right to have records of that counselling secure from production to defence in sexual assault prosecutions.

76. The Coalition submits that this Court should hold that, in the context of a sex-unequal legal and social culture, production of complainants' counselling records will

aggravate women's inequality by perpetuating the discriminatory stereotyping and discrediting of women and will undermine the integrity of the justice system by deterring reporting and distorting the fact finding process. As a consequence, vindication of complainants' constitutional rights and the interests of justice can only be achieved by an absolute prohibition against the production of complainants' counselling records in sexual offence proceedings.

PART IV: NATURE OF ORDER SOUGHT

77. The Coalition respectfully requests:

(a) that the Appeal be allowed;

(b) that the Order for Production of the records be quashed; and

(c) that Orders for Production of complainants' counselling records in sexual offence cases be declared a violation of the sex-equality guarantees in the Charter.

All of which is respectfully submitted.

THE OUTCOME

Head Notes—A.(L.L.) v. Beharriell

The A.(L.L.) decision was based on two issues: whether L.L.A. and the other applicants had the right to appeal the original disclosure order, and what was the appropriate test for disclosing complainants' personal records. The Coalition and LEAF did not deal with the first issue, and it is therefore only briefly presented. With respect to the second issue, the Court relied upon its rulings in the O'Connor case.

First Issue: Jurisdiction

The seven-member Court (Lamer, La Forest, L'Heureux-Dubé, Sopinka, Gonthier, Cory, and Major JJ) ruled unanimously that orders made with respect to third parties in criminal proceedings are final with respect to those parties and may be appealed, with leave, to the Supreme Court. Consequently, the Court granted itself jurisdiction to hear the appeal.

Second Issue: Production of Medical Records Held by Third Parties

Per Lamer CJ and Sopinka, Cory, and Major JJ: [para. 2] The procedure and substantive law to be followed where the accused seeks the production of therapeutic records in the hands of third parties is set out in *R v. O'Connor*. The appeal must be allowed as respondent failed to follow the requisite procedure and substantive law but without prejudice to his right to renew his request for production via the procedures developed by this Court in *O'Connor*.

Per La Forest, L'Heureux-Dubé, and Gonthier JJ: Private records, or records in which a reasonable expectation of privacy lies, may include medical or therapeutic records, school records, private diaries, social worker activity logs, and so on.

A class privilege should not be recognized for private records. A better approach is that advocated in *R v. O'Connor*, involving a balancing of the sexual assault complainant's Charter rights to privacy and equality with the accused's Charter rights to a fair trial and to full answer and defence.

[L'Heureux-Dubé then proceeds to apply the O'Connor test to the facts of this case.]

[As] set out in O'Connor, in determining the likely relevance of the private records, the trial judge cannot rely upon illegitimate purposes or discriminatory and stereotypical reasoning. For instance, an application based on credibility "at large," based on unsupported assertions of "recent complaint" or of "allegations of sexual abuse by other people," or based on the mere fact that a witness has a past psychiatric history or that he or she received counselling after a sexual assault are all insufficient grounds to meet the threshold of likely relevance. In the case at hand, the respondent argued that "the records have to be reviewed to determine if there is any information in there which would be relevant to the trial, credibility of the complainant, [and] how the information was extracted prior to them going to the police." These grounds do not meet the test for an application for production of private records held by third parties (see O'Connor). This should have been amply sufficient either to dismiss the respondent's application for production or to allow the Crown's application to quash the subpoena duces tecum.

Given that the respondent has not established the first element of the test for production, namely the likely relevance of the private records held by the appellant third parties either to the issues at trial or to the competence of the witness, and that his request constituted nothing more than a fishing expedition, the trial judge's order directing the production of those records by the appellants must be quashed. (pp. 589-90)

IN THE SUPREME COURT OF CANADA

(ON APPEAL FROM THE COURT OF APPEAL FOR SASKATCHEWAN)

BETWEEN:

ROBIN JAMES GOERTZ

Appellant

(Respondent)

AND:

JANET RITA GORDON

(FORMERLY JANETTE RITA GOERTZ)

Respondent

(Petitioner)

AND:

WOMEN'S LEGAL EDUCATION AND ACTION FUND (LEAF)

Intervenor

AND:

MINISTRY OF THE ATTORNEY GENERAL FOR ONTARIO
OFFICE OF THE CHILDREN'S LAWYER

Intervenor

Factum of Women's Legal Education and Action Fund (LEAF)

Goertz v. Gordon

INTRODUCTION

In 1993, Janet Gordon and Robin Goertz divorced after 20 years of marriage. Following a bitter custody battle, Gordon was awarded custody of the couple's 5-year-old daughter Samantha, with access arrangements provided for the father. In November 1994, Gordon sought to vary the access arrangements to enable her to move, with Samantha, to Australia to enter into a three-year Master's program in Orthodontics. Her application was successful and she and Samantha moved in February 1995. In allowing the original access order to be varied so that Gordon could move, the Saskatchewan Court of Queen's Bench relied heavily upon the trial judge's findings of fact that Gordon was the proper custodial parent of Samantha.

Robin Goertz appealed unsuccessfully to the Saskatchewan Court of Appeal. He then appealed to the Supreme Court of Canada. LEAF and the Attorney General for Ontario (Office of the Children's Lawyer) intervened in the appeal.

FACTUM

PART I: FACTS

1. The Women's Legal Education and Action Fund (LEAF) adopts the facts as set out in the Respondent's factum.

PART II: ISSUES

2. The issue in this appeal is the interpretation of the best interests of the child test under sections 16 and 17 of the Divorce Act in relocation cases.

PART III: ARGUMENT

Women's Social and Economic Disadvantage Flowing from Primary Responsibility for Children Is a Sex Equality Issue

The Gender-Based Division of Labour Prior to Separation

3. Historically, women have been almost exclusively responsible for the unpaid labour of childcare, whether or not they have also been employed in paid work. Currently, women in marital and non-marital relationships (hereinafter "spousal relationships") continue to bear prime responsibility for the childcare, regardless of employment.

Moge v. Moge, [1992] 3 SCR 813, at 861.

M. Gunderson, L. Muszynski, and J. Kleck, *Women and Labour Market Poverty* (Ottawa: Canadian Advisory Council on the Status of Women, 1990), at 13, 14, 20, 22, and 24-27.

Statistics Canada, *Women in Canada: A Statistical Report*, 3rd ed., Target Groups Project, Cat. no. 89-503E, at 70 and 83.

4. Childcare is largely treated as a private responsibility. The work world is generally unresponsive to family needs, having been historically structured on the assumption of the mother taking responsibility for domestic work and childcare at home.

Moge, supra, at 861.

L. Duxbury and C. Higgins, "Families in the Economy," chapter 3 in M. Baker, ed., *Canada's Changing Families: Challenges to Public Policy* (Ottawa: The Vanier Institute of the Family, 1994), at 34-35.

Rosalie Abella, *Report of the Commission on Equality in Employment*, Royal Commission on Equality in Employment (1984), at 28-29.

5. Women's primary responsibility for childcare has socially defined women as secondary earners who are likely to limit their paid work force participation. This division of labour has exacerbated women's inequality in the paid work force by contributing to systemic pay and employment inequity.

Abella, supra, at 28-32.

6. At the same time, the division of labour during spousal relationships is gender-based in large part because it has frequently been economical for women to limit their paid work force participation to address childcare needs. In response to the conflicting physical and emotional demands of paid work and responsibilities for home and family, women make sacrifices affecting their paid work opportunities. Women are much more likely than men to interrupt their work force participation, work part time, or disrupt their workday to accommodate childcare responsibilities.

Moge, supra, at 861.

Willick v. Willick, [1994] 3 SCR 670, at 723.

N. Zukewich Ghalam, "Women in the Workplace" in *Canadian Social Trends: A Canadian Studies Reader*, Volume 2 (Toronto: Thompson Educational Publishing, 1994), 141, at 145.

E. Diane Pask and M.L. (Marnie) McCall, eds., *How Much and Why? Economic Implications of Marriage Breakdown: Spousal and Child Support* (Calgary: Canadian Research Institute for Law and the Family, 1989), at 56-72.

Statistics Canada, *Women in Canada: A Statistical Report*, supra, at 69, 70, and 74.

Susan B. Boyd, "Potentialities and Perils of the Primary Caregiver Presumption" (1990), *Canadian Journal of Family Law Quarterly* 1-30, at 3-11 and 19.

The Gendered Nature of Childcare Following Separation

7. For most women, the assumption of primary childcare responsibilities after separation is simply a continuation of the responsibilities held by them prior to separation.

Young v. Young, [1993] 4 SCR 3, at 49.

Eleanor E. Maccoby and Robert H. Mnookin, *Dividing the Child: Social and Legal Dilemmas of Custody* (Cambridge, Mass.: Harvard University Press, 1992), at 268.

"Fatherhood" (1989), 3 *Canadian Journal of Women and the Law* 69, at 83-85.

Custodial Parents Are Primarily Women

8. When married and unmarried spouses separate, it is overwhelmingly mothers that have sole custody of their children, usually by agreement of the parties. In 1991, mothers were awarded custody in 74% of all custody decisions settled in court, and 77% of single parent families were headed by separated and divorced women.

Young, supra, at 49.

Statistics Canada, *Women in Canada: A Statistical Report*, supra, at 18 and 25.

Federal/Provincial/Territorial Family Law Committee, Department of Justice, Canada, *Custody and Access: Public Discussion Paper* (Ottawa: Supply and Services, 1993), at 13.

C. James Richardson, *Divorce and Family Mediation Research Study in Three Canadian Cities* (Ottawa: Supply and Services, 1988), at 268-70.

Women Have Primary Responsibility for Children in Joint Custody Arrangements

9. In recent years, there has been an increased number of "joint custody" awards and agreements. In joint custody arrangements, mothers usually continue to assume primary responsibility for their children by providing most of the day-to-day care and decision making. As well, children continue to reside primarily with their mothers.

Young, supra, at 49 and 50.

Lapointe v. Lapointe (October 20, 1995), unreported, Man. CA, at 20 and 21.

Richardson, *Divorce and Family Mediation Research Study in Three Canadian Cities*, supra, at 320.

Maccoby and Mnookin, supra, at 268.

Federal/Provincial/Territorial Family Law Committee, supra, at 13.

Statistics Canada, *Women in Canada: A Statistical Report*, supra, at 18 and 25.

10. Absent changes in social structures, it is highly predictable that women will continue to be primarily responsible for children following separation, whether in sole or joint custody arrangements.

Young, supra, at 49.

Maccoby and Mnookin, supra, at 279.

The Social and Economic Disadvantage of Women with Sole or Primary Custodial Responsibility After Separation

11. The employment compromises made by women, before and after separation, impede their ability to support themselves and their children following separation. Women who interrupt their employment experience losses in numerous employment-related areas, including seniority, opportunity for advancement, development of job skills, keeping skills up to date, fringe benefits, and the ability to accumulate future benefits such as pensions and disability insurance.

Moge, supra, at 861.

Pask and McCall, supra, at 56-65.

12. Custodial mothers have difficulty meeting their childcare responsibilities because of the work world's unwillingness to accommodate family responsibilities, and the lack of affordable, quality childcare and other social support systems, which are continually being eroded by government fiscal restraint.

Willick, supra, at 714, 715, and 720.

Brockie v. Brockie (1987), 5 RFL (3d) 440 (Man. QB), at 447-48.

Janine Brodie, *Politics on the Margins: Restructuring and the Canadian Women's Movement* (Halifax: Fernwood Publishing, 1995), at 57-58.

Helen McKenzie and Vivian Shalla, *Poverty in Canada* (Library of Parliament Research Branch, 1994), at 5.

National Council of Welfare, *Women & Poverty Revisited* (Ottawa: Supply and Services, 1990), at 49-52.

13. Custodial mothers who face additional levels of discrimination beyond sex and family status, experience even greater difficulty in finding employment. Women with disabilities, immigrant women, aboriginal women and visible minority women experience higher levels of unemployment, and have lower incomes than other women in Canada.

Statistics Canada, supra, at 9, 121, 122, 131, 137, 138, 145, 146, 152, 160, and 166.

National Council of Welfare, supra, at 112-27.

14. When single mothers are unable to obtain paid work, a life of poverty is virtually unavoidable. Ninety-three percent of single mothers who had no employment earnings were below the poverty cut-offs in 1993.

Punam Khosla, *Review of the Situation of Women in Canada* (Ottawa: National Action Committee on the Status of Women, 1993) (drawing on Statistics Canada, *Perspectives*, Spring, 1993, Cat. no. 75-001E), at 27.

15. Single-parent mothers are 5 to 6 times more likely to live in poverty than are mothers raising their children with a male partner. Three years after separation, the incomes of women and children had dropped by at least 30%; while on average, men's incomes more than doubled those of their former wives.

"Robert Glossop on the Canadian Family" in *Canadian Social Trends* no. 35, Winter 1994, Statistics Canada, at 9.

National Council of Welfare, *Poverty Profile 1992* (Ottawa: Supply and Services, 1994), at 4, 13, 14, and 70.

C.A. Gorlick, "Divorce: Options Available, Constraints Faced, Pathways Taken," chapter 7 in N. Mandell and A. Duffy, *Canadian Families: Diversity, Conflict and Change* (Toronto: Harcourt Brace Canada, 1995), at 216 and 225.

McKenzie and Shalla, supra, at 5.

16. The difficulty in meeting their childcare responsibilities is magnified for custodial mothers, particularly low-income custodial mothers, who are socially isolated or geographically removed from family and community. Many women, such as immigrant women and aboriginal women, face additional disadvantage due to extreme social and physical isolation from family and community, language differences, and lack of accessible support systems.

Ontario Advisory Council on Women's Issues, *Brief to the Ontario Government on Sole Support Mothers* (Toronto, 1987), at 16.

Statistics Canada, supra, at 9, 121, 122, 131, 137, 138, 145, 146, 152, 160, and 166.

Marlee Kline, "Complicating the Ideology of Motherhood: Child Welfare Law and First Nations Women" (1993), 18 *Queen's Law Journal* 306-42, at 312, 324-326, and 339.

Canadian Advisory Council on the Status of Women, *Sharing our Experience* (Ottawa: Supply and Services, 1993), at 19-29.

Custodial Mothers and Abuse

17. Twenty-nine percent of women who have been married or in a common law relationship have been physically or sexually assaulted by their partners on at least one

occasion. One-fifth of women reported that the violence continued after separation. For some women, the assaults began at the time of separation, while for others, the violence escalated during separation.

Statistics Canada, supra, at 104, 105, and 113.

18. Legal processes are sometimes used by men as a means to harass women. One American study estimates that at least one-half of contested child custody cases involve families with a history of some form of family violence. Those men who cannot disconnect from the women they abuse, use the legal system as a new arena of combat.

Final Report of the Canadian Panel on Violence Against Women, *Changing the Landscape: Ending Violence—Achieving Equality* (Ottawa: Supply and Services, 1993), at 229-31.

L.E. Walker and G.E. Edwall, "Domestic Violence and Determination of Visitation in Divorce," chapter 8 in D.J. Sonkin, ed., *Domestic Violence on Trial: Psychological and Legal Dimensions of Family Violence* (New York: Springer Publishing Co, 1987), at 127-33.

The Interpretation of Sections 16 and 17 of the Divorce Act Must Be Consistent with the Charter's Guarantees of Sex Equality

19. The Charter is the supreme law of Canada and, accordingly, statutes must be interpreted and applied in a manner consistent with the fundamental values enshrined therein. Where a statute is capable of more than one interpretation, the interpretation which most closely accords with Charter values should be favoured.

Young, supra, at 92 and 107.

P.(D.) v. S.(C.), [1993] 4 SCR 141, at 181.

Slaight Communications Inc. v. Davidson, [1989] 1 SCR 1038, at 1078.

Hills et al. v. AG Canada, [1988] 1 SCR 513, at 558.

AG Canada v. Mossop, [1993] 1 SCR 544, at 581-82.

20. In accordance with this Court's evolving jurisprudence, while section 15 does not itself guarantee social equality, equal law is seen as a means of attaining an equal society. Thus, the purpose of section 15 is to ensure equality in the formulation and application of the law.

Andrews v. Law Society of British Columbia, [1989] 1 SCR 143, at 171.

Willick, supra, at 705.

21. "An assessment of whether a particular interpretation of a statute is consistent with ... Charter values necessitates a contextual approach which contemplates the social framework in which the Act operates." "The social context of divorce is an evolving concept. So, too, are our understandings of the economic consequences thereof."

Willick, supra, at 679, 699, and 706.

Moge, supra, at 861-64.

22. It is submitted that the Divorce Act provisions concerning custody, like those concerning support, must be interpreted so as to promote the values of substantive, rather than formal equality.

Willick, supra, at 705-6.

Moge, supra, at 866-75.

Andrews, supra, at 174.

23. This Court has recognized that the legal treatment of women following separation has a significant impact on the social and economic status of women and their children, and as such, their substantive equality. It is submitted that the section 15 guarantee of sex equality requires that principles for determining the best interests of a child not impose a detrimental burden on women, by virtue of women's primary responsibility for care of children before and after separation. Restrictions on relocation perpetuate the relative disadvantage of women and their children.

Moge, supra, at 861.

24. LEAF submits that with regard to issues of relocation, an interpretation of the custody provisions of the Divorce Act in a manner consistent with the Charter's equality provisions, recognizes:

(a) the relationship between the continuing gender-based division of labour before separation and women's post-separation custodial responsibilities;

(b) the impact of their pre-separation role on women's ability to support themselves and their children after separation; and

(c) the particular difficulties for single mothers in caring for themselves and their children within a social context of a work world that is largely unresponsive to their needs and responsibilities.

Custody and Relocation

Evolution of the Law

25. At common law and until the mid-19th century, fathers were entitled to sole custody of their legitimate children as a matter of right, based on the view that fathers owned their wives and children. The exclusive right to custody included the right to determine where the child would live. Fathers' absolute rights to custody were gradually eroded due in part to legislation, and in part to the emergence of the equitable principle of the best interests of the child.

Lapointe, supra, at 7-8.

26. As Canadian custody jurisprudence developed, as set out in *Lapointe v. Lapointe*, the following propositions evolved concerning a parent's wish to relocate with a child in his or her care:

(a) a custodial parent was free to change the place of residence of a child in his or her custody without prior approval unless the power to make the decision to do so was restricted by court order or agreement;

(b) on an application by an access parent to forbid such a change, the onus was on the parent to show that the change was motivated by an intention to defeat his or her access rights, was unreasonable, or was contrary to the best interests of the child;

(c) in deciding the best interests of a child, a judge would ordinarily defer to the decision of the parent to whom the ultimate decision-making power with respect to that child had been entrusted; this, of course, assuming that the custodial parent's decision was bona fide and reasonable;

(d) a custodial parent whose decision-making power with respect to residence was restricted could nonetheless apply to a court for an order permitting a proposed move;

(e) on such an application, the custodial parent had to show a sufficient change in circumstances to justify the removal of the restriction and the bestowal of the decision-making power with respect to residence on him or her; and

(f) where such a custodial parent discharged his or her burden, the other parent was in exactly the same position as he or she would have been in on an application to forbid a change by a custodial parent whose decision-making power was unrestricted.

Lapointe, supra, at 15 and 16.

Custody and Relocation Under the Divorce Act

27. Today, questions of custody of and access to a child are determined based solely on the best interests of the child.

Divorce Act, RSC 1985, c. 3 (2nd Supp.), as amended, ss. 16(8) and 17(5).

Young, supra, at 26 and 117.

Lapointe, supra, at 17.

28. Section 16(7) of the *Divorce Act* contemplates that a custodial parent can relocate without court approval.

Lapointe, supra, at 16.

29. Under section 16(10) of the Divorce Act, the principle that a child is to have as much contact with each parent as is in the child's best interests, reflects that the focus is on the child's best interests, rather than on maximizing contact per se as a legislative goal. The concept of maximum contact was influenced by the principle of presumptive joint custody, which has been firmly rejected throughout Canada by federal and provincial legislatures.

Divorce Act, supra, s. 16(10).

Lapointe, supra, at 17.

Federal/Provincial/Territorial Family Law Committee, supra, at 29-31.

Interpretation and Application of the "Best Interests of the Child" Test

Generally

30. The best interests test requires a judge to decide what is in the best interests of a particular child at the time the custody decision is made. While recognized factors are to be considered, the weighing of each factor is left to the discretion of the judge, and there are no presumptions to aid in this decision.

Young, supra, at 117.

E. Diane Pask and M. L. (Marnie) McCall, "K.(M.M.) v. K.(U.) and the Primary Care Giver" (1991), 33 RFL (3d) 418, at 421.

Best Interests and Relocation

31. In interpreting sections 16 and 17 of the Divorce Act, the courts have adopted various approaches to relocation cases. In *Carter v. Brooks*, the Ontario Court of Appeal stated the following considerations:

(a) the only principle that governs is the best interests of the child;

(b) the best interests test cannot be implemented by the devising of a code of substantive rules, even if this could be done within the confines of a single case;

(c) the process should not begin with a general rule that one of the parties will be unsuccessful unless he or she satisfies a specified burden of proof;

(d) at the end of the process, if it is not possible for the court to conclude on a result which better accords with the best interests of the child, then the result must necessarily be in accordance with the legal status quo on the issue to be decided;

(e) an important factor to take into account, in favour of the custodial parent, is that the existing custody decision (by order or by agreement) shows that from a day-to-day point of view, the best interests of the child lie with the child's being with the custodial parent;

(f) an incident of custody includes the determination by the custodial parent of where the parent and the child shall live;

(g) if there is a new family unit as a result of a custodial parent having remarried, the well-being of that family unit bears on the best interests of the child;

(h) the nature of the relationship between the child and the access parent will always be of importance;

(i) the reason for the move is important. If the move is necessary, this would count in favour of the move;

(j) the distance of the move is of basic concern. The greater the distance, the more severe the impact of the proposed move will be on the relationship with the access parent;

(k) the degree of severity of impact of the proposed move is also likely to be effected rather directly by the financial resources of the access parent;

(l) the child's views are relevant; and

(m) the very general principle expressed in section 16(10) of the Divorce Act (the maximum contact provision) should be taken into account, whether or not it is expressed in statutory form.

Carter v. Brooks (1991), 30 RFL (3d) 53 (Ont. CA), at 61-65.

32. *Carter v. Brooks* effectively relied on only one of the considerations, that being, the test of necessity (as set out in paragraph 31(i) above). By placing the onus on the custodial mother to justify that a move is necessary, and by reviewing the reasons for her decision to relocate, the court eroded her ability to make decisions in the child's best interests.

33. More recently, an interpretation of sections 16 and 17 of the Divorce Act has emerged which reaffirms that custody is a package of responsibilities, including the responsibility to decide where a child lives. The most recent Court of Appeal cases reaffirm the principle in prior jurisprudence of giving deference to the custodial parent's ability to determine and act in the child's best interests.

Levesque v. Lapointe (1993), 44 RFL (3d) 316 (BC CA).

MacGyver v. Richards (1995), 11 RFL (4th) 432 (Ont. CA).

Lapointe, supra.

Factors Relevant to Issues of Relocation

The Custodial Parent Is in the Best Position To Determine the Child's Best Interests

34. The person in the best position to make decisions about the child's well-being is the custodial parent. As the person responsible for exercising judgment on a daily basis, who is most familiar with the child's needs, and who will live with the reality of decisions, the custodial parent is better situated than a judge to determine what is in the child's best interests, including residence.

Lapointe, supra, at 18.

Young, supra, at 41-42.

MacGyver, supra, at 444-45.

In the marriage of I and I (1995), 19 Fam. LR 147 (Fam. Ct. of Australia), at 158.

James C. McLeod, annotation to *Hines v. Hines* (1992), 40 RFL (3d) 274 (NS SCTD), at 277.

Karen M. Munro, "The Inapplicability of Rights Analysis in Post-Divorce Child Custody Decision Making" (1992), 30 *Alberta Law Review* 852-99, at 893-99.

Custody Is a Significant Responsibility

35. Custody is an enormous undertaking for the custodial parent. The high level and constancy of the responsibility for custody is far greater than that of the parent who sees the child intermittently and exercises access.

Young, supra, at 51.

Thomson v. Thomson, [1994] 3 SCR 551, at 589.

MacGyver, supra, at 445.

Lapointe, supra, at 22.

I and I, supra, at 164.

The Best Interests of the Child Are Linked to the Well-Being of the Custodial Parent

36. The child's best interests are inextricably linked to the well-being of the custodial parent.

Moge, supra, at 871.

Young, supra, at 70.

Levesque, supra, at 328.

MacGyver, supra, at 446.

Lapointe, supra, at 19.

I and I, supra, at 156.

Frank Furstenberg Jr. and Andrew J. Cherlin, *Divided Families: What Happens to Children When Parents Part* (Cambridge, MA: Harvard University Press, 1991), at 71-72.

Frank F. Furstenberg, S. Philip Morgan, and Paul D. Allison, "Paternal Participation and Children's Well-Being After Marital Dissolution" (1987), 52 *American Sociology Review* 695-701, at 697 and 698.

Jeanne M. Tschann, Janet R. Johnston, Marsha Kline, and Judith S. Wallerstein, "Conflict, Loss, Change and Parent-Child Relationships: Predicting Children's Adjustment During Divorce" (1990), 13(4) *Journal of Divorce* 1-22, at 18-20.

Department of Justice Canada, *Response to 99 Steps*, released November 17, 1995, at 8 and 9.

37. The child's best interests are not only intimately intertwined with the well-being of the custodial parent, but with any new family unit. The custodial parent and the child are a new family unit on separation. The court must consider the effect on the mother, and thus on the family unit, of restricting where she can live. The goal of maintaining present access may be desirable, but not at the cost of the well-being of the custodial mother and the child in her care.

Korpesho v. Korpesho (1982), 31 RFL (2d) 449 (Man. CA), at 451 and 452.

Carter, supra, at 63.

MacGyver, supra, at 446.

Lapointe, supra, at 22.

I and I, supra, at 164.

James C. McLeod, annotation to *Axam v. Séguin* (1994), 5 RFL (4th) 186 (Ont. Ct. Gen. Div.), at 187.

Susan B. Boyd, "Is There an Ideology of Motherhood in (Post) Modern Child Custody?" paper presented at the Learned Societies Conference, Ottawa 1993, revised 1995, at 11-12.

Access—Assumptions and Realities

38. Access, including its nature and duration, is determined solely on the basis of the best interests of the child rather than the needs and desires of the access parent. Custodial parents are expected and obliged to make decisions and to conduct their lives consistent with the child's best interests, not with the needs and desires of the access parent.

Thomson, supra, at 589.

M.(B.P.) v. M.(B.L.D.E.) (1992), 42 RFL (3d) 349 (Ont. CA), leave to appeal to SCC refused (1993), 48 RFL (3d) 232, at 360.

MacGyver, supra, at 446 and 448.

Lapointe, supra, at 17.

39. Principles of interpretation that restrict the relocation of custodial parents have been based on certain assumptions and myths regarding access. These assumptions regarding access are not accurate, or are usually unexamined in relation to the facts of a particular case:

(a) the assumption that maximum contact with both parents is beneficial for all children. The reality is that maximum contact with both parents is not necessarily beneficial for all children, and therefore, ordering or agreeing to it is not necessarily in the best interests of all children. The majority of studies based on large national surveys in the United States, found little association between father visitation and children's well being;

MacGyver, supra, at 446.

Lapointe, supra, at 17.

Valerie King, "Variation in the Consequences of Non-Resident Father Involvement for Child's Well-Being" (1994), 56 *Journal of Marriage and the Family* 963-72, at 963.

Denise Donnelly and David Finkelhor, "Does Equality in Custody Arrangement Improve the Parent-Child Relationship?" (1992), 54 *Journal of Marriage and the Family*, at 837 and 842-44.

Richardson, *Divorce and Family Mediation Research Study in Three Canadian Cities*, supra, at 31-32.

Federal/Provincial/Territorial Family Law Committee, supra, at 29-31.

(b) the assumption that where access has diminished, the problem is with the custodial parent interfering with access. The reality is that access parents do not necessarily exercise their access. In women's experience, the major problem with access is that men do not always exercise their access rights or that they do so erratically or unpredictably;

C. James Richardson, *Court-Based Divorce Mediation in Four Canadian Cities: An Overview of Research Results*, A Report Prepared for the Department of Justice Canada, February 1988 (Ottawa: Supply and Services, 1988), at 36, 38-39.

Richardson, *Divorce and Family Mediation Research Study in Three Canadian Cities*, supra, at 287-88.

Frank F. Furstenberg Jr., Christine Winquist Nord, James L. Peterson, and Nicholas Zill, "The Life Course of Children of Divorce: Marital Disruption and Parental Contact" (1983), 48 *American Sociological Review*, 656-68, Table 6, at 663.

Federal/Provincial/Territorial Family Law Committee, supra, at 17.

(c) the assumption that frequent access is more beneficial. The reality is that frequent access as opposed to amount of time spent, is not necessarily more beneficial for a child (that is, that one day per week for 7 weeks is not necessarily better than 1 full week). What counts is not the quantity of time, but the extent to which the access parent and child have a relationship in which the child feels valued. The regularity and predictability of visits is more important than frequency of visits;

M.B. Isaacs, B. Montalvo, and D. Abelsohn, *The Difficult Divorce: Therapy for Children and Families* (New York: Basic Books, 1986), at 273.

Judith S. Wallerstein and Sandra Blakeslee, *Second Chances: Men, Women and Children a Decade after Divorce* (New York: Ticknor & Fields, 1989), at 238.

(d) the assumption that proximity is a predictor of regular contact. The reality is that proximity is not always a predictor of regular contact. More significant is the commitment of the access parent to exercising access, and the relationship between the access parent and the child;

Furstenberg Jr., Nord, Peterson, and Zill, supra, Table 7, at 665 and 666.

(e) the assumption that the standard access arrangement is the most beneficial. The reality is that the overwhelming number of boiler-plate access arrangements in orders and agreements indicates a bias toward a standard structure. Underlying that bias is an assumption that this arrangement is in the best interests of the child. The standard access structure (every other weekend, plus one week night) is not necessarily the best arrangement simply because it is typical;

(f) the assumption that the original access arrangement is the appropriate access arrangement for all time. The reality is that the access arrangement agreed to (or court ordered) at one time is not always the most suitable arrangement for all time. Access appropriate for a 2-year old child may not be appropriate for a 7-year old or a 13-year old. In reality, access is restructured on an on-going basis by parents, to take into account the ages and stages of the child.

MacGyver, supra, at 443.

Lapointe, supra at 22.

Courtney v. Courtney (1992), 42 RFL (3d) 450 (Ont. Ct. Gen. Div.), at 451-53.

Maccoby and Mnookin, supra, at 198-202.

(g) the assumption that the post-separation arrangement should follow the pre-separation arrangement as closely as possible. The reality is that post-separation arrangements cannot and should not attempt to look like the pre-separation arrangements. It is an impossible ideal, unrealistic, ignores any conflicts that exist between the parents, and assumes such an arrangement could work;

Martha A. Fineman, "Dominant Discourse, Professional Language, and Legal Changes in Child Custody Decision-Making" (1988), 101 *Harv. L Rev.* 727-44, at 769.

(h) the assumption that change is bad for children. The reality is that change, by definition, is not necessarily bad for children. If a child has stability of care, the child can deal with and accept change.

David Gately and Andrew I. Schwebel, "Favourable Outcomes in Children After Parental Divorce" in Craig A. Everett, ed., *Divorce and the Next Generation* (New York: The Haworth Press, 1992), at 57 and 61.

Principles for Determining What Is in the Child's Best Interests in Accordance with Charter Values

40. While the best interests of the child must be a child-centred test, it is submitted that the inextricable link between the well-being of the child and the custodial mother, requires a recognition of the realities and interests of the custodial mother. Promoting women's substantive equality is fundamental to the well-being of women and the children in their care. Accordingly, it is submitted that the concept of the best interests of the child should be interpreted in a manner consistent with the constitutional goal of promoting women's substantive equality.

41. It is submitted that an interpretative approach to the best interests of the child that reaffirms the decision to relocate as an incident of custodial responsibility, and that defers to the decision making of the custodial parent, as set out in the most recent Court of Appeal decisions (*Levesque v. Lapointe*, *MacGyver v. Richards*, and *Lapointe v. Lapointe*), more closely accords with the values enshrined in section 15 of the Charter.

42. As a result of the social and economic disadvantage experienced by custodial mothers and their children, they will need to move in order to:

(a) obtain employment or better employment to become as self-supporting as possible. Improved employment includes employment with sufficient flexibility to enable custodial mothers to meet their children's needs;

(b) obtain adequate and affordable childcare so as to allow women to work and accommodate their child rearing responsibilities;

(c) obtain support or create distance if the post-separation relationship is abusive;

(d) seek or maintain support from family, friends, or new family units so as to best meet their children's needs;

(e) obtain adequate and affordable housing; and

(f) attend school or retraining, to improve their chances of finding a job.

These needs occur within a social context of a highly mobile society, especially in relation to work.

Bali Ram, Y. Edwards Shin, and Michel Pouliot, *Canadians on the Move* (Statistics Canada and Prentice Hall Canada Inc., 1994), Cat. no. 96-309E, at 1, 3, 7, and 16.

Korpesho, supra, at 451.

43. It is submitted that deference to the relocation decisions of custodial parents is consistent with the modern philosophy of family breakdown, which aims at encouraging and facilitating the ability of former spouses to get on with their lives.

Korpesho, supra, at 451 and 452.

44. It is submitted that in considering the best interests of the child with respect to issues of relocation, a large measure of deference should be accorded to the custodial mother's judgment. This deference is based upon, and should be exercised to include recognition:

(a) that the custodial mother is in a better position to judge the child's best interests, relative to the court or the access parent;

(b) of the significant responsibilities involved in caring for a child as a custodial mother;

(c) of the social and economic disadvantage experienced by custodial mothers that limit their ability to meet their childcare responsibilities and make it necessary for them to move;

(d) of the importance to the child of supporting the custodial mother in meeting her responsibilities; and,

(e) that caution should be exercised in second-guessing the custodial mother's judgment that a move is in the child's best interests.

45. It is submitted that, in interpreting sections 16 and 17 of the Divorce Act, a failure to recognize the substantive differences between custody and access in terms of the significance to the child's well-being and in terms of the nature and extent of parental responsibilities, is inconsistent with the Charter guarantee of substantive

equality for women and reflects a formal equality approach, which was rejected by this Court in *Andrews*.

Andrews, supra, at 174.

46. When a court considers whether a relocation by a custodial mother is "necessary" (as in *Carter v. Brooks*), it exercises judgment and applies a standard to the custodial mother that it does not apply to an access parent making a similar decision. No court orders are made forcing access parents to move, to stay, or to exercise their access. Courts do not restrict the relocation of an access parent for the sake of the child's best interests, whether the motivation to relocate was benign, or whether the change in access was harmful to the child.

MacGyver, supra, at 447.

47. A request to relocate ought not to be determined on the grounds of whether an access parent is exercising access, or has fulfilled his legal or moral obligations. By exercising access and paying support the access parent is doing what he is required to do. Courts should be wary of introducing an analysis that rewards access parents for visiting their children and paying support, to the detriment of the custodial parent.

James G. McLeod, annotation to *Wainio v. Gilmour* (1994), 2 RFL (4th) 116 (Ont. CA), at 117-18.

48. The fact that a child will be affected by a relocation decision, like many other decisions of a custodial parent, does not mean that a court should interfere with or change that decision. On relocation, access can be restructured in accordance with the child's overall interests. An assumption that it cannot be restructured in this way, places too much significance on the status quo as to access, as:

(a) there are situations where the distances involved and the economic circumstances of the parents require radical restructuring, and even limiting access. However, access is not restricted to in-person contact. Technology offers parents and children various opportunities for contact; and

(b) access options and arrangements that are in the child's best interests will continue to evolve as the circumstances of the child and the parents change.

MacGyver, supra, at 445.

Lapointe, supra, at 18 and 19.

I and I, supra, at 164.

Maccoby and Mnookin, supra, at 295.

McLeod, supra, at 187.

49. It is submitted that to interpret sections 16 and 17 of the Divorce Act in a manner consistent with section 15 of the Charter, the court should apply the following test: where a parent with sole custody seeks to relocate, the move, in and of itself, is a material change in circumstances with respect to access only, but not with respect to custody. Accordingly, a sole custodial parent's decision to relocate is not subject to the

court's review, as the relocation decision is an incident of custody. However, access may be restructured by the court.

Joint Custody

Evolution of the Law

50. Joint custody is a relatively new legal concept in Canada.

Baker v. Baker (1979), 8 RFL (2d) 236, at 244.

Kruger v. Kruger (1979), 11 RFL (2d) 52, at 78.

Julian Payne and Brenda Edwards, "Co-operative Parenting after Divorce: A Canadian Perspective" (1989), 11 *Advocates' Quarterly* 1-30, at 1.

51. Section 16(4) of the Divorce Act allows the court to make an order granting custody or access "to any one or more persons." Although it does not use the words joint custody, this is referred to as the joint custody provision of the Divorce Act. Neither this section, the remainder of the Divorce Act, nor any other legislative provision contains a definition of joint custody.

52. Initially, joint custody was only ordered in the rare circumstance where both parties agreed. Courts are no longer as reluctant to impose joint custody on parents as they once were, and indeed, joint custody orders take many forms. The meaning of the phrase joint custody is indeterminate. At one end of the continuum is joint legal custody, with sole caregiving provided by one parent and minimal contact by the other parent. In the middle is joint legal custody, with primary caregiving provided by one parent and contact by the other parent that looks like "liberal access" described in sole custody and access circumstances. At the extreme other end of the continuum is joint legal custody, which also includes joint physical custody, where both parents provide equal caregiving of the child and make decisions about the child on a consensus basis. All of these arrangements are called "joint custody." As a result, it is impossible to determine the factual reality of a legal joint custody order without reference to the practical circumstances of the care for the child. Most joint custody orders include an award of "primary residence" or "primary care and control" to one parent, and fixed specified time for the other parent to see the child. Only occasionally do joint custody orders set out areas of joint decision making. Orders for joint legal custody combined with joint physical custody are the exception.

Baker, supra, at 246.

Kruger, supra, at 79 and 80.

Hines v. Hines (1992), 40 RFL (3d) 274 (NS SCTD), at 289-90.

Kaemmle v. Jewson (1993), 50 RFL (3d) 70 (Ont. Ct. Gen. Div.), at 74-75.

Hussein v. Hussein (1994), 3 RFL (4th) 375 (NB QB), at 384-85.

Tweel v. Tweel (1994), 7 RFL (4th) 204 (PEI TD), at 216.

Keown v. Keown, [1995] BCJ no. 26 (SC, Master, January 4, 1995).

Radford v. Cassiano, [1995] OJ no. 105 (Prov. Ct., January 18, 1995).

Woodland v. Ceeco, [1995] BCJ no. 226 (SC, February 8, 1995).

Julian Payne and Brenda Edwards, supra, at 5-7.

Furstenberg Jr. and Cherlin, supra, at 74 and 76.

Donnelly and Finkelhor, supra, at 837.

Maccoby and Mnookin, supra, at 269.

Joint Custody and Relocation

53. Most joint custody arrangements, whether by order or agreement, are *in fact* more akin to the traditional sole custody and access arrangements, regardless of legal attribution of rights and responsibilities. Further, women in joint custody arrangements usually have, *in fact*, the primary custodial responsibility. Even with joint physical custody, women still find themselves making most of the day-to-day decisions about the child, and assuming responsibility for most daily child-related tasks. Accordingly, it is necessary to distinguish between the legal description of the arrangement and the factual reality of the arrangement.

Young, supra, at 49-50.

Levesque, supra, at 325.

Lapointe, supra, at 20.

I and I, supra, at 161.

Statistics Canada, supra, at 18, 69, and 70.

Richardson, *Court-based Divorce Mediation in Four Canadian Cities: An Overview of Research Results*, supra, at 35.

Richardson, *Divorce and Family Mediation Research Study in Three Canadian Cities*, supra, at 320.

Maccoby and Mnookin, supra, at 268, 269, and 279.

Pask and McCall, supra, at 427-28.

54. It is submitted that courts must analyze each situation to determine whether a joint custody arrangement, in law, is in fact true equal parenting, in roles and responsibilities, or one more akin to sole custody. In contrast to the situation where each parent has sole responsibility for the day-to-day management of the child's life while the child is living with that parent, for equal periods of time, the primary custodial parent is the person who has primary day-to-day experience of and contact with the child, and who has the most information available to determine issues regarding the child's well-being. The following are factors to determine who is a primary custodial parent:

(a) custodial responsibility involves not only arranging the child's life, but arranging one's life around the child;

(b) custodial responsibility is not necessarily a question of quantum of time spent with the child. Although quantum of time spent may be an indicator, it is an over simplification to look only at time spent;

(c) custodial responsibility is to be examined over the entire life of the child, not simply the period post-separation;

(d) custodial responsibility is about taking responsibility for ensuring the child's daily needs are met, not solely doing various tasks related to the child;

(e) custodial responsibility is about determining which parent tracks the child's movement during the day, and whom the child keeps informed of her whereabouts; and,

(f) custodial responsibility is about which parent has primary management of the child's daily life, and of the organization of the child's daily life.

Levesque, supra, at 328.

Lapointe, supra, at 20-21.

55. The primary custodial parent performs her childcare responsibilities in the same social context and generally in the same manner as sole custodial parents, and the same principles regarding relocation should accordingly apply. It is submitted that where a joint custodial parent *in fact*, assumes the responsibilities of a sole custodial parent, a relocation is a material change in circumstances with regard to access only, but not with regard to custody and the test in paragraph 49 applies. It is submitted that a failure to interpret the best interests concept in this way is to put form over substance in a manner inconsistent with the equality values enshrined in the Charter.

56. If all the indicia of true equal parenting are met, a decision to relocate is a material change in circumstances with respect to custody, and the court must re-examine the custody arrangement itself, not whether one parent can move.

Levesque, supra, at 325.

Lapointe, supra, at 20-21.

Separation Agreements and Court Orders with Relocation Restrictions

57. Where a separation agreement or court order contains a relocation restriction, it is submitted that the relocation of a parent with sole or primary custodial responsibility amounts to a material change in circumstances with regard to residence and access, but not with respect to custody. The relocation restriction, by virtue of the court order or agreement, is subject to the court's review. It is submitted that in determining the best interests of the child, the onus should be on the access parent to establish that the move is contrary to the child's best interests, and the principles enunciated in paragraphs 34-39 should be applied on the review.

58. A relocation restriction in a separation agreement is not determinative of the child's best interests, and should be given little weight in that:

(a) a court is obliged to consider only the best interests of the child as it exists at the time of the application, both at first instance and on variation;

(b) while a relocation restriction may have been appropriate at the time the agreement was entered into, it may be inappropriate at a later date, on an analysis of the child's best interests; and

(c) any analysis of the significance or validity of relocation restrictions in agreements must include an analysis of women's unequal bargaining power in post-separation negotiations, and why such a clause was entered into. The choices that women make post-separation are tied to the social context and the circumstances in which they find themselves before and after separation. A relocation restriction may not reflect any real consensus that a relocation would not be in the best interests of a child.

Divorce Act, supra, ss. 16(8) and 17(5).

Richardson v. Richardson, [1987] 1 SCR 857, at 869-70.

Willick, supra, at 686 and 727-29.

Levesque, supra, at 323.

Marcia Neave, "Resolving the Dilemma of Difference: A Critique of "The Role of Private Ordering in Family Law" (1994), 44 *University of Toronto Law Journal* 90-131, at 110-31.

Donald Poirier and Michelle Boudreau, "Formal Versus Real Equality in Separation Agreements in New Brunswick" (1992), 10 *Canadian Journal of Family Law* 239-56, at 251-56.

Conclusion

59. It is submitted that the test to be applied in determining relocation applications is as follows:

(a) *Sole Custody*: Where a parent with sole custody seeks to relocate, the move, in and of itself, is a material change in circumstances with respect to access only, but not with respect to custody. Accordingly, a sole custodial parent's decision to relocate is not subject to the court's review, as the relocation decision is an incident of custody. However, access may be restructured by the court.

(b) *Legal Joint Custody with a Primary Custodial Parent*: Where a parent with primary custodial responsibility, in a legal joint custody arrangement, seeks to relocate, the test for a parent with sole custody should be applied.

(c) *Legal Joint Custody: True Equal Parenting*: Where a parent with legal joint custody, in a true equal parenting situation, seeks to relocate, the move is a material change in circumstances with respect to custody, and the court must re-examine the custody arrangement itself, and not the decision to relocate.

(d) *Relocation Restrictions in Orders or Agreements*: Where an order or agreement contains a relocation restriction, the decision of a parent with sole or primary custodial responsibility to relocate is a material change in circumstances with respect to residence and access, but not with respect to custody. The relocation restriction, by virtue of the order or agreement, is subject to the court's review. In determining the best interests of the child, the onus is on the access parent to establish that the move is contrary to the child's best interests, and the principles set out in paragraphs 34-39 must be applied.

PART IV: NATURE OF ORDER SOUGHT

60. Based on the principles of interpretation outlined above, LEAF submits that this appeal should be dismissed.

All of which is respectfully submitted.

THE OUTCOME

Head Notes—Goertz v. Gordon

The decision was released on May 2, 1996. The Court unanimously dismissed the appeal. However, the Court split on the proper test to be applied. The principal judgment was written by McLachlin and concurred in by Lamer CJ, Sopinka, Cory, Iacobucci and Major. A concurring judgment was written by L'Heureux-Dubé and adopted by La Forest. Gonthier wrote a brief concurring judgment in which he agreed with parts of L'Heureux-Dubé's decision but not her findings regarding the burden of proof.

Per Lamer CJ and Sopinka, Cory, McLachlin, Iacobucci and Major JJ: The parent applying for a change in the custody or access order must meet the threshold requirement of demonstrating a material change in the circumstances affecting the child. For that threshold to be met, the judge must be satisfied of (1) a change in the condition, means, needs or circumstances of the child or in the ability of the parents to meet the needs of the child, (2) which materially affects the child, and (3) which was either not foreseen or could not have been reasonably contemplated by the judge who made the initial order. An application to vary custody cannot serve as an indirect route of appeal from the initial custody order. The judge must assume the correctness of the initial order and consider only the change in circumstances since the order was issued.

The threshold condition of a material change in circumstance satisfied, the court should consider the matter afresh without defaulting to the existing arrangement. The earlier conclusion that the custodial parent was the best person to have custody is no longer determinative, since the existence of material change presupposes that the terms of the earlier order might have been different had the change been known at the time.

If the threshold is met, the judge on the application must embark on a fresh inquiry into the best interests of the child, having regard to all the relevant circumstances relating to the child's needs and the ability of the respective parents to satisfy them. The focus of the inquiry is not the interests and rights of the parents.

Under the Divorce Act, the custodial parent's conduct can be considered only if relevant to his or her ability to act as parent of the child. Usually, the reasons or motives for moving will not be relevant to the custodial parent's parenting ability. Occasionally, however, the motive may reflect adversely on the parent's perception of the needs of the child or the parent's judgment about how they may best be fulfilled. For example, the decision of a custodial parent to move solely to thwart salutary contact between the child and access parent might be argued to show a lack of appreciation for the child's best interests. However, absent a connection to parenting ability, the custodial parent's reason for moving should not enter into the inquiry.

Each case turns on its own unique circumstances and the only issue is the best interest of the child in the particular circumstances of the case. Section 17(5) of the Divorce Act directs that the judge must consider the child's best interests "by reference" to the material change in circumstances. However, the inquiry cannot be confined to that change alone, isolated from the other factors bearing on the child's best interests.

The child's mother argues that the inquiry into the best interests of the child should begin with a presumption in favour of the custodial parent. This would place the onus on the access parent to show why remaining with the custodial parent is not in the child's best interest. I have concluded that this submission must fail. Once the applicant has discharged the burden of showing a material change in circumstances, both parents should bear the evidentiary burden of demonstrating where the best interests of the child lie.

It is no answer to an inquiry into the best interests of the child triggered by the material change to argue that the custodial parent has the right and responsibility to decide where the child shall live. The demonstration of a material change places that right at issue. The judge will normally place great weight on the views of the custodial parent, who may be expected to have the most intimate and perceptive knowledge of what is in the child's interest. The judge's ultimate task, however, is to determine where, in light of the material change, the best interests of the child lie.

The wording of the Divorce Act belies the need to defer to the custodial parent; rather, the Act has expressly stipulated that the judge hearing the application should be concerned only with the best interests of the child. The rights and interests of the parents, except as they impact on the best interests of the child, are irrelevant. Material change established, the question is not whether the rights of custodial parents can be restricted; the only question is the best interests of the child. Nor does the great burden borne by custodial parents justify a presumption in their favour. Custodial responsibilities curb the personal freedom of parents in many ways. The Act is clear. Once a material change is established, the judge must review the matter a new to determine the best interests of the child.

The argument that a presumption would render the law more predictable in a way which would do justice in the majority of cases and reduce conflict damaging to the child between the former spouses also founders on the rock of the Divorce Act. The Act contemplates individual justice. The judge is obliged to consider the best interests of the particular child in the particular circumstance of the case. Had Parliament wished to impose general rules at the expense of individual justice, it could have done so. It did not. The manner in which Parliament has chosen to resolve situations which may not be in the child's best interests should not be lightly abjured. Even if it could be shown that a presumption in favour of the custodial parent would reduce litigation that would not imply a reduction in conflict. The short-term pain of litigation may be preferable to the long-term pain of unresolved conflict. Foreclosing an avenue of legal redress exacts a price; it may, in extreme cases, even impel desperate parents to desperate measures in contravention of the law. A presumption would do little to reduce the underlying conflict endemic in custody disputes.

In assessing the best interests of the child, the judge should more particularly consider, inter alia: (a) the existing custody arrangement and relationship between the child and the custodial parent; (b) the existing access arrangement and relationship between the child and the access parent; (c) the desirability of maximizing contact between the child and both parents; (d) the views of the child; (e) the custodial parent's reason for moving, only in the exceptional ease where it is relevant to that parent's ability to meet the needs of the child; (f) disruption to the child of a change in custody; and (g) disruption to the child consequent on removal from family, schools, and the community he or she has come to know. The "maximum contact" principle mentioned in ss. 16(10) and 17(9) of the Divorce Act is mandatory but not absolute and the judge is only obliged to respect it to the extent that such contact is consistent with the child's best interests. As set out in s. 16(9) of the Act, parental conduct does not enter the analysis unless it relates to the ability of the parent to meet the needs of the child. In the end, the importance of the child's remaining with the parent to whose custody it has become accustomed in the new location must be weighed against the continuance of full contact with the child's access parent, its extended family and its community. The ultimate question in every case is this: what is in the best interests of the child in all the circumstances, old as well as new?

Where, as here, the child enjoyed frequent and meaningful contact with the access parent, a move that would seriously curtail that contact suffices to establish the necessary connection between the change and the needs and circumstances of the child. Further, since the terms of the previous order were premised on the child's residence remaining within a reasonable distance of the access parent, the move to Australia would clearly breach this provision. The judge was thus required to embark on a fresh appraisal of the best interests of the child. While he failed to give sufficient weight to all relevant factors, when all these factors are taken into account, the judge was correct in continuing the mother's custody of the child, despite her intended move to Australia. There is no support in the evidence, however, for restricting the father's access to Australia. Access in Canada would have the advantage of making the father's limited time with the child more natural while allowing the child to maintain contact with friends and extended family. Accordingly, the custody order should be upheld and the access order should be varied to provide for access to be exercisable in Canada.

Per Gonthier J: The reasons of McLachlin J are agreed with. There is also agreement with L'Heureux-Dubé J's explanations of factors pertinent to assessing the best interests of the child that are to be considered, though her views on onus of proof are not shared.

Per La Forest and L'Heureux-Dubé JJ: The notion of custody under the Divorce Act encompasses the right to choose the child's place of residence. Absent an agreement or a court order restricting the incidents of custody, such as the child's place of residence, it is thus within the custodial parent's powers to decide such a change of residence, subject to the right of the non-custodial parent to oppose such choice by seeking a variation of the custody or access terms under s. 17(5) of the Act. Parental agreements as to any right of the child should be encouraged since parents are generally in a better position to assess the best interests of the child, but these agreements are not binding on courts. Restrictions on the rights of custodial parents should be the exception, not the rule, and such restrictions should not be inferred from generous or specified access provisions without more.

The first consideration in an application for variation of custody or access orders under s. 17(5) of the Act is whether there has been a material change of circumstances in accordance with the guidelines in *Willick*. Once this threshold is reached, the next step is whether the change is such as to trigger a re-appraisal of the whole situation of the parties and the children or only necessitates an assessment of the impact of the alleged change or changes on the custody of the child. It is only where the alleged change or changes are of such a nature or magnitude as to make the original order irrelevant or no longer appropriate that an assessment of the whole situation is warranted.

In assessing the merits of a variation application linked to the change of residence of the child by the custodial parent, the following guidelines must inform the courts:

1. All decisions as to custody and access must be made in the best interests of children, assessed from a child-centred perspective. The Divorce Act makes it clear that the best interests of the child [are] the only consideration to be taken into account in making orders concerning children. The objective of promoting maximum contact with the non-custodial parent, inasmuch as it is consistent with such interests, is an important consideration.

2. In the absence of explicit restrictions on the incidents of custody, such as the child's place of residence, it must be assumed that an existing custody order or agreement reflects the best interests of the child and that the appropriate decision-making authority lies with the custodial parent. The attribution of custody to one parent carries with it the presumption that such parent is the most able to ensure the best interests of the child. Before custody can be entrusted to one of the parents in divorce proceedings, a number of factors play a role in the assessment of the best interests of the child. The desirability of maintaining maximum contact between the child and both parents is an important factor, but the court must also balance such considerations as the child's physical, emotional, social and economic needs in light of the quality of his or her relationship with both parents, their respective ability to look after the child's best interests and, where the child is old and mature enough, his or her wishes and preferences. The assessment of the child's best interests also involves a consideration of the particular role and emotional bonding the child enjoys with his or her primary caregiver. If, after such an inquiry is conducted, or by mutual consent of the parties, a child's custody is entrusted to one of the parents, it necessarily follows that such parent has

been found to be best able to ensure the best interests of the child, taking into account all the circumstances of the parties and the child. Given that day-to-day decisions affecting the child are clearly left to the custodial parent, there is no reason not to defer to his or her ability and responsibility to act in the child's best interests when it comes to other decisions, such as the change of residence of the child, which will necessarily take into account the impact of access to the non-custodial parent by the child. In both cases, if the decision constitutes a material change of circumstances, s. 17(5) allows for a variation in as much as such a decision will be found to impact on either the custody of the child or the access by the non-custodial parent.

3. In determining the best interests of the child under s. 17(5), courts must focus on the impact of the change of residence on the existing custody order and the appropriate modifications to access as the case may be, and generally not proceed to a de novo appraisal of all the circumstances of the child and the parties, since s. 17(5) of the Act provides that "the court shall take into consideration only the best interests of the child as determined by reference to that change." This particular wording is indicative that where the change consists of the proposed relocation of the child by the custodial parent, what must be ascertained is the impact of such relocation on the existing custody order which must be assumed to properly ensure the child's best interests. The best interests of the child are rightly presumed to lie with the custodial parent.

4. The non-custodial parent bears the onus of showing that the proposed change of residence will be detrimental to the best interests of the child to the extent that custody should be varied or, exceptionally, where there is cogent evidence that the child's best interests could not in any reasonable way be otherwise accommodated, that the child should remain in the jurisdiction. The proposed change of residence of the child by the custodial parent will not justify a variation in custody unless the non-custodial parent adduces cogent evidence that the child's relocation with the custodial parent will prejudice the child's best interests and, further, that the quality of the non-custodial parent's relationship with the child is of such importance to the child's best interests that prohibiting the change of residence will not cause detriment to the child that is comparable to or greater than that caused by an order to vary custody. Where there is an agreement or court order explicitly restricting the child's change of residence, the onus should shift to the custodial parent to establish that the decision to relocate is not made in order to undermine the access rights of the non-custodial parent and that he or she is willing to make arrangements with the non-custodial parent to restructure access, when appropriate, in light of the change of residence of the child.

The proposition that the determination of the best interests of the child under s. 17(5) is best left to the discretionary realm of questions of fact where each relevant factor is to be equally considered and where no party bears any specified burden of proof must be rejected because it fosters uncertainty in the application of the law and encourages litigation and ongoing parental conflict which clearly are not in the best interest of the children.

Here, the change of residence, which involves moving to another country and was also unforeseen at the time the custody order was originally made, constitutes a material change in the circumstances of the child. The judge applied the correct test and, upon the evidence before him, properly concluded that the threshold upon which the merits of the application for variation could be considered had been met. Despite the father's alleged increased involvement in his child's life since the initial custody order, the custody challenge was essentially based on the inevitable limitation to his access rights the child's change of residence would involve. Since less than two years had elapsed between the date of the order entrusting custody of the child to the mother and her projected change of residence, this initial order clearly remains highly relevant upon consideration of the merits of the application for variation. All other considerations being equal, in such circumstances a variation application would normally be restricted to an appraisal of the impact of the child's change of residence on the prior custody determination as well as the appropriate modification to access as the case may be.

On the merits of the application, the judge did not err in law in concluding that the mother should be allowed to move with the child to Australia. The evidence supports his conclusion that the best interests of the child required upholding the custody of the mother. It was entirely proper for him to "rely heavily" on the divorce judge's determination that the best interests of the child were best served by entrusting custody to the mother and, accordingly, to examine the impact of the change of residence on such determination as well as the possible modifications to access. On the evidence, the judgment, in spite of its brevity, makes clear that the father did not satisfy the judge that the impact of the chance of residence of the child was such as to warrant a variation of custody, particularly in light of the possibility of accommodating the father's access and contact with the child. The judge was thus correct in upholding the mother's custody of the child despite her intended move to Australia. He erred, however, in confining the exercise of the father's access to the child to Australia. The evidence does not support such a conclusion. The access order should be varied to provide for access to be exercisable in Canada.

Appendices

APPENDIX A

LEAF Board of Directors

Carol Allen
Denise Arsenault
Beth Atcheson
Leslie Belloc-Pinder
Phyllis Berck
Stephanie Bernstein
Alison Brewer
Beverly Britton-Clarke
Rosemary Brown
Flora Buchan
Joyce Burpee
Dawn Butler
Colleen Cattell
Susan Clarke
Pat Cooper
Andrée Côté
Rachel Cox
Linda Coyle
Elizabeth Cusack-Walsh
Mary Margaret Dauphinee
Diane Davies
Joan Dawkins
Doreen Demas
Raminder Dosanjh
Coreen Douglas
Daphne Dumont
Mary Eberts
Ertrice Eddy
Maria Eriksen
Frances Ewing
Judith Finlayson
Halyna Freeland
Stéphanie Gagné
Fern Gaspar
Lynn Gaudet
Dale Gibson
Linda Gaudet
Kim Gilson
Frances Gordon
Sheila Greene
Barbara Hackett
Suzanne Heron-Herbert
Mary Lue Hinds
Betty Hopkins
Jessie Horner
Shelly Howell
Agnes Huang
Betty Lou Huculak
Sherron Hughes
Patricia Hughes
Wendy Hutchinson
Joan Jones
Ritu Khullar
Pat Lalonde
Lucie Lamarche
Hélène Lebel
Dominique Leclercq
Betty Lee

Shelagh M'Gonigle
Heather McFadgen
Corinne Matte
Shauna MacKenzie
Jean McBean
Gayle McDonald
Sandra Hunt McDonald
Vera Asp McGinty
Marilou McPhedran
Lee Ann Montgomery
Odette Montigny
Lisa Murphy
Sylvia Neschokat
Lise Novack
Brigid O'Reilly
Pat Paradis
Brenda Parris
Eloise Perles-Spitzer
Yvonne Peters
Frances Piercey
Marilyn Pilon
Dagmar Rinne
Eve Roberts
Linda Robinson
Nancy Ruth (Jackman)
Magda Seydegart
Jane Shackell
Virginia Schuler
Elizabeth Shilton
Fabienne Simon
Lynn Smith
Starr Solomon
Freda Steel
Mary Lou Stirling
Madeleine Dion Stout
Deborah Strachan
Diane Sturino
Susan Tanner
Linda Taylor
Chantal Tie
Susan McCrae Vander Voet
Ruth Welsh
Charla Williams
Vera Marie Wolfe
Carolyn Woloski
Pat Wouters

APPENDIX B

Members of LEAF's National Legal Committee (1985-1995)

Co-Chairs
Carol Allen
Mary Eberts
Jean McBean
Pat Paradis
Elizabeth Shilton
Lynn Smith
Eloise Spitzer
Elizabeth Thomas
Chantal Tie

Volunteers
Jenny Abell
Carol Allen
Himani Bannerji
Suzanne Boivin
Christine Boyle
Karen Busby
Michelle Caron
Andrée Côté
Anne Derrick
Penny Desjarlais
Daphne Dumont
Mary Eaton
Mary Eberts
Catherine Frazee
Dale Gibson
Yola Grant
Victoria Gray
Lucie LaMarche
Dominique LeClercq
Catharine MacKinnon
Kathleen Mahoney
Jean McBean
Sheila McIntyre
Sharon McIvor
Helena Orton
Yvonne Peters
Elizabeth Shilton
Lynn Smith
Eloise Spitzer
Joanne St. Lewis
Freda Steel
Beth Symes
Kathryn Thomson
Elizabeth Cusack Walsh

Staff
Gwen Brodsky
Annie Bunting

Shelagh Day
Mary Teresa Devlin
Lynn Gaudet
Leslie Hardy
Jan Hatch
Christie Jefferson
Susan Joanis
Carissima Mathen
Connie Nakatsu
Helena Orton
Jane Rounthwaite
Jennifer Scott
Erin Shaw
Joanne St. Lewis

APPENDIX C

LEAF National Staff

Anneli Ahonen
Colleen Albiston
Marian Ali
Carol Allen
Elaine Atkinson
Melaine Aucoin
Marion Bloom
Gwen Brodsky
Joanne Brown
Annie Bunting
Dudu Chan
Jane Craig
Shelagh Day
Mary Teresa Devlin
Daphne Dworatzek
Ana Ellis
Kate Erikson
Joan Flood
Lynn Gaudet
Stephaine Grace
Penelopi Gramatikopoulos
Trish Haddad
Gail Hanney
Leslie Hardy
Alexandra Horsky
Fatum Hussein
Christie Jefferson
Susan Joanis
Leslie Knight
Barbara Kosowan
Stelle Kynlestakis
Cathy Laurier
Charmaine Lawrence
Anna Luca
Mary Elizabeth Luka
Carissima Mathen
Bert McBain
Jodi McCandless
Diane Miles
Mary Anne Moore
Jennifer Mulrain
Connie Naskatsu
Azadeh Navim
Helena Orton
Elaine Penelegan
Jane Rounthwaite
Jennifer Scott
Pirkko Shalden
Erin Shaw
Michelle Sherwood
Arlene Skagfeld
Joanne St. Lewis
Kim Tang
Marwin Tin
Elizabeth Topp
Susan McCrae Vander Voet
Go Yao Yao
Andrea York
Margot Young

APPENDIX D

LEAF Counsel in Supreme Court of Canada Cases

Date	Case	Counsel
1988	*Canadian Newspapers*	Elizabeth Shilton Helena Orton
1989	*Andrews*	Mary Eberts Gwen Brodsky
	Borowski	Mary Eberts Helena Orton
	Brooks	Lynn Smith Kathryn Thomson
	Daigle	Suzanne Boivin
	Janzen	Louise Lamb
1990	*Keegstra*	Kathleen Mahoney Linda Taylor
	Taylor	Kathleen Mahoney Linda Taylor
1991	*Canadian Council of Churches*	Mary Eberts Dulcie McCallum
	Seaboyer and Gayme	Elizabeth Shilton Anne Derrick
	Sullivan and Lemay	Lynn Smith Mary Eberts
1992	*Butler*	Kathleen Mahoney Linda Taylor
	Moge	Helena Orton Alison Diduck
	M.(K) v. M.(H)	Elizabeth McIntyre Nicole Tellier

1992	*Norberg*	Victoria Gray
	Schacter	Mary Eberts Jennifer Aitken
1993	*Conway*	Elizabeth Shilton Arleen Huggins Karen Schucher
1994	*Whitley and Mowers*	Diane Oleskiw Chantal Tie Laurie Joe
	R v. M.L.M.	Chantal Tie Jean Whalen
1995	*Thibaudeau*	Katherine Hardie
	O'Connor	Sharon McIvor Elizabeth Shilton
	A.(L.L.) v. Beharriell	Anne Derrick Sharon McIvor
1996	*Goertz v. Gordon*	Carole Curtis Donna Wilson

APPENDIX E

Coalition Partners in Supreme Court of Canada Cases

Canadian Newspapers v. Canada

Barbra Schlifer Commemorative Clinic

Women's College Hospital Sexual Assault Care Centre

Metropolitan Toronto Special Committee on Child Abuse

Metro Action Committee on Public Violence Against Women and Children

Ontario Coalition of Rape Crisis Centres

Broadside Communications Ltd.

WomenHealthSharing Inc.

Seaboyer and Gayme v. The Queen

Barbra Schlifer Commemorative Clinic

Women's College Hospital Sexual Assault Care Centre

Metropolitan Toronto Special Committee on Child Abuse

Metro Action Committee on Public Violence Against Women and Children

Ontario Coalition of Rape Crisis Centres

Canadian Council of Churches v. The Queen

Canadian Disability Rights Council (CDRC)

R v. Thibaudeau

Charter Committee on Poverty Issues

Federated Anti-Poverty Groups of BC

National Action Committee on the Status of Women (NAC)

O'Connor v. The Queen

DisAbled Women's Network Canada

Aboriginal Women's Council

Canadian Association of Sexual Assault Centres

A.(L.L.) v. Beharriell

DisAbled Women's Network Ontario

Aboriginal Women's Council

Canadian Association of Sexual Assault Centres

APPENDIX F

LEAF Foundation Board of Directors

Pat Adams
Denise Arsenault
Beth Atcheson
Phyllis Berck
Pat Bowles
Joyce Burpee
Susan Clarke
Catherine Delaney
Marie DunSeith
Mary Eberts
Judy Erola
Valerie Fine
Sally Flintoft
Barbara Gory
Mary Lue Hinds
Shoba Khetrapal
Pam Medjuck
Marilou McPhedran
Joan Neville
Gail Paech
Nancy Ruth (Jackman)
Helen Ryane
Jean Sheen
Elizabeth Shilton
Joy Shuchat
Vara Singh
Lynn Smith
Susan McCrae Vander Voet
Elizabeth Wolfe

Staff

Karen Cairney
Mary Chrow
Jan-Marie Divok
Oksana Kucil

APPENDIX G

LEAF Foundation Branching Out Endowment Campaign

Honourary Chair
Nancy Ruth (Jackman)

National Co-Chairs
Judy Erola & John Tory

National Executive
Judy Erola
Milt Harris
John Tory
Pam Medjuck
Nancy Ruth (Jackman)

National Leadership Committee
Isabel Bassett (Toronto)
The Honourable Monique Bégin (Ottawa)
Rosemary Brown (Ottawa)
The Honourable Pat Carney (Vancouver)
Adrienne Clarkson (Toronto)
Martha Cohen (Calgary)
Erminie Cohen (Saint John)
Madeleine Dion Stout (Ottawa)
Rose Ellen Ghiz (Charlottetown)
Susan Fish (Toronto)
Lynn Gaudet (Whitehorse)
Reva Gerstein (Toronto)
Ruth Goldbloom (Halifax)
Marguerite Hale (Ottawa)
Marsha Hanen (Winnipeg)
Lois Hoegg (St. John's)
Chaviva Hosek (Toronto)
Shelley Howell (Yellowknife)
Hal Jackman (Toronto)
Marion McCain (Florenceville)
The Honourable Pauline McGibbon (Toronto)
Maureen McTeer (Calgary)
Maria Minna (Toronto)
Lucie Pépin (Montreal)
John Reynolds (Charlottetown)
Tannis Richardson (Winnipeg)
Vara Singh (Toronto)
Joan Sutton Straus (Toronto)
The Honourable Tillie Taylor (Saskatoon)
Wendy Williams (St. John's)

Alberta

Calgary
Anna DiPede
Maria Eriksen
Lauren Johnson

Leah Kovitz
Marilyn Palmer

Edmonton
Betty Hewes
Jean McBean

British Columbia
Colleen Cattell
Ani Feuermann
Janet Kee
Joy Leach
Heather MacFadgen
Janet McMynn
Lynn Smith
Sharlein Smith
Bonnie Theemes
Gayle Webster

Manitoba
Elaine Adam
Laurie Allen
Gail Asper
Jeri Bjornson
Marjorie Blankstein
Dianne Bourbonnaif
Shirley Bradshaw
Renate Bublick
Marilyn Gault
Barbara Hendrickson
Betty Hopkins
Daria Kiperchuk
Nancy Leitch
Shelley Marshall
Betty-Ann McPhedran
Maggie Nishimura
Doris Mae Oulton
Marilyn Pilon
Marlene Roy
Joan Scott
Muriel Smith
Susan Thompson

New Brunswick
Allison Brewer
Judy Budovitch
Lynne Burnham
Deborah Doherty
Marguerite Henderson-Davis
Ellen King
Lorraine King
Betty Lee
Judy MacPherson
Mary Lou Stirling

Newfoundland
Joan Marie Aylward
Kathryn Crosbie
Anne Fegan
Sheila Greene
Luanne Leamon
Irene Muzychka
Dorothy Robbins
Eve Roberts
Mary Visentine

Nova Scotia
Laura Bennet
Camille Cameron
Camille Cameron
Lisa Campbell
Lorenne Clark
Mary Cooley
Liz Crocker
Karen Willis Duerden
Ruth Epstein
Gerry Godsoe
Gus Grant

Anne Jackman
Lucy Kerr
Bernadette Macdonald
Peg MacInnis
Monica Maloney
Shirlee Medjuck
Jackie Mullenger
Heather Robertson
Rosemarie Sampson
Allison Scott
Robbie Shaw
Mary Sparling
Marie De Young

Ontario
Ottawa
Ruth Bell
Ruth Berger
Penny Collenette
Jocelyn Côté-O'Hara
Shirley Greenberg
Shelagh M'Gonigle
Wendy Porteous
Starr Solomon

Toronto
Sandra Anstey
Mona Bandeen
Jalynn Bennett
Phyllis Berck
Sam Bulte
Julie Davis
Michael Doran
Anne Dubin
Valerie Elia
Valerie Fine
Florence Minz Geneen
Tom Hodgson
Dorothy Krauskie
Marian Maloney
Marcia McClung
Penny Offman
Marilyn Roycroft
Lawrence Tanenbaum
Rose Wolfe

Prince Edward Island
Dianne Porter

Quebec
Bunnie Berke
Pauline Couture
Rita Dionne-Marsolais
Lorraine Duguay
Diana Dunford
Nicole Duval Hesler
Libby Lubell
Nancy Lydon
Marissa Nuss
Dorothy Reitman
Pierrette Sevigny-McCollamy
Jennifer Stoddart

Saskatchewan
Mae Boa
Lorraine Hill
Janet McMurtry
Roberta Mireau
Mary Bain Reid
Peggy Wakeling

APPENDIX H

Other LEAF Litigation Outside the Supreme Court of Canada (1985-1995)

A.L. v. The Crimes Compensation Board (Saskatchewan)
Denial of full compensation in spousal assault
LEAF intervention in the Saskatchewan Court of Queen's Bench (1991) and Saskatchewan Court of Appeal (1992)

Albrecht v. Albrecht
Division of Canada pension credits on separation or divorce
LEAF intervention in Supreme Court of Ontario—Divisional Court (1990)

Attorney-General of Canada v. Daniels
Incarceration of federally sentenced Saskatchewan native women
LEAF intervention in Saskatchewan Court of Appeal (1991)

Re: "Baby R"
Control of pregnant women through child welfare legislation
LEAF intervention in Supreme Court of British Columbia (1988)

Beaudette v. The Director of the Income Maintenance Branch of the Ministry of Community and Social Services and A-G of Ontario; Horvath v. The Director of the Income Maintenance Branch of the Ministry of Community and Social Services and A-G of Ontario
Constitutional validity of Ontario "man in the house rule" under welfare law
LEAF sponsorship of complainants in Supreme Court of Ontario—Divisional Court (1986)

Blainey v. The Ontario Hockey Association and Ontario Human Rights Commission
Constitutional validity of exclusion in Ontario human rights legislation from protection against discrimination in sport for girls
LEAF sponsorship and intervention in Ontario Weekly Court (1985) and Ontario Court of Appeal (1986)

Caron v. Sa Majeste La Reine

Prosecution for welfare fraud under "man in the house rule" under Quebec welfare legislation

LEAF intervention in Quebec Court of Appeal (1991)

Celik v. Wen-do Women's Self Defence Inc.

Same-sex organization

LEAF sponsorship of Wen-do before Ontario Human Rights Commission (1991)

Century Oils (Canada) Inc. v. Davies

Pregnancy discrimination as sex discrimination

LEAF sponsorship of respondent (Davies) in Supreme Court of British Columbia (1988)

Melita M. Chittenden, Avelina M. Villanueva, The Toronto Organization for Domestic Workers' Rights v. AG of Ontario

Exclusion of domestic workers from minimum wage protections

LEAF sponsorship in Supreme Court of Ontario—Divisional Court (1986)

Re: "Colgate Palmolive" (Workers' Compensation Board)

Availability of workers' compensation for injuries due to sexual and racial harassment in the course of employment

LEAF sponsorship of injured worker before Workers' Compensation Board (1990)

Jane Doe v. Board of Commissioners of Police for the Municipality of Metropolitan Toronto, Jack Marks, Kim Derry & William Cameron

Civil action for breach of sections 7, 15, and 28 of the Charter, and for negligence, based on police investigation and treatment of sexual assault

LEAF sponsorship of complainant and intervention in Ontario Weekly Court (1989) and Ontario Court of Appeal (1990)

Haldimand-Norfolk Regional Board of Commissioners of Police et al. v. Ontario Nurses' Association of Ontario et al.

Application of Ontario pay equity legislation

LEAF sponsorship of the Equal Pay Coalition in Ontario Court of Appeal (1990)

Kane et al. v. Church of Jesus Christ Christian-Aryan Nations et al.

Human Rights Board of Inquiry addressing racist symbols and constitutional validity of legislation prohibiting same

Joint intervention of LEAF and the Canadian Congress of Black Women before Alberta Human Rights Commission Board of Inquiry (1992)

*The Queen v. O'Connor**
Disclosure obligations of complainants in sexual assault cases
Coalition intervention in BC Court of Appeal (1994)

"D.P."
Application for admission to the bar by man convicted of sexual assault of two children, including his daughter
LEAF intervention before Tribunal of the Law Society of Upper Canada (1989)

George Ramdial, Nilufar Ramdial and Lana Salmon v. Metropolitan Toronto Condominium Corporation No. 624
Protection against adult-only housing under human rights legislation
LEAF sponsorship of complainant Salmon before Ontario Human Rights Commission Board of Inquiry (1990)

*The Queen v. Schachter**
Maternity and childcare benefits under the Unemployment Insurance Act and remedies under the Charter
LEAF intervention as a party in Federal Court Trial Division (1988) and Federal Court (1990)

*The Queen v. Seaboyer and Gayme**
Sexual assault and rape shield law
Coalition intervention in Ontario Court of Appeal (1986)

Shewchuk v. Ricard
Constitutional validity of the Child Paternity and Support Act allowing child support claims against putative fathers
Coalition intervention in British Columbia Court of Appeal (1986)

Vinogradov v. Governors of University of Calgary et al.
Analysis of complaint of systemic sex discrimination in employment
LEAF sponsorship of complaint before Board of Inquiry, Alberta Court of Queen's Bench, and Alberta Court of Appeal (1990)

* These cases were ultimately heard by the Supreme Court of Canada and the relevant facta are reproduced in full elsewhere in this book.

Submissions, Reports, Position Papers, Etc.**

1. Submission to the [Ontario] Standing Committee on the Administration of Justice concerning Bill 7 and The Family Benefits Act, February 1986

2. Submission to the Department of Justice about reform of the Canadian Human Rights Act, June 1986

3. Submission to the Canadian Human Rights Commission concerning the Commission's policy guidelines about pregnancy and childbirth discrimination, October 1986

4. Submission to the Ontario Task Force on Mandatory Retirement (Ianni Commission) about the impact of mandatory retirement on women, March 1987

5. Submission to the Standing Committee on the Secretary of State Women's Program, March 1987 (transcript of oral submission only)

6. Submission to the Joint Committee of the Senate and the House of Commons on the 1987 Constitutional Accord (Meech Lake Accord), September 1987

7. Submission to the Senate of Canada on the Meech Lake Constitutional Accord, March 1988

8. Submission to the Standing Committee on Human Rights and the Status of Disabled Persons concerning the future of the Court Challenges Program, October 1989

9. Submission to the Legislative Committee of Parliament on the constitutional validity of Bill C-43, An Act Respecting Abortion. January 1990

10. Submission to the Royal Commission of Inquiry into the response of the Newfoundland criminal justice system to complaints about treatment of sexual assault of children and women (Hughes Commission), June 1990

11. Submission to the Legislative Committee of Parliament on Bill C-49, An Act Respecting Sexual Assault, May 1992

12. Submission to the Boyer Committee on the review of federal laws and regulations for compliance with the Charter, April 17, 1985 (transcript of oral submission only)

13. Submission to Special Senate Committee on National Defence re OSSOMM—right to organize and needs of spouses of members of the Canadian Armed Forces, June 12, 1986

14. Submission re the rules governing the intervention of public-interest groups in Charter litigation at the Supreme Court of Canada, June 1986

15. Submission to Ontario Women's Directorate—an examination of alternatives available to amend the Criminal Code after the decision of the Supreme Court of Canada in *Seaboyer and Gayme*, January 1992

16. Litigating for Lesbians—LEAF's Report on Consultations with the Lesbian Community, June 1993

17. LEAF and Pornography: Litigating on Equality and Sexual Representations—position paper re follow-up to *Butler* decision, September 1993

18. Submission to Minister of National Revenue—Canada Customs' seizure of lesbian and gay materials, September 1994

19. Submission on Proposed Cross-Gender Staffing at the New Regional Institutions for Federally Sentenced Women (Arbour Commission), January 1996

20. Submission on the Classification of Federally Sentenced Women (Arbour Commission), January 1996

21. Submission on Federally Sentenced Aboriginal Women and The Healing Lodge (Arbour Commission), January 1996

22. Submission re Guaranteed Available Income for Need (GAIN) Act, February 1996 (prepared by WestCoast LEAF)

** This list includes the submissions, reports, or position papers on file at the National Office. It may not include all submissions, reports, or position papers of the provincial legal committees.

APPENDIX I

Table of Cases